CAREER OPPORTUNITIES in

LIBRARY AND INFORMATION SCIENCE

D0573292

CAREER OPPORTUNITIES

in

LIBRARY AND INFORMATION SCIENCE

ALLAN TAYLOR
JAMES ROBERT PARISH

Foreword by NANCY RODERER

Checkmark Books®

An imprint of Infobase Publishing

Career Opportunities in Library and Information Science

Checkmark Books
An imprint of Infobase Publishing, Inc.
132 West 31st Street
New York NY 10001

Library of Congress Cataloging-in-Publication Data

Taylor, T. Allan.
  Career opportunities in library and information science / by Allan Taylor and James Robert Parish ; foreword by Nancy Roderer.
       p. cm.
  Includes bibliographical references and index.
  ISBN-13: 978-0-8160-7546-1 (hardcover : acid-free paper)
  ISBN-10: 0-8160-7546-8 (hardcover : acid-free paper)
  ISBN-13: 978-0-8160-7547-8 (pbk. : acid-free paper)
  ISBN-10: 0-8160-7547-6 (pbk. : acid-free paper)
1. Library science—Vocational guidance—United States—Juvenile literature. 2. Information science—Vocational guidance—United States—Juvenile literature. 3. Librarians—Employment—United States—Juvenile literature. 4. Librarians—Job descriptions—United States—Juvenile literature. I. Parish, James Robert. II. Title.
  Z682.35.V62T39 2009
  020.23'73—dc22   2008039466

Checkmark Books are available at special discounts when purchased in bulk quantities for businesses, associations, institutions, or sales promotions. Please call our Special Sales Department in New York at (212) 967-8800 or (800) 322-8755.

You can find Infobase Publishing on the World Wide Web at http://www.infobasepublishing.com

Cover design by Takeshi Takahashi

Printed in the United States of America

VB Hermitage 10 9 8 7 6 5 4 3 2 1

This book is printed on acid-free paper.

To Barbara Meyers Ford
For her continuous helpful sharing of information, time, and encouragement
and
To Mary Ellen Padin
For her support and aid to so many information professionals

CONTENTS

FOREWORD

The term *library and information sciences* was not in widespread use in my formative years, and it took some serendipity to find my way to it. Much has changed since then, but in some ways, I believe, the field is still evolving and still not well enough defined. Let me tell you first how I found my way to it and then tell you where I think we are today. Along the way, I hope to expand your view of the field and the exciting opportunities available within it.

It seems that I have always been interested in how people find and use information. Among my earliest memories are happy times spent with my grandfather, a retired teacher/entrepreneur, who somehow managed to convey his zeal for acquiring the latest facts in our frequent trips to the library in the park across the street from our house in Elmhurst, Illinois. These adventures got across to me a connection between the library and information, a recurring theme in my life.

Another area of interest entered my life in high school, when a friend's father went to a seminar on automatic data processing, as it was then called, and its use in actuarial work. He gave me the big binder of information he received and told me that this was the field for me. I found the contents fascinating and added computer science to my interests.

Undergraduate majors at the University of Dayton—which I attended—included mathematics and computer sciences, which in those days were closely linked since computer science had an emphasis on the approaches to analyzing numerical data. I enjoyed both mathematics and computer science but also found pleasure in a broad range of other subjects. Whatever I studied, I found myself most interested in how information was generated, how it was accessed, and what people did with it. Thus,

it was reasonably clear to me at graduation from the University of Dayton that I wanted to work with information but not so clear how to do that. It was my good fortune to find an article about a field called *information science* and to have the author of that article answer my inquiry about prospects in the field with a long letter of advice. There were, in fact, he said, graduate schools at which I could learn about information science and a wide variety of jobs available to me after completing my graduate studies. It seemed that I was on track. I chose one of the schools that he had recommended, the University of Maryland, and obtained a wonderful education at the School of Library and Information Sciences there.

Fast forward to today, and it is now considerably easier to find information programs at colleges and universities. Most schools of library science have broadened their curricula to be more encompassing of information activities within and outside of libraries and have changed their titles to *library and information science, information science, information studies,* or just *information*. Other educational programs have emerged that deal with information, especially in schools of computer science, business, communication, and medicine. While computers provided the original stimulus for the emergence of information professions, there has been a gradual evolution of the information professions toward being focused primarily on the information content of computer and other systems, considered, of course, in relation to the people and the technologies involved.

It is curious to me that, despite the considerable evolution of the field, the term *information profession* is not in widespread use. As noted above, there are a number of academic programs in this area, but their graduates tend to go into a broad range of jobs with more specific job titles. While the title of this book, *Career Opportunities in Library and Information Science*, continues the distinction between work in libraries and work elsewhere involving information, the authors acknowledge the many similarities and shared elements between the two disciplines and indicate the extent to which they interact in the everyday life and work of librarians in particular. That said, I believe that it will be a considerable step forward in the evolution of this field when we acknowledge those similarities by using the umbrella term *information professions* and work together to advance the field.

Marcia Bates, a prominent contributor to both theory and practice in the information world, has described the information professions in several of her publications. In 2007, she published an excellent article on the subject (http://informationr.net/ir/12-4/colis/colis29.html) basing her analysis on the work she did with Mary Niles Maack on the *Encyclopedia of Library and Information Science*. Bates lays out a broad spectrum of information disciplines falling under the general categories of the disciplines of a cultural nature, associated with the arts and humanities, and the sciences of information, associated with the social and natural sciences. She indicates many areas of information professional work, including publishing, various types of librarianship, archival work, information management, database development, and information retrieval. With this study, she has made a major contribution to defining the information professions and their relationships to one another. As she indicates, there is a wealth of information professions with much in common, easing the movement of individuals among the related professions.

* * * *

For me, a career in the information professions has encompassed several different roles. After graduation from the University of Maryland, I joined a statistical consulting firm based in Rockville, Maryland, that had a specialization in library and information studies. Over a period of more than a decade, I consulted primarily with federal and state agencies on their information problems. My work ranged considerably in scope, from studies of individual libraries, to planning for the future of scientific and technical publishing in the United States, to specific information functions considered from creation, to storage, to retrieval, to use. Along the way, I had the opportunity to observe literally hundreds of organizations involved in information and to gain a sense of how they operated.

Around the pivotal age of 40, I began to feel that it was time for a professional change. Here the many organizations and activities I had observed over the years became grist for the mill of determining my next position. I found myself drawn toward academe, where I could at once continue in an intellectually stimulating environment but become part of an organization that I could help move forward. Searching for my preference in subject areas, I noted that my work in medicine had been noteworthy in terms of both the rapid growth of medical information and also the importance of medical information to people's lives. Of course, I wanted to continue to work with information, and I thought some combination of library and other information work would be ideal.

With these specifications, I determined that an academic medical center would best fit my profile. I am fortunate to have been employed by three stellar academic medical centers, those of Columbia, Yale, and Johns Hopkins Universities, in roles that combined medical librarianship with medical informatics. The position at Columbia came about through contacts made in my consulting work, especially at the National Library of Medicine, and through my professional networks. These factors contributed to my obtaining subsequent positions at Yale and Hopkins, as well as my growing résumé of accomplishments, including publications and presentations.

A key factor in my career progressions has been drawing upon my professional networks, most especially through the American Society for Information Science and Technology (ASIS&T). ASIS&T is a focal point for sharing information and promoting the information professions (http://www.asis.org). Founded in 1937, ASIS&T defines its membership as "information professionals leading the search for new and better theories, techniques and technologies to improve access to information." For me, ASIS&T has provided a circle of colleagues and much intellectual stimulation since I first joined it in 1972. As its current president, I am using the opportunity of leadership to promote the information professions. As you pursue your career in an information profession, you would be most welcome to join us in ASIS&T.

Nancy Roderer
Baltimore, Md., 2008

Nancy Roderer holds a B.S. in mathematics and computer science from the University of Dayton and an M.L.I.S. in information retrieval from the University of Maryland. She has worked as a consultant, librarian, and medical informatician in Washington, D.C., New York, N.Y., New Haven, Conn., and Baltimore, Md. Her family includes three grandsons, whom she is encouraging to become information professionals.

INDUSTRY OUTLOOK

Traditionally, libraries have been the official information repository of the record of a culture and a nation. They are places where people go to conduct research and to learn. According to the American Library Association (ALA), there are an estimated 130,000 libraries of all types in the United States. These facilities range in size from small libraries with several hundred books (and accompanying periodical literature), a single part-time staff member, and limited operating hours to the world's largest library facility, the Library of Congress, with more than 120 million items and thousands of employees. The ALA estimates that the number of people working in libraries may approach 500,000. The library workforce includes librarians and other professionals, paraprofessionals, and clerical and technical personnel. Types of libraries include public libraries, school libraries (or school library media centers), academic libraries (found in public and private postsecondary institutions of higher education), and special libraries (which include corporate, medical, law, religious, governmental, prison, non-for-profit organizations, and many other highly specialized collections).

Most librarian positions incorporate three major aspects of library work: user services, technical services, and administrative management. Even librarians specializing in one of these areas frequently perform other tasks. Librarians in user services (which include reference, circulation, and computer service) aid the public in finding information. Librarians in technical services are involved in acquisitions and cataloging, and their work in the acquisition and preparation of library materials seldom leads them into interaction directly with the public. Librarians in administrative posts oversee the management and planning of libraries, includ-ing the preparation of budgets and the negotiation of contracts for services, materials, and equipment; supervise library employees; and perform public relations and fundraising duties. In small libraries or information centers, librarians generally handle all types of jobs, including selection, acquisition, and supervision. In large facilities, librarians typically specialize in a single area (such as acquisitions, cataloging, reference, or administration). Increasingly, librarians have found they can apply their information management and research skills in areas outside libraries, including publishing, the creation of information systems, database development, marketing, and the training of database users. They may hold management positions in institutions or corporate posts or even start their own information-related businesses.

* * * *

As libraries develop new roles and goals of service, their staffing needs will change. One constant is that computer literacy is essential in almost every position. Staff needs vary greatly depending on the size of a library and its location.

A public library staff ranges from a one- or two-person branch to a main library with 50 to 100 or more staff workers. Medium to large size libraries usually have a large range of library positions at all levels filled with appropriately trained personnel. They typically have many specialized librarians responsible for administration, reference and readers' advisory services, collection development, and programming. Paraprofessional library technicians and clerical staff perform supportive tasks in such areas as children's services, bookmobiles, outreach, and technical services. Smaller libraries may have only one or two librarians to handle reference and children's services. In very small facilities or branches and on bookmobiles, the staff members tend to be generalists who share all the jobs, from checking out materials to customer services.

As libraries grow in size and complexity, their staff members tend to become more specialized in their responsibilities. Many of them have advanced education, though not necessarily master's degrees in library and information science. Their academic backgrounds and training are often in specialties other than library science. In addition, it is not unusual for library employees to work many years in a particular area of either public or technical services. For example, in the circulation department, one clerk may be responsible for reserves, one for overdue collections, one for stack maintenance, and others for checking materials in and out. The clerks often may be supervised by a library technician or by a librarian, and they may be supported by library pages and aides.

School library media programs serve as the hub of educational activity in a school, addressing the information needs of the entire school curriculum. The role of the school media specialist is to manage a library media center at the elementary, middle, or high school level. Responsibilities are numerous, and library media specialists often must act as the budget director, staff supervisor, purchaser, cataloger, archivist, and repairer of equipment. They are also responsible for teaching library and research skills to both the student body and the teaching faculty. They collaborate with the school's faculty and administration in planning programs in support of the teaching curriculum and the school's goal of achieving the learning standards required by each state and the federal government. This library profession has been growing steadily as parents and school administrators recognize the value of a well-funded, well-staffed school library media center. Studies have shown a direct correlation between the availability of quality library resources and student achievement. Studies show that test scores rise in elementary and middle schools when library media specialists and teachers collaborate to promote information literacy.

Academic library work is by far the most eclectic area of librarianship. Work settings vary greatly, from small community college libraries to major research libraries within universities. Academic libraries primarily serve the academic community of the institution, which includes undergraduate students, graduate students, faculty, administration, and staff. Smaller college libraries usually focus on service to the student body by supporting the curriculum, while large university libraries not only support the curriculum but also provide graduate students and faculty with material to support their research. Job opportunities vary according to the interests and expertise of individual librarians. While some academic librarians are involved with management or administration, others may work in acquisitions, archives, circulation, collection management, computer and information systems, documents, instruction, reference, serials, or subject specialization. It is common today for many academic librarians to divide their work among several areas of expertise. In addition, academic librarians are considered to be scholars in their own right and must fulfill certain scholarly expectations. On many campuses, academic librarians are appointed faculty and are able to secure tenure. As faculty members, they are expected to pursue further formal education, to do research, and to publish.

Special libraries include corporate, medical, law, religious, governmental, prison, non-for-profit institutions, and many other highly specialized collections. Often, the designation is used as a catchall term for any library that is not a public, school, or academic library. A common element, however, is that the collections and services of these types of libraries are very narrowly focused to support the activities of the parent organization. Of the characteristics that are most common to these facilities, the primary one is that their collections include materials relating to specialized subject areas. Second, these libraries gather their collections and design their services to directly support and further the objectives of their parent organizations. Finally, these libraries are primarily concerned with actively seeking and providing information that the parent organization's clients or patrons need rather than building general information collections. They must provide special and even individualized services for their patrons. The management and staffing of special libraries and information centers are more varied and distinct than are those found in other types of libraries. Often, the administrator responsible for the library or information center is not a librarian at all, but a director or officer of the organization. In addition, personnel working in special libraries and information centers usually have more varied backgrounds than do staff in other types of libraries. The special librarian or information specialist must have a degree in a subject specialty as well as in library and information science. In fact, this subject expertise may be so vital to companies and businesses that they may prefer a technician with subject specialization to a professional with a master's degree in library or information science. Large special libraries often include professional librarians or information specialists backed up by subject specialists, technicians, programmers, and clerks.

* * * *

Over the years, the book has played the central role in the transmission of information and was central to the concept of a traditional library. With the significant proliferation of scientific and technical information in the 20th century, an emphasis grew away from the book to information itself. Such data were often stored in media other than books: in periodicals, documents, research reports, and on microfilm. It became clear that the package in which the information was contained was less important than locating specific information stored within these media. This was substantially different from the way libraries had customarily satisfied the information needs of their patrons, namely providing a physical item (a book). Thus, this shift in emphasis away from the item that held the information to a concentration on accessing the information itself presented a significant challenge to modern librarianship. Then, the development of personal computers, with their increased capacity to store information without the need of a physical document, presented a further challenge for librarianship by offering a different means of information retrieval. Libraries began to be redefined from places to locate books and electronically stored data records to places that house the most advanced media as well as remote access to a wide range of information resources.

* * * *

A library's primary purpose is to acquire, store, organize, disseminate, and provide access to the vast bodies of available knowledge and information. Information does *not* organize itself, and it has a tendency toward randomness. Unless there are ways to organize it effectively, it quickly becomes chaos. The primary purpose of systematizing library collections is to meet the various and growing information needs of library users. Organizing knowledge in libraries means organizing and managing many types of information and media: data stored in physical items such as books, video recordings, or pictures, as well as information stored electronically in words, sounds, or images. It also means organizing efficiently the records that serve as representations of these items, such as catalog cards or the electronic bibliographic records in libraries' computerized catalogs.

The impact of the Internet and the World Wide Web, the maturity and widespread use of electronic periodical indexes and full-text databases, and the use of automated holdings catalogs have greatly impacted libraries, whether they are rural or urban, small or large, specialized or general. No longer are libraries defined by the size of their physical collections but rather by the amount of information to which they can provide users access. These dramatic changes have greatly impacted people employed in the library and information profession. Whether in an elementary school media center or in a university research library, the job environment is faster paced than ever, with continuing retraining needed as the newest information storage media become available. Few libraries or information centers are tied to only a single medium of information storage anymore. Rather, multiple formats are in use simultaneously, such as microforms, paper, optical discs, and digital data. As such, there is a continuous learning curve for staff and, correspondingly, for library patrons and researchers. Increasingly, the role of librarians and library technicians (let alone other information professionals) is that of trainer and navigator in their instruction of customers on the use of tools and their recommending of relevant resources among the welter of available information.

For library and information center personnel, the emphasis on computer skills is extremely important, with the focus on using the computer as a tool to unlock the world of electronic information and transmitting the appropriate information to library patrons and end users whether or not they are physically present in the library, center, or office. In addition, automation of the behind-the-scenes processes in libraries has been gaining momentum. Repetitive routines have been greatly reduced to a set of programmable instructions that a computer can execute. With each step of this process, the tasks of library staff members have become less routine and more reliant on the ability to manipulate computers to extract needed data.

Another challenge for librarians is helping library users become skillful in evaluating the usefulness and reliability of the wide array of information now available. Until the advent of the Internet and the World Wide Web, information available from libraries went through two evaluation processes. First, publishers, to some extent, vetted materials before publishing them, and, second, libraries made selection choices based on their budgets and what appeared to best meet their customers' unique information needs. Web-based information, however, does not meet such scrutiny. This electronic tool that allows brilliant insight to be communicated worldwide at nearly the speed of light also permits any individual to broadcast lesser thoughts just as effectively.

One of the greatest new challenges for librarians and information professionals is the evaluation of online data. Many of their patrons and end users require assistance and training in how to gain access to electronic data, but they also need guidance in assessing the information they find. In school and academic libraries, this responsibility is shared with classroom teachers. In special libraries, staff has a duty to sift through and evaluate such data for other professional colleagues within their organizations. In public libraries, the way is not as clear, as public librarians must balance access to information with the frequent demand by patrons to control materials considered offensive by some.

* * * *

The growth of new information technologies as represented by the World Wide Web has provided a considerable impetus to explore and understand information science. Information science has been defined as "the science that investigates the properties and behavior of information, the forces governing the flow of information, and the means of processing information for optimum accessibility and usability. The processes include the origination, dissemination, collection, organization, storage, retrieval, interpretation and use of information."[1] Information science studies the application and usage of knowledge in organizations and the interaction between people, organizations, and information systems. It is a broad, interdisciplinary field, incorporating not only aspects of computer science but also library science, cognitive studies, and social sciences. Information science focuses on understanding problems from the perspective of the users (of that information) involved and then applying information (and other) technology as needed. It tackles systemic problems first rather than individual pieces of technology within the system. The efforts of information scientists and specialists have contributed much to the understanding of how information is generated, organized, disseminated, and used. Areas of interest for information scientists include data modeling (the process of creating a model to structure and organize data), document management (devising a computer system to track and store electronic documents and/or images of paper documents), groupware (the development of software designed to help people involved in a common task achieve their goal), human-computer interaction (the study of the interaction between people, or users, and computers), information architecture (the practice of structuring information for a purpose), information ethics (which investigates the ethical issues arising from the development and application of information technologies), information retrieval (the science of searching for information in documents, searching for documents themselves, searching for metadata that describe documents, or searching within databases), information society (the study of a society in which the creation, distribution, diffusion, use, and manipulation of information is a significant economic, political, and cultural activity), informa-

---

[1] Taylor, Robert S. "Professional Aspects of Information Science and Technology." *Annual Review of Information Science and Technology*, vol. 1. Edited by Carlos A. Cuadra. New York: Wiley, 1966, pg. 15–40.

tion systems (concerned with the development, use, application, and influence of information technologies), knowledge engineering (the building, maintaining, and development of knowledge-based systems), knowledge management (concerned with the range of practices used by organizations to identify, create, represent, and distribute knowledge of reuse, awareness, and learning purposes between organizations), semantic web (the evolving extension of the World Wide Web in which Web content can be expressed not only in natural language but also in a form that can be understood, interpreted, and used by software agents, permitting them to find, share, and integrate information more easily), and user-centered design (concerning the techniques used to develop information systems that take into account the needs, wants, and limitations of the end user).

The goal of information science is to provide information to individuals who need it. There is a significant difference between the terms *data* and *information.* Superficially, information results from the processing of raw data. However, the real issue is getting the right information to the right person at the right time and in a usable form. Information science's emphasis on usability and accessibility is very similar to one of the major objectives of librarianship.

For librarians, this goal of information science is personified by the services they render to facility users. Thus, the librarian and the information scientist or professional both facilitate the transmission of information to people to meet their needs, be they practical, theoretical, religious, or aesthetic. An understanding of how to define information needs and wants, how individuals behave when they search for information, and how information systems can best be designed and used to satisfy information needs is critical to both information science and librarianship.

Information technicians and professionals can be found in all types of institutions. Present-day organizations increasingly rely on information gathering to perform their functions effectively. Making the best management decisions relies, in part, on an organization's ability to acquire, access, and evaluate a wide assortment of pertinent information in a timely fashion. As organizations became increasingly complex and their reliance on rapid access to high-quality information grew, a field known as information resources management (IRM), or information management, emerged. In many cases, managing information has become a task with the same significance as managing the fiscal and human resources of an organization. It is the mission of information specialists and professionals to ensure that the sought-after information is provided in a timely manner and that the acquisition of appropriate information systems is cost-effective. The growth of such new positions as chief information officers (CIOs) is testimony to the increasing recognition of how crucial information resource management (IRM) is to the survival of organizations, both public and private.

* * * *

New generations of younger librarians moving into library workplaces face some unique factors. The flattening of workplace hierarchies and the rise of participative management leads the way for younger and less experienced librarians to participate on equal ground (to some extent, at least) with their elder colleagues. Technological change has brought the need for a whole new set of skills and a new way of looking at library services. Growing up with this new technology affects the perspectives of incoming generations of librarians. What is unique is the way this technology is now integrated with their lives. With this background, next-generation librarians may bring in new ideas and are often better able to relate to younger groups of patrons, drawing them in and involving them in their libraries. Above all, in order for traditional libraries to keep their younger workers, they will need to find ways to remain attractive in the face of increased nontraditional job opportunities, particularly in the field of information science and technology.

With all the technological changes occurring at breakneck speed in today's society—and their tremendous impact on what individuals and organizations require in the way of information portals, structure, and systems—the duties and roles of librarians and information specialists, scientists, and technicians will continue to alter, expand, and provide exciting career challenges for coming generations.

ACKNOWLEDGMENTS

First and foremost, we acknowledge and gratefully thank James Chambers and Sarah Fogarty at Facts On File, Inc., for their enthusiastic guidance on this project. They both have been concerned, enthusiastic, and unfailingly helpful to us. We also thank our agent, Stuart Bernstein, for his help and suggestions on this project. Furthermore, we feel greatly indebted to Nancy Roderer for her wonderfully informative foreword to this book.

Additionally, we thank the following individuals for their assistance with this project: Barbara Meyers Ford, Alex Gildzen, Kimberly O'Quinn, Steven Whitney, and Blair Whittington.

HOW TO USE THIS BOOK

Purpose

Ours is an age of information. More and more information becomes available daily, particularly through the use of ever-expanding electronic technologies. The management of all this information—from its accumulation to its categorization, its storage, and its dissemination—becomes more challenging each day. These are the tasks that librarians and information professionals perform all the time.

The 86 or so careers described in *Career Opportunities in Library and Information Science* make it one of the most inclusive directories of jobs in the fields of library science and the information profession available in a single volume. While most people picture the job of "librarian" from their experience with college librarians or the librarians at their local public library, there are actually a wide variety of jobs open to people interested in librarianship. Similarly, careers for information professionals expand far beyond the library to include jobs in business, professional organizations, and government. All these careers are involved in some of the most exciting technological developments as applied to information. Whether our current environment is labeled the "information age" or the "electronic era," the impact that technological advancements have made in these two fields of information research and service is immense.

The practice, service, and research aspects of librarianship have been drastically modified by the introduction of computer technology. The information industry has greatly expanded its influence through advancements in computer technology and the application of information techniques and technology to business, government, and science and technology. In both these areas, however, the underlying critical factor still is people. The continual technical, communicative, and service expansion of these industries relies on trained librarians and information professionals: talented programmers, systems technicians, and persevering clerical workers.

The purpose of *Career Opportunities in Library and Information Science* is to serve as a guide to the varied occupations within these fields. By consulting this volume, high school and college students interested in a career in librarianship or in the application of information science to business institutions, professional organizations in such fields as law or medicine, or government can learn who does what within the organizational superstructures of these industries. Librarians and information specialists who are currently employed in their professional capacities will also find the information contained in this book helpful as they expand and/or redefine their career paths.

In *Career Opportunities in Library and Information Science*, jobs are not merely summarized in a few paragraphs but are explained in detail, including duties, alternate titles, salary ranges, employment and advancement prospects (with a Career Ladder detailing typical routes to and from the position), prerequisites (including education and training, experience, and skills requirements), organizations to join, and helpful tips for entering the job arena under discussion or expanding capabilities with a view to career advancement. This volume is geared to assist both those seeking to start a career as a librarian or information specialist and to those experienced and working librarians and information specialists who are looking to make career shifts or advancements within their professions.

Many of the jobs detailed in this volume are available to individuals with appropriate educational credentials (typically a high school diploma and a bachelor's degree, as well as a master's degree for most librarian and information specialist positions) and from one to five or more years of experience. Job positions discussed in this volume cover entry- and mid-level posts and those that require more training and/or education as well as more years of seasoning within their field, and these are both mid-level and high-end posts.

Sources of Information

Research for this book includes the authors' own experiences; interviews with professionals in various positions within the librarian and information specialists fields; and facts, reports, surveys, and other data obtained from job data banks, professional guilds and associations, the federal government, and educational institutions. The job descriptions provided are based on representative samples of actual job posts, employment documents, research studies, salary surveys, and tables of organization from many sources. Thus, the career descriptions detailed are not theoretical. They represent current practice and reflect the actual structure of jobs in both of these fields.

How the Book Is Organized

The 70 job profiles (which actually cover more than 86 jobs) in *Career Opportunities in Library and Information Science* are organized into three main sections: Library Science, Information Science, and Education. The Library Science section contains four subsections: Librarians, Special Librarians, Library Assistants, and Library Technicians. The Information Science section contains two subsections: Information Managers, and Information Scientists, Technicians, and Support Staff. The Edu-

cation section covers both library science and information science education. This organization is designed to reflect the different aspects and job levels in all three of these areas. A Foreword provides an overview of these related (and sometimes overlapping but somewhat different) fields of library science and information science, and the career opportunities available in both of them.

While the careers discussed in this book are the most frequent job positions found within these industries, job titles and responsibilities are not universally consistent, and their definitions vary and often overlap from setting to setting. While most of the job positions involve functions specific to librarianship or to information science, some positions may overlap. Most present-day librarians are involved in some form of information processing (whether in research or in the day-to-day activities of aiding library patrons in finding information), and most information specialists are involved in researching information from many of the same sources that librarians use as well as using technologies used by both fields. Each job description notes when there are opportunities for a position in other related areas.

The Job Profile

Each job profile starts with a Career Profile, which includes a brief description of the position's major duties; any alternate job titles for the post; salary ranges; employment prospects; opportunities for promotion; and the job prerequisites insofar as education and training, job experience, special skills, and personality traits are concerned. A Career Ladder graphically illustrates a typical career path to and from the position described, including the positions below and above each job. The rest of the profile is in an extended narrative format with more detailed information on the job that contains the following:

- Position description, including typical major duties and responsibilities and any optional duties that may or may not be part of the given job
- Salary ranges from entry-level to top earnings, including the factors (such as individual skills and experience or geographic location) that often affect how much a particular position may pay

- Employment expectations or job forecast, indicating how difficult the post may be to obtain
- Possibilities and suggestions for advancement and whether such work progression is unusually difficult
- Education required and any special training necessary for the particular job
- Whether any licensing or certification training may be required
- Necessary and/or useful experience, skills, and personal attributes that enhance the potential for success in the job
- Whether there are any union or guild requirements for holding the particular job and/or suggested professional associations related to the job that may be useful
- Tips and practical suggestions for obtaining the initial job in this job category

Appendixes

Four Appendixes offer further resources for individuals seeking any of the more than 86 job positions described in *Career Opportunities in Library and Information Science*. Appendix I, Educational Institutions, lists colleges, universities, and educational institutions in every state and the District of Columbia that offer undergraduate degrees (four-year programs) in such areas as cognitive science and computer/information science—general, data processing technology, human resources management, information systems, information resources management, information technology, library science, management information systems, statistics, and system administration. The listing does *not* include such overlapping general majors as computer science, marketing, or word processing, which most colleges/universities offer. The listings provide each institution's address, telephone number, fax number, e-mail address, and Web site as well as the major programs relevant to the fields of library science and information science.

Appendix II, Periodicals, Directories, and Annuals, offers a useful resource list of magazines, directories, and annual volumes concerned with topics of interest to librarians and information professionals. (Note that books are not included in this appendix but are part of the Bibliography.)

Appendix III, Professional, Industry, and Trade Associations, Guilds, Unions, and Government Agencies, lists professional trade associations, guilds and unions, and government agencies related to the fields of library science and information science. For each entry, the address, telephone number, fax number, e-mail, and Web site are provided.

Appendix IV, Useful Web Sites, offers a wide range of Internet resources in many categories that are useful for job searching, trade news and information, and networking as well as a list of general search engines that will help in researching these industries.

A Glossary of terms relevant to both fields includes frequently used technical terminology, buzzwords, and names. The Glossary is followed by a Bibliography, which includes sources used in researching this book as well as an extended list of current useful books on careers in library and information science and some of the expanding technological innovations now pervasive throughout both fields.

The Index provides a quick source for locating particular job titles (including cross-references to alternate job names), organizations cited in the text (but not in the Appendixes), and other relevant information appearing in the chapters.

Finally, please keep in mind that the Internet is in a constant state of flux, and Web sites sometimes change their Web address or, on occasion, cease to exist. If a URL given in this book—each of which was verified as this volume was written—does not produce the desired Web site, it may be necessary to do a search engine query using the name of the Web site to locate its new home.

LIBRARY SCIENCE

LIBRARIANS

ACADEMIC LIBRARIAN

Duties: Provide public and technical services, instruction, and collection development in postsecondary educational institutions and oversee library automation in college and university libraries

Alternate Title(s): College Librarian; University Librarian

Salary Range: $28,900 to $70,200

Employment Prospects: Good

Advancement Prospects: Fair to good

Prerequisites:

Education or Training—Master of Library Science (M.L.S) degree or Master of Library and Information Science (M.L.I.S.) required; additional master's degree in some specialty area is recommended; Academic Librarians who want to teach or hold top administrative positions should have a Ph.D. in library or information science

Experience—Solid experience with computers and some experience in teaching will prove to be helpful

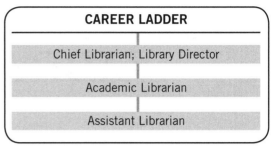

Special Skills and Personality Traits—Ability to work in a team environment; superior communication and technical skills; flexibility; good interpersonal talents and above-average academic ability; intellectual curiosity; love of books and information retrieval; service orientation

Special Requirements—Certification may be required by some states at their state-run educational institutions

Position Description

Academic libraries are found in public and private colleges and universities. Academic libraries make up nearly 4,000 of the approximately 130,000 libraries in the United States. The primary mission of an academic library is to support the research needs of faculty, students, and staff at such institutions. As an example, community colleges generally prepare students to transfer to upper-division programs at four-year colleges and provide vocational training programs to assist students to enter the workforce. Community colleges have also expanded to include support of lifelong learning and support of community economic development. As such, a community college library has expanded from just classroom support to include community users enrolled in noncredit courses and other tailor-made training classes and must keep pace with the information needs of geographically distant students.

On the other hand, academic libraries for four-year educational institutions have a much different focus than those of two-year college libraries. The funding levels, scope of collections, and often highly technical materials will be quite different. Many large universities maintain separate departmental libraries servicing a particular faculty (such as the science departments or even just the physics department). Many different types, sizes, and collections are found in academic libraries, and some Academic Librarians are specialists in these collections, archives, and fields of knowledge.

The number and level of degrees granted by an academic institution greatly impact its library development as well as the extent to which the institution emphasizes the creation of new knowledge. While all colleges/universities are engaged in disseminating knowledge, some support cutting-edge research, which demands a far different library collection and library service than does just supporting beginning learners. Researchers at the forward boundary of their specialty need to know everything possible about their area of expertise, including what has happened in just the last five minutes. This requires very specialized sources of information for not just the general discipline (say physics), but also for the narrow subdiscipline within which a scholar is working. These focused needs greatly impact the academic library and the librarian. On the other hand, lower-level undergraduates are just learning about their discipline and some of its basic vocabulary and concepts. They need much more fundamental information, and the

Academic Librarian who services their information needs must have a much smaller but tailored collection of research materials (books, periodicals, and Internet resources).

Academic libraries at universities or colleges may require their librarians to have a position on the faculty. In those cases, the university or college may stipulate that the library faculty meet the institution's requirements for promotion and tenure, which usually includes continuation of their formal education, research, publishing, and service components. (Faculty appointment brings additional benefits such as vacation, retirement plans, health and life insurance, and tuition remission.) Whatever the type of academic library, Academic Librarians usually work side by side with paraprofessionals and student workers.

Librarians in academic settings often focus on instruction, such as teaching students how to analyze and synthesize data. Through group classes and tutoring sessions, they help students hone their research skills. As such, Academic Librarians must keep up to date with the latest technological advances in storage, research, and retrieval of library materials in a wide variety of media formats. Most Academic Librarians are also involved in collection development that must be relevant to the special needs of their type of library. Thus, they must be completely familiar with the curricula of their institutions, the types of classroom assignments given, and the courses students are required to take. To keep aware of curriculum changes, Academic Librarians must maintain close faculty ties, particularly with heads of departments, often through the establishment of faculty-library committees.

Academic Librarians usually work in several areas or, at the least, rotate through several areas during the academic year. Academic librarianship consists of public and technical services, instruction, collection development, and library automation. The size of operations may vary from a one-person branch operation to a major research facility, and the focus may range from undergraduate students to research professors.

College library staffs generally tend to be much smaller than those of university libraries. College libraries are usually staffed by five to 10 Academic Librarian professionals, who are supported by clerical and student personnel. University libraries usually require more staff members, often highly specialized (in discipline and/or information-retrieval expertise), to acquire, process, and disseminate the information contained in much larger collections, which can range from several hundred thousand volumes to millions of volumes (as well as voluminous electronic information resources).

These larger libraries may be staffed by as few as 25 and as many as 100 or more professional, associate, technical, and clerical personnel who are supported by sometimes hundreds of student helpers. In addition, university libraries generally have large collections in almost every subject area, whereas college libraries tend to concentrate on the general arts and sciences with a strong emphasis on humanities, social sciences, and the physical and biological sciences.

Salaries

Salaries for this post vary greatly depending on the specific job responsibilities and the type of academic library involved. According to the latest (2007) data from the American Library Association (ALA), salaries for Academic Librarians ranged from $22,048 (starting yearly salaries) to $225,000 (for highly experienced senior librarians). The median annual salary for Academic Librarians was $53,000.

Employment Prospects

Employment of Academic Librarians is expected to continue to grow steadily as technological advances continue to expand through the next decade. New positions, especially for accredited librarians with the requisite technical skills and background, will continue to be available. The increasing use of computerized information storage and retrieval systems within the academic library environment frees the Academic Librarian from the more mundane tasks (such as cataloging, which now can be handled by library technicians) to concentrate on the specific contribution that their academic library adds to the goals and philosophy of its parent institution.

In addition, Academic Librarians will always be needed to manage staff, help users of the library to develop database searching techniques, address complicated reference requests, and aid in defining users' needs.

Advancement Prospects

Opportunities for advancement vary according to the interests and expertise of individual Academic Librarians. Many can use their specialty backgrounds to develop the library's collection (along the guidelines of the needs of their parent institution), provide specialized services, or devote their career to the development of technical services or library automation. Some may decide to advance within the management structure of the library to such higher posts as chief librarian or library director, which entails both being the administrator of the library department but also being active in the council and administration of the university or college as a whole. The more experience, time, and additional education an individual has, the better the chances for advancement become.

Education and Training

A master of library science (M.L.S.) or a master of library and information science (M.L.I.S.) degree from a graduate program accredited by the American Library Association (ALA) is a basic required professional degree for employment as an Academic Librarian. Many colleges and universities also require Academic Librarians to have an additional advanced degree (master's or Ph.D.) in a particular subject area of importance to the institution. Most librarians who have faculty status are required to have a Ph.D. in their specialty.

Special Requirements

Some states require a state certification (based on the educational degree of the individual) for Academic Librarians at their state-run educational institutions.

Experience, Skills, and Personality Traits

Academic Librarians must have leadership abilities and be able to manage a diverse staff of professional, paraprofessional, clerical, and student personnel. They need to have particularly strong communication and interpersonal skills, the ability to work within a team environment, good technical proficiency, and an understanding of the complex issues facing libraries and higher education. They must be familiar with all aspects of librarianship, from reference work to technical services. Experience in teaching and knowledge of Web development and technical advances in information retrieval are also key. Flexibility in adjusting to change and a service orientation are important. Their administrative duties in making their libraries more productive, innovative, and entrepreneurial in developing information-literate students are primary, and their skills in accomplishing these goals are critical to their success.

Unions and Associations

At some universities, Academic Librarians are tenured members of the faculty. At other institutions, they are unionized. They also can belong to a variety of trade associations that provide educational guidance, support, conferences, and information to their members. Such associations include the American Library Association (ALA), the Association of College and Research Libraries (ACRL), and the Library Administration and Management Association (LAMA). The latter two are divisions of the ALA.

Tips for Entry

1. While studying for your degree, work in an academic library, even as an unpaid intern or volunteer. Internships at well-known libraries, such as the Library of Congress and the National Library of Medicine, may lead to a future job (and add experience in your given field of expertise).
2. College placement services (and online job sites) can be great resources in finding a job. Check these venues for advice and job leads. Join various professional librarian organizations and online groups/blogs to keep in touch with other librarians you have met to provide a network to learn about job opportunities.
3. State and national library industry trade associations (such as the American Library Association [ALA], the American Society for Information Science and Technology [ASIS&T], the Council on Library/Media Technicians [COLT], the Medical Library Association [MLA], and the Special Libraries Association [SLA]), typically have free job information centers or placement services.
4. In looking for jobs on the Internet, beyond checking the Web sites of the professional associations already mentioned, also visit the Web site of the Association for Library and Information Science Education (ALISE). It has links to all library schools, each of which has state and national employment listings.
5. Check out the *American Library Directory*, which lists a wide variety of libraries, or look at the *Guide to Employment Sources in the Library and Information Professions*, which is available online at the American Library Association (ALA) Web site.

ARCHIVIST

CAREER PROFILE

Duties: Assess, buy and collect, organize, preserve, maintain control over, and provide access to information determined to be of value and to be used by the library or institution in exhibitions, publications, and educational programs

Alternate Title(s): Archival Manager; Archives Director; Collections Manager or Director; Historical Manuscript Curator; Manuscripts Curator; Museum Archivist; Records Manager

Salary Range: $29,000 to $51,000

Employment Prospects: Fair to good

Advancement Prospects: Fair to good

Prerequisites:

Education or Training—Both a bachelor's degree in English language and literature or history and a master's degree in archival science, history, library science, or library and information science usually required; Ph.D. degree in library science or library and information science is recommended

Experience—Work as an intern, volunteer, or part-time worker in a museum or archive for one to two years

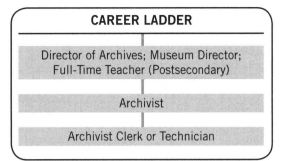

CAREER LADDER

Director of Archives; Museum Director; Full-Time Teacher (Postsecondary)

Archivist

Archivist Clerk or Technician

Special Skills and Personality Traits—Basic knowledge of document and artifact conservation; detail oriented; excellent research and computer skills; forward looking and technologically proficient; good communication and interpersonal skills; logical and organized in work activities

Special Requirements—Certification is available from the Academy of Certified Archivists (ACA) and sometimes may be a requirement

Position Description

An Archivist is a professional who assesses, collects, organizes, preserves, supervises, and provides access to information determined to have long-term value. Data maintained by an Archivist can be of any type of media (including documents, electronic records, letters, photographs, and video or sound recordings). Determining what materials have enduring value is not always an easy task. Archivists must select items valuable enough to justify the costs of storage and preservation as well as the labor-intensive expenses of arrangement, description (cataloging), and reference service.

Archivists' duties include acquiring and appraising new collections, arranging and describing data records, monitoring and maintaining a current inventory of all archived documents, data records, computer hardware and/or electronic media used onsite, providing reference services to users of archived items, and the active preservation of materials. In arranging the collection, Archivists apply two main principles: provenance and original order. Provenance refers to the origin of the material being archived, essentially who created the material and when. Order refers to keeping the recorded materials in their original chronological sequence as established and maintained by the creator(s). This also means that data records from one corporate body should not be mixed with records from another. However, original order is not always the best way to maintain some collections, and Archivists must use their own experience and knowledge of current best practices to determine a correct way to keep a collection of, say, mixed media or a collection lacking a clear original arrangement.

Archivists are also guided in their work by a code of ethics. Alongside their work behind the scenes arranging and caring for collections, Archivists assist users in interpreting collections and answering their inquiries. This reference work may be just part of an Archivist's job in a smaller organization, or it may be the major part of his or her occupation in a larger archive (where the specific tasks of processing and referencing may be handled by separate individuals).

Archivists analyze documents, such as government records, minutes of corporate board meetings, letters of famous persons, and charters of nonprofit foundations by ascertaining date of writing, author(s), or original recipient to appraise the material's value to posterity or to the entity employing the archivist to organize the material. In their work, Archivists direct the activities of workers engaged in the cataloging and safekeeping (preservation) of materials and prepare (or direct the preparation of) document descriptions and reference aids for use of the archives, such as abstracts, accession lists, bibliographies, guides, indexes, and microfilmed (or scanned to online) copies of documents. They direct the filing and cross-indexing of archived materials and establish, write, and administer policy guidelines concerning public access and use of materials. They also frequently are required to transfer information from one medium to another, such as transferring written information into a digital format.

Archivists are engaged by a variety of organizations, including government agencies, local authorities, museums, hospitals, historical societies, businesses, charities, corporations, colleges and universities—basically, any institution whose records may potentially be of value to researchers, exhibitors, genealogists, or others. Alternatively, Archivists may also work on the collection of a large family or a single individual. Often, they may be educators as well. Some universities and colleges use Archivists to lecture on a subject related to their archived collection(s). Archivists employed at cultural institutions or for local government organizations frequently design educational or outreach programs to further the ability of archive users to understand and access information within the collection. These activities might also include managing exhibitions, promotional events, and even media coverage.

Salaries

According to a salary survey report on Archivists done by PayScale, Inc., in 2007, median annual salaries (other than those for government archivists, who usually have the highest salaries) ranged from $30,000 to $55,000 or more, with starting yearly salaries usually ranging from $22,000 to $25,000.

Employment Prospects

While applications for archives jobs sometimes outnumber the positions available, there still is an ongoing need for trained professional Archivists in businesses, charities, corporations, historical societies, hospitals, museums, historical societies, and other institutions whose records and documents are deemed valuable.

The U.S. Department of Labor's Bureau of Labor Statistics estimates that the projected growth of employment for Archivists through 2014 will be between 10 and 20 percent, which is about average for employment growth overall during that same period.

Advancement Prospects

Many archives are very small and have limited opportunities for advancement. Archivists in such situations usually advance by transferring to a larger archive. Larger facilities provide opportunities to work as a supervisor, managing people and multiple collections. Depending on their field of specialty, some Archivists may decide to concentrate their careers on teaching at a college or university or on the administration of an established archive as a director of archives. Archivists within a museum environment may trade upon their knowledge of the museum's holdings to advance into the administration of that institution.

Education and Training

Typically, Archivists need an American Library Association (ALA)–accredited master of library science (M.L.S.) degree, a master of archival administration (M.A.A.) degree, a master of archival science/studies (M.A.S.) degree, or a master of history (or another related humanities field) degree with an emphasis on archival administration. In addition, many archival positions require extensive technological knowledge in order for the Archivist to create Internet-accessible collections and referencing aids.

Knowledge of archival descriptive practices often required of Archivists include USMARC (United States standard for machine readable cataloging) and electronic access tools such as Hypertext Markup Language (HTML, used to structure text and multimedia documents and to set up hypertext links between documents), Encoded Archival Description (EAD), and Standard Generalized Markup Language (SGML).

Special Requirements

Certification as an Archivist may be a requirement for some positions. The Academy of Certified Archivists offers supplemental archival training within their certification program. This program, however, does have yearly membership fees, with members required to recertify every five years. Some states require a certification in the form of an M.L.S. degree.

Experience, Skills, and Personality Traits

Archivists who work in reference and access-oriented posts need to have excellent interpersonal and communication skills in order to assist individuals with their research. Because of the amount of sorting and listing of materials and documents, Archivists have to be very logical, well organized, and able to pay extremely close attention to detail. They should have research skills to aid them when cataloging records or when assisting users. They may need to have a background in historical research to help them in selecting materials to be archived.

In addition, an ability to apply basic knowledge of conservation (preservation) of documents and artifacts is needed. Many different types of media (such as photographs, acidic papers, and unstable copy processes) can deteriorate unless stored and maintained properly. While many archival collections consist of paper records, increasingly Archivists must confront the new challenges posed by the preservation of electronic records, so they need to be forward looking and technologically proficient.

Unions and Associations

Many Archivists belong to a professional organization, such as the Society of American Archivists (SAA) or the American Society for Information Science and Technology (ASIS&T), besides joining professional associations that deal with their particular specialty, such as the American Historical Society (AHS).

Tips for Entry

1. While completing your master's degree, gain work experience as an Archivist by volunteering or working as an intern at a local museum, genealogical society, or historical society.

2. Both course work in computer science and practical experience with the development of Web sites using HTML and EAD programming tools should prove valuable in obtaining employment in today's electronically oriented environment.

3. Include both social science and communication courses in your college studies, as these skills will be essential in your career as an Archivist.

4. Look for job opportunities posted on the Society of American Archivists' online employment bulletin (http://www.archivists.org/employment/index.asp).

5. Jobs in most federal libraries require that you establish your civil service eligibility. Contact the U.S. government's Office of Personnel Management (OPM) at http://www.usajobs.opm.gov for help.

ASSISTANT LIBRARY DIRECTOR

Duties: Assist the Library Director with hiring and training of staff, maintain the facility, plan for new equipment or renovations to library facilities, attend meetings, scheduling, budgeting, and supervise public relations

Alternate Title(s): Associate Library Director; Head Librarian; Library Administrator; Library Manager

Salary Range: $30,000 to $85,000 or more

Employment Prospects: Good

Advancement Prospects: Good

Prerequisites:

Education and Training—Bachelor's degree in the social sciences, public administration, or a related field plus a master's degree in library science (M.L.S.) or in library and information science (M.L.I.S.) is usually required

Experience—Six or more years of increasingly responsible professional librarianship experience, including administration, adult and children's programs, budgeting, community relations, employee

CAREER LADDER

Library Director
Assistant Library Director
Librarian; Supervising Librarian

supervision, reference services, resource acquisitions, and technical resources

Special Skills and Personality Traits—Analytic skills; demonstrated administrative and supervisory abilities; excellent computer proficiency; good verbal and written communication talents; great interpersonal abilities; substantial knowledge of the principles and practices of library science and the provision of library services to specialized patron groups, such as children, students, and unsophisticated or nonusers of library facilities

Position Description

Under the general supervision of the library director, the Assistant Library Director has the broad responsibility for the administration and management of all the system-wide support areas of the library as well as those of any branch libraries and departments. These task areas include administration, technology support, and assistance with maintaining and building the library's collection(s). Management encompasses developing short- and long-range planning, overseeing staff and coordination of budget preparation as well as presenting justifications for budget requests and monitoring expenditures, interpreting library policies and procedures and providing staff with advice and assistance about same, monitoring the staff personnel evaluation system, participating in and leading task forces and special projects, and assisting the library director in accomplishing library administrative and management goals.

Technology support includes management and coordination of library technology; developing short- and long-range planning to ensure that the library does not fall behind on future technology (including new media and software); and planning for existing and future staffing, equipment, and materials needs. Collection support takes in management and coordination of collection development, cataloging, processing, and receiving procedures; overseeing presentation of budget requests and their justification for collection expansion; monitoring budget expenditures; and assisting in bid specification preparation and bid proposal evaluations for library materials contracts.

In addition, Assistant Library Directors coordinate and implement special programs and displays as well as coordinate and supervise interdepartmental activities and projects. They gather data and perform statistical analyses for the library director to assist in short- and long-range planning. They oversee building maintenance and housekeeping requests. They may also fill in on the reference desk or assist patrons.

In addition, Assistant Library Directors perform public relations duties and have fundraising tasks. They may coordinate operations and projects with library divisions and other city departments and library groups. They may be asked to represent the library director at state, regional, and national professional organizational meetings and conferences. In academic libraries, they may work closely with campus trustees and faculty on matters concerning collection and funding. Assistant Library Directors act on behalf of the library director during the latter's absences and perform related duties as assigned by the library director.

Salaries

Salaries for this position vary depending on the size and location of the library and the depth of the responsibilities of the position. According to PayScale, Inc.'s, salary survey report (updated in October 2007) for this post, median annual salaries ranged from $32,028 to $77,965. Generally, the average yearly salary for Assistant Library Directors ranges from $40,000 to $45,000.

Employment Prospects

Opportunities for employment as Assistant Library Directors remain good for experienced librarians as technological advancements open new opportunities in academic, public, and special libraries. Librarians who have the technological skills and have gained experience in the various aspects of library science, including reference techniques, collection development, readers' advisement, cataloging and classification, and online services have the best potential for advancement.

Advancement Prospects

After gaining experience applying the principles and practices of library science to the reality of working within a library and after acquiring the administrative and supervisory experience involved in carrying out the position as Assistant Library Director, the logical next career step is to move into a directorship of a library. Assistant Library Directors who pursue further education and technical advancement will find many opportunities to move into the higher administrative post. Such promotions usually come after Assistant Library Directors have demonstrated their management and supervisory skills and their knowledge of library automation and have pursued additional training.

Education and Training

Most academic and public library positions require a master's degree in library science (M.L.S.) or in library and information science (M.L.I.S.), preferably from a school or university accredited by the American Library Association (ALA). While undergraduate degrees in almost any subject area are appropriate, it is highly recommended that such a degree be earned in social science or business and/or public administration. Several years of experience as a librarian in all aspects of library practice is typically necessary, as is some administrative or supervisory experience.

Experience, Skills, and Personality Traits

Assistant Library Directors must have a thorough knowledge of modern library organizations, procedures, policies, aims, and services as well as a meticulous grounding in the principles and practices of library science. They need a substantial knowledge of the applications of computer technology to library operations and a good understanding of library administration practices. They must have solid oral and written communication abilities with both individuals and groups. Their supervisory and training talents must be exemplary, and they must be able to plan, coordinate, and supervise the work of other staff. They should have knowledge of public service management theories and practice; strategic planning using goals and objectives; staff development methods; time management, organizational skills; community relations; and publicity, promotion, and marketing techniques. They must have good research skills and effective analytical abilities. They need to be able to exercise leadership in dealing with both staff and the public.

Unions and Associations

Assistant Library Directors often belong to a variety of trade organizations that provide educational guidance, conferences, and information. Such groups include the American Library Association (ALA), the American Society of Information Science and Technology (ASIS&T), the Association for Library Collections and Technical Services (ALCTS), the Association of Records Managers and Administrators (ARMA), and the Library Administration and Management Association (LAMA).

Tips for Entry

1. During your undergraduate education, include courses in both business administration and psychology, as these will be useful in your duties as Assistant Library Director.
2. Join professional organizations to gain support and knowledge about your library administrative duties, and learn about job opportunities.
3. Attend library conventions or conferences and check job boards and placement services that list library-related positions. In addition, in your search as a librarian for a higher administrative position, check out the *American Library Directory* or the *Guide to Employment Sources in the Library and Information Professions* (available online at http://www.ala.org/ala/hrdr/libraryemp resources/employmentguide05.htm).

BIBLIOGRAPHER

Duties: Help develop a library's collections in support of the library's goals or, if an academic library, in support of the research and curricula interests of the educational institution of which it is a part

Alternate Title(s): Subject Specialist

Salary Range: $25,000 to $50,000 or more

Employment Prospects: Fair to good

Advancement Prospects: Fair

Prerequisites:

Education or Training—Bachelor's degree and a master's degree in library science (M.L.S.) or in library and information science (M.L.I.S.) are required; in some instances, a master's degree or a doctorate degree in the specialty field of Bibliographer may be required as well

Experience—Basic knowledge of and experience with the bibliographic process and collection development policies; demonstrated successful reference and instructional library experience; some acquaintance with statistical analysis (to aid in control of the collection and to devise reports in support of collection development policies)

CAREER LADDER

```
Senior Bibliographer; Collections
Development Librarian; Systems
Librarian
            |
      Bibliographer
            |
Reference Assistant; Technical Assistant;
Acquisitions Technician
```

Special Skills and Personality Traits—Ability to adapt to rapidly changing library environment; detail oriented; excellent research skills; good communication and computer skills; knowledge of electronic and traditional information processes and sources; public service orientation

Special Requirements—No certification beyond an M.L.S or M.L.I.S. degree usually demanded

Position Description

Bibliographers are subject specialists. This includes both area and language specialists. They help develop libraries' collections in support of the libraries' goals or in support of the research and instructional missions of the university or college to which the facilities belong. They accomplish these tasks through making recommendations for purchase, the identification of special acquisition opportunities, and interaction with donors. They may decide questions of selection, development, and management on their own (as in public libraries) or in consultation with faculty, both individually and officially, with departmental library liaisons and chairpersons, through students, and with the library director (as in academic libraries).

Generally, Bibliographers are not expected to have the depth of knowledge of a field or fields necessary for faculty teaching in that area. As a generalist, however, a Bibliographer is expected to strive for a balanced view of a specific discipline while responding to specific academic needs and interests or with the wants and

interests of the public library's customers and goals. Based on their subject knowledge, familiarity with the specific collection, and an awareness of the university's (or college's) curriculum, programs, and research needs that the library supports, Bibliographers are responsible for developing and implementing a collection management strategy that will best meet user needs within the framework of the library's goals, priorities, and available resources. This responsibility involves collection evaluation, monitoring the use of the collection, checking the preservation needs of material within the collection, and bibliographic control (designed to provide information about the organization of and methods of access to the collection). As a part of helping users attain access to materials that best satisfy their needs, Bibliographers frequently prepare bibliographies or other guides to the contents of their collection as well as user guides for physical access.

In the pursuit of their job responsibilities, Bibliographers must have a thorough ongoing knowledge of the specific collection(s). They must maintain a current awareness of the curricular, programmatic, research, and other user needs relating to the collection(s). They usually are responsible for monitoring and allocating individual budgets for the collection(s) as well as developing and implementing (under the guidance of the collections development director/librarian) collection development policies, programs, and procedures. They work with the library's acquisition services to establish and monitor gathering and collecting plans appropriate for specific subject areas and to maintain effective vendor and donor relations.

With the advent of automated collection processes (such as the one linking academic libraries in Ohio to a new kind of library consortium, known as OhioLINK, or OL [http://www.ohiolink.edu]), the role of Bibliographers is enhanced, but it also forces them to revise fundamentally their understanding of their job. With such systems, collection mapping becomes as, or more, important than collection building. In a true virtual library (such as that envisioned by OL), collection materials all in one place becomes less important than knowing where all the needed materials are located. In addition, rather than the traditional need to cover all areas needed for the local library's research and instruction requirements, Bibliographers in such a special consortium focus on maintaining a core in-depth collection with narrowly defined specialty areas related to the specific research needs of their institutions. Access that will cover the full subject needs are met by the collections of other libraries in the consortium (some of which may be accessible electronically, while others may be available through interlibrary loan). Thus, a critical new task for Bibliographers is not just to map the consortium collection but also to ensure that research material desired to supplement the core collection is accessible and available. These responsibilities involve keeping up with coordinated collection development groups, serial cancellation projects, commercial information services, and resource-sharing agreements. Finally, Bibliographers involved in such a consortium need to provide ongoing education and training in technical areas to library staff and be able to explain this "virtual" library to faculty, students, and any other users of the library.

Even when not involved in such a consortium, it is recommended that Bibliographers set up a Web page that will supplement their library collection by linking with supplementary resources. Examples of such links would be association pages, outstanding Web sites in the subject area, and specialized library catalogs. This enhanced technical expertise on the part of Bibliographers extends to both the public and academic library environment.

Furthermore, they may be responsible for helping students and other users learn how to use effectively the library's collections and services. In academic libraries, Bibliographers may serve on committees; hold leadership positions within the library and the general academic community; conduct research; publish; and actively participate in the work of academic, professional, and community service organizations. Some Bibliographers have a direct obligation for allocating, expending, and monitoring the budget(s) for their area(s) of responsibility. Most Bibliographers are responsible for evaluating the strengths and weaknesses of a collection to verify the effectiveness of collection development policies or to identify areas for retrospective development.

Salaries

Salaries for Bibliographers vary according to the depth and variety of their responsibilities as well as the size of the collection for which they are accountable. Annual earnings may range from $20,000 to $50,000 or more. Experienced Bibliographers may have a yearly income as high as $80,000.

Employment Prospects

Bibliographers are essential to the working process of a library and, thus, are in demand in academic, government, institutional, and public libraries. Many positions will open up when an existing Bibliographer leaves, resigns, or otherwise becomes unable to continue bibliographic duties. In addition, as businesses expand their research needs and seek to build their company information resources, the need of a Bibliographer will become apparent. Governmental bibliographic needs are usually fulfilled by promotion from within a given department or organization. Some Bibliographers advance from technical or assistant positions in a library after earning an advanced degree in their subject area. In other instances, librarians within the system may be asked to serve as a Bibliographer, or a librarian may volunteer to take on bibliographic responsibilities.

Advancement Prospects

Bibliographers of smaller institutions may advance their careers by moving to larger businesses or governmental agencies or organizations or by transferring from the public library sector to a larger academic library. Some may advance further into a higher library management position, such as collections development manager, or use their technological expertise to become systems librarians.

Education and Training

Educational qualifications for becoming a subject Bibliographer may be filled in a variety of ways. Besides the basic master's degree in library science (M.L.S.) or in library and information science (M.L.I.S.), an advanced degree in their subject area is generally preferred, but other education and experience may be acceptable. The basic knowledge of the bibliographic process, which is an important part of the educational process to gain a librarianship degree, generally transfers well from one discipline to another. Bibliographers in academic libraries may be required to be members of the academic faculty, in which case they may have to meet the institution's requirements for promotion and tenure, which usually includes additional formal education, research, and publishing.

Special Requirements

Some states require a state certification as a librarian, but usually the achievement of an M.L.S. or an M.L.I.S. degree, along with an advanced degree in the area of specialty for the librarian, is sufficient.

Experience, Skills, and Personality Traits

Bibliographers must have a basic knowledge of and experience with the bibliographic process and collection development policies in general. They should be able to demonstrate successful reference and instructional library experience. Their computer skills must be excellent, and they need to have some acquaintance with statistical analysis procedures (as a means of analyzing collection usage). They must be detail oriented, have excellent communication and research abilities, and be knowledgeable in both electronic and traditional information processes. They also should exhibit a strong public service orientation.

Unions and Associations

Most Bibliographers find it obligatory to belong to the Bibliographical Society of America (BSA), which is the only scholarly society in the United States whose primary focus is the study of books and manuscripts as physical objects. In addition, like most librarians, Bibliographers should belong to the American Library Association (ALA). They may also want to join the American Society for Information Science and Technology (ASIS&T), the Modern Language Association (MLA), or the Special Libraries Association (SLA).

Tips for Entry

1. While earning your master's degree in library science, volunteer (or seek an internship) at a library, public or academic, to gain practical experience.
2. During your internship or volunteer work, ask to work at the circulation desk to perfect your people skills in dealing with users of the library.
3. Take computer courses to gain knowledge of information processing systems that you will have to use in your work as a Bibliographer.

CATALOGER

CAREER PROFILE

Duties: Describe (list) library materials (usually in computerized catalogs) by author, title, and subject or keyword so library users can easily identify material they want to see

Alternate Title(s): Catalog Librarian; Descriptive Catalog Librarian

Salary Range: $30,000 to $57,000 or more

Employment Prospects: Good

Advancement Prospects: Good

Prerequisites:

Education and Training—Master's degree in library science (M.L.S.) or in library and information science (M.L.I.S.) required; a second master's degree in another subject desirable

Experience—Previous experience as a volunteer or intern in a library, archive, or museum is helpful

Special Skills and Personality Traits—Ability to work independently; capacity for formulating and communicating complex verbal and written procedures; excellent verbal and written communication skills; foreign language proficiency; good interpersonal skills and presentation abilities; meticulous and logical in work habits; well organized

Special Requirements—Some states require certification for librarians working in public schools and local libraries

CAREER LADDER

Cataloger in Larger Public or Academic Library; Director of Cataloging Services

Cataloger

Assistant Cataloger; Entry-Level Librarian

Position Description

A Cataloger, or catalog librarian, compiles information on library materials in all bibliographic formats (books, monographs, serials, periodicals, other documents, electronic resources, videos, DVDs, CD-ROMs, microforms, and other items) and prepares cards (or computer records) to identify these materials and to integrate this information into a library catalog so that staff and library patrons can locate the material available in the library. Catalogers verify author, title, and classification number on sample catalog cards prepared by library assistants (known as classifiers) against the corresponding data on the title page, table of contents, or other document information. Catalogers then fill in additional information, such as the presence of bibliographies, illustrations, maps, and appendixes (if a book) or serial information (if a periodical) and describe the material by subject covered, date published (or produced), format, and other physical characteristics of the item. Thus, a record (card or computer entry) is completed for the material, providing a shelf address or location in the library for each book, CD, video, periodical, or other item as well as providing specific data about the material for the library holdings files (catalog files or a database of computer records).

In classifying library materials, Catalogers describe materials by subject, date published, format, author, title, and other characteristics (depending on the type of collection in which the material will reside). Cataloging, however, is not always so straightforward. Catalogers must make constant distinctions and decisions about materials, such as whether to group maps in a separate location or list them, instead, in the library's general card (or online) catalog. Two types of cataloging take place for each item. *Descriptive cataloging* describes the physical characteristics of a book, video, CD, data file, or other type of item. *Subject cataloging* focuses on identifying the primary subject or subjects and then assigns the best subject headings and classification number to reflect this.

Catalogers have traditionally recorded all the information on cards that were maintained in card files. Today, most Catalogers use computerized database retrieval systems. After classification numbers (usually known as call numbers) are assigned to the material (typically by technical assistants), Catalogers determine the subject headings for the material and provide descriptive information on each item, which then is entered into the library's database, known as an OPAC (online public access catalog). This database provides a master inventory of the library's holdings and allows library users to search the automated catalog, whether on or off site.

The two most common classification systems in use are LC and Dewey decimal. LC evolved from the original organizing scheme that Thomas Jefferson, third president of the United States, used for his own book collection before selling it to the new national library (now known as the Library of Congress). This alpha-numeric system is in use at most large libraries (public and academic) and many smaller specialized libraries (such as those at research facilities). Melvin Dewey's decimal-based scheme was introduced in 1876 and remains the standard among many public and school libraries. There are other more specialized classification schemes, such as the SuDocs (Superintendent of Documents) system, which is employed for large government document collections. This scheme divides a collection into subgroups of documents based on the agency that issued (or produced) the item.

The automation of library bibliographic records began with the invention of the MARC (machine-readable catalog) record. MARC records are a standard method of recording and sharing information about a bibliographic item. By using standard content designators, the information is stored electronically and can be retrieved and interpreted by any other computer that is programmed to read MARC records. The MARC record can contain all the information displayed in a library's OPAC as well as other information about the item that may prove useful to librarians. Once a library has cataloged a book or another real or virtual bibliographic item and has coded the resulting cataloging data into MARC format, this data can be passed on to other libraries and read by their cataloging software. This allows libraries to acquire cataloging data from the Library of Congress and other libraries or library networks (such as the Online Computer Library Center [OCLC of Ohio], the Western Library Network [WLN], or the Research Libraries Information Network [RLIN]) without repeating the labor-intensive effort of original cataloging by its own Catalogers. While the MARC format was originally developed by the Library of Congress, it has quickly evolved into the international standard for exchanging bibliographic data.

Catalogers search bibliographic databases to determine the relationship of materials in their library to existing bibliographic records. They apply cataloging rules to characterize the item, describe its subject content, and establish or modify personal names, corporate names, uniform title(s), series and subject headings, access points, and classification and content designa-

tion. In academic libraries, Catalogers need to work intensively with bibliographers to learn on what topics faculty and students (in academic libraries) or library patrons (in public libraries) are working and then design workflows that will make these material available as quickly as needed. They may participate in collection development, prepare and provide statistical and other reports to library administration, assist in the preparation and implementation of cataloging procedures and documentation, take part in liaison activities with the faculty, and serve on committees within the library and the educational institution.

While Catalogers seldom have much interaction on the job with the public, they must work with acquisitions staff to answer questions about what is being ordered for the library or what has been received and where to shelve it, as well as work with preservation staff to handle items that are fragile or material damaged in transit. They confer with other Catalogers about tricky cataloging situations and work with them and technicians in planning and implementing priorities and strategies. They may also recommend changes or additions in descriptive and subject cataloging rules. The sheer volume of their tasks can be overwhelming as materials often come into a public or academic library far faster than they can be cataloged. Thus, this type of library job can be highly stressful.

Salaries

According to the 2007 salary survey reports on the library field compiled by PayScale, Inc., annual salaries for Catalogers range from $30,000 to $60,000 or more, with median salaries ranging from $37,000 to $56,000. For Catalogers working for the federal government, the median yearly salary was found to be $76,475, and law firms had a higher median salary ($64,098) than most other employers.

Employment Prospects

While employment of librarians is expected to grow more slowly than the average for all occupations through 2014 (according the U.S. Department of Labor's Bureau of Labor Statistics), job opportunities are expected to be very good because a large number of librarians (including Catalogers) are expected to retire in the coming decade. Although the availability of cataloging information from sources other than a library's Cataloger makes it possible for many cataloging tasks to be carried out by technical assistants, there is always a need for original cataloging. Computerized catalogs allow patrons to search for material by author, title, subject, or keyword. Since these patrons are now able to conduct these searches from home, the necessity of correct cataloging is even more crucial. As Richard A. Murray (catalog librarian for Spanish & Portuguese Languages at Duke University) points out (in his 2002 article *The Whimsy of Cataloging*), "Even though the things we catalog and the methods we use are changing in the digital age, the basic concepts of organizing and providing access to information will always be in demand."

Advancement Prospects

Experienced Catalogers can advance to larger libraries or special libraries (for Catalogers with particular areas of expertise). They can also move up to supervisory or management posts either in cataloging or in other areas of the library or at other public, private, academic, or museum facilities. Additionally, they can apply their methodical and analytical skills to other fields, such as bibliography or history. Promotions for Catalogers usually come with experience and the display of administrative abilities, demonstrated knowledge of automated systems, and additional training.

Education and Training

Catalogers need a master's degree in library science or in library and information studies, along with a bachelor's degree in the humanities, English, or general arts. Catalogers should supplement their studies with courses in computers and business. Many libraries offer additional on-the-job training to teach the specifics of cataloging and the use of computer technology in cataloging. It is also highly recommended that prospective Catalogers volunteer with a library, archive, or museum to gain experience within the field.

Catalogers in school libraries usually need a bachelor's degree in education and courses in library and information science. Some schools require an M.L.S. degree with a focus in school library media. Other schools may require a master's degree in education with a focus in school library or educational media.

Special Requirements

Some states require licensing of librarians (including Catalogers) as both teachers and school librarians in order to work within a school system.

Experience, Skills, and Personality Traits

Catalogers must have a command of cataloging and organizational theory. Computer proficiency is a neces-

sity and Catalogers should be familiar with ongoing trends in information technology. They must have excellent interpersonal, analytical, and communication skills, both oral and written. They should have a demonstrable ability to work collaboratively and have some experience functioning on committees or teams. They must be able to assess new and emerging technologies for the delivery of library services and have an awareness of (inter)national trends and developments in cataloging, metadata standards, and information methods. They need to be heavily detail oriented and should enjoy research and be able to work independently in a systematic manner. It is recommended that they have a reading knowledge of at least one foreign language and have some skills in special knowledge areas.

Unions and Associations

Catalogers working in either public, academic, special, or school libraries may belong to a variety of trade associations that provide support, conferences, educational guidance, and information to their members. Such organizations include the American Library Association (ALA), the American Association of School Librarians (AASL), the American Society for Information Science and Technology (ASIS&T), the Association for Library Collections and Technical Services (ALCTS), the Association of College and Research Libraries (ACRL), the Association of Research Libraries (ARL), and the Special Libraries Association (SLA).

Tips for Entry

1. While attending library school, take every opportunity to work as a student assistant in the campus library, do a practicum (course of study devoted to practical experience) or internship in another library, or volunteer in the cataloging department of the library.
2. Join professional organizations for librarians and keep in touch with library and information science associates by networking, through which you may learn about job opportunities.
3. Subscribe to the major library trade publications, such as *Library Journal* and *American Libraries*, as well as targeted online newsletters and blogs.
4. Attend library conventions or conferences and check their job boards and network with other catalog and reference librarians.

CHIEF LIBRARIAN

Duties: Coordinate activities of a library branch or department; train and direct library assistants in their tasks; assist in selection and purchasing of material for library; aid patrons in selection and location of books, audiovisual materials, and other items; manage technology employed at the library

Alternate Title(s): Principal Librarian; Public Librarian; Senior Librarian; Senior Manager or Supervision Librarian; University Librarian

Salary Range: $30,000 to $80,000 or more

Employment Prospects: Good

Advancement Prospects: Good

Prerequisites:

Education and Training—Master's degree in library science (M.L.S.) or library and information science (M.L.I.S.)

Experience—Student internship or volunteer experience in a library is highly recommended

Special Skills and Personality Traits—Ability to delegate professional assignments to subordinates and evaluate their work; attention to detail; com-

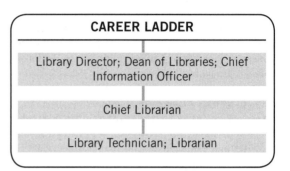

CAREER LADDER

Library Director; Dean of Libraries; Chief Information Officer

Chief Librarian

Library Technician; Librarian

puter proficiency; excellent interpersonal and communication abilities; familiarity and experience in the use of technical location and access services and ability to use and integrate new technologies into the library; organizational talents

Special Requirements—Most states require that senior librarian staff employed in municipal, county, or regional library systems be certified; in addition, librarians working within a state university system usually must be certified by the state

Position Description

Chief Librarians (as senior supervising librarians) coordinate and manage the activities of a library branch or department and assist library patrons in the selection and location of books, audio and audiovisual materials, periodical and serial resources, and other library media. They train and supervise library support staff in the performance of such tasks as receiving, shelving, and locating materials. They may search catalog files, biographical dictionaries and indexes, and the content of reference materials to assist library patrons in locating and selecting information of interest to them. They aid them in using it effectively for their personal and/or professional purposes.

Chief Librarians usually manage the acquisitions budget, planning acquisitions in all topic areas consistent with the library holdings and goals. In so doing, they must follow trends in publishing, computer technology, and the media to oversee effectively the selection and organization of library materials. This commitment to their own continuing education includes their maintaining and expanding their knowledge of current local,

states, and federal events as well as contemporary societal themes.

The traditional idea of a library is in the process of being redefined from a place of access to books, periodicals, and research materials to one that also houses the most advanced technical media, including CD-ROMs, the Internet, virtual libraries, and remote access to a wide variety of online resources. Consequently, Chief Librarians and their staff must combine their traditional duties with work involving quickly changing technology that affects the ways they can provide service to library patrons. The most significant example of how technology has altered the role of librarians has been the move away from traditional card catalogs to online public access catalogs (OPACs). Not only did librarians have to develop the software and the machine-readable cataloging (MARC) standards for cataloging records electronically, they also had to purchase and run the computers necessary to operate the software; they also had to educate the public on how to use the new technologies and how to move to more virtual working environments. Other technology developments, from electronic databases (including the Internet) to logistical functions (such as bar codes or the newer radio frequency identification codes, or RFIDs), have impacted the workload of librarians—from Chief Librarians to all types of support staff. Many librarians now provide virtual reference services (via Web-based chat, instant messaging, text messaging, and e-mail), pursue digitalization initiatives for works in the public domain, teach technology classes to users, and participate in the development of information architectures for improving access and search functionality. Thus, Chief Librarians and the librarians they supervise are using ever-changing technology to fulfill and expand on their historical roles.

The position of Chief Librarian is a senior administrative post in public, academic, and governmental libraries. In state library systems, they may work in tandem with local government officials, library trustees, and librarians in acquiring state and federal aid, interpreting and applying state laws relating to public library administration, and identifying and coordinating programs of cooperative interlibrary projects. Within academic libraries, Chief Librarians (sometimes called *university librarians*) are responsible for the library within the college or university structure and may be called the dean of libraries. Some postsecondary institutions treat many librarians, including Chief Librarians, as faculty, and they may be called professors or have some other academic rank.

Salaries
According to PayScale, Inc. (in the salary survey report updated as of September 2007), median annual salaries for Chief Librarians ranged from $56,192 to $77,765 based on job location and type of employer. In their 2007 salary survey, the American Library Association-Allied Professional Association found that the annual salaries for senior management positions (which includes that of Chief Librarian) ranged from $31,366 to $104,000 in academic libraries and from $30,000 to $120,768 in public libraries. Median annual salaries were $42,584 and $57,374, respectively.

Employment Prospects
Although employment of librarians is expected to grow more slowly than the average for all occupations through 2014, according to the U.S. Department of Labor's Bureau of Labor Statistics, job opportunities are expected to be very good because a large number of librarians are expected to retire in the coming decade. More than three in five librarians are age 45 or older and will become eligible for retirement in the next 10 years.

Thus, librarians who have had experience in reference work, user services, technical services, and administrative services and have demonstrated information and people management skills will have the opportunity to advance to the higher-level administrative position as Chief Librarian, whether of a department in a large library (university or otherwise) or a branch library in a citywide or countywide library system.

Advancement Prospects
As head of a branch library or a department head, Chief Librarians can advance to becoming Chief Librarian of the library system. Those Chief Librarians in a senior position within a library system have only one avenue of advancement within library administration open to them, primarily to that of library director or chief information officer. Advancement opportunities tend to be better in larger library systems.

Education and Training
Most library positions require a master of library science (M.L.S.) or library and information science (M.L.I.S.) degree, preferably from a school accredited by the American Library Association (ALA). Undergraduate degrees in almost any subject are appropriate.

Most M.L.S. and M.L.I.S. programs take one to two years to complete. Computer-related coursework is a very important part of these degrees, and most programs offer interdisciplinary degrees combining technical coursework in information science and information delivery systems with traditional training in library science and procedures. Most librarians continue their training once they are employed in order to keep abreast of new information systems and other technology applicable to library work. Chief Librarians usually rise through the ranks of library administration and, as such, have had years of training and work as librarians in the various aspects of library work, from systems and acquisitions to cataloging and reference work.

Special Requirements
Many states require that public librarians employed in municipal, county, or regional library systems be certified. Academic librarians employed in state university systems usually also have to be certified. While specific requirements vary from state to state, generally graduates of an ALA-certified program can submit their applications to the state librarian based on their educational degree.

Experience, Skills, and Personality Traits
Chief Librarians must have extensive experience in supervision and administration and be able to use and

integrate new technologies into a library. They should be proficient in a modern computing environment (word processing, database management, spreadsheets, and so forth), including the use of Internet resources and Web content creation and management. In addition, they must have a thorough knowledge of the principles of library administration (public or academic) and of library techniques, systems, and procedures.

They must be able to delegate professional assignments to subordinates and evaluate their work and be able to establish and maintain effective working relationships with county and city administrators, librarians, department personnel, and library patrons. They must be able to speak and write effectively about library services and promote concepts of the high quality of such services. They should have demonstrated an ability to be a team player during their career as a librarian.

Chief Librarians must be highly organized, have a strong attention to detail, be well read, and have a love of books, research, and education. Above all, as service is the cornerstone of librarianship, they must be very people oriented and keep that orientation in the forefront of the long-range planning for library growth and expansion.

Unions and Associations

The primary trade associations for librarians are the American Library Association (ALA), the American Society for Information Science and Technology (ASIS&T), and the Special Libraries Association (SLA). They may also belong to associations specifically devised to provide educational guidance, support, conferences, and information to library administrative personnel, such as the Library Administration and Management Association (LAMA) and the Library and Information Technology Association (LITA) of the ALA.

Tips for Entry

1. While attending library school, take every opportunity to work as a student assistant in the college or university library. In addition, investigate doing a practicum (a course of study devoted to practical experience in the field) or internship in another library, or volunteer in the type of facility that interests you. Experience counts when library administrators are looking at your résumé.

2. Work at making contacts by joining various professional organizations for librarians, and keep in touch with them to provide a network through which you may hear of job opportunities and, later, with whom you may well work as a library administrator.

3. E-mail discussion groups such as LIBjobs and LISjobs are excellent sources for job postings. Also, check the job lines at the Web sites of the professional associations related to library work: the ALA, SLA, and ASIS&T.

4. Subscribe to the major library trade publications, *Library Journal* and *American Libraries*, to keep abreast of trends, new technologies, and potential administrative job openings, and read online newsletters and blogs devoted to librarianship.

CHILDREN'S LIBRARIAN

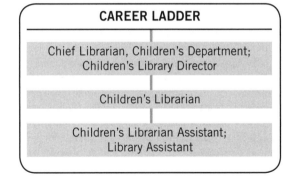

Position Description

Children's Librarians are responsible for the children's program for the libraries in elementary, middle, or high schools as well as those collections in public libraries. As experts in children's literature and books aimed at youngsters, they assist young patrons in selecting and locating appropriate library materials. They decide on books, audiovisual materials, and other items of interest to children to be acquired by the library. They plan and conduct programs for children to encourage reading, viewing, listening, and use of library materials and facilities. They confer with teachers, parents, and community groups to assist in developing programs to encourage and improve youngsters' communication skills. They compile lists of materials of interest to children and arrange attractive library displays. Their activities with children may include storytelling, book talks, puppet shows, and film and multimedia programs. In school libraries, Children's Librarians may also teach library and research skills and provide computer technology assistance.

Just as in adult public libraries, children's libraries have changed considerably over the past 15 years or so from an institution housing paper records and books to a center offering a full range of special media, such as CD-ROMs, computers, data files, films, DVDs, recordings, and other multimedia materials (such as video games). Thus, Children's Librarians also serve as information specialists, instructors, and program administrators in their development of appropriate strategies, programs, and teaching methods to promote the integration of all this relatively new technology into a school's curriculum and into the use patterns of the library.

Effective library service for children entails a broad range of experience and professional skills. The librarian serving children must be fully knowledgeable about the theories, practices, and emerging trends of librarianship and information retrieval but must also have a specialized understanding of the particular needs of child library users. The assignment of responsibilities for planning, managing, and delivering library services to children varies in relation to the size and staffing pattern of the school library or the local public library. Some libraries may have only one librarian responsible for providing all services to children; others will have more than one professional Children's Librarian sharing the duties. In larger public libraries with multiple outlets, there may be a coordinator or manager of children's services who oversees the planning, training, design, and delivery of services to children by a number of librarians.

The Association for Library Services for Children (ALSC) has recommended a set of competencies for librarians serving children in public libraries. These include (1) Understand theories of infant, child, and adolescent learning and development and their implications for library service; (2) recognize the effects of societal developments on the needs of children as well as the needs of an ethnically diverse community; (3) maintain regular communication with other agencies, institutions, and organizations serving children in the community; (4) participate in all aspects of the library's planning process to represent and support children's services and analyze the costs of library services to children in order to develop, justify, administer, and evaluate planned budgets; (5) define and communicate the needs of children so that administrators, other library staff, and members of the larger community understand the basis for children's services; (6) demonstrate a knowledge of and appreciation for children's literature, periodicals, audiovisual materials, Web sites and other electronic media, and other materials that constitute a diverse, current, and relevant children's collection, keeping abreast of new materials by consulting a wide range of reviewing sources and publishers' catalogs as well as by attending professional meetings and keeping up with literature in the field; (7) be aware of adult reference materials and other library resources, which may (also) serve the needs of children and their caregivers; (8) evaluate and recommend collection development, selection, and weeding policies for management of the children's collection; (9) acquire materials that reflect the ethnic diversity of the community as well as the need of children to become familiar with other ethnic groups and cultures; (10) match children and their families with materials appropriate to their interests and abilities and provide help when needed, respecting children's right to browse, and answer their questions regardless of their nature or purpose; (11) understand and apply search strategies to give children full and equitable access to information from the widest possible range of sources and compile and maintain information about community resources so that children and adults working with children can be referred to appropriate sources of assistance; (12) design, promote, execute, and evaluate programs for children of all ages, based on their developmental needs and interests and the goals of the library, as well as provide outreach programs commensurate with community needs and library goals and objectives; (13) promote an awareness of and support for meeting children's library and information needs through all media as well as understand library governance and the political process and lobby on behalf of children's services; (14) keep abreast of current trends and emerging technologies, issues, and research in librarianship, child development, education, and allied fields; and (15) convey a nonjudgmental attitude toward patrons and their requests and demonstrate an understanding of and respect for diversity in cultural and ethnic values.

Salaries

Salaries for a Children's Librarian differ among schools according to the district, union regulations, number of graduate or in-service credits held by the librarian, and the individual's experience. Often Children's Librarians are hired on the same type of salary schedule as teachers. Starting annual salaries for school librarians may range from $20,000 to $25,000 and may range as high as $65,000 or more, usually for a nine-month contract and dependent on type of advanced degree and years of experience in both teaching and library work. In public libraries, Children's Librarians who head children's departments may expect yearly salaries ranging from $35,000 to $65,000 or more, with benefits, depending on experience.

Employment Prospects

Employment possibilities for Children's Librarians are good for seasoned, professional individuals, both within school systems and public libraries. The demand for Children's Librarians with an M.L.S. degree (and the knowledge of technological advances in library service) continues to grow.

Advancement Prospects

Children's Librarians can advance into larger school or public libraries. With years of experience, increased knowledge of library automated systems, and additional training to enhance administrative skills, they may move into higher administrative ranks as library directors or chief information officers.

Education and Training

Children's Librarians should have a master's degree in librarianship from a program accredited by the American Library Association (ALA) or a master's degree with a specialty in school library media from an educational institution accredited by the National Council for the Accreditation of Teacher Education (NCATE). Undergraduate degrees in almost any subject are appropriate. Many Children's Librarians continue their education throughout their career, particularly in new media technology as applied to library work.

Special Requirements

State certification for all Children's Librarians who teach in a school system is usually necessary, with a certification as both a librarian and a teacher. Requirements vary from state to state, but Children's Librarians who work in schools are usually expected to have some coursework in child psychology, education, and teaching methods. Most have had internships. Many states have reciprocity agreements wherein Children's Librarians who have earned certification in one state can be certified in another state by providing proof of their previous certification.

Experience, Skills, and Personality Traits

Children's Librarians should have a deep, abiding love of children's literature (both fiction and nonfiction) and other media devoted to children and take great pleasure in working with youths, parents, teachers, and community leaders. They should have excellent communication skills, both written and verbal, and love to tell stories. They must be well organized, have good administrative and public relations talents, and be comfortable with computer technology. They need to be able to set long- and short-range goals, objectives, and priorities for their library and demonstrate problem-solving, decision-making, and mediation techniques. They may be required to identify outside sources of funding and write effective grant applications. They should be good listeners and communicate constructively with both children and their parents and relatives.

Unions and Associations

Children's Librarians working in K-12 school libraries may or may not belong to a union, but they also may belong to a variety of trade associations that provide conferences, educational guidelines, support, and information to members. Primary among these groups are the Association for Library Service to Children (ALSC) and the Young Adult Library Services Association (YALSA), both of which are divisions of the American Library Association (ALA). Other general associations of interest to Children's Librarians include the American Library Association (ALA), the American Society of Information Science and Technology (ASIS&T), and the Special Libraries Association (SLA).

Tips for Entry

1. While completing your education (bachelor's and master's degrees), take every opportunity to work as a student assistant in either college/university libraries or local public libraries. Consider doing an internship or a practicum (a course of study devoted to practical experience in the field) in another library to gain practical experience in library work.

2. Subscribe to major library trade publications, such as *Library Journal* and *American Libraries,* to look for job opportunities in either public libraries or school systems looking for Children's Librarians. Also, check out *Jobs for Librarians and Information Professionals* (http://www.lisjobs.com), a comprehensive guide to online job resources for librarians and information professionals, as well as read relevant online newsletters and blogs.

3. For a position as a Children's Librarian in a school system, contact school superintendents in the areas in which you would like to work to find jobs in school libraries within the age groups with whom you want to work.

CIRCULATION/INTERLIBRARY LOAN LIBRARIAN

Position Description

Circulation/Interlibrary Loan Librarians manage all functions of the circulation department, interacting constantly with library staff and with library patrons of all ages and oversee the facility's interlibrary loan services. In their supervision of the circulation of the library's collection of books and nonbook materials, Circulation librarians oversee the department's staff, help library patrons use library services and facilities, follow and interpret library policies, and coordinate circulation activities with other departments. Besides performing routine circulation desk duties when required, they also oversee the return of books and other materials to shelves or storage areas and supervise billing and collections operations.

Under the general supervision of the director of the circulation department, Circulation Librarians administer the procedures of the circulation department and help interview, train, and evaluate the performance of circulation and shelving staff. As a part of these personnel duties, they keep track of vacations and meeting schedules for the department's staff to ensure proper coverage at all times in all areas of the department and aid in preparing weekly schedules for both circulation and shelving personnel. They must be aware of all events, shows, and classes held at the library at any given time in order to dispense this information to all members of the circulation staff so that they, in turn, can respond to any questions that library patrons or the public may have and be able to register interested individuals in such activities.

The efficient operation of the circulation desk is a primary concern for Circulation Librarians. They evaluate circulation operating procedures and suggest (and carry out) adjustments to these processes to improve efficiency. They oversee the enrollment of new patrons to the library and provide information and advice about the library's book and media collections and its best use to new and current patrons. They also oversee the book reserve system (which is maintained at the circulation desk), whereby patrons can reserve books that are presently in circulation. In academic and school libraries, reserve materials tend to be high-use items required for study by classes during a semester or school term. The number of available copies of these items is usually less than the number of students, so shared use must be enforced through the reserve system. In addition, Circulation Librarians supervise the receiving and recording of overdue fines and the inspection of any damaged circulation materials, whether books, media, or equipment. They track any cataloging errors that are discovered, oversee the performance and repair of circulation equipment, and recommend equipment improvements or replacements. One other task of a Circulation librarian is to maintain the circulation data and prepare regular statistical reports on a weekly, monthly, or yearly basis.

Interlibrary loan (abbreviated ILL and sometimes called interloan, document delivery, or document supply) is a service whereby a user of one library can borrow books, videos, DVDs, sound recordings, microfilms, and other media materials or receive photocopies of articles in magazines that are owned by another library. Sometimes for a small fee, or possibly for no cost, a library that has the item will loan or copy it, and the item is transported to the requestor's library to be checked out or just used within the library. Policies vary about whether the user is charged for the request. Loans between branch libraries in the same system may take one or two days, while loans between library systems may require a week or more to be delivered. If an item is rare or difficult to find, interlibrary loan does not guarantee that the lending library will send the requested item to the borrowing library, as some collections and volumes may be noncirculating.

Libraries have formed voluntary associations with one another to provide an online union catalog of all the items held by all member libraries. Whenever a library adds a new item to its catalog, a copy of the record is sent electronically to update the union list. This allows libraries to find out quickly which other libraries hold a particular item, and software/online communication can facilitate the requesting and supplying of interlibrary loans. In the United States, OCLC (Online Computer Library Center) is typically used by public and academic libraries, and RLIN (Research Libraries Information Network) is employed primarily by academic libraries, although some libraries are members of both. Journals are not usually lent, but a photocopy or a digital scan is made of the article requested instead. Policies vary about whether the cost of the duplication is passed on to the patron.

Circulation Librarians are frequently also in charge of the interlibrary loan services of the facility at which they are employed. Thus, they oversee the operation (and supervise the staff) of the interlibrary loan services and the transmission of requests either electronically (through OCLC or other networks) or using the American Library Association (ALA)–approved interlibrary loan forms. Their duties typically include OCLC searching, researching, and tracking; processing all orders; returning all loaned items in a timely fashion and communicating with patrons; negotiating and administering any bills or fines for services as necessary; and maintaining the library's reputation as a viable and trustworthy interlibrary loan service provider.

Salaries

Salaries for Circulation/Interlibrary Loan Librarians vary considerably depending on the experience and responsibilities of the librarian and the location and size of the library. Beginning Circulation/Interlibrary Loan Librarians with a master's degree in library or information studies accredited by the American Library Association (ALA) can expect an annual salary range from $31,000 to $40,000. According to the 2007 salary survey compiled jointly by the ALA and Allied Professional Association (APA), yearly salaries for librarians who manage support staff range from a low of $31,000 to a high of $98,304, with a median salary of $45,562.

Employment Prospects

It is estimated that the need for experienced Circulation/Interlibrary Loan Librarians will grow due to the increasing diversity and growing population of library users, both in public and academic libraries, and because more Circulation/Interlibrary Loan Librarians will reach retirement age in the next decade. Likewise, competition for this highly responsible post will increase. Those applicants who have had experience in circulation and are familiar with computer applications in library service will have the better job prospects.

Advancement Prospects

Circulation Librarians who have displayed administrative skills and who have gained seasoning in library automated systems can advance to become head of circulation departments and then, with additional training, advance to more senior administrative positions, such as library directors or chief information officers. Career advancement opportunities are better in the larger library systems or at the larger university libraries.

Education and Training

Circulation/Interlibrary Loan Librarians must have a master's degree in library science (M.L.S.) or in library and information science (M.L.I.S.) from one of the approximately 60 schools accredited by the American Library Association (ALA). Coursework with an emphasis on reference or public service is helpful. In addition, several years of increasingly responsible work within a library, preferably including experience in circulation control, is highly recommended.

Experience, Skills, and Personality Traits

Circulation/Interlibrary Loan Librarians are expected to have some background with library circulation practices, procedures, and standards as a library assistant and must be able to relate effectively to library patrons and coworkers. They should have experience in supervisory and staff training, in cash management, and in the preparation of concise statistical and narrative reports. They should have strong research skills to locate difficult requests, be familiar with current practices for copyright compliance, and be competent with computer applications in library searches, networks, and operations. They must have excellent written and oral communication abilities, good analytical skills, a strong public service orientation, and the capacity to work independently but also effectively in a team environment. Experience with an integrated library management system is important.

Unions and Associations

Circulation/Interlibrary Loan Librarians may belong to a variety of trade associations that provide educational guidance, support, and information to their members. Primary among these organizations is the American Library Association (ALA). Others include the American Society for Information Science and Technology (ASIS&T), the Association for Library Collections and Technical Services (ALCTS), the Library Administration and Management Association (LAMA), the Reference and User Services Association (RUSA), and the Special Libraries Association (SLA).

Tips for Entry

1. While earning your master's degree (M.L.S. or M.L.I.S.), take additional courses in public service and psychology, as they will prove useful in your interaction with library staff and patrons.

2. When applying for a library assistant position, request work within the circulation department and seek experience doing searches for interlibrary requests to aid in your training for a full-time post as a Circulation/Interlibrary Loan Librarian.

3. Make contacts within local libraries while studying for your degree, as often part-time jobs open up unexpectedly and need to be filled quickly. By joining professional organizations for librarians, you will make contacts, and by keeping them, you will have a network through which you can learn about part-time opportunities when they arise.

COLLECTIONS DEVELOPMENT DIRECTOR

Position Description

Collection development of a library includes selecting research resources in a wide variety of formats and languages, providing instructional and reference assistance in the use of these materials, evaluating the current collections and weeding where necessary, planning for future growth, and preserving library resources. Libraries, generally, attempt to maintain a well-balanced and broad collection with the goal of supporting lifelong learning and responding to community needs for information, encouraging a desire to read, and enriching the quality of life in the community. A variety of sources is used to select materials for most collections. Professional journals, reviews, bibliographies, patron and staff recommendations, well-known book clubs and their recommendations, and personal expertise are balanced as equal factors in selection decisions. Other factors frequently considered include content accuracy, contribution to the balance and diversity of the collection, coverage of current events and popular culture, nomination or receipt of awards or prizes, affordability, quality, and Internet accessibility.

Most libraries and information centers (as well as museums and other institutions that employ collection development personnel, usually called curators) have a written mission statement that enumerates their vision and their policies for developing their collection. Such statements include both a materials collection policy and a collection development policy. The former deals with the purchase (or gift acceptance) of books, journals, CDs, videos, and so forth. A collection development policy extends to include the criteria for selecting materials, policies on collection assessment, weeding out criteria, preservation and conservation methods employed, the balance of monographs to serials, switching formats (print to CD to Internet Web-based files), liaison to academic departments (if an academic library), serials cancellation projects, and so forth. Criteria for selection may include topic (is this a subject area that the library collection currently focuses on?), reading level (is the level appropriate for the library's patrons?), currency (is the information up-to-date and timely?), demand (is much interest in the material anticipated for the topic or the author?), cost (what items will provide the best value for the collection?), author's credentials, publisher or producer's reputation, features (does it have an index, bibliographies, special appendixes, a CD-ROM, a companion Web site, and so forth?), resource sharing (will other local libraries purchase it and make it thus available via interlibrary loan?), and availability in other media (which version would be most appropriate for the collection: print, multimedia, or electronic?).

Collections Development Directors are responsible for the entire selection process (including supervising staff) and usually are tasked with the planning or updating of the library's collection development policy. Large university and research libraries with collections numbering in the millions of items will have many subject specialists, resource coordinators, and bibliographers who are expert in their disciplines. All of these specialists report to a Collections Development Director. In smaller libraries, areas of responsibility may be delegated among staff librarians, again reporting to the Collections Development Director. Branch librarians may have direct responsibility for building their own collections, or they may coordinate with a centralized systemwide selection team.

Besides their supervisory duties, Collections Development Directors develop budgets; gather and analyze statistical data on their collection and its use; and provide researchers, media, and the public with information and assistance pertaining to their institution's collection. They strive to improve donor relations, provide reference and research services, create exhibits, and oversee preservation and conservation efforts. Most directors use computer databases to catalog and organize their institution's collection and may be involved in grant writing and fund-raising to support their collection projects.

Collections Development Directors are often called curators and may oversee collections in a wide variety of institutions other than libraries, including museums, zoos, aquariums, botanical gardens, nature centers, and historic sites. They may work for either private institutions or government departments.

With the advent of the digital age, Collections Development Directors face new challenges. As Robert G. Sewell, associate university librarian for collection development and management at Rutgers University Library, states, "In this age of the hybrid library, the great challenge is to find the proper but ever-shifting balance between the new media and traditional resources." He says of his work activities: "Another feature of my position is that Special Collections and University Archives report to me. I love to jump from deciding about what electronic resources we will acquire for the system, to allocating and monitoring the collections budget, to dealing with vendors, to acquiring and conserving rare books and manuscripts, to working with donors."

Salaries

Earnings of Collections Development Directors vary considerably depending on their experience, their specialty, their responsibilities, and the size of the institution. Salaries in large public and academic libraries are considerably higher than those for smaller libraries in either area. According to a joint American Library Association–Allied Professional Association salary survey, median annual salaries for supervisory department managers in public libraries in 2007 ranged from $42,000 to $62,000. For academic libraries, the median yearly salary in 2007 ranged from $57,000 to $65,000.

Employment Prospects

Job opportunities for librarians with the requisite experience in collection development should be good due to an increasing number of staff reaching retirement age within the next decade. However, the competition for this post of great responsibility is heavy, and those librarians with the experience and capacity to cope with continuous learning and constant change (as technological innovations further challenge standard collection procedures) have the best chances for employment.

Advancement Prospects

The advancement path for Collections Development Directors is usually upward into the higher management levels of the library, particularly the position of assistant library director, which, in turn, may lead to the position of library director or chief information officer.

Education and Training

A master's degree in library science (M.L.S.) or in library and information science (M.L.I.S.) is requisite for Collections Development Directors, as it is with most library administrative positions. In addition, librarians coming into the field of collection development and management, especially in academic libraries, should have a strong educational background (a bachelor's degree or higher) in some specialty discipline. As

Robert Sewell points out, such a background "provides a foundation for understanding the ways knowledge is organized and the way researchers do their work," which also "will enable the librarian to relate more effectively with students and faculty [and the general public] to determine their needs."

Special Requirements

Some academic libraries require Collections Development Directors to take teaching positions at the college or university of which the library is a part. In some cases, particularly at state university systems, teaching posts require a teacher's certificate for employment.

Experience, Skills, and Personality Traits

Collections Development Directors must have three to five years of experience in collection development and should have management, supervisory, and budgetary backgrounds. They must be able to establish priorities and see projects through to completion. They need excellent oral, written, planning, and interpersonal skills and a capacity for leadership in a library setting, which includes the ability to manage a department with professional staff. They should be technologically sophisticated and be able to use a personal computer and computer software programs at the level of proficiency required for a development office (which often includes ease in using MS Office Suite and database programs). They may be required to have grant writing abilities and have some knowledge of the principles of major gift fund-raising.

Unions and Associations

Besides belonging to the major trade association for librarians, the American Library Association (ALA), Collection Development Directors and librarians should be members of the Association for Library Collections and Technical Services (ALCTS). They may also find it useful to belong to other industry trade groups, such as the American Association for Information Science and Technology (ASIS&T) and the Special Libraries Association (SLA).

Tips for Entry

1. For your bachelor's degree, choose a field of interest to you that will be a useful discipline to compliment your master's degree in library and information science. This is particularly beneficial if you plan to work in an academic library environment.

2. In the process of earning your master's degree in library and information science, take courses in budgeting and statistics, as a knowledge of these processes will be vital in your collections development career.

3. Take every opportunity to work as an intern, do a curator practicum (a course of study devoted to practical experience in the field), or volunteer in a library (public or academic) and request work in the collection development area to provide you with relevant background experience.

FINANCIAL OFFICER

Duties: Responsible for all financial accounting and record keeping of library income, expenses, insurance, and investments; aids in budget preparation and analysis

Alternate Title(s): Chief Financial Officer; Controller; Director of Finances; Financial Manager; Financial Operations Officer

Salary Range: $45,000 to $85,000 or more

Employment Prospects: Fair to good

Advancement Prospects: Fair

Prerequisites:

    Education and Training—Bachelor's degree in business or accounting required; master's degree in library and information science recommended

    Experience—Five to 10 years of background in the administration of the business and financial operations of an organization, including experience in bookkeeping and accounting work that includes accounts payable, payroll and benefits, and purchasing; nonprofit business and grant funding experience helpful

---

CAREER LADDER

Library Director; Chief of Financial Operations
Financial Officer
Business Operations Officer; Accountant

Special Skills and Personality Traits—Capacity to effectively coordinate multiple, complex functions; demonstrated oral and written communication skills; detail oriented; excellent interpersonal skills and a public service manner; familiarity with municipal and state financial, compliance, and reporting practices; problem-solving abilities; strong computer and Internet abilities

Special Requirements—Certification as a certified public accountant (CPA) may be required; eligibility to be bonded may also be needed

---

Position Description

Financial Officers in a library are the primary individuals responsible for managing the financial risks and procedures of the business side of the library. They are also responsible for financial planning and record keeping as well as financial reporting to higher management. In some smaller libraries, they may be the higher management, as the position of library director may include financial management of the facility along with other administrative duties.

Financial Officers maintain current cash flow statements to scrutinize cash activity and monitor bank account balances and budget balances. They check current investments and purchases and redeem investments when appropriate. Most important, they monitor deposit of all library receipts. They calculate monthly bills to be paid, verify receipt of materials being billed, and prepare checks and vouchers, paying interim bills between board meetings as necessary and reconciling all bank statements monthly as required by statute and library regulations. They generate end-of-month financial reports and maintain all financial records

as demanded by statute and library rules. They prepare monthly financial reports for board meetings and attend board meetings chaired by the library director or director of libraries (if an academic library).

Financial Officers usually coordinate and supervise the preparation of the library's budget(s) and manage and monitor the expenditure levels of funds designated by the budget. This monitoring includes but is not limited to: the acceptances of invoices and supporting documentation from library departments and processing of payments; the maintenance of machine and manual ledgers and files to track and report authorized payments; the preservation of complete files of purchase and trust fund orders and requisitions; the preparation of annual balancing, closing, and reporting on each individual fund; and the planning and oversight of the library's annual audit.

Financial Officers sometimes are tasked with overseeing all aspects of the library's contracting activities, which typically include the drafting, advertising, and awarding of contracts for goods and services according to accepted policies and practices, as well as the maintenance of complete files on contracts both let and advertised. This supervision usually includes the administering of executed contracts, with the Financial Officer serving as a liaison to existing and potential contractors in order to ensure compliance with the provisions of existing contracts.

Financial Officers are usually required to maintain up-to-date employee files that include federal and state tax withholding, federal I-9 forms, insurance, public employee retirement fund (PERF) files (when appropriate), employee change notices, and other documentation that is part of the payroll process. They may be asked to assist in yearly reviews of health/life/dental/vision insurance benefits and initiate application processes when the library changes insurance carriers.

Throughout, Financial Officers must follow the legal requirements for employee record keeping and state and federal audits as well as ensure that the accounting procedures used comply with state and federal regulations and that employee practices follow state and federal wage and hour laws.

Salaries
Yearly earnings for Financial Officers in libraries range from $45,000 to $85,000 or more, depending on the size of the library, its type (public, academic, or special), whether it is a part of a state system, the extent of its revenues, and the scope of responsibilities that this post entails.

Employment Prospects
According to the U.S. Department of Labor's Bureau of Labor Statistics, employment of financial managers generally is expected to grow about as fast as the average for all occupations through 2014. As in other managerial occupations, job seekers are likely to face competition because the number of job openings will most likely be less than the number of applicants. For those financial managers looking for employment in libraries, a master's degree in library and information science should enhance their chances. In addition, job opportunities may improve as a large number of librarians (including Financial Officers) are expected to retire in the coming decade. More than three in five librarians are now age 45 or older and will become eligible for retirement in the next 10 years.

Advancement Prospects
Financial Officers looking for advancement within their library environment have only a few options, mainly becoming library director (the position of which encompasses much more than just financial knowledge

and thus would require additional training and experience) or chief information officer (a position in which Financial Officers can use their technical and computer expertise). Financial Officers may find better prospects by transferring to another business occupation possibly related to library work, such as publishing, or any one of many media fields.

Education and Training
Financial Officers should have a bachelor's degree in business or accounting. Some larger libraries may also require a master's degree in these fields as well. It is recommended that a Financial Officer working in a library environment have, in addition, a master's degree in library and information science to be acquainted with library practices, procedures, rules, and regulations. In addition, continuing education is vital to financial managers, who must cope with changes in federal and state laws and regulations and the proliferation of new and complex financial procedures.

Special Requirements
In some instances, libraries may require their Financial Officers to be certified public accountants (CPAs) or certified management accountants (CMAs). Many associations offer professional certification programs. For example, the CFA (Chartered Financial Analyst) Institute confers the chartered financial analyst designation on investment professionals, the Association for Financial Professionals (AFP) awards the certified cash manager credential to those who pass a computer-based exam and have relevant experience, and the Institute of Management Accountants offers a certified in financial management designation to members with a bachelor's degree with at least two years of work experience and who pass the institute's four-part examination.

Experience, Skills, and Personality Traits
Financial Officers must have excellent oral and written communication skills as well as the ability to interact harmoniously and communicate well with library staff, board members, and library patrons. They must have excellent oral and written communication skills and, from their knowledge of and experience with automated business support systems, have the facility to learn and efficiently operate library computer systems, peripheral equipment, and software programs. They must be familiar with municipal and state financial, compliance, and reporting practices. They must be able to handle confidential and sensitive information with discretion and trust and have proven talents in initiating and managing change. They must have excellent

organizational, problem-solving, and facilitation skills and have a basic public service manner. They should have the specific ability to handle and accurately balance daily cash receipts and work precisely with exceptional attention to detail.

Unions and Associations

Besides the trade organizations associated with library work, the American Library Association (ALA), the American Society for Information Science and Technology (ASIS&T), and the Special Libraries Association (SLA), Financial Officers should also belong to associations related to the specifics of their work, such as the American Management Association (AMA), the American Association of Grant Professionals (AAGP), the Association for Financial Professionals (AFP), and the National Conference of CPA Practitioners (NCCPAP).

Tips for Entry

1. Look for an internship where you can gain experience in the practicalities of everyday finance and to learn about the responsibilities and issues specific to Financial Officers.

2. To supplement your courses in business, finance, and accounting (where you become familiar with financial terms and principles), read publications such as the *Wall Street Journal* to become better acquainted with the specifics of investing and fund accounting.

3. Work three to five years in bookkeeping and accounting positions, experience that should include accounts payable, payroll, benefits, and purchasing, for a nonprofit business. Look to gain experience in grant funding as well, as that may frequently be part of your job as a library Financial Officer.

4. In your employment search, check out the *American Library Directory*, which lists a wide variety of libraries, or look at the *Guide to Employment Sources in the Library and Information* Professions, which is available online at the American Library Association (ALA) Web site.

HUMAN RESOURCES DIRECTOR

CAREER PROFILE

Duties: Manage employee relations functions for a library or library system, including benefits, compensation, recruiting, staffing, terminations, and policies and procedures

Alternate Title(s): Associate Director, Library Human Resource; Director of Library Personnel; Employment Manager (or Director); Executive Director, Human Resources; Human Resources Manager; Personnel Director; Recruitment Manager; Training and Development Director

Salary Range: $40,000 to $95,000 or more

Employment Prospects: Good

Advancement Prospects: Fair to good

Prerequisites:

Education and Training—Bachelor's degree in human resource management or allied field; master's degree in library and information science usually required as well

Experience—Two to three years of office experience; three to five years of human resource management and supervisory experience; background in library or nonprofit environment usually preferred

Special Skills and Personality Traits—Ability and judgment to deal with sensitive matters

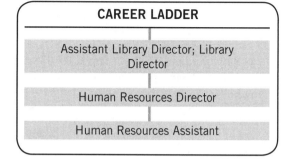

CAREER LADDER

```
Assistant Library Director; Library
Director
          |
Human Resources Director
          |
Human Resources Assistant
```

on a confidential basis and collaborate effectively with diverse groups; commitment to service and teamwork as well as to professional growth and development of library staff; computer proficiency; detailed oriented; excellent oral and written communication skills; outstanding analytical, organizational, and problem solving abilities

Special Requirements—Professional in human resources (PHR) or senior professional in human resources (SPHR) certification often required; in addition, if position is with an academic library as a member of the teaching staff, a teaching certification may be required

Position Description

Human Resources Directors serve as a crucial link between library management and library staff. The primary goal of human resource management is to help an organization meet its strategic goals by attracting and maintaining employees and managing them effectively. They plan, direct, and carry out policies relating to all phases of personnel activity. They recruit, interview, and aid in the selection of employees to fill vacant library posts. They organize and conduct new employee orientation to foster a positive commitment toward the library's policies and objectives. In addition, they evaluate personnel policies and training programs. They make sure employees have the required information about their benefit and retirement plans. They regularly discuss benefits, pension plans, and policies with employees. They post notices for job openings so library staff will have the opportunity to apply for such jobs. They conduct exit interviews for staff who leave.

Human Resources Directors keep records of insurance coverage, pension plans, and personnel transactions, such as hires, promotions, transfers, and terminations. They investigate accidents and prepare reports for the library's insurance carrier. They conduct wage surveys to determine competitive salary rates and meet with library employees and management to resolve grievances and disputes. They prepare reports and recommendations to reduce absenteeism and turnover. They may represent the library at personnel-related hearings and investigations. They may be tasked with contracting with outside suppliers to provide employee services, such as canteen, transportation, and relocation. They advise library managers on organizational policy matters such as equal employment opportunity and sexual harassment and recommend any needed changes. They analyze and modify compensation and benefits policies to establish competitive programs and ensure compliance with legal requirements. They prepare budgets for human resources and personnel work and attend budgeting and strategic planning meetings.

In smaller academic or public libraries, the Human Resources Director may work alone in handling all aspects of human resources activities and thus need to have an extensive range of knowledge. In some smaller facilities, the library director may even act as the Human Resources Director. In the largest libraries or statewide library systems, the Human Resources Director may supervise several departments, each headed by an experienced human resources manager or assistant manager who, most likely, would be a specialist in one type of human resource activity, such as benefits, compensation, employee relations, employment and recruitment, performance management, or training and development.

Salaries

Earnings for Human Resources Directors vary considerably according to the size of the library and the number of responsibilities as well as geographic location. In its 2007 salary survey reports on Human Resources Directors and managers, PayScale, Inc., determined that the median annual salaries for this position varied from $40,398 to $97,287. According to a 2005 salary survey conducted by the National Association of Colleges and Employers, bachelor's degree candidates majoring in human resources received starting salary offers averaging $36,967 per year.

Employment Prospects

According to the U.S. Bureau of Labor's Office of Labor Statistics, it is expected that overall employment of human resources managers and specialists will grow faster than the average for all occupations through 2014, even though the abundant supply of qualified college graduates and experienced workers should create keen competition for jobs. A general understanding of the workings of a library will give an individual an edge in a job application for a human resources position, but libraries also often look "outside the library world" to fill such posts.

Advancement Prospects

At times, some Human Resources Directors feel they must focus too much on the financial aspects of their duties to allow them to provide the assistance they want to give staff. Such individuals who leave the profession often go into career counseling, psychology, and guidance counseling and even labor relations. Individuals who prefer the financial side go into budgeting, inventory control, and quality control management. Those

Human Resources Directors who prefer to remain within the library environment may advance to higher management positions, such as assistant library director and then library director.

In larger libraries (or library systems), the human resources work may be spread into several specialized departments, such as information technology, which would have a department head. In some cases, individuals who start out in an area such as human resources technology may have an interest in and an opportunity to become a full-fledged librarian, library manager, or library director, with the necessary additional training.

Education and Training

A bachelor's degree in human resources management or a related field is the usual requirement for human resources personnel. A master's degree in human resource management, industrial relations, organization behavior, or business administration also is considered worthwhile. Many libraries prefer that candidates have a master's degree in library science (M.L.S.) or in library and information science (M.L.I.S.) as well.

It is critical for Human Resources Directors to keep up to date on state and federal requirements concerning personnel matters (such as discrimination, sexual harassment, taxes, and so forth). For this reason, continuing education is an essential part of a Human Resources Director's job.

Special Requirements

Many organizations require a candidate for Human Resources Director to have a certification in human resources management. The most common certifications are professional in human resources (PHR) and senior professional in human resources (SPHR). These certifications are awarded by the Human Resources Certification Institute of the Society for Human Resource Management (SHRM) (http://www.shrm.org). Another organization that offers certification is the American Society for Training and Development Certification Institute (ASTD) (http://www.astd.org). In addition, the International Foundation of Employee Benefit Plans (IFEBP) (http://www.ifebp.org) confers a designation to individuals who complete a series of college-level courses and pass exams covering employee benefit plans. One other organization that can provide information on certification for Human Resources Directors is World at Work (http://www.worldatwork.org). Academic libraries may require their Human Resources Directors to be a part of the college's or university's teaching staff and hence require teaching certifications of them.

Experience, Skills, and Personality Traits

For many specialized jobs in the human resources field, previous experience is an asset; for the position of Human Resources Director, it is *essential*. Human Resources Directors must have the ability to work with individuals as well as have a commitment to the library's goals and policies. They must be able to speak and write effectively. They need to be able to work with or supervise people with various cultural backgrounds, levels of education, and work experience. They must be able to cope with conflicting points of view; function well under pressure; and demonstrate discretion, integrity, fair-mindedness, and a persuasive, congenial personality.

Human Resources Directors must be adept with computers and be familiar with database user interfaces and query software (such as Microsoft Access), document management software (such as Atlas Business Solutions Staff Files), human resources software (such as Human Resources Information System, or HRIS), time accounting software (such as Exact Software Macola ES Labor Performance), and word processing software (such as Microsoft Word).

In addition, they should be fully knowledgeable (and preferably have had some practical application experience) with such employment laws as the Americans with Disabilities Act (ADA), the Equal Employment Opportunity Commission (EEOC), and the Family Medical Leave Act (FMLA). They should have several years of human resources management and supervisory experience, usually as a human resources assistant. They need to have a strong commitment to service and teamwork, exhibit solid organizational and analytical skills, and have a dedication to the professional growth and development of the library staff.

Unions and Associations

Outside the major professional associations for librarians (the American Library Association, or ALA, the American Society for Information Science and Technology, or ASIS&T; and the Special Libraries Association, or SLA), Human Resources Directors may find it useful to belong to such professional organizations of their field as the American Society for Training and Development (ASTD), the International Public Management Association for Human Resources (IPMA-HR), and, above all, the Society for Human Resource Management (SHRM).

Tips for Entry

1. Consider participating in an internship or work-study program while obtaining your bachelor's degree. An internship is frequently part of a four-year degree program, and it offers you a chance to apply what you have learned in the classroom to an actual work situation as well as build your skills and make contacts with people within the field.

2. Consider taking a position as an interviewer, a compensation specialist, or a trainer, as many Human Resource Directors have worked in these posts to gain expertise before becoming managers.

3. Consider a part-time job in a library to gain a general understanding of the workings of a library, which may well give you an edge (and add to your experience in human resources) in your job application.

LIBRARY CONSULTANT

Duties: Assist individual libraries, regional library service systems, governmental departments, educational institutions, or special libraries in library development and specialty areas; provide consultation, continuing education, and facilitation on operations, management, and services to all types of libraries; plan, implement, and evaluate programs for the improvement of library information services

Alternate Title(s): Business Analyst; Online Resources Consultant; Program Management Analyst; Project Management Consultant

Salary Range: $30,000 to $75,000 or more

Employment Prospects: Fair to good

Advancement Prospects: Fair to good

Prerequisites:

    Education and Training—Master's degree in library and information science from an American Library Association (ALA)-accredited program, or comparable combination of education and experience; degrees in specialty subject areas may be required as well

    Experience—Considerable experience with professional principles and practices of library and information science and current trends in library services; background in planning and evaluation projects, programs, and/or services within a library setting

    Special Skills and Personality Traits—Ability to get along with a wide range of people and work in a team environment; analytical skills; creativity; familiarity with problem-solving techniques with groups; good judgment and time management talents; strong oral and written communication expertise

    Special Requirements—In some instances, a state license or certification as a library consultant may be required

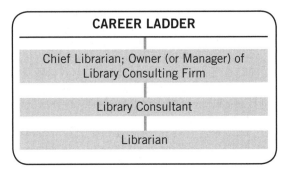

CAREER LADDER

Chief Librarian; Owner (or Manager) of Library Consulting Firm

Library Consultant

Librarian

Position Description

Library Consultants are either librarians who have developed their expertise by running or working in libraries or individuals from outside the field of library science who have specific knowledge relevant to libraries and information systems. Library organizations might need a consultant when they have no expertise in a particular area or when the time of need is considered short term, usually less than a year, with a general start and stop time frame, or when the organization members continue to disagree about how to meet their perceived need and feel that by bringing in a consultant to provide expertise or facilitation skills they will come to a consensus. They may also want an objective perspective from someone without any strong biases about the organization's past and current issues.

    Library Consultants analyze administrative policies, observe work procedures, and review data relative to book, media, and other collections to determine the effectiveness of the library service to its public. They conduct organizational studies and evaluations, design systems and procedures, conduct work measurement studies, and prepare operations and procedures manuals to assist library management in functioning more efficiently and effectively. They compare allocations for building funds, salaries, and collections with statewide and national standards to determine the effectiveness of the facility's fiscal operations. They gather statistical data, such as population and community growth rates, and analyze building plans to determine the adequacy of the institution's programs for expansion. They may be asked to promote, coordinate, and develop public library services to children, young adults, the elderly, persons with disabilities, and the unserved so that these special groups receive equal access to high-quality public library services by conducting needs assessments, publishing information, conducting workshops, and consulting with public and regional library staff and community organizations. They prepare their evaluation of a library's system based on observation and surveys and recommend measures to improve the organization and administration of the library.

Library Consultants may be hired for specific needs, such as coordinating and conducting conferences and workshops related to youth services, or overseeing the development and production of summer library programs, or managing online resources and user interface programs presently in use at a library and planning for future development of such resources. Special libraries, such as medical and law libraries, may hire consultants with specific types of backgrounds to provide specialized information and advice. For example, professional law Library Consultants may supply legal information and advice on library laws to librarians and trustees.

Local or state government departments or agencies may engage Library Consultants to develop, implement, and evaluate statewide continuing education programs for public library development. In so doing, they commonly work on such statewide projects as children's services, literacy, library service to non-English speakers, and the library's leadership with their local economic development community and learning programs. They may serve as the state library liaison to other state agencies concerned with telecommunications, automation, and networking. In some instances, library consulting firms are contracted to offer comprehensive library director (or library staff) recruitment services that expedite the hiring process by forwarding a qualified pool of candidates for a library board (or director) to review. Thus, library boards may save valuable time by focusing on just the finalists who meet their predetermined criteria.

Salaries

Yearly salaries may range from $33,000 to $80,000, depending on the scope of the consulting work and the size of the library (or library system). In its 2007 salary survey of Library Consultants, PayScale, Inc., found that the median annual salaries ranged from $49,841 to $52,893, depending on such factors as the type of employer and years of experience held by the consultant.

Employment Prospects

As with management analysts, the employment of Library Consultants is expected to grow as fast as or faster than the average of all occupations through 2014, according the U.S. Department of Labor's Bureau of Labor Statistics, as libraries seek to improve and expand their organization and services in response to the challenges of the digital age and their patrons' changing needs. Consultants with strong computer backgrounds

and experience in the application of computer technology in library work and service will have the best chance at employment.

Advancement Prospects

Library Consultants who have gained the requisite experience and have some business background as well may decide to set up their own consulting firm or may look for a managerial post in an already existing firm. Some Library Consultants may choose to leave the consulting business and further their careers in library service as full-time librarians.

Education and Training

A master's degree in library science (M.L.S.) or in library and information science (M.L.I.S.) from an accredited school is a basic requirement for consulting work for libraries. In addition, two to three years of full-time professional librarian experience in library networking and systems, library construction or renovation, continuing education programs for library personnel, children's and other special services for library patrons, and a basic understanding of professional standards for librarians are required. In some cases, a master's degree in education or computer science may be substituted for the master's degree in library science, as long as the candidate has the equivalent background within a library environment, particularly training and experience in library automation systems.

Special Requirements

Some states require certification of librarians, particularly those working in statewide systems or in statewide academic institutions and may require the same of Library Consultants hired to work within such systems.

Experience, Skills, and Personality Traits

Library Consultants must have considerable knowledge of the organization, administration, and operation of public and academic libraries. They must be familiar with library planning concepts and techniques, library materials, methods, and the staff organization of library personnel. They should have knowledge of library networking and resource sharing methodologies, library service delivery systems to children and special populations (such as the elderly and persons with disabilities), library construction and renovation, and the legal requirements relating to the accessibility of library services.

Library Consultants must have a thorough understanding of computer technology and the ability to adapt and apply it to library networking activities and automation needs. They must have excellent oral and written communication skills and the ability to establish and maintain cooperative relationships with department and civic officials, educators, subject specialists, database vendors, librarians, and library technical database staff. They should demonstrate careful attention to detail and display a high level of initiative, effort, and commitment toward completing their assignments efficiently. They need to be able to listen to others and respond appropriately to their comments.

In addition, Library Consultants should have a working knowledge of small group dynamics and facilitation techniques, of the consulting process (and have skill in practicing it), and of continuing education techniques and practices. They need to have the ability to develop long-term goals and objectives, to organize and implement complex service programs effectively in cooperation with others, and to plan and evaluate programs.

Unions and Associations

The American Library Association (ALA) is the primary professional association for librarians and, as such, should be of interest and use for Library Consultants. In addition, they may find it useful to be a member of such professional groups in the management consulting industry as the Association of Management Consulting Firms (AMCF) and the Institute of Management Consultants USA, Inc. (IMCUSA).

Tips for Entry

1. In addition to a master's degree in library and information science, a bachelor's degree in business administration should prove useful to you in your career as a Library Consultant.

2. Add some psychology courses to your curriculum to better understand group dynamics and leadership techniques in dealing with a wide variety of people.

3. Gain experience working in both public and academic libraries before becoming a Library Consultant, as you will need a working knowledge of various library standards, practices, and procedures.

LIBRARY DIRECTOR

CAREER PROFILE

Duties: Serving as head of the library, responsible for all library functions within the framework of the library's goals and objectives, policies, and budget

Alternate Title(s): Chief Officer, Library (or Library System); Dean of Libraries; Director of Library and Information Services; Head Librarian

Salary Range: $23,500 to $179,000 or more

Employment Prospects: Good

Advancement Prospects: Good

Prerequisites:

Education and Training—Four-year undergraduate degree in any field; master's degree in library science (M.L.S.) or library and information science (M.L.I.S.) required; a second master's degree, such as a law or business degree, is recommended; a Ph.D. or D.L.S. (doctor of library sciences) may be necessary to obtain a post as director in a large top academic or public library

Experience—May vary greatly according to the size of the library and scope of responsibilities, but usually a background of eight to 10 years as a librarian, with five years of managerial or administrative experience

CAREER LADDER

Library Director of Large Library

Library Director

Assistant Library Director; Associate Library Director; Library Administrator; Library Manager

Special Skills and Personality Traits—Ability to meet people easily, to motivate others, and to work effectively with library staff and boards; capable of interacting well as part of a team; good communication skills, imagination, creativity, and talent for organization; knowledge of emerging technologies and their applications to libraries is *essential*

Special Requirements—Directors of academic and school libraries usually must have a teaching certificate; for directors of public or special libraries, a teaching certificate seldom is necessary but is an additional bonus

Position Description

Library Director positions perhaps offer the largest range of duties in the library world. A Library Director has overall authority and responsibility for the planning, direction, and operation of a library or a group of libraries. In a rural setting, the director may be the only regularly scheduled employee. In large urban operations, the director may oversee a staff of hundreds and more than 50 branch libraries. In the small facility, the director may handle everything from locking the doors, to cataloging new acquisitions, to paying the bills. In a major library, the director most likely will have maintenance, librarian, and accounting staff members to accomplish these tasks.

Library Directors plan and carry out library service objectives, prepare budgets, purchase print and nonprint materials and equipment to run the library, supervise employees, arrange for maintenance of library buildings and grounds, create publicity for the library, prepare grant applications, collect statistical data to evaluate the efficiency and success of the library, and establish cooperative relationships with the library board or any other governing authorities. Library Directors are also the lead professional librarians who are knowledgeable about a wide range of library practices and procedures. They set an example for others in the delivery of reference and patrons' services as well as in the application of technology to advance library operations.

They analyze, select, and effect recommendations as to personnel, such as department chiefs or branch library supervisors. They coordinate the activities of branch libraries or department libraries. They analyze and coordinate departmental budget estimates and control expenditures to keep within the limits of approved budgets. They review and evaluate purchases of books, nonprint materials, and equipment, examining trade publications and materials, interviewing publishers' representatives, and consulting with others in order to select materials appropriate for their library's collection(s). They may review and select materials to be discarded, repaired, or replaced.

They administer personnel regulations, interview and appoint most job applicants, rate staff performances, and promote and discharge employees. They encourage and support staff members in their professional development, recommending opportunities for additional staff education and career enhancement. They plan and conduct staff meetings and participate in community, professional, and educational staff conferences to discuss and act on library problems and responses to community or university/college needs. They usually are responsible for fund development through grant writing, annual appeals, planned giving, memorial programs, and requests to municipalities, legislators, and community service organizations.

They constantly evaluate their library as to how successful the facility is in presenting services that meet community (or college/university) needs and interests, whether the library is keeping pace with new technology, whether the institution's collection meets community (or educational) expectations and needs, and what other segments of the community need to be introduced to the library and its services. Today, building broad community support means reaching a population that is often online and interacting on the Internet. As Rush Miller, University Librarian at Hillman Library at the University of Pittsburgh, states, "It's not about books anymore and it's not about organizing information. It's about connecting people to what they want to learn." Thus, Library Directors need to visit local community groups, business organizations, civic associations, and churches (or, as academic or university Library Directors, the various departments, committees, and study groups of the educational institution). They must use surveys—both paper and online—as well as new tools such as blogs and social networks. Above all, Library Directors (whatever type of facility they head) have to articulate and support the vision, mission, and strategic goals of their library and the institution of which it is a part, be it a college or university, a citywide library system, or a special library connected to a business or other professional organization.

Salaries
The ALA-APA (American Library Association–Allied Professional Association) in their 2007 salary survey found that Library Directors in public libraries had annual earnings ranging from $23,500 to $179,627, depending on the size of the library. Median yearly incomes for public Library Directors ranged from $44,722 to $97,566, again depending on the size of

the facility. For Library Directors of academic libraries, salaries ranged from a minimum of $28,500 to a maximum of $225,000, depending on the size and type of educational institution. Median annual salaries ranged from $59,849 to $102,075.

Employment Prospects
Employment prospects for Library Directors in public, academic, and special libraries are good, as every library needs a director, particularly well experienced individuals who can manage the ever-increasing and ever-changing resources (both print and nonprint) of libraries and can respond to the needs of patrons. In addition, continual attrition due to retirement will lead to more openings for Library Director positions through 2014.

Advancement Prospects
As new technology impacts the mission and responsibilities of libraries, opportunities continue to improve for Library Directors, who have both education in and experience with the ever-increasing technological areas, to move into larger and more responsible administrative positions in larger public, academic, or university libraries.

Education and Training
Most public, academic, and special library positions require a master's of library and information science (M.L.I.S.) degree, preferably from a school accredited by the American Library Association (ALA). Undergraduate degrees in almost any subject area are appropriate, particularly those in business administration. Many college and university Library Director positions require a doctoral degree in library science or an advanced business degree. Those Library Directors working in special libraries, such as law or medical libraries, may need a master's (or other advanced) degree in those disciplines. Five to 10 years of experience in progressively administrative or supervisory positions are generally required as well.

Special Requirements
Library Directors of many academic libraries and most university, college, and school libraries are members of the teaching staff of their institutions. As such, they usually need a state certification as a teacher.

Experience, Skills, and Personality Traits
Library Directors must have a comprehensive knowledge of the principles and practices of library administration and of library operations, aims, and services.

Their knowledge of and experience with excellent customer service is paramount. Along with their superior communication talents, they must have imagination, creativity, leadership skills, a talent for organization and administration, and excellent negotiating abilities. They need to be able to meet people easily, to motivate individuals, to work well as part of a team, and to interact effectively with both library staff and library boards. They should have successful experience in strategic planning and a background in general management (including fiscal management and contract negotiations with vendors). They should be able to work with multiple constituencies collaboratively and have a high level of energy and enthusiasm. An ongoing knowledge of emerging technologies and their applications to both library processes and services is vital. Familiarity with local area networks and PC-based applications software and library MARC formats are important as well as a knowledge of library Web design and scripting languages.

In addition, they must be completely familiar with laws pertaining to the administration of libraries: city and county ordinances pertaining to development, the Americans with Disabilities Act (ADA) requirements as applied to employment applications, the Fair Labor Standards Act (FLSA), the Family Medical Leave Act (FMLA), the Equal Employment Opportunity Commission (EEOC) Sexual Harassment Regulations, the Title VII Civil Rights Act of 1964 pertaining to antidiscrimination matters, the Emergency Evacuation/Workplace Safety Rules, and local ordinances on buildings and safety.

Unions and Associations

Besides belonging to the premier professional association for librarians, the American Library Association (ALA), Library Directors may find it helpful to belong to a variety of other trade groups that provide educational guidance and support, conferences, and information to their members. Such organizations include the American Society for Information Science and Technology (ASIS&T), the Association for Library Collections and Technical Services (ALCTS, a division of the ALA), the Association for Library and Information Science Education (ALISE), the Association for Library Trustees and Advocates (ALTA, a division of the ALA), the Association of College and Research Libraries (ACRL, a division of the ALA), the Association of Record Managers and Administrators (ARMA), and the Library Administration and Management Association (LAMA).

Tips for Entry

1. During your undergraduate college years, seek out courses in business administration and psychology, as these skills will be crucial in your work as Library Director in managing both the operation of your library or library system and gaining the trust and backing of your staff(s).

2. Join various professional organizations for Library Directors to provide you with a network through which you may hear of job opportunities.

3. In any job search you do, check out the *American Library Directory*, which lists a wide variety of libraries, or the *Guide to Employment Sources in Library and Information Professions*, which is available online at the ALA Web site (http://www. ala.org/ala/hrdr/libraryempresources/employmentguide05.cfm.

4. Attend library conventions and conferences and check job boards as well as investigate the placement services that list library-related positions at annual ALA conventions.

MEDIA LIBRARIAN

Position Description

The traditional concept of a library is fast changing from a place to access paper records, recordings, books, or microfilm/microfiche to one that also houses the most advanced multimedia equipment and materials, which may include CD-ROM, the Internet, virtual libraries, and remote access to a wide range of multimedia nonprint resources. Today's library media centers reflect this dramatic change in the concept of a library, in that along with book collections and other print collections (such as photo and microfilm/microfiche), it also holds in its collection video, DVD, software, CD-ROM, and other nonprint materials for patrons and students to use. They also have multimedia workstations available so that users can take advantage of electronic resources such as the Internet. Media Librarians are the professional specialists who manage these increasingly in-demand centers.

Within the library community, there seems to be some confusion about the term *Media Librarian*. Some

librarians consider individuals working in libraries who have been trained in educational technology, instructional communication techniques and design, and audiovisual education to be Media Librarians. Others consider only Media Librarians working in a school or higher education environment to be "real" Media Librarians. Still others consider specialists employed in libraries who have a degree in the areas of video, music, photography, film, or graphics to be Media Librarians.

As Dr. John W. Ellison, associate professor in the Department of Library and Information Studies at the New York State University at Buffalo, points out, "Persons educated (through course work or real world experience) in exclusively one medium such as film, video, print, or photography should be called film, video, print, or photography specialists. Those persons educated in educational technology, instructional communication, instructional design, or audiovisual education may well be knowledgeable in several non-print formats, but lacking the print education or knowledge gained from experience, would prevent them from being considered media librarians." His point is that those librarians who truly should be considered Media Librarians typically have an excellent background in traditional library work combined with nonprint library services backgrounds and experience. By the very nature of their educational training, they are knowledgeable about nonprint formats and the selection, organization, management, and programming that are necessary to develop nonprint library services. As Ellison notes, "Most media librarians will see the broader aspects of services rather than the limited 'educational' view often possessed by nonprint generalists or the extremely narrow perspective of some film specialists."

While Media Librarians are leading the way, all library positions have been altered by the advent of the Internet and its e-communication technology and by the widening of the library profession to encompass *all* aspects of organizing, processing, using, and analyzing information. Media Librarians can be found in companies and government as well as schools and colleges and public library systems. They are involved in a variety of activities, depending on the type of library in which they work, the identified needs of its patrons, and the scope of their responsibilities.

As managers, Media Librarians develop staff (and the criteria used to select media personnel) and evolve the administrative manuals used by them. They conduct evaluations of the adequacy and suitability of facilities, equipment, nonprint materials, and services. They schedule inventory of equipment and establish policies for the maintenance of materials and equipment. They determine the library's goals regarding media services and develop criteria for evaluating materials and equipment. On the one hand, they plan the arrangements of space and furniture for media areas of the library and on the other hand, conduct training of personnel and administer patron tours and orientation programs in the use of media equipment and technology. They may be required to develop grant proposals for federal, state, and privately funded projects and programs and plan and implement community relations activities in relation to the library's media programs, as well as prepare a media services bulletin (newsletter or blog) and prepare other promotional materials.

Media Librarians conduct research on existing and emerging technologies that may impact the library's media equipment and services. They develop a plan of assessment and evaluation of the media program based on the library's established objectives and disseminate their research information and findings, ultimately applying their conclusions to the department's

operation. They research, preview, evaluate, select, and acquire materials and equipment for their media services department. Upon acquisition, they assign accession or inventory numbers to materials and equipment purchased (or gained through donations). They set up equipment and give instruction on the use of it as well as demonstrate the effective use of nonprint media materials.

Furthermore, Media Librarians establish library policy for distribution of nonprint media materials and equipment, schedule the use of materials and equipment, and maintain distribution files and records. They establish the cataloging procedures for materials and equipment and establish classification procedures. They compile a materials list and prepare annotations for in-house publications concerning the media services available. In addition, they may write reviews for professional publications. By fostering collection-building practices that assure access to sources of electronic information, Media Librarians help libraries represent the increasingly diverse spectrum of perspectives and formats available in the ever-changing digital age. They aid libraries in reacting to the growing importance and influence of new and emerging interactive social media such as blogs, social networks, and wikis (collaborative Web sites whose content can be edited by anyone who has access to it) that have quickly gained a foothold in the culture and are popular with many patrons of libraries and with students. Media Librarians have the task of finding information systems and technology applications that incorporate the basic library tenet of free access to information and that help their libraries build diverse digital collections.

Salaries

Annual earnings for Media Librarians ranged from $32,000 to $55,000 or more according to a September 2007 salary survey report made by PayScale, Inc. The highest-paid Media Librarians tended to be at academic libraries serving major colleges and universities.

Employment Prospects

Library use is increasing in both academic/school and public libraries. Libraries today respond to the new technologies and means of information processing available to the public. They teach and make accessible the skills, materials, and equipment to help their patrons make effective use of information in all formats. Thus, libraries have a tremendous need to have media specialists as part of their staff. Job growth for Media Librarians is on the upswing and will continue to grow in the foreseeable future in public, academic, and school libraries; in private industry; and in such special libraries as health and law media centers.

Advancement Prospects

Many Media Librarians obtain advancement through increases in pay. When there is more than one staff member, Media Librarians can move to supervisory and management positions. By obtaining further licensing, Media Librarians can advance further into the ranks of library management by applying for positions as library directors, library supervisors or coordinators at the district (or central office) level in statewide systems, or chief information officers in their corporate or special libraries. Those with higher educational administrative ambitions can look for positions as principals (of schools), program directors, assistant superintendents, and school superintendents.

Education and Training

A standard master's degree in library and information science (M.L.I.S.) is a basic requirement for Media Librarians. In addition, it is recommended that library students interested in new technologies applied to the library environment should seek multidisciplinary programs that prepare individuals for what is now a multichannel information society. For Media Librarians working in school or academic libraries, it is recommended that they have either a standard M.L.S. degree or a master's degree with a specialty in school library media from an educational institution accredited by the National Council for the Accreditation of Teacher Education (NCATE).

Special Requirements

Media Librarians who are employed by school systems (and in some cases, those who work in academic libraries) may be required by states to be certified as teachers, particularly those working within state university or library systems.

Experience, Skills, and Personality Traits

Media Librarians should have a solid foundation and passion for technology in all its forms. They must be extremely adept at computer technology and software. They need to have excellent teaching and communication skills (both written and oral), and interpersonal, management, and problem-solving capabilities. In addition, attention to detail and good organizational talents are essential components of this post. Media Librarians should be enthusiastic in nature; warm and positive in their response to patrons and students; and caring, creative, and flexible in their commitment to help patrons and students.

Unions and Associations

The single most important professional association for Media Librarians is the American Library Association (ALA). In addition, they may find it beneficial to have membership in such organizations as the American Society for Information Science and Technology (ASIS&T), the Association for Educational Communications and Technology (AECT), the Library and Information Technology Association (LITA), the Special Libraries Association (SLA), and, especially, the Council on Library/Media Technicians (COLT).

Tips for Entry

1. While earning your undergraduate and M.L.S. degrees, volunteer or intern at a school or public library media center to learn firsthand about what such a center and its librarians do.
2. Upon being hired as a Media Librarian, continue your professional development through self-study, networking with colleagues, attending professional conferences, and enrolling in continuing education courses devoted to new media technology.
3. Investigate the informative Web site entitled Digital Media and the Library at http://www.nmrls. org/ce/digitalmedia.htm.

PUBLIC RELATIONS DIRECTOR

Duties: Supervise the planning, development, and implementation of diversified programs designed to inform and serve library users, the public, local and national media, legislators, private donors, and civic organizations in order to support fund-raising and other goals of a library

Alternate Title(s): Media Outreach Coordinator; Public Information Officer; Public Relations Coordinator; Public Relations Manager; Public Relations Specialist

Salary Range: $32,000 to $65,000 or more

Employment Prospects: Fair

Advancement Prospects: Fair to good

Prerequisites:

    Education and Training—Bachelor's degree in advertising, communications, marketing, public relations, or a related area; master's degree in library science (M.L.S.) or in library and information science (M.L.I.S.) seldom required, though desirable

    Experience—Two to three years of experience supervising public relations specialists engaged in the preparation of promotional and informational material, preferably for a library; some background

in the creation of library promotional and informational pieces

    Special Skills and Personality Traits—Ability to communicate effectively, both verbally and in writing; excellent analytical and computer skills; creativity, initiative, and good judgment; excellent decision-making, problem-solving, and research capabilities; leadership ability and positive, outgoing personality; solid organizational talents

    Special Requirements—Certifications as public relations specialists are available but seldom required

---

CAREER LADDER

```
Public Relations Consultant; Public
Relations Company Manager
              |
Public Relations Director
              |
Public Relations Assistant
```

Position Description

Barron's Marketing Dictionary defines public relations as a "form of communication that is primarily directed toward gaining public understanding and acceptance." The definition states that public relations usually deals with issues, not products or services, and "uses publicity that does not necessitate payment in a wide variety of media and is often placed as news or items of public interest." Public relations, or PR, is used to establish and support rapport with the various publics that an organization may have. Its main purpose is to generate goodwill.

As such, public relations is often thought of as a principal management function in any organization through which public and private organizations and institutions seek to win and retain the understanding, sympathy, and support of those who may be concerned. It is an essential element in the communication system that informs the public on many aspects of library services that may affect their lives.

The public relations process includes an analysis of the current situation within the library and/or library system, which is helpful in establishing the library's current strengths, weaknesses, and potential. It also helps in assessing the institution's public image and constituency. In turn, the process helps to formulate an action program of public relations objectives as well as an allocation of a budget. The final step is a measurement and evaluation of the success of this program and a reanalysis of the library's current situation.

The primary objectives of most library public relations programs are to promote community awareness of library service, to stimulate public interest in and usage of the library, and to develop a public understanding and support of the library and its role within the community. As a means of accomplishing these objectives, Public Relations Directors at libraries often develop an annual plan of specific goals and activities and detail the funds that should be allocated to carry out the agenda and the periodic evaluation of the program. They may set up training sessions, workshops, and other aids in which library staff members can participate to assure courteous, efficient, and friendly contact with library patrons and the public. Personal and informational group contacts are set up and maintained with government officials, opinion leaders, service clubs, civic associations, and other community organizations by both library staff and library board members. Public Relations Directors also frequently conduct surveys of the community to assure the effectiveness of the library's responsiveness to the interests and needs of the public. As a means of communication, Public Relations Directors use the local media to keep the public aware of and informed about the library's resources and services and produce newsletters, brochures, and other promotional materials to be distributed to the public. They also help the library sponsor programs, classes, exhibits, and other library-centered activities and set up the means of cooperating with other community groups in organizing these activities to fulfill the community's needs for educational, cultural, informational, or recreational opportunities.

Public Relations Directors generate positive publicity for the library and its programs with the media, on the library's Web site, and through other new media outlets. They are tasked with tracking, quantifying, and reporting on the success (or failure) of library public relations programs and are responsible for coordinating the development and publication of all library-generated brochures, calendars, and Web materials. In their work, they must follow all library policies, guidelines, and procedures and may directly supervise any receptionist staff. In small public, school, or special libraries, public relations may be the sole concern and responsibility of the facility's director. In many academic and most larger public libraries and library systems, a separate staff position for a Public Relations Director is more typical.

Salaries

Depending on the size of the library and the scope of duties, annual salaries for Public Relations Directors may range from $32,000 to as high as $65,000 for experienced PR directors. This range of earnings for Public Relations Directors within the library community is lower than that of most Public Relations Directors working for business organizations, telecommunications companies, and government agencies.

Employment Prospects

As many people are attracted to the profession of public relations because of the high-profile nature of the work,

keen competition exists for most entry-level positions. In addition, most public relations applicants tend to look for positions at public relations firms, in companies, or in government. Individuals with an interest in librarianship who are also interested in public relations work may find employment as assistants in larger libraries or library systems. Opportunities are best for college graduates who have combined a degree in journalism, public relations, advertising, or another communications-related field with a PR internship or other related work experience. From being an assistant, the next step upward to becoming Public Relations Director may depend on attrition or transferring to another library or library system to obtain the post.

Advancement Prospects

Public Relations Directors in libraries who wish to escalate further in library administration must gain further education (an M.L.S. degree) and training. Some Public Relations Directors may decide to join a public relations firm as its top PR specialist or even set up their own public relations company and include in their client list smaller libraries who need guidance in their public relations efforts.

Education and Training

The usual requirement for public relations specialists (and Public Relations Directors) is an undergraduate degree in advertising, communications, journalism, or public relations. Regardless of their specific major, their curriculum should include courses in advertising, business administration, public affairs, public speaking, and creative and technical writing. It is also highly recommended that they gain practical experience in public relations through internship programs while in college. Additionally, specific experience working within a library will help to familiarize them with library policies, practices, and procedures.

Special Requirements

Accredited certifications for Public Relations Directors are seldom requested or required. However, for professional satisfaction, Public Relations Directors and their specialists who are members of the Public Relations Society of America (PRSA) can participate in an examination for accreditation. The Universal Accreditations Board gives the Accredited in Public Relations (APR) designation to those who have at least five years of full-time public relations work and a bachelor's degree in a communications-related field. In addition, the International Association of Business Communicators (IABC) has an accreditation program, resulting in the earning of the Accredited Business Communicator (ABC) designation.

Experience, Skills, and Personality Traits

Public Relations Directors must have the ability to communicate persuasively, both orally and in writing, with other members of their staff, the public, the media, and governing library boards. They need tact, good judgment, and an exceptional ability to establish and maintain effective work-related rapport. They should be creative, highly motivated, resistant to stress, and both flexible and decisive. They must have excellent analytical and computer abilities as well as be proficient at problem solving and research. They need to be well organized and be able to supervise and guide their staffs.

Unions and Associations

Public Relations Directors and their staffs may find it useful to belong to the primary association of the public relations profession, the Public Relations Society of America (PRSA), as well as the American Marketing Association (AMA). In addition, as they must be familiar with the library and information community. Membership in such associations as the American Society for Information Science and Technology (ASIS&T) and the American Library Association (ALA) may prove useful as well.

Tips for Entry

1. Practice your public relations skills while in college by volunteering to publicize school events or act as a "media contact" for a campus organization.

2. When taking classes in journalism and business communications, focus on how public relations individuals "manage" the media in order to plant favorable ideas about their projects, services, and key personnel.

3. Increase your interest in the expanding potentials of the Internet and the creation of blogs, as these new communication technologies may prove to be essential in your PR efforts on behalf of the library or library system for which you work.

PUBLIC SERVICES LIBRARIAN

Duties: Assist library patrons in locating and obtaining material; instruct patrons in the use of library materials and technologies; promote library services and answer telephone (and e-mail) reference and information inquiries; supervise library assistants and aid in the selection, purchase, and preparation of new materials

Alternate Title(s): Adult Service Librarian; Information Specialist; Librarian; Public Librarian

Salary Range: $25,000 to $90,000 or more

Employment Prospects: Good

Advancement Prospects: Good to excellent

Prerequisites:

Education or Training—Bachelor's degree and a master's degree in library or information science (M.L.S.) required; additional degrees may be mandatory when working as a Public Services Librarian within an academic library or university environment

Experience—Volunteer background in a library or a student internship is recommended

Special Skills and Personality Traits—Detail oriented with strong organizational abilities; excellent interpersonal and communication skills; computer proficiency and willingness to work independently; service orientation

Special Requirements—Most states require Public Services Librarians employed by city, county, or regional library systems to be certified

Position Description

Public libraries are institutions created through legislation within the jurisdiction they serve. As such, they receive taxpayer funding but must adhere to service standards and meet a wide group of (ever-changing) patron needs. They are usually overseen by a board of directors or library commission from the community. Public libraries provide a wider range of needs and objectives than most other such facilities. They serve the leisure-reading wants of people from children to senior citizens and the information needs of patrons from first graders to scholars. In addition, they provide Internet access. Occasionally, private lending libraries serve the public in the same manner as public libraries. Academic libraries, on the other hand, primarily serve a specific postsecondary educational institution.

Public Services Librarians work directly with the public. Librarians who work within public facilities may specialize in one area of work (such as circulation and interlibrary loan or reference and research) or perform many types of jobs, depending on the character and size of the library. In all cases, service is the key word. Public

Services Librarians assist patrons in finding information and using it effectively for personal and professional purposes, so they have to be familiar with a wide variety of scholarly and public information resources. They talk to library users to learn what information they need and then help them conduct a search. This may involve teaching users how to use computers to search for items based in the library or on the Internet. Librarians may help users locate materials in the library. If the item the library patron needs is not housed at the particular institution, Public Services Librarians will search other libraries to see if the item(s) can be located at other facilities. They oversee and coordinate interlibrary loan and document delivery services. They also explain library activities, rules, and services to users. They demonstrate library equipment to patrons, explain library procedures, and detail how to use library facilities. If a patron makes a complaint, they take action to resolve the problem.

A second part of being a Public Services Librarian involves technical work. They order and receive library materials. When the items arrive, they classify them by subject matter and may enter (or supervise the entering of) the information about the materials into the online catalog system. They check the condition of books when they are returned by library patrons and ensure that those that are worn are repaired. They may work at circulation desks where they check out items to customers and accept payment of any overdue fines.

A third area of Public Services Librarians' work is administrative. They supervise other employees and plan activities for library patrons. They may organize book sales, children's storytelling hours, book discussions for adults, and other special events. They order supplies and equipment and prepare budgets as well as monitor income and expenses. They may also be responsible for negotiating contracts for services, such as cleaning. They may hire, direct, and train library staff. In addition, they usually are involved in the library's education of the public about the institution and its services and may put together fund-raising events. They may confer with local schoolteachers, administrators, and community members to develop, plan, and conduct programs involving the library and the community.

In large facilities, librarians often specialize in a single area, such as acquisitions, cataloging, reference, special collections, or administration. In smaller libraries, they may do all of these tasks. They may also be tasked with compiling lists of books, periodicals, articles, audiovisual materials, and other nonprint resources on particular subjects and with analyzing the library's collection and recommending further materials.

Public Services Librarians may also work in academic libraries, where the emphasis is less on the public and more on the particular information needs of students, teachers, and scholars. The marketing of library services in academic libraries is to the faculty and administration of the institution rather than the general public. Nonetheless, much of the work of the Public Services Librarian is the same in both cases, as they provide assistance in such library functions as circulation; e-reference; aid in the use of print, nonprint, and electronic sources; and other patron services.

Public Services Librarians must understand and work with both the standard Dewey decimal system of classifying library materials and computer databases as well as keep abreast of current technological trends that apply to library work. Automated registration of borrowers (of library materials), circulation of materials, ordering, and cataloging are now common in all types of public libraries. Many libraries have access to remote databases and maintain their own computerized databases. The widespread use of automation in libraries makes it critically important for Public Services Librarians to develop their database searching skills. Librari-

ans develop and index databases and help train users to develop search skills. Some public libraries and library systems are forming consortiums with other libraries (and systems) through e-mail and sharing of files, allowing library patrons to submit information requests simultaneously to several libraries (or systems).

Work schedules for Public Services Librarians may be busy, demanding, and stressful, since answering questions and teaching library patrons how to use library resources can be taxing. They may be required to work evenings and weekends and may be required to do much standing, stooping, bending, and reaching.

Salaries

Salaries for Public Services Librarians vary a great deal depending on the specific job responsibilities as well as the size and location of the library. Librarians with primarily administrative duties (which include supervisory duties) often earn more than other librarians. According to the 2007 joint ALA-APA salary survey of public library positions, annual income for librarians of all regions who supervise support staff ranged from a minimum of $25,896 to a maximum of $112,710, with the median salary being $48,432. For those public librarians of all regions who do not supervise, yearly salaries ranged from a minimum of $22,048 to a maximum of $89,572, with the median salary being $46,471.

Employment Prospects

According to the U.S. Department of Labor's Bureau of Labor Statistics, employment of librarians in general is expected to grow more slowly than the average for all occupations through 2014. However, job openings are expected to be very good because a large number of librarians are expected to retire during this period. More than three in five librarians will become eligible for retirement during this time, which will result in many job vacancies.

However, as the Department's *Occupational Outlook Handbook, 2007–08* states, further growth in the number of librarians will be limited (to some extent) by the increasing use of computerized information storage and retrieval systems and the hiring instead of less costly library technicians and assistants. Computerized systems make cataloging easier, allowing library technicians to perform the work. In addition, many libraries are equipped for users to access library computers directly from their homes or offices. In this way, users can bypass librarians altogether and conduct research on their own. Nonetheless, librarians will be needed to manage staff, help users with database searching, address complicated reference requests (either by phone, e-mail, or in person), and define users' needs.

Advancement Prospects

Public Services Librarians can advance to administrative positions, possibly leading to becoming library director. Promotions typically come with the acquisition of experience and administrative skills, full knowledge of the library's automated systems, and additional training.

Public Services Librarians may apply their information management and research skills to arenas outside libraries, for example, database development, reference tool development, information systems, publishing, Internet coordination, marketing, and training of database users. Librarians with entrepreneurial instincts may sometimes start their own consulting practices, acting as freelance librarians or information brokers and servicing libraries, businesses, and government agencies.

Education and Training

Most public library positions require a bachelor's degree and a master's degree in library science (M.L.S.) or library and information science (M.L.I.S.), preferably from a school accredited by the American Library Association (ALA). Bachelor's degrees in almost any subject are appropriate.

Most M.L.S. and M.L.I.S. programs take one to two years to complete. Computer-related course work is becoming an increasingly important part of an M.L.S. degree. Some programs offer interdisciplinary degrees that combine technical courses in information processing and science with traditional training in library science. The M.L.S. degree provides general preparation for library work, but individuals often specialize in a particular area, such as reference, technical services, or children's services. Librarians usually participate in continuing training and education throughout their careers to keep abreast of new information systems brought about by constantly changing technology.

Special Requirements

States generally have certification requirements for Public Services Librarians in public schools and local libraries, though there are wide variations among states. Some 24 states require librarians employed in local library systems to be certified, while several other states have voluntary certification guidelines.

Experience, Skills, and Personality Traits

Public Services Librarians must have strong interpersonal, computer, organizational, communication, and instruction skills. They need to show initiative, commitment, creativity, and attention to detail. They have to be open to considering new ideas, new concepts, and differing opinions. They should be curious and exhibit a love of books, research, and education, particularly in the area of library and database instruction. They should be team players and be willing to do a variety of tasks, possibly all within the same day's work. They need to be extremely patient, good listeners, and very customer oriented.

They need to be fully knowledgeable about the principles, practices, and theory of collection development including selection, deselection, and evaluation tools and methods. They need to be familiar with the role serial and book vendors play in the acquisition process. They should have some experience in the principles, theories, and practices of adult learning and how library users process and use information. They must be knowledgeable of the principles and practices of online searching, including search construction and strategy, search commands and syntax, index structure, use of controlled vocabularies, and natural language searching. They need to gain experience in the content and structure of a variety of databases to determine the most appropriate and cost-effective one for providing the required information to the library user.

Finally, they must have proven supervisory skills, as they usually will be required to supervise a wide variety of library staff. They need to have the ability to train other members of the library staff in technologies related to the library's information systems.

Unions and Associations

The primary professional organizations of interest to Public Services Librarians are the American Library Association (ALA) and the American Society of Information Science and Technology (ASIS&T). They may also join such groups as the Public Library Association (PLA) and the Association of College and Research Libraries (ACRL) if they work in an academic library. In addition, the International Federation of Library Associations and Institutions (IFLA) represents the interests of libraries and librarians internationally.

Tips for Entry

1. While earning your bachelor's and master's degrees, volunteer at your school or a local library to gain familiarity with library practices.
2. Start working as a library technical assistant, as this is excellent background for all library work.
3. Look for jobs on the Internet (such as at http://www.lisjobs.com and http://www.libraryjobpostings.org) and on job bulletin boards at placement services that list library-related jobs.

REFERENCE LIBRARIAN

Duties: Analyze library patrons' research requests to determine needed information and assist in furnishing or locating that data; use standard reference materials, including online databases and the Internet, to answer reference questions; explain to patrons how to use the facility's resources

Alternate Title(s): Electronic Resource and Reference Librarian; Head of Information and Reference Services; Library Media Research Specialist; Reference and Electronic Services Librarian; Research Librarian

Salary Range: $22,048 to $60,000 or more

Employment Prospects: Excellent

Advancement Prospects: Good to excellent

Prerequisites:

Education or Training—Bachelor's degree and master's degree in library science (M.L.S.) or in library and information science (M.L.I.S.) required

Experience—Student internship or volunteer experience in a library is recommended

CAREER LADDER

Reference Librarian at Larger Library; Library Director; Independent Information Broker

↑

Reference Librarian

↑

Assistant Reference Librarian; Library Reference Assistant

Special Skills and Personality Traits—Attention to detail; excellent people skills; communication and computer proficiency; organizational ability; willingness to work independently

Special Requirements—State certification may be necessary; licensing for school library media research specialists is often required

Position Description

Reference Librarians, usually working at a reference desk (sometimes called an information desk), help individuals doing research to locate the information they need through a structured conversation called a reference interview, in which the Reference Librarian responds to the library user's initial explanation of his or her information needs by first attempting to clarify the patron's request, then by determining what information sources will fill that need and directing the user to the appropriate resources. The assistance may take the form of research on a specific question, providing direction on the use of databases and other electronic information resources, obtaining specialized materials from other library and information sources, or providing access to and care of delicate or expensive library-held materials. In one or more of these services, help may be sometimes provided by other library staff members who have been given special training. The services that are provided at a reference desk may vary depending on the type of library, its purpose, its resources, its size, and its staff.

Typically, a reference desk can be consulted either in person, by telephone, through e-mail, or by online chat.

The increasing role of technology in libraries has had a significant impact on the roles of various library jobs, including those of Reference Librarians. New technologies are dramatically increasing the accessibility of information, and Reference Librarians have found they need to adopt such technologies to adapt to the evolving needs of today's library users. The most significant example of how technology has altered the role of the librarian in the last 50 years has been the move from traditional card catalogs of the library's resources to online public access catalogs (OPACs).

Increasingly, the job of a Reference Librarian is changing due to the Internet. Requests for a specific bit of information, such as the address of a government agency or where to obtain tax forms, are declining, as much of that kind of information is relatively easy now to find online. Reference questions are becoming more complex, requiring more in-depth and time-consuming investigation. In addition, the wonderful explosion of information access can also translate into a confusing welter of options for a customer. As Walter Gregner, supervisor of the art, music, and video department at the Minneapolis Public Library, states, "When people call us now with reference questions, it's increasingly prefaced with a statement like, 'I've been trying to find this on the Internet for the last three hours.'" Gregner goes on to say, "They're not very savvy yet about the best way to access information. Increasingly, the role of the reference librarian is becoming one of being an instructor or adviser on how to find something on the Internet. We give them advice on different search engines to use, or we've already bookmarked certain sites that we know are useful for certain types of information." A survey conducted for the Urban Libraries Council in 2000 indicated that the Internet is not driving people away from libraries. On the contrary, of the 3,087 adults surveyed, 75.2 percent of Internet users said they also use the library, and 60.3 percent of library users also used the Internet. An additional incentive for Internet users to tap into their local library is cost. Large library systems—especially those in large cities and at many universities—subscribe to online journals and databases that charge fees that library patrons, in turn, can typically access free of charge. As an information adviser, today's Reference Librarian is well equipped to direct library users to the best tool for their research needs, saving time and providing a less frustrating experience for the library patron.

Another changing facet of the Reference Librarian's job is e-mail requests for information. It is becoming increasingly common for a Reference Librarian to receive such a request, find the relevant data, and send it to the library user as an e-mail attachment. (Many libraries, such as the New York Public Library, have even created a new online library position to handle such e-mail requests.) Many Reference Librarians now provide virtual reference services (via Web-based chat, instant messaging, text messaging, and e-mail), teach technology classes to their users, and work on the development of information architectures for improving access and search functionality.

Besides the reference and research aspects of their positions, Reference Librarians select and suggest materials for purchase and then prepare those items by classifying them according to subject matter. They supervise library assistants who prepare cards, computer records, or other access tools that direct library patrons to resources. They compile lists of books, periodicals, articles, audiovisual materials, and electronic resources on particular subjects and are frequently asked to analyze the library's collections and recommend additions for them. Depending on their subject specialty, Reference Librarians may be assigned to collect and organize books, pamphlets, manuscripts, and other print materials in their specific field and to recommend electronic resources for easy access to other materials relevant to potential research in their specialty field. Many Reference Librarians are given responsibility for service in other departments, such as circulation, interlibrary loan, and computer services, depending on the size and needs of their institutions.

Those Reference Librarians in senior positions, such as "head of reference," are responsible for the overall management of the reference department. This encompasses the supervision and evaluation of staff, scheduling and staffing of the reference desk(s), development of the reference collection, compiling of reference department statistics on a scheduled basis, and participation in budget allocation procedures.

Salaries

The earnings of Reference Librarians vary a great deal depending on their responsibilities, experience and expertise, and the size and location of the library. Starting annual salaries for Reference Librarians with M.L.S. degrees but no experience can range from $25,000 to $36,000 or more. Median yearly salaries for Reference Librarians range from $35,546 to $59,063, depending on location and type of library, according to PayScale, Inc.'s, 2007 Salary Survey Report. Experienced Reference Librarians can expect annual incomes ranging upward to $70,000 or more.

Employment Prospects

Chances of employment as a Reference Librarian are good to excellent. According to Market Data Retrieval, a subsidiary of Dun & Bradstreet that provides information on the education market (including public libraries), the number of reference specialists working in public libraries increased by 56 percent from 1995 to 2002. The need for technologically adept Reference Librarians is only escalating along with the expansion of available data resources. Additionally, the large number of expected retirements in the next decade is anticipated to result in many job openings for librarians in general and Reference Librarians in particular to replace those who leave.

Advancement Prospects

Reference Librarians can progress to administrative positions or to work that is more specialized. Promotions usually come from the acquisition of experience and administrative skills, the knowledge of automated library systems, and additional training. Advancement opportunities tend to be greater in larger library systems.

In addition, librarians are increasingly applying their information management and research skills to arenas outside libraries, such as database development, reference tool development, information systems, publishing, Internet coordination, marketing, and training of database users. Reference Librarians with entrepreneurial skills and ambitions sometimes start their own consulting practices, acting as freelance librarians or information brokers and providing services to libraries, businesses, and governmental agencies.

Education and Training
Although many schools offer master's degrees in library science (M.L.S.), most libraries prefer graduates of the approximately 60 schools accredited by the American Library Association (ALA). Reference Librarians should have a master's degree in library science (M.L.S.) or library and information science (M.L.I.S.) and a bachelor's degree (B.A.) in almost any field. Reference Librarians often combine their M.L.S. degree with a master's degree (in business administration, law, medicine, or other field), or a Ph.D. in their own specialized field, particularly if they wish to work within any of the larger public library systems or in academic libraries.

The ALA, Special Libraries Association (SLA), and American Association of Law Libraries (AALL) as well as additional organizations have various scholarships to assist library students. Some library science departments also offer graduate student assistantships and scholarships.

Special Requirements
Most states require that public librarians (including Reference Librarians) employed by city, county, or regional library systems be certified. Reference Librarians employed in academic libraries who become members of the teaching staff of their educational institution usually are required to be certified as teachers. Those employed in public libraries not a part of regional library systems usually are not required to be certified.

Experience, Skills, and Personality Traits
Reference Librarians must possess excellent research, writing, and editing skills. They must exhibit extraordinary customer service abilities with strong interpersonal and communication talents. They must be able to interact diplomatically with customers and staff at all levels. They have to demonstrate an understanding of the critical need to turn information into useful knowledge. They must possess a strong work ethic and demonstrate critical thinking and teaching skills. Their analytical skills should include subject analysis and the ability to organize and describe resources. They need to be able to handle a number of tasks simultaneously, manage multiple projects, and be flexible enough to deal with constantly changing priorities and deadlines.

Reference Librarians must be heavily detail oriented and highly organized. They should be able to work independently but also work well in a team environment. They should be able to demonstrate effective conflict resolution management and have the ability to take a lead role by displaying initiative and seeking and communicating service improvements. They should have outstanding computer and Internet skills, including know-how with electronic resources and content evaluation techniques. They need to be highly proficient with but not limited to Microsoft Office applications and Adobe Acrobat and have a working knowledge of Web-based information and library database systems.

Unions and Associations
Reference Librarians may belong to a variety of trade associations that provide educational guidance and professional support through conferences and various other informational means to their members. Primary for Reference Librarians is the Reference and User Services Association (RUSA), an arm of the American Library Association (ALA). Other pertinent organizations include the ALA itself, the American Society for Information Science and Technology (ASIS&T), and the Special Libraries Association (SLA).

Tips for Entry
1. To see firsthand how a typical reference department operates, visit the reference department of a large local library or a university, college, or central public library. Observe the reference desk and pose sample research questions to gain insight into what a Reference Librarian deals with on a daily basis.
2. While earning your bachelor's and master's degrees, consider student internship programs in libraries or volunteer in your local public or school library to gain seasoning within a library environment.
3. It is important to remember that membership in professional associations keeps librarians aware of the constantly changing array of technology that is reshaping library services.

SCHOOL LIBRARIAN

Duties: Manage, develop, and promote a library within a school to ensure that it provides an effective resource and information source for the institution's pupils and staff

Alternate Title(s): Coordinator, Media Resources—Library; Information Technology Specialist; Library Media Teacher; Media Center Director; School Library Media Specialist

Salary Range: $30,000 to $80,000 or more

Employment Prospects: Good

Advancement Prospects: Good

Prerequisites:

Education or Training—Bachelor's degree, preferably in education; master's degree in library science (M.L.S.) or in library and information science (M.L.I.S.) usually needed; additional education degree typically also necessary

Experience—Knowledge of and experience with information technology and library skills; some teaching background helpful

CAREER LADDER

Library Administrator; Media Specialist at Larger College, University, or School System; Teacher, Library School

School Librarian

Library or Media Assistant

Special Skills and Personality Traits—Ability to facilitate groups and communicate effectively; excellent writing and speaking talents and leadership abilities; good organizational and planning skills; solid understanding of the information needs of children or young adults and some knowledge of children and adolescent behavior and development

Special Requirements—Certification as a school library media specialist required; additional education certification may be necessary as well

Position Description

Elementary schools, junior and senior high schools, and colleges and universities all employ librarians, who select and order books, audiovisual materials, computer equipment and databases, and other print and nonprint materials in order to support their institutions' educational programs. They maintain their collections so students (and faculty) can access them easily, and they also teach students how to use them effectively.

In colleges and universities, School Librarians are typically called academic librarians. Most college and university librarians have master's degrees in library science. Top administrative posts, however, generally go to those who have doctoral degrees as well. Librarians who work in large university libraries are frequently required to have master's degrees in the subject areas of the faculties they represent as well as master's degrees in library and/or information science. Some academic libraries may even require proficiency in foreign languages.

Actual duties in elementary, junior, and senior high school libraries vary according to the size of the facility and the needs of the students. High school libraries are generally bigger than those in elementary schools

because older students need more extensive resources for research. Elementary and secondary school librarians often work alone, while librarians in larger school systems, colleges, and universities may be members of sizable staffs that include technical assistants and clerks. The tasks of cataloging new materials, returning materials to their shelves or bins, and the repair of damaged books are usually accomplished by these support staff, but in smaller libraries, it often is librarians themselves who do these chores.

Elementary School Librarians usually teach basic library skills and the use of basic reference materials in regularly scheduled classes in the library. They teach students how to distinguish the various kinds of books and how to use the library's classification systems for locating books and other materials. They promote the use of the library for information and research while making it an interesting and important part of the school day.

It usually is in junior and senior high school (or equivalent private school) that students learn more extensively about research techniques, so that School Librarians often hold orientation sessions to explain the use of library card or automated catalogs, computer databases, reference books, indexes to periodicals, and audiovisual and other nonprint materials. School Librarians may set up exhibits designed to make students aware of the library's holdings or connect the exhibits to historical events or holidays.

In their mission to support an institution's educational programs, School Librarians perform separate but overlapping roles to link the information resources and services of the library media programs to the information needs and interests of the school's students and faculty. As program administrators, they guide and direct all activities related to the library program, such as the management of staff, budgets, equipment, and facilities. They plan, execute, and evaluate the library program to ensure its quality both at a general level and on a day-to-day basis. They work with the school's administration and technology coordinator on establishing policies for use of electronic hardware and software within the library and supervise and maintain all ongoing and daily functions of the school library media center. They maintain circulation and usage records, which provide detail for support of ongoing library programs. They supervise the library facilities and make recommendations for media center budget expenditures and all proposals for improvement of library and media services. School Librarians usually submit monthly reports to the school's principal or administration detailing library statistics with notes, commentary, reports, and recommendations.

As information specialists, School Librarians provide their expertise in acquiring and evaluating information resources in all types of formats and in bringing an awareness of information issues to teachers, administrators, students, and others as well as providing a model for students in the effective locating, accessing, and evaluating of information within and beyond the library media center. They continually evaluate the library's collections and programs in terms of the needs of the students and faculty, accepted standards of quality, and the expansion and availability of appropriate technology.

As a teacher, the School Librarian works with students and other members of the academic community to analyze learning and information needs, the location and use of resources that will meet those needs, and the understanding and communication of the data these resources provide. As such, the School Librarian must be knowledgeable about current research on teaching and learning and be skilled in applying the research to a variety of situations, particularly those that call for students to access, evaluate, and use information from multiple sources (and by various means) in order to learn, think, create, and apply new knowledge. School Librarians may design and implement formal and informal in-service education for library and teaching staff on matters relating to the library's materials and the use of the library facilities. They often promote reading and literature appreciation through such activities as book talks, displays, author/illustrator presentations, and special events.

As an instructional partner with the school's teaching staff, School Librarians join with teachers and administrators to identify links regarding student information needs; curricular content; learning outcomes; and a wide range of print, nonprint, and electronic information resources. They frequently participate in district, building, department, and grade-level curriculum design and assessment of projects and work on integrating curriculum needs into the library media program. They often serve as a resource consultant for teachers, providing ideas and materials for classroom curricula, aiding in the interpretation and communication of intellectual content and suggesting materials for the professional growth of the school's teachers. In addition, they often consult with parents or parent groups on the reading and information needs of their children.

School Librarians are responsible for optimizing the use of information technology (IT) services within the library, which may include online data systems and in-house databases. They may develop training packages for staff and pupils on the use of IT materials and services as effective information retrieval tools. They supervise the proper arrangement of materials for effective retrieval, including the systematic indexing, classification, and cataloging of all library resources. They must maintain a library environment that is inviting, and conducive to learning. They establish and maintain standards of behavior for students to ensure a positive learning climate within the library. They supervise the library clerical and technical staffs and train student assistants and parent volunteers in facility procedures and practices.

Throughout their careers as School Librarians, they must keep abreast of new books, nonprint and technology-based materials, and current developments in curricula and educational technology through wide professional reading and attendance at professional conferences. They usually attend faculty meetings and often serve on school and district committees and may participate in monthly or quarterly programs and idea-sharing meetings with other librarians from the school's district and from local public libraries.

Salaries

Salaries vary by school, location, education, and experience. Starting salaries for School Librarians are comparable to initial salaries for teachers who have also earned master's degrees. Salaries typically increase with experience and education. In the National Education Association's *Estimates of School Statistics 2005*, the average classroom teacher's annual salary was estimated at $47,750 for the 2004–2005 year.

According to PayScale, Inc.'s, 2007 survey report on School Librarian jobs, median annual salaries for School Librarians and library media specialists ranged from a low of $31,914 to a high of $79,166, depending on location, educational level of the school, experience, and scope of responsibilities of the position.

Employment Prospects

The U.S. Department of Labor's Bureau of Labor Statistics projects that the growth of employment for librarians will be slower than the average for all jobs through 2014. However, census data and surveys also project a large percentage of librarians will retire in the next 10 to 12 years, creating a critical demand for new professionals.

A 2000 survey by the American Association of School Librarians (AASL) showed only 21 percent (approximately 800 graduates of accredited programs in the United States and Canada) of library school graduates went on to school librarianship or school media careers each year. Yet data from the same period indicated that there were more than 66,000 state-certified library media specialists in public and private schools throughout the United States. Still, competition for School Librarian jobs may be stiff in schools at all levels, especially those in urban areas. In addition, according to the National Center for Education Statistics (NCES), just 87 percent of public secondary schools in the United States have school libraries, and only 79 percent of public secondary schools have a paid full-time state-certified School Librarian.

Advancement Prospects

School Librarians often find advancement with additional education. With advanced degrees in library and information science or with second subject master's degrees, they may transfer to large college or university libraries or become library administrators where they can employ their administrative and organizational skills. They may also choose to become teachers at library schools.

Education and Training

It is recommended that applicants for School Librarian positions have a bachelor's degree in education and a master's degree in library science (M.L.S.) or library and information science (M.L.I.S.) from a program accredited by the American Library Association (ALA). Some 32 states have ALA-accredited programs. An example of specialized college degree courses that provide both an M.L.I.S. with a school library certification program is one given at the School of Information Sciences at the University of Pittsburgh (http://www2.sis.pitt.edu). Other programs are more often found in educational units accredited by the National Council for Accreditation of Teacher Education (NCATE).

Special Requirements

Depending on the state, elementary and secondary School Librarians usually need to be certified both as librarians and as teachers. To be certified as a School Librarian, they generally must earn a bachelor's degree and a master's degree in library science or library and information science and pass written examinations.

Most states require state certification for teachers and may require a library media teaching certification for their School Librarians as well as bonding and/or drug testing. Information about the National Board for Professional Teaching Standards' (NBPTS) certification in the area of library media can be found on its Web site at http://www.ala.org/aasltemplate.cfm?section=nationalboardcer. Another Web site that has data about certification of School Librarians is http://www.sldirectory.com/libsf/resf/jobs.html.

Experience, Skills, and Personality Traits

School Librarians must have experience and training in library practices and procedures. They should be familiar with computerized information retrieval systems and online catalogs. They must have excellent communication and interpersonal talents, as they must exhibit a good rapport with staff and students, usually of a diverse school population. They need to have superior organizational and planning skills and an ability to collaborate well with faculty, administrative staff, and other community-based groups. They should have some experience in teaching and a good understanding of the information requirements of children or young adults as well as an awareness of the behavior and development of children and adolescents.

Unions and Associations

Professional organizations of primary interest for School Librarians, other than the American Library Association (ALA), include the American Association of School Librarians (AASL), the Association for Library Service to Children (ALSC), and the American Society for Information Science and Technology (ASIS&T). Other professional associations of interest include the Association for Educational Communications and Technology (AECT), the Association for Supervision and Curriculum Development (ASCD), the Education and Library Networks Coalition (EdLiNC), the International Association of School Librarianship (IASL), the International Society for Technology in Education (ISTE), the International Federation of Library Associations and Institutions (IFLA), and the Young Adult Library Services Association (YALSA).

Tips for Entry

1. During your pursuit of your bachelor's and master's degrees, consider volunteering at local libraries or taking a student internship at a school or academic library to earn practical experience while gaining your degrees.

2. In your search for a job as a School Librarian, consult the AASL and their Web site (at http://www.ala.org/ala/aasl/aaslindex.cfm), which provide a collection of online resources for job postings throughout the United States.

3. In addition, the AASL offers a variety of books and other publications to assist school library media specialists and teachers in their collaborative library information programs for students.

SERIALS AND ACQUISITIONS LIBRARIAN

Position Description

Serials and Acquisitions Librarians are responsible for all the steps involved with the ordering and receipt of materials (print and nonprint) housed within the library or accessed electronically. The acquisitions process is the nuts and bolts of procuring items and paying the publishing companies that produce them. Acquisitions is usually part of the technical services department of the library. There are many types and sizes of publishers, with many of them now offering multimedia and electronic works in addition to the more traditional print titles.

While some publishing companies still depend exclusively on regional sales personnel to market and sell their products, most publishers work directly with libraries or through intermediaries known as jobbers to sell their products. These are industry middlemen who supply books, magazines, videos, CDs, DVDs, and other materials from hundreds of individual publishers. They pass on to libraries a discount from the publisher on the suggested retail or list price of an item. Typically,

discounts range from a low of 5 percent to a high of 40 percent. Other services offered by wholesalers include customized processing and cataloging of materials, special heavy-duty bindings, library MARC records on tape, catalog card sets, and bar codes. Most libraries work with a number of different wholesalers to acquire the range of materials their collections demand. Even so, there are occasions when a library makes purchases from their community or online bookseller because of immediate need, exclusive distribution, or other considerations.

Many jobbers (and individual publishers) offer an acquisitions service known as an approval plan. A library submits a detailed profile of its selection criteria to the jobber, who then automatically ships materials matching the profile to the library. Items are still subject to approval by the Serials and Acquisitions Librarian. Standing orders or continuation plans are another time-saver for libraries. With a standing-order contract, a library indicates that it will automatically purchase each new edition of a title. Another service offered by some companies is the rental of books whereby the Serials and Acquisitions Librarian (or staff under his or her supervision) preselect titles from a monthly catalog of forthcoming titles. This provides a steady infusion of new titles that can either be returned when their popularity has waned or, if needed, purchased to add to the permanent collection. In addition, many business, financial, and marketing publications, such as telephone directories, criss-cross directories, and corporate directories, have long been available to library collections not through outright purchase but through a lease agreement.

As the reliance of libraries on electronic sources of information, or e-collections, grows, so does the negotiation of the licensing agreement with the publisher become an important part of the acquisition process. Commonplace with personal computer software, then with CD-ROM products, and later with Web-delivered sources, licensing is a growing area of responsibility for the Serials and Acquisitions Librarian. The procurement of online sources is often handled directly with the company that produces the database, periodical index, full-text books, or other electronic information product, as jobbers and subscription agents have not yet entered into this market in any significant way. When library consortia, such as academic library systems, have negotiated group purchase deals, an intermediary agent may have been involved. (Publishers use licensing as a legal means of controlling the use of their products, and libraries may run the risk of narrowing or giving up the fair use rights that they and their patrons usually enjoy. That is why great care has to be taken on the part of the Serials and Acquisitions Librarian in negotiating such licenses.)

Other duties of most Serials and Acquisitions Librarians include managing the budget for books, journals, and electronic materials. They establish policies and procedures for the acquisitions department and monitor expenditures and encumbrances to ensure that funds are being expended at an appropriate rate. They supervise the verification, ordering, and receipt of materials and train all staff in the use of the acquisitions system and other departmental procedures. They provide statistical and/or financial reports to library administration on a regular basis and maintain patron use statistics of the print, serial, and electronic collections. They review gift materials and make certain that acknowledgments for gifts are sent out. They conduct use and cost studies to determine which journal subscriptions should be added or dropped, and they solicit feedback from library users to determine changing informational needs of the facility's patrons. They

may serve on committees within their library or their institution. They participate in liaison activities with the faculty of an institution or local community groups and businesses.

Usually, Serials and Acquisitions Librarians are also assigned reference or circulation duties on a regular basis, which includes helping patrons, students, or faculty access book, periodical, and electronic resources. In addition, as they manage all aspect of the library's book, journal, and electronic materials collections, they must keep abreast of new acquisitions technologies and equipment as well as such legal matters as access versus ownership problems and other issues that particularly concern the ongoing development and use of electronic formats of information.

Some libraries, particularly those in academic institutions, are finding that they need to create a separate position for an electronic resources librarian because the exploding electronic environment has complicated the nature of collection management. Such posts take on the specific acquisitions tasks of licensing electronic content and serve as the point person for electronic resource inquiries from faculty, staff, students, and library patrons.

Salaries

Salaries for this position vary a great deal depending on the responsibilities of the librarian and the location of the library. In general, annual salaries range from a low of $30,000 to as much as $60,000 depending on experience. Median yearly salaries for this position typically span from $40,000 to $50,000.

Employment Prospects

While employment of librarians in general is expected to grow more slowly than the average for all occupations through 2014 and beyond, job opportunities for qualified Serials and Acquisitions Librarians, particularly those with seasoning in electronic resources, is good, especially in academic facilities, as technological advances make their special skills vital in an increasingly complex information environment.

Advancement Prospects

Opportunities for advancement vary according to the interests and expertise of individual Serials and Acquisitions Librarians. Generally, the more education and specialized know-how an individual has, the better the prospects for advancement. Some may decide to advance further into library management: first to head the acquisitions department and then to become the director of the library. Those who focus on electronic resources may decide to apply their skills to arenas outside of libraries, such as database development, information systems, electronic publishing, or the marketing of electronic materials and information.

Education and Training

A master's degree in library science (M.L.S.) or in library and information science (M.L.I.S.) from an institution accredited by the American Library Association (ALA) is an absolute necessity. Many colleges and universities also require an additional master's degree in a particular subject area of importance to the institution and often combine the librarian job with a teaching position at the institution.

Special Requirements

Serials and Acquisitions Librarians who work in academic libraries often have teaching positions at the library's college or university. As such, besides their academic credentials, they may be required to hold teaching certifications.

Experience, Skills, and Personality Traits

Serials and Acquisitions Librarians must be fully knowledgeable about library acquisitions procedures, budget management, and fiscal control. They should have a working knowledge of database management and spreadsheet software. They must have hands-on work experience with one or more integrated library management systems, as well as the Online Computer Library Center (OCLC) network system. They must have a thorough knowledge of U.S. and foreign publishing industries, and experience negotiating with vendors and publishers is extremely helpful. Increasingly, knowledge of and experience with the purchasing, licensing, management, and technological aspects of electronic resources as well as the process of digitization of materials is becoming vital for Serials and Acquisitions Librarians.

They also must have excellent analytical, organizational, interpersonal, and communication skills. They need close attention to detail and must exhibit flexibility and initiative. They must be able to work independently as well as within a team environment and have the flexibility to work in rapidly changing, high-paced surroundings. Academic libraries may also require a potential candidate for the position to meet tenure requirements in the performance of primary responsibilities as well as a strong desire for professional and creative development.

Unions and Associations

Besides membership in the American Library Association (ALA), Serials and Acquisitions Librarians may want to join specific divisions or groupings within that professional organization, such as the Association for Library Collections and Technical Services (ALCTS) and the North American Serials Interest Group (NASIG). Additionally, they may find value in membership in such groups as the American Society of Information Science and Technology (ASIS&T), the Association of College and Research Libraries (ACRL), the Association of Subscription Agents (ASA), and the Special Libraries Association (SLA).

Tips for Entry

1. As employers seek librarians who are experienced with computers, expand your know-how with the Internet and electronic database structure while earning your library degree(s).

2. While completing your education, seek experience working in a library, such as restocking books or doing other similar duties, as these types of library jobs are often available to college students.

3. Join various professional organizations, such as the North American Serials Interest Group of the American Library Association or, if you are interested in a career in academic libraries, the Association of College and Research Libraries to provide a growing network through which you may learn about job and advancement opportunities.

SPECIAL COLLECTIONS LIBRARIAN

Duties: Supervise and manage all aspects of acquisitions operations (including cataloging, preservation, and promotion) relating to special collections of books and archival and other materials on specific subjects to be used primarily for research

Alternate Title(s): Collection Management Librarian; Collections Specialist; Curator of Special Collections; Head of Special Collections; Special Collections Archivist

Salary Range: $33,000 to $70,000 or more

Employment Prospects: Good

Advancement Prospects: Good

Prerequisites:

Education or Training—Bachelor's degree in any subject; master's degree in library science (M.L.S.) or master's degree in library and information science (M.L.I.S.); advanced degree in specialty area may be required

Experience—Several years of successful post-M.L.S. library experience (including archives and special collections management) in an academic or research setting often required

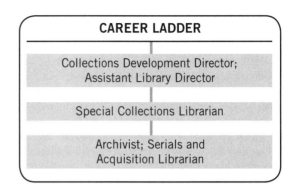

CAREER LADDER

Collections Development Director; Assistant Library Director

Special Collections Librarian

Archivist; Serials and Acquisition Librarian

Special Skills and Personality Traits—Ability to work independently; demonstrated organizational and planning abilities; excellent computer skills; flexibility, creativity, and initiative; good interpersonal and communication skills coupled with an ability to work effectively with a variety of library patrons and to interact favorably with potential donors; strong supervisory skills

Special Requirements—Special Collections Librarians in an academic library environment may be required to have a teaching certificate

Position Description

Special collections may include rare books, manuscripts, pamphlets, archival material, personal correspondence and photographs, or in-depth assortments of materials devoted to one or more related subjects. In academic libraries, such collections are often used to enhance the college's or university's curriculum and teaching programs as well as the larger scholarly community. Special collections can also be found in nonacademic areas, such as museums, medical institutions, and governmental agencies. Many collections are assembled to add prestige to the organization to which they are connected or are brought together for the purposes of an exhibit. Many others are designed to be held and not made available until a given period of time passes, as in collections of correspondence that must await the death of the originator of that correspondence.

Special Collections Librarians supervise the acquisition, cataloging, preservation, organization, and management of such specific subject collections. They manage the materials budget, monitor expenditures,

ensure the correct ordering and receipt of library materials in all types of formats and media for the collection, review and implement collection management policies, and oversee vendor relations and purchasing agreements. They must maintain accurate acquisitions data, statistics, reports, and policies. In some cases, Special Collections Librarians may have had the original idea of contacting a particular person or group of people in order to gain a predominant collection in a particular area, such as the writings of a specific author or playwright. In some instances, they may actively pursue possible "celebrity" donors, courting them, getting them to donate, adhering to the donor's requirements (as to the availability of the collection to the public, for example), promoting exhibits (if allowed) from the collection, keeping the donor happy, and so forth, as well as targeting other potential donors to build the library's reputation of housing distinguished special collections.

They examine reference works and consult specialists preparatory to selection of materials for their collection. They appraise books and other materials using references such as bibliographies, book auction records, and special catalogs on incunabula (printings prior to the year 1501). They may produce press releases announcing the acquisition of collections as well as compile bibliographies and publish papers concerning their special collection to notify scholars of available materials. They frequently lecture on book lore, act as consultants, and may plan and arrange special displays for library exhibits and produce related exhibition catalogs. They may be required to index and reproduce materials for sale to other libraries.

Within college and university libraries, Special Collections Librarians coordinate special collections with the development of the educational institution's library and archives for historical and scholarly information purposes. They usually participate in library-wide design, planning, management, and assessment of information and education services provided by the library. They maintain active liaison relationships with appropriate faculty members to ensure that the library's special collections continually anticipate and support new directions in the curriculum relating to the subject area of their special collection.

Special Collections Librarians may be involved in their library's electronic resources acquisitions programs and, as such, aid in devising efficient and responsive processes for acquiring needed digital resources and for maintaining and configuring them to maximize their utility. In addition, they may be involved in the process of gathering and analyzing usage data for subscribed electronic journals and databases that relate to the special collection under their care. They negotiate with vendors and publishers of commercially produced resources on pricing and access terms. They monitor the changing patterns of scholarly communication and publishing in their field of expertise to assess their impact on the acquisition and delivery of information from their special collection. They frequently work closely with library consortium partners of their library to coordinate collections and to expand the breadth of information resources and services that are available to their library patrons, students, faculty, or scholars.

Special collections often have great monetary as well as documentary and aesthetic value. Special Collections Librarians must take caution in situations when there is a potential for them to profit personally from library-related activities. They also must be sure that the special collection does not compete with the main library in the process of acquisition or in any other library activity. Special Collections Librarians' first responsibility is to the library as a whole, but they also must protect the confidentiality of researchers and any materials

from their collection as required by legal statutes, donor agreements, or policies of the library. They also must be very cognizant of security for the material and books in their special collection. The Association of College and Research Libraries (ACRL), a division of the American Library Association (ALA), recommends that special collections appoint a library security officer (LSO) and develop a security policy that ensures that all library staff members are aware of their legal and procedural responsibilities in applying security measures.

Salaries

Salaries of Special Collections Librarians are usually based on their experience and qualifications and may also vary according to the size and policy requirements of the special collection. Annual wages range from a minimum of $33,000 to a high of $70,000 or more, depending on the extent of their responsibilities; the size, type, and prestige of the special collection(s) under their control; and their library background.

Employment Prospects

While employment of librarians in general is expected to grow more slowly than the average for all occupations through 2014 and beyond, job opportunities for librarians are expected to be very good because a large number of librarians are expected to retire during this period. More than three in five librarians are age 45 or older and will become eligible for retirement in the next decade, resulting in many job openings. In addition, there have been a smaller number of people entering this profession in recent years, resulting in more jobs than applicants in many cases.

Those librarians with special interests who have had from two to four years of library experience in collections and acquisitions, particularly in an academic environment, should find ample opportunities to use their expertise in their field of interest by applying for positions as Special Collections Librarians.

Advancement Prospects

Special Collections Librarians in the larger academic libraries may look for promotion within the collections area of the library to the higher administrative position of collections development director, or they may decide to move into higher administrative positions within the library, such as assistant library director or library director.

Education and Training

As with librarians in general, Special Collections Librarians are required to have a bachelor's degree in a field of interest to them and a master's degree in library science (M.L.S.) or in library and information science (M.L.I.S.). Some libraries with special collections may also require advanced degrees (other master's degrees or Ph.D. degrees) in the subject area of the collection.

Special Requirements

Special Collections Librarians who also teach within the college or university in which the library resides may be required to have a teaching certificate in addition to their regular library degree qualifications.

Experience, Skills, and Personality Traits

Usually, a minimum of three to six years of progressively responsible experience in a library with an emphasis on collection development and collection assessment is recommended. College or university libraries usually require the collections experience be gained in an academic library. This background should include the training and supervision of students and volunteers as well as developing working partnerships with either academic departments or other professionals related to the use of special collections. Some experience in developing public programs and outreach strategies for a library collection is also important background for Special Collections Librarians.

They must have a strong service orientation; have excellent oral and written communication skills; possess a positive interpersonal style; have the ability to work both independently and as part of a team; and exhibit flexibility, initiative, and creativity. They should have shown a capacity for leadership and have excellent time management talents. They need to have a working knowledge of professional theories, techniques, terminology, and standards related to the arrangement and description of manuscripts, photographs, official records, and other source materials.

Special Collections Librarians should have a technical working knowledge of a wide variety of information technology applications, including working with metadata and digital projects, experience with integrated library systems, and know-how with MARC cataloging procedures. While not usually required, familiarity with collections management software, digitization of library resource material, and grant writing is highly recommended. In addition, experience in managing, licensing, and troubleshooting electronic resources and knowledge of recent trends in electronic preservation and access should be helpful. In order to pursue actively collections for their libraries, they also need the requisite skills, connections, and initiative to court the potential donors (who may be celebrities).

Unions and Associations

The primary professional association for Special Collections Librarians is the Association of College and Research Libraries (ACRL), a division of the American Library Association (ALA). Additionally, they may find value in membership in the Association for Library Collections and Technical Services (ALCTS) and the Association of Specialized and Cooperative Library Agencies (ASCLA), both divisions of the ALA, as well as the Rare Book and Manuscript Section (RBMS) of that association. Additionally, membership in the Special Libraries Association (SLA) may be valuable. Depending on their specialty, they may also want to join associations related to specific types of special libraries, such as the American Association of Law Libraries (AALL) or the Medical Library Association (MLA).

Tips for Entry

1. While earning your bachelor's and master's degrees, consider student internship programs in libraries, or volunteer to work in your local public, academic, or school library to gain seasoning within a library environment.
2. Include both social science and communication courses in your college studies, as these skills will be essential for you as a Special Collections Librarian.
3. In addition to your M.L.S. degree, supplement your education with greater depth of knowledge of your field of interest, to the extent of earning a master's, doctoral, or professional degree in the given subject.

SYSTEMS LIBRARIAN

Duties: Responsible for the administration and overall maintenance of the library's integrated library system as well as any computer-related systems or equipment used by library staff or patrons

Alternate Title(s): Automation Librarian; Automation Specialist; Electronic Services and Systems Librarian; Head of Information Technology/Systems Librarian; Information Services Librarian; Information Systems Librarian; Library Technology Officer; Network Manager; Web Development Management Librarian

Salary Range: $40,000 to $65,000 or more

Employment Prospects: Excellent

Advancement Prospects: Good

Prerequisites:

Education or Training—Master's degree in library science (M.L.S.) or in library and information science (M.L.I.S.) required; undergraduate degree in computer science or technology recommended

Experience—Experience as a team player who can multitask, set priorities, solve problems, and collaborate in establishing goals; strong background in computer science and technology, database management, and content management systems

Special Skills and Personality Traits—Ability to work independently and as a team member in developing services and completing projects; attention to detail; customer-service orientation; excellent communication (both vocal and written) and interpersonal talents; exceptional planning and project management abilities; good organizational skills; strong problem-solving and analytical skills

Special Requirements—May be required to be certified as a professional librarian

Position Description

Systems librarianship is a technical field that focuses on computing and networking in a library context and is a mix of technical and nontechnical elements. As important as the nontechnical portions are for effective public service in the library profession, they should not overshadow the need for a strong technical aptitude on the part of the Systems Librarian. The best Systems Librarians combine expertise in both professional areas in ways that serve both their organizations and constituencies.

Systems Librarians' main mission is to work with constantly advancing technology and to respond to the rapidly changing information needs and technology skills of library users and staff. They manage and support the implementation, operation, integration, and enhancement of the library's automated information system. The functioning of most present-day libraries, from circulation to cataloging to public services, depends on the efficient operation of an integrated library system that automates all functions of the facility and manages all its vital information systems.

Systems Librarians manage, coordinate, plan, budget, implement, and service the library's information systems operations, including the integrated library system itself. They provide technical expertise, support, and training for library automation planning and development. They coordinate the training of library staff and patrons in the use of hardware, software, networking, database management, Internet search, and other information technologies. They manage the library's workstations and develop Internet, network, and Web-based applications used in the institution. Their project planning includes budgeting; selecting hardware, software, and vendors; purchasing equipment or services (including contract negotiations with vendors or service providers); and installing both hardware (including networking cables and devices) and software (customizing programs when necessary). They continuously research and evaluate new applicable technologies, consulting with other computing and technology personnel and upgrading their own skills. They document and inventory current technologies used in the library, prepare reports for library management, and attend meetings and conferences when required.

Systems Librarians may also be responsible for overseeing upgrades and the implementation of (new) equipment and software and preparing and releasing necessary documentation. They usually aid in strategic planning and in evaluating and recommending services, products, and projects. They provide the communication link between system vendor(s) and relevant library staff, making sure departments responsible for the various modules of the system are informed of vendor changes and keeping the vendor informed of the needs and concerns of the constituent departments.

Usually, a large amount of their time is spent diagnosing and repairing malfunctions of both hardware (such as workstations, printers, card readers, and computers) and software. They investigate network faults and answer complex technological questions. They typically also oversee the library's digital printing network and the facility's public photocopying equipment used by patrons.

In addition, Systems Librarians may be responsible for the library's Web site development, overseeing the management of the organization, content, and design of its Web pages. In some instances, this job may be filled by a nonlibrarian (a Web development manager). Nonetheless, most library administrations seem to prefer a trained librarian to fill this position of Web development librarian, sometimes known as a Web and digital library specialist. In academic libraries, besides overseeing the library's Web site, a Web development librarian may be responsible for designing, developing and implementing Web-enabled solutions for grant and nongrant funded projects and for providing technical expertise to support digital conversion and delivery projects. In addition, this position may also be responsible for maintaining and updating existing Web applications, for testing and implementing scan and post processing strategies, and for monitoring the performance of digital conversion equipment, contacting system vendors for problem resolution and upgrades.

Systems Librarians at academic libraries often are nontenured professionals with academic rank and are tasked with collection development, university service, and their own professional development. They frequently act as liaisons between the library and the campus computing services department. At the same time, most Systems Librarians at academic libraries are expected to work at the reference desk and, like most other academic librarians, fulfill the many responsibilities of a tenure-track faculty position.

Salaries

Annual salaries of Systems Librarians range from $40,000 to $65,000 or more, depending on their experience, the scope of their responsibilities, and the library's size, location, and the extent of its reliance on technology.

Employment Prospects

As the highly technical world of computer applications and electronic information processing continue to alter the way in which libraries do business and deal with patrons' information needs, the necessity for Systems Librarians to monitor and manage these complex systems will only increase. Applicants with both a solid understanding of basic librarianship and a varied and current knowledge of emerging library technologies will have the best chances of gaining a position.

Advancement Prospects

Systems Librarians may move into a broad range of administrative and supervisory posts. While the technical aspects of smaller public and academic libraries may be administered by a single professional Systems Librarian (with a small support staff), the larger public and academic libraries usually have senior management positions or department heads responsible for budget, equipment, facilities, and personnel.

Education and Training

Systems Librarians combine their librarianship with their love of technology. They generally need to have a master's degree in library science (M.L.S.) or in library and information science (M.L.I.S.) combined with a bachelor's degree in computer science or technology. Alternatively, Systems Librarians may supplement their M.L.S. degree with courses in computer science and technology and business studies.

Systems Librarians should be knowledgeable about available library automation systems and library database development processes. They should have experience with server administration and management and current and emerging content-linking and authentications standards (such as OpenURL, DOI, and Z39.50), archival metadata applications (such as Digitool), library Web-based digital and electronic link resolver systems (such as SFX and ILLiad), online database searching tools (such as OVID, PubMed, and BIOSIS), HTML procedures, Microsoft Office, and Internet applications.

Systems Librarian Marshall Breeding of Vanderbilt University recommends particularly the use of Perl programming language since, as he says, "it thrives on tasks related to text processing, Web interfaces, and database access—all staples of the typical library technical environment."

Special Requirements

Most states require that public librarians (including Systems Librarians) employed in municipal, county, or regional library systems be certified by submitting an application to the state librarian.

Experience, Skills, and Personality Traits

Systems Librarians must be well informed about the theories, objectives, principles, and techniques of library and information science and about the planning, design, implementation, and use of automated systems within a library environment. They should be familiar with current and emerging information technologies to retrieve, develop, and disseminate information. They should have experience in systems analysis, design techniques, database management across a variety of platforms, various operating systems, and the application of library automation software. Background with automated integrated library systems used for cataloging and classification, serials, circulation, acquisitions, and public access catalogs is important, as is knowledge of local and wide area networks, electronic mail, spreadsheet, word processing, and data management software systems. They should be well grounded in HTML, Java, and other coding principles as well as the structure of HTML documents. They need to be well informed about both database management and content management systems and should have experience with Online Computer Library Center (OCLC) services.

Systems Librarians must be very detail oriented and have excellent analytical and organizational abilities. They should exhibit outstanding communication and interpersonal skills coupled with an interest in working with the public and a basic understanding of human nature. In carrying out their duties, Systems Librarians must be able to move from issue to issue and project to project with equal aplomb, sometimes at a moment's notice. At the same time, they need to keep in mind the relative priority of the duties at hand and a sense of the interdependence among projects. They must exhibit sound judgment and a sense of curiosity and risk taking coupled with persistence and drive to follow through each project to completion. They should have excellent time and resource management skills and a technical realism related to their awareness of the organizational needs and goals.

Unions and Associations

The American Library Association (ALA) is a resource for all librarians. Membership in one division, the Library and Information Technology Association (LITA), should prove valuable for Systems Librarians, in that it provides up-to-date information through both the *LITA Newsletter* and the more scholarly journal *Information Technology and Libraries*. Another ALA division of interest to Systems Librarians is the Association for Library Collections and Technical Services (ALCTS), as well as the American Society of Information Science and Technology (ASIS&T). The Association for Computing Machinery (ACM) supports a number of special interest groups that might be of interest for Systems Librarians. In addition, the Council on Library and Information Resources (CLIR), the Technology Resource Consortium (TRC), and the National Information Standards Organization (NISO) are other groups of potential interest to Systems Librarians.

Those Systems Librarians employed in academic libraries may find it advantageous to be members of the ALA's Association of College and Research Libraries (ACRL), the Association of Research Libraries (ARL) of the ALA, the Association for Educational Communication and Technology (AECT), and the Association for the Management of Information Technology in Higher Education (AMITHE). Similarly, there are professional groups for medical librarians, law librarians, public librarians, special librarians, and so on that should be useful to Systems Librarians working in those areas.

Tips for Entry

1. While attending library school, take the opportunity to work as a student assistant in the university library, do a practicum or internship in another library, or volunteer as a Systems Librarian assistant to gain necessary experience.

2. While studying for your degree, learn about the profession's current trends and activities and make useful contacts by joining a professional association such as the American Society for Information Science and Technology. In addition, visit the placement service job list on the ASIS&T Web site (http://www.jobtarget.com/home/index.cfm?site_id=180).

3. In addition to your library and computer studies, include some business courses, as you will most likely be responsible for budget preparations and monitoring of business expenses on projects with which you will be involved as a Systems Librarian.

TECHNICAL SERVICES LIBRARIAN

CAREER PROFILE

Duties: Plan, develop, and direct the technical services functions of acquisitions, cataloging, accessing, maintaining, and processing of the library's collections and coordinate technical services functions with the public service activities of the facility

Alternate Title(s): Senior Library Technician; Technical Services System Administrator

Salary Range: $35,000 to $60,000 or more

Employment Prospects: Fair to good

Advancement Prospects: Good

Prerequisites:

Education or Training—Master's degree in library science (M.L.S.) or in library and information science (M.L.I.S.) from an educational institution accredited by the American Library Association (ALA)

Experience—Acquisitions and cataloging background; familiarity with an integrated library system and demonstrated ability to apply technological approaches to meet traditional and emerging user needs in a dynamic library environment; supervisory experience usually required

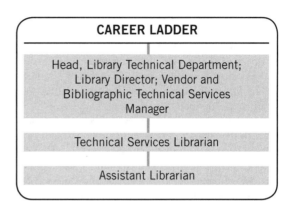

CAREER LADDER

Head, Library Technical Department; Library Director; Vendor and Bibliographic Technical Services Manager

Technical Services Librarian

Assistant Librarian

Special Skills and Personality Traits—Ability to work independently and as a team member in a problem-solving context; excellent oral, written, and interpersonal communication skills; good analytical and organizational abilities; strong computer proficiency

Special Requirements—Academic libraries may require a teacher's certificate; some states may demand certifications for Technical Services Librarians in public schools and local libraries

Position Description

Today, a library's collection is no longer just what the institution physically owns but, increasingly, what it provides access to, regardless of the format. Collections now consist of hard-copy books, magazines, newspapers, videos, CDs, CD-ROMs, and DVDs along with free and subscription-based documents, periodicals, images, and multimedia that are available electronically to the library's patrons. Yet, regardless of the delivery format, library materials are acquired, cataloged, processed, and supplied to customers based on well thought-out collection development policies, user profiles, and organizational principles. Typically, the division of the library in which these activities take place is called the technical services department.

Providing access to library resources is a complex process that combines a knowledge of bibliographic and metadata (data about data, as in a library catalog, which is data describing publications) control. Technical Services Librarians perform the tasks that pertain to resource management, including acquisitions, catalog-

ing, processing, accessing, and maintaining holdings of library resources (both print and nonprint). They are responsible for the planning, directing, and conducting of these technical services operations, managing and maintaining these functions and the library's database maintenance projects.

For collection development, they identify and select materials to be added to the collection according to the library's policies and maintain all appropriate statistics. They assist in the weeding out of library materials (called deacquisition) and conduct periodic inventories of library materials. Concerning acquisitions, Technical Services Librarians order and receive new, replacement, and gift materials for the facility. They maintain the library's subscriptions and preparations of the serial and periodical holdings. Usually, they are responsible for the accounting of the library's materials budget and oversee the allocation of funds according to subject areas, departments, materials format, and so forth. From their understanding of the principles of descriptive and subject cataloging rules, they administer the cataloging of all types of library materials according to AACRII and MARC codes, tags, and other relevant standards, providing a level of descriptive cataloging, classification, and subject analysis appropriate to their library and its community of users. In addition, they provide and maintain bibliographic links in the library's catalog to electronic and other remote resources.

They identify, establish, and apply proper procedures for the physical processing of library materials as well as supervise the mending, binding, and preservation processes for materials. They review processing procedures by the library's clerical staff as well as what data is entered into the library's automated system by technical support staff, checking for quality of processing and accuracy of inputting. They assist in the library's database management, including development and maintenance of local authority files and holdings deletions in both their library catalog and the Online Computer Library Center (OCLC) database. They recommend procedural and workflow changes in the operation of the technical services department and assist in developing and maintaining department procedure manuals. They may assist the systems librarian in the development and maintenance of the library's Web page. They work closely with other librarians in planning library-wide operations and programs and provide reference assistance when needed.

In academic libraries, Technical Services Librarians frequently serve as faculty liaisons to one or more colleges or departments of the university or college. They usually participate in library, university, and professional committees. In public libraries and public library systems, Technical Services Librarians often serve on system bibliographic support committees, which meet regularly to address public access concerns. In both cases, they are responsible for performing ongoing analyses of community or educational needs to recommend any needed modifications to the library's services, collections, or programs. They review technical services policies to ensure that they meet the needs of the library's community and to verify that policies and practices are in agreement. In smaller libraries, the Technical Services Librarian may perform all the duties of technical services (including acquisitions, cataloging, and processing) with the assistance of a small technical staff. In larger libraries and library systems, the technical services work often is divided among librarians with distinct titles and training, such as catalogers, acquisitions librarians, and serials librarians. Though historically the position of Technical Services Librarian involves little direct contact with the public, it is becoming more common for librarians in technical ser-

vices to be assigned reference or other public service duties as well.

Salaries

The mean average annual income of Technical Services Librarians is $50,000, and salaries range from $35,000 to $60,000 or more depending on experience; the scope and range of their responsibilities; and the library's size, location, and extent of its reliance on technology.

Employment Prospects

Employment of librarians in general is expected to grow more slowly than the average for all occupations through 2014. However, job opportunities in general are expected to be good because a large number of librarians are expected to retire during this period. Yet, in the case of Technical Services Librarians, there is another job-seeking obstacle: the outsourcing of technical service operations in public libraries, consisting primarily of the acquisition, cataloging, authority control, and physical processing of materials. Now, many libraries purchase and copy records from databases at OCLC or other bibliographic utilities for the majority of new materials. When replacing traditional card catalogs with online catalogs, libraries have hired contractors to convert their records to digital formats. Now this outsourcing is being applied to other technical functions, mainly in public libraries (as the special needs of academic libraries may not be met by many vendors who may reject including alternative press materials, local materials, and local publishers). Outsourcing is used to cut the high salary overhead of Technical Services Librarians and to reduce backlogs of materials that need to be cataloged and processed. Thus, in some instances, mainly in the public library sector, there may be less demand for Technical Services Librarians in the coming years.

Advancement Prospects

Technical Services Librarians typically progress to become head of the technical services department of their facility or move to a larger library or library system as technical services head or supervisor. Some may choose to graduate into higher positions in library administration, such as library director. Others may look outside the field of librarianship to use their expertise in management positions with vendors and other services that supply libraries.

Education and Training

A master's degree in library science (M.L.S.) or in library and information science (M.L.I.S.) from an ALA-accredited institution is a major requirement for this post. In addition, three to five years of library experience—primarily in acquisitions and cataloging—is usually required, along with knowledge of the LC classification system and current cataloging standards (AACR2, MARC, and LCSH) and of OCLC systems and functions. Familiarity with one or more integrated library systems is highly recommended.

Special Requirements

Academic libraries frequently require a teacher's certificate, as librarians are understood to be faculty members. In addition, some states demand certifications as professional librarians of Technical Services Librarians working in public schools and local libraries.

Experience, Skills, and Personality Traits

Technical Services Librarians should have several years of experience in acquisitions and cataloging. They should have an awareness of new trends, standards, practices, and emerging technologies in cataloging and technical services, including those related to digital libraries, such as AACR2R, LCSH, LC classification, USMARC formats, metadata standards and their functions in libraries, and OCLC applications. They need to have knowledge of database design and management. They should exhibit strong computer and technology skills, including Web design, development, and management, and a basic knowledge of such programming/scripting languages as Perl, HTML, XML, C++, or MySQL. They should be familiar with digital image and text creation and digital production using national standards.

Technical Services Librarians must have excellent oral and written communication abilities as well as excellent analytical, organizational, and interpersonal talents. They need to be able to document procedures and have a thorough understanding of how information is organized, accessed, and used to support the mission of the library. They should have a strong commitment to customer service and proven supervisory and leadership experience. They must be able to work independently but also as a team member in a problem-solving context.

Unions and Associations

General membership in the American Library Association is highly recommended. In addition, two divisions of the ALA are of special interest for Technical Services Librarians: the Association for Library Collections and Technical Services (ALCTS) and the Public Library Association (PLA). Furthermore, membership in either the American Society for Information Science and Technology (ASIS&T) or the Special Libraries Association (SLA) may prove beneficial.

Tips for Entry

1. While earning your undergraduate and graduate degrees, take every opportunity to work as a student assistant in the school or university library, do a practicum or internship in another library, or volunteer in the cataloging department of the library.

2. During your years of initial library work, gain as much experience as you can in cataloging all types of library materials and in the physical processing of materials.

3. It is important to remember that membership in library and information science professional associations keep Technical Services Librarians aware of the constantly changing array of technology that is reshaping library services in general and technical services in particular.

YOUNG ADULT LIBRARIAN

Duties: Work closely with students and other young adults to fulfill their homework assignments and other reference needs and prepare library programs for young adults

Alternate Title(s): Reference/Young Adult Services Librarian; Young Adult Reference Librarian

Salary Range: $30,000 to $58,000 or more

Employment Prospects: Good

Advancement Prospects: Good

Prerequisites:

    Education or Training—Master's degree in library science (M.L.S.) from a program accredited by the American Library Association (ALA) required, with course work/emphasis on young adult literature and youth services

    Experience—Experience with young adults (ages 12 to 18) in a library setting; familiarity with online circulation systems and online search techniques; one to three years of reference background, preferably in an automated system; some supervisory and administrative experience in a library setting may be required

    Special Skills and Personality Traits—Ability to work independently, prioritize, and manage numer-

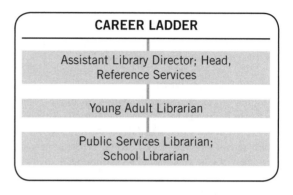

CAREER LADDER

Assistant Library Director; Head, Reference Services

Young Adult Librarian

Public Services Librarian; School Librarian

ous diverse tasks at one time; capacity to interact tactfully with library patrons, staff, and volunteers; full understanding of reference sources and research techniques and a working knowledge of common computer applications and use of the Internet; good communication, persuasion, and conflict resolution abilities; knowledge of and appreciation for young adult development and thorough familiarity with young adult literature and materials

Special Requirements—A teaching certificate may be necessary in some cases, and some states demand a professional librarian certificate in order to work in a state library system as well

Position Description

The primary responsibility of Young Adult Librarians is for young adult materials and services. They develop and maintain collections of books, DVDs, audiocassettes, CDs, and other material for young adults (ages 12 to 18). They recommend goals and objectives for the young adult collection and support services. They provide reference and reader advisory services to young adults, parents, and educators. They develop and implement programs for young adults, working with school personnel to coordinate programs, conduct library tours, and make presentations at schools. They collaborate with local businesses to encourage support of young adult programs, developing press releases and other materials to publicize these offerings, and supervise volunteer opportunities for members of the community. They plan and implement special events, including grant projects and fund-raising and other local events involving young adults and volunteers.

Young Adult Librarians aid students and other teenagers in the use of library tools such as indexes, bibliographies, and standard reference books as well as the computerized library catalog, online databases, and educational CD-ROMs. They instruct young adults in basic information gathering and research skills and in the use of the Internet, assisting them in online searching. They compile bibliographies in areas of special interest for young adults based on their requests and patterns of use of materials. They plan and present young adult programs and lead book discussion groups. They involve young adults in setting up services targeted for their age group. At all times, they maintain a pleasant and safe environment for young adults.

They train and support other staff members in the provision of service for young adults and coordinate the activities of volunteers assigned to young adult areas. They are responsible for the allocated budget of the young adults collection. They monitor expenditures and approve purchases for the department. They research grant possibilities and seek funds to support the young adult collection and programs. They compile, review, and interpret statistical data regarding use of young adults services, preparing regular management reports for review by the library director and other facility management staff.

They keep up to date with trends in library reference services by attending professional library conferences, seminars, workshops, and committee meetings. They read the professional literature and participate in the development of goals, policies, and procedures related to young adult services by attending and participating in staff meeting discussions. They may provide material classification and cataloging services when needed.

Salaries

Annual salaries for Young Adult Librarians range from $30,000 as a starting salary to $55,000 or more, depending on the scope of their duties and the size and location of the library. The mean average yearly salary is usually between $39,000 and $45,000.

Employment Prospects

The U.S. Department of Labor's Bureau of Labor Statistics projects that the growth of employment for librarians will be slower than the average for all jobs through 2014. However, census data and surveys also project a large percentage of librarians will retire in the next 10 to 12 years, creating a critical demand for new professionals.

Advancement Prospects

Young Adult Librarians may decide to advance into a higher supervisory position in their department by becoming head of the reference department of their library or move into higher ranks of library administration by advancing to the post of assistant library director and, eventually, library director. On the other hand, they may decide to capitalize on their experience with young adults by applying for positions as school librarians.

Education and Training

The basic requirement for Young Adult Librarians is a master's degree in library science (M.L.S.) or library and information science (M.L.I.S.) from a college or university accredited by the American Library Association (ALA), supplemented by one to three or more years of reference and other public library work, including some supervisory and administrative experience. Young Adult Librarians are encouraged to seek degree

programs that have an emphasis on young adult literature and youth services. Any equivalent combination of education, training, and experience that provides the required knowledge, skills, and abilities may be acceptable. Practical experience with young adults is important background for this position.

Young Adult Librarians should have a thorough knowledge of library operations and services; of new trends in library services for young adults; of current young adult literature and other materials; of library policies and procedures concerning the explaination of programs and services to teenagers, parents, and educators; of reference sources and research techniques; and of common computer applications and use of the Internet.

Special Requirements

In cases when Young Adult Librarians are tasked with teaching classes in the use of library resources, they may be required to have a teaching certificate. Some states also demand that Young Adult Librarians who work within state library systems be certified as professional librarians.

Experience, Skills, and Personality Traits

Young Adult Librarians must be knowledgeable of all library operations and programs, collections policies, cataloging systems (including automated ones), books and literature in general, standard reference sources, and online information databases. They must be familiar with library-specific and work processing software and be expert at Internet searching and in the use of personal computers. In addition, they should be skilled in the use of audiovisual equipment. They should have some experience in bookkeeping practices and be acquainted with budgetary principles and procedures.

Young Adult Librarians must have excellent communication talents and demonstrate effective interpersonal skills with young adults and other professionals who work with teenagers. They must have knowledge of and appreciation for literature for young adults, appropriate audiovisual (AV) material, and a solid familiarity with current reading, viewing, and listening interests of young adults. As Dora Ho, Young Adult Librarian at the North Hollywood Regional Branch of the Los Angeles Public Library, states, "Recently, manga [Japanese comics and graphic novels] has gained popularity with teens, and it is important to be aware of popular trends in teen materials in addition to knowing about homework assignment material and literary classics." She suggests, "Talk to teens in your library. They are forthcoming in sharing their interests, their likes and dislikes."

It is important for Young Adult Librarians to plan and manage library programs in conjunction and consultation with local schools' guidance or careers classes and instructors in order to provide programs that will appeal to young adults. As Ho further explains, "Our library creates and sponsors a variety of programs of interest to teens, including a Sidewalk Astronomy Program, Drawing Comics and Animation Workshops, and Wildlife on Wheels to name a few. . . . I try to strike a balance between serious and fun programs."

In addition, Young Adult Librarians typically coordinate active volunteer programs for their libraries. They recruit, train, supervise, and evaluate students, young adults, and adult volunteers; establish work schedules and assignments; provide orientation programs; and interact with library staff to integrate volunteers into the library's activities. As such, they must have administrative and management skills as well as excellent persuasion, negotiating, and conflict resolution abilities.

Unions and Associations

The primary professional association for Young Adult Librarians is the Young Adult Library Services Association (YALSA), a division of the American Library Association (ALA). The association has developed a set of competencies for librarians serving young adults that are available from the association as well as a quarterly journal: *Young Adult Library Services*. Other professional organizations of interest include the American Society for Information Science and Technology (ASIS&T), the Association for Library Service to Children (ALSC), and the Special Libraries Association (SLA) as well as area and state library groups and federations.

Tips for Entry

1. While earning your library degree, consider volunteering for local outreach groups that interact with young adults (teens) to gain experience working with, listening to, and gaining an understanding of their interests and goals.

2. Include sociology and psychology courses during your undergraduate education experience, as an understanding gained from these classes will aid you in your work with both teens and adults.

3. As a Young Adult Librarian, consult *The Alan Review* (http://scholar.lib.vt.edu/ejournals/ALAN/) and the Virtual Young Adult Index (http://www.infopeople.org/trainingpast/2004/youngadult/cg2_Webliography_for_YA.pdf) for data about young adult literature and for links to libraries with young adult Web pages. In addition, many states have online resource pages for Young Adult Librarians.

SPECIAL
LIBRARIANS

ART LIBRARIAN

Duties: Collect, organize, and provide access to information (both print and nonprint) and other materials relating to the visual arts, architecture, and design

Alternate Title(s): Art and Design Librarian; Art Catalog Librarian; Visual and Digital Materials Archivist; Visual Resources Librarian

Salary Range: $35,000 to $60,000 or more

Employment Prospects: Fair

Advancement Prospects: Fair

Prerequisites:

Education or Training—Undergraduate degree in art, art history, humanities, or the social sciences; master's degree in library science (M.L.S.) and a master's degree or Ph.D. degree in art history usually required

Experience—Background in information technology and media literacy programs; familiarity with methods of scholarly research in art, architecture, and design; knowledge of principles in library collection development and reference work; archival experience with visual material processes; three to five years of professional library experience, including some managerial and/or supervisory

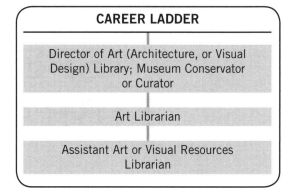

involvement; working experience in application of technology to library services, particularly digital technology systems

Special Skills and Personality Traits—Ability to work collaboratively, independently, or under supervision; interpersonal, verbal (including presentation and teaching), and written skills; strong project management proficiency; reading knowledge of at least two languages other than English; strong service orientation

Special Requirements—Teaching certificate may be necessary

Position Description

Special libraries are facilities containing distinctive materials used by industrial, commercial, or governmental organizations or by such institutions as schools, universities, museums, or hospitals. Special librarians are responsible for ordering, cataloging, and classifying targeted collections of books, manufacturers' catalogs, technical specifications and manuals, periodicals and serials, magazines, newspapers, audiovisual material, microforms, rare collectibles, art forms, and other items.

Art Librarians and visual resources librarians are specialists skilled in organizing and providing access to data and materials on the visual arts. They support research, provide instruction, catalog their subject-specific collection, and promote public awareness of the arts to students, teachers, scholars, curators, artists, and other patrons of their libraries. The scope of their collections may include the entire field of visual cul-

ture or be focused on certain special areas such as art, architecture, design, film, or photography. Art information specialists and librarians handle all types of formats including the printed page (books, periodicals, and serials), electronic media, film, graphic materials, slides, and video. They use this material and their own knowledge to meet the specific information needs of their libraries' users, aiding them in their research, understanding, and enjoyment of the visual arts.

Art Librarians and visual resources professionals are employed in a diversity of educational institutions, such as public, college, and university libraries and art departments; art museums; fashion and design institutes; and art schools. They may find employment in architecture and design firms, art galleries and bookshops, picture research agencies, and corporate art collections. They may catalog slides for a university art department, conduct database searches for museum curators, manage a historical photographic collection, create and maintain Web sites for art departments, or teach preservation and processing methods on a college or university campus. Some Art Librarians and information professionals may be found in archives, historical societies, and anthropological institutions that have collections of special visual interest.

Art Librarians may be required to manage day-to-day operations of an art library, including staffing, services, collections, and facilities. They may supervise staff members and graduate student research assistants. For historical collections of rare books, manuscripts, and artwork, Art Librarians create, enhance, and maintain original and complex copy cataloging records for a wide range of materials in a variety of formats, including books, maps, manuscripts, archives, serials, and ephemera.

Art Librarians in academic libraries may specialize in specific areas. One example is visual arts resources. As visual arts resources librarians, they may manage the educational institution's slide and digital image collections. They collaborate with faculty in preparing, editing, and presenting images within the classroom setting. They are responsible for the overall acquisition, processing, cataloging, and maintenance of both slide and digital images and act as the reference librarian to the visual arts department of the college or university.

Salaries

Salaries vary greatly for Art Librarians depending on their specific type and amount of job responsibilities and the size and location of the library or collection. Beginning Art Librarians may start at annual salaries ranging from $35,000 to $40,000. The average yearly salary of Art Librarians with little to no supervisory responsibilities spans from $45,000 to $55,000. Experienced Art Librarians with supervisory responsibilities may have annual incomes of $60,000 or more.

Employment Prospects

Art librarianship is a highly specialized career area. Job opportunities occur, but only for those with appropriate experience and background. Many Art Librarians combine their work with other part-time art activities and/or employment.

Advancement Prospects

For seasoned Art Librarians, opportunities for advancement are usually within a broad range of administrative and supervisory posts. Smaller art collections typically have a single professional Art Librarian and a small support staff. In major collections and the bigger public and academic libraries, Art Librarians may hold management positions as assistant directors or department heads and have budget, personnel, facilities, and collection management responsibilities. Some Art Librarians may specialize and obtain future education and training in order to become conservators or curators in a large educational library or a museum.

Education and Training

It is recommended that Art Librarians have a bachelor's degree (B.A.) in art or art history and a master's degrees in library science (M.L.S.) or library and information science (M.L.I.S.). Some institutions prefer an additional master's degree in art or art history as well. It is recommended that they have had several years of training in reference work and/or bibliographic cataloging in an academic or public library.

Undergraduate work should include a wide background in the humanities, as Art Librarians will be called on to be familiar with the relationship of art to other disciplines. In addition, a reading knowledge of one to two languages other than English is highly suggested. (Basic cataloging and bibliographic research in art, architecture, and design require a working knowledge of German and at least French or Italian.)

Special Requirements

Academic libraries frequently require a teacher's certificate, as librarians in general are understood to be faculty members. In addition, some states demand certifications as professional librarians of Art Librarians in public school and local library systems.

Experience, Skills, and Personality Traits

Art Librarians should have knowledge of the historiography of art history and a basic knowledge of materials, techniques, and terminology employed in the fields of art, architecture, and design. They should be familiar with current modes of cultural analysis and have a knowledge of traditional and electronic reference resources. They should be fully acquainted with the principles of library collection development and have a working knowledge of the applications of technology to library services, particularly digital technology systems. An understanding of photographic techniques and practices is desirable, and proficiency with computers, the Internet, electronic media, and database management is increasingly vital. They need to have a thorough knowledge of current cataloging standards (AACR2, Library of Congress Subject Headings, OCLC, MARC, Dublin Core, and other metadata processes).

Art Librarians must be able to work both independently and collegially in a demanding and rapidly changing environment. They should have excellent interpersonal, communication, organizational, and project management skills. They must have a strong commitment to service and an aptitude to work successfully with faculty, staff, students, and other library users.

Unions and Associations

Art Librarians have a variety of trade associations that provide educational guidance, career support, conferences, and information to their members. Primary among these groups is the Arts Libraries Society of North America (ARLIS/NA). Other organizations include the American Institute for Conservation of Historic and Artistic Works (AIC), the American Library Association (ALA), and the Special Libraries Association (SLA).

Tips for Entry

1. Both in your undergraduate and graduate years, consider volunteer work (or a student internship) in your school library (or a local library) to gain hands-on experience in and knowledge of library policies, practices, and procedures.

2. As a reading knowledge of German is very important in art research, take language courses in German starting in your undergraduate years, and consider adding another language, such as French, Italian, or Spanish, to your curriculum.

3. Employment in this field may be found in the job listings posted by the American Library Association and, in particular, those posted by the Arts Libraries Society of North America on their Web site (http://www.arlisna.org/jobs.html).

BUSINESS LIBRARIAN

Duties: Find, collect and analyze information and data relevant to a company or the business department of a library; supervise a research staff

Alternate Title(s): Business Information Specialist; Business Institutional Librarian; Corporate Information Specialist; Corporate Librarian; Economics, Finance and Data Librarian; In-House Information Specialist

Salary Range: $35,000 to $65,000 or more

Employment Prospects: Good to excellent

Advancement Prospects: Good

Prerequisites:

Education or Training—Undergraduate degree in business; master's degree in library science (M.L.S.) or in library and information science (M.L.I.S.)

Experience—Some public library background working with the business sector or experience in an academic or research library often required; some experience in the business world and a second language are helpful

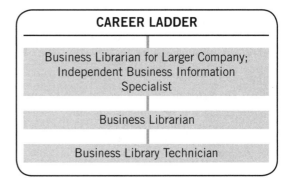

Special Skills and Personality Traits—Comfortable working both independently and as a team member; detail oriented with strong organizational abilities; excellent computer skills; good communication and interpersonal abilities; self-motivated

Special Requirements—Some states require a library certification for business librarians working within state library systems

Position Description

Business Librarians manage a corporate library or a business section in a public, academic, or research library that specializes in materials relevant to commerce and management. They collect, build, and arrange the information resources of the organization (or library section). They catalog and classify technical books, manufacturers' catalogs and specifications, periodicals, series, newspapers, audiovisual material, microforms, journal reprints, electronic media materials, business and financial databases, and other materials relevant to their collection. They often prepare abstracts and indexes of current material, organize bibliographies, and analyze background information, preparing reports on areas of particular interest. For example, a corporate librarian would likely provide the sales department with data about competitors and their products as well as governmental policies and regulations that may affect the corporation.

Business Librarians' responsibilities include collection development, maintaining the online subject guide (for the firm or the library), answering reference questions, and conducting library instruction sessions. If

employed by a business, they serve as a companywide information resource for its staff. They train staff in cataloging, locating, and processing materials that support the business information needs of the organization's management or that fulfills the collection policies of the library in general and its business section specifically.

Business Librarians conduct literature searches, which may include articles and reports from real-time (online) news feeds, newspapers, broadcast transcripts and trade publications, research reports and analyst notes in support of financial decision making, and in-depth repositories of scientific and technical data about patents, trademarks, and other intellectual property. These searches may come from online data, automated library systems, CD-ROM databases, or automated research sources and vendors, such as LexisNexis and WealthEngine. Business Librarians identify the best sources for their staff and optimize search strategies through controlled vocabulary, ontology, and related terms development. They often assist in the maintenance of the company's Web site(s) and the creation of subject guides for users of the Web site(s).

When working within a research or academic library, they assist students, faculty, staff, and other researchers in identifying the library's business holdings. They solve complex reference problems, or refer them to other units or specialists, and aid library patrons in the organization of data resources. When functioning within a corporation, Business Librarians research technology trends, study consumer issues, and profile companies and the industry sector for employees and management.

Salaries

Salaries for this position vary depending on job responsibilities, the size of the company (or library), and its location. Starting annual salaries range from $35,000 to $40,000 and may rise as high as $60,000 or more for Librarians who manage large business collections at larger research libraries or corporations.

Employment Prospects

The rise of the Internet and the resultant technology revolution in business have created tremendous demands for Business Librarians who can research, find, collect, analyze, and organize the information available from the Internet for easy corporate consumption and for the use of library patrons researching business topics. Thus, the role of the Business Librarian has expanded and evolved. For individuals with the technical expertise, job possibilities in libraries and the corporate world are extremely good.

Advancement Prospects

Business Librarians can use their talent in a range of related jobs, particularly with larger companies or bigger research and academic libraries. On the other hand, many corporate information libraries and specialists become freelance consultants in establishing and maintaining research facilities for firms.

Education and Training

Most business library positions (in either libraries or corporations) require a master's degree in library science (M.L.S.) or in library and information science (M.L.I.S.). Undergraduate degrees may vary, but special expertise in business, the social sciences, or the company's area of specialization is recommended. Computer-related coursework is vital for Business Librarians.

Many companies seek librarians who have had reference experience in an academic or research library as well as work experience (or educational background) in an economic/business/data reference setting. Experience and training in library management and records management processes are also important.

Special Requirements

In some states and state library systems, librarians, including Business Librarians, may need to be certified as professional librarians. In some academic libraries, if Business Librarians have instructional duties, they may need to be certified as teachers.

Experience, Skills, and Personality Traits

Business Librarians need a strong familiarity with research strategies in economics, finance, and business data and be conversant with standard statistical software packages and trends in scholarly research and communication. Experience with content-management systems, search engines, and other relevant technical applications (and relational databases) is useful.

Business Librarians work closely with employees of their firm or with library patrons conducting research, so they need strong interpersonal and communication skills. They must have excellent analytical and organizational talents, be highly self-motivated and detail oriented, and be able to work well independently or as part of a team. Their computer abilities must be very strong.

Unions and Associations

The Business and Reference and Services Section (BRASS) of the American Library Association (ALA) is key for Business Librarians. In addition, membership in the ALA, the American Society for Information Science and Technology (ASIS&T), the Association For Library Collections and Technical Services (ALCTS), the Association of Independent Information Professionals (AIIP), and the Special Libraries Association (SLA) should prove to be extremely beneficial.

Tips for Entry

1. As a Business Librarian, become familiar with your facility's sources and your business department's needs. If you work at a research or academic library, get to know the business faculty, their research areas, and what classes they teach.

2. Make contact with other Business Librarians in your institution, at nearby libraries, or at conferences—all of whom can be a resource when you must handle tough research queries—and learn what types of questions you might be asked and what sources are best for answering them.

3. For collection development ideas, study business magazines (such as *Harvard Business Review*, and *Business Week*) and publishers' catalogs. To keep current on topics in business, read the *Wall Street Journal* and the business sections of newspapers (such as the *New York Times*, the *Chicago Times*, and the *Los Angeles Times*), as well as subscribe to pertinent (online) newsletters.

DOCUMENT SPECIALISTS

Duties: <u>Document Delivery Specialist</u>: For libraries or clients, acquire, organize, manage, maintain, and make available document materials such as annual reports; dissertations; industrial, federal, and military regulations and established standards; government documents (federal, state, and local); market research studies; patents; and photocopies of journal articles; <u>Government Document Specialist</u>: Aid library patrons, students, and other library users in locating, evaluating, and organizing information published by government agencies and other government bodies

Alternate Title(s): <u>Document Delivery Specialist</u>: Access Services Librarian; Document Accessibility Specialist; Document Coordinator; Documents Information Delivery Specialist; Records Information Manager/Specialist; <u>Government Document Specialist</u>; Government Documents Information Specialist; Government Documents Librarian

Salary Range: <u>Document Delivery Specialist</u>: within library, $30,000 to $45,000 or more; as independent consultant, $40 to $100 per hour; <u>Government Document Specialist</u>: $28,000 to $55,000 or more

Employment Prospects: Good

Advancement Prospects: Good

Prerequisites:

Education or Training—Master's degree in library science (M.L.S.) or library and information sci-

CAREER LADDER

Owner or Manager of Document Delivery Company, Research Librarian; Chief Information Officer, Government Librarian

Document Delivery Specialist; Government Document Specialist

Library Assistant, Library Technician

ence (M.L.I.S.) from a university or college accredited by the American Library Association (ALA) is required; additional graduate degree in specialty area recommended

Experience—Familiarity with integrated library systems; some supervisory experience and some years of direct working experience with federal government information at a professional level may be required

Special Skills and Personality Traits—Ability to work independently; attention to detail; computer proficiency and statistical abilities; effective oral and written communication talents; excellent research skills; flexibility and patience; strong organizational and interpersonal aptitude

---

Position Description

Document Delivery Specialists are librarians who specialize in the finding, acquiring, managing, organizing, handling, and delivery of documents to library patrons or business clients. Some Document Delivery Specialists may concentrate on the handling of government documents only. Others work in public, academic, and special libraries, but many are employed by document delivery companies that complement the services of online researchers in libraries in locating and obtaining various kinds of documents: from market research reports and papers from conferences to journal articles and government documents. Others in this profession work for specific types of organizations or businesses,

such as pharmaceutical and medical companies, financial services companies, and consulting firms.

The document delivery process typically involves a fixed project with a specific deadline and budget, although some Document Delivery Specialists function as consultants on a continuing basis. Many typical research projects may have numerous research citations for material cogent to the project, but much of this material (e.g., the actual article or report) may not be available online, either from the Internet or from fee- or free-based databases. Most document delivery services include interlibrary loan and electronic reserve services as well as photocopy and print services. Document delivery firms are often located in communities with large academic or research libraries. Examples of major, established document delivery vendors include Ingenta (http://www.ingenta.com), the U.S. Department of Commerce National Technical Information Service (NTIS) (http://www.ntis.gov), ISI Document Solution (http://ids.isinet.com), and Information Express (http://www.ieonline.com/docdel.html). Like many other vendors in the library business, document delivery companies may themselves be specialized. Some may supply only medical sources, others may specialize in patent data, and still other firms may provide access to a wider array of subject area materials, ranging from newspaper and periodical articles to monographs to foreign language materials.

Document Delivery Specialists working in academic or public libraries are usually responsible for both document delivery service areas (which typically cover lending, borrowing, and electronic reserves) and interlibrary loan request processing (which includes searching, receiving, and shipping tasks). As such, they may or may not supervise staff and/or student volunteers; recruit, screen, hire, and train staff; and evaluate employees and provide guidance and feedback to assigned staff and volunteers. They schedule, assign, and prioritize workloads on a daily basis. They assist library patrons in using electronic databases, electronic journals, and electronic reference materials, helping them identify and locate appropriate discipline-specific and interdisciplinary resources, demonstrating search techniques, and aiding them in interpreting results.

Document delivery companies complement the online research services of libraries by locating and obtaining assorted kinds of documents, usually for smaller companies that have no researchers on staff. Document Delivery Specialist in these firms provide documents to clients, such as other librarians, human resource professionals, marketing and managing supervisors, legal consultants, accounting experts, scientists, and other advisers. They provide assistance by offering customized support services, such as document delivery, book and journal acquisition, and specialized searches. Information access is now much easier with the use of sophisticated tools such as OPACS (online public access catalogs) and the Internet. Many database producers supply copies of documents cited on their online databases. Independent brokerage firms provide documents from in-house collections from various database producers that choose to house their collections with commercial suppliers. In addition to these traditional avenues of delivery, independent document delivery firms now have access to full text in a growing variety of modes and delivery options. The number of data-

bases providing ASCII full text is expanding exponentially, and the advent of electronic imaging technologies has created an explosion of options and opportunities for searching and retrieving documents. Full text with graphics and images can be retrieved immediately and delivered to the desktop or fax machine of the end user, copyright-cleared, without the document delivery expert having to see or touch the original hard copy. All of this can enable Document Delivery Specialists to locate and offer a wide range of materials and provide information solutions keyed to their clients' needs.

Government Document Specialists concentrate on helping library patrons and/or business clients locate and evaluate documents and other information published by the government. This material may include both published and unpublished government data that may appear in print, on CD-ROMs, online at a Web site or in an electronic database, and in other multimedia formats. They access, evaluate, and select documents, reference works, maps, geographic or geologic information systems, and other resources that are not part of a library's depository program. They must process documents classified according to the unique schemes contained in the Superintendent of Documents (SuDoc) Classification Systems. They need to be fully familiar with this system and work closely with the cataloging department or their libraries to ensure that they follow the system's rules. They also coordinate and oversee the daily operations of their departments, create procedures manuals for support staff, keep appropriate statistics, and write reports for library administrators.

An important aspect of Government Document Specialists' job is to design and implement educational and outreach programs to let students, library patrons, and, if with an academic library, faculty members know about available government document services and resources. They often conduct instructional sessions in the use of documents and in the accessing of documents in various electronic formats. They may do some cataloging related to these documents and participate in their libraries reference service, bibliographic instruction, and collection development programs.

Government documents are obtained by a number of means, including the Internet, government printing offices, commercial book dealers, or membership in depository library programs that acquire government informational materials for free. The Federal Depository Library Program is the depository program of the U.S. government, and a federal depository library is a facility in the United States that holds documents printed by the Government Printing Office (GPO), provides access online to government material, and, through other programs, collects and makes available documents of the different state and local governments and those of foreign countries. Government Document Specialists administer the federal and state government document depository programs as related to their libraries.

As Cindy Page, government document librarian at the Houston (Texas) Public Library states, "Any of our varied patrons could be directed to government sources if that is what it takes to answer their question. I find that, very often, people do not realize it is government information that they need." She goes on to give an example whereby she helped make a young student's day by finding an army technical manual explaining how a tuba is constructed and how to take care of one. "We don't often deal with musical instrument questions in the Business Library," she says, "but this technical manual proved to be exactly what was needed."

Salaries

Salaries for both these positions vary a great deal depending on the specific job responsibilities and the location of the library or consulting firm. As independent consultants, Document Delivery Specialists may charge between $40 and $100 an hour, depending on the specific type of information being sought and their expertise. It should be noted, however, that many of the resources that Document Delivery Specialists use have costs attached to their availability, which may come out of the specialist's fee.

Government Document Specialists with a master's degree from an educational institution accredited by the ALA may expect an annual salary range from $35,000 to $55,000 or more. Those with no professional experience may have starting salaries ranging from $28,000 to $35,000 yearly depending on the geographic location of the library. With experience, annual incomes for Government Document Specialists may exceed $68,000.

Employment Prospects

With the expansion of library technology allowing easy access to documents, the value of Document Delivery Specialists has increased. While computers and the Internet are now a part of almost everyone's life, serious research is still a specialty that is most efficiently performed by a professional, particularly when it comes to accessing research materials beyond the usual books or Web sites. In addition, with the economic necessity of outsourcing some library work, the availability of document delivery services has become more attractive and financially viable.

Advancement Prospects

Many Document Delivery Specialists begin their careers by working for a document delivery consulting firm. After several years of hands-on experience, they may advance to become manager of the firm or set up their own businesses. For Document Delivery Specialists working within a library or library system, advancement may come with additional training to such positions as reference or circulation librarians.

Government document librarians may be able to move into administrative positions such as department head or chief information officer after gaining more seasoning and specific additional training in administrative skills. As expected, advancement opportunities tend to be better in large public or academic library systems in urban areas, which, however, is where the competition is strongest.

Education and Training

Most Document Delivery Specialists have a master's degree in library science (M.L.S.) or in library and information science (M.L.I.S.) and have had some experience and training while working in a library setting. In addition, they may be required to have advanced degrees in such specialty areas as law, medicine, or business.

Most Government Document Specialists have a master's of library science (M.L.S.) or master's of library and information science (M.L.I.S.) from a school accredited by the American Library Association (ALA). Additional on-the-job training in researching, locating, and evaluating government documents is usual.

Experience, Skills, and Personality Traits

Both Document Delivery Specialists and Government Document Specialists should have previous customer service experience, preferably in a library setting. They should have backgrounds in interlibrary loan and document delivery processes within an automated library environment, a working knowledge of both information technologies used in interlibrary loan and current interlibrary loan practices, protocols, and national codes. A year or two of supervisory experience of full-time staff (including hiring, scheduling, and training) is helpful.

Applicants for either of these positions should have effective oral and written communication and interpersonal skills and the ability to work collaboratively with individuals and small groups. They need to plan, implement, evaluate, and report on work activities and manage multiple tasks. They must have excellent research skills along with good computer knowledge and organizational abilities. They must exhibit patience and be able to work with details and statistics.

Document Delivery Specialists who plan to run their own businesses must have the facility to work well with customers as well as have the separate set of skills required to operate a business, including marketing, advertising, public relations, financial planning, and time management.

For Government Document Specialists, several years of experience working with federal and state government information at a professional level is often a basic requisite. Knowledge of emerging technologies in libraries and their applications in the use of government information resources and services is essential. In addition, the ability to accept and work with change is an important characteristic of this job.

Unions and Associations

Document Delivery Specialists may belong to a variety of trade associations that provide educational and professional guidance, support, conferences, and information. These include the American Library Association (ALA), the International Federation of Library Associations (IFLA) Section on Document Delivery and Interlending, the American Society for Information Science and Technology (ASIS&T), and the Special Libraries Association (SLA).

In addition to those already mentioned, Government Document Specialists may find membership in the National Association of Government Archives and Records Administrators (NAGARA) professionally useful.

Tips for Entry

1. While earning your bachelor's and master's degrees, an internship experience in a government documents collection is excellent preparation for a position as a Government Document Specialist as well as valuable background for a Document Delivery Specialist post.

2. Additionally, internship or doing a practicum with a reference department in a large academic or public library will give you experience in practical reference work that is essential to both Document Delivery Specialists and Government Document Specialists.

3. When looking for positions, consult *Jobs for Librarians and Information Professionals* (http://www.lisjobs.com), which is a comprehensive guide to online job resources for librarians and information professionals.

FILM/VIDEO/DVD LIBRARIAN AND AUDIOVISUAL LIBRARIAN

Duties: Collect, organize, catalog, and process film, video, DVD, and other audiovisual materials in a library's collection; answer reference inquiries on this material and plan all library audiovisual programs

Alternate Title(s): Audiovisual Specialist; Film Librarian; Media Librarian; Media Specialist

Salary Range: $35,000 to $60,000 or more

Employment Prospects: Good

Advancement Prospects: Good

Prerequisites:

    Education or Training—Bachelor's degree in communication recommended; master's degree in library science (M.L.S.) or library and information science (M.L.I.S.) required

    Experience—Familiarity with preservation issues pertaining to media resources; knowledge of licensing and copyright issues for media materials; subject expertise in film, video/DVD, or media/cinema studies; two to three years of reference and/or collec-

tion work in a public or academic library; working knowledge of audiovisual and other media equipment materials, including basic maintenance

Special Skills and Personality Traits—Detail-oriented; excellent communication and interpersonal talents; good organizational skills and ability to work independently; managerial and leadership abilities; some training as an instructor or teacher recommended

Position Description

Film/Video/DVD Librarians are often called media librarians, as are Audiovisual Librarians. Media, in these cases, refers to nonprint library materials, such as films, videos, DVDs, music CDs (and MP3 downloads), audiobooks, microforms, and a variety of computer interactive multimedia. Strictly speaking, however, all print and nonprint library materials are medias by which librarians transfer information to patrons. Nonetheless, media is commonly thought of as pertaining to nonprint materials.

Film/Video/DVD Librarians develop and evaluate film/video/DVD collections in libraries and the services that make them available to patrons. They work in all types of institutions: academic, governmental, public, and special libraries. They organize, catalog, and maintain these collections. They coordinate with appropriate subject specialists and participate with them in the selection of audio, video, and digital media materials for their libraries, as well as supporting material in other formats (such as print materials). They teach users how

to search and use the collection and answer reference questions pertaining to the material. They supervise a staff of technical assistants and direct the booking of any film rental services or circulation services for the film/video/DVD collection. They advise on the maintenance and preservation of the materials in the media collection and on their proper housing.

Film/Video/DVD Librarians must be knowledgeable not only about the history of film and other entertainment media (such as television) but also the full range of educational videos, including consumer health and fitness videos and documentaries. They must be aware of and address the licensing and copyright issues for films and other media materials.

Another type of media librarian is Audiovisual Librarians. While they oversee collections that may include films, videos, and DVDs, their collections usually also include audio CDs, audiobooks, and other nonprint materials. They assist library patrons in their choices of materials, using their understanding of the collection. They advise other library personnel on audiovisual materials and the appropriate selections for particular needs and uses. They establish and maintain contact with film distributors and other resources for procurement of tapes, videos, DVDs, audiobooks, and other nonprint materials. They prepare and arrange audiovisual programs for presentation to groups and may lead discussions after the programs. They advise on the planning of audiovisual programs, their technical problems (such as acoustics and lighting), and their program content. They evaluate audiovisual equipment and give advice on the selection of equipment, taking into consideration such factors as intended use, quality of the equipment, and price. They may be required to operate film projectors, splicers, film inspection equipment, and tape and CD or record playing equipment. In addition, they may train personnel in the operation and maintenance of audiovisual equipment. As such, they must be well informed about audiovisual resources for use in their libraries, and be aware of copyright laws pertaining to those resources.

Audiovisual Librarians in academic libraries confer with teachers to select course materials and to determine which training aids are best suited to particular classroom situations. They may develop manuals, texts, workbooks, or related materials for use in conjunction with multimedia materials.

Salaries

The earnings of both Film/Video/DVD Librarians and Audiovisual Librarians vary considerably depending on the scope of their responsibilities, the location and size of the library, and the extent and scope of the library's collection. Annual salaries for Film/Video/DVD Librarians range from approximately $35,000 to as high as $60,000 or more. Yearly incomes for Audiovisual Librarians range from $30,000 to $60,000 or more, particularly in libraries in larger urban areas.

Employment Prospects

Most academic and public libraries have media (nonprint) collections and active audiovisual programs. There is always a need for specially trained librarians to manage these collections and to administer these programs. Like many other library positions, there are expected to be a large number of retirements in the coming decade, opening up posts in all fields of library work, including that of media librarians.

Advancement Prospects

Film/Video/DVD Librarians may progress into a number of supervisory and administrative positions. Smaller collections typically are administered by a single librar-

ian supported by a small staff. Larger academic and public libraries are better avenues for advancement, as they generally have a greater number of librarians in the department and a bigger support staff. Film/Video/DVD Librarians who move into administrative posts head such departments, overseeing budgets, personnel, facilities, and the management of the library's media collection.

Education and Training

Undergraduate training for Film/Video/DVD Librarians should include as broad an education as possible, with a concentration in film and liberal arts. They then will need to earn a master's degree in library science (M.L.S.) or in library and information science (M.L.I.S.). It is recommended that their M.L.S. degree have a concentration in nonprint media or television/broadcasting/mass communications. For Audiovisual Librarians, it is recommended that they acquire a bachelor's degree in education and/or instructional technology in addition to their master's degree in library science or library and information science. In addition, most libraries expect their Film/Video/DVD Librarians to have several years of background in reference work (and thus interactive work with the public), either in academic or public library environments.

Experience, Skills, and Personality Traits

Film/Video/DVD Librarians must have an expertise in film, video/DVD, or media and cinema studies. They must be familiar with preservation issues pertaining to all types of media resources and be well aware of licensing and copyright issues pertaining to media materials. They should have at least two to three years of reference, cataloging, and collection work in a public or academic library. Audiovisual Librarians must have a working knowledge of audiovisual and other media equipment materials, including basic maintenance.

Both Film/Video/DVD Librarians and Audiovisual Librarians must be detail oriented and have excellent communication, interpersonal, and organizational skills. They need to have good computer and managerial/leadership abilities. They should be able to work independently, and it is recommended that they have some training as an instructor or teacher.

Unions and Associations

The primary association of interest for Film/Video/DVD Librarians and Audiovisual Librarians is the American Library Association (ALA) and its Video Round Table (VRT) division. VRT provides leadership within the larger association on all issues related to film/video collections, programs, and services in libraries. In addition, a variety of other trade associations of interest to media librarians provide educational guidance, support, conferences, and information to their members. These include the American Institute for Conservation of Historic and Artistic Works (AIC), the American Film Institute (AFI), the American Society of Information Science and Technology (ASIS&T), the Association for Information Media and Equipment (AIME), the Audio Publishers Association (APA), and the National Association of Media and Technology Centers (NAMTC).

Tips for Entry

1. While earning your bachelor's and master's degrees, investigate working part time or volunteering in a film production company to gain expertise that should prove valuable in your career.

2. Join specific professional media associations, such as the Association for Information Media and Equipment (AIME) and the National Association of Media and Technology Centers (NAMTC) to network about vacancies in the library media field.

3. Attend conventions and conferences, read media trade journals, and communicate with media professionals through your associations to keep abreast of industry developments.

GOVERNMENT ARCHIVIST

Duties: Assess, collect, organize, preserve, maintain, provide access to, and store valuable materials that can be used in exhibitions, publications, research, and educational programs

Alternate Title(s): Archival Manager; Conservator; Docent Coordinator; Government Librarian; Historical Editor; Outreach Coordinator; Preservationist

Salary Range: $35,000 to $75,000 or more

Employment Prospects: Fair

Advancement Prospects: Fair to good

Prerequisites:

    Education or Training—Undergraduate and graduate (usually master's) degrees in archival science, history, library science, or library and information science usually required, but exact type of degree can vary

    Experience—Three to five years of professional archival background, including project management, with experience managing budgets and bidding for funds usually preferred

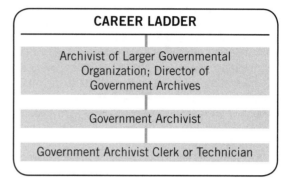

CAREER LADDER

Archivist of Larger Governmental Organization; Director of Government Archives

Government Archivist

Government Archivist Clerk or Technician

Special Skills and Personality Traits—Detail oriented; excellent organizational and interpersonal abilities; good communication and computer skills; research proficiency

Special Requirements—Voluntary certification available from the Academy of Certified Archivists (ACA)

Position Description

An archivist is a professional who evaluates, collects, organizes, preserves, maintains, provides access to, and stores information and/or materials determined to have long-term value. Deciding what records have enduring value is not always easy. Archivists must also select materials valuable enough to justify the costs of storage and preservation plus the labor-intensive expenses of arranging, describing, and making them available for reference use. The theory and scholarly work underpinning archives practices is called archival science. The materials maintained by archivists can be any form of media (photographs, video or sound recordings, letters, documents, published materials, or electronic files).

Federal, state, and local governments all maintain their own archives (mostly of governmental documents and other related materials). These archives may be a part of a library, museum, or historical society, or they may exist as a completely separate unit based in a governmental building. They can range from large, well-funded enterprises providing a variety of archival services to small and limited operations dependent mostly on part-time volunteer staffs.

Government Archivists preserve the paper and other documents that constitute the heritage of a government, a people, or a region. They acquire, appraise, arrange, and catalog government archives as well as assist patrons of the archives and plan exhibitions. They participate in research activities involved with archival materials and directly manage the disposition, preservation, and safekeeping of governmental archive materials.

Archive materials can be in the form of papers, books, blueprints, photographs, drawings, maps, films, video and audio tapes, and electronic data. These materials may also include historical documents, institutional records and documents, or works of art—namely any document or material thing that reflects transactions or procedures can be considered an archival record. Records may be saved on any medium, from paper, film, videotape, and audiotape to electronic disk or computer file. In addition, a backup copy of them may be placed onto some other medium to protect the originals and to make them more accessible to researchers who use the records.

On a daily basis, Government Archivists are involved in classification processes: the indexing, cataloging, and listing of the material so that the archive staff and the public can locate the material with little trouble. In arranging archival records and materials, archivists apply two important principles: provenance and original order. Provenance refers to the origin of the records, essentially who created them. Order refers to the process of keeping archival records in their original order as established and maintained by the creator(s). Original order, however, is not always the best way to maintain some collections, and archivists must use their own experience and current best practices to determine the correct way to keep collections of mixed media or those lacking a clear original arrangement.

Archivists respond to personal, telephone, e-mail, and written inquiries from members of the public and governmental agencies, advising them how best to access, use, and interpret governmental archives. They facilitate access through user-friendly computer-aided searches and by exploring ways of networking archives and other means of facilitating remote access. They frequently coordinate educational and public outreach programs, such as exhibitions, talks, visits to government archives, workshops, lectures, and classes. They may produce teaching materials on the use of archival materials and facilitate training sessions on archival procedures for both the public and governmental personnel. Senior Governmental Archivists also carry out traditional management tasks, such as overseeing budget, staff, strategy, and funding activities.

In addition, Government Archivists develop and implement procedures for the processing and preservation of archival materials. Archivists have time-honored methods for preserving items and information in climate-controlled storage facilities, which involves both the cataloging and accession of items into a collection archive, their retrieval, and their safe handling. However, the advent of digital documents and items along with the development of electronic databases has caused a reevaluation of these traditional procedures. For example, at the National Archives, whose goal is the ensure the preservation of the documentation of U.S. history and government, new solutions are sought for the preservation challenge presented by electronic records, which include the documentation of presidents, vital national security documents (such as battle plans, weapons designs, and intelligence information), records of immigration and citizenships, property ownership, voter registration, and census data. The archives has set up an Electronic Records Archives, or ERA, whose goal is, as Allen Weinstein, archivist of the United States, says, "to provide access to all types of electronic records via the Internet to anyone, anywhere, anytime—regardless of the hardware and software that was used to create the records or that will be available in the future."

Salaries

Salaries for Government Archivists tend to be higher than those of most other archivists. According to PayScale, Inc.'s, October 2007 salary survey report on archivists, the median annual salary for Government Archivists employed in state and local government was $39,051 (which is in line with most other archivists). However, the median yearly income for Government Archivists employed in the federal government was $71,093. Most Government Archivists have civil service status.

Employment Prospects

Nearly a third of all archivists work in federal, state, and local governments, and about half of these jobs are in the Washington, D.C., area. Many federal archivists work for the National Archives and Records Administration (NARA). All state governments have archival or historical records sections that hire archivists.

Some archivists may begin their career working on grant-funded projects and eventually achieve long-term job positions. However, as qualified applicants usually outnumber job openings, the competition for these governmental positions is stiff. Those with the best chances for employment are graduates with a concentration in archives or records management and who have solid computer skills.

Openings for Government Archivists are greatly dependent on available funds and may improve as governmental organizations and agencies continue to emphasize the necessity of establishing archives and organizing records and information on the local and state levels. While archivists tend not to leave their jobs once they find them, the need to replace those Government Archivists who retire will create additional job openings.

Advancement Prospects

Eligibility for advancement for many civil service jobs is based on experience. Qualified workers must take written and oral tests for advanced positions. Most local and state governmental archives are small, with restricted resources and staff and limited opportunities for promotion. Archivists at these facilities typically advance by transferring to a larger unit that has supervisory posts. Federal archives, however, usually offer many more opportunities of career progression for archivists. Some senior Government Archivist positions (such as director of a large state or federal archive) typically require a doctorate degree in history, library science, or a related field.

Education and Training

Individuals can prepare for a career in archives through a variety of educational programs. Most entry-level positions require an undergraduate and a graduate degree together with archival coursework and a practicum (a school or college course that is designed to give students supervised practical application of previously studied theory). Although archivists have a variety of undergraduate majors, most receive graduate degrees in history, library science, or library and information science. Some have degrees in both fields. Still others may obtain a master's degree in archival science/studies (M.A.S.). Other useful specializations include public administration and political science. For higher-ranking positions, a Ph.D. is often demanded, particularly in academic institutions.

An educational resource available to Government Archivists and preservationists is the Northeast Document Conservation Center (NEDCC), which provides organizations and individuals with help in learning proper care and procedures in the preservation of materials as well as the digitization of materials. They also offer courses online. (Its Web site is at http://www.nedcc.org/home.php.)

Special Requirements

The Academy of Certified Archivists (ACA) offers voluntary certification for archivists. The designation "Certified Archivist" is obtained by those with at least a master's degree and a year of appropriate archival experience. The certification process requires candidates to pass a written examination, and they must renew their certification on a periodic basis.

Experience, Skills, and Personality Traits

Because of the highly varied nature of the job and work environment, Government Archivists need to have a corresponding wide range of talents. They must have excellent communication and interpersonal skills in order to aid those individuals doing research. They must be well versed in the basic knowledge of conservation of documents and cultural artifacts. Many different types of media can deteriorate if not stored and maintained properly. They must have the requisite computer proficiency to confront the new challenges posed by the preservation of electronic records. Because of the amount of sorting and listing required, they need to be very logical and organized and be able to pay close attention to detail. They need basic research skills to catalog records and assist users.

Unions and Associations

Besides membership in the American Library Association (ALA), the American Society of Information Science and Technology (ASIS&T), and the Special Libraries Association (SLA), Government Archivists find membership in the National Association of Government Archives and Records Administrators (NAGARA) and in the Society of American Archivists (SAA) to be of special interest and usefulness. Among the various professional organizations concerned with preservation techniques and education are the American Institute for Conservation of Historic and Artistic Works (AICHAW), the Association for Information and Image Management (AIIM), and the Association for Recorded Sound Collections (ARSC).

Tips for Entry

1. Among useful business background courses that you may take while earning your undergraduate and graduate degrees, those in records management are particularly vital to your future career as a Government Archivist.
2. To gain archival seasoning, consider working during the summer as an intern, volunteer, or part-time worker in a museum or archive.
3. Jobs in most federal libraries require that you pass civil service examinations. Contact the Office of Personnel Management (OPM) through USAJOBS, the federal government's official employment information system, at http://www.usajobs.opm.gov, for help.

GOVERNMENT LIBRARIAN

Duties: Locate, acquire, evaluate, and organize federal (or state and local) government documents and other relevant materials for federal and state libraries and archives; guide patrons (including government officials and sometimes the general public) on how to access information resources; supervise library assistants and manage the technology used for information research and retrieval

Alternate Title(s): Government Document/Legislative Librarian; Government Documents Librarian; Government Information Specialist/Librarian; Library Supervisor, Government Center

Salary Range: $35,000 to $80,000 or more

Employment Prospects: Fair to good

Advancement Prospects: Good

Prerequisites:

Education or Training—Master's degree in library science (M.L.S.) or library and information science (M.L.I.S.) required; undergraduate degree may be in any area of choice

Experience—Student internship in a library or volunteer background, particularly in library reference or research, is helpful

CAREER LADDER

Government Library Director; Government Chief Information Officer

Government Librarian

Librarian Assistant; Librarian Technician

Special Skills and Personality Traits—Dedicated customer service attitude and demonstrated project management abilities; detail oriented, with statistical abilities; excellent communication (both written and verbal) and interpersonal talents; energetic and flexible; good computer skills; strong organizational and prioritization abilities

Special Requirements—Some states require certification of librarians employed at state government libraries; federal Government Librarians may have to pass civil service exams before employment

Position Description

Libraries of government departments provide information to policy makers, to government staff and employees, and sometimes to the general public. Government libraries are any facilities that are established and fully supported by government to serve government with the primary audience being government, although the actual audience served may be broader than government. Their primary function is to assist government at different levels by making available all kinds of information published by government and nongovernment bodies and individuals. Government libraries are found in all shapes and sizes and operate in every setting imaginable, from the large urban federal court library to the relatively isolated county law library, from the small library serving a department of the federal government to the largest depository of print, nonprint, and audio materials in the United States, the Library of Congress.

Most Government Librarians, like other librarians, have a variety of tasks and projects, including attend-

ing to the reference desk, aiding with research, conducting training sessions, and supervising staff. Most library duties involve organizing, such as classifying and cataloging materials or coordinating projects. Like most librarian positions, Government Librarians are involved in three basic aspects of library work: user services, technical services, and administrative services. Even those librarians that specialize in one of these areas perform all the other responsibilities as well.

In small government libraries or information centers, Government Librarians typically handle all aspects of the work, from keeping current with literature and other available resources on government and political matters to selecting materials from publishers, wholesalers, and distributors to add to the collection at the library or center. They prepare these new materials for classification (usually by subject matter) and cataloging. They supervise assistants who prepare cards or computer records that direct library users to resources.

Large libraries or information centers usually have large professional support staffs, and Government Librarians often specialize in a single area, such as acquisitions, cataloging, reference, or administration. In all cases, teamwork is essential to maintain quality service to the public.

Another type of Government Librarian is government documents librarians. They work in federal and state libraries and archives, specializing in locating and evaluating data published by government bodies. U.S. government agencies provide information on a wide variety of topics, from nutrition and health care to gardening and saving money on utility bills. For more than 140 years, the Government Printing Office (GPO) has produced and distributed federal government information products. Both published and unpublished government information appears in print, CD-ROM, online, and multimedia formats. In addition, the GPO provides public access to government materials and information online, mainly through the Federal Depository Library Program (FDLP).

A federal depository library is a library in the United States that holds documents printed by the GPO, provides access online to government material, and through other programs collects and makes available documents of the different state and local governments and for those of foreign countries. There are approximately 1,250 such libraries located in all 50 states. The mission of the FDLP is to disseminate information products from all three branches of the federal government (and many state and local governments as well) to the federal depository libraries, which maintain this data as part of their existing collections and are responsible for assuring that the public has free access to all this material. Anyone can visit federal depository libraries and use the federal depository collections, which are filled with information on careers, business opportunities, consumer information, health and nutrition, legal and regulatory information, and demographics, among numerous other subjects. Government Librarians manage the depository collections and ensure that library staff and users follow the rules of these programs. They evaluate and select documents, reference materials, and Internet resources, both those that are available from the GPO and those that are not provided as part of the library's depository programs.

The Internet is increasing access to government information as well as making it easier for users to interact with Government Librarians who may be based in other parts of the country. Government Information Online (GIO) is a national pilot project sponsored by the Illinois State Library, the Online Computer Library Center (OCLC) in Ohio, and the University of Illinois at Chicago. The GPO is participating in the pilot along with more than 30 of the federal depository libraries. Users of the service can interact online with Government Librarians across the country during a weekly chat, or users can submit questions at any time via an e-mail interface.

Government Librarians are responsible for the processing of government documents, many of which are classified according to unique schemes contained in the Superintendent of Documents Classification System (SuDoc). Government Librarians must be thoroughly knowledgeable about this system and work closely with their cataloging staff to guarantee that they follow the rules. As part of the public service, Government Librarians often design and implement educational and outreach programs to inform public users about the services and resources available to them.

One obstacle government libraries face is that governmental priorities can change radically with a shift of the political party in power. Government libraries are long-term entities and must span many such shifts in power. This results in government libraries competing for limited resources and monies with shorter-term pressing issues in government departments. Building alliances with care is therefore critical to the success and even the survival of the government library. Key to building these coalitions is the identification and fulfillment of users' needs. The primary users of government libraries are typically government staff, but there can be conflicting priorities if, for example, in-depth research for ongoing programs is not given a defined place in relation to urgent requests from senior officers in a government department. There also can be tension about using resources for secondary users of the library, such as the public, particularly when budgets for resources and staff get tighter. Thus, Government Librarians must continually assess and understand the needs of their patrons in order to set priorities.

Salaries

Incomes for Government Librarians vary a great deal depending on their specific job responsibilities, their experience, and the location of the library. According to PayScale, Inc., median annual salaries for Government Librarians in 2007 ranged from a low for state and local government libraries of $38,818 to a high of $64,868 for federal government nonsupervisory positions. Supervisory and managerial posts in federal libraries, such as the Smithsonian Institute or the Library of Congress, have yearly salaries spanning from $45,000 to $100,000 or more.

Employment Prospects

The increasing use of computerized information storage and retrieval systems continues to contribute to slow growth in the demand for librarians of all sorts. Nonetheless, libraries in general (and government libraries in particular) recognize the need to have information specialists on staff to help patrons (both public and government officials) with statistical datasets, geographic information systems, and electronic access to government information. While there are fewer positions specifically titled government information librarian, positions are still available for individuals qualified in the area of government information, especially for those with technological backgrounds.

Advancement Prospects

Eligibility for promotion and tenure in many civil service jobs is based on experience, and qualified workers must take written and oral tests to be eligible for advanced positions. Experienced Government Librarians may be able to advance to administrative positions, such as library director or chief information officer.

Education and Training

The federal government and most state and local governments require a master's degree in library science (M.L.S.) or library and information science (M.L.I.S.) for most Government Librarian positions. Computer-related coursework is an extremely important part of an M.L.S. degree, as is the use of new resources such as online reference systems, Internet search methods, and automated circulation systems. Librarians usually take continuing training courses once they are employed to keep abreast of new information systems brought about by changing technology.

Special Requirements

Some states demand certification of librarians employed in municipal, county, and regional library systems. Government Librarians employed by the federal government may be required to take civil service exams before they are employed.

Experience, Skills, and Personality Traits

Government Librarians must demonstrate a strong customer service attitude and display excellent project management capabilities. They need to be flexible and able to handle change well. They should be personable and patient and have excellent communication skills. They need to be able to work with details, have statistical abilities, and possess solid computer knowledge. They must be highly organized and able to set priorities easily.

Unions and Associations

Government Librarians are civil service employees and thus do not belong to unions. However, there are a variety of trade associations that can provide educational guidance, professional support, and conferences and information useful for Government Librarians. These groups include the American Library Association (ALA), the American Society for Information Science and Technology (ASIS&T), the National Association of Government Archives and Records Administrators (NAGARA), and the Special Libraries Association (SLA).

Tips for Entry

1. During your undergraduate and graduate years, gain experience by working as a student assistant, volunteer in the college or university library, or do a practicum or internship at another library.
2. Jobs in most federal libraries require that you pass civil service examinations. Contact the Office of Personnel Management (OPM) at http://www.usajobs.opm.gov for help. Federal jobs that can be obtained without the use of OPM include, among others, the U.S. Foreign Service, the judicial and legislative branches of government, the Library of Congress, the National Science Foundation, the United Nations Secretariat, and the U.S. Postal Service.
3. To locate federal job openings around the world, contact OPM's Career American Connection at (912) 757-3000, or check out the federal jobs Web site at http://usajobs.opm.gov.

LAW LIBRARIAN

Duties: Develop and administer law information programs and systems at governmental, corporate, or academic libraries to ensure information and materials are organized to meet users' needs; provide reference services for attorneys, clerks, judges, and other patrons; purchase, prepare, and systematize printed materials; supervise law library technicians

Alternate Title(s): Corporate Law Librarian; Government Law Librarian; Law Library Cataloging Librarian; Law Reference Librarian

Salary Range: $40,000 to $75,000 or more

Employment Prospects: Good

Advancement Prospects: Good

Prerequisites:

    Education or Training—Most law libraries require a master's degree in library science (M.L.S.) or in library and information science (M.L.I.S.) from an American Library Association (ALA)–accredited institution; many Law Librarians also have a J.D. (Doctor of Jurisprudence) or L.L.B. (Bachelor of Laws) degree as well, and some employers may require this degree

    Experience—Background working in a law library is highly recommended; library reference work

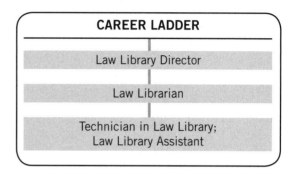

often required as well as a working familiarity with print and electronic resources

    Special Skills and Personality Traits—Capacity to work independently and as a member of a team; detail oriented; good organizational abilities; proficiency with computers, software, the Internet, and library-relevant information technology applications; strong interpersonal and oral and written communication skills; substantial legal research talents

    Special Requirements—Law Librarians employed in academic libraries may have teaching responsibilities, for which certification may be required

Position Description

Law Librarians are professionally trained individuals who function in various legal settings. Some may be lawyers who attended law school and practiced law for a while before they moved to law librarianship. Some Law Librarians may begin as library paraprofessionals who make a transition to librarianship. Some Law Librarians may have initiated their careers in other types of libraries, from school and academic libraries to special libraries, and then just happened to be employed at a law library.

There are different types of law libraries: those serving law firms and corporate law departments and those providing library services for government agencies, law schools, and judicial courts. There are different sizes of law libraries, from a one-person facility serving a small or moderate sized law firm to the law library of the U.S. Congress. Similarly, there are diverse Law Librarian positions (from catalog librarians and reference and

research librarians to library directors, from computer services librarians to rare books librarians).

Many Law Librarians juggle many different duties and projects. They may work at the reference desk of the institution or undertake research for a law partner, a professor, or a government official. They may serve on a university or government committee, edit a newsletter, catalog books or other materials, conduct training sessions, supervise library assistants or technicians who check in serials, negotiate a contract with a bibliographic utility supplying electronic data to the library, or write policy manuals.

Like most other librarians, Law Librarians are involved in setting library policy and make decisions about personnel and resources, organizing materials (cataloging and classifying) and information (creating bibliographies). They organize people and projects. They tend to think institutionally about policies and procedures, for example, setting up a system for assigning study carrels that will be fair for all law students or setting up a checkout system for a law firm library that will attract use by all the attorneys. In addition, they actively create, coordinate, and promote library services with instructional services and educational programs that familiarize students, faculty, law partners, or employees of government agencies or businesses (depending on where the law library resides) with the facility's resources in both print and electronic formats. Academic Law Librarians may teach legal research and writing courses and lecture on legal research to various classes within or outside the educational environment.

Law Librarians have to be fully acquainted with all types of research resources, from print to electronic media. Particularly for law firms or university law libraries, when information is needed quickly (and cost may not be a primary concern), electronic resources such as LexisNexis or Westlaw frequently are used. Many of these database services are expensive, so Law Librarians need to be able to research both from print and electronic media. Then, too, not everything may be found on the Internet. There are pockets of information, known as "deep Web," that cannot be reached by most search engines unless some advanced commands are known. In addition, search techniques, like the Internet itself, are constantly changing. Part of a Law Librarian's job is to know what is available electronically, what is not, and what print resources can be used to supplement electronic search strategies.

Nonetheless, electronic searches can yield fruit. As Sybil Turner, Law Librarian at the law firm of Arnall Golden Gregory, indicates, "A partner might say 'I want to find out the number of companies with sales between $100 and $200 million headquartered in Georgia in X industry' and ask for addresses and the names of the top executives. Ten years ago, that was much harder and more expensive to do, especially at smaller firms, because there were only a few databases that tracked it. Or an attorney might say 'I'm meeting with so and so. Can you find any information on him?' I might find out he won a golf tournament last year, and the attorney can sneak that in."

As law librarianship and legal research are always changing, it is crucial for Law Librarians, as professionals, to devote substantial amounts of their time to continuing self-education. This includes reading professional publications, monitoring online discussions of issues and practices of the profession, and attending training sessions. One example of these changes affecting the law library world is the move to go partially or entirely digital by implementing Internet resources via an online provider or in-house intranet (a privately maintained computer network that can be accessed only by authorized persons, such as members or employees of the organization that owns it). There are economies and efficiencies possible from virtual resources that are critically selected and acquired by Law Librarians. Such a virtual law library still requires acquisitions, organization, training, and instruction on effectively using its resources. Virtual Law Librarians must negotiate contracts, develop virtual knowledge resources, and perform in-person services for clients.

Salaries

According to an October 2007 salary survey report compiled by PayScale, Inc., median annual salaries for Law Librarians ranged from $47,589 to $72,433, depending on the geographic location of the library. Median yearly salaries for various types of Law Librarians were as follows: at law schools, $48,288; at law firms, $57,736; in government, $71,908; at legal services firms, $52,487; at law departments of college or university libraries, $45,139; and at legal research and analysis firms, $62,985.

Employment Prospects

Employment possibilities are good for Law Librarians, even though it is often true that they may have to change employers to gain a desired position. Nonetheless, in larger urban areas, there are plenty of opportunities with corporate law firms; with county, state, and court libraries; and with law school academic libraries, many of them advertised and filled locally.

Advancement Prospects

Experienced Law Librarians may look for advancement to the higher administrative posts of director of the law library or chief information officer in their business firm. Eligibility for promotion in many civil service jobs is based on experience and the successful completion of written and oral tests. Experienced Law Librarians in governmental institutions may progress to administrative positions, such as department heads or chief information officers.

Education and Training

To qualify for virtually any professional job in a law library, whether governmental, academic, or corporate, Law Librarians must have a master's degree in library science (M.L.S.) or in library and information science (M.L.I.S.) from an American Library Association (ALA)–accredited institution.

Not all Law Librarians need to have law degrees. However, many large law firms, judicial courts, government libraries, and academic law libraries do require a J.D. or L.L.B. degree for reference Law Librarians and most middle management and directorship positions in their facilities. Most positions that require a law degree insist that it be earned from a law school accredited by the American Bar Association (ABA). Since academic law library directors are usually members of the law school faculty, almost all of them must have law degrees. A law degree is less important for other posts, such as cataloging, acquisitions, circulation, control of government documents, and computer services, although some individual Law Librarians in these positions do have law degrees.

Special Requirements

Law Librarians in academic libraries or at law schools frequently have teaching duties as well, which often necessitates having a teaching certificate. In some instances, these teaching duties are critical for attaining tenure on the faculty.

Experience, Skills, and Personality Traits

Librarianship is fundamentally a service profession. Law Librarians, therefore, must have a strong service orientation with excellent communication and interpersonal skills. They must have substantial legal research abilities and a solid knowledge of print and electronic resources. They must be able to develop productive working relationships and function as effective team members as well as carry out duties independently. They need to be familiar with current trends in legal publishing, education, and research and have a thorough knowledge of the U.S. legal information market. A reading knowledge of at least one modern foreign language is an additional asset for Law Librarians.

If they are in charge of cataloging, they need to have a working knowledge in the application of the Anglo-American Cataloging Rules (AACR2r), the Library of Congress Subject Headings (LCSH) and classification, and MARC 21 formats for bibliographic and authority data. They should also have background in cataloging materials through a cataloging utility, such as the Online Computer Library Center (OCLC) or Research Libraries Information Network (RLIN) in an integrated library system environment.

Unions and Associations

Professional associations of interest for Law Librarians include the American Association of Law Libraries (AALL), which has a special interest section and Web site for both academic law libraries and public Law Librarians, the American Bar Association (ABA), the American Library Association (ALA), the Association of Record Management Administrators (ARMA), the Law and Technology Resources for Legal Professionals (LLRX), and the Legal Division of the Special Libraries Association (SLA). For government Law Librarians, the Special Interest Section (SIS) of AALL is particularly key.

Tips for Entry

1. While earning your library degree and/or your law degree, explore the possibilities of summer internships at your state's legal aid society to give you practical experience in going to court and taking depositions.
2. One way to gain a better sense of what Law Librarians do is to talk with them. Talk to the librarians at the law library you use or contact your local chapter of the American Association of Law Libraries (AALL).
3. The AALL has published a booklet entitled *Finding Your Way in the Information Age* that explains the many roles of Law Librarians as well as the types of skills needed to be successful in this profession. You can request a free copy from the AALL at their Web site (http://www.aallnet.org).

MAP LIBRARIAN

Duties: Classify, catalog, and interpret map collections; handle reference questions about maps; select maps or map collections for purchase

Alternate Title(s): Geoscience and Map Librarian; Map/Geographic Information System (GIS) Librarian

Salary Range: $35,000 to $55,000 or more

Employment Prospects: Good

Advancement Prospects: Good

Prerequisites:

Education or Training—Undergraduate degree in geography or geoscience; master's degree in library science (M.L.S.) or library and information science (M.L.I.S.)

Experience—Academic background or experience in geography or related field; experience in reference, instruction, and collection development in an academic, research, or public library; familiarity with geographic information system (GIS) applications used in education and research; training in the use of statistical sources and government information resources

CAREER LADDER

Director of Map Library at Larger Academic or Research Library

↑

Map Librarian

↑

Assistant Map Librarian

Special Skills and Personality Traits—Ability to work both independently and in a collaborative, team-oriented environment; excellent oral and written communication talents; good interpersonal and organizational abilities; strong computer proficiency and the ability to employ technology in the delivery of library services

Special Requirements—Map Librarians hired by academic libraries may have teaching duties and, as such, may be required to have a teaching certificate

Position Description

Maps are, of course, valuable in everyday life, but they also have considerable historical significance in that they can describe the geography of the past. They can aid in research for land use and future real estate development as well as in mining and engineering projects. Maps report the state of the Earth's surface, a plan for the Earth's surface, a report of people and resources on the Earth, or a projection of what space within and outside the solar system may look like. They are cartographic reports of scientific information.

A library's map collection typically consists of government and commercially produced print maps, atlases, reference materials, microforms, and digital space data. Much of this digital data is for use in a geographic information system (GIS), a collection of computer hardware, software, and geographic data for capturing, storing, manipulating, analyzing, and displaying all forms of geographic and spatial information. Data can be information about population, zoning, or topology and can provide aerial photographs that can

have a wide-scale range. Data produced for use in a GIS are created by local, state, federal, international, and commercial agencies.

Primary responsibilities of Map Librarians include providing subject-specific reference, consultation, and instruction for library patrons needing assistance with digital and print cartographic and geospatial resources and geography collections. They usually participate in collection development, selecting, organizing, and evaluating materials in all formats, and in all management activities related to the map collection and associated materials. They plan library services and user education programs related to maps and geospatial data.

Map Librarians may develop the library's map collection Web pages that provide access to map-related Internet resources. They generally supervise all cataloging of maps to provide bibliographic access through their facility's online catalog. They work in conjunction with other library units to assure consistent policies for the cataloging of maps, remote sensing imagery, aerial photographs, and data sets, creating and reviewing metadata for digital geospatial data and data sets as needed.

Map Librarians in academic libraries may collaborate with academic departments to integrate GIS into the particular teaching and research needs of the school. They may perform public services for campus and community patrons using the full collection of cartographic materials held by the library. They may provide course-related instruction and participate in other user education activities.

Salaries

Annual earnings for this position vary to a degree depending on the Map Librarian's responsibilities and the type and location of the library. Most beginning Map Librarians have starting yearly salaries in the range of $35,000 to $40,000, and salaries for seasoned Map Librarians (whose duties include little to no supervisory responsibilities) range from $45,000 to $55,000 or higher. (Those Map Librarians who are also tasked with supervisory duties will generally earn more.)

Employment Prospects

As with many other library positions, there will be an increase of retirements in the coming years. Thus, prospects for Map Librarians are generally good, as more positions should open up than there will be librarians to fill them through this period.

Advancement Prospects

Map Librarians may move into supervisory or administrative posts. Smaller collections are usually administered by a single Map Librarian with a small support staff. Map Librarians in larger academic, research, or public libraries may head the map department and be responsible for budgets, personnel, facilities, and collection management.

Education and Training

For their undergraduate degree, Map Librarians should major in geography, geoscience, or a related field. They then will need to earn a master's degree in library science (M.L.S.) or in library and information science (M.L.I.S.). It is important that they have some training in the application of GIS services in libraries and/or education or research.

Special Requirements

Map Librarians employed at academic libraries may have teaching responsibilities at the college or university. As such, they may have to have a teaching certificate. Some may be appointed to the rank of assistant or associate professor, depending on their qualifications.

Experience, Skills, and Personality Traits

In terms of librarianship, the main difference between a Map Librarian and the more conventional reference librarian is the ability to think graphically. Reference inquiries are spatially related, and, given that author and title are largely redundant (except for accompanying reference material such as book or serial literature), when searching for maps or spatial information, the need to interpret queries in terms of place and scale is absolutely paramount.

Map Librarians should have some experience with user instruction, professional library reference work, and knowledge of cataloging standards and practices concerning cartographic materials. They need to have strong computer skills, especially in a networked environment. They should have some familiarity with Web site design, development, and maintenance. They also need to be aware of all the latest advances in digital cartography and its availability on the Internet, such as those available from MapQuest, the Internet mapping business located at http://www.mapquest.com. (MapQuest has become the largest map publisher in the history of cartography.) MapQuest, among other sources, uses maps as navigational tools, but mapping is also a powerful visualization aid. As data visualization continues to grow as a process, maps are being integrated into information standards, all of which Map Librarians must be cognizant of and aware that the cataloging of maps and the cataloging of spatial data are changing and evolving along with the development of spatial metadata standards.

Map Librarians need to have a strong sense of public service and the ability to interact positively and work productively with colleagues. They must have excellent oral and written communication skills, outstanding organizational abilities, and a potential as an instructor and trainer. In addition, they should exhibit a commitment to scholarship and their own professional growth.

Unions and Associations

There are various trade associations of interest to Map Librarians. They include the American Library Association (ALA) and its Map and Geography Round Table group, the American Society for Information Science and Technology (ASIS&T), the Association of American Geographers (AAG) and their component group, the Geomorphology Specialty Group (GSG), and the North American Cartographic Information Society (NACIS). Regional groups include the North East Map

Organization (NEMO) and the Western Association of Map Libraries (WAML).

Tips for Entry

1. A useful way to learn about map and cartography's current activities and concerns, as well as a way to make useful career contacts, is to join the North American Cartographic Information Society (NACIS) as a student member.

2. As every librarian today with a connection to the Internet now has access to several hundred thousand maps in digital form, the chief limitation on providing map reference service is a lack of information about pertinent Web sites. For driving directions and street maps, use your favorite search engine to locate and check out MapQuest, EarthaMaps, or MapBlast. For topographic maps, look up TerraServer-USA or Trails.com.

3. Note that Odden's Bookmarks (http://oddens. geog.uu.nl/index.php) is the most comprehensive collection of links for all aspects of cartography and is particularly useful for areas outside the United States, whereas Infomine (http://infomine.ucr.edu) has a more selective collection of map and GIS links focusing on the United States.

MEDICAL LIBRARIAN

CAREER PROFILE

Duties: Provide health information about new medical treatments, clinical trials and standard trials procedures, tests, and equipment to physicians, allied health professionals, patients and their families, corporations, and the public

Alternate Title(s): Clinical Medical Librarian; Health Information Specialist; Health Science Librarian; Hospital Librarian; Medical Reference and Education Librarian; Medical Research Librarian

Salary Range: $37,000 to $65,000 or more

Employment Prospects: Good

Advancement Prospects: Good to excellent

Prerequisites:

Education or Training—Undergraduate degree in a medical field recommended; master's degree in library science (M.L.S.) or library and information science (M.L.I.S.) required

Experience—A background in science, health sciences, or allied health is useful; some practical experience in medical research or within a medical laboratory is recommended as well

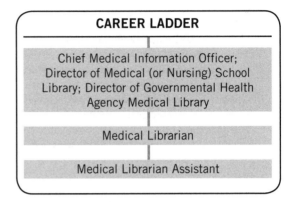

CAREER LADDER

Chief Medical Information Officer; Director of Medical (or Nursing) School Library; Director of Governmental Health Agency Medical Library

Medical Librarian

Medical Librarian Assistant

Special Skills and Personality Traits—Creativity and flexibility; detail oriented; energetic self-starter who can be a team player as well; good organizational and problem-solving abilities; excellent oral and written communication talents; solid interpersonal skills with emphasis on customer service; computer proficiency

Special Requirements—Medical Librarians (particularly those in medical school libraries) who have teaching duties may need teaching certificates

Position Description

Medical Librarians provide health information about new medical treatments, clinical trials and standard trials procedures, tests, and equipment to physicians, medical students, government employees, corporate employees and corporations, patients and their families, and the public. They help physicians provide information about quality care to patients, help patients find information, answer consumers' questions, and provide available data to the health care industries. They teach physicians, medical students, and other allied health professionals how to use medical-related software programs, online resources, search engines, and the Internet to obtain the latest data on medical topics.

Medical Librarians hold a wide variety of jobs in heath information sciences. Work settings for Medical Librarians include academic medical centers, ambulatory centers, clinics, colleges, consumer health libraries, hospitals, research centers, universities, and medical schools. They can be library directors, Medical Librarians, Web managers at an academic medical center, collection development and/or catalog librarians at a university or medical college library, reference librarians at a hospital or a government agency, nursing school library directors, information architects for a pharmaceutical company, or consumer health librarians at a large medical center.

Medical Librarians work with a variety of health care providers: doctors, nurses, occupational therapists, physical therapists, patients, medical faculty, health professions students, health care consumers, and corporations. They use computers and personal digital assistants (PDAs) frequently in their work. Some Medical Librarians are systems librarians, responsible for fixing computers, running local area networks (LANs), or for training other to use technology. They frequently create Web pages for their libraries and may even be responsible for the Web site for their hospitals, universities, or medical schools. Medical Librarians look for information from many sources and, in the process, communicate with physicians and hospital administrators, professors and university chancellors, and corporate administrators.

An example of such a Medical Librarian is Kate Oliver, a reference librarian at the National Institutes of Health in Bethesda, Maryland. The tools of her work include a variety of high-speed, high-tech electronic resources, some 60,000 books, and thousands of medical and scientific journals. "Searching for biomedical information is," says Oliver, "a bit like the scientific process: you try and retry different approaches. The most important thing—more important than knowing specific information about a subject—is to understand how the literature is indexed in a database, that is, the 'structure' of the record. When you understand how data are put into a database, you then can visualize how best to find and pull out the kinds of information that you need."

Medical Librarians need to be familiar with key databases that cover biomedical literature, such as MEDLINE, a massive index of some 7 million articles published since 1966 that is the standard searching tool for medical literature, and Dialog, a database vendor that allows a user to search through many databases. Such databases include Biosis (abstracts of scientific articles in the fields of biology and biomedicine), Chem Abstracts (abstracts of articles specifically dealing with chemistry), and Science Citation Index (abstracts of articles in a wide range of magazines and journals).

Medical Librarians often serve on the faculty of health care and biomedical degree programs, where they instruct health care providers on how to access and evaluate information. They also may participate on university or pharmaceutical company research teams, where they can have an impact on the development of new treatments, products, and services. They may collaborate with health care colleagues on a variety of institution-related tasks, such as fund-raising, marketing, business, and information technology systems.

Consumer health Medical Librarians commonly serve the health information needs of patrons in public libraries. With the present-day emphasis on patient health education, consumers now engage in research of their own to increase their knowledge of treatments and procedures and to reduce fear and anxiety about their conditions. This has resulted in a demand for quality data written in lay terminology, which in turn has increased the demand for librarians specially trained to locate and disseminate this type of information.

Salaries

The salaries of Medical Librarians vary according to the type and location of their institutions, the level of their responsibilities, and the length of their employ-

ment. The Medical Library Association (MLA) reported in 2005 that the average starting yearly salary for a Medical Librarian was $40,832, and the overall average annual salary was $57,982. Furthermore, medical library directors earned up to $158,000 per year. According to PayScale, Inc.'s, 2007 survey of Medical Librarian salaries, median annual salaries ranged from $37,853 to $59,768, depending on the type of employer and location. Annual salaries for Medical Librarians at research facilities range from $50,000 to $62,000.

Employment Prospects

Job prospects for Medical Librarians are good. It is estimated that more than 50 percent of Medical Librarians currently employed will be retiring within the next decade. Applicants for Medical Librarian posts in large metropolitan areas, where most graduates prefer to work, usually face stiff competition. Those candidates willing to work in rural areas should have better job prospects.

Advancement Prospects

Opportunities for advancement vary according to the interests and expertise of the individual Medical Librarian. The more time, experience, and additional education an individual has, the better the advancement prospects. Some may use their particular subject backgrounds to develop collections and provide specialized services. Others may choose to specialize in library management and decide to advance to library directorships.

Because Medical Librarians have a number of highly marketable skills, they can move forward to a variety of positions, such as Web manager for a medical center, a medical informatics expert for a research facility, or a chief medical information officer for a pharmaceutical company. On the other hand, they may prefer to branch out to work as community outreach coordinators for a public health agency, reference librarians at a hospital, or directors of a nursing school library.

Education and Training

It is recommended that Medical Librarians have a bachelor's degree in some field or specialty of medicine (though in many cases, a liberal arts major, with some course work in medical terminology, biology, or other science, may be entirely appropriate), and also a master's degree in library science (M.L.S.) or library and information science (M.L.I.S.). A Ph.D. degree in library and information science is advantageous for a college teaching position in a medical school or a top administrative job in a college or university library or major library system. Most Medical Librarians participate in continuing training and education once they are on the job to keep abreast of new information systems brought about by changing technology.

Special Requirements

For those Medical Librarians based at colleges, medical schools, and universities, their responsibilities may include teaching, and, therefore, they may have to have gained teaching certifications. In addition, the Medical Library Association (MLA) offers certification examinations, which are designed to aid Medical Librarians to advance to higher positions.

Experience, Skills, and Personality Traits

As Medical Librarians spend much of their time working with people, they need to have strong communication and interpersonal talents. They must be detail oriented and highly organized and have excellent computer skills. They need to have a solid basis and interest in medicine and health-related issues and be extremely service oriented. They should be good at sharing knowledge and teaching people one at a time or in small groups. They need to be both creative and energetic self-starters and demonstrate an ability to work as team players. Fluency in one or more languages other than English (especially Spanish or German) is a definite advantage.

Medical Librarians need to demonstrate their familiarity with appropriate use of a core collection of medical reference tools for fact finding and gathering information. They should have experience with database searching techniques, particularly PubMed, Scopus, and other National Library of Medicine resources. They may need to have a familiarity with bibliographic management software programs such as EndNote and Reference Manager or at least a clear ability to become familiar with these research products.

Unions and Associations

The two primary professional organizations for Medical Librarians are the American Library Association (ALA) and the Medical Library Association (MLA), with its Academy of Health Information Professionals (AHIP), the MLA's peer-reviewed professional development and career recognition program. In addition, there are other professional groups of interest to Medical Librarians, such as the American Medical Informatics Association (AMIA), the Association of Academic Health Sciences Libraries (AAHSL), the Health and Science Communications Association (HSCA), and the National Network of Libraries of Medicine (NN/LM). (The NN/LM provides timely and convenient access to biomedical and health care information resources for its members as well as a means of searching for medical libraries in each state.) For students, there is the Health Occupations Students of America (HOSA).

Tips for Entry

1. While earning your degrees, investigate doing an internship in a medical library or volunteering at a hospital information desk as a good way to learn more about the profession and to gain work experience at the same time.
2. During your undergraduate years, seek courses in Web design and development, informatics, computer or information systems, research techniques, statistics, education, communication, and biosciences.
3. Become familiar with as many different computer programs as possible.
4. Explore Web sites and publications that profile Medical Librarians and their work, such as the Medical Library Association (http://www.mlanet.org), the National Library of Medicine (http://www.nlm.nih.gov), and the National Network/Libraries of Medicine (http://www.nnlm.nih.gov).

MUSIC LIBRARIAN

Duties: Organize, catalog, and maintain music collections; answer reference inquiries; select appropriate music, books, journals, recordings, microforms, and sometimes manuscripts and other rare materials for acquisition; recommend means of preservation and housing of music materials

Alternate Title(s): Director of Music Library; Head—Music Library; Music Archivist Librarian; Music and Media Cataloger; Music Director (radio-TV broadcasting)

Salary Range: $32,000 to $65,000 or more

Employment Prospects: Good

Advancement Prospects: Good

Prerequisites:

Education or Training—Undergraduate degree in music performance, music theory, or music history and master's degree in library science (M.L.S.) or library and information science (M.L.I.S.); master's degree or Ph.D. degree in music may be required

Experience—Two to three years of public service experience in an academic, research, or public library, including reference, cataloging, and instruction experience

Special Skills and Personality Traits—Ability to interact effectively with faculty, students, staff,

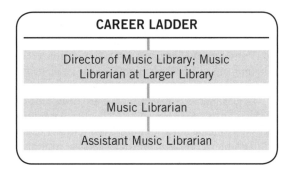

CAREER LADDER

Director of Music Library; Music Librarian at Larger Library

Music Librarian

Assistant Music Librarian

and the public from diverse cultural backgrounds; capacity for working collaboratively within a team; demonstrated organizational and time management skills; detailed knowledge of music literature and music reference sources; excellent oral and written communication abilities; familiarity with the latest technology and trends in the field of music librarianship, such as digital audio formats, with respect to preservation and access; strong customer service orientation

Special Requirements—Music Librarians employed at academic libraries typically are members of the faculty and, as such, usually need to have teaching certifications

Position Description

A Music Librarian is a special librarian qualified to concentrate in the field of music. A broad musical background is essential, for music of any style, medium, or era can find a place in most music collections. Music Librarians work in large research libraries such as the Library of Congress or the New York Public Library; in the music section or branch library in universities, colleges, and music conservatories; in public libraries; in radio and television station libraries; with music publishers and dealers; with musical societies and foundations; and with bands and orchestras. In addition, some Music Librarians, besides their duties in their library, develop online resources, set up freelance music businesses, are audio archivists, or are experts in audio digitization.

Traditional responsibilities of librarians in general are at the heart of a Music Librarian's activities: organiz-

ing, cataloging, and maintaining collections; providing instruction to library patrons on the use of the library; answering reference questions; and selecting music, books, recordings (CDs and DVDs), microforms, and sometimes manuscripts as well as rare materials for acquisition. In addition, they have to be knowledgeable about the means of preserving and housing the materials of the collection and the use of electronic bibliographic and reference resources in their work.

Depending on the type and nature of the institution where they are employed, Music Librarians may also plan exhibits and concerts and collaborate with other institutions in organizing lectures, classes, or other public programs. In a conservatory or university school of music, Music Librarians usually order or rent the music needed by student performing ensembles, from orchestra to band to opera workshop to chamber groups to individual instrumental performers. Music Librarians employed by symphony orchestras and broadcasting stations organize and maintain libraries of performance materials or recordings for use only by those particular organizations. Those employed by music publishers may have editorial duties or be responsible for maintaining the inventory of rental music to be licensed out. Those employed by music dealers acquire materials from numerous publishers worldwide for retail sale to over-the-counter or mail-order and Internet customers.

Music Librarians may also take an active role in music scholarship by compiling bibliographies; pursuing research; or writing reviews of new music related-publications, recordings, or other music materials. Particularly in academic libraries, they often teach music bibliography and other classroom subjects within their areas of specialization. As members of library or music professional organizations, they may serve on local, national, or international committees devoted to issues such as electronic information storage and retrieval, cataloging standards, education for librarianship, preservation practices, and library management. Within their library, they may be responsible for organizing training programs for staff, researchers, or interns.

Administrative tasks are another important part of a Music Librarian's job. They are often responsible for soliciting gifts and bringing in donations to their libraries. Their management duties may include formulating and implementing goals, objectives, policies, and procedures for their libraries, as well as setting priorities and allocating financial, staff, and space resources. Most Music Librarians work with the public, whether they hold full-time positions or interact with the public on a part-time basis in addition to their other duties. Those librarians involved with technical services (acquisitions, cataloging, and organizing the collection) may have little contact with the public.

Salaries

Earnings for this position vary depending on the extent of the Music Librarian's responsibilities and the type, size, and location of the library. Annual salaries range from the low $30,000s to the mid-$50,000s. For Music Librarians in academic settings, their ranking and status as members of the faculty help to determine their annual salaries, with salaries ranging from $42,000 to more than $65,000, again depending greatly on their experience and capabilities.

Employment Prospects

Employment opportunities for Music Librarians in academic and public libraries are good, whether they work full time in a larger library or on a part-time basis in a smaller library. Those working in businesses, such as music publishers and broadcasting stations, may be musicians who find that they can combine their library jobs with part-time second careers as a performers.

Advancement Prospects

Music Librarians in academic, public, or research libraries typically advance their careers by promotion to supervisory positions, including that of the director of the music library. While music collections in smaller libraries may be administered by a single Music Librarian with support staff, in the larger music libraries in universities, music conservatories, and the bigger public and research libraries they may have posts as assistant heads or department heads and have budget, personnel, facilities, and collection acquisitions and management responsibilities.

Education and Training

Training for music librarianship should include as broad an education as possible in both music and the liberal arts. Undergraduates need a wide background in the humanities, as Music Librarians must be familiar with the relationship of music to other disciplines. In addition, basic music cataloging and bibliographic research usually necessitates a working knowledge of German and at least one Romance language (French, Italian, or Spanish).

A master's degree in library science (M.L.S.) or library and information science (M.L.I.S.) is required by most employers. Because Music Librarians need a thorough knowledge of music history and repertory, a second master's degree in music is required or highly desired as well. Libraries specializing in folk music or music of non-Western cultures demand training in ethnomusicology, archives management, and other additional languages. In libraries where music is combined with other subjects, such as fine arts or dance, backgrounds in those subjects may also be expected.

While Music Librarians who work for broadcasting stations, orchestras, or bands may have only a bachelor's degree in music, in academic libraries it is not uncommon to find a Music Librarian with a Ph.D. Many earn their advanced degrees while working full time as librarians.

Special Requirements

For those academic Music Librarians who have teaching duties as well or are members of an institution's teaching faculty, teaching certification may be a requirement. For most other Music Librarians, no certification is necessary.

Experience, Skills, and Personality Traits

To be a successful Music Librarian, a solid general knowledge of music is paramount, coupled with a strong commitment to public service. This deep interest in music should extend to books about, recordings of, and research into music. Music Librarians must be able to work well with others and have excellent oral and written communication skills. They should be both flexible and creative. They should have some seasoning in developing and maintaining a research library collection, have some supervisory experience, and be familiar with the latest technology and trends in the field of music librarianship regarding both the preservation and maintenance of music materials.

In addition, Music Librarians need to be highly organized, have great attention to detail, and have a demonstrated ability to work both independently and collaboratively on a team. Specifically, they should have some background in music performance or composition—some Music Librarians are musicians as well. Music Librarians need to be familiar with music copyright and licensing issues and have experience in budgeting and project management. Knowledge of one or more languages other than English may be necessary, particularly in research.

Unions and Associations

The most important professional association for Music Librarians is the Music Library Association (MLA).

Other professional groups of interest include the American Library Association (ALA), the American Society for Information Science and Technology (ASIS&T), the Association of Research Libraries (ARL), the Center for Research Libraries (CRL), the Digital Library Federation (DLF), the Special Libraries Association (SLA), and the American Federation of Musicians (AFM) (http://www.afm.org) if the librarians are performers as well as librarians.

Tips for Entry

1. During your undergraduate and/or graduate years while earning your degrees, investigate internships or practicums in a music library. Many students gain experience by working in the music library of their college or university. Alternatively, you might investigate part-time work with a music publisher or a performance ensemble.

2. Joining the Music Library Association as a student member can provide you with the means of making valuable contacts in the music library field.

3. When searching for a position as a Music Librarian, visit the placement service job list on the Music Library Association (MLA) Web site at http://www.musiclibraryassoc.org.

NEWS LIBRARIAN

Duties: Use online databases, personal interviews, print resources, and other research outlets to fill the information needs of news reporters, producers, writers, and other newsroom staff in publishing establishments such as newspaper and magazine publishers and in broadcasting establishments such as radio and television stations as well as Internet news sites

Alternate Title(s): Director of Information Services; Director of News Research, Archives, and Archive Sales; Information Resources Specialist; Media Archive Director; Media Archivist/Librarian; Media Resource Center Coordinator; News Archives Coordinator; News Archivist; News Information Center Director; News Information Resource Library Director; News Library Director; Print and Visual News Researcher

Salary Range: $14,000 to $56,000 or more

Employment Prospects: Fair

Advancement Prospects: Good

Prerequisites:

   Education or Training—Undergraduate degree in communications, English, journalism, or liberal arts; master's degree in library science (M.L.S.)

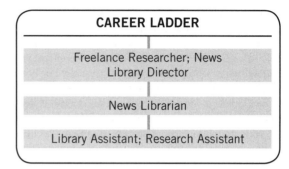

CAREER LADDER

Freelance Researcher; News Library Director

News Librarian

Library Assistant; Research Assistant

or in library and information science (M.L.I.S.) required

   Experience—Some professional work in an information organization usually preferred; in addition, professional research background necessary; knowledge of newsroom operations helpful

   Special Skills and Personality Traits—Ability to work well under pressure and to meet deadlines; computer proficiency required, usually with both PC and Macintosh programs; knowledge of additional database programs or Web design programs such as Dreamweaver is considered a plus; good communication, interpersonal talents, and organizational habits

Position Description

Once a job filled by journalists near retirement (hence the traditional name for a news library as a morgue) or newsroom managers looking for additional tasks to do, all the traditional roles for news libraries changed as new technology opened new vistas from the 1970s onward. By the late 1980s, advanced technology, such as computer-output microfiche, optical disks, computerized indexing, automated full-text retrieval systems, digital photo archiving, online database searching, spreadsheets, computer-assisted reporting, and media polling had appeared on the newspaper scene. Papers were now using commercial electronic systems for full-text storage and retrieval of newspaper stories.

Whereas News Librarians used to handle simply folders of clippings, today's News Librarians and researchers manage the information resources library that is stored on files, on tape or microfilm, or in computers for use by news and editorial staffs. As Nora

Paul, library director of the Poynter Institute of Media Studies in St. Petersburg, Florida, states, News Librarians "are the collectors, managers, and redistributors of the organization's primary product, information. This is critical in all stages of information's flow through the organization—initial information gathering for use in news reporting, in the collection of the news product into databases, in the repackaging of information created by the organization into new products."

News Librarians are responsible for both short-term and long-term research projects and must be equipped to meet the research needs of news reporters and editors who need information immediately. News Librarians develop, organize, and maintain a variety of resources, from a physical collection of clippings to the creation and maintenance of online databases or intranets (private computer networks that use Internet protocols and network connectivity to share securely part of an organization's information or operations with its employees). They maintain records and statistics on the use of databases and information services that they provide. The majority of News Librarians' research is now conducted online via the Internet as well as subscription databases such as Lexis/Nexis. However, other materials such as clippings files, hard-copy photos, microfilm, microfiche, pamphlets, magazines, and books are still essential resources.

News Librarians may hire, train, schedule, and evaluate library support staff (including interns and assistants) and direct the activities of those assistants engaged in clipping, classifying, cataloging, indexing, storing, editing, and retrieving information or do these activities themselves if they lack the support staff. They train newsroom associates in the use of the internal archive, the Internet, and searchable databases, such as LexisNexis, Factiva, and ProQuest. They may be responsible for the digital archiving and indexing of photos and PDF (portable document format) files using such programs as Merlin. They may process, catalog, and assign appropriate indexing terms to both edited and raw video generated by the news production team. They often develop databases for data storage and retrieval according to the needs of the news staff. They may prepare library budgets and promote and market library products and services to the public.

News Librarians exercise quality control over the news archive and assume responsibility for its accuracy and completeness. They must stay abreast of new research and public records sources. They may use their research to compile, edit, and write information pieces, profiles, and chronologies for publication. They typically are tasked with the weeding and reorganization of the collective archive on a regular basis. They may participate in or direct library projects to improve video archive and research services that include but are not limited to intranet Web page design and creation, tape selection, maintaining the accuracy and consistency of the thesaurus (used for researching materials), prepping materials for off-site storage, and backing up online databases created in-house.

News Libraries differ from many other types of libraries in that they are largely for-profit entities. They make money on commercial database services as well as other research services and products. The high-pressure, fast-paced atmosphere that results can lead some librarians to question their own ethical standards in order to get the job done. Additionally, the rapidly changing media landscape as more readers turn to online products from printed products has created much turmoil and uncertainty at many media companies. The decline in traditional classified advertising revenues is also putting great cost-cutting pressure on newspaper companies in particular. This, in turn, affects the jobs and resources available to News Librarians. Marketing library services and proving the library's value to management is on ongoing issue. Finally, copyright is a tricky subject, including encouraging reporters and news editors to follow good copyright practices, managing reprint permissions, and developing revenue from the repackaging of editorial content for online purposes.

Salaries

Earnings vary greatly for News Librarians based on their experience, the scope of their duties, their geographic location, and even their job titles. These job designations can range from starting positions to managerial posts. In a survey by the Special Libraries Association, the average annual salary for special librarians, including News Librarians, in the United States in 2005 was roughly $65,500. In a survey of wages of news information librarians in 2007, PayScale, Inc., found that their median annual income was $67,928 and that their median hourly rate ranged from $16.81 to $20.94, depending on their years of experience. For News Librarians represented by the Newspaper Guild, top minimum annual salaries ranged from a low of $14,000 at the *Chattanooga (Tennessee) Times* to a high of $56,000 for research/librarian at the *New York Times* and $71,168 for the chief News Librarian at the *New York Times*.

Employment Prospects

Salaries and demand for experienced News Librarians is increasing, and these information professionals are becoming increasingly vital assets in newsrooms due to today's digital world. Professionals who know how to manipulate and find information fast in the new media of Internet search and online databases are becoming more valuable than ever before. However, it is not an easy field to break into, as jobs tend to be scarce as media companies continue to downsize their staffs and reorganize their operations. Market pressures, disappointed revenue expectations by management, rising costs, and lowered profits (particularly from advertisers who are migrating to the Internet from print media) have affected newsrooms (both print and broadcasting) with dramatic cuts in staffs and budgets.

Nonetheless, News Librarians and their adjunct staff are still much in demand to help with needed information structures as news organizations merge or combine their newsprint (and even their television) with online operations. The News Librarian has the advantage of expertise in information architecture and evaluation, access to available digital technology, control of the archive (which can prove to be a source of revenue), and a useful interaction among all departments of a newspaper or a broadcasting station. The best sources for positions within newspaper (or broadcasting) library departments, as well as that of a News Librarian, remains with the larger daily and national journalist organizations.

Advancement Prospects

The right combination of skills and experience can be a tremendous boost for a News Librarian's advancement into a position as new library director, though such moves are often more dependent on job attrition and being at the right place at the right time. Some News Librarians may decide against advancing into library management and instead choose to use their research skills to move into freelance book research or other research jobs within publishing or business organizations.

Education and Training

For News Librarians, undergraduate degrees may be in journalism, English, communications, or any other liberal arts field of their interest, but they will need to have a master's degree in library science (M.L.S.) or in library and information science (M.L.I.S.). For News Librarians who wish to concentrate on archivist duties exclusively, they may not be required to have an M.L.S or M.L.I.S. degree.

Experience, Skills, and Personality Traits

In addition to superior research talents, News Librarians need to have excellent communication (both oral and written) and interviewing skills. They must be able to work well with people, communicate about what information is wanted and what they can deliver, and query reporters to figure out what information would really be of most use to them. They need to be creative and have good problem solving abilities. There is no single best way to research a question. Good News Librarians need to think of creative ways to answer questions when the usual resources fail. They need excellent computer and technical skills. This computer proficiency should include PC and extensive Web knowledge and experience with word processing, spreadsheet software, and such database programs as SQL, MySQL, PHP, AP, Capio, Dreamweaver, and MediaWiki. Their research skills should include experience with commercial information sources, such as LexisNexis, Factiva, Dow Jones, PACER, ChoicePoint, and Accurint. They should be familiar with Boolean logic, relevance, precision, and recall as used in Internet search techniques.

In addition to knowing how to use technology, they also must be able to teach others how to use it. They need to be able to learn new technologies quickly and be able to juggle multiple tasks at once. They require excellent attention to detail and flexibility. Newsrooms (print or broadcast) can be tense and hectic at times, and getting flustered is not an option. They must be accurate and consistent in their work, and a sense of humor is a useful personal trait.

Technology has had a large impact on the process of archiving as well. Originally, archives consisted only of text materials. Now they have expanded to include items such as photos, PDF files of pages, multimedia files, graphics, and so forth. News Librarians, in their archival duties, have had to learn how to manage these new data types.

Unions and Associations

Beyond the obvious professional groups (mentioned below) most likely to be useful for News Librarians, there is the Special Libraries Association (SLA), which has its own separate division just for news libraries, as well as the American Library Association (ALA) and the American Society for Information Science and Technology (ASIS&T). Some News Librarians at unionized newspapers are also represented by The Newspaper Guild (TNG).

The many professional journalism organizations include the American Press Institute (API), the Association for Education in Journalism and Mass Communication (AEJMC), the Association for Women in Communications (AWC), the Newspaper Association of America (NAA), the Online News Association (ONA), and the Society of Professional Journalists (SPJ).

Tips for Entry

1. During your undergraduate work, seek employment with the school library (or a local library) to familiarize yourself with library methodology and potential research resources.
2. Add to your computer knowledge with additional course work (or actual job experience during the college year or in summer internships).
3. Consider taking an archiving job in a news library as a means of getting your foot in the door. It can be a great way to show off your technical skills and then work your way up.
4. Do not forget to network. Go to conferences, ask to tour various news libraries near you, and do informational interviews with News Librarians.

LIBRARY ASSISTANTS

BOOKMOBILE DRIVER

CAREER PROFILE

Duties: Drive and maintain in good working order a library bookmobile; assist patrons and answer their questions; perform circulation duties; maintain the book collection, shelving materials as needed

Alternate Title(s): Bookmobile Assistant Librarian; Bookmobile Clerk/Driver; Bookmobile Librarian; Library Assistant/Bookmobile Driver

Salary Range: $16,000 to $39,000 or more

Employment Prospects: Good

Advancement Prospects: Fair to good

Prerequisites:

Education or Training—High school diploma; commercial driver's license usually required; usually receives training on the job

Experience—One to two years of commercial driving background with public contact and customer service duties; some experience with library work is helpful

Special Skills and Personality Traits—Ability to work well with minimum supervision; basic library skills; good communication and interpersonal talents; interest in books and other library materials and media; knowledge and abilities necessary to drive and maintain library motor vehicles and capacity for doing preventive maintenance and minor vehicle repairs; public service attitude

Special Requirements—Commercial driver's license (class A or class B with air brake certification) and clean driver's record for at least a year usually obligatory

CAREER LADDER

```
Library Assistant; Library Technician
                  |
         Bookmobile Driver
                  |
   High School Graduate; Retiree
```

Position Description

Some libraries provide an extended library service to their communities by operating bookmobiles, trucks or vans stocked with books and other materials that travel to designated sites on a regular schedule. Typically, bookmobiles take library materials to hospitals and nursing homes, schools and other educational facilities, senior citizen centers, neighborhoods without a library branch, and, in some cases, patrons living in remote areas.

Bookmobile Drivers (sometimes called bookmobile librarians) are a library's primary outreach staff. Because Bookmobile Drivers may be the only link some people have to a library, much of their work is helping the public. They may assist handicapped people or people with disabilities get to the bookmobile or shovel snow to ensure their safety. They often enter hospitals or nursing homes to deliver books and other library materials to patrons who are bedridden. The schedules of Bookmobile Drivers depend on the size of the area being served. Some of them go out on their routes daily, while others go only on certain days. On these other days, they may be on duty at the library. Some also work evenings and weekends to give patrons as much access to the library as possible. Flexible schedules are usually available, as many Bookmobile Drivers are on part-time scheduling as it is.

They drive the bookmobile (or the light truck that pulls the book trailer) to and from assigned locations. They maintain the bookmobile in a clean and operative condition, washing the exterior and detailing the interior of the vehicle on a periodic basis. They ensure that routine vehicle maintenance (such as oil changes, tune-ups, and safety inspections) and needed repairs are performed in a timely manner. (They may perform minor vehicle troubleshooting and repairs to handle emergency breakdowns to ensure that the bookmobile schedule is followed.)

Drivers may work alone or be accompanied by a library assistant or technician. When they work alone, they perform many of the same duties as do library assistants. They provide information about library policies and services. They assist patrons in locating materials or take requests for particular items. They advise and/or recommend books or other materials when appropriate and provide routine reference information, making note of any nonroutine reference questions to ask the library's reference or adult services librarians and then ensure that the correct answers are conveyed back to the patron. They receive and check out library materials available for loan, collect fines, maintain the book collection, and shelve materials, and they may operate cameras to take photos for library cards.

Bookmobile Drivers keep track of their mileage, the materials lent out, and the amount of fines collected. They record statistics on circulation and the number of people who visit the bookmobile. They may also record requests for special items from the main library and arrange for the materials to be mailed or delivered to a patron during the next scheduled visit. They may also be responsible for any photocopying equipment or other library equipment on board the bookmobile. Many bookmobiles are equipped with personal computers and CD-ROM systems linked to the main library system, which allows Bookmobile Drivers to process library card applications by keying information into the library's database and to issue new cards as well as reserve or locate library materials immediately. Some bookmobiles even now offer Internet access to patrons.

In addition to their regular duties, they may occasionally operate audiovisual equipment to show slides or films. They often assist in planning and carrying out programs sponsored by the library such as reader advisory sessions or used book sales and may aid in promoting library services through community awareness drives, fund-raising, and other activities.

Salaries

Salaries for Bookmobile Drivers vary considerably depending on the extent of their responsibilities, their experience, the region of the country, the size of the city, and the type and size of the library. The level of technical expertise (including mechanical ability) may also affect earnings. In general, yearly salaries for Bookmobile Drivers range from $16,000 to as much as $39,000, with the average annual salary being about $24,000. Many Bookmobile Driver positions are offered by libraries as part time or flextime.

Employment Prospects

Job opportunities for Bookmobile Drivers should be good, as turnover among these workers tends to be high. This position tends to attract retirees and others who prefer a part-time schedule. Thus, there is considerable movement into and out of this occupation, opening up positions to replace those who have transferred to another occupation, moved on to a full-time library career, or left the labor force altogether. In general, it is expected that employment for Bookmobile Drives should grow about as fast as the average for all occupations. While the majority of Bookmobile Drivers work in public libraries, there are some academic libraries that have outreach bookmobile programs in need of drivers.

Advancement Prospects

For Bookmobile Drivers who wish to progress to positions as library assistants or technicians, additional education is necessary. Advancement depends greatly on how much an individual is willing to work toward a library career.

Education and Training

A college education is *not* required for this position, though a high school diploma is mandatory. Some experience in library work is generally preferred. As an alternative, some two-year schools offer an associate's degree in library technology. In this type of program, students learn to order, process, catalog, locate, and circulate library materials as well as how to operate library computer systems. Most Bookmobile Drivers receive training on the job from experienced library assistants or technicians.

Special Requirements

The possession of a commercial driver's license (CDL) is a basic requirement. Some states may demand successful completion of a training program. In addition, a clean driver's record is essential.

Experience, Skills, and Personality Traits

Bookmobile Drivers should have one to two years of commercial driving experience that includes direct public contact and customer service duties or a combination of related education, training, and experience coupled with the required commercial driver's license.

Bookmobile Drivers should be computer proficient and be capable of learning the computer software applicable to library systems. They need to accurately enter and retrieve data on a computer terminal. They should be familiar with approved library methods and procedures. They need to have good communication skills, both oral and written, and show courtesy in dealing with library staff and the public. They should have a likable personality and enjoy interacting with and serving customers of all ages. They must be able to work well without supervision, be well organized, and have good time management skills.

They should be physically fit and able to carry armloads or boxes of books, of 30 to 50 pounds to and from the bookmobile. They must be knowledgeable of safe and defensive driving practices. They should have the know-how necessary to drive and maintain library motor vehicles and skill at doing preventive maintenance and minor vehicle repairs.

Unions and Associations

There is one specific professional association of interest to Bookmobile Drivers, the Association of Bookmobile and Outreach Services (ABOS), whose goal is to support and encourage government officials, library administrators, trustees, and library staff in the provision of quality bookmobile and outreach services to meet diverse community information needs. In addition, the American Library Association (ALA) has an Outreach Services/Bookmobile section for its members.

Tips for Entry

1. While gaining your high school education, volunteer at your school library, community library, or local public library to become familiar with library practices and procedures.
2. A helpful high school course is driver education. In addition, take some business courses, particularly those involving office procedures, as good background for your work as a Bookmobile Driver.
3. Consider a summer job with a manufacturer where you can learn how to drive commercial trucks on an everyday basis.

HUMAN RESOURCES ASSISTANT

Duties: Under the guidance of the human resources director, aid in all personnel matters, including recruitment, payroll, employee benefits, skills management, personnel development, performance management, and discharging

Alternate Title(s): Human Resources Clerk; Personnel Assistant; Personnel Clerk

Salary Range: $25,000 to $40,000 or more

Employment Prospects: Fair to good

Advancement Prospects: Good

Prerequisites:

Education or Training—High school diploma or general equivalency diploma (GED) required; training in computers, in filing and filing systems, in organizing, and in human resources practices desirable; in some cases, an associate's degree in library science, human resources, or records management may be required

Experience—Interactive experience with individuals in a business setting recommended

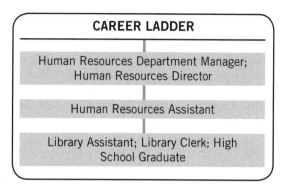

CAREER LADDER

Human Resources Department Manager;
Human Resources Director

Human Resources Assistant

Library Assistant; Library Clerk; High
School Graduate

Special Skills and Personality Traits—Ability to interact and communicate well with individuals at all levels of a library's organization; ability to demonstrate poise, tactfulness, diplomacy, and good interpersonal abilities; aptitude for working in a team and multitask environment; good computer and problem solving skills; initiative and adaptability; strong attention to detail and excellent conflict resolution talents

Position Description

The primary goal of human resource management is to help an organization meet its strategic goals by attracting and maintaining employees and managing them effectively, so the primary goal of Human Resources Assistants is to aid the human resources director in accomplishing this objective. Their main responsibility usually is to ensure that the library's personnel records are up to date by keeping track of address changes; alterations in job titles due to promotion, performance reviews, or evaluations; health insurance and other benefits (such as pension and retirement plans); salaries; and terminations. Frequently, this process involves entering data into computer files as well as paper files. They may be required to create reports on personnel matters for the director.

Some Human Resources Assistants aid in hiring library clerical and assistant staff. In this process, they conduct research on the Internet or talk to staffing firms and consulting firms to find qualified applicants for specific staff positions. They screen job applicants by eliciting information from them about their education and work experience and frequently ask for refer-

ences from present or past employers, researching these references to aid in the process of choosing appropriate staff for the library. They are typically the individual who calls or writes applicants to tell them they have or do not have a job. In addition, they are usually the person who provides employees with information about their work benefits. They may explain how employee assistance plans and worker compensation programs work and help employees use the programs. They often set up training programs for new library employees and current employees who want to update their skills.

In smaller academic or public libraries that have a human resources director, there may be only one Human Resources Assistant. In such cases, they usually perform a variety of other clerical duties, such as answering telephone or written (including e-mailed) inquiries from the public, sending out announcements of job openings, issuing application forms, and maintaining files of records. When credit bureaus and finance companies request confirmation of a person's employment at the library, Human Resources Assistants provide authorized information from employees' personnel records. They also may contact payroll departments and insurance companies to verify changes to records.

In larger libraries or statewide library systems, there may be several sections within the human resources department under the direction of the human resources director. Each of these groups may be headed by an experienced Human Resources Assistant or assistant manager who usually is a specialist in one type of human resources activity, such as benefits, compensation, employee relations, employment and recruitment, performance management, or training and development.

Salaries

Pay scales for this position vary depending on the scope of the Human Resources Assistant's responsibilities and experience as well as the geographic location of the library.

According to the PayScale, Inc., October 2007 salary survey, Human Resources Assistants had median annual salaries ranging from $28,534 to $41,034.

Employment Prospects

Employment of Human Resources Assistants is expected to grow about as fast as the average for all occupations through 2014, according to the U.S. Bureau of Labor's *Occupational Outlook Handbook, 2007–08.* Beginning assistant positions may become available as Human Resources Assistants advance within the human resources department, transfer to a larger library or library system with an expanded human resources department, take jobs unrelated to human resources administration, or leave the labor force.

Advancement Prospects

Human Resources Assistants progress in human resources administration by becoming managers of specific sections of a human resources department or by becoming employed at a larger library or in a library system with an expanded human resources department where their skills and talents can be used in an administrative post. The ultimate job goal for many Human Resources Assistants is to become a human resources director. For such a position, they may have to earn a certification in human resource management. The two most common certifications are Professional in Human Resources (PHR) and Senior Professional in Human Resources (SPHR). After the completion of course work and the successful passing of an examination, these certifications are awarded by the Human Resources Certification Institute of the Society for Human Resource Management (SHRM) or by the American Society for Training and Development Certification Institute (ASTD).

Education and Training

Human Resources Assistants must have at a minimum a high school diploma or a general equivalency diploma (GED). Generally, training beyond high school is not required. Many libraries, however, prefer assistants to have had formal training in computers, in filing and maintaining filing systems, in organizing, and in human resources practices. These skills can be learned in a vocational high school program aimed at office careers, and the rest can be acquired on the job. Formal training is available at a small number of community colleges, most of which offer diploma programs in office automation. Many proprietary schools (postsecondary schools that teach vocational or occupational skills but do not grant degrees) also offer such programs.

Some libraries or library systems may require Human Resources Assistants to have an associate's degree (from an accredited college or university) in library science, human resources, or records management as well as several years of relevant experience in records management.

Experience, Skills, and Personality Traits

Some libraries may require that Human Resources Assistants have a background of several years of relevant experience in records management as well as experience with automated library systems. Generally, Human Resources Assistants should have excellent computer skills, and know-how with Word, Excel, and Access database software is recommended.

They must have solid communication skills, both written and oral, and be able to deal with all library staff with diplomacy and tact. They will have to develop good conflict-resolution skills. They need excellent interpersonal skills to handle sensitive and confidential business situations. They should be neat, well dressed, and have a pleasing personality. A clear speaking voice is important, particularly for their work with telephones. They must be detail oriented, be able to handle multiple tasks with differing priorities, and be excellent problem solvers.

In their research for appropriate library staff, Human Resources Assistants must be able to scan résumés of job candidates quickly and efficiently, and they must be increasingly sensitive to confidential information such as salaries and Social Security numbers. They must also be fully conversant with fair employment practices including, but not limited to, Equal Employment Opportunity and Affirmative Action.

Unions and Associations

Outside the major professional associations for librarians (the American Library Association, or ALA, the American Society for Information Science and Technology, or ASIS&T, and the Special Libraries Association, or SLA), Human Resources Assistants who are intent on a career in human resources will find it useful to belong to such groups as the American Society for Training and Development (ASTD), and, most important, the Society for Human Resource Management (SHRM).

Tips for Entry

1. Consider a part-time job (or summer position) in a library to gain a general understanding of the practices and procedures of a library, which may well give you an edge (and add to your experience in human resources) in your job application.

2. Join a student association of a human resources professional organization to learn more about the field and network with human resources professionals about a career in human resources administration.

3. Knowledge of the latest trends in staffing and in safety and health issues is extremely important for human resources professionals. The Society for Human Resource Management (SHRM) provides statistics to human resources personnel on these and other issues relevant to the profession.

LIBRARY AIDE

CAREER PROFILE

Duties: Under general supervision, perform a variety of manual and related entry-level clerical tasks in support of library services, including the unpacking, sorting, delivering, and shelving of library materials

Alternate Title(s): Circulation Aide; Circulation Clerk; Desk Attendant; Library Attendant; Library Helper; Page; Runner; Shelver; Shelving Clerk; Stack Clerk

Salary Range: $7.25 per hour to $9.00 per hour or more

Employment Prospects: Good to excellent

Advancement Prospects: Good

Prerequisites:

Education or Training—High school diploma or general education diploma (GED) required; in some cases, one year or more of post–high school education may be required; bilingual skills useful

Experience—Some background working with the public and in general office clerical work; previous library experience recommended

Special Skills and Personality Traits—Ability to communicate effectively both orally and in writing with diverse customers and library employees; knowledge of office equipment including typewriters, adding machines, copy machines, and computer workstations; basic math proficiency; excellent alphabetical and numerical filing skills; physically fit and dependable work and attendance habits

Special Requirements—Candidates for Library Aide positions in school systems, which include providing instructional assistance, may be required to pass a proficiency test and possess a certificate of completion from a library aide certificate program

CAREER LADDER

Library Assistant; Library Clerk
Library Aide
High School Graduate; Library Volunteer

Position Description

Library Aides perform clerical work involved in the operation of a school library media center or academic or public library and provide library services for students, teachers, and patrons who do not necessarily require the application of library skills. It is the entry-level post in the library support staff. As experience and adeptness are gained, assignments become more varied and may require the use of judgment and independence within established guidelines. Library Aides may be assigned to one task (such as the circulation desk) or may alternate among duties as the need arises. Library Aides are distinguished from library assistants in that the latter independently perform more responsible clerical support tasks and usually have had specific training in library practices and procedures.

Library Aides perform a variety of routine manual support tasks including sorting, shelving, stacking, and retrieving a wide assortment of library materials. They also process returned items and maintain such materials according to alphabetical, numerical, and categorical systems. They conduct shelf checks for accuracy in shelving and shift and transport books and other library materials to assigned areas of the library as directed. They run errands, assisting in keeping all areas of the library in a clean, neat, and orderly condition, and may assist others in activities related to opening and closing the facility. They sort and route mail, books, and periodicals to their proper library destinations.

Library Aides perform basic clerical tasks to assist technical support services, including simple mending, labeling, jacketing in preparation for circulation, and undertaking minor repairs on a variety of library materials. When working in the circulation area of the library, they check out materials and register patrons for library cards. They assess, collect, and tally damage and late fees from library patrons, using their judgment to reduce or eliminate charges as appropriate. Under the guidance of circulation librarians, they reconcile cash balances. They assist patrons with the use of library equipment and respond to questions regarding policies and procedures. They answer inquiries of a nonprofessional nature on the telephone, via e-mail, and in person and refer persons requiring professional assistance to the appropriate librarian. In addition, they may do routine bibliographic checking and perform basic reference assistance to library patrons or students.

They may be assigned to place orders for library materials using electronic ordering, telephone, fax, or mail. In such cases, they process these orders by entering them into the library's computer system using established procedures. They may process interlibrary loans according to established guidelines and maintain public bulletin boards in the library. They may maintain statistical records and data for staff members and librarians and may undertake routine typing, keyboarding, copying, and maintenance of files. In addition, they assist with library public service programs and displays as well as aid with special projects and services.

Salaries

According to PayScale, Inc.'s, October 2007 salary survey report on Library Aides (helpers), their median hourly salary rate ranged from $7.28 to $8.92, depending on the type of library and the geographic location. Many Library Aide jobs start as part-time positions and only later may become full-time jobs.

Employment Prospects

As the job of Library Aide is an entry-level post (either part time or full time), and since there is much turnover for this position (as Library Aides move on to a college education or advance to assistant posts at the library), the potential for employment is good to excellent.

Advancement Prospects

With the acquisition of new skills, experience, and training, full-time Library Aides may find career progress by transferring to positions of more responsibility in the library paraprofessional staff, such as library clerks or library assistants. Advancement opportunities tend to be better in the larger public libraries and library systems. Most libraries fill their office and administrative support job positions by promoting individuals within their organizations, so promotion prospects can be good.

Education and Training

Most libraries require a high school diploma or a general education diploma (GED) for employment as a Library Aide. Standard computer and secretarial skills gained from business education courses in high school or at community colleges are also highly desirable. In addition, many employers require some experience working with the public, a background in general office work, and some previous library work experience or familiarity in using a library. Extensive training in library procedures and practices usually takes place on the job under the guidance of a senior librarian or a library assistant.

Special Requirements

Library Aides who are employed in school district systems assist teachers in teaching information retrieving skills and assist students in the selection of books and other learning resources. They may need to pass an instructional assistance test and receive a library aide certificate before working in the school library media center.

Experience, Skills, and Personality Traits

Library Aides need to have basic mathematics skills and be knowledgeable about alphabetical, numerical, and subject filing systems. They should understand the basic operation of standard office equipment, including copying machines, adding machines, microfiche and microfilm readers and printers, and computer workstations. They should have an excellent knowledge of English grammar, spelling, and usage. They should have good computer skills, and a familiarity with word-processing and spreadsheet programs is valuable.

Library Aides must be able to establish and maintain tactful and effective working relationships with library coworkers and the public. They should have strong communication skills to be able to deal effectively with diverse library customers and employees. They should pay close attention to detail, be well organized, and be able to understand and carry out oral, verbal, and written instructions. They should be physically fit, as they will have to perform a wide range of physical motions, which may include routine and repetitive bending, reaching, pushing, moving, and carrying library books and other materials.

Unions and Associations

While there are no specific professional associations geared toward Library Aides, those aides wanting to continue to develop a career in library science should consider belonging to one or more of the general professional associations of the library field, such as the American Library Association (ALA), the American Society for Information Science and Technology (ASIS&T), and the Special Libraries Association (SLA).

Tips for Entry

1. While in high school, volunteer in the school library or at a local public library to gain experience in library practices and procedures.
2. A summer job as a part-time office assistant or clerk will familiarize you with filing methods and with the type of office equipment used in libraries as well.
3. Learning a second language is a valuable asset and is particularly useful in assisting library patrons and/or students of diverse backgrounds.

LIBRARY CLERK

CAREER PROFILE

Duties: Compile and update records, issue and receive library materials, sort and shelve books, provide general library information to patrons, and perform general clerical functions

Alternate Title(s): Administrative Support Clerk; Circulation Clerk; Document Control Clerk; Interlibrary Loan Clerk; Library Assistant, Clerical; Library File Clerk; Library Media Clerk; Library Page; Periodicals Clerk; Records Clerk; Reference Clerk; Shelving Clerk

Salary Range: $15,000 to $30,000 or more

Employment Prospects: Excellent

Advancement Prospects: Good

Prerequisites:

Education or Training—High school diploma or equivalent

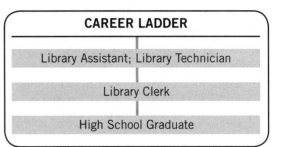

Experience—Familiarity with library procedures usually preferred; secretarial experience helpful

Special Skills and Personality Traits—Attention to detail; computer proficiency; good judgment with the capacity to make minor decisions in accordance with established procedures; organizational talent; strong communication and interpersonal skills

Position Description

Library Clerks receive and check out library materials to library patrons, register new patrons for library cards, respond to patrons' questions regarding the physical location of library resources, assist patrons in the use of library materials and facilities, receive and collect fines from patrons on overdue library resources, assist library users in accessing basic library materials and making interlibrary loan requests, process publications for circulation, sort and shelve books and other library materials, answer phones and route calls as necessary, perform basic reference work or refer more complex questions to reference librarians, perform all facility opening and closing procedures (including attending to the book drop and equipment, such as copiers, fax machines, printers, and computers) in the work and public areas of the library, and conduct routine clerical activities as requested by library staff.

Upon receipt of returned library books, materials, and equipment, they check them for damage and may make minor repairs to books, documents, periodicals, and other materials as needed. They return equipment to storage and maintain records and logs of materials borrowed, as well as other statistical information for monthly reports as needed.

In addition, Library Clerks may use their typing and computer skills to process materials orders and to update library catalogs or purge online and/or paper records by removing title records of resources that have been withdrawn from the library's collection. They may aid librarians in preparing posters, bulletins, and newsletters (both paper and online) to promote use of the library and its materials. They often perform varied clerical cataloging and clerical administrative work in the library's technical services department. Under the direction of the acquisitions librarians, they may perform clerical work involved in materials acquisitions by locating and verifying bibliographic data, filling out order forms, figuring costs, and following up on problem orders. They may be responsible for maintaining subscriptions to publications.

In large public and academic libraries, the various duties of the Library Clerk may be assigned to specific clerks who have those duties as their main, if not only, responsibility. In these cases, these clerks may be known by their function, such as records clerk, circulation clerk, reference clerk, periodicals clerk, shelving clerk, file clerk, and so forth. In smaller libraries, the clerical staff may be tasked with all these functions with no distinction in job title.

Salaries

Salaries for this position vary considerably depending on the scope of job responsibilities and the geographic location of the library. Annual earnings for Library Clerks range from the lows of beginning salaries of $15,000 to highs of $30,000 or more for seasoned clerks with a larger range of duties or years of experience in their specific duties.

Employment Prospects

Library clerical jobs are often part-time positions and, as such, are attractive to both high school students and retired individuals seeking part-time work. For this reason, there tends to be a lot of movement in and out of this type of post. Hence, opportunities remain excellent for people interested in jobs as Library Clerks. Library Clerks are employed in academic, public, and special libraries; school and postsecondary institution libraries; large business firms that have libraries; and government departmental libraries.

Advancement Prospects

With the acquisition of new skills, experience, and training, Library Clerks may find advancement by transferring to positions of more responsibility, such as library assistants or library technicians. Career progression opportunities tend to be better in larger public libraries and library systems. Most libraries fill their office and administrative support job positions by promoting individuals within their organizations, so advancement prospects can be good.

Education and Training

Successful completion of a high school education is the usual requirement for a position as a Library Clerk. In addition, standard computer and secretarial skills gained from business education courses in high school or at community colleges are highly desirable. Training in library procedures and practices usually takes place on the job under the guidance of a senior librarian or an experienced assistant.

Experience, Skills, and Personality Traits

Library Clerks must exhibit patience and have a strong customer service orientation, be flexible and resourceful, and be team players. They need to be highly organized and able to update files as well as keep accurate records and files. They should have excellent interper-

sonal skills, as they deal with the public continuously, and be able to communicate effectively and pleasantly. Among their technical skills, they need to know how to use a computer terminal and a personal computer, be able to key accurately with moderate speed, have knowledge of and some skill in data entry, and be able to operate copying equipment.

They should be familiar with the principles, practices, and techniques of library operations as well as general office procedures. They should be comfortable answering the phone and using a public address system. They need to have an appreciation for detail and the ability to maintain accuracy and persevere at tasks that are repetitive. In addition, they have to be physically fit and able to lift and carry boxes of library materials when needed.

Unions and Associations

Library Clerks may find it advantageous to belong to a variety of trade associations that provide educational guidance, support, conferences, and information to their members. Such groups include the American Library Association (ALA), the American Society for Information Science and Technology (ASIS&T), the Association of Part-Time Librarians (APTL), the Library Assistants and Technicians Group section of the ALA, and the Special Libraries Association (SLA). In addition, some states have library associations organized to aid library support staff, such as the New York State Library Assistants' Association (NYSLAA).

Tips for Entry

1. While completing your high school education, volunteer in the school library or at a local public library to gain experience in library practices and procedures.
2. A summer job in an office as a part-time office assistant or clerk will familiarize you with office filing methods and acquaint you with the types of office equipment used in libraries as well.
3. Consider taking postsecondary education courses in secretarial training, which cover word processing, bookkeeping, office procedures, telephone skills, and interpersonal communication.

OTHER LIBRARY ASSISTANTS

Position Description

Library Assistants assist librarians with the operation of a library, which includes such tasks as selection and organization of library materials; circulation of library materials to patrons; helping patrons with research; providing services to patrons; and, in some cases, acquisitions and the technical services of ordering, processing, classifying, and cataloging of newly acquired library materials. Job titles associated with particular levels vary from library to library, but generally Library Assistants are classified into a clerical level (and may even be called library clerks in some cases) and a more skilled and higher-paid paraprofessional level. Library Assistants at this rank act more independently and may be involved in the supervision of other library employees (mainly clerks, aides, and volunteers). Library Assistants are also employed in school libraries to aid school librarians in selecting and organizing materials and assisting students and teachers with research. These assistants also may coordinate and implement children's programming and services, such as story hours.

Clerical Library Assistants perform many of the library duties related to record keeping. In the circulation department, where they are often referred to as circulation assistants, they reserve, circulate, renew, and discharge books and other materials. They issue to library patrons identification cards according to established procedures and enter and update their records on the facility's computer. When necessary, they may send out notices and collect money for lost or overdue books. They may also be responsible for shelving books and other library materials as well as compiling library statistics and updating book lists. At the circulation desk, they answer the telephones and provide routine information or refer and transfer calls to appropriate library personnel.

In the acquisitions department, where they are usually called acquisitions assistants, they assist in the procurement of books, pamphlets, periodicals, audiovisual materials, and other library items by checking prices, figuring costs, and preparing appropriate order forms. They are often responsible for entering data into the library's automated ordering and cataloging systems.

Paraprofessional Library Assistants are generally assigned more complex responsibilities and/or supervisory duties due to their enhanced library training and experience. In the circulation department, where they also are usually referred to as circulation assistants, they may deal with problems and handle complaints concerning fines as well as supervise volunteers, library aides, and student helpers. They may also be tasked with scheduling and supervising the work of library clerks and aides.

In reference departments, paraprofessional Library Assistants, known as reference assistants, respond to reference questions requiring minimal research. In addition, they help people locate library materials and teach them how to use reference sources, indexes, card catalogs, and library automated systems. Some library assistants have special training to help patrons who have vision problems. They aid such library patrons in finding their desired materials or closely related substitutes from the facility's collection of large type or braille volumes and tape cassettes and CDs (including audiobooks).

With their knowledge of library policies and procedures, paraprofessional Library Assistants, known as library services assistants, often are responsible for working with the interlibrary loan system. They do bibliographic searching, prepare cataloging information from the Online Computer Library Center (OCLC) database, and check in periodicals and serial microforms. They identify any errors on book requests (such as duplicate orders) and provide correct bibliographic data for book orders. They assist patrons in the location of library materials, in the use of the library's online system, and in the use of audiovisual equipment and computers. They prepare library materials for technical processing and cataloging and maintain records associated with items sent for cataloging. With additional training, library services assistants may be responsible for a department's function, such as processing overdue charges, or coordinating interlibrary loan borrowing, or providing (without senior librarian supervision) evening and weekend service at a public service desk. They may be responsible for compiling, monitoring, and preparing a public services and serials statistical report, usually on a weekly basis. They may be assigned to function as a liaison with publishers, vendors, outside service providers, and administrative offices service supervisors when problems occur with invoices of materials being acquired by the library. In this capacity, they input invoices into the library's automated system, matching the correct order record with books and other materials as they are received. They process these library items and select those that need binding.

At higher levels, experienced Library Assistants who understand the policies, procedures, standards, systems, and basic resources of the library may be placed in charge of the entire operation of a small branch library

answering to a librarian supervisor who is usually off-site. They may supervise, evaluate, and recommend hiring and firing of student volunteers or entry-level library aides and clerks. As such, they must maintain records and compile statistics related to the functioning of their branch libraries. They may be required to analyze statistics and prepare summary reports and recommendations based on their analysis.

In addition, they may be responsible for the operation of a variety of library equipment (including computers, printers, copiers, fax machines, microfiche readers, and document delivery and imaging equipment), troubleshooting problems, and contacting and following up with vendors for repair as appropriate. They must be capable of performing complex duties and problem resolution associated with ordering, receiving, sorting, processing, arranging for access, cataloging, circulating, preserving, storing, and transporting of library materials in a variety of traditional and electronic formats. They may participate in formulating policies and procedures for improving work processes as well as aid in the creation and updating of policy and procedures manuals and other written documentation.

Salaries

Salaries for Library Assistants vary greatly based on the location of the library and the variety and amount of their responsibilities, which, in turn, depend on their background, training, and knowledge. Library Assistants with college associate's degrees are more likely to start at higher salaries and advance more easily than those without such educational background. According to PayScale, Inc.'s, October 2007 salary survey report on Library Assistants, median salaries ranged from a low of $20,219 to a high of $37,365.

Employment Prospects

The job outlook for Library Assistants is good. According to the U.S. Bureau of Labor's *Occupational Outlook Handbook, 2007–08 Edition*, employment of library assistants is expected to grow as fast as the average for all occupations through 2014. Efforts to contain costs in local governments (which control the budgets of public libraries) and academic institutions of all types may result in more hiring of library support staff than librarians. In addition, due to changing roles within libraries, Library Assistants are taking on more responsibility commensurate with their additional training.

Many Library Assistants start out as part-time workers and then leave this relatively low-paying occupation for other jobs that offer higher incomes or full-time work, so job opportunities to fill these positions should be good. Some beginning positions become available as Library Assistants move to full-time posts or gain further experience and advance within the library organization.

Advancement Prospects

Library Assistants can advance to positions that are more specialized, and, in some library systems, clerical Library Assistants can move up to paraprofessional Library Assistants based on experience. Paraprofessionals can progress to supervisory positions or to more specialized work, such as library technicians. Promotions usually come with the acquisition of experience and supervisory skills, knowledge of library automated systems, and additional training. Advancement opportunities tend to be greater in larger libraries or library systems. Library Assistants looking to make library science their careers and advance to positions as librarians will need to pursue a master's degree in library science (M.L.S.) or in library and information science (M.L.I.S.).

Education and Training

Education and training requirements for Library Assistants vary from employer to employer. The minimum requirement for clerical library assistants is usually a high school diploma and some clerical experience. Knowledge of library operations, such as filing and indexing, and a broad knowledge of information sources, such as almanacs, atlases, and encyclopedias, can be helpful. For paraprofessional Library Assistant positions, an associate of arts degree with a specialization in library technology is usually preferred. Many of these library technology programs are available through community colleges and vocational schools and usually include courses in library technical services, cataloging, and library media materials and equipment. Usually, a certificate or associate's degree in library assistance or library technical assistance can be earned with the successful completion of the program. Appropriate library clerical experience can sometimes be substituted for part or all of the education requirement.

Some academic libraries require a bachelor's degree and as much as three years of experience in library work. Some technical and special libraries demand specialized training in such fields as law, science, medicine, or foreign languages.

Experience, Skills, and Personality Traits

Library Assistants must be able to perform their clerical or paraprofessional tasks with limited supervision. They should be able to exercise good judgment in evaluating situations and making decisions. They need to have excellent communication skills (both oral and written) and solid interpersonal abilities. As they deal directly with the public, they should project a professional appearance and a pleasant personality. A clear speaking voice and fluency in English are important, as they frequently use the telephone and may be required to use public address systems.

They should be familiar with computers and applicable software, as their work involves considerable computer use. They should be familiar with basic office equipment as used in libraries and be able to troubleshoot problems with them. They need to be able to handle multiple tasks and projects and be able to prioritize their work schedules. They should be detail oriented and organized in their work habits. They must be able to work both independently and in tandem with other library staff.

Unions and Associations

Professional trade associations of interest to Library Assistants include the American Library Association (ALA), the Library Assistants and Technicians Group (a division of the ALA), the Association of Part-Time Librarians (APTL), the American Society of Information Science and Technology (ASIS&T), and the Special Libraries Association (SLA).

Tips for Entry

1. During your high school years, volunteer in your school library or at a local public library to become acquainted with its practices and procedures. Library administrators tend to select candidates who have some relevant library experience over those who do not.

2. Some Library Assistant associate's degree programs offer practicum courses. These classes give you hands-on experience working in a library under the supervision of a librarian or a library technician.

3. Some office clerical work experience is advisable. A summer job in a local business will give you that seasoning.

TECHNICAL ASSISTANT

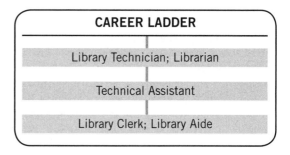

CAREER LADDER

Library Technician; Librarian

Technical Assistant

Library Clerk; Library Aide

Position Description

Library Technical Assistants (sometimes referred to as LTAs) perform many duties, which may vary from facility to facility and may overlap those of other types of library assistants. Libraries frequently have differing administrative staff structures. Libraries that have Technical Assistants often may not use other types of library assistants, such as circulation assistants and acquisitions assistants, as their job duties overlap too much.

As the job title suggests, Technical Assistants handle some of the technical duties in the library. While clerical skills are part of Technical Assistants' jobs, the emphasis of their work is on their special technical abilities. For example, they show patrons how to use the library's computer system. They also assign new books, audiovisual materials, and other library materials to topics in the library's classification system. Then they enter this information into the facility's computers. They often set up and maintain the periodical and reference sections. They demonstrate to patrons how to use audiovisual equipment and maintain this hardware.

They aid librarians in ordering, preparing, and processing print and nonprint library materials. Increasingly, libraries have become havens for new technology.

Besides lending books through interlibrary loan systems, libraries offer many services, such as CD-ROMs, DVDs, and the Internet. In some libraries, patrons can check out books (and some other selected library materials) themselves by placing them on a sensor, pushing a button, and waiting for the return slip to print out. However, all this technology can sometimes be difficult to navigate for patrons. Thus, Technical Assistants aid patrons in the use of all the services that libraries have to offer. They answer questions about the library card catalog and assist patrons in the use of bibliographic tools.

Among their other tasks, Technical Assistants may issue library cards and check out books, magazines, tapes, and other materials. They may update patron accounts on computers as well as issue and collect fines when necessary (a job that a circulation assistant in another library may do as well). They answer patrons' questions about the library and may teach them how to use the reference materials. In addition, Technical Assistants may sort returned library materials and place them back on their proper shelves or cabinets. Technical Assistants who work in schools create posters and displays that encourage library use. They may also help teachers and students with special projects.

Many Technical Assistants perform administrative jobs as well. They may perform routine descriptive cataloging, such as fiction and children's literature. They may verify bibliographic information on order requests. They may supervise other library assistants, aides, and volunteers. In so doing, they direct the activities of library staff in the maintenance of library materials on shelves or materials in a section of a department or division, such as in the ordering or receiving section of the acquisitions department or card preparation activities in the cataloging department. They compile reports about the library. For example, they may determine how many books are borrowed each month.

Technical Assistants may assist with the development of library policies and procedures, such as those that affect Internet access. They may also use their computer skills to design and maintain special databases and Web pages for the facility. Technical Assistants often order new materials at the request of librarians and prepare the order forms. They may also monitor and maintain library supplies.

Some library Technical Assistants work for businesses such as law firms. In these offices, Technical Assistants search for books and articles on particular topics at the request of members of the firm or employees. Occasionally, they may write summaries of books and articles for employees of the business or members of the firm.

Salaries

According to their salary survey report for library Technical Assistants (last updated in October 2007), PayScale, Inc., found that median annual salaries for this position ranged from $18,000 to $37,000 depending on the type of library (school, company, government, academic, or public) and the extent of an individual's educational background.

Employment Prospects

As is true for most library assistant positions, the job outlook for Technical Assistants is good. According to the U.S. Bureau of Labor's *Occupational Outlook Handbook, 2007–08 Edition*, employment of library assistants in general is expected to grow as fast as the average for all occupations through 2014. Efforts to contain costs in local governments (which control the budgets of public libraries), businesses, and academic institutions of all types may result in more hiring of library support staff than librarians. In addition, due to changing roles within libraries, library assistants are taking on more responsibilities commensurate with their additional training. The increased use of computers in libraries

is producing job growth for Technical Assistants. With their technical background, they are well positioned to handle the challenges of the new technologies increasingly used by libraries to provide better services for a technologically minded public.

Advancement Prospects

Technical Assistants usually advance by taking on added responsibilities. They can be promoted to supervisory positions. Enrolling in continuing education courses may increase their chances for advancement. Those who pursue a master's degree in library science (M.L.S.) or in library and information science (M.L.I.S.) may advance to librarian posts.

Education and Training

A high school degree is essential, and an associate of arts (A.A.) or of science (A.S.) (two-year) degree is often a requirement. Frequently, libraries now look for Technical Assistants who have an A.A. or A.S. degree in a computer-related field or a minimum of three years of experience with PC and Windows-based systems, networking, multimedia, audiovisual equipment, and work in a public or academic library. In some cases, a bachelor's degree in a computer-related field is preferred.

Experience, Skills, and Personality Traits

Technical Assistants must have a solid background in the use of computers and be able to make use of library automated systems. They need to have a good understanding of library materials, procedures, and techniques as well as a working knowledge of both bibliographic tools and sources and reference tools (which includes computerized systems). They should have a clear comprehension of the Dewey decimal and Library of Congress systems of cataloging library materials and a familiarity with copyright law. They should have exemplary data entry and typing skills and be good in basic mathematics.

Technical Assistants must have an excellent customer service orientation and the ability to work with a diverse public in a teaching and coaching environment. They must have solid organizational, communication (both oral and written), and interpersonal skills. They should display initiative and be able to work independently.

Unions and Associations

Technical Assistants should find it useful to belong to the Library Assistants and Technicians Group of the American Library Association (ALA) as well as the American Society of Information Science and Technology (ASIS&T) for educational guidance, support, conferences, and information. In addition, the Council on Library/Media Technicians (COLT) represents all areas of service in public and academic libraries with an emphasis on library support staff. Members include librarians, library support staff, administrators, and educators.

Tips for Entry

1. During your high school years and while you are earning your associate's degree, take every opportunity to gain library experience by volunteering in the type of library that interests you.

2. In your job search, e-mail discussion groups such as LIBjobs (http://www.ifla.org/II/lists/lib-jobs.htm) and LISjobs (http://www.lisjobs.com), which are good sources for job postings. Topical groups are also useful places for finding potential job listings in a particular field of librarianship.

3. By joining professional associations for librarians, such as the ALA and COLT, you can access their job placement services and job lines. COLT, in particular, maintains job lines for library support staff.

LIBRARY TECHNICIANS

ACQUISITIONS TECHNICIAN

Duties: Provide technical support for the acquisitions or collection development librarian; use the library's online system to process and expedite procurement, receipt, and payment of acquisitions for the library's collection

Alternate Title(s): Acquisitions Assistant; Library Collections Technician; Library Media Acquisitions Technician; Library Technician–Acquisitions and Processing; Ordering Specialist; Serials Technician

Salary Range: $18,000 to $45,000 or more

Employment Prospects: Good

Advancement Prospects: Good

Prerequisites:

Education or Training—High school diploma or general equivalency diploma (GED) required; at least two years of library and/or information science course work (and/or an associate's degree in library science or a two-year library technician diploma) from an accredited college or university usually preferred

Experience—Two to four years of general paraprofessional library background; experience working

CAREER LADDER

Senior Library Assistant; Senior Library Technician; Collections Development Director

Acquisitions Technician

Library Aide; Library Clerk; High School Graduate

with online catalogs and computerized record keeping systems desirable

Special Skills and Personality Traits—Ability to work independently and take guidance from supervisor; accuracy, attention to detail, and good organizational abilities; excellent interpersonal and communication skills (both oral and written); good math and computer skills

Position Description

As paraprofessional library assistants, library technicians employ their technical expertise to aid librarians in ordering, preparing, and organizing materials for the use of library patrons. As the job title suggests, library technicians handle many of the technical duties at the facility as well as aid patrons in the use of the technical equipment and materials in the library.

Under the guidance of the special collections librarian (or the acquisitions librarian), Acquisitions Technicians are responsible for the purchasing and processing of print and nonprint materials for the library collection. They use the facility's online integrated library system (ILS) and established procedures to procure and process orders for books, media materials, equipment, and other library materials. They verify orders against existing vendor online files as well as input codes, project numbers, requisitions, and purchase orders into the library's purchasing system. They process orders, maintain databases of purchased materials, and monitor warranties and agreements. They maintain liaisons with vendors, publishers, and subject specialists and use

a variety of databases to resolve billing and order fulfillment problems (which may include either duplicates or nonreceipt of materials). expedite special requests, verify and authorize billings and invoices, verify and update library records, and coordinate equipment repair and related services.

Acquisitions Technicians check materials received from vendors and other sources for accuracy of what was ordered as well as maintain and update records for the payment of invoices and the allocation of collections funds. They supervise and train library student employees, volunteers, and aides and assistants in collections development standards and procedures. They monitor collections funds accounting in the library's automated system, keeping daily records, and create monthly and year-end statistical reports on the status of library materials purchased and processed.

Acquisitions Technicians are usually heavily involved with bibliographic control of library materials. They search such national databases as OCLC (Online Computer Library Center, a subscription library database) to verify information regarding requested materials (using their knowledge of cataloging standards) and to create and edit bibliography and authority records for export into their library's database used in the processing and cataloging of purchased materials.

They may also be responsible for sorting library mail to ensure proper distribution to individual librarians and departments. They may prepare monographs and theses for binding and process gift items for inclusion in the facility's collections. They may be involved in the identification and recommendation of current and retrospective acquisition needs and may survey patrons (and/or faculty) for desired library materials. They may research indexes and other sources for the availability of desired library acquisitions. They may participate in committees related to the library's automated system and collection development plans and procedures.

Salaries

According to PayScale, Inc.'s, October 2007 salary survey, median annual earnings for library technicians in general (and Acquisitions Technicians in particular) ranged from a low of $18,657 (as a beginning salary) to a high of $51,434 (for an experienced technician), depending on geographic location and type of library (school, academic, public, government, or special).

Employment Prospects

The use of computers in the acquisition, processing, cataloging, and maintenance of library materials has increased exponentially and has produced job openings and job growth for library technicians in general and Acquisitions Technicians in particular. The widespread use of computerized information storage and retrieval systems within libraries has meant that Acquisitions Technicians now handle these more technical jobs, such as entering catalog information into the library's computer and procuring library materials for the library's collection(s) that were once administered by librarians. Opportunities for job employment should be best for those applicants with at least two years of college, excellent computer skills, and some training in library technology. According to the U.S. Department of Labor's *Occupational Outlook Handbook, 2008–09 Edition*, employment of library technicians, including Acquisition Technicians, is expected to grow about as fast as the average for all occupations through 2014. The increasing use of library automation is expected to continue to spur job growth for library technicians, in particular those involved in automated purchasing and processing systems. In addition, escalation in the number of professionals and other patrons who use

special libraries should result in good job opportunities for library technicians in those settings.

Advancement Prospects

Acquisitions Technicians can progress to senior technician and/or supervisory positions. Experienced technicians who continue their educations and gain master's degrees in library science (M.L.S.) or in library and information science (M.L.I.S.) may be able to advance to specific librarian positions, such as acquisitions librarian or collections development director.

Education and Training

Besides the basic requirement of a high school diploma, many libraries request applicants to possess a two-year post-secondary library science or library technician diploma or the equivalent of two or more years of working in a library setting.

Experience, Skills, and Personality Traits

Most library employers typically require of applicants for this position that they have two to four years of general library seasoning, including keying/typing and ordering, preparing, shelving, and maintaining library materials. Some libraries insist on a working knowledge of library classification systems, filing procedures, and the processing of library acquisitions as well as some experience working in an integrated library system environment. They should also be knowledgeable of computerized record keeping systems and databases. They should have knowledge of library cataloging practices, including the Dewey decimal system and Library of Congress subject headings. Some basic bookkeeping experience is helpful.

Acquisitions Technicians must be very detail oriented and well organized. They should demonstrate excellent interpersonal and communication skills (both oral and written). They must be able to work independently while recognizing situations that require their supervising librarian's attention and be able to function well in a team environment as well. A high degree of computer literacy is essential, including familiarity with the Microsoft Office suite of applications. A strong knowledge of computer concepts, operations, and functions as applied to automated library catalog systems is a welcome bonus. They should have good math skills and some comprehension of accounting and budgeting practices.

Unions and Associations

Besides membership in the American Library Association (ALA), Acquisitions Technicians may wish to join specific divisions or groupings within that professional organization, such as the Association for Library

Collections and Technical Services (ALCTS) and the North American Serials Interest Group (NASIG), both of which may be beneficial in their career development. Additionally, they may find value in membership in such groups as the American Society of Information Science and Technology (ASIS&T), the Association of College and Research Libraries (ACRL), the Association of Subscription Agents (ASA), and the Special Libraries Association (SLA).

Tips for Entry

1. During your high school years, do volunteer work in your school library or at a local public library to become acquainted with library practices and procedures. Many library administrators tend to prefer candidates who have some relevant library experience over those who do not.
2. Some library assistant and library technician associate's degree programs offer practicum courses. These classes provide hands-on experience working in a library under the supervision of an acquisitions or collection development librarian or a library Acquisitions Technician.
3. As a summer job, look for a position in a bookstore, at an online print/nonprint sales firm, or with a book vendor in order to gain a practical understanding of procurement practices and procedures.

CATALOGING TECHNICIAN

Duties: Assist in the daily operations of the library's cataloging department by compiling data on written matter (such as books, periodicals, serials, monographs, and nonprint materials) and prepare catalog cards/computer records to identify materials and to integrate information into the facility's catalog

Alternate Title(s): Assistant Cataloger; Cataloging Assistant; Descriptive Catalog Assistant/Technician

Salary Range: $18,000 to $42,000 or more

Employment Prospects: Good

Advancement Prospects: Fair to good

Prerequisites:

Education or Training—High school diploma and associate's degree in library studies usually required; often, bachelor's degree desired; in some cases, master's degree in library science (M.L.S.) or in library and information science (M.L.I.S.) also desired

Experience—Two to five years of library background with minimum of one to two years of

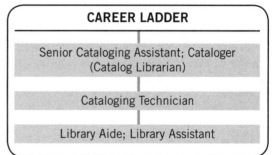

CAREER LADDER

Senior Cataloging Assistant; Cataloger (Catalog Librarian)

↑

Cataloging Technician

↑

Library Aide; Library Assistant

cataloging experience; knowledge of cataloging standards and practices necessary; proficiency with automated library systems desirable

Special Skills and Personality Traits—Ability to interact collaboratively and work effectively in teams; excellent interpersonal and communication abilities; computer proficiency; service orientation; strong analytical talents

Position Description

A library catalog is a register of all bibliographic items found in a particular library or group of libraries (such as those belonging to a university system spread over several geographic locations). A bibliographic item can be any information entity (such as books, computer files, graphics or art objects, and cartographic materials) that is considered library material or as linked to the catalog (such as a Web page) as long as it is relevant to the catalog and to the patrons of the library.

The card catalog has been a familiar sight in libraries for generations, but it has been effectively replaced (except in some of the smallest libraries) by the Online Public Access Catalog (OPAC). There are several catalog types, such as an author catalog (sorted alphabetically by the author's—or authors'—or editor's names), a title catalog (sorted alphabetically by the titles of the entries), a dictionary catalog (in which all entries—author, title, subject, series—are interfiled into a single alphabetical order), a keyword catalog (a subject listing sorted alphabetically according to some system of keywords), a systematic or classified catalog (a subject catalog sorted according to some systematic subdivision of subjects), and a shelf list catalog (a formal catalog with

entries sorted in the same order as the library items are shelved). The latter type of catalog can also function as the primary inventory for the library.

Creating and producing formal catalogs is relatively easy, as the cataloger can follow a set of cataloging rules. However, only a subject catalog can detail which works about a given subject the library has or has access to, and this type of catalog is much more difficult to produce, as the cataloger must provide an accurate impression of the contents of the bibliographic item being cataloged. The most commonly used set of cataloging rules in the English-speaking world are the *Anglo-American Cataloging Rules, Second Edition* (or AACR2).

Online cataloging has greatly enhanced the usability of library catalogs thanks to the introduction of Machine Readable Cataloging (MARC) standards. Rules governing the creation of catalog MARC records include not only formal cataloging rules such as AACR2 but also special rules specific to MARC, available from the Library of Congress and also the Online Computer Library Center (OCLC) system.

Catalog Technicians assist in the daily operation of the library's cataloging area or department. Generally, their cataloging work is of limited scope and difficulty, as they are usually assigned to catalog library materials for which a bibliographic record is already available. They perform searches on such databases as the OCLC system for new bibliographic records to meet the library's cataloging needs. They check materials to be cataloged against computer printouts from these searches to verify the accuracy of the bibliographic records. They consult standard reference materials, such as the Library of Congress Subject Headings book and subject authority file, to determine the appropriateness of the subject heading to the materials to be cataloged and revise the subject heading if required. They assign unique call numbers to the cataloged items; check the library's shelf lists to determine the uniqueness of the newly derived call numbers, modifying them if necessary; code the bibliographic records for computer input into the library's automated system; and prepare catalog cards from this system if their library still uses a card catalog.

Experienced Catalog Technicians may be responsible for all the library's cataloging operations. They perform edits of existing Library of Congress bibliographic records or member records on the OCLC system. In this process, they download OCLC records into their library's automated system, editing and updating the library's bibliographic records. They record statistical counts of titles that have been cataloged or withdrawn from the library's collection and provide monthly reports. They correct any reported typographical errors in their library's OPAC records. They may be assigned to update periodically the library's automated records in accordance with changes in the AACR2 cataloging rules and updated cataloging practices and procedures. In so doing, they consult automated authority files, the National Union Catalog, and other reference materials to verify the accuracy of format and content of their library's existing records, making revisions as necessary.

Catalog Technicians also process library materials for inclusion into the collection by labeling, stamping, bar-coding, and affixing security strips to all materials and take processed library materials to the circulation area for filing. They may also prepare donated books and other library materials for library administrators to determine whether they should be retained in the collection. Additionally, they may assist in the training of new library aides and technicians on technical service tasks and provide support for circulation and reference desks as needed.

Salaries

Annual incomes for Cataloging Technicians range from beginning salaries of $18,000 to $21,000 to those for experienced technicians (who accomplish more difficult cataloging tasks) of $35,000 to $42,000 or more.

Employment Prospects

Employment opportunities for all library technicians are expected to grow about as fast as the average for all occupations through 2014, according to the U.S. Department of Labor's Bureau of Labor Statistics. Continuing library automation is expected to spur job growth among library technicians, particularly Cataloging Technicians, as computerized information systems have simplified descriptive cataloging procedures in making bibliographic information easily retrievable from a central database (such as OCLC). Such tasks can be handled by Cataloging Technicians (with a resultant savings in terms of salary) instead of catalog librarians.

Advancement Prospects

Cataloging Technicians may progress to senior positions in larger libraries or library systems. Such posts usually include supervisory duties over library staff. With additional education, a master's degree in library science (M.L.S.) or library and information science (M.L.I.S.), Cataloging Technicians may move up to full-fledged librarian careers.

Education and Training

The minimum requirement for beginning Cataloging Technicians is a high school diploma and three to four years of library experience, which should include providing reader services for patrons or performing book processing procedures such as searching, accessioning, and shelf listing books and other library materials. Additionally, the completion of an associate's degree in library studies or a library technician certificate and associate of applied science (A.A.S.) degree is highly recommended. The latter degree program prepares students to work in a variety of library environments, including school media centers as well as public and academic libraries.

Experience, Skills, and Personality Traits

Most library technicians have had prior library experience whereby they have learned basic library principles, practices, and techniques. They should have know-how with conducting searches online using a major bibliographic utility; be aware of library filing rules and inventory procedures; and be knowledgeable of proper

English usage, spelling, grammar, and punctuation. Their library experience should include book ordering, cataloging (using the Dewey decimal system, the Sears List of Subject Headings, and MARC Records), and circulation. They should be familiar with automated library systems and know cataloging standards and practices.

Library Technicians have to be very detail oriented, have excellent time management and organizational abilities, and be able to communicate effectively both orally and in writing. They must be able to prioritize duties when faced with interruptions, distractions, and fluctuating workloads and complete their tasks in a timely manner. They should be able to work effectively as part of a team but also function well with little supervision. They must have good math skills, strong keying/typing ability, and a proficiency in using computer word processing applications. They should have an exceptional customer service attitude and excellent interpersonal talents. They must be able to follow detailed procedures and be receptive to feedback. They should be physically fit, able to bend, reach, lift, and carry up to 30 to 50 pounds (as well as push and pull book carts weighing up to 200 pounds) and spend extended time at a computer terminal.

Unions and Associations

Cataloging Technicians should find membership in the American Library Association (ALA) to be useful (particularly the work of its Committee on Cataloging: Description and Access, which is responsible for developing official ALA positions on additions to and revisions of the AACR2 rules), as well as the cataloging section group of the International Federation of Library Associations and Institutions (IFLA). In addition, they may find value in participating in such groups as the American Society of Information Science and Technology (ASIS&T), the Association for Library Collections and Technical Services (ALCTS), the Association of College and Research Libraries (ACRL), and the Special Libraries Association (SLA).

Tips for Entry

1. While completing your education, take every opportunity available to gain library experience by volunteering in your school library or at a local public library or by taking a summer internship position with a library.

2. It is important to make contacts by joining various professional organizations for librarians and keeping in touch with your contacts to provide a network through which you may learn about job opportunities or receive answers to your professional questions.

3. Consider obtaining at least a reading knowledge of a language other than English as an additional useful tool for your cataloging profession.

CIRCULATION TECHNICIAN

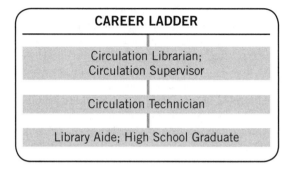

Position Description

With the rapid spread of automation and computerized information systems in libraries, certain tasks, such as descriptive cataloging and circulation (or access services), are now frequently handled by library technicians instead of librarians. At the outset, Circulation Technicians may act as circulation assistants, working at the public service desk (once known as the circulation desk and now frequently referred to as the access services desk). There they are responsible for such duties as checking out books and other library materials to patrons, answering and directing incoming telephone calls and messages, providing directional information to facility users, assisting patrons in the use of the library's (card or online) catalogs and indexes, aiding users in locating library materials, and answering routine reference inquiries (referring patrons needing further assistance to the appropriate librarian). They issue library cards, transfer library cards from other libraries, process overdue notices, handle patron user inquiries concerning overdue fines and lost library material fees, collect and record fines for overdue books and other library materials, contact patrons about library materials placed on hold for them, and maintain and update confidential patron records.

They may shelve library materials, maintain reading areas and displays in a neat and organized manner, ready shelves to maintain materials in appropriate locations and order, and weed out materials as requested by librarians. They assist library patrons with photocopying equipment and remove money from photocopiers, handling it according to established library procedures. They may also be responsible for making regular bank deposits of and managing the fine and book sale income for the library. They assist librarians with special projects involving data entry into the library's computer catalog system or its Web server. They monitor the use of public computers and assist with procedures to prepare and open the library for its daily activities.

Circulation Technicians usually oversee the use of the automated circulation system and its computers, software, printers, bar code readers, and other peripheral equipment. This involves communication and contact with the service provider for the equipment software. Operational responsibilities usually also include the many functions of the computerized system for electronic patron records, borrowing records, fines and over-dues as well as uploading data, updating records, and records backup procedures.

Experienced Circulation Technicians typically have supervisory tasks as well as their other access services work. In many cases, they become the primary supervisor of the circulation department of the library, supervising student assistants and other aides. In this capacity, they train and schedule full-time and part-time circulation staff and may manage the budget for student workers. In consultation with the library director and circulation librarian or systems librarian, they establish, disseminate, and enforce circulation procedures. They may also be responsible for carrying out interlibrary loan procedures for incoming and outgoing library materials.

Salaries

Like most other library technicians, annual salaries for Circulation Technicians range from $20,000 (as a beginning salary) to $45,000 or more (for more experienced technicians who have supervisory duties). According to PayScale, Inc.'s, 2007 salary survey report , the median yearly salaries for library technicians ranged from $23,196 to $51,434 depending on geographic location as well as type and size of the library.

Employment Prospects

According to the U.S. Bureau of Labor's *Occupational Outlook Handbook, 2007–08 Edition*, employment of library technicians in general (and Circulation Technicians in particular) is expected to grow about as fast as the average for all occupations through 2014. The escalating use of library automation is expected to continue to spur job growth among library technicians. Computerized information systems now used by libraries have simplified many tasks, including circulation. These duties are now often handled by library technicians instead of librarians. Although efforts to contain costs could dampen employment growth of library technicians in school, public, and college and university libraries, cost containment efforts could also result in hiring more library technicians than librarians.

Advancement Prospects

Circulation Technicians usually progress by assuming added responsibilities. While they typically start at the circulation (or access services) desk, checking books and other library materials in and out, after gaining seasoning, they may become responsible for storing and verifying library patron information. As they advance, they may become involved in budget and personnel matters in their departments. The next advancement step is to supervisory posts whereby they are put in charge of the day-to-day operation of the circulation department.

Some Circulation Technicians may decide to pursue further education and earn master's degrees in library science (M.L.S.) or in library and information science (M.L.I.S.) to use their technical knowledge in furthering a career in library science.

Education and Training

Circulation Technicians must have a high school diploma, and many libraries insist on an associate's degree as well. Some community colleges offer an associate's degree or certificate program designed for library technicians. These programs usually include both liberal arts and library-related study. Students learn about library and media organization and operation as well as how to order, process, catalog, locate, and circulate library materials, which includes working with library automation systems. Many libraries and all library associations offer support for continuing education courses to keep library technicians abreast of new developments in the field. Some libraries or library systems may require that Circulation Technicians have a B.A. or B.S. as well as one to two years of experience in library and information services and customer services.

Experience, Skills, and Personality Traits

Most public, academic, and special libraries insist that their Circulation Technicians have from one to three years of previous library experience. They must have a general knowledge of practices of library service, classification, and organizational functions and a working knowledge of library automated systems. They must be able to use data processing applications as they apply to library functions. They need to be able to type and input computer data as well. They should be adept at using photocopying equipment as well and have a basic mechanical aptitude and strong analytical and organizational skills.

Circulation Technicians must be able to provide friendly, high-quality customer service and maintain a professional demeanor and composure when dealing with difficult library patrons. They must pay attention to detail and must understand and follow written and oral directions and complete projects with minimum supervision. They should have excellent verbal and written communication skills and problem-solving abilities. They should be able to multitask in a fast-paced environment and be physically fit to walk and stand for extended periods, place books and other library materials on shelves of varying height (frequently bending, kneeling, squatting, or reaching to do so), and lift boxes weighing up to 30 pounds.

Unions and Associations

Circulation Technicians may find it useful to belong to a variety of trade associations that provide educational guidance, support, and information to their members. Primary among these organizations is the American Library Association (ALA). Others include the American Society for Information Science and Technology (ASIS&T), the Association for Library Collections and Technical Services (ALCTS), the Council on Library/Media Technicians (COLT), the Library Administration and Management Association (LAMA), and the Special Libraries Association (SLA).

Tips for Entry

1. During high school, consider taking a summer job with or volunteer at your local library to gain practical knowledge of library practices and procedures.
2. Volunteer to work at your school library to gain hands-on experience providing services to a variety of library users.
3. While gaining your associate's degree (or library technician certificate), take courses in public service and human psychology, as they will prove useful in your interaction with library staff and patrons.

CLASSIFIER

CAREER PROFILE

Duties: Classify library materials according to subject areas in preparation for cataloging

Alternate Title(s): Cataloger/Classifier; Cataloging Assistant; Classifying Technician

Salary Range: $20,000 to $45,000 or more

Employment Prospects: Fair

Advancement Prospects: Fair to good

Prerequisites:

Education or Training—Bachelor of arts degree and master's degree in library science (M.L.S.) or library and information science (M.L.I.S.) usually required; broad educational background preferred

Experience—Two to four years of experience cataloging in academic, public, or special libraries

Special Skills and Personality Traits—Capacity to work with close attention to detail; excellent communication (particularly writing) abilities; good interpersonal skills; knowledge of library automated systems and Internet protocols; thorough understanding of the Dewey decimal system and the Library of Congress classification schedules

Special Requirement—Security clearance may be needed to work at a government library

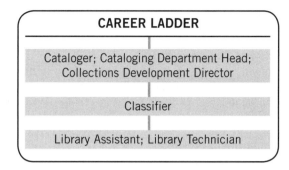

CAREER LADDER

Cataloger; Cataloging Department Head; Collections Development Director

Classifier

Library Assistant; Library Technician

Position Description

According to *Webster's College Dictionary* (2005 edition), to classify is "to arrange or organize by classes, or to order according to class." A Classifier is one who creates classifications. As a knowledge organization mechanism, classification is a way that humans understand the world by aggregating (collecting together) like entities. The World Wide Web is a good example of knowledge/information distribution, whereby Web sites generally serve narrow information topics and form information and knowledge communities through hyperlinks. Within the library world, the Dewey decimal system and the Library of Congress cataloging system used in cataloging books, serials, and most other library materials are classification schemes to arrange library materials by providing a shelf address, or location, for each item and to provide specific information on each item for the facility's holdings database.

Library Classifiers are specialized technicians within the library's technical services department who categorize library materials according to their subject matter in preparation for cataloging and entrance into the facility's collection. They review the materials to be classified and search information sources to determine the proper subject matter of the materials. They may explore such reliable databases as the Online Computer Library Center (OCLC) for an already completed MARC (machine readable cataloging) bibliographic record for the item they are classifying. They select appropriate classification numbers and descriptive headings according to the Dewey decimal, Library of Congress, or other classification systems (such as the Superintendent of Documents, or SuDocs, System employed for government document collections). They make sample cards (or create preliminary computer records) containing author, title, classification number, descriptive heading, and explanatory summary to guide library catalogers in preparing bibliographic records.

This bibliographic record contains the descriptive cataloging (physical description of the date of publication or creation, dimensions, number of pages, types and quantity of illustrations), a bibliographic description of elements necessary to identify the item (author[s], title, edition, place of publication or creation, any series statement, and notes), and a subject cataloging. The latter focuses on identifying the primary subject or subjects of the item and then assigning the best subject headings and classification number to reflect this. It is this subject analysis (description of the content of the item, the subject heading that will represent that content, and a classification number, or call number, that will signify that subject) that is the specific task of a Classifier. Classifiers also compose annotations of the content of the item, as well as keywords to guide the subject cataloging of it. Classifiers are usually found in the larger public library systems, academic library systems, and specialized libraries to aid the cataloging process. With smaller library collections, their subject tasks are usually undertaken by the cataloging librarian.

Salaries

As with most types of library technicians, median annual salaries for Classifiers range from a low of $20,000 to a high of $45,000 or more for experienced Classifiers.

Employment Prospects

Employment opportunities for Classifiers are best at academic or public libraries (or library systems) with significant multidisciplinary collections or with specialized libraries or government libraries. Classifiers are sometimes hired for their subject expertise when a library or library system is converting their collection from a manual (card) system to a digitized (computer accessible) system, when a collection has been cataloged according to the Dewey decimal classification scheme and is being converted to the more flexible Library of Congress classification schedule, or when a facility has acquired a large acquisition of new materials.

Advancement Prospects

Classifiers may progress in their careers to become cataloging librarians and, with further experience and training, heads of a library's cataloging department. Conversely, they may decide to move into another allied management area of the library, that of the collections development department.

Education and Training

Classifiers must have a master's of library science (M.L.S.) or a master's of library and information science (M.L.I.S.) degree from an educational institution accredited by the American Library Association (ALA). A broad liberal arts undergraduate education is preferable, and language skills beyond English are desirable.

Special Requirements

Classifiers working in government libraries (such as the National Archives) may be required to obtain and maintain a government security clearance.

Experience, Skills, and Personality Traits

Classifiers should have a minimum of one to two years of progressively responsible experience in a library that involves performing assorted library support activities (such as circulation work, processing orders for library materials, and locating and verifying bibliographic information) and requires the application of library technology, practices, policies, and procedures. Their library backgrounds must reflect their knowledge and understanding of the various elements related to the organization of library materials, including elements of bibliographic description, catalog card data and general format, standard library tools and reference sources (such as the Library of Congress Subject Headings and *Readers' Guide to Periodical Literature*), classification schemes (e.g., Dewey decimal, Library of Congress), and the nature of diverse types of publications and library materials.

Above all, Classifiers must be thoroughly familiar with the library classification schemes of the Dewey decimal system and the Library of Congress (LOC) classification schedule. Understanding the LOC Voyager Integrated Library System (ILS) is useful when needing to access Library of Congress bibliographic records. Classifiers must demonstrate great attention to detail. They must be extremely organized, have excellent interpersonal talents, and exhibit good communication abilities. Their computer proficiency must be strong.

Unions and Associations

Classifiers working in either public, academic, or special libraries may belong to a variety of trade associations that provide support, conferences, educational guidance, and information to their members. Primary among these groups are the American Library Association (ALA) and the Special Libraries Association (SLA). In addition, membership in the American Society for Information Science and Technology (ASIS&T), the Association for Library Collections and Technical Services (ALCTS), and the Association of College and Research Libraries (ACRL) should prove beneficial.

Tips for Entry

1. Working at your school or community library is a good introductory experience in library duties. Ask to work with the cataloging department.
2. Consider becoming proficient in languages beyond English, as you will be processing materials published abroad.
3. Think about specializing in a specific branch of liberal arts studies, such as history, law, medicine, economics, or psychology, to enhance your employment potential as an expert Classifier.

CONSERVATION TECHNICIAN

Duties: Evaluate library materials in need of mending and perform basic and complex repair and conservation treatment

Alternate Title(s): Binding and Conservation Technician; Book Binder Technician; Book Conservator; Book Repair Technician; Library Conservation Technician; Library Materials Conservation Technician; Preservation Technician; Restorer Technician

Salary Range: $16,000 to $35,000 or more

Employment Prospects: Fair to good

Advancement Prospects: Fair

Prerequisites:

Education or Training—High school diploma or equivalent required; in some cases, associate's degree or bachelor's degree also required

Experience—Several months of experience and training in library or archives conservation and/or bookbinding, with one to two years of library background

CAREER LADDER

Conservator, or Conservation Administrator; Freelance Preservation Specialist

Conservation Technician

Library Technician; Library Assistant

Special Skills and Personality Traits—Ability to work independently and with others and meet deadlines; excellent manual dexterity and visual and spatial skills; computer proficiency; knowledge of conservation techniques and practices dealing with library and archives materials; outstanding communication talents; strong organizational abilities

Position Description

Conservation Technicians are responsible for treating books, manuscripts, and other materials in their library's collections. They evaluate library materials that have been selected for repair, identify and assess repair options, and supervise assigned library staff with regard to treatment choices. They perform a wide variety of treatments on paper, cloth, and leather bindings, following established standards and procedures. They construct bindings in various styles and materials, including pamphlet bindings, case bindings, and post bindings. They make pockets for loose materials such as maps or charts. They mend binding structures, including making repairs to textblocks (the body of a book, consisting of the leaves, or sections, of the unit to be bound, rebound, or restored) prior to sending them out for commercial binding; flattening of rolled or distorted pages; reparation of tears, reattachment of book spines, covers, or loose leaves; tightening hinges; cloth (or leather) case rebacking; resewing; endpaper replacement; tipping in replacement pages.

Conservation Technicians dry-clean (by sprinkling crumbled art gum or draft power over a surface and rotating a soft cloth over the cleaning agent to absorb the soiling material) and repair books and periodical pages, maps, drawings, and other flat paper materials, using Japanese tissue and paste. They may preserve by immersing paper in deacidification baths to remove acidity from papers and ink to prevent deterioration and seal documents in cellulose cases and pass sealed objects through heated rollers to laminate them. They construct protective enclosures (such as drop spine boxes, four-flap portfolios, phase wrappers, and custom-designed boxes) and use Mylar (thin polyester film) to encapsulate maps, drawings, posters, and other flat work. They restore objects by such methods as immersing papers in mild bleach solution to brighten faded backgrounds, removing old varnish from such artworks as engravings and mezzotints, and fortifying papers by resizing them in a bath of gelatin solution. They mend tears with adhesive and tissue, and retouch stained, faded, or blurred watercolors, prints, or documents using colors and strokes to reproduce those of the original artist or writer.

Conservation Technicians track all materials during the treatment process, maintaining statistical spreadsheets and using conservation treatment log databases to track document and special collection materials being treated. They compile totals of work completed from the databases to present to library administrators. They charge and discharge materials to ensure accountability and access. They maintain inventories of conservation supplies, tools, and equipment and order supplies and equipment.

Conservation Technicians may be required to spray objects, storage containers, or areas with fungicides, insecticides, or pesticides and control the temperature, humidity, and exposure to natural or artificial light in areas where valuable library materials are displayed or stored. They may assist in preparing library materials for exhibition and may train library staff in methods of handling such items as well as train and supervise student assistants in minor and intermediate conservation procedures. They assist with the salvage of damaged library materials. Finally, they may be responsible for preservation reformatting of library materials to a variety of media (such as photocopies or microfilm) or even converting library materials to digital form.

Salaries

Annual salaries for Conservation Technicians start as low as $15,000 to $20,000 for beginners and go as high as $35,000 or more for experienced technicians.

Employment Prospects

Employment of library technicians (including Conservation Technicians) is expected to grow about as fast as the average for all occupations through 2014, according to the U.S. Bureau of Labor Statistics. Some job openings will result from the need to replace those who transfer to other fields or retire. There is a growing awareness in the library community about the need for the preservation and conservation of library materials, which should increase employment opportunities.

Advancement Prospects

Conservation Technicians may become head of the library conservation department, frequently known as a conservator or preservation specialist. Conversely, they may work as freelancers under contract to treat particular types of materials for libraries, museums, or other businesses.

Education and Training

For beginning Conservation Technicians, besides a high school diploma (or its equivalent), a bachelor's degree (or at least an associate's degree) is often demanded by library employers. In addition, formal or on-the-job training in bookbinding and/or book repair and conservation is a basic requirement. One to two years working in the collections department of a library is another frequent prerequisite.

Most employers expect Conservation Technicians to keep current with bookbinding and conservation techniques by reading and attending lectures and workshops. An excellent source of online links to preservation and conservation sources and groups is maintained by the Book Arts Web at http://www.philabiblon.com/pressite.shtml.

Experience, Skills, and Personality Traits

Most libraries require their Conservation Technicians to have prior background (from two to five years) in bookbinding, book repair, and book conservation acquired through apprenticeship or hands-on experience in private practice or library conservation programs. Conservation Technicians need excellent manual dexterity coupled with strong visual and spatial skills. They must demonstrate their understanding of book structures and standard conservation procedures for the treatment of paper-based materials.

They must have effective communication talents and be familiar with automated library information systems. They need excellent math and computer skills, must be familiar with the maintenance of statistics and inventory control, and knowledgeable in both the English and metric measuring systems. In addition, they must be able to use word processing and spreadsheet software and be familiar with imaging and graphics applications. They should have some supervisory experience and be able to work independently as well as with others. They need to have solid time management and organizational skills.

Unions and Associations

Besides belonging to one or both of the primary organizations for libraries, the American Library Association (ALA) or the Special Libraries Association (SLA), Conservation Technicians may want to join such groups as the American Institute for Conservation of Historic and Artistic Works (AIC), and the Core Activity Group on Preservation and Conservation (PAC) of the International Federation of Library Associations and Institutions (IFLA).

Tips for Entry

1. Consider taking a summer job or internship at a book bindery to gain experience in the field.
2. Access http://mysite.verizon.net/sgaither/preservation/BkPprPrs.htm for valuable data on book and paper conservation and preservation resources.
3. Check out such publications as *Archival Products News* or the *International Preservation News (IPN)*, published by IFLA.

INFORMATION SERVICES TECHNICIAN

Duties: Perform a variety of technical work providing information about publications and resources and perform reference and other centralized information/library/communication services

Alternate Title(s): Electronic Services Library Associate; Information Services Coordinator

Salary Range: $20,000 to $45,000 or more

Employment Prospects: Good

Advancement Prospects: Fair to good

Prerequisites:

Education or Training—High school diploma required; associate's degree or other postsecondary training in library technology often preferred; bachelor's degree may be required

Experience—One to three years of library work, including customer service; background using electronic information services and automated library systems

Special Skills and Personality Traits—Ability to manage multiple tasks and work with minimal supervision; advanced knowledge of print and electronic library and information resources;

CAREER LADDER

```
Technical Services Librarian;
Systems Librarian; Freelance
Computer Technician
            │
Information Services Technician
            │
Library Aide; Library Assistant;
Library Clerk
```

proficiency in written and spoken English and excellent oral and written communication skills; adeptness with Microsoft Windows, word processing, spreadsheet, e-mail, and Web browsing applications, with a capacity to adapt to evolving technology; strong public service experience and positive attitude

Special Requirement—Government security clearance may be necessary if working at a government library

Position Description

The Information Technology Association of America (ITAA) defines information technology as "the study, design, development, implementation, support or management of computer-based information systems, particularly software applications and computer hardware." The association further notes that "completing tasks using information technology results in rapid processing and information mobility, as well as improved reliability and integrity of processed information."

In support of the technical and information services department of a library, Information Services Technicians perform technical work, providing information for library patrons and requests from centralized information/library/communications services by accessing and processing data through electronic networks, the Internet, and various software programs. They advise and assist library patrons in the selection and use of information resources available at their library; give

technical help; and provide information about facility services, policies, and collections. They assist technical services librarians with the organization, scheduling, training, delivery, communication, and record keeping associated with the information services offered by the library. They may supervise and coordinate the work of student employees.

Information Services Technicians often assist the systems librarian in the design and maintenance of the library's Web pages, keeping the information current and accurate, as well as undertake other technical services. They may perform routine preventive maintenance tasks (for instance, updating virus protection) as well as routine software installations. They usually maintain an inventory control of computers and related equipment in the library. They may be called on to assist other library staff members with the operation and maintenance of office equipment as well as with the various publicly used equipment. They may lend a hand with circulation duties as appropriate. They usually compile and maintain statistics and other data on the use of technical equipment by both staff and patrons. They may also help out reference librarians in answering interlibrary loan and technical reference queries at the reference desk or via the telephone or e-mail. They may aid the collections development department in searching electronic resources for additions to the library's holdings as well as the processing of electronic orders for such.

Information Services Technicians working in academic libraries may be involved in outreach programs to both faculty and students that teach and inform about new electronic resources that may assist them in their information retrieval needs. As so many more resources are now available electronically, learning about these new research options is becoming significantly more important for students, faculty, and researchers.

Salaries
Similar to most other library technicians, annual income for Information Services Technicians range from $20,000 to $45,000 or more, with the average yearly salary being about $32,000.

Employment Prospects
According to the U.S. Department of Labor's *Occupational Outlook Handbook, 2007–08 Edition*, employment of library technicians (including Information Services Technicians) is expected to grow about as fast as the average for all occupations through 2014. In addition to jobs opening up through employment growth, some vacancies will result from the need to replace library technicians who transfer to other fields or retire.

The increasing use of library automation and computerized information systems is expected to continue to spur job growth among library technicians. Although efforts to contain costs possibly could dampen employment growth for library technicians in both public and academic libraries, cost containment efforts could also result in the hiring of more library technicians than librarians. Growth in the number of professionals and other workers who use special libraries should result in good job opportunities for library technicians in general and Information Services Technicians in particular in those settings.

Advancement Prospects
Experienced Information Services Technicians may decide to pursue their careers in librarianship by further education (a master's degree in library or library and information science) and seasoning (including supervisory experience). Job positions in librarianship for which their technical expertise would provide them with a natural advancement include either technical services or systems librarians. Other Information Services Technicians may choose to further their careers in business or government by becoming freelance computer technicians or by being hired by a computer service bureau.

Education and Training
A high school diploma plus some postsecondary training to the extent of an associate's degree designed specifically for library technicians are usually basic requirements for Information Services Technicians. Some libraries or library systems may require that these library technicians have a Bachelor of Arts (B.A.) or Bachelor of Science (B.S.) degree in a technical field relevant to library automation and computerized information services as well as one to two years of experience in library work (including customer services).

Special Requirements
Information Services Technicians working in government agencies or libraries may be required to obtain and maintain a government security clearance.

Experience, Skills, and Personality Traits
Information Services Technicians should have experience gained through employment in a position providing technical information to the public or employment in a clerical position involving the use of computer equipment and software. They need to be proficient in Microsoft Windows, word processing, spreadsheet, e-mail, and Web browsing applications as well as have a demonstrable knowledge of PC operating systems, hardware, and related peripherals (printers, scanners, and so forth). They should have know-how in networking, client-server technology, and the Internet and have the facility to adapt to evolving technology. They need to have a thorough knowledge of print and electronic library and information resources. In addition, they should be able to perform simple routine repairs to equipment and have sufficient computer expertise to handle routine downloading of software and routine maintenance.

Information Services Technicians should be proficient in written and spoken English, have excellent oral and written communication skills, be able to manage multiple tasks with minimal supervision, and be detail oriented. They should have some background working skillfully with library patrons and have a positive public attitude.

Unions and Associations

Besides belong to one or more of the primary associations for librarians, such as the American Library Association (ALA), the Association of College and Research Librarians (ACRL), and the Special Libraries Association (SLA), Information Services Technicians may find it useful to belong to one or more of the professional groups devoted to information processing, such as the American Society for Information Science and Technology (ASIS&T), the Association of Information System Professionals (AISP), and the Information Technology Association of America (ITA).

Tips for Entry

1. While earning your high school diploma, volunteer to help in your local or school library with such tasks as shelving books and other library materials or doing other library aide work as an opportunity to learn about library work while developing contacts that could lead to a job.

2. Look for summer jobs that will involve working with the public to develop your customer service skills and a situation that will provide you with experience in performing simple routine repairs to computers and other electronic equipment.

3. Volunteer to work on your school's Web site and other information processing systems to gain practical technical knowledge and experience.

LIBRARY TECHNICIAN

Duties: Assist librarians in acquiring, preparing, and organizing library materials; assist library patrons in locating information

Alternate Title(s): Cataloger/Technical Services Specialist; Library Technical Assistant; Library Technical Specialist; Media Technician; Technical Services Assistant; Technical Services Specialist

Salary Range: $16,000 to $45,000 or more

Employment Prospects: Good to excellent

Advancement Prospects: Good

Prerequisites:

Education or Training—High school diploma and an associate's degree or a certificate from a library diploma program (called "library and information technician") from a community college or institute required; a bachelor's degree may be required in some instances

Experience—Training in library procedures and practices necessary and some familiarity with a library environment

Special Skills and Personality Traits—Ability to follow library policies and procedures, especially

as related to circulation and processing of materials; aptitude for computers and know-how to work with software applications; attention to detail and good organizational abilities; capable of using office machines and troubleshooting equipment problems; excellent communication skills (both written and oral); strong people skills; willingness to attend conferences and workshops

Special Requirements—Working in government libraries may require a security clearance

Position Description

A technician is an individual skilled in the performance of the technical or procedural aspects of a profession. Library Technicians are highly trained in library procedures and practices, enabling them to provide technical support and assistant to librarians in all types of libraries. They must be able to assume responsibility for overseeing most library services.

Library Technicians' work covers all facets of library functions including acquisitions, cataloging, circulation, reference, and audiovisual. They usually work under the supervision of librarians but may also supervise other library paraprofessional or clerical staff. The tasks carried out by Library Technicians vary with the size and type of library. In small facilities, they typically handle a range of duties. In large institutions, they generally specialize in one or more areas (such as acquisitions, cataloging, children's services, circulation, online services, or reference). They may also work in school or special libraries such as business or law libraries or in governmental libraries.

Library Technicians both help librarians acquire, prepare and organize library materials and assist patrons in locating information. As libraries increase their use of new technologies, such as CD-ROM, the Internet, virtual libraries, and automated databases, the duties of library technicians expand and evolve accordingly. Increasingly, Library Technicians are assuming greater responsibilities, in some cases taking on tasks previously performed by librarians. The now widespread use of computerized information storage and retrieval systems has resulted in Library Technicians handling technical services—such as entering catalog information into the library's computer, or overseeing the use of the library's automated circulation system—that were once performed by librarians. Library Technicians assist technical services librarians with customizing databases. In addition, they instruct library patrons on using computer systems to access the facility's data and data available online.

The increased automation of library record keeping has reduced the amount of clerical work performed by Library Technicians. Many libraries now offer self-service registration and circulation areas with computers, decreasing the time Library Technicians have to spend manually recording and inputting information on library patrons and circulation data. Some Library Technicians operate and maintain audiovisual equipment, such as film projectors, tape and CD players, and DVD and videocassette players and assist library patrons with microfilm and microfiche readers. They may also design posters, bulletin boards, and displays.

Library Technicians may enter cataloging details onto networked online cataloging databases and search online databases for cataloging data to be used in their libraries' cataloging and classification of new materials. They often provide research from commercial databases as well as supply research from Internet searches and online databases. They may be asked to compile lists of books, periodicals, articles, and audiovisual materials on particular subjects as well as analyze the library's collection and recommend items for purchase.

Library Technicians frequently assist reference librarians in answering loan and reference queries at the reference desk or via telephone or e-mail. They guide library patrons in finding and using library resources including reference materials (such as dictionaries, encyclopedias, almanacs, indexes, handbooks, directories, and yearbooks), audiovisual equipment, computers, and electronic resources. They may assist librarians in arranging loans to and from other libraries and use Internet resources to provide interlibrary loan services to patrons. In addition, their duties may include organizing periodicals, creating invoices, preparing books for binding, and conducting library tours and reader education.

Library Technicians in school facilities assist librarians in acquiring, preparing, and organizing instructional and other library materials and, most important, encourage and teach students to use the library and media center. They assist pupils with special assignments and educate them on how to use computer systems to access data. Some Library Technicians work for businesses, such as law firms or research organizations. In these offices, they search online databases for books and articles about particular topics. They occasionally may be required to write summaries of books and articles.

Many Library Technicians perform administrative tasks. They supervise library aides, assistants, and other staff members. They compile reports about the library, such as determining how many books are borrowed each month. They may assist with the development of library policies and procedures, such as those that affect Internet access. They may also monitor and maintain library supplies.

Salaries

According to the second quarter 2007 salary statistics compiled by the Occupational Employment Statistics (OES) program in cooperation with the U.S. Bureau of Labor Statistics, hourly wages throughout the United States for Library Technicians ranged from a low of $7.91 (annual wage: $16,453) to a high of $21.45 (annual wage: $44,616). The average hourly wage was $13.97 (annual wage: $29,058). According to salary statistics (as of November 2007) compiled by PayScale, Inc., median yearly income for Library Technicians ranged from a low of $18,804 to a high of $45,525 depending on the type and location of the library. Federal libraries had a mean annual wage of $39,587, whereas academic libraries had a mean annual wage of $29,001, public libraries a mean annual wage of $31,532, and business libraries a mean annual wage of $45,503.

Employment Prospects

The employment outlook for Library Technicians is extremely good. Increasing use of computerized circulation and information systems should continue to spur job growth of Library Technicians, although some libraries' budget constraints may moderate this expansion. Nonetheless, the need to replace Library Technicians as they advance to administrative or librarian posts or leave the profession mean that there will be continuous job openings. In addition, escalation in the number of professional persons and other workers who use special libraries (government, law, medical, museum) will result in good job opportunities for Library Technicians in those settings. Information on acquiring a job as a Library Technician with the federal government may be obtained from the Office of Personnel Management, available on the Internet at http://www.usajobs.opm.gov. Library Technicians working for public libraries are usually considered employees of the city or town where the facility is located, so local classified advertisement listings are a good place to check.

Advancement Prospects

Library Technicians usually progress by assuming added responsibilities. Many start at the circulation desk, checking books in and out, or work in the cataloging department, researching data online for catalogers. After gaining seasoning, they may become responsible for storing and verifying circulation, acquisition, or cataloging information. As they advance, they often become involved in budget and personnel matters within their departments. Some Library Technicians move up to supervisory positions and are placed in charge of the day-to-day operation of their departments. Some may decide to further their careers in librarianship by continuing their education and earning a master's degree in library science (M.L.S.) or in library and information science (M.L.I.S.).

Education and Training

Many libraries require their Library Technician applicants to have both a high school diploma and a library technician certificate or an associate's degree. Associate of applied science degrees in library information technology are offered by some two-year institutions. These programs are composed of library-related study as well as liberal arts courses. Students graduate with knowledge of library and media organization and operation as well as the skills of ordering, processing, cataloging, locating, and circulating library materials.

Some libraries prefer to hire potential Library Technicians who have little training and teach them on the job, while others may prefer their Library Technicians to have a bachelor's degree. Because of the rapid development of technology in the library environment, computer skills have become necessary, and knowledge of databases, library automation systems, and circulation systems can be very helpful skills for job applicants.

Special Requirements

Library Technicians looking for employment in federal government libraries may be required to obtain a security clearance.

Experience, Skills, and Personality Traits

Library Technicians must have a strong customer service orientation and be able to communicate clearly with library patrons, coworkers, and their librarian supervisors. They need to be able to follow library policies and procedures, especially relating to circulation matters and to the processing of new library materials. They must take a methodical approach to their work, be detail oriented, exhibit excellent organizational know-how, have good English writing and speaking skills, and be excellent problem solvers.

Library Technicians require a strong aptitude for computers and proficiency in software applications, with knowledge of databases, library automation systems, online library systems, online public access systems, and circulation systems being particularly valuable skills. They should be able to use various office machines (such a photocopiers and microfilm/microfiche equipment) and troubleshoot problems. They should have a proven ability to multitask and meet deadlines and an ability to operate under minimal supervision, exercising their strong decision-making talents. They should have a willingness to attend conferences and workshops and continue to learn new skills.

Unions and Associations

Besides belonging to the premier professional association of the library field, the American Library Association (ALA) and, in particular, its Library Support Staff Interests Round Table (LSSIRT) section, other groups of interest for Library Technicians include the American Society for Information Science and Technology (ASIS&T), the Association for Library Collections and Technical Services (ALCTS), the Council on Library/Media Technicians (COLT), the Library Administration and Management Association (LAMA), and the Special Libraries Association (SLA).

Tips for Entry

1. During high school, volunteer or seek an internship at your school or local public library to gain a working knowledge of library practices, policies, and procedures.
2. Besides your computer expertise, knowledge of literature is a good basic preparation for most library jobs. Thus, you should consider taking as many literature classes as possible.
3. Because many public library (and some special library) positions are advertised and filled only at the local level, check out the classified ad sections of newspapers, and particularly their online versions, as you can then search the classifieds by keywords.

INFORMATION
SCIENCE

INFORMATION MANAGERS

CHIEF INFORMATION OFFICER

CAREER PROFILE

Duties: As the senior information services executive for a major corporation, business, or library, oversee the management, implementation, and usability of information and computer-related activities as well as long-term planning and setting of organizational standards for information services

Alternate Title(s): Chief Knowledge Officer (CKO); Information Resources Director; Information Resources Manager (IRM); Information Systems (IS) Director; Senior Information Officer; Vice President, Information Systems

Salary Range: $90,000 to $200,000 or more (including nonsalary benefits)

Employment Prospects: Poor

Advancement Prospects: Poor to fair

Prerequisites:

   Education or Training—Master's in business administration (MBA) plus graduate degree in information systems and technology

   Experience—Ten to 15 or more years of business background, including computer operations, infor-

CAREER LADDER

Chief Information Officer (CIO) in Larger Company; Senior Management Position; Chief Executive Officer (CEO)

Chief Information Officer

Manager, Information Systems; Systems Librarian

mation systems analysis and research, and management duties with increasing responsibilities

Special Skills and Personality Traits—Ability to delegate responsibilities and oversee multiple operations; excellent visionary and strategic thinking; good communication skills; outstanding business acumen; strong leadership abilities and exceptional self-confidence

Position Description

Chief Information Officer (CIO) is a job title usually given to persons in a business or enterprise who are responsible for the information technology and frequently the computer systems that support the goals of the business or enterprise. They are accountable for the vision, strategy, and oversight of the overall technological direction of their organizations. As information technology and systems have become more important and business and technology strategies increasingly become intertwined, CIOs are more and more viewed as major contributors in formulating strategic plans and goals for their companies. Information technology is an integral component in enabling business model innovation and in building a strong foundation for future business competitiveness and flexibility. In many organizations, CIOs report directly to the chief executive officer (CEO) and may sit on the organization's executive board. CIOs propose the information technology and systems that an enterprise will need to achieve its goals and then work with a technical staff and a budget to implement the plan. The role of CIOs is sometimes used interchangeably with the role of chief technology officers (CTO), although they are somewhat different jobs. CTOs are responsible for technological research and development as part of products and services, whereas CIOs deal primarily with information technology as infrastructure.

Typically, Chief Information Officers are involved with analyzing and reworking existing business processes, with identifying and developing a company's capability in using new tools related to information systems and processes, with reshaping an enterprise's physical infrastructure and network access, and with identifying and exploiting an enterprise's knowledge resources. In many cases, CIOs head a company's efforts to integrate the Internet and the World Wide Web into both its long-term strategy and its immediate business plans.

Specifically, CIOs create a resource acquisition and management strategy for needed capital and operational investment in the company's information technology (IT) infrastructure and services. As such, they develop and cultivate entrepreneurial strategic relationships with internal and external partners, work with appropriate collaborators to build policies and standards needed to achieve an integrated IT environment within their firms, and promote a customer-service orientation within the information technology department or section of their companies. Chief Information Officers are frequently responsible for the management of multiple information and communications systems and projects, including voice, data, imaging, multimedia, and office automation. They ensure that IT services and operations are continuous, secure, accurate, current, and well used. In so doing, they facilitate communication among staff, management, vendors, and other technology resources within their organizations.

As senior executives, CIOs must have a thorough knowledge of administrative procedures. They propose budgets for projects and programs and make decisions as to staff training and equipment purchases. They hire and assign computer specialists, information technology employees, and support personnel to carry out specific parts of projects or take charge of managing specific projects. They supervise the work of all these employees, review their output, and establish administrative procedures and policies.

As an ongoing part of their positions, CIOs must continually monitor how their companies' competitors are using information technology. When and if their firms contemplate expansion, they may also research possible mergers that would bring new technology or resources to their companies. Additionally, CIOs set policies that will ensure uniform standards for information technology operations (including computer activities) in such areas as data integrity and security, plans for recovery from natural disasters, and standards for training of new employees or the continuing training and education of professional employees.

In some business organizations, the post of CIO has been expanded into a position known as the chief knowledge officer (CKO), who is responsible for ensuring that the organization maximizes the value it achieves through "knowledge." CKOs help organizations achieve the best possible returns on investment in knowledge (people, processes, and intellectual capital), exploit their intangible assets (know-how, patents, and customer relationships), repeat successes, share best practices, improve innovation, and avoid knowledge loss after organizational restructuring. In performing their duties, they must be good at developing and understanding the big picture, advocacy (articulation, promotion, and justification of the knowledge agenda, sometimes against cynicism or even open hostility), project and people management (oversight of a variety of activities, atten-

tion to detail, and ability to motivate), communications (communicating clearly the knowledge agenda, having good listening skills, and being sensitive to organizational opportunities and obstacles), leadership, teamworking, influencing, and interpersonal skills.

Within the library field, there is a move on the part of some professionals to reshape senior librarian positions into Chief Information Officer posts in order to better manage and apply the accelerating crush of knowledge and technology to meet the expanding information needs of library users. If, as the American Association of School Librarians and the Association for Educational Communications Technology stated in 1998, the mission of library media programs is "to ensure that students (and other patrons of libraries) are effective users of ideas and information," then librarians are truly information officers. They are teachers of information skills, advocates of reading proficiency, and information managers. Particularly in schools, as more resource-based learning is used (instead of textbooks), computer networks are becoming the information lifeblood of such facilities. Thus, it is librarians who are becoming the information managers of this technology and the effective guides to its use by students and library patrons.

Salaries

While still a relatively new position within most corporate organizational structures, Chief Information Officers are gaining recognition in the corporate world because of the crucial role that information technology plays in business success. Some CIO positions at smaller firms may still just be departmental manger jobs, while those at many larger companies have already achieved the importance of other traditional corporate positions such as senior vice presidents and chief financial officers (CFOs). In their November 2007 salary survey of Chief Information Officers, PayScale, Inc., found that median annual salaries ranged from $90,752 to $175,456, depending on years of experience, geographic location, and type of industry.

Employment Prospects

Since the Chief Information Officer is usually a top-level executive post, there are few such openings at any given time. Managers who have compiled an impressive record and who have the requisite business and technological background may be well positioned to move up to the post of CIO when it is created by the company or when an already created position becomes vacant. However, competition for such high executive positions usually is severe and involves nationwide searches.

Advancement Prospects

As the position of CIO is the top IT post within an organization, advancement possibilities may consist mainly of moving into similar CIO jobs in larger companies. In some fairly rare cases, CIOs may have the opportunity to become the chief executive officer (CEO) of their (or another) organization.

Education and Training

In order to reach the level of CIO, an individual must have a solid background built up over many years. The foundation must be a strong undergraduate and graduate background in both information systems and technology (or computer science) and business management. Ideally, a master's degree in business administration (MBA) should be coupled with a graduate degree in information science, systems, or technology.

Experience, Skills, and Personality Traits

Candidates for a position as CIO should have seasoning supervising and managing information systems (IS) operations, including networking, database management, training of information employees, and systems support. This background usually leads to a position as department information services manager or director of information services. The advancement process to become CIO usually takes from 10 to 15 years.

Management and leadership abilities are of primary importance for Chief Information Officers. They must have strong interpersonal and communication skills, excellent business acumen, integrity, and the ability to think and act strategically. They need superior project management talents and must have the capacity to set and manage priorities effectively. They should have proven records of implementing business vision through short- and long-term planning and have had experience with complex project management and system(s) integration. They should have very strong research and analytical capabilities and the ability to inspire people to share a common vision and goals. They must be able to work effectively with top management, establishing and maintaining effective working relationships with others, and be able to delegate authority and exercise control over the successful completion of projects.

Unions and Associations

Chief Information Officers, as business managers, should find membership in such professional organizations as the American Management Association (AMA) and the National Management Association (NMA) to be useful. Groups devoted to information systems and technologies include the American Society of Information Science and Technology (ASIS&T), the Information Technology Association of America (ITAA), and the Society for Information Management (SIM).

Two organizations designed specifically for CIOs are CIO Today (which produces a newsletter for its members on information technology) and the CIO Executive Council (which consists of several hundred of the world's leading chief information officers and focuses on regional issues coupled with support and influence throughout the global community). In addition, for Chief Information Officers working within the federal government, there is the Chief Information Officers (CIO) Council, which serves as the principal governmental interagency forum for improving information resources. Its role includes developing recommendations for information technology management policies, procedures, and standards as well as identifying opportunities for the sharing of information resources between agencies of the federal government.

Tips for Entry

1. You will need both extensive information technology and business management experience before you can apply for a position as CIO. Try to find jobs that have extensive management responsibilities while keeping up to date on technical issues within the information field.

2. Contacts and professional connections will be useful in both advancing within your company and in finding other organizations that are expanding their top executive management with the addition of a CIO position.

3. Because you will be responsible for many things, you must remain focused on the business objectives of the use of information technology and not get sidetracked by areas of particular personal interest. During your business studies, focus on learning time management techniques that you can use to run your IT department in an effective manner.

CHIEF TECHNOLOGY OFFICER

CAREER PROFILE

Duties: Be responsible for the technical direction of an organization and for technological research and development as part of products and services, and provide a technical voice in the strategic planning for an organization

Alternate Title(s): Chief Technical Officer (CTO)

Salary Range: $75,000 to $150,000 or more

Employment Prospects: Fair to good

Advancement Prospects: Poor to fair

Prerequisites:

Education or Training—Bachelor of science (B.S.) in computer science or similar engineering degree required; master's degree in a field such as systems management, computer science, information science and technology, or equivalent usually demanded as well; in some cases, doctoral degree recommended

Experience—Eight to 15 years of successful, progressive, and applicable work in the management of information technology services and in managing network infrastructure with significant senior-level management responsibilities; extensive experience in software development often required

Special Skills and Personality Traits—Ability to recruit and retain a team with engineering and prod-

CAREER LADDER

Chief Executive Officer; Director of Technology; Vice President, Technical Services

Chief Technology Officer

Computer and Information Scientist/ Engineer; Director of Research and Development

uct management expertise; demonstrated facility to balance multiple priorities; excellent leadership and strategic management skills; outstanding computer abilities; sound business and problem-solving aptitude, including know-how to interact with higher executive levels; strong project management talents, including budgeting; superior analytical skills; written and verbal communication proficiency

Special Requirements—Certification as a computing professional usually required as part of professional background

Position Description

The increasingly significant role of technology in strategic business decisions has created the need for executives—Chief Technology Officers (CTOs)—who understand technology and recognize profitable applications to products, services, and processes for businesses, corporations, government agencies, and library systems. They are operational executives who are responsible for technological research and development. They provide reliable advice on its applications to products and services, customers and revenues, and the competitive positioning of their organizations in the marketplace. In this respect, they differ from chief information officers (CIOs), who deal primarily with the application of information technology to an organization's infrastructure. In contrast, the CTO's primary responsibility is contributing to the strategic direction of the organization by identifying the role that specific technologies will play in its future growth.

Chief Technology Officers monitor new technologies and assess their potential to become new products or services provided by their organizations, oversee the selection of research projects to ensure that they have the potential to add value to an organization, and provide reliable technical assessments of potential mergers and acquisitions. In addition, they frequently have the further duties of explaining company products and future plans to the trade media and of participating in government, academic, and industry groups in which there are opportunities to promote their organizations' reputation as well as capture or elicit data valuable to the organizations' future plans.

The position of Chief Technology Officer is relatively new, emerging from the post of research and development (R&D) laboratory director in the 1980s. The definition of what a CTO is and how this person should contribute to an organization varies widely. Each organization has unique requirements for its CTO and provides a distinctive organizational structure into which the person fits. Nonetheless, the most prominent responsibilities of this position include monitoring and assessing new technologies. The rate of technological change guarantees that knowledge and expertise gained several years ago will no longer be completely valid today or tomorrow. This fact creates the need for a technologically current person (the CTO) to serve as an adviser to senior executives during strategic decision making. Furthermore, in some industries, new products based on new technology are vital to the company, whereas in other industries, core products remain unchanged for decades, but the processes used to create them are continually evolving and becoming more efficient. One of the primary roles of the CTO is to provide the technical vision to complement the business vision and to define what the organization's products and/or services will look like in two or more years.

Another responsibility is to provide technical and business insight regarding the value of potential company mergers and acquisitions. Such insight might include evaluating patents, reviewing technical publications, and studying trade data in order to determine the worth of the target company and to rank it against its competitors. CTOs also have a role in marketing and media relations, in that their technical expertise is needed to translate accurately product details into terms that can be marketed.

In addition, they may serve as media spokespersons for their organization. In their function as the technical voice for their organizations, CTOs are able to create in-house a technology-friendly culture that is aligned with their organizations' business strategies.

CTOs frequently are tasked with participating in professional groups and their associated meetings, to project a positive image of their organizations, and to communicate information about their organizations to other members of the profession. In another public arena, CTOs may be called on to provide services to government, academic, and professional associations. Since most CTOs possess advanced college degrees, they tend to have multiple relationships with members of academia. These ties often lead to partnerships and funding for research that is of mutual interest. As a businessperson, the CTO must be certain that money and time spent on such projects are aligned with his or her organization's corporate strategy and that they have a realistic potential of contributing to the organization's competitive advantage in the foreseeable future.

Since part of CTOs' management tasks is to direct and supervise a support staff, they often are required to negotiate and maintain responsibility for managing vendor contracts as well as manage budgets and provide monthly revenue and expense reports. Thus, CTOs are not just senior technologists of an organization but are primarily senior business executives with a focus on technology.

In some business and financial organizations, a number of the duties of the CTO have been assigned to a subordinate supporting position known as a chief data officer (CDO), who is both a member of the organization's executive management team and also the manager of the data processing and data mining operations. This high-level individual guides the creation and implementation of data strategy. Besides revenue opportunities, acquisition strategy, and customer data policies, the CDO is charged with explaining to executives, employees, and customers the strategic value of data and its important role as a business asset and revenue driver.

Salaries

In its November 2007 salary survey report on Chief Technology Officers, PayScale, Inc., found that median annual salaries varied from a low of $80,816 to a high of $152,921, depending on the type of employer, scope of responsibilities of the position, number of years of experience, and geographic location. A yearly salary of $200,000 plus benefits for a CTO at a large corporation is not unusual.

Employment Prospects

CTO positions are usually top-level executive posts, and, as such, there tend to be few openings at any given time. Many future CTOs come from a research and development laboratory, where, as a leading scientist or researcher, they have shown a talent for organization, handling exceptional people, and envisioning the future. If such individuals are willing to give up direct, hands-on research in order to create an environment in which others are enabled to do outstanding and valuable work, they may become the director of R&D and future CTOs. (In some companies, the title CTO is a direct substitute for director of R&D, whereas in other operations, the CTO is an additional position designed to bridge the gap between the company's strategies and its research activities.)

Companies began adding CTOs to the executive ranks in the 1980s because technology was becoming an integral part of many strategic decisions and future plans. Thus, this position is new to the executive ranks and is much more dependent on the type and phase of the organization involved. Research scientists/engineers who have compiled an impressive record and who have the requisite business and technological backgrounds may be in good situations to move up to position of CTOs when they are created by their organizations or when these posts becomes vacant. However, competition for this executive job usually is severe and may include nationwide searches, not just promotion from within.

Advancement Prospects

As Chief Technology Officer is a top executive ranking within an organization, advancement possibilities frequently consist mainly of moving into a similar CTO post in a larger company, government agency, or library system, where he or she may become director of the technology division or vice presidents of technical services. In some atypical cases, CTOs may have the opportunity to become the chief executive officers (CEO) of their (or other) organizations.

Education and Training

Many organizations require their CTOs to have, at the very least, a bachelor's degree in computer science or technology. Most organizations demand, in addition, a master's degree in information technology and a master's degree in business administration (MBA) or equivalent experience. Some companies may also require a doctoral degree due to the specific nature of their products, processes, or services.

Special Requirements

As part of their technology background, most CTOs are computer experts. As such, they may be required to have certification as computer professionals.

Experience, Skills, and Personality Traits

CTOs must have superior analytical and problem-solving skills, excellent written and oral communication abilities, and the capacity to effectively recognize and prioritize critical issues. Strong management skills are needed to develop, coordinate, budget, and supervise project plans. They must be able to build and motivate teams, forging diverse numbers of people into a successful and innovative group and fostering a team- and goal-oriented environment.

They must be methodical and logical in their application of technology to business strategies and display business acumen and technical adeptness that inspires confidence. They should have a demonstrated facility to balance multiple priorities, such as prototype development, new product development, and maintenance of an existing product or service. They must have strong software process experience, including the ability to estimate accurately the resources needed for software-driven projects. Specific knowledge of the best practices and tools for automated testing of such computer processes as cross-browser Web applications and relational databases are a bonus. Many CTOs have both a technological and business background, which gives them an appreciation for and understanding of both the technical aspects and the financial impacts of technical issues.

Unions and Associations

Besides memberships in such business groups as the American Management Association (AMA) and the National Management Association (NMA), CTOs should find it useful to belong to such information systems and technology organizations as the American Society of Information Science and Technology (ASIS&T), the Information Technology Association of America (ITAA), and the Society for Information Management (SIM).

Professional associations devoted to computing technology of interest to CTOs include the Association for Computing Machinery (ACM), the Computing Technology Industry Association (CTIA), and the Institute of Electrical and Electronics Engineers (IEEE) Computer Society.

Tips for Entry

1. To gain wide professional experience in computer applications, consider applying for a position with a computer service bureau as a first step toward becoming a CTO.
2. To learn more about the role of CTOs, subscribe to publications that focus on CTOs, such as *Research-Technology Management* (the publication of the Industrial Research Institute, which focuses on CTOs in the pharmaceuticals, consumer products, and electronics industries) and *InfoWorld* (which focuses on CTOs of companies that provide information technology products and services and those serving in government agencies).
3. Web sites of particular interest for CTOs include the Chief Technology Officer network (http://www.ctonet.org), the Chief Technology Officer Weblog (http://ww.ctoweblog.com), and StartupCTO for CTOs of small start-ups (http://www.startupcto.com).

DATABASE ADMINISTRATOR

Duties: Be responsible for the overall operation and security of an organization's database systems; supervise and coordinate the development and use of data resources

Alternate Title(s): Database Analyst; Database Coordinator; Database Design Analyst; Database Manager; Data Systems Manager

Salary Range: $40,000 to $98,000 or more

Employment Prospects: Good

Advancement Prospects: Fair

Prerequisites:

Education or Training—In some instances, an associate's degree in computer science or related information technology field acceptable minimum requirement; bachelor's degree in computer science, information science, or management information systems (MIS) more usually required; master's degree in business administration (MBA) recommended

Experience—Four to five years of practical programming and computer systems background, including designing and programming with major database software packages and with database security programs; management experience helpful

Special Skills and Personality Traits—Ability to think logically and concentrate attention on details; good communication and management skills; responsible and consistent work habits and facility to adapt to changing needs and technology; strong database design and computer proficiency, including working knowledge of Structured Query Language (SQL)

Special Requirements—Certification as a computer professional highly recommended; certification in specific types of programming and/or database management recommended as well

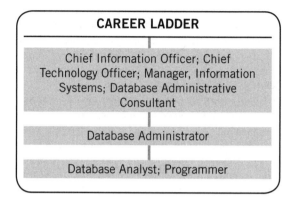

CAREER LADDER

Chief Information Officer; Chief Technology Officer; Manager, Information Systems; Database Administrative Consultant

Database Administrator

Database Analyst; Programmer

Position Description

Databases, collections of information organized electronically, are central to information processing in the business, governmental, and library worlds. They typically contain information used in activities such as sales transactions, inventories, and mailing lists as well as data about customers, orders, vendors, products, research, and bibliographic collections.

One of the primary responsibilities of Database Administrators (DBAs) is to manage databases, working with database management systems software and determining effective storage methods while supervising all the tasks involved with a database environment. For their work, they must be familiar with database management products, such as Structured Query Language (SQL), server application programming (SAP), and Oracle-based database management software.

DBAs identify user needs, set up computer databases to meet those needs, and test systems. In ensuring optimum performance of database systems, DBAs

must have an understanding of the various platforms and operating systems involved. Another important element of their jobs is the planning, designing, and implementation of database security. As the world continues toward becoming an entirely "wired" society, data integrity and backup systems have moved to the forefront of a DBA's responsibilities.

Since DBAs are in charge of all aspects of database operations, their duties typically include:

- developing standards and guidelines for the use and acquisition of pertinent programming software and to protect vulnerable information and reviewing the description of changes to database design to understand how changes affect the database
- designing or modifying the structure of databases and database management systems, the input forms used to gather data to be entered into the database, and the reports to be generated for managers or executives, and supervising database analysts or other

programmers in these tasks

- testing programs and/or databases, correcting errors and making necessary modifications
- planning, coordinating, and implementing security measures to safeguard information against accidental or unauthorized damage, modification, or disclosure, and making contingency plans (such as for backup or recovery) to deal with these threats
- configuring and maintaining the server computers that allow access to the database across the local area network (LAN), usually within the confines of the company
- approving, scheduling, planning, and supervising the installation and testing of new products and improvements to computer systems (such as the installation of new databases)
- creating the processes that bring together data generated by many different departments or users into a form that can be used for evaluation of operations and for executive decision making
- training users and answering any questions
- specifying user access levels for each segment of the database
- developing methods for integrating different products so they work properly together (such as customizing commercial databases to fit specific needs or creating Internet accessibility so that product specifications can be retrieved by potential customers)

DBAs must regularly run software to verify the consistency and correctness of data formats and the relationships between databases, as different users and departments may use the same database and update different parts of the same records within the database. Programs that access the database or change/add data must follow the same protocols. DBAs frequently modify database programs to increase the processing performance, usually called "performance tuning."

DBAs must always be vigilant to ensure that software developers follow good programming practices. As most DBAs assign programming tasks to database analysts, supervision and training of these analysts is crucial. In addition, they should confer with coworkers to determine the impact database changes may make on the system (or other interacting systems) and the staff cost of making these changes.

In interdepartmental meetings, DBAs represent the data processing department and explain database operations to other managers and top administrators. In turn, they listen to the information needs of managers and administrators in order to make necessary changes to the database system.

DBAs must be familiar with many types of computers and database operating systems. These include mainframes, Windows, and UNIX systems. They may work with databases such as Oracle, Ingres, and Access. Because database technology changes quickly, DBAs must keep their skills and knowledge up to date by attending classes, reading magazines, and communicating with other computer specialists.

Salaries

As the position Database Administrators is an extremely important and heavily responsible one, they tend to be well paid. Large organizations with more complex data needs generally pay higher salaries than smaller organizations (which may not even have a separate person for this position but, rather, include it in system administration). According to PayScale, Inc.'s, November 2007 salary survey of Database Administrators, their median annual salaries ranged from $46,000 to $100,000 or more, depending on type of the employer and geographic location. According to Salary.com, the median expected yearly salary for a typical Database Administrator in the United States is $85,760.

Employment Prospects

As databases have become more integral to business, the position of Database Administrator has become increasingly vital. According to the U.S. Bureau of Labor Statistics, computer scientists and Database Administrators are expected to be among the fastest growing occupations through 2014 as organizations continue to adopt and integrate increasingly sophisticated database technologies. The demand for networking to facilitate the sharing of information, the expansion of client-server environments, and the need for computer specialists to use their knowledge and skills in a problem-solving capacity will be major factors in the rising demand for computer scientists and Database Administrators. Applicants for this position who have extensive experience with the most popular database systems and strong computer skills will have the best chances. Many such applicants may be successful database analysts who can make this career advance when a Database Administrator in an organization retires or moves on.

Advancement Prospects

As the position of Database Administrator is at the top of most database-related career paths, advancement usually is either to the manager of an organization's information systems department or into a high-level technical management post, such as chief technology officer (CTO).

A growing number of Database Administrators work on a contract or temporary basis. Many work independently or are self-employed as consultants. Organizations may hire administrators with specific skills or experience with specific types of databases to carry out a particular project. These projects may last from several months to several years.

Education and Training

While some jobs as Database Administrator require only a two-year degree in computer or information science, the vast majority of Database Administrator positions require a bachelor's degree in computer science, information science, or management information systems (MIS). MIS programs usually are part of a business school, and they differ quite a bit from computer science programs in that they focus on business and management-oriented course work and business computing courses. Many employers seek Database Administrators who have the requisite computer technology background but also have a master's degree in business administration (MBA) with a concentration in information systems.

Special Requirements

Certification as a computer professional is a way for an applicant for the post of Database Administrator to demonstrate a level of competence. One way is to become certified in a specific type of database management. Some software manufacturers offer certification that indicates that an individual has mastered the use of their particular system. In addition, voluntary certification is available through organizations associated with computer specialists. Such certification assures potential employers that a candidate's skills are up to date.

Experience, Skills, and Personality Traits

Database Administrators must have solid backgrounds in the theory of database design and the detailed operations of the most commonly used database software packages. They may be tasked with supervising the development of Internet-accessible databases using such languages as Java, CGI (common gateway interface) scripts, Visual Basic, HTML (hypertext mark-up language), and XML (extensible mark-up language). They must have an extensive knowledge of computer software applications and experience with data analysis as well as an ability to understand high-level programming languages. They should have a working knowledge of database security protocols and be able to read and interpret technical manuals and specification documents.

Database Administrators must be able to think logically. Because they often deal with a number of tasks simultaneously, the ability to concentrate and pay attention to detail is key. Database Administrators need to communicate effectively with computer personnel, such as programmers and managers, as well as with users, other staff, and top management, who may have no technical computer background.

In addition, Database Administrators should demonstrate leadership capacity and a facility to manage priorities. They must be able to work independently at times yet also function closely within a team at other times. They must have a strong sense of responsibility and the willingness to expand their knowledge in order to keep up with new challenges and changing needs.

Unions and Associations

Database Administrators usually find it useful to belong to computer science–related professional groups, such as the Association for Computing Machinery (ACM), the Computing Technology Industry Association (CTIA), and the Institute of Electrical and Electronics Engineers (IEEE) Computer Society. In addition, membership in such business organizations as the American Management Association (AMA) and the National Management Association (NMA) as well as such other information systems and technology associations as the American Society of Information Science and Technology (ASIS&T), the Information Technology Association of America (ITAA), and the Society for Information Management (SIM) is highly recommended.

Tips for Entry

1. Seriously consider participating in an internship (say, in a data processing or data design service bureau) while in college. An internship is usually part of a four-year degree program and offers you a chance to apply what you have learned in the classroom to a work situation. It allows you to build skills and make valuable contacts with people in your field.
2. In addition to your computer courses, include classes in mathematics and business administration and management, as these will be necessary skills for your career as Database Administrator.
3. After graduation, look for entry-level programming jobs that will reinforce your database skills and will provide you the years of practical experience needed before moving up into a position as a Database Administrator.

INFORMATION ARCHITECT

CAREER PROFILE

Duties: Design the organization and navigation systems of a Web site to help users find and manage information successfully

Alternate Title(s): Information Technology Architect; Interaction Designer; Interactive Designer; Prototyper; Usability Designer; User-Centered Information Designer; User Experience Designer; User Interface Designer

Salary Range: $40,000 to $100,000 or more

Employment Prospects: Good

Advancement Prospects: Fair

Prerequisites:

Education or Training—Bachelor's degree with computer-related major or library science degree required; master's degree in information science and technology, industrial design, graphic design, or related field often necessary

Experience—Five or more years of background as an information architect, interaction designer, or experience designer; know-how designing interactive experiences both in traditional and non-traditional online Web experience or software; some business knowledge; seasoning in defining user experience with Web sites as well as developing and documenting usage cases, task flows, and detailed interaction designs; internal or external client service experience in software design,

CAREER LADDER

```
┌─────────────────────────────────────┐
│   Chief Information Officer;         │
│   Database Administrator; Freelance  │
│   Information Specialist             │
└─────────────────────────────────────┘
              │
┌─────────────────────────────────────┐
│   Information Architect               │
└─────────────────────────────────────┘
              │
┌─────────────────────────────────────┐
│   Systems Programmer; Interface Web   │
│   Designer; Information Technician    │
└─────────────────────────────────────┘
```

instructional technologies, interaction design, and/or Web development

Special Skills and Personality Traits—Ability to resolve complex design and implementation issues and negotiate the adoption of those design solutions; advanced proficiency in design tools; excellent oral and written communication and presentation skills; capacity for working both independently and as a team member; understanding of human factors, user-centered design processes, interaction design guidelines, usability methodologies, industry standards and trends, platform standards, and software development; thorough understanding of graphic design principles

Special Requirements—Certification as an Information Architect is recommended

Position Description

Information architecture is the art and science of expressing a model or concept for information. The Information Architecture Institute goes on to define information architecture (IA) as the structural design of shared information environments as well as the art and science of organizing and labeling Web sites, intranets, online communities, and software to support usability and findability. IA describes a specialized skill set that relates to the interpretation of information and expression of distinctions between signs and systems of signs. It relates to library science, and many library schools teach IA. The core of its discipline is creating information structures that facilitate effective and efficient communication.

In the context of information systems design, IA refers to the analysis and design of the data stored by information systems, concentrating on entities, their attributes, and their interrelationships. It is the modeling of data for an individual database and for the corporate data models an organization may use to coordinate the definition of data in several (or even hundreds) of distinct databases. Information design draws on a wide range of competencies that are seldom possessed by a single person. For this reason, information designers tend to work on information products in teams that include specialists and other information architects. Their tasks involve using, commissioning, coordinating, and understanding research (including business process investigation and analysis, academic research into such topics as ergonomics and cognitive and perceptual psychology, knowledge of what has been tried before, and qualitative and quantitative user research).

Other elements of their skill sets include transforming a given product or Web site employing words, diagrams, type, and sequencing to restructure information messages so that they tell their story more effectively, as well as writing and/or editing to make such messages clear, unambiguous, and understandable by their intended audience(s). Information Architects' graphic and typographic design skills include the designing of the appearance of an information product so that users can best locate what they want and better understand it when they do find it.

Information Architects play an integral role in the development of clients' Web sites. Working closely with the team involved in the Web development process, Information Architects contribute to the planning stage by organizing information, developing Web site architectures, and building labeling and search systems. They often employ user-centered design (UCD) principles, structuring the architecture around the needs and capabilities of the intended user audience. (This is in contrast to more traditional/academic approaches of organizing information, where the focus is on some internal consistency or internal logic.) Some Information Architects specialize in developing such deliverables as site maps, flow diagrams, and screen-level design prototypes to represent the structure of a Web site or interactive application.

As the World Wide Web emerged in the mid-1990s, the term *information architecture* began to take on a shade of meaning that described an evolving set of Web design practices. The explosive growth of the Web design industry in the late 1990s fueled a growing demand for professional Information Architects. Information Architects use a range of tools and techniques from other fields, including human-computer interaction, anthropology, information management, and library and information science. When a Web site or help system lacks definition and structure, users can become lost in the content. As content providers, Information Architects organize and interrelate content so the user remains oriented and gets needed answers. By defining formal design patterns for information architecture, content providers can apply tested architectures to improve a user's experience. In this context, Information Architects help define such things as the division of topics and setting the specialization of content types as well as developing guidelines and setting examples for the type of information that goes into specific content object types. The creation of categories and taxonomies (techniques of classification) is inherent in IA. This type of information is often designed for a high level of reuse, with the intent that a single content object can be deployed to different media types, including print, online help, marketing materials, and on Web pages.

Information Architects often work closely with software and Web teams, but typically they focus on navigation schemes and usability rather than pure design or hard-core program coding. Their usual first step is to detail the content and organization of a Web site. They and their team then inventory all existing content, describe what new content is required, and define the organizational structure of the site. Once this content architecture has been sketched out, small prototypes of parts of the site are built to test what it feels like to move around within the proposed design for the site. These site protoypes are the best way to test site navigation and develop effective user interfaces. In addition, creating a prototype allows graphic designers on the team to develop relations between how the Web site looks and how the navigation interface supports the information design.

Information systems are dynamic and, ideally, should adapt to specific users' actions. A well-developed IA means that users will spend less time finding information and are less likely to miss locating what they need altogether.

Because IA practices and techniques became popular with the advent of the World Wide Web, some Information Architects may lack experience designing information systems that are *not* Web-based and where browsing is less related. Users of business systems typically have different goals (such as providing users with tools to expedite required business tasks) than nonprofessional users. In contrast, commerce sites and news sites invite users to explore and browse information, in many cases to support their business model. For these reasons, Information Architects are finding it important to understand the specific business and user requirements rather than just apply the same techniques to shape a system's information.

While work on the design of Web sites is the hub of the Information Architect's profession, it has become clear to some Information Architects that the audiences to which they (as information designers) cater may be very broad (such as the signs in airports that are designed to inform everybody) or very specific (as in information products such as telephone bills, which can be personalized for individual customers using market segmentation and information management techniques and technologies similar to those used in direct marketing). There is a growing demand on the part of clients using Information Architects for them also to serve as bridges between strategy and interface and to play active roles in product development. The Information

Architecture Institute's business plan has been designed to extend the practice of IA beyond just the Web to include a wide variety of shared information spaces, including virtual (e.g., software, Web sites), physical (e.g., museums, libraries, hospitals), and procedural (e.g., flows of information in work processes). In addition, the institute is striving to make both customers and beginning Information Architects aware of relevant cost and value propositions, such as the cost of finding information, the cost of *not* finding information, the cost of using information, the cost of building and managing information systems, the value of creating knowledge networks, the value of educating employees and customers, the value of strengthening brand (product), and the value of fostering innovation.

Salaries

In their November 2007 salary survey report for jobs of Information Architects, PayScale, Inc., found that median annual salaries ranged from $42,500 for those with less than one year of experience to $101,800 for those with 20 years or more seasoning. In terms of geographic location and types of employer, median yearly salaries ranged from a low of $50,000 to a high of $107,500.

Employment Prospects

With the growing information needs of the public, businesses, government, and other organizations, the demand for professionals to manage information systems and to design them and their Web counterparts will continue to grow. As has been pointed out by Jesse James Garrett, author of *The Elements of User Experience: User-Centered Design for the Web*, most working Information Architects get to be Information Architects by doing IA work as part of some other job they had. While the IA part of their duties was never defined as such, they take an interest in it, and they manage to persuade their organizations (or others) to let them take responsibility for this type of work. Many Information Architects move into full-time roles from positions as programmers, interface designers, HTML coders, and other Web team members (which may also include content producers and writers).

The main point, as made by Louis Rosenfeld, coauthor of *Information Architecture for the World Wide Web*, is that the field of IA is still a new one. He states, "To break in, you won't be expected to have 20 years' experience or even any sort of certification. . . . To [have] the ability to sell is important. You will continually be asked to justify yourself and the field of IA to business and professional colleagues who still think it's too new and

abstract to have concrete value." A further challenge for Information Architects is to serve organizations where information is spread among dozens or hundreds of business units, making it difficult for users to find what they need, as well as to work for global companies with multicultural and multilingual audiences.

Advancement Prospects

Some Information Architects work freelance or set up their own consulting firms. Others may advance their careers within an organization's management structure to become database administrators or the more all-inclusive position of chief information officer.

Education and Training

The minimum educational requirement is a bachelor of science or bachelor of arts degree (with a master's degree usually preferred) in a technology-related field (such as computer science, user interface design, or information technology) with multidisciplinary backgrounds such as psychology, computer science, information sciences, commerce and business, library science, human-computer interaction, and graphic design. A bachelor's degree (and/or a master's degree) in information technology, while giving mainly a background in computer hardware, software, networking, and general computer science concepts, also teaches students how to solve information technology problems and how to teach people the best ways to use computer technology. Many four-year colleges and universities offer bachelor's degrees in information technology. Some community colleges offer two-year programs that can be transferred to four-year schools.

Special Requirements

Certification as an Information Architect is available from the Society for the Certification of Information Architects (SCIA), an association of certified (enterprise) information, IT (information technology)-business, and IT architects. Certification is voluntary and usually is not required by companies, but it does convey a sense that the applicant has been well trained and is knowledgeable about the latest technology and technological processes in IA.

Experience, Skills, and Personality Traits

Most organizations look for Information Architects to have at least two years of related industry experience in new media, information technology, or library and information science. They should have backgrounds in applying research and analysis to the development of Web sites. They should have some experience with user-centered design techniques, the development of organizational and structural concepts for Web sites, and documentation requirements for Web development teamwork. They should be schooled in the techniques of information representation, hypertext design, and the technologies of metadata (data modeling, XML). Familiarity with Flash, HTML, JavaScript, and CSS design capabilities is useful as well. They should have some background in relational databases, general client-server architecture, and a strong understanding of the Web and associated Internet technologies. Above all, Information Architects must blend the technical and visual with a keen sense for organizational structures and usability.

Information Architects must have the capacity for strategic and associative thinking, a strong business sense, superior organizational and logic skills, effective communication talents (both orally and in a variety of written and diagrammatic forms), proven interpersonal aptitude (including client-relation skills and the ability to work within a team environment), and creative thinking and problem-solving abilities. They must be detail oriented, thorough, and able to multitask and meet tight deadlines.

Unions and Associations

Professional groups of interest to Information Architects include the American Society for Information Science and Technology (ASIS&T), the Association for Computing Machinery (ACM), the Computing Technology Industry Association (CTIA), and the Society for Technical Communication (STC).

Tips for Entry

1. Facts on, advice about, and knowledge of information architecture as a career can be found by contacting the Information Architecture Institute (IAI) (http://iainstitute.org) or the International Institute of Information Design (IIID) (http://www.iiid.net).

2. Besides your studies in information architecture and interaction design, include courses in business, psychology, sociology, computer-human interaction, and communication, as your career in IA will be enhanced by your multidisciplinary background.

3. The online publication *Boxes and Arrows* (http://www.boxesandarrows.com) as well as the blogs of authors Jesse James Garrett (http://blog.jjg.net) and Louis Rosenfeld (http://www.louisrosenfeld.com) provide many resources for Information Architects.

INFORMATION RESOURCES DIRECTOR

CAREER PROFILE

Duties: Responsible for all information (acquisition, storage, retrieval, and transmission) and communication resources at a company, government body, academic institution, library system, or other organization

Alternate Title(s): Director, Information Resources; Director of Academic Information Resources; Director of Information Resource Management; Director of Information Resources; Director of Information Services; Director of Information Technology

Salary Range: $60,000 to $115,000 or more

Employment Prospects: Fair to good

Advancement Prospects: Fair

Prerequisites:

　Education or Training—Bachelor's degree in information management, computer science, or business administration required; master's degree in library or library and information science (M.L.S. or M.L.I.S.) or business administration (M.B.A.) preferred

　Experience—Minimum of five to eight years of experience in academic and/or administrative infor-

---

CAREER LADDER

Senior Management Positions
Information Resources Director
Information Scientist; Systems Administrator; Systems Technician

---

mation systems, with three or more years in a management/leadership capacity

　Special Skills and Personality Traits—Ability to organize, prioritize, and manage multiple projects; capacity for making decisions in difficult situations while building a consensus in support of institutional strategies and working within a team environment; excellent communication and interpersonal skills; in-depth understanding of key issues in development and use of administrative information systems; knowledge of information technology trends and applications

---

Position Description

Information Resources Directors serve as the strategic partner for senior management regarding information acquisition, storage, retrieval, and transmission. They often assume responsibility for all information and communications resources of an organization. They develop plans and systems to support its information and technology needs. They may work in companies, libraries or library systems, educational institutions, health systems, and government agencies.

They plan the investment in information resources (IR), operations, and support. They may manage a department of information resources and its human, technological, and financial assets. They may direct the planning, implementation, and maintenance of software programs and review software needs and purchases and may be responsible for the functionality of software used. They often serve as liaisons with outside software vendors. In addition, they may direct planning, implementation, and maintenance of the organization's

computer hardware. In so doing, they review computer hardware needs and purchases and make recommendations to senior management.

Information Resources Directors may be responsible for the development of specialty content databases (such as a membership database to facilitate mailings and registrations for a professional society). In a governmental agency, Information Resources Directors usually are tasked with infrastructure management, project and process management, records and information management, and software development and maintenance. In library systems they may be responsible for assessing and transforming existing technical service workflow processes, and developing and implementing projects and initiatives related to the integration of next-generation discovery, access, and resource management technologies into library operations. In university settings, they may work with senior librarians in planning, specifying, and recommending equipment and systems as well as in developing and implementing services within the library structure that support research and instruction. This work includes the acquisition and availability of library collections and computing hardware and software, developing training and support programs for academic uses of computers, and establishing policies to guide the use of academic information resources. They may also be involved in the university's publishing services.

Salaries

With their wide duties, Information Resources Directors tend to have high salaries. Depending on the type of organization for which they work and its geographic location, they may earn median annual salaries ranging from a low of $60,000 to a high of $115,000 or more.

Employment Prospects

Most Information Resources Directors advance from the ranks of information technicians, computer programmers, or systems technicians. They should have five to eight years work with information systems and technology in their fields of endeavor, such as in a research library or in a health services information organization. In addition to other information systems managers, Information Resources Directors can expect a 16 percent growth rate in employment possibilities through 2016, which is faster than the average for all occupations, according to the U.S. Department of Labor's *Occupational Outlook Handbook, 2007–08 Edition*.

Advancement Prospects

As the post of Information Resources Director is a senior one in most firms, career advancement often occurs by transferring to a larger organization with added responsibilities and a higher salary. Some may be able to advance into other senior management positions. In the library field, that might mean becoming chief librarian or dean of the library. In a business or governmental organization, that might mean becoming a vice president in charge of information resources or head of technical services of a government agency.

Education and Training

Most employers expect the applicants for this position to have a bachelor's degree in computer science or the equivalent with a concentration in programming as a minimum requirement. In addition, they usually prefer a master's degree in library science or library and information science (M.L.S. or M.L.I.S.). In some cases, a master's degree in business administration (M.B.A.) may be required.

As Information Resources Directors must keep up with changing technology, both hardware and software,

continuing education is a vital part of their work. Moreover, they must keep current with the evolving information and technological needs of their organization.

Experience, Skills, and Personality Traits

Information Resources Directors should have five to eight years of progressively responsible experience in management of information technology. They should have a record of successful implementation and management of emerging technologies. They must have a record of success in leading and managing organizational change, in meeting deadlines, and in taking initiative in the development and completion of concurrent projects.

Information Resources Directors must exhibit extensive knowledge of information technology trends and applications, scholarly communication patterns, best practices and current trends in digital resource management and operations, as well as traditional technical services. They should have a facility to lead and collaborate with colleagues and be experienced in team-oriented project management. They must have excellent analytical aptitude, interpersonal skills, written and oral communication talents, and be an articulate spokesperson/presenter. They should be able to make decisions in difficult situations while building a consensus in support of institutional strategies. For Information Resources Directors in the library field, they should have experience in collection building and management as well as knowledge of archives and records management theory and practice.

Unions and Associations

Professional associations of interest to Information Resources Directors include the American Society for Information Science and Technology (ASIS&T), the Council on Library and Information Resources (CLIR), and the Association of Professional Researchers for Advancement (APRA), the last of which is a major international organization for fund-raisers who specialize in research and information management.

Tips for Entry

1. As this post requires a strong computer programming background, familiarize yourself with many programming languages as well as systems designs, network topologies, and applicable hardware.
2. As business applications are key elements of this position, consider earning a master's degree in business administration (M.B.A.).
3. Consider working as an information technician in a research library or university to develop your knowledge of information technology.

INFORMATION SYSTEMS (IS) MANAGER

Duties: Manages all operations in an information systems department, planning, directing, and coordinating activities in such areas as electronic data processing, information systems, systems analysis, computer programming, voice and/or data communication systems, security, and disaster recovery

Alternate Title(s): Computer Systems Manager; Data Center Manager; Data Processing Manager; Director of Data Operations; Information Systems (IS) Director; Information Technology (IT) Manager; Information Technology Systems (ITS) Manager; Management Information Systems (MIS) Manager; Technical Services Manager

Salary Range: $45,000 to $100,000 or more

Employment Prospects: Good to excellent

Advancement Prospects: Good

Prerequisites:

   Education or Training—Bachelor's degree in computer science, business administration with emphasis on computer technology, or related technology area required; master's degree in library and information science (M.L.I.S.) or master's degree in business administration (M.B.A.) with information technology as a core component recommended

   Experience—Five to 10 years of experience in systems analysis, data administration, software engineering, network design, or computer programming, including supervisory responsibilities, usually

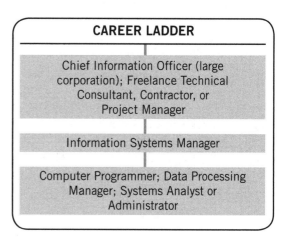

CAREER LADDER

Chief Information Officer (large corporation); Freelance Technical Consultant, Contractor, or Project Manager

↑

Information Systems Manager

↑

Computer Programmer; Data Processing Manager; Systems Analyst or Administrator

required; project management experience in a fast-paced environment

Special Skills and Personality Traits—Ability to multitask with several complex and concurrent projects and schedule and prioritize duties; excellent interpersonal and leadership abilities; familiarity with the relevant operating systems and commonly used software; good analytical and problem-solving skills; strong verbal and written communication talents; thorough working knowledge of programming and systems analysis

Special Requirements—Certification as a computer professional not required but recommended

Position Description

Organizations are constantly challenged to make greater use of new technologies to stay competitive. Important issues involving the use of online commerce (e-commerce) and information systems include when and how a company (or, for example, government agency or library) incorporates these new technologies. Information Systems Managers are essential in planning an organization's future, maintaining Internet support, and supervising data security operations. They are in charge of all planning and development phases of a firm's activities. They consult with executive managers about plans and goals for the future as well as needs

of the organization from an operational and strategic perspective while working with teams in the conceptual capacity and developmental processes of particular products or services.

The vast majority of information systems are developed for and used by people in functional areas (such as accounting, finance, human resources, manufacturing, and marketing). To build information systems that address the needs of organizations, Information Systems Managers (ISMs) must possess a solid mix of business and technical knowledge and be experienced with the technical aspects of computer hardware and networking systems. They need to understand organizational structures, objectives, operations (including processes and the flows of data between processes), and the financial implications related to these factors so they can design systems that support the needs of a wide variety of individuals within the corporation, government agency or department, laboratory, library, or other institution.

The duties of Information Systems Managers can be quite diverse. They include setting up networks (including the installation of lines), the installation and upgrading of hardware and software, administering servers, programming and systems design, development of computer networks, and the implementation of Internet and intranet sites. In some instances, they may be called on to do Web page design. They assign and review the work of systems and business analysts, computer programmers, support specialists, and other computer-related workers. They consult with users, management, vendors, and technicians to assess technology needs and system requirements. They develop information technology resources, providing for data security and control, strategic computing, and disaster recovery. They evaluate data processing proposals to assess project feasibility and requirements (including financial). They document and record information on work progress and employee performance for executive management.

While planning and synthesizing a global information systems vision for the future of their organization, Information Systems Managers leverage the existing systems to achieve and maintain cost efficiencies to help improve the quality of products and services companywide. They coach and direct staff in operational activities to ensure compliance with departmental goals, objectives of the organization, external regulations (if any), and budgetary requirements. They supervise the daily operations of an information systems department, analyzing workflow, establishing priorities, developing standards, and setting deadlines. They usually control the operational budget and expenditures of the department and of specific projects assigned to the department. They review and approve all systems charts and programs prior to implementation. They often are required to manage backup, security, and user help systems.

Salaries

The high salaries for this position reflect the complexity of the duties and the level of responsibility that an Information Systems Manager has. In their November 2007 salary survey report for this position, PayScale, Inc., found that median annual salaries for this position varied from $47,000 to $85,000 depending on years of experience, type of organization, and geographic location. In addition, Information Systems Managers, especially those with large organizations, often receive more employment-related benefits (such as expense accounts, stock option plans, and bonuses) than do nonmanagerial employees in their organizations.

Employment Prospects

There is a strong demand for candidates for the position of Information Systems Manager who have the right mix of technical and managerial skills. According to the U.S. Bureau of Labor Statistics, their employment is expected to grow 16 percent through 2016, which is faster than the average for all occupations. New applications of technology in the workplace will continue to drive demand for workers, fueling the need for more managers. To remain competitive, firms continue to install sophisticated computer information networks and set up more complex intranets, the Internet, and Web sites. Installing a successful computer network and keeping it running smoothly is essential to almost every organization. Thus, prospects for qualified IS Managers are excellent. Those with management proficiency and an understanding of business practices and principles along with specialized technical knowledge and strong communication skills will have the best odds in the workplace.

Many Information Systems Managers begin their careers as systems analysts, computer programmers, or in other computer-related posts. With training in business operations and management techniques, they may advance to mid-level managerial positions, such as data processing managers, and then move on to become Information Systems Managers for their organizations or transfer to other firms for such positions.

Advancement Prospects

Information Systems Managers in larger organizations who demonstrate outstanding ability and achieve successful results are in a good situation to advance into key executive job tracks (such as vice president positions) or shift to a larger organization to become director of information services in the role as chief information officer, supervising all information systems throughout the organization. Some organizations may offer structured career paths, with increasing management and technical responsibilities. The role of Information Systems Managers in smaller groups is likely to cover a wide range of responsibilities, and some may choose to enhance their programming and development skills, customizing their roles to satisfy their career interests while meeting the needs of the organization. They may stay with that organization or use their skills to move to larger operations.

Some Information Systems Managers may choose to transfer into technical consultancy, contracting, or project management, capitalizing on their specialist technical information. However, such a move to freelance status does require a substantial technical and business background.

Education and Training

A bachelor's degree in computer science, management information systems, or business administration with a heavy component of computer programming is usually required. Many organizations prefer to hire candidates with a master's degree in computer science, library and information science (M.L.I.S.), or business administration (M.B.A.) with technology as a core component (which differs from a traditional M.B.A. in that there is a heavy emphasis on information technology in addition to the standard business curriculum). Some educational institutions offer a master's degree in information systems management (M.I.S.M.) that integrates information technology practices with applied business methods. As with most information technology careers, Information Systems Managers must keep current with all new advancements in technology, usually by taking additional courses, especially in the market-leading technologies such as Oracle (http://www.oracle.com) and Microsoft (http://www.microscoft.com) and the operating systems on which they function.

Special Requirements

Certification is not usually a requirement for Information Systems Managers. However, a growing number of organizations are recommending that their computer-related employees become certified. There are many certifications available to network and computer systems administrators, usually offered through community colleges or adult education training programs as well as a variety of vendors and product makers.

For Information Systems Managers who have information security management responsibilities, there is a specific certification, the Certified Information Security Manager (CISM), available from the Cisco Company (http://www.isaca.org/Template.cfm?Section=CISM_Certification). The certification is for individuals who manage, design, oversee, and/or assess an organization's information security.

Experience, Skills, and Personality Traits

Information Systems Managers need to be experienced with the technical aspects of computer hardware and software and networking systems. Besides their thorough working knowledge of programming and systems analysis, they must have general management ability as well as specific comprehension of their organizations' computer systems. Their daily work usually involves managing a team of information technology workers, so leadership and management skills are a key qualification. They usually interact regularly with staff, other units, upper management, and scientists, so that proficiency in oral and written communication is vital. In addition, they need strong budgeting skills and the ability to communicate with contractors, suppliers, and financial groups, as they are involved in making decisions concerning equipment purchases.

Information Systems Managers must be experienced in data analysis, data modeling, and needs assessment techniques as well as designing and implementing processes for capturing and using information. Familiarity with developing detailed technical specification documents for project managers and departmental teams is a valued trait. Excellent time management and strong problem solving skills are required, as is the ability to multitask with several complex and concurrent projects.

Generally, candidates seeking to become Information Systems Managers should have backgrounds of five to 10 years in systems analysis, data administration, software engineering, network design, and computer programming, including increasing supervisory responsibilities and some project management experience. Employers tend to look favorably on potential Information Systems Managers with backgrounds in both software and other specific technology and business. The importance of their decisions that affect the business has only been augmented by the growth in electronic commerce (e-commerce). In general, Information Systems Managers exercise an important role in representing an organization when interacting with outside individuals.

Unions and Associations

Professional groups of particular interest to Information Systems Managers include the American Business Association (ABA), the American Society for Information Science and Technology (ASIS&T), the Association for Computing Machinery (ACM), the Association for Information Systems (AIS), the Computing Technology Industry Association (CTIA), the Information Technology Association of America (ITAA), and the Institute of Electrical and Electronic Engineers (IEEE) Computer Society.

Tips for Entry

1. Helpful elective courses in high school that will prepare you for both your college education and for your occupation as an information systems specialist include computer applications, computer programming, computer science, electronics, and network technology. Consult your school counselor to see if work-based learning opportunities are available in your school and community.

2. Consider participating in a computer-based internship while in college. An internship is usually part of a four-year degree program, and it offers you a chance to apply what you have learned in the classroom to a work situation. In addition, it allows you to build skills and make contacts with people in the field.

3. Your college placement office can help you find a job in an information technology company that has an executive training program. There are employment agencies that specialize in placing information professionals that can offer you job leads. In addition, you can contact computer manufacturers and organizations with large computer centers, such as insurance companies, utilities, universities, and colleges. If you are interested in a government job, you should apply to take the necessary civil service examination.

KNOWLEDGE ENGINEER

CAREER PROFILE

Duties: Receiving information from domain experts, interpret the information and relay it to computer programmers, who code the data into systems databases to be accessed by end users

Alternate Title(s): Knowledge Manager; Artificial Intelligence Programmer; Expert Systems Programmer; Knowledge/Content Manager; Knowledge Management Specialist; Knowledge Strategy Analyst; Knowledge Systems Analyst

Salary Range: From $47,000 for trainees, to $85,000 or more for experienced programmers, to $105,000 or more for senior top experts

Employment Prospects: Fair

Advancement Prospects: Fair

Prerequisites:

Education or Training—Bachelor's degree in computer science, information management, library and information science, or management information systems required; master's degree (preferably in computer science) often recommended; for some scientific applications, a Ph.D. in a relevant scientific field may be demanded

Experience—Four to seven years of experience working in an information technology consulting, systems implementation, and information-sharing environment or in the knowledge management/content management fields

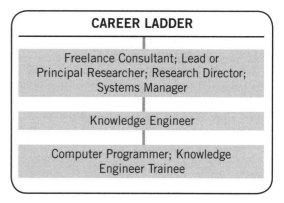

CAREER LADDER

Freelance Consultant; Lead or Principal Researcher; Research Director; Systems Manager

Knowledge Engineer

Computer Programmer; Knowledge Engineer Trainee

Special Skills and Personality Traits—Ability to work independently and as part of a team; capacity for innovative, self-motivated problem solving and critical thinking; excellent oral and written communication skills, including the ability to give formal presentations to various audiences; strong leadership abilities and proven managerial and supervisory skills; superior interpersonal talents and professional demeanor; willingness and ability to work closely with clients

Special Requirements—Certification as a professional computer programmer may be necessary; government jobs frequently require security clearance

Position Description

Today most organizations rely on computer and information technology to conduct business and operate more efficiently. The rapid spread of technology across all industries has generated a need for highly trained technicians to help organizations incorporate new technologies. The tasks performed by technical individuals known as computer systems analysts (which include information analysts) evolved rapidly, reflecting new areas of specialization or changes in technology as well as the preferences and practices of employers.

Computer systems analysts solve computer problems and apply computer technology to meet the individual needs of organizations. Systems analysts may plan and develop new computer systems or devise ways to apply existing systems' resources to additional opera-

tions. Most systems analysts work with specific types of systems (such as accounting, business, or scientific and engineering systems) that vary with the type of organization. Some systems analysts are known as systems developers or systems architects.

Knowledge Engineers are computer systems experts or are trained in the field of expert systems. They receive information from experts in a particular field of thought, interpret the data, and relay it to programmers who code the information into a systems database that can be accessed by end users. As such, Knowledge Engineers construct a meaningful, useful, and simplistic knowledge-based system (the expert system) whereby the received knowledge and information is structured according to how humans reason and use logic. This process acknowledges that there are various types of knowledge and that different approaches and techniques should be used for the particular knowledge required. In addition, it recognizes that there are different types of experts and expertise, so the methods of structuring information and knowledge received from them should be chosen appropriately. Further, Knowledge Engineers appreciate that there are assorted ways of representing knowledge (which can aid in the task of acquiring, validating, and reusing knowledge) and that there are various ways of using knowledge (so that the acquisition process of knowledge from experts can be guided by the aims of the end user, or a goal-oriented approach).

Often, Knowledge Engineers are employed to break down the data received from the subject experts into more simplistic terms (which cannot be easily communicated to end users by the highly technical subject expert) to aid in the process of constructing a computer system. In some instances, Knowledge Engineers need to "tease apart" highly complicated expert knowledge because the expert is too familiar with the area of expertise to break the knowledge down into its logical components. Thus, Knowledge Engineers interpret and organize internal information that will be used to make decisions on the design and creation of a computer system.

Knowledge engineering is a relatively new profession, and the purpose of the job of a Knowledge Engineer is to work with clients who want expert computer systems created for them or their businesses. The Knowledge Engineer collects the information that a client wants in the system and interprets it for a computer programmer, who creates the program to organize, process, evaluate, and utilize the information for end use.

The most common form of expert systems is a program made up of a set of rules that analyze data (supplied by the use of the system or researched by the Knowledge Engineer) about a specific class of problems as well as provide mathematical analysis of the problem(s) and, depending on their design, recommend a course of user action. Commonly, expert systems are designed and created to facilitate tasks in such fields as accounting, financial services, human resources, medicine, process control, and production.

Salaries

Salaries for Knowledge Engineers depend considerably on the project and the employer. Those working within academic institutions may earn salaries similar to those paid other scientists or professors. Those employed on corporation projects are likely to be paid more, but this is very dependent on the financial viability of the project. Those working for govern-ment projects are subject to the terms and processes of government-funded projects.

Generally, trainees with less than one year of experience may expect annual salaries around $47,000. Experienced Knowledge Engineers with more than 20 years in the field may anticipate yearly incomes of $85,000 or more, and senior top experts may receive $100,000 or more per year.

Employment Prospects

While employment of computer systems analysts and computer software engineers is expected to grow much faster than the average for all occupations through 2014, according to the U.S. Department of Labor's Bureau of Labor Statistics, the position of Knowledge Engineer is extremely specialized and such a new profession that job openings are not yet common. Nonetheless, the growing demand for networking to facilitate the sharing of data from one computer system to another, the expansion of client-server environments, and the need to find computer specialists who can use their knowledge and skills in a problem-solving capacity in developing usable computer systems of information will be major factors in the rising demand for computer systems analysts in general and for Knowledge Engineers to aid in the process.

Advancement Prospects

Experienced and successful Knowledge Engineers may find career progression by becoming senior research project leaders in large data processing departments of major corporations or governmental agencies. Those who display leadership abilities may be able to advance to general managers of systems analysis or data processing departments. Knowledge Engineers with several years of seasoning may turn freelance and open their own consulting firms.

Education and Training

A bachelor's degree in computer science, information management, library and information science, or management information systems is a basic necessity for the position of Knowledge Engineer. In addition, a master's degree (usually in computer science or an equivalent field) is recommended. Experienced Knowledge Engineers working on scientific projects may be required to have a Ph.D. in the relevant scientific field.

Special Requirements

While not often demanded, certification as a professional computer programmer provides an employer with an assurance of expertise on the part of the applicant. Knowledge Engineers who seek employment with government agencies usually must obtain security clearances.

Experience, Skills, and Personality Traits

There is a wide range of skills that Knowledge Engineers must have. Many of these proficiencies are needed to ensure that Knowledge Engineers will be able to create the documentation required, such as analyses, overviews, feedback reports, and knowledge database frequently asked questions (FAQs). They must have some background working with established information technology operations methodologies for systems management. Knowledge Engineers also need to be educated in several different computer languages and applications so they can create expert systems with great ease and with minimum potential errors. Specifically,

- They need to be able to create such documentation as procedure-oriented sheets and network designs. This means that they need to have excellent written and verbal communication abilities. They also need to be able to select the most pertinent pieces of information from all the data they receive from the experts. In addition, they must be able to give formal presentations to widely different audiences.
- They need to be able to analyze and apply problem-solving techniques so they can document trouble-shooting processes to be used in testing the resultant computer systems. While they are required to carry out data collection and data entry, they must use validation and verification techniques to ensure that the data they collect and then enter into their knowledge-based systems fall within the accepted boundaries of the application.
- They will be working under pressure and must meet tight deadlines. They need to be able to manage and work independently, efficiently, and quickly on multiple tasks of various sizes and topics.
- They should be familiar with Web-based knowledge management systems and search engine technologies (such as Microsoft's SharePoint Portal Server).
- They must be well versed in assorted types of programming languages, such as standard generalized markup language (SGML), XML, and HTML. Addi-

tionally, they should have a general knowledge of such programs as JavaScript and UNIX.

- They need to be familiar with such software applications as Microsoft Office, Microsoft FrontPage, Microsoft Visio, Adobe Acrobat, and other graphics software applications.
- They need to have knowledge of requirements and systems implementation tools, information-sharing and file-sharing applications, online collaboration tools, and data mining tools.

Above all, Knowledge Engineers should be innovative, detail-oriented, self-motivated, problem-solving, and critical-thinking individuals with strong organizational talents. They should have a high energy level to allow them to react to situations quickly and decisively and not be afraid to take positions and make decisions.

Unions and Associations

Relevant professional groups for Knowledge Engineers include the American Society for Information Science and Technology (ASIS&T), the Association for Computing Machinery (ACM), the Computing Technology Industry Association (CTIA), the Institute of Electronics and Electrical Engineers (IEEE) Computer Society, and the National Workforce Center for Emerging Technologies (NWCET).

Tips for Entry

1. As a means of gaining a broad background in the study of intelligence and human knowledge processes, take courses in fields such as anthropology, linguistics, philosophy, and psychology (cognition).
2. Mathematics and logic have as important a part to play in the development of knowledge-based systems as does computer science, so include a solid background in both areas in your educational curriculum.
3. Look for internships or co-op programs with computer service bureaus offered through your school to obtain practical experience in the use of specific computer languages and processes and to develop contacts with professionals in the field.

MANAGEMENT INFORMATION SYSTEMS (MIS) DIRECTOR

Position Description

Today, business organizations, institutions, and government departments realize their need for an effective management information systems for their managers to use for all phases of management, including planning, organizing, directing, and controlling. Management information systems (MIS) allow managers to make decisions for the successful operation of their businesses and organizations. Management information systems consist of computer resources, people, and procedures employed in the modern business and organization enterprises. MIS refers to the organization (and people) that develops and maintains most or all of the computer systems in the enterprise so that managers can make decisions. The goal of an MIS organization is to deliver information systems to the various levels of corporate, institutional, or governmental managers. MIS professionals create and support the computer system and its components throughout the organization, from the largest mainframe to desktop and portable PCs.

Management information systems can be used in a variety of functional ways to support managers. Major types of management information systems include those for accounting management, financial information management, manufacturing operations, marketing management (including product development, distribution, promotion, and sales forecasting), and human resources (including workforce analysis and planning, hiring, training, and job assignments). Management information systems are distinct from other information systems in that they analyze other information systems used in the operational activities of the organization, and they concentrate primarily on the integration of computer systems to fit the aims of the organization.

Management Information Systems (MIS) Directors control the information systems and computer resources for their organizations. They usually work under the chief information officer and plan and direct the work of subordinate information technology employees. They oversee a variety of user services, such as an organization's help desk, which employees can contact with questions or problems. In addition, MIS Directors typically are responsible for making hardware and software upgrade recommendations based on their technical background and their experience with their organizations' technological needs. Helping to ensure the availability, continuity, and security of data and information technology services for their organizations is their primary goal.

The specific responsibilities of Management Information Systems (MIS) Directors include establishing standards for computer products to make certain there is compatibility throughout their organizations' computer systems. They coordinate the acquisition, installation, and testing of hardware and software as required or contracted and make sure there is compliance with all software licenses and all applicable copyright laws. They administer the organizations' network databases and files to guarantee that adequate security and data integrity are maintained. They implement and control necessary security backup procedures. They evaluate, negotiate, and monitor purchases and service agreements to maximize the cost-effectiveness of vendor contracts according to established standards. They coordinate and provide computer software and hardware training, documentation, and reference materials to personnel within the organization who are involved with the MIS system in any form. They troubleshoot and maintain all data processing and information systems, software, hardware, and networks and perform systems analysis in identifying further data processing needs and developing situations. They design customized programs to meet these needs and plan and implement the budget for the management and information system as well as the computer systems.

Management Information Systems (MIS) Directors are found in charge of medical records and paperless systems, Web site design and development, consulting, security risk assessment processes, Internet marketing, financial and business analysis, customer relationship management consulting, e-commerce enterprises, legal forensics enterprise resource planning, and supply chain management. They are uniquely qualified in that they have both a widespread technology-oriented background but also a solid grounding in basic business concepts.

Salaries

Reflecting the degree of responsibility that this position holds, Management Information Systems (MIS) Directors are compensated well. In their November 2007 salary survey report on directors of information systems, PayScale, Inc., found that median annual salaries for this position ranged from $67,667 to $112,558, depending on the type of organization for which they worked, and/or the geographic location of the organization.

Employment Prospects

While the necessity of an effective management information system is of primary concern for present-day organizations, there are relatively few openings for this top management post at any given time. Individuals with solid experience as information technology managers and records of success at their technical work can be promoted from within the ranks of the organization, but there is often a nationwide search for candidates when such positions open up. As a result, there is strong competition for such job openings. Those who are promoted from within the ranks must have demonstrated that they can cross over from being technicians to becoming managers. Their jobs change from being technicians to being systems managers who supervise other people's technical work.

Advancement Prospects

The potential for advancement for Management Information Systems (MIS) Directors is narrow in that this is a top information systems position in most organizations. Individuals with strong business and management skills may be able to move on to the main executive advancement track of their organizations (into posts such as vice presidents) or transfer to larger organizations that have chief information officer (CIO) positions available.

Education and Training

Most MIS Directors have solid technology and business backgrounds, usually graduate degrees in information systems or information management, and often master's degrees in business administration (M.B.A.) as well. MIS Directors who work in academic institutions and government departments or agencies may have computer science backgrounds instead. Some MIS Directors have specific education and training in management information systems and in the design and management of information technology, as some educational institutions are now offering curricula in this area. Many MIS Directors specialize in specific areas of information science, such as scientific or engineering research, or in particular disciplines, such as business, education, finance, government, library science, or medicine.

Special Requirements

Certification as a computer or information science professional is highly recommended. Industry certification for the major computer networks and computer operating systems is available from both educational institutions and from specific computer manufacturers.

Experience, Skills, and Personality Traits

As MIS Directors and managers are the communication bridges between information technology (IT) and the business community, they need to understand business processes in order to analyze how to improve the business process using IT. MIS Directors must be able to demonstrate strong application development implementation and support know-how. They should have three to five years of management experience, particularly in the areas of software testing, systems development and analysis, and systems operations. Their strong technical backgrounds should include a deep understanding of relational databases, SQL (structured query language), data warehousing, and technical application infrastructure. They must have excellent communication skills (both verbal and written) and good interpersonal abilities, as they will have to relate to colleagues and carry out human resources related activities such as interviewing job applicants and completing performance evaluations.

They need to be able to demonstrate their expertise in troubleshooting, maintaining, and repairing computers, hardware, and networking equipment as well as evaluating software capabilities. They should have excellent problem-solving, decision-making, and project planning and management skills.

As top management, they must have outstanding talents in leadership and people management. Their business and administrative backgrounds must include strong budget and finance experience.

Unions and Associations

At this level of management, MIS Directors are likely to belong to management and executive organizations as well as technical professional associations. Some of these may include the American Society for Information Science and Technology (ASIS&T), the Association for Computing Machinery (ACM), the Association for Information Systems (AIS), the Association for Information Technology Professionals (AITP), the Computing Research Association (CRA), the Institute for Operations Research and Management Sciences (INFORMS), the Institute for the Management of Information Systems (IMIS), the Institute of Operations Management (IOM), and the Society for Information Management (SIM).

Tips for Entry

1. While in college, volunteer to work in your school's computing center, even to the extent of getting a work-study position or internship through which you can learn about operations and technical support procedures.

2. Needless to say, you will need extensive information systems and management experience before you can apply for the position of MIS Director. Try always to find positions that have the potential of growing management responsibilities while always keeping up to date on technical issues.

3. Regardless of what specific advantages you have established for yourself, when you apply for the position of MIS Director, you will be competing with top candidates from all over the country (or possibly the world). Skills and experience that closely match the priorities of your prospective employer may make the difference. Do research to help you identify and highlight how your background matches with the needs and priorities of the organization you are hoping to join.

NETWORK ADMINISTRATOR

Duties: Manage the operation and planning of a local area network (LAN) or wide area network (WAN); select an appropriate network operating system and accompanying software tools; deal with the connection between networks and the Internet; establish procedures for support staff and users; organize technical support and training for network features (such as data backup and security protections, performance monitoring, and modem connections); supervise technicians and programmers

Alternate Title(s): Information Technology (IT) Manager; LAN/WAN Manager (or Administrator); Network Engineer; Networking Systems and Distributed Systems Engineer; Network Manager; Network Systems Administrator

Salary Range: $40,000 to $60,000 for small local area networks; $65,000 to $85,000 or more for large or wide area networks

Employment Prospects: Good

Advancement Prospects: Fair to good

Prerequisites:

   Education or Training—Bachelor's degree in computer science, information science, or information systems management, with a business and communication concentration required; master's degree in

CAREER LADDER

Information Systems Director

Network Administrator

Network Analyst; Network Control Operator; Applications Programmer

computer science or information science recommended

   Experience—Three to six years of experience helping run information systems and network operations, with evidence of increasing responsibilities

   Special Skills and Personality Traits—Ability to manage multiple projects, activities, and tasks simultaneously and assume accountability; excellent management, problem-solving, troubleshooting, and documentation skills; good programming and systems analysis abilities; highly developed verbal and written communication proficiency; self-starter and service-oriented attitude

   Special Requirements—Industry certifications (such as Certified Network Associate [CNA]) usually required

Position Description

In most modern office environments, individual computers, each containing its own disk drive and processor, are set up to communicate with one another by way of a local area network (LAN), which is a computer network that covers a small geographical area (usually a single building or a group of buildings). In addition, the LAN may also connect the network of computers with a series of printers, a mainframe computer or file server with even greater processing power and memory storage, and other devices that can transmit messages from the network over telephone lines to another location. As the name suggests, a LAN is local, meaning that it is a proprietary system limited to a finite number of users. It also is a network system that affords users both functional and communicative diversity through a distribution of resources. A LAN permits employees, isolated in separate offices,

to operate off the same system as if they were all sitting around a single computer.

One of the great attributes of LANs is that they can be installed simply, upgraded or expanded with little difficulty, and moved or rearranged without disruption. They are useful because they can transmit data quickly. Perhaps more important, any individual familiar with the use of a personal computer can be trained quickly to communicate or perform work over a LAN. LANs function because their transmission capacity is greater than any single terminal in the system. As a result, each station terminal can be offered a certain amount of time on the LAN, like a timesharing arrangement.

The connection of two or more LANs over any distance (such as throughout a state, a country, or the world) using telecommunications (telephone lines or radio waves) for the purpose of simultaneously sharing files and organizational information is called a wide area network (WAN). WANs necessitate the use of special software programs in the operating system to enable the telecommunications links that connect LANs and other types of networks together, so that users and computers in one location can communicate effectively with users and computers in other locations. Many WANs are built for one particular organization and are private. Others, built by Internet service providers, enable connections from an organization's LAN to the Internet.

Network Administrators are the individuals who manage LANs within an organization (as well as any WAN used by the organization or institution), maintaining the hardware and software that make up the network. They function as company managers, systems administrators, and technical problem solvers. Their primary duties include network security, the installation of new applications, the distributing of software upgrades, the monitoring of daily activity on the network, the enforcement of licensing agreements, the development of storage management programs, and the provision of routine backups to the data and information in the system.

They participate in the configuration of networks, research technical manuals and brochures, and recommend purchases of application servers, peripherals (such as computer terminals), and software. They test and evaluate hardware and software to determine efficiency, reliability, and compatibility with the system and upgrade components when necessary. As part of their administrative duties, they direct the work of network technicians and computer support staff.

Network Administrators develop plans to safeguard computer files against accidental or unauthorized modification, destruction, or disclosure and to meet emergency data processing needs. They coordinate the implementation of computer system plans with organization personnel and outside vendors. They test systems to ensure the correct functioning of data processing activities and all security measures, modifying computer security files to incorporate new software, correct errors, and change individual access status. They confer with organizations' personnel to discuss issues such as computer data access needs, security violations, and programming changes. They monitor the use of data files and regulate access to safeguard information in the computer files. They write reports to document computer security and emergency measures policies, procedures, and test results. They help prepare budget requests and make reports to upper management.

They may install and maintain Web servers, providing networking assistance to users of the system, including help with network connections and pass-words. They assist with linking Web servers to database systems, manage remote client dial-in access, and use various Web-based scripting languages to create online forms that link users to databases. They manage all upgrades and backups and may manage the setup and maintenance of intranets related to system administration functions. Above all, they establish and follow procedures to keep the computing and network systems running in excellent condition.

Salaries

Network Administrators of small LANs, such as those that serve a single company office or work group, usually receive the lowest annual salaries, ranging from $40,000 to around $60,000. Administrators of large LANs typically get intermediate salaries ranging from $55,000 to $65,000 per year, and the highest annual salaries ($70,000 to $80,000 or more) go to administrators of WANs, such as those run by corporations with nationwide and/or international branches and some state and federal government agencies.

Employment Prospects

Most desktop computers (and, in some cases, personal notebook computers) used in business (even small operations), organizations, and governmental departments and agencies are part of a LAN, or internal computer network system, known as an intranet. With the extensive use of the ever-expanding Internet, electronic mail (and such present-day extensions as blogs and Facebook sites) as instant communicators, and networked databases for ease of information search, the need and demand for experienced Network Administrators has increased greatly, especially for administrators capable of managing larger and more complex networks. According to the U.S. Department of Labor's Bureau of Labor Statistics, it is estimated that the employment of information systems managers is expected to grow as much as 16 percent by 2016, which is faster than the average for all occupations. Technicians who work on network systems, such as network analysts and network control operators, may find career promotion by advancing into the position of Network Administrators if they have demonstrated not just their technical skills but also their leadership and management abilities.

Advancement Prospects

Career progressions open to Network Administrators are usually into higher management levels (such as information systems director) or to the supervision of larger or more complex networks. In either case, competition for such posts tends to be high, particularly with each step of advancement.

Education and Training

While some seasoned computer programmers may find themselves elevated to Network Administrators on the strength of their computer skills and accomplishments, most corporations, organizations, and governmental bodies seek candidates who have solid technical educational backgrounds (four-year and, more likely, graduate degrees in computer science, information science, or information management systems, with courses in network design and engineering). In addition, applicants need to have the requisite technical skills and knowledge about electric circuit boards, servers, processors, chips, databases, computer systems, computer hardware and software, and applications and programming. Some management and business administration courses should prove helpful in their duties as administrators.

Special Requirements

Most employers require Network Administrators to have the appropriate certification as professionals. Many certification programs are available from Learning Tree International (http://www.learningtree.com), including Certified Local Area Network Professional, Certified Wide Area Network Professional, and Certified Internet-working Professional. Other certification programs include those from Novell (Certified Novell Engineer, or CNE, and Master Certified Novell Engineer, or MCNE) (http://www.novell.com/training), from Microsoft (Microsoft Certified Systems Engineer) (http://www.microsoft.com/learning/mcp/mcse), and various Cisco network certifications (http://www.cisco.com/web/learning/le3/le2/le0/l9/learning_certification_type-home.html).

Experience, Skills, and Personality Traits

Network Administrators usually have from three to six or more years of experience as information technology (IT) professionals, typically working as network technicians or assistants. Basic requirements for this position include basic programming (or script writing) skills and working knowledge of network utilities and configuration menus (including a thorough understanding of basic network architecture and Internet protocols along with the developing applications based on these protocols). They should have solid know-how in configuring, deploying, and maintaining a wide array of networking devices (such load balancers, routers, switching, firewalls) and background working with server farms.

They should be able to demonstrate their knowledge of Microsoft Windows servers and desktop products and their ability to support networked printers. They should have prior experience in technical analysis, systems programming, and computer service and repair.

Network Administrators must have strong personal organization and time management skills as well as great verbal and written communication and documentation abilities. They should be able to manage multiple projects and tasks simultaneously. They need good interpersonal talents, as they will have to interface effectively with computer vendors and computer technicians as well as upper management personnel. They must have excellent troubleshooting capabilities and strong project management skills with a well-honed ability to prioritize. In addition, they should be able to learn new technology with minimal or no formal training.

Unions and Associations

Many Network Administrators belong to the Association for Computing Machinery (ACM), the Institute of Electrical and Electronics Engineers (IEEE) Computer Society, and the System Administrators Guild (SAGE) as a matter of course and join special interest groups devoted to networking issues important to them, such as security, user training, and Internet/Network interface. Membership in professional groups that attract information systems management professionals, such as the American Society of Information Science and Technology (ASIS&T), may also be beneficial.

Tips for Entry

1. Be sure that your educational program includes courses in all of the following areas: computer science and computer operations (including network architecture, programming, and systems analysis), management (including both budgeting and business administration), and communications (including both employee relations and technical writing). You may be able to concentrate on networking and Internet development in your computer course structure.

2. Consider internship possibilities whereby you can work on the network at your school or at a local business.

3. It is very important that you earn the most appropriate certification for the type of network systems on which you are looking to work. Check with the Association for Computing Machinery (ACM) (http://www.acm.org), which has student chapters at some colleges and universities.

RECORDS MANAGER

Duties: Responsible for the effective and appropriate management and maintenance of information produced in and received by organizations, irrespective of the media in which the data exist

Alternate Title(s): Archivist; Files Supervisor; Records Management Analyst; Records Management Specialist; Records Specialist; Records-Section Supervisor

Salary Range: $35,000 to $85,000 or more

Employment Prospects: Fair to good

Advancement Prospects: Fair

Prerequisites:

Education or Training—Bachelor's degree in computer science or business with strong computer component desirable; master's degree in library and information science from a program accredited by the American Library Association (ALA) recommended

Experience—Three to five years of experience in records management; information technology background as it relates to records management, including a working understanding of databases, e-mail systems, and network file servers, recommended

CAREER LADDER

Independent Records Management Consultant; Information Systems Manager

Records Manager

Assistant Records Manager; Information Technician

Special Skills and Personality Traits—Ability to work both independently and as part of a team; effective written, oral, and consensus-building communication skills; excellent analytical and organizational abilities; good interpersonal talents; strong service orientation and excellent presentation and customer service skills

Special Requirements—Certification as a Records Manager required

Position Description

Records management (RM) is the practice of identifying, classifying, archiving, preserving, and/or destroying records. The International Standards Organization (ISO) standard (15489:2001) defines it as "The field of management responsible for the efficient and systematic control of the creation, receipt, maintenance, use and disposition of records, including the processes for capturing and maintaining evidence of and information about business activities and transactions in the form of records." The standard goes on to identify records as "information created, received, and maintained as evidence and information by an organization or person, in pursuance of legal obligations or in the transaction of business." The International Council on Archives (ICA) Committee on Electronic Records terms a record as "a recorded information produced or received in the initiation, conduct or completion of an institutional or individual activity and that comprises content, context and structure sufficient to provide evidence of the activity." While the description of a record is usually related to a document, a record can

be either a tangible object or digital information that has value to an organization. For example, birth certificates, medical X-rays, office documents, databases, application data, and e-mail are all examples of records.

Records management involves

- creating, approving, and enforcing records policies, including a classification system (encompassing categorization and indexing) and a records retention policy
- developing a records storage plan, which includes the short- and long-term storing of physical records and of digital information in such a way that they are both sufficiently accessible and are safeguarded against environmental damage (physical records) or unwarranted intrusion (digital records)
- identifying existing and newly created records, classifying them and then sorting them according to standard operating procedures
- coordinating the access and circulation of records within and outside the organization

- executing a retention policy to archive and/or destroy records according to operational needs, operating procedures, statutes, regulations, and organizational policies

Records Managers are the individuals responsible for the development, implementation, and administration of directives and standard operating procedures for the creation, retrieval, protection, preservation, and destruction of the records (both hard copy and electronic) for their organizations. They facilitate the development of filing systems and retention and disposal schedules, maintaining these to meet administrative, legal, and financial requirements. They analyze any records management problems and design strategies and procedures to meet ongoing records management needs of their organizations.

They appraise existing records retention programs and schedules and, upon researching regulatory, statutory, and industry requirements, recommend modifications and revisions. They arrange for off-site storage of the organizations' records (hard copy and data backup files for protection) when necessary and manage all associated vendor relationships. They arrange for the secure destruction of records and generally are responsible for overseeing the use of automated information systems for search and retrieval, data entry, and reporting on records archives. They provide semimonthly orientation and training sessions on records retention and other records management topics (such as classification, indexing, and abstracting of records for ease of retrieval) for staff.

Recent dramatic headlines have made it quite apparent that records management (or the lack thereof) is an essential activity to ascertain and confirm the credibility of many business transactions and government activities. The proliferation of electronic documents (especially e-mails) and the potential litigation exposure that they cause are becoming the bane of legal advisers and Record Managers in many corporations and government agencies. Additionally, there are other types of records than e-mail (such as paper, electronic image files, video tapes, and voice recordings) that have the potential to become evidence in litigation. Making sure that all the relevant data are accessible in a timely fashion—should an organization need to defend itself in a lawsuit—is another part of the job of Records Managers.

Records Managers are present in virtually every type of organization. For example, in the health care industry, health information management involves not only maintaining patient files but also coding the

files to reflect the diagnoses and treatments of the conditions suffered by patients. Records Managers in the pharmaceutical industry are responsible for maintaining laboratory research information, clinical trials data, and manufacturing documentation. Records Managers in law firms often have the responsibility for managing any conflicts over agreement with the firm's records management policy as well as maintaining client material files. In the various energy industries, Records Managers specialize in compliance with government regulations regarding the production of oil, gas, and electrical power and the handling of nuclear materials. The demands of legislation, such as the Data Protection Act, have also broadened the environment in which records and information professionals work.

Salaries

According to a salary survey in December 2007 conducted by Salary.com., the median expected annual salary for a typical Records Manager in the United States is $77,141. Median yearly salaries in this survey ranged from $57,359 to $101,934. In their November 2007 salary survey, PayScale, Inc., found that the median annual income for Records Managers ranged from $37,983 to $78,723, depending on the type and the geographic location of the organization and the extent of the responsibilities of the individual position.

Employment Prospects

With the increase in compliance regulations and statutes, many companies have realized the necessity for effective records management. While government, legal, health care, and library organizations have a strong historical records management discipline, general record keeping of corporate data has a history of being poorly standardized and implemented. Statutes such as the U.S. Sarbanes-Oxley Act have created new concerns among corporate "compliance officers," so that more standardization of records management practices within organizations has become a major requirement. In addition, the role of the Records Manager in the protection of an organization's records has gained attention on the part of information technology managers and other executives. Furthermore, the need to ensure that certain information about individuals is not retained has brought greater focus on records retention schedules and records destruction timetables.

For all these reasons, there is a rising call for records management professionals due to the increased recognition within most business sectors of the value and need of knowledge and information management. Presently, employment opportunities are fair and should improve over the next several years with the increased pressure to comply with regulations and the need to maintain and access an organization's information. Increasingly, Records Managers are employed both to establish a new records management system and to oversee it in the long term.

Advancement Prospects

As records management is a relatively new profession so far as most businesses are concerned, there is no clearly defined career path, so career advancement will depend much upon the inclinations of each Records Manager. Qualified individuals seeking higher levels of management within an organization may aim at information management posts, such as that of information systems (IS) manager. Others may be more attracted to the range of freelance and consultancy work (though these types of positions are usually open only to senior professionals with years of seasoning). There are considerable opportunities for consultancy work, occasionally involving overseas travel, as employers identify the need for expertise they lack in-house.

Education and Training

A bachelor's degree in computer science or business administration is a basic requirement for this position. In addition, a master's degree in library and information science from an educational program accredited by the American Library Association (ALA) with course instruction in records management is becoming desirable. Furthermore, most employers are looking for individuals who have had two to five years of records management experience, with some of that time spent in a supervisory role. As information management procedures and legislation relating to them change fast, it is important for Records Managers to update their professional skills and knowledge through additional education and membership in associations devoted to the profession.

Special Requirements

Certification as a certified records manager (CRM) is an absolute requirement for this position. Certifications are available from the Institute of Certified Records Manager (ICRM) (http://www.icrm.org), an international certifying organization of and for professional records and information managers. Its primary objective is to develop and administer the program for professional certification of records managers, including certification examinations and certification maintenance program.

Experience, Skills, and Personality Traits

Records management, being a complex process, involves many years of education and practice for full mastery. A thorough knowledge of records management and archival management principles and methodologies is critical as is an awareness of current trends in electronic records management. An information technology (IT) background as it relates to records management, including a working understanding of databases, e-mail systems, and network file servers, is valuable, as is a comprehension of legal requirements related to records management. Familiarity with the Freedom of Information Act and Data Protection Act is of additional value.

Records Managers must have effective written, oral, and consensus-building communication skills. They should have a strong service orientation and be able to function within a team environment. They should have excellent analytical, organizational, and leadership abilities. They need excellent interpersonal skills, as they have to work tactfully and effectively with all levels of personnel.

Unions and Associations

The primary professional group for Records Managers is the Association of Records Managers and Administrators International (ARMA International), whose membership includes Records Managers, archivists, corporate librarians, imaging specialists, legal professionals, IT managers, consultants, and educators. Additional professional associations of interest include the American Society of Information Science and Technology (ASIS&T), the Association for Information and Image Management (AIIM), the Enterprise Content Management Association (ECM), and Professional Records and Information Services Management (PRISM).

Tips for Entry

1. During college, look for a work-study position or internship with a library system or an information services consulting firm to gain experience with at least one automated information system.
2. In addition, look for volunteer work in your educational institution's computer lab or the school library where you can become familiar with data storage, retrieval, and automated filing systems.
3. Information about obtaining a job as a records management technician with the federal government is available from the Office of Personnel Management, available on the Internet at http://www.usajobs.opm.gov.

SYSTEMS ADMINISTRATOR

Duties: Manage the operation of an organization's multiuser computer system or network so that it runs smoothly and reliably and meets users' needs; responsible for application installations and upgrades of both software and hardware; work with security personnel on system safeguards; perform systems programming activities as needed

Alternate Title(s): Computer Systems Manager; Information Technology (IT) Specialist

Salary Range: $40,000 to $85,000 or more

Employment Prospects: Good

Advancement Prospects: Good

Prerequisites:

    Education or Training—Bachelor's degree in computer science, computer engineering, information system management, or management information systems (MIS) is a basic requirement; employers with complex systems may necessitate a master's degree, and jobs in research laboratories or educational institutions may demand a Ph.D.

    Experience—Three to five years of experience with computer operating systems (such as UNIX or Microsoft Windows) and/or networking; working knowledge of utility software, backup, and secondary procedures; file and system maintenance procedures;

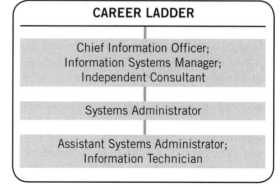

    software installation and upgrading procedures; and basic programming and/or scripting

    Special Skills and Personality Traits—Ability to communicate and work well with others (such as other computer and support personnel, managers, and customers); attention to detail; excellent analytical, problem-solving, and troubleshooting skills; good organizational talents to balance and prioritize work and multitask; strong writing and documentation capabilities

    Special Requirements—Industry certification relating to the operating system or networking software usually required

Position Description

Systems Administrators are responsible for running technically advanced information systems, whereas a network administrator is an engineer involved in computer networks, and database administrators are responsible for the environmental aspects of computer databases. The duties of a Systems Administrator and a network administrator often overlap. However, the Systems Administrator is more geared to the computer hardware and less on the network, although, in many cases, Systems and network Administrators are one and the same, especially in smaller companies. A Systems Administrator usually is involved with operational software and hardware installations and configurations, may be concerned with application installations and upgrades, and may also perform systems programming activities.

The duties of Systems Administrators are wide-ranging and vary broadly from one organization to another. They are typically charged with installing, supporting, and maintaining servers or other computer systems and planning for and responding to service outages and other problems. Other duties may include scripting or light programming, project management for systems-related projects, supervising and training computer operators, and being the consultant for computer problems beyond the knowledge of technical support staff. Thus, a Systems Administrator must demonstrate a blend of technical skills and responsibility.

Systems Administrators install computers and their operating systems, but their most important responsibility is to monitor the operation of the systems and fix any problems that arise, whether with data storage, network communications, or the running of the software. They must keep track of user accounts, setting up accounts for new users and answering questions about systems operations and procedures. If resources (such as disk space or printers) are limited, Systems Administrators must allocate their use according to various priorities. Above all, they must ensure that the design of organizations' computer sites allows all the components, including computers, the network, and software, to fit together and work properly. Furthermore, they must monitor and adjust the performance of existing networks and continually survey current computer sites to determine future network needs. Additionally, they must troubleshoot problems reported by users and by automated network monitoring systems, making recommendations for enhancements in the implementation of future servers and networks, and work with security personnel to safeguard and protect the operations of the network systems.

Systems Administrators set up and maintain the assorted services on which users depend. This may include file servers, databases, access to the Internet and to any internal network of the organizations (intranets), and software applications than run on individual users' computers or on central servers. Many pieces of software that run in conjunction with Web servers need to be installed, maintained, and configured to deliver different kinds of content to Web pages. Then, there are issues of maintenance, upgrades, and compatibility. The Internet was essentially invented by UNIX professionals, and much of the Internet is run on UNIX (an operating system like Windows). Versions of UNIX are free (such as Linux) or commercial (such as Sun Microsystems, Hewlett-Packard, IBM, and Silicon Graphics). Though there are Web sites running on other systems, most Systems Administrators use UNIX-based systems.

Systems Administrators' duties may include programming database applications and performing database administration duties for production and non-production systems, such as work order tracking and hardware and software inventory custom database systems. They often provide backup support for local area network (LAN) installations, configurations, maintenance, and administration.

In addition, they usually coordinate all the activities of vendors and contractors and interface with hardware and software vendors in areas of product support, troubleshooting, and new product purchases.

Salaries

Salaries for Systems Administrators depend largely on the size and complexity of the installations for which they are responsible as well as the duties involved and the skills required. Systems Administrators who work in large corporate organizations usually receive higher earnings than those in academic or government settings. While salaries are decent, they tend to be lower than those of other computer professionals because many individuals see this position as a way to gain experience before moving forward to more lucrative managerial or specialist posts. In addition, many Systems Administrators work freelance.

According to PayScale, Inc.'s, December 2007 salary survey on this position, median annual salaries for Systems Administrators ranged from a low of $43,005 to a high of $63,929, depending on their years of experience, the geographic location of the organization for which they worked, and the type of industry within which they worked. The median yearly income of senior Systems Administrators ranged from $58,809 to $86,878, again dependent on geographic location, years of experience, and type of industry.

Employment Prospects

The need for capable Systems Administrators is constant. According to the U.S. Bureau of Labor Statistics, employment of computer support specialists (of which Systems Administrators are a primary example) is expected to increase faster than the average for all occupations through 2014, particularly for college graduates who are up to date with the latest skills and technologies and who also have relevant work experience. Candidates with specific knowledge of operating systems (such as UNIX/Linux and Microsoft Windows XP) will be more competitive, as will those with backgrounds in networking and Web applications. Newly hired assistant Systems Administrators usually work under the guidance of experienced administrators, performing routine maintenance of computer systems and other "behind the scenes" work for training periods that may last up to three months.

Advancement Prospects

Systems Administrators who have demonstrated their ability to handle increasing responsibility have excellent chances of moving up the administrative ranks (in large institutions) or of qualifying for more advanced positions in organizations larger than the ones in which they are employed. One route to career progression is to aim at becoming a manager or director of information systems. Another possibility is to specialize in a particular area (such as networking, or security, or a particular operating system) with a view to becoming a well-paid industry consultant. Almost invariably, job promotions depend more on performance than on additional formal education.

Education and Training

Most organizations prefer to hire Systems Administrators who have bachelor's degrees in computer science or information systems and who have supplemented their education with hands-on experience with operating systems. For more complex jobs, many employers favor hiring applicants who have graduate degrees. Sometimes, a master's degree in computer science or computer engineering is sufficient. However, most research laboratories and many educational institutions require Ph.D.'s. In addition, many employers who conduct business buying and selling products online prefer candidates for the position of Systems Administrator to have a working knowledge of e-commerce and Internet security technologies and procedures.

Special Requirements

The successful completion of an industry certification training program, especially in operating system or networking software (and the earning of such designations as Microsoft Certified System Engineer, or MCSE, or Apple Certified Systems Administrator, or ACSAO) often helps individuals quality for entry-level positions in computer systems administration. Certifications are available from industry certification programs allied with specific operating systems (such as Red Hat's certification curriculum or the Linux Professional Institute) or from such organizations as Systems Administration, Networking, and Security (http://www.sans.org). Certification is a critical part of the viability of an individual's application for this post.

Experience, Skills, and Personality Traits

Systems Administrators must have excellent organizational skills in order to balance and prioritize work as well as good analytical, critical thinking, and problem-solving abilities to troubleshoot systems problems. They must have effective communication talents (both written and oral) to work successfully with support personnel, customers, and managers. Their technical aptitude must be exceptional, and they need to be able to work independently (or as part of a team) and under pressure to meet tight schedules. Employers often seek self-starters who can rapidly navigate a wide variety of technical problems and interpersonal interactions.

Their specific technical backgrounds should include working knowledge of UNIX/Linux and/or Sun Solaris operating systems administration and experience with multiuser, multihost, multi–operating system (OS) server environments. Programming know-how with such high-level languages as Perl and UNIX shell scripts is useful. The ability to administer a network of Windows (workstation and server)- and UNIX-based systems, such as user accounts, directories, and security, is an addition plus.

Unions and Associations

Systems Administrators who work in government (and a few private) installations may belong to clerical or office worker unions, such as the Communication Workers of America (http://www.cwa-union.org). Most Systems Administrators, however, do not belong to unions but usually find it helpful to join general computer-related groups such as the Association for Computing Machinery (ACM), the Association of Computer Support Specialists (ACSS), the Computing Technology Industry Association (CTIA), and the Institute of Electrical and Electronics Engineers (IEEE) Computer Society. In addition, there are a few professional organizations specifically organized for Systems Administrators, such as the League of Professional System Administrators (LOPSA), the Network and Systems Professionals Association, Inc. (NASPA), and specific operating systems associations, such as USENIX Association's Special Interest Group, the Systems Administrator Guild (known as SAGE).

Tips for Entry

1. During your education years, volunteer to help local nonprofit groups (or your own school) set up or maintain their computer systems, or help minorities or senior citizens connect to the Internet. Document whatever experience you gain for future use on your résumé.

2. Decide which of the two major computing environments (UNIX/Linux or Microsoft Windows) most interests you, and delve into the details of that operating system. One way to do this is to obtain an inexpensive computer, acquire free software from either of these systems (such as free UNIX clone software such as BSD or Windows programs that are available free) and install it. Get a manual and learn how to use it. This job is all about problem solving, and you need to be a "tinkerer at heart," as one systems administrator has phrased it.

3. When deciding on what type of certification to get, check articles on the computer industry to find out which certifications are most in demand and which one(s) would be most appropriate for your job experience and career.

INFORMATION SCIENTISTS, TECHNICIANS, AND SUPPORT STAFF

COMPUTER SCIENTIST

Duties: Conduct research into fundamental computer and information science as a theorist, designer, or inventor; solve or develop solutions to problems in the field of computer hardware and software

Alternate Title(s): Computer Communications Specialist; Computer Engineer; Computer Research Analyst

Salary Range: $60,000 to $115,000 or more

Employment Prospects: Good

Advancement Prospects: Fair to good

Prerequisites:

Education or Training—Bachelor's degree necessary for most positions; master's degree in management information systems (M.I.S.) or business administration (M.B.A.) often required; doctoral degree in computer or information science recommended

Experience—Two to four years of hands-on experience in software and general software applications as well as with specific software applications for information systems; working knowledge of computer system architecture and system software organization and modeling techniques

CAREER LADDER

Chief Technology Officer; Management Information Systems (MIS) Director; University Computer Research Department Head; Independent Computer/Systems Consultant

↑

Computer Scientist

↑

Computer Programmer; College Graduate

Special Skills and Personality Traits—Ability to think logically and pay close attention to detail; capacity for working independently as well as with a team; effective communication skills, both oral and written; excellent analytical and problem-solving capabilities

Special Requirements—Programmer certification may be required and is highly recommended

Position Description

Computer science deals with the theoretical foundations of information and computation and their implications and applications in computer systems. Primarily, it is the study of computers and their design and uses in computation, data processing, and systems control (which includes the design and development of computer hardware and software and programming). The field encompasses theory, mathematical activities such as design and analysis of algorithms, performance studies of systems and their components, and estimations of the reliability and availability of systems by probabilistic techniques. Computer science has many subfields. Some of them emphasize the computation of specific results (such as computer graphics), while others relate to properties of computational problems (such as computational complexity theory). Others focus on the challenges of implementing computations, such as programming language theory (which studies approaches to describing computations) and computer programming (which applies specific programming languages to solve specific computational problems). Another subfield, human-computer interaction, focuses on the challenges in making computers and computations useful, usable, and universally accessible to people.

Computer Scientists work as theorists, researchers, and inventors. Their jobs are distinguished by the high level of theoretical expertise and innovation they apply to complex problems and the creation (or application) of new technology. Those employed by academic institutions function in areas ranging from complexity theory, to hardware architecture, to programming-language design. Some work on multidisciplinary projects, such as developing and advancing uses of virtual reality, extending human-computer interaction, or the designing of robots. Their counterparts in private industry work in areas such as applying theory to practical management and manufacturing problems, developing specialized programming languages and information technologies, and designing specific types of applications (such as programming tools, knowledge-based systems, and even computer games).

Computer science is a constantly evolving field. Due to its highly dynamic nature, competent and qualified computer science professionals are needed constantly. As software stability becomes the crux (and the critical component) of comfortable modern-day living, organizations (and the government) look for professionals who can create software systems that ensure stability. Computer science graduates can work with all kinds of industries (or government institutions) as technical administrators, or they can work in research areas of the computer industry.

Computer science graduates can choose to be software developers, whereby they will be required to have sufficient knowledge of various operating systems and software applications as well as a thorough understanding of the particular industries for which they are developing software. They can be computer communications specialists, aiding in the integration of telecommunications and computer systems to deliver robust and accurate business and transaction solutions. They can decide to be research analysts, aiding senior staff (in industry and government organizations) in carrying out research-led activities. They can become systems and security administrators, since many systems and security issues have occurred as networked computing and the Internet have become a way of life. Or, if their primary interest is in hardware development, they can become computer engineers, working with systems manufacturers and high-end technical industries that involve a high level of computerization.

Salaries

Due to their highly technical background and knowledge, salaries for experienced and qualified Computer Scientists tend to be high. According to the U.S. Department of Labor's Bureau of Labor Statistics, the median annual earnings of computer scientists in May 2006 were $93,950. The middle 50 percent earned between $71,930 and $119,100. The lowest 10 percent earned yearly less than $53,590, and the highest 10 percent had incomes of more than $144,880. In their December 2007 salary survey report, PayScale, Inc., confirmed these high earnings and found that median annual salaries for Computer Scientists ranged from $79,220 (for those who had one to four years of experience) to $111,443 (for those with 20 or more years of experience). Furthermore, while beginning annual median salaries may start as low as $35,000, they may climb as high as $119,900, depending on the type of employer and the geographic location of the employer.

Employment Prospects

The U. S. Department of Labor's *Occupational Outlook Handbook, 2007–08 Edition* states that the Computer Sci-
entist occupation is expected to grow 37 percent through 2016, much faster than the average for all occupations in the United States. Job increases will be driven by the very rapid growth in computer systems design and related services, which is projected to be one of the fastest growing industries in the U.S. economy. Thus, Computer Scientists should enjoy excellent job prospects.

For computer science jobs in business environments, many employers want Computer Scientists and systems analysts to have business management or closely related skills, while a background in the physical sciences, applied mathematics, or engineering is preferred for work in scientifically oriented organizations.

Advancement Prospects

Computer Scientists often progress into managerial or project leadership positions. Those having advanced degrees may choose to leave private industry (or the government) for academic posts. Computer Scientists who have made a career in a particular field or a certain application may find lucrative opportunities as independent consultants or may opt to start their own computer consulting firms.

Education and Training

A bachelor's degree in computer science or information technology is a prerequisite for most Computer Scientist jobs. Relevant work experience is also vital. For more technically complex jobs, individuals with graduate degrees are usually preferred. Most Computer Scientist positions require a Ph.D. degree, as one of the primary functions is research. Computer Scientists with only a bachelor's or master's degree are generally limited in their ability to advance their career. Most four-year colleges and universities offer bachelor's degrees in computer science. Most community colleges have two-year programs that can be transferred to four-year schools. In addition, many schools offer graduate degree programs in computer science. Some universities teach computer science as a theoretical study of computation and algorithmic reasoning. These programs typically also teach computer programming but treat it as a vessel for the support of other fields of computer science rather than a central focus of high-level study. Other colleges and universities as well as secondary schools and vocational programs that teach computer science emphasize the practice of advanced computer programming rather than the theory of algorithms and computation in their computer science curricula. Such curricula tend to focus on skills that are important to workers entering the software industry rather than the research and advanced study of computer science.

Special Requirements

Certification as a computer professional may not be required, but it is highly recommended. In addition, many certifications are related to specific products (both hardware and software), and, often, training for them is available from the manufacturers of these products. For information about available certification programs, the Institute for Certification of Computing Professionals (ICCP) should be contacted. Their Web site is at http://www.iccp.org.

Experience, Skills, and Personality Traits

The professional background of Computer Scientists should include competence in the application of the theoretical foundations of computer science, including computer systems architecture, systems software organization, and modeling of the representation and transformation of information structure. An understanding of design characteristics, limitations, and potential applications of information systems as well as of broad areas of applications of computing that have common structures, processes, and techniques is useful. A strong mathematical background is necessary.

Computer Scientists need to have strong problem-solving and analytical skills as well as good interpersonal abilities. They must be able to think logically and have excellent communication talents, particularly writing abilities. Often, the difference between good programmers and great programmers is *not* how many programming languages they know but rather whether they can communicate their ideas. If they can write clear comments and technical specifications, then other programmers can understand their code, use it, and work with it instead of rewriting it. In addition, by preparing clear documentation for end users, Computer Scientists allow users to figure out what their computer code is supposed to do, which is the only way those users can see the value in the code.

Because Computer Scientists often deal with a number of tasks simultaneously, they must have the ability to concentrate and pay close attention to detail.

While they may sometimes work independently, they frequently work in teams on large projects, so they must be able to communicate effectively with computer personnel such as programmers and managers as well as with users or other staff who may have no technical computer backgrounds.

They must have excellent time management skills and be able to assign and schedule tasks in order to meet work priorities and goals. A positive attitude and a customer service orientation are additional abilities that many employers require.

Unions and Associations

The primary professional groups for Computer Scientists include the Association for Computing Machinery (ACM), the Computing Research Association (CRA), the Computing Technology Industry Association (CTIA), and the Institute of Electrical and Electronics Engineers (IEEE) Computer Society.

Tips for Entry

1. While earning your degree in computer science, do not neglect business and economics courses. An understanding of microeconomics will provide an understanding of supply and demand and how and why business works the way it does.

2. As software developer Joel Spolsky suggests, during your college work, take programming-intensive courses, including working with the C programming language (which is more closely aligned to a computer machine than most other computer languages), so that you will be able to create efficient computer code in higher-level languages.

3. Search out good summer internships at software companies, and practice your programming skills by writing, say, a content management system for your campus newspaper. All these activities will improve your résumé and are what employment recruiters look for in applicants.

COMPUTER SUPPORT SPECIALIST

Duties: Provide technical assistance to computer systems users; answer questions or resolve computer problems for clients in person, via telephone or e-mail, and from remote locations

Alternate Title(s): Computer Technical Support Specialist; Desktop Support Technician; Help Desk Analyst; Help Desk Technician; Information Technology (IT) Specialist; Office Systems Coordinator

Salary Range: $35,000 to $55,000 or more

Employment Prospects: Good

Advancement Prospects: Fair to good

Prerequisites:

Education or Training—Bachelor's degree in computer science or computer-related field preferred

Experience—Working familiarity with common software and operating systems through part-time or summer work or internship programs

Special Skills and Personality Traits—Excellent communication (both written and oral) and listen-

ing skills; good research abilities (including print and online); strong analytical thinking, problem-solving, and troubleshooting talents; well organized and able to manage time well

Special Requirements—Certification as a computer professional may be required

CAREER LADDER

Computer Applications Developer; Manager, Technical Support; Quality Control Computer Engineer; Systems Administrator

Computer Support Specialist

Computer Technician; Information Technician

Position Description

Computer Support Specialists provide technical assistance to computer systems users. These specialists may work either within an organization that uses computer systems or directly for a computer hardware or software vendor. They may also work for help desk or support services firms, for which they provide computer support to clients on a contract basis.

Some Computer Support Specialists (often called help desk technicians) field phone calls and e-mails or make house calls to people who are having difficulty with a particular piece of computer hardware or software or answer questions that are not addressed in a product's instruction manual. Many of the people who need assistance have no technical expertise, so Computer Support Specialists must ask them to describe the problem as well as the commands that were entered or steps taken that led up to the problem. If the difficulty was caused by user error, the specialist explains how the situation occurred and how to fix it. If the problem is due to a fault with the software or hardware, the specialist tries to determine its cause, which may require consultation with supervisors or computer programmers. Once the cause has been determined, Computer

Support Specialists can walk the user through the steps required to fix the problem. In responding to these requests for guidance, they must deal with both inexperienced users and computer-smart programmers and software designers. They must be able to reduce technical information to simple language. In addition, they document the type of questions they answer each day and the type of support they provide. They solicit customer feedback and use the information to improve the quality of their service.

Other Computer Support Specialists (usually known as technical support specialists) provide support to individuals in the information processing department of an organization. They may run automatic diagnostics programs to resolve problems; work on monitors, keyboards, printers, and input devices; and install, modify, clean, and repair computer hardware and software. These repairs may mean reinstalling software or replacing nonfunctioning hardware. They may refer major hardware or software problems or defective products to vendors or technicians for service. Once changes have been made, Computer Support Specialists test computers to make sure they work. They may continue to monitor computers to see if the changes remedy the trouble or if more work needs to be done. They document what repairs they made and what hardware and/or software they used.

They may also write training manuals and instruct computer users in how to use new computer hardware and software. In addition, they may even oversee the daily performance of their organizations' computer systems and evaluate software programs as to their effectiveness. They may be called on to evaluate computer systems to determine if they need to be expanded or upgraded. They may also modify software produced by other computer firms to meet the requirements of their organizations or clients.

Still other Computer Support Specialists concentrate on setting up computer systems that are delivered to customers. This includes installing the operation systems and any software the client will need. They may train personnel at clients' offices on how to use the computer systems and answer questions about getting started with the systems. A Computer Support Specialist may be assigned to user support for a particular client, taking all calls from that customer to resolve computer problems that arise.

Yet another area of support is computer security. Computer Support Specialists who concentrate on security are playing an increasingly important role in firms that provide support services on a contract basis. Computer hackers are becoming more sophisticated, and the number and complexity of computer viruses is growing. These specialists may be called on to educate users on computer security. They may install security software, monitor networks for security breaches, respond to cyber attacks, and even, in some cases, gather data and evidence that may be used in prosecuting cyber crimes.

Salaries

Salaries depend somewhat on the complexity of the support to be provided. Entry-level positions for specialists who answer basic user questions provide annual incomes of $35,000 or so. More experienced Computer Support Specialists (and those who provide technical support in an organization) may earn $40,000 to $50,000 or so yearly. According to their December 2007 salary survey report, PayScale, Inc., found that the median annual salaries earned by Computer Support Specialists ranged from $35,909 to $60,231, depending on the type of employer, years of experience, and geographic location.

Employment Prospects

As computers have become an integral part of everyday life, there has been an escalating demand for specialists to provide advice to users and to solve the inevitable problems, whether the disaster of a crashing hard drive or the annoyance of a forgotten password. Even with the increasing installation of online help in the form of "frequently asked questions" (FAQs) files and the interactive troubleshooting "wizards" within the software itself, there is still a need for experienced specialists to deal with the tougher problems.

Most computer hardware and software companies maintain their own in-house technical support staff. Often, this is a basic entry-level post within the company. Large organizations that use computers extensively may also have an in-house support group and may provide its own training program to newly hired Computer Support Specialists. According to the U.S. Bureau of Labor Statistics, employment of Computer Support Specialists is expected to increase faster than the average for all occupations through 2014. Although many help desk technician jobs are being outsourced abroad, developments in new technology and the need for in-house technical support staffs will help guarantee new jobs based in the United States.

Advancement Prospects

Technical Computer Support Specialists may progress to supervisory positions in which they oversee the work of support staffs and handle more complicated problems. Seasoned support specialists can look for a position as a manger of a help desk or support department. With additional training or education, Computer Support Specialists may pursue careers as quality assurance computer engineers who test computer programs for problems or design software to perform such tests. Alternatively, experience gained in technical work can help them toward careers as systems administrators or systems analysts.

Beginning Computer Support Specialists often work for organizations that deal directly with customers or in-house computer users. Then they may advance into more responsible jobs in which they use what they have learned from customers to improve the design and efficiency of future products. Eventually, some Computer Support Specialists become applications developers, who design products rather than assist users. Computer Support Specialists at hardware and software companies generally enjoy greater upward mobility than those who work in independent consulting firms.

Education and Training

A four-year bachelor's degree with a major in computer science, information systems, or other computer-related areas is a standard requirement for this position.

College programs in math and sciences are valuable, as are courses that develop communication skills. Most vendor firms that make computer software or hardware train their support specialist employees to provide assistance for each of their products.

As technology continues to change and improve, Computer Support Specialists must keep their skills current and acquire new ones. Many continuing education programs are provided by employers, hardware and software vendors, colleges and universities, and private training institutions. In addition, professional development seminars offered by computer service firms can aid in enhancing skills and advancement opportunities.

Special Requirements

A certificate indicating expertise in particular software or particular hardware products can be helpful and may be required by some employers. The completion of a certification training program, offered by a variety of computer vendors, product makers, and software firms, may aid in qualifying for entry-level positions as Computer Support Specialists. The Institute for Certification of Computing Professionals (ICCP) provides information about available certification programs. Their Web site is at http://www.iccp.org.

Experience, Skills, and Personality Traits

Employers search for evidence that applicants for positions as Computer Support Specialists have had hands-on experience with software and computer systems similar to those they use and need to be supported. All Computer Support Specialist jobs require strong analytical thinking and problem-solving abilities. Computer Support Specialists must have excellent communication skills, as they must write technical reports about the problems they encounter and be able to communicate clearly with users. The constant interaction with other computer personnel, customers, and employees requires Computer Support Specialists to communicate effectively on paper, via e-mail, and in person. In addition, strong writing skills are useful in preparing manuals for employees and customers.

Computer Support Specialists should have a thorough knowledge of a variety of network and operating systems as well as programming logic and database concepts. Basic experience or training in C or Visual Basic programming is useful as well. They must have strong attention to detail and the ability to work independently. They should demonstrate customer service skills as well as excellent time management and project implementation abilities.

Unions and Associations

Professional groups of interest to Computer Support Specialists include the Association for Computing Machinery (ACM), the Association of Computer Support Specialists (ACSS), the Computing Technology Industry Association (CTIA), the Institute of Electrical and Electronics Engineers (IEEE) Computer Society, and SAGE, the special interest group of the USENIX Association.

Tips for Entry

1. Check with your teachers or counselors to learn if work-based learning opportunities in the computer industry or computer-related organizations are available in your school or community. These might include internship programs or part-time employment.

2. When you run into problems on your own computer, call the technical support number and note how they treat you. Did their representative understand your problem or ask the appropriate questions? Learn how to deal with the public from their mistakes.

3. Further information about computer careers and, specifically, about becoming a Computer Support Specialist, is available by contacting the National Workforce Center for Emerging Technologies (NWCET). Their Web site is at http://www.nwcet.org.

DATABASE ANALYSTS (INCLUDING DATA COMMUNICATIONS ANALYST AND DATABASE INFORMATION ANALYST)

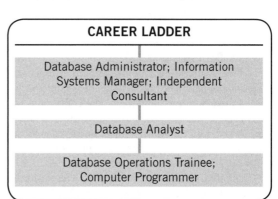

Position Description

A database is a collection of related information accessed and managed by its database management system (DBMS). As has been often stated, database work is the "bread and butter" of today's Information Age. Most businesses, governments, and other institutions need to keep track of large amounts of data (such as customer information, inventory of materials, and medical and insurance records). Database Information Analysts are responsible for

- analyzing organizations' database needs through discussion with computer users and other technical staff
- designing one or more databases for each type of information that organizations use
- allocating database storage and planning for future storage requirements of organizations' database systems
- making modifications in database systems already in place to reflect changes in business or information gathering practices, new standards, and new regulations

- providing the information reports that organizations' managers and analysts need to use the information most effectively
- communicating with organizations' internal technical, applications, and operational staff, as appropriate, to ensure database integrity, security, and availability
- preparing all necessary documentation
- reviewing database use and performing basic analysis and fine tuning to ensure its optimal performance as well as responding to system problems that may affect the database
- implementing and ensuring adherence to database backup, restart, recover, and reorganization standards
- coordinating testing activities for appropriate application systems development with relevant technical staff
- monitoring and tracking application systems development progress in order to provide and/or recommend the appropriate application of database resources and/or technology to meet organizations' development and support requirements

In addition, Database Analysts may be tasked with installations, upgrades, and decommissions of server products and application development programs. They usually are responsible for creating and maintaining database storage structures (tablespaces) and primary objects (tables, views, indexes, triggers, clusters, memory structures, rollback segments, redo logs, archives, control files, and initialization and configuration parameters). They interact with and assist database systems administrators to provide a compatible and usable database environment and assist in the development and implementation of data and database related standards, procedures, and guidelines. They may be asked to train staff in database procedures.

Data Communications Analysts are Data Analyst specialists who design, test, and evaluate computer network systems. They work with both local area networks (LANs) and wide area networks (WANs). They also work with Internet, intranet (a business's internal internet), and other data communication systems. To find out an organization's needs, they survey users of the network and talk with the organization's staff. If there is an existing network system, they monitor its performance and identify areas that need upgrades. In researching potential hardware and software products, they may visit vendors or study the vendors' technical manuals. They test products to determine whether they will function with the existing system and then evalu-

ate the results of their research and testing. They may recommend certain products for purchase, or they may make changes to current software or even design their own software. In any of these instances, Data Communication Analysts integrate the new products into the existing system as well as develop and write procedures for users to follow. In many organizations, they set up user accounts and train users in the use of the hardware and software as well as educate them in basic network problem solving. They monitor the new (or redesigned) networks to ensure that they operate properly. When problems occur, they identify and solve them, ensuring that information is made available to all authorized users of the network.

Salaries

According to the May 2008 salary survey conducted by PayScale, Inc., median annual salaries for Database Analysts ranged from $43,985 to $65,000, according to the type of employer and employer location. The median yearly salary for Database Analysts with less than one year of experience was $42,907, whereas the median annual salary for those with 10 to 19 years of experience was $64,921.

Employment Prospects

Because databases and database development are so central to modern businesses, governments, and other institutions, the growth in demand for Database Analysts is constant and steady. Since most positions require thorough knowledge of specific database software and operating systems, it is critical for Database Analysts to keep their skills up to date in order to have the best job opportunities.

Advancement Prospects

Advancement for Database Analysts usually comes through the gaining of specialized skills. Some may go into consulting (or set up their own consulting firms). Others may enter the managerial track and advance to positions as database administrators for an entire company or department, and, from there, on to the higher management level of information systems managers.

Education and Training

An undergraduate degree (preferably in computer science, computer programming, database administration, or management of information systems) is usually required for the position of Database Analyst. In addition, some employers want their applicants to have either a bachelor's or master's degree in business administration (coupled with programming and operating systems courses).

Special Requirements
Certification as a computer or information professional is desirable, if not required. Information on available certification programs (many of which are offered by computer and software manufacturers) may be obtained by contacting the Institute for Certification of Computing Professionals (ICCP) at its Web site: http://www.iccp.org.

Experience, Skills, and Personality Traits
Database Analysts must be proficient in database management systems (DBMS), such as DB2/UDB, IM, MSSQL, and Oracle. They need to be familiar with the knowledge data dictionary concepts for relational database management systems and be proficient in data analysis techniques. They must be skilled in technical writing for the documentation of all programming and technical efforts and be adept at both physical database design and entity relationship diagramming at a logical or conceptual level. They must be efficient in troubleshooting and solving problems in a maintenance mode and be effective in enforcing database standards and guidelines in regard to data, data analysis, data modeling, and physical database change management. They need to have the ability to understand the structure and relationships among different items of information as well as the workflow and procedures used by the individuals who carry out the business functions of organizations. Experience in a variety of business settings can be helpful in this regard, allowing them to comfortably facilitate both technical and business discussions.

Database Analysts must be able to effectively balance and weigh competing priorities and determine the appropriate course of action. They must have excellent analytical and problem-solving skills, be resourceful, and show initiative. Their communication abilities must include clear and concise presentation skills with an ability to fashion technical material and explanations for various types of audiences. They must be consistent in applications work and have close attention to detail. They must be persistent, able to work under pressure, and able to work both independently and as part of a team.

Unions and Associations
Of primary interest to Database Analysts (as with other software developer positions) is the Association for Computing Machinery (ACM) and its special interest groups (SIGs) devoted to database issues. Other professional associations of interest to Database Analysts include the American Society for Information Science and Technology (ASIS&T), the Computing Technology Industry Association (CTIA), the Institute of Electrical and Electronic Engineers (IEEE) Computer Society, and the Information Technology Association of America (ITAA).

Tips for Entry
1. Besides your course work in database languages and systems, take classes in business administration and information science, as knowledge gained from them will be useful in your career as a Database Analyst.
2. Look for volunteer or part-time experience helping local nonprofit groups with their database needs, all of which will be valuable additions to your résumé.
3. Be mindful that it is critical to maintain and extend your competencies as well as develop new skills in emerging technological modifications in database development. Continuing education courses are an integral part of your continued growth and professional success.

DATA MINER

Duties: Explore and analyze databases covering business, government, or scientific applications to extract additional useful information or to discover data patterns and relationships

Alternate Title(s): Chief Data Officer (CDO); Database Analyst (Specialist); Data Mining Analyst; Data Mining Developer; Data Mining Manager; Data Mining Researcher; Machine Learning Scientist

Salary Range: $65,000 to $85,000 or more

Employment Prospects: Good

Advancement Prospects: Good

Prerequisites:

Education or Training—Graduate degree (such as a master of science or Ph.D. in computer science, econometrics, information retrieval, machine learning, statistics, or a related field) usually required; a master's degree in business administration (M.B.A.) or a degree in market research or psychology is recommended

Experience—Demonstrated expertise with major database software and machine learning methods and tools; familiarity with data warehousing and data mining tools, technologies, and techniques; know-how with statistical and database applications

in a particular area (such as biostatistics, economics, marketing, or physical science); project management background

Special Skills and Personality Traits—Creative and results-oriented with high attention to detail; excellent communication (both verbal and written) and computer skills; good analytical and problem-solving abilities

Special Requirements—Certification as a computer professional not required but useful as background detail on résumé

Position Description

Data mining is the process of analyzing data from different perspectives and summarizing it into information that can be used in numerous ways. For example, customer purchase data can be correlated to create profiles of typical types of buyers so they can be targeted by marketing and promotional efforts, or tax returns can be analyzed to find patterns that relate to various types of fraud so a profile can be developed for identifying and auditing potentially suspect returns. Data mining is increasingly being employed in the sciences to extract information from the enormous data sets generated by modern experimental and observational methods.

As data sets have grown in size and complexity, the modern technologies of computers, networks, and automated sensors have made data collection and organization far easier. However, the captured data need to be converted into information and knowledge in order to become useful. Data mining describes the entire process of applying computer-based methodology to data and identifying trends within data that go beyond simple analysis.

Data have been defined as any facts, numbers, or text that can be processed by a computer. In today's complex world, organizations are accumulating vast and growing amounts of data in different formats and assorted databases. This includes

- operational or transactional data such as sales, costs, inventory, payroll, and accounting
- nonoperational data such as industry sales, forecast data, and macroeconomic data
- metadata, that is, data about data itself, such as logical database design and data dictionary definitions

The patterns, associations, and relationships among all this data can provide useful information. For example, analysis of retail point-of-sale transaction data can yield information on which products are selling and when. Information, in turn, can be converted into knowledge about historical patterns and future trends. For instance, information on retail supermarket sales can be analyzed in light of promotional efforts to provide knowledge of consumer buying habits. Data mining in customer relationship management (CRM) applications can contribute significantly to the bottom line of businesses and other organizations. In addition, data mining can be helpful to human resources departments in identifying the characteristics of their most successful employees. Other uses include the study of human genetics, in which the important goal is to understand the mapping relationships among the individual variations in human DNA sequences and variability in disease susceptibility. In the area of electrical power engineering, data mining techniques have been widely applied for condition monitoring of high voltage electrical equipment to determine when parts need to be repaired or replaced. Data mining is also used for security and risk assessments in industries such as banking that are vulnerable to criminal attack.

Dramatic advances in data capture, processing power, data transmission, and storage capabilities are now enabling organizations to integrate their various databases into data warehouses. (Data warehousing is a process of centralized data management and retrieval.) Centralization of data is needed to maximize user access and analysis. Much of the work in implementing a data warehouse is devoted to making similar data consistent when they are stored in the data warehouse. (For example, one operational system feeding data into the data warehouse may use "M" and "F" to denote the sex of an employee, while another operational system may use "Male" and "Female" instead.) Equally dramatic advances in data analysis software permit users to access this refined data freely. Data mining software analyzes relationships and patterns in stored transaction data based on open-ended user queries. Generally, any or all of four types of relationships are sought:

- *Classes*—Stored data are used to locate data in predetermined groups. For example, a restaurant chain could mine customer purchase data to determine when customers visit and what they typically order. This information could be used to increase customer traffic by having daily specials.
- *Clusters*—Data items are grouped according to logical relationships or preferences. For instance, data can be mined to identify market segments or consumer affinities.

- *Associations*—Data can be mined to identify associations. For example, one Midwest grocery chain used this mining capacity to analyze local buying patterns. It was discovered that when men bought diapers on Thursdays and Saturdays, they also tended to buy beer. Further analysis showed that these shoppers typically did their weekly grocery shopping on Saturdays, while, on Thursdays they bought only a few items. The retailer concluded that they purchased the beer to have it available for the upcoming weekend. Thus, they increased their revenues by moving the beer display closer to the diaper display and making sure that beer and diapers sold at full price on Thursdays.
- *Sequential patterns*—Data are mined to anticipate behavior patterns and trends. For example, an outdoor equipment retailer can profit from the likelihood of a backpack being purchased based on a consumer's purchase of sleeping bags and hiking shoes.

The process of data mining usually consists of five major elements: (1) extract, transform, and load transaction data onto a data warehouse system; (2) store and manage the data in a multidimensional database system; (3) provide data access to business analysts and information technology professionals; (4) analyze the data by application software; and (5) present the data in a useful format, such as a graph or table. Data mining begins with formulating a problem or objective and selecting suitable databases to be examined. The data may have to be cleansed to remove erroneous or incomplete records. Because of the huge size of many of the databases involved, Data Miners may do their preliminary assessment using a small portion of the data to bring the number of variables to a manageable range. Data Miners can then apply a variety of software tools and algorithms from such fields as statistics, pattern recognition, expert systems, or other forms of artificial intelligence. While many of these software tools are now available, many Data Miners prefer to write their own software to handle more advanced or particular applications.

The next step consists of modeling, which is building a model in one situation in which the answer is known and then applying it to another situation where it is not. The final stage of the data mining process involves using the model selected as the best in the previous stage of validation and applying it to new data to generate estimates of the outcome of whatever is needed by the organization and reports summarizing the results of the analysis in a simple form for business, institutional, or governmental users.

Thus, Data Miners have the potential for an interesting and challenging career. However, the growing use of data mining by corporations and government agencies as related to data collected about individuals also raises privacy, civil liberties, and ethical concerns. The development and application of ethical standards to this field presents a great challenge for Data Miners and their profession.

Salaries

Due to the advanced skills needed and the growing demand for data mining applications in nearly every sector of the economy and culture, specialists in this field can command high salaries. While individuals with limited experience may not expect annual incomes exceeding $60,000, those with significant experience and background may expect salaries of $120,000 or more. According to a 2007 survey of Data Miners' salaries, the median annual nationwide salary was $71,000, and median yearly salaries varied from $64,000 to $89,000, depending on geographic location.

Employment Prospects

The mounting demand for data mining skills from e-commerce firms and traditional businesses such as banks, insurance companies, and health care providers (all of whom are using data mining to devise marketing programs to reach new customers while keeping existing customers satisfied) has meant a steady demand for seasoned Data Miners. However, individuals starting a career in data mining should realize that employment may be relatively short-lived—just for the length of a particular project. Becoming an independent consultant may be an alternate and attractive possibility, particularly for successful individuals with advanced skills.

Advancement Prospects

While the data mining field is still a new and relatively open-ended profession, data mining specialists have great potential for advancement, particularly if they keep their skills up to date with new and emerging tools in the field. Career progression can occur through gaining increasing responsibility beyond the specific project as a manager or executive involved with data mining programs. Alternatively, their increased skills may generate high demand for them as independent consultants who, in turn, can demand higher salaries or fees.

Education and Training

Data mining is a demanding multidisciplinary job. During high school, students interested in this field should take introductory programming or computer science classes as well as courses in statistics and advanced mathematics. In college, a solid bachelor of science degree in computer science is recommended, including courses in programming, database design, algorithms, computational mathematics, and knowledge engineering (or artificial intelligence).

In addition, it is recommended that prospective Data Miners earn a second degree in fields in which they would like to apply their data mining skills. For example, Data Miners interested in the life sciences should have a degree in biology (including courses in biostatistics or bioinformatics), while those interested in commercial applications should consider a master's degree in business administration (M.B.A.). Courses specifically in data mining are starting to be offered in some computer science programs, and it may not be long before degrees and professional certifications in data mining will also become available.

Special Requirements

Usually, basic certification as a computer professional is not a requirement, but it always enhances an individual's résumé, particularly as a starting point in this highly technical field.

Experience, Skills, and Personality Traits

Data mining as a profession is still being developed. Thus, Data Miners must have the discipline to master new and challenging techniques and applications while also possessing the flexibility and imagination to find the potential in the vast resources of the databases with which they work. They need strong analytical and problem-solving abilities and strict attention to detail. They should be adventurous, creative, and results-oriented. Most of their potential employers and/or clients have specific objectives or problems they want solved, but it is usually necessary for Data Miners to clarify them before beginning their work. Thus, excellent verbal communication skills are essential, as are writing abilities needed for compiling reports. They must be able to work smoothly with other professionals as well as work independently, usually on strict or tight deadlines.

Unions and Associations

Data Miners typically join professional organizations in the computer field, such as the Association for Computing Machinery (ACM) and its special interest groups (SIGs) devoted to database issues, the Computing Technology Industry Association (CompTIA), and the Institute of Electrical and Electronic Engineers (IEEE) Computer Society. Of more general interest may be such professional groups as the American Society for Information Science and Technology (ASIS&T) and the Information Technology Association of America (ITAA).

Tips for Entry

1. Use your high school years (and possibly the first years in college) to take a broad range of computer, mathematics, and science- and/or business-related courses to help you decide on the particular interest areas or applications for your data mining career.

2. During college, search out internships or summer jobs (such as with a research laboratory, a computer consulting firm, or a marketing company) that will give you an opportunity to work with database systems and the analytical tools used for them.

3. A solid business background is beneficial, so consider earning a master's degree in business administration (M.B.A.), which will have the further virtue of preparing you for easy communication with potential business employers.

INFORMATION CLERK

Duties: Classify, store, retrieve, and update information and records generated by an organization; may perform data entry and word processing duties as well as other office clerical activities, including providing information about the organization to the visiting public

Alternate Title(s): Administrative Assistant; Documentation Specialist; File Clerk; Office Assistant; Records Clerk

Salary Range: $20,000 to $35,000 or more

Employment Prospects: Good to excellent

Advancement Prospects: Fair to good

Prerequisites:

Education or Training—High school diploma or its equivalent required or a mix of education and related work experience; usually trained on the job under close supervision of seasoned employees

Experience—Some office background recommended; proficiency with computers and desktop computer software often required

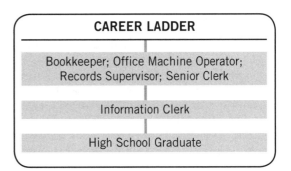

Special Skills and Personality Traits—Ability to read accurately and rapidly; accuracy and facility with making quick decisions; capacity for working well with others; excellent computer skills; readable handwriting and good English and spelling skills; willingness to do routine and detailed tasks

Position Description

The amount of information generated by organizations today continues to expand rapidly. Information Clerks (often called file clerks or record clerks) classify, store, retrieve, and update this data. In small offices, they may have additional responsibilities, such as entering data, performing word processing duties, sorting mail, and operating office equipment, such as copy and fax machines. They examine incoming material and code it numerically, alphabetically, or by subject matter. They then store paper forms, letters, receipts, and reports or enter necessary information into other storage devices, such as computer databases. Some clerks operate mechanized files that rotate to bring the needed records to them, while others convert documents to film that is then stored on microforms (such as microfilm or microfiche). Another method is for Information Clerks to use imaging systems that scan paper files, paper reports, and film and store the material on computer files.

Records must be kept up to date and accurate, and Information Clerks ensure that new information is added to files in a timely manner. They may discard outdated file materials or transfer them to inactive storage areas (or computer files). They must check files at regular intervals to ensure that all items are correctly sequenced and placed. When records seem to be missing, Information Clerks must search to locate the missing materials. As an organization's needs for information change, Information Clerks implement alterations to the filing system.

When records or other filed material are requested, Information Clerks locate them and give them to the individual in the organization who requested them. A record may be a sheet of paper stored in a file cabinet, an image on a microform, or a document on a computer file. In all cases, clerks retrieve the document either by hand or by displaying it on a microform reader and printing it out or retrieving it from the computerized storage (which may be a mainframe computer, a CD-ROM, or a floppy disk). To retrieve the latter type, Information Clerks must enter the document's identification code into a computer to get the location of the document and make a copy for the requesting individual. Even when files and records are stored electronically, it is common practice to retain a backup paper copy (and even additional electronic copies). Information Clerks may be made responsible for the maintenance of more complex central records systems, with requirements to establish and maintain various cross-reference indexes and to prepare a large volume and variety of records for permanent storage (either as paper or computer files).

Other kinds of Information Clerks are responsible for answering inquiries from individuals visiting the organizations for which they work. These clerks provide information regarding activities conducted by the organizations, or the location of departments, offices, and employees within the organizations. If they work for retail establishments, they may inform customers of the location of store merchandise. These clerks receive and answer requests for information from company officials and other employees. For more substantive questions, they may have to call specific employees or officials to their information desks to answer inquiries. They may be required to keep records of the questions asked and the types of information given out. In some cases, this type of Information Clerk may be called a receptionist, who may have the additional duties of answering phones, routing phone calls, greeting visitors or patients if in a doctor's office or in a hospital, and coordinating all mail into and out of the organization.

Salaries

As most Information Clerk jobs are entry-level positions, salaries tend to be low. According to PayScale, Inc.'s, November 2007 salary survey of Information Clerk positions, median annual salaries ranged from $22,012 to $33,750, depending on the type of employer and geographic location. For Information Clerks employed by the federal government, median yearly salaries ranged from $25,228 to $41,957.

Employment Prospects

According to the U.S. Department of Labor's *Occupational Outlook Handbook, 2007–08 Edition*, employment of Information Clerks is expected to grow faster than the average for all occupations through 2014. This increase is a result of the rapid growth of service-providing industries, with their expansion of information-gathering activities. In addition, turnover in this large occupation will create numerous openings as Information Clerks transfer to other jobs or leave the labor force altogether. Opportunities should be best for individuals with a wide range of clerical and technical skills.

Advancement Prospects

Information Clerk (or file clerk) positions are considered entry-level jobs for individuals with little work experience. Large companies and government agencies hire many levels of clerks depending on the complexity of the work. These levels allow clerks to advance within the clerical field as their skills and experience increase. Many Information Clerks advance in this way to become data input operators, other office machine operators, or bookkeepers. Those who remain in filing and record-keeping work may become supervisors or trainers.

Education and Training

Most employers prefer applicants for this position to have either a high school diploma, a general equivalency diploma (GED), or a mix of education and related work experience. Some may even require an associate business degree, with course work in computer applications and records management. Some schools provide certificates or diplomas to those who satisfactorily complete their business training programs. Applicants for civil service jobs such as Information Clerks usually are required to take a written and oral examination.

Most employers give Information Clerks on-the-job training regardless of their educational preparation because each organization has its own policies and procedures. Employers are looking as well for Information Clerks who are proficient with desktop computers and their software, as more files and records are now being stored electronically.

Experience, Skills, and Personality Traits

Information Clerks must be (or become) knowledgeable about modern office practices, procedures, and equipment. They must understand the principles and procedures used in maintaining and controlling a complete filing system and have the ability to keep privileged information confidential. They should be able to work independently and under pressure and be able to function well with others. They need to have good interpersonal abilities and have excellent communication skills, including legible handwriting and a clear speaking voice. They must be able to read accurately and rapidly, be alert, extremely accurate in their work, and be able to make quick decisions. They must be willing to do routine and detailed work and be eager to learn new skills.

Unions and Associations

Generally, Information Clerks are not union members, though some who work with word processing equipment in government agencies may belong to clerical unions. Information Clerks who look to make careers in records management may find it useful to join the Association of Records Managers and Administrators (ARMA) International and the American Society of Information Science and Technology (ASIS&T) to enhance their career potentials and make contacts with other professionals in that field.

Tips for Entry

1. Use a part-time or summer job to gain experience as an office assistant. This work will help to prepare you for the office workplace as well as make future employers more confident that you will be able to fit in well in their organizations.

2. In addition, explore work-study programs in your high school or local community colleges, which can provide you with excellent part-time job opportunities that may lead to full-time positions after graduation. You should contact your school counselor to inquire about such programs.

3. Upgrading your computer skills is important (perhaps at night school). Also, if you are looking to advance your career into management, look for opportunities to help coordinate work within your organization or even supervise and train other employees. This experience will make you a better candidate for management positions that may become available.

INFORMATION SCIENTIST

Duties: Conduct research into fundamental issues concerning information science as a theorist, designer, or inventor; design information systems, using electronic data processing principles, mathematics, and computer processes

Alternate Title(s): Information Research Scientist; Information Technology Analyst

Salary Range: $55,000 to $110,000 or more

Employment Prospects: Poor to fair

Advancement Prospects: Poor

Prerequisites:

Education or Training—Bachelor's degree in computer science, computational science, or information science and master's degree in library and information science (M.L.I.S.) from an American Library Association (ALA)–accredited institution usually required; in some cases, a Ph.D. in a related subject or specialty field (such as engineering, chemistry, or bioinformatics) may be necessary as well

Experience—Background in creating and applying the use of controlled vocabularies and taxonomies; familiarity with researching scientific or other literature on commercial databases; strong understanding of online information retrieval practices and procedures

Special Skills and Personality Traits—Ability to manage multiple priorities and work well both independently and collaboratively as part of a team; attention to detail; basic computer proficiency and strong database research skills; excellent interpersonal and communication talents; strong critical thinking, analytical, and organizational skills

Special Requirements—Positions with federal government agencies may require security clearance

CAREER LADDER

Chief Information Officer; Independent Consultant; Information Systems Director

↑

Information Scientist

↑

Graduate Student; Information Technician

Position Description

Information science is concerned with the collection, organization, and use of data. Students in this discipline learn about computer data storage and processing, about systems planning and design, and about how to design and develop databases that meet a wide variety of user needs. It is the aspect of computer science that studies how information is used by individuals and the technology that makes it happen.

The work of Information Scientists is distinguished by the high level of theoretical expertise and innovation they apply to complex problems and the creation or application of new technology. Those employed by academic institutions focus on areas ranging from complexity theory to hardware and programming language design. Some work on multidisciplinary projects such as developing and advancing the uses of virtual reality or extending human-computer interaction. Their counterparts in private industry concentrate on areas such as applying information theory, developing specialized languages or information technologies, and designing programming tools and knowledge-based systems.

They develop and design methods and procedures for collecting, organizing, interpreting, and classifying information for input into their clients' computer systems, as well as for the retrieval of specific information from computer systems. In their duties, they use their knowledge of symbolic language and optical or pattern recognition principles. They conduct logical analyses of business, scientific, engineering, and other technical problems, formulating mathematical models of the problems and their potential solutions by computers. In addition, they develop alternate designs to resolve problems in the input, storage, and retrieval of information.

Their online research may encompass the identification and evaluation of scientific literature and publications relating to clients' specific fields (such as pharmaceutical products or biodiversity and ecosystems information). They may index specialized literature (journal articles, theses, books, and abstracts) with internally maintained thesauri. In so doing, they develop and produce on-demand retrospective searches of information databases and maintain current awareness searches. They must ensure that correct and useful indexing and record structures support quality standards for access and retrieval of this data.

In addition to online research, their work may be specifically directed toward document identification and retrieval, collection management, bibliographic database management, or ongoing developments in the field of information resources and technology. Their work requires an understanding of digital formats, conversion alternatives, and metadata standards. Regardless of the specific information goals of their organizations, Information Scientists build content, respond to user requirements, and construct the knowledge structures needed by organizations, including the selection and implementation of content standards and conduction of user testing. Most Information Scientists specialize in specific fields of information science, such as scientific or engineering research, or in particular fields, such as business, education, library science, or medicine.

Salaries

Wage earnings by Information Scientists tend to be high due to their technical expertise and training. According to the U.S. Department of Labor's Bureau of Labor Statistics, the yearly salaries for Information Scientists in May 2006 ranged from a low of $53,590 to a high of $144,880, with a median annual wage being $93,950. In its December 2007 salary survey report on computer and Information Scientists, PayScale, Inc., found that median annual salaries ranged from $58,049 to $119,994, depending on the type of employer, years of experience, and geographic location.

Employment Prospects

It is estimated that computer and Information Scientist positions will be among the fastest growing occupations through 2012. Although they are increasingly employed in every sector of the economy (particularly the medical and scientific fields), their greatest concentration is in computer systems design and related service industries. Job increases are expected to be driven by the very rapid growth in this sector, which is projected to be one of the quickest-expanding industries in the U.S. economy. In addition, many job openings will arise annually from the need to replace individuals who move into managerial positions or other technical occupations or who leave the labor force.

Advancement Prospects

Information Scientists employed in private industry may progress into managerial or project leadership positions. Those employed in academic institutions may become heads of research departments as well as published authorities in their fields. Some Information Scientists may further their research careers by becoming independent consultants.

Education and Training

Initially, a bachelor's degree in computer science, computational science, or information science is compulsory for an Information Scientist. Then, a master's degree in library and information science (M.L.I.S.) from an American Library Association (ALA)–accredited institution is required. Many specialty fields (such as engineering, chemistry, biology, medicine, and pharmaceuticals) also demand a Ph.D. from their Information Scientists to be able to apply their expertise to the needs, requirements, and processes of their fields. Additionally, as rapidly changing technology demands increasing levels of skill and education from Information Scientists, continuing education is a critical component of their career paths.

Special Requirements

Certification as computer professionals may be required by some employers of their Information Scientists. The Institute for Certification of Computing Professionals (ICCP) provides extensive information about a variety of certification programs. (Their Web site is at http://www.iccp.org.) Information Scientists employed by government agencies or organizations that have government contracts usually are subject to security clearances and must meet eligibility requirements for access to classified information.

Experience, Skills, and Personality Traits

As part of their computer technical backgrounds, Information Scientists should have some know-how with Linux and other UNIX operating systems as well as hands-on familiarity with modern programming languages. The more experience they have working with a wide variety of database systems, the better are their chances for employment. In addition, they should be able to prepare and deliver technical presentations and training on specialized topics, which means their communication and interpersonal abilities must be exemplary.

Information Scientists should have some background in creating and applying the use of controlled vocabularies and taxonomies. They should be familiar with research techniques for searching scientific and other literature on commercial databases coupled with a strong understanding of online information retrieval practices and processes. They need to be able to manage multiple priorities and have strong attention to detail. They must be able to work independently as well as function as members of team efforts. They must be capable of critical thinking and have strong analytical and organizational talents. Additionally, many large corporations and organizations prefer their Information Scientists (and specialists) to have multidisciplinary technical backgrounds.

Unions and Associations

Professional groups of primary interest to Information Scientists include the Association for Computing Machinery (ACM), the Computing Research Association (CRA), the Computing Technology Industry Association (CTIA), the Institute of Electrical and Electronics Engineers (IEEE) Computer Society, and the National Workforce Center for Emerging Technologies (NWCET).

Tips for Entry

1. While in college, seek summer internships with computer service bureaus or consultants to hone your programming skills and gain experience with a variety of programming languages.
2. If you have a special field of interest (such as chemistry, biology, engineering, or medicine), consider earning an additional degree in that field, which you can apply to your work as an Information Scientist.
3. Besides your technical course work in college, take a business class and/or a psychology class to provide you with some management skills to better handle the direction of projects of which you will be in charge as an Information Scientist.

INFORMATION TECHNICIAN

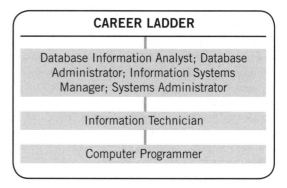

Position Description

Information technology (IT) is defined by the Information Technology Association of America (ITAA) as "the study, design, development, implementation, support or management of computer-based information systems, particularly software applications and computer hardware." Encompassing the computer and information sciences industries, IT is the capability to electronically convert, input, process, store, protect, output, retrieve, transmit, and receive data and information securely, including text, graphics, sound, and video, as well as the ability to control machines of all kinds electronically. Broadly speaking, IT comprises computers, networks, satellite communications, robotics, videotext, cable/satellite television, electronic mail (e-mail), electronic games, and automated office equipment. The industry consists of all computer, communications, and electronics-related organizations, including hardware, software, and services.

With today's sophisticated hardware, software, and communications technologies, it is often difficult to classify a computer system as belonging uniquely to one specific application program and process. Increasingly, organizations are consolidating their information needs into a single, integrated system. One example is a German software program called SAP, which runs on mainframe computers and is a database that enables companies to organize all their data (information) into a single database, then choose only the program modules (which are freestanding and customized to fit each customer's needs) or tables they want at any given time.

Information Technicians plan, implement, operate, and maintain IT systems. An information system (IS) is the system of persons, data records, and activities that process the data and information in an organization, including both manual and automated processes. Computer-based ISs are the IT component of such a system. Information Technicians install, configure, modify, maintain, troubleshoot, diagnose, and repair computer hardware and software to assure the smooth running of computer-based ISs. They set up new systems and modify existing ones to accommodate new hardware and software. They also troubleshoot, diagnose, and resolve problems with peripheral equipment (including printers) and investigate and resolve problems with e-mail configurations. They connect an organization's computers to network systems and assure proper connectivity. They back up data files in accordance with established procedures, configure antivirus programs, and restore user files when necessary. They respond to inquiries from an organization's staff about the IS and provide technical data concerning related standards, requirements, practices, and procedures. They install software, test its applications to assure proper operation, and configure hardware and software to provide proper network access. They check switches, cables, and other network components to assure functionality and perform a variety of network administration activities, including establishing and maintaining user accounts, e-mail accounts, and Internet connectivity. They operate an assortment of tools and equipment to maintain and repair computer systems.

In many organizations, Information Technicians assemble data sets and other documentation (such as data management, procedure writing, and the writing of job setup instructions) needed to build information databases and assist in deciding how the information is to be presented in the database. They aid in designing and coordinating the development of integrated IS databases as well as help maintain Internet and intranet Web sites. They may be responsible for the maintenance of the organization's telecommunications systems as well as their local area networks (LANs) and/or their wide area networks (WANs). Additionally, Information Technicians may conduct training and provide ongoing technical support to end users as well as work with the organization's staff to evaluate the IT requirements of the organization.

Salaries

According to a 2006 *InfoWorld* Compensation Survey, annual salaries for IT professionals were up 4.8 percent that year, the best showing in five years and indicating a trend upward. In their December 2007 salary survey report on Information Technicians and technology specialists, PayScale, Inc., found that yearly median salaries ranged from a low of $37,204 to a high of $79,590, depending on the type of employer and the number of years in the field.

Employment Prospects

Most businesses and many organizations have computer systems that they need to protect, maintain, or expand. In addition, there are other organizations that

need to add computer systems and to develop information databases. Because of technological advances and the competition between businesses as well as the continuous need for information databases by scientific and medical organizations (and governmental agencies), it is unlikely that the demand for Information Technicians and computer technicians will slow any time soon. Organizations will continue to invest heavily in their computer database systems and, in turn, hire technicians to develop and maintain these systems.

Advancement Prospects

With additional training in management practices and processes, Information Technicians interested in an information management career may progress into middle manager positions in the IT field (such as database or systems administrators). They may decide to expand their analytical skills by moving up to positions as database information analysts.

Education and Training

Most employers require their Information Technicians to have a high school diploma or a general equivalency diploma, or GED, supplemented by college-level course work (or an associate's degree) in computer science or a related field, coupled with one to three years of experience in the installation, maintenance, and repair of computer hardware, software, peripherals, and related equipment. Some employers demand a bachelor's degree in information systems, computer science, or computer engineering or an equivalent four years of hands-on experience in an IT-related environment.

Special Requirements

A certification as a computer professional may be required by some employers and, in any case, is a valuable addition to the résumé of an Information Technician. The Institute for Certification of Computing Professionals (ICCP) provides extensive information about a variety of computer certification programs. (Their Web site is located at http://www.iccp.org.) Information Technicians employed by governmental agencies or organizations who have government contracts often are subject to a security investigation and may be required to meet eligibility requirements for access to classified data.

Experience, Skills, and Personality Traits

Information Technicians must have considerable proficiency in computer technology. They need to be completely familiar with methods and techniques used in troubleshooting various computer hardware and software problems and the principles and practices of technical problem solving. They should be able to read and interpret technical documents (including computer software programs, hardware installation instructions, computer operating and maintenance instructions, and procedures manuals). They need to have good writing skills, as they will have to formulate reports on a routine basis. They may be required to write simple correspondence and present information to individuals (or small groups of persons) involved with their organizations. Their verbal communication skills must be excellent as well, since they will have to communicate successfully with other technology professionals within and outside their organizations and outside technical support providers. In addition, they will need to respond to customers and to staff database users and address their complaints and problems in a timely, accurate, and courteous manner. They will be required to provide technical guidance and assistance to users, customers, and team members in the use of the computer system hardware and software.

Information Technicians must possess excellent analytical talents and possess strong attention to detail along with a capacity for following through on their tasks effectively. They must maintain organized and accurate records, including clear and concise program documentation, user procedures, reports of work performed, and other written material. They must be able to prioritize their tasks and handle multiple tasks simultaneously. Finally, Information Technicians must be physically fit, as this position often requires moderate physical activity and the ability to lift equipment and other items (which may weigh up to 50 pounds). They may be required to climb ladders or access equipment in cabinets or underneath office furniture.

Unions and Associations

Of primary professional interest to Information Technicians is the Information Technology Association of America (ITAA), the industry trade group for many U.S. IT organizations. For those Information Technicians who work for multinational corporations, the World Information Technology and Services Alliance (WITSA) will be useful, as it is a consortium of more than 60 IT industry associations from economies around the world. Besides these umbrella organizations, Information Technicians may find it useful to belong to the Association for Computing Machinery (ACM), the Computing Research Association (CRA), the Computing Technology Industry Association (CTIA), the Institute for Electrical and Electronics Engineers (IEEE) Computer Society, and the National Workforce Center for Emerging Technologies (NWCET).

Tips for Entry

1. During high school or college, seek internships or work experience programs that will allow you to work in a computer consulting firm where you can gain firsthand experience and apply what you have learned in your computer courses.
2. As computer database and IT is constantly being modified and expanded, it is important to research your field and stay updated on the latest technology through additional course work and reading.
3. Besides your computer courses, take some business management courses, as they will provide you with useful background in your daily work within your professional environment.

PRIVATE INDUSTRY INFORMATION BROKER

CAREER LADDER

Director or Owner of Information Brokerage Firm

Private Industry Information Broker

Research Librarian; Beginner Information Broker

business firm, law library, or health services firm); function well with others and work well under pressure; computer literacy; excellent interpersonal, communication, and organizational skills; outstanding research abilities; strong business sense

Position Description

Information Brokers search for specified information for clients. They may use various resources, including the Internet, online services that specialize in databases, public and private libraries, books, CD-ROMs, and personal contacts via telephone or e-mail. They supply—for a fee—information retrieval from publicly accessible data sources and often private sources as well.

Many Information Brokers (or independent information professionals, as they are sometimes called) serve businesses, organizations, and the professions directly, providing information services or products ranging from research on demand, to market or research analysis, to software products. Others serve libraries and information centers by providing publications for the profession, consulting services, or temporary staffing on- or off-site. There is a large virtual network within the Information Broker professional community that encourages subcontracting among members when one Information Broker has a client but does not have the time or special expertise to perform the assignment. Thus, Information Brokers can be clients of fellow Information Brokers.

Many Information Brokers specialize in specific fields of information, such as the law, health services, business and financial services, or scientific and technical information. Legal services Information Brokers often have advanced degrees in law and have had some experience working within a law library. They are usually affiliated with law firms and perform legal research writing, manage law libraries, and offer litigation support. They search documented law cases, legal statutes and decisions, and other sources of law and are able to draft legal memoranda, pleadings, motions, and briefs. They may also be responsible for updating law library collections, organizing and arranging these libraries, monitoring expenditures, and recommending acquisitions. In addition, legal services Information Brokers find information about products, ownership of subsidiaries, and expert witnesses. Usually their services are for a fixed project with a deadline and a specific budget, although some legal services Information Brokers work on a continuing basis.

Health services Information Brokers provide crucial information to the health care industry using online searching, library research, competitor intelligence (monitoring of a competitor's business initiatives and plans), and similar provenances. They take the raw data from all their sources and present only those that are pertinent to their client. The entire health care industry is built on a framework of information, enabling doctors, nurses, and other health care professionals to provide appropriate care to their patients as well as to know about product safety and the most effective drugs and medical devices available from manufacturers. This information is available from the U.S. government, professional associations, books, professional journals, information databases, and the Internet and requires the health services Information Broker to fully understand and be knowledgeable of medical terminology. Typical clients include smaller medical corporations and drug companies without staff researchers. For example, a pharmaceutical company working on a drug that has the potential for treating a number of different disorders may use a health services Information Broker to research the number of patients afflicted with each disorder as well as the current methods and costs of treatment in order to determine whether the current treatments are lacking and whether its drug might be more cost effective and useful.

Financial services Information Brokers offer a variety of services to consumer banks, investment banks, and stock brokerage firms. They have the expertise to locate data and analyze detailed financial data about competitors, aid in providing information for potential merger and acquisition efforts, and provide solutions that are understandable to members of the institutions for whom they work. For example, if a bank has provisionally decided to stop certain financial services to a local market, an Information Broker can perform a zip code analysis of direct-mail or in-branch promotions. The result of this data mining may reveal a new market segment on which to focus future promotions, thus providing new avenues of revenue for the bank while at the same time identifying desired demographics of potential customers.

Most financial institutions have their own market analyses, forecasts, and other expert research. However, such information usually is spread throughout many different offices on different servers and is, essentially, inaccessible to easy usability. Financial services Information Brokers can apply their organizational talents to create a data library integrating all potential data sources within one company and help with drafting a routing policy for print materials that will provide the needed usability. Additionally, they can provide information about trends, innovative products, new types of banking services, and delivery methods required by small businesses for brokerage firm analysis. Some financial services Information Brokers also offer consulting services in financial technical writing or translation services. Many are generalists who can provide all types of financial information for their clients.

Science and technology Information Brokers serve various types of clients, often specializing in chemistry, engineering, patent searching, or computer programming and software design. These customers include other consultants and research firms, laboratories, petrochemical and energy companies, as well as other high-technology organizations. Most information professionals who provide such services have scientific backgrounds themselves (and may have advanced degrees in specific fields) in addition to their library science training and research backgrounds. Unlike ordinary researchers, science and technology Information Brokers are more interested in resources than answers. They work at perfecting their ability to know where to find specific scientific and technical data so as to know where to investigate when such information may be needed again. They provide summaries and evaluations of scientific literature for their clients, frequently searching the patent literature, which contains a great deal of information not published anywhere else.

With access to more than 2,500 international databases and information centers worldwide, science and technology Information Brokers can provide information on demand, as well as document delivery services in addition to their regular consulting services. Moreover, some offer the ability to index full-text documents so they can access pertinent indexed materials for specific questions and problems posed by their clients. Information Brokers are uniquely trained for this type of research work.

Salaries

Private Industry Information Brokers often charge between $45 and $100 an hour for their services, depending on the specific type of information being sought and the difficulty of providing it. The annual income of experienced Information Brokers may exceed $150,000. However, many of the services and databases used by Information Brokers charge hourly fees, which must be deducted, along with other operating expenses, from the broker's ultimate compensation.

Employment Prospects

The sheer amount of available industry information— be it financial, medical, legal, or scientific and either inside or outside a company—creates a tremendous demand for information professionals who are adept at locating the correct data efficiently and presenting it to the client in the desired format and within the required time restraints. This explosion of information on the Internet and in specialized databases worldwide has forced organizations to turn to the services of Information Brokers who have the research and computer skills to satisfy their information needs, which has made this profession one of the fastest-growing job areas in information science.

Advancement Prospects

Many, if not most, Information Brokers sign up at first with large information brokerage firms that specialize in their particular field of interest. Eventually, after gaining seasoning and a reputation for successful work, many start their own independent consulting businesses. They may begin their own consulting brokerage firms on a part-time basis while maintaining full-time jobs elsewhere. Thus, they can develop their businesses slowly, concentrating on their growing lists of clients and building their businesses through referrals from satisfied clients. As Mary Ellen Bates, principal of Bates Information Services, has put it: "The best way to build your business is through referrals. The only way to get referrals is to do a better job than anyone else. Not cheaper . . . better." At some point, part-time Information Brokers often find it difficult to maintain full-time work elsewhere, and most will decide to work full-time at their own firm, spending a great deal of time and energy on building their operations.

Education and Training

Most Private Industry Information Brokers have a master's degree in library science (M.L.S.) or, preferably, in library and information science (M.L.I.S.) as well as a business degree (and, ideally, some financial background). Information Brokers who specialize in particular types of industry should have practical experience in those industries: Health services Information Brokers should have some medical experience and some time spent working in a medical library; legal services Information Brokers may not need law degrees, but should have worked in law libraries; financial services Information Brokers should have business degrees and some financial experience (possibly even working in banks or brokerage firms); science and technology Information Brokers need degrees in their fields of expertise and should have some laboratory experience as well.

Experience, Skills, and Personality Traits

The most important professional attribute of Information Brokers is their outstanding researching abilities coupled with their computer proficiency. Organizational skills and good business sense (for those who will be running their own consulting firms) are equally key. The ability to work well with clients is critical, and Information Brokers need to develop the ability to serve as tactful intermediaries between their clients and their information sources. They must know how to ask pertinent questions effectively and elicit needed data from these sources without antagonizing them. They must be able to define their goals and implement them, be willing to take calculated risks, and be amenable to new ideas and potential business relationships. They need to be creative, determined, disciplined, and dedicated to providing the best information service they can.

In addition to their specific research skills (including knowing where to obtain needed information), Information Brokers who manage their own consulting firms must be able to market and sell their services. Operating a business requires different skills, such as the ability to write business plans, create advertising and marketing campaigns, manage the financial and accounting aspects of running a business, and supervise necessary staff.

Unions and Associations

Private Industry Information Brokers may belong to a variety of professional organizations that can provide them with educational guidance, support, conferences and meetings with professional colleagues, and basic and career information. Groups of interest include the American Society for Information Science and Technology (ASIS&T), the Association for Information Professionals (AIP), the Association of Independent Information Professionals (AIIP), the Library and Information Technology Association (LITA, a division of the American Library Association), the Public Record Retrievers Network (PRRN), and the Society for Competitor Intelligence Professionals (SCIP). In addition, Information Brokers who specialize in particular industries may find it beneficial to belong to specific professional groups associated with those areas, such as the American Association of Law Libraries (AALL), the Medical Library Association (MLA), the American Business Association (ABA), and various scientific and technology organizations.

Information on national standards in information resources is available from the National Information Standards Organization (NISO), which is the U.S. nonprofit standards organization that develops, maintains, and publishes technical standards related to bibliographic and library applications. Its Web site is located at http://www.niso.org.

Tips for Entry

1. It is critical for you to gain experience and to establish yourself in the Information Brokerage profession by working for an employer before setting out on your own. Consider working for an information brokerage firm for several years. Consult the *Burwell World Directory of Information Brokers* (http://www.burwellinc.com) to locate more than 1,800 information brokerages listed in the directory.

2. After several years of experience, you may be ready to set up your own consulting firm, but first develop a solid business and marketing plan. During your first several years of business, be sure you have an alternate means of financial support, as it takes time to make real money and set your business on a sound financial keel.

3. Consider setting up a Web site to advertise your services as an Information Broker. In addition, contact local organizations in your field of expertise to discuss how your particular research skills may benefit them.

4. As it is critical for you to maintain your computer, research, and information technology skills, consult continuing education seminars at local community colleges, universities, or other educational institutions.

PUBLIC POLICY AND PUBLIC RECORDS INFORMATION BROKERS

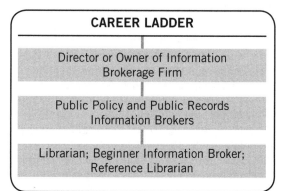

CAREER LADDER

Director or Owner of Information Brokerage Firm

Public Policy and Public Records Information Brokers

Librarian; Beginner Information Broker; Reference Librarian

Position Description

Public Policy and Public Records Information Brokers are individuals who search for specified information requested by their clients. They use various resources, including the Internet, online services that specialize in databases, public and private libraries, books, CD-ROMs, and personal contacts via telephone and e-mail. They provide, for a fee, information retrieval from publicly accessible data sources and often private sources as well.

Public Policy Information Brokers often serve governmental agencies at federal, state, or local levels. These agencies often need examples of policies that have been developed, implemented, and reviewed by other governmental jurisdictions to help develop and implement their own. In addition, they often need to know about technology trends and specific data in order to design their own information databases and information systems as well as to guide them in setting up their own workplace situations. Public Policy Information Brokers collect examples through online

research and primary interviews with other agencies in order to identify what has worked in similar agencies (or what has *not* worked) as well as to research human resource policies and procedures.

Public Policy Information Brokers bring to bear their unique abilities to know where to find specific public policy data, which distinguishes them from other types of researchers who collect facts, rather than discovering where to find such facts (or similar facts) again when needed. Thus, brokers are flexible in that they do not have to spend time building elaborate databases but must be able to present information so that it is understandable and accessible to their clients.

While government agencies and their employees have access to online resources, many of them have discovered that searching for information is a complicated, frustrating, and time-consuming process. That is why they often turn over the more complex parts of their information seeking to professional brokers. For example, a local government agency is considering new ordinances concerning changing traffic patterns.

It most likely would hire a Public Policy Information Broker to locate examples of similar ordinances in other jurisdictions (cities, states, or counties) and identify potential resources in national organizations or regional governments that might aid it in setting up its own policies and ordinances. Government human resource departments and divisions often request the help of Public Policy Information Brokers before they establish or revise their own policies relating to sexual or gender discrimination, disability access, or acceptable Internet use by their employees. In this case, information brokers research and collect current legal writings and examples of successful policies of other government agencies as well as contact public interest associations and groups that might offer pertinent information.

Public Records Information Brokers provide their clients with data about specific businesses, corporations, individuals, and properties by searching public documents, such as bankruptcy filings, professional licenses, vital statistics records (for birth, death, marriage, divorce, and adoption information), civil and criminal court records, property ownership records, tax liens, Uniform Commercial Code (UCC) filings, and vehicle registrations. Legislation such as the federal Freedom of Information Act and states' public records acts allow for public access to government records, and Public Records Information Brokers are familiar with the access process of obtaining information from these sources. They also can provide manual, telephone, and online research for their clients through their access to research libraries and online databases (from both the United States and abroad). In addition, much potential information that clients might need from public records is usually found buried in county courthouse files, which brokers can access through their network of local researchers. Their clients may require them to provide large or small studies, comprehensive reports, or answers to specific questions. The ability of Public Records Information Brokers to locate specific public records information distinguishes them from other research agencies that collect facts without bothering to learn where they can get these and similar facts when needed in the future.

For example, a citizens' group desiring to find out information about a rash of residents' illnesses may use a Public Records Information broker to learn more about local power plants or neighborhood industrial facilities. (This might include the broker checking with federal and state agencies such as the Environmental Protection Agency, local departments of transportation, and the Occupational Safety and Health Administration for compliance information and potential issues.)

Small business owners (and even corporations) may hire Public Records Information Brokers to conduct preemployment screening of potential employees who will be responsible for handling goods and cash, making sure that they do not have a history of theft, unsafe driving, or drug usage. Public Records Information Brokers can also verify previous job positions that the applicants have held.

Both Public Policy Information Brokers and Public Records Information Brokers often operate as temporary contractors or consultants, and when their clients are government agencies or large corporations, they often work through a public competitive bidding framework for acquiring jobs. Typically, these assignments are a single project with a deadline and a specific budget, although some information brokers work on an ongoing basis for their client(s).

Salaries

Independent Public Policy and Public Records Information Brokers may charge between $40 and $85 per hour (which translates potentially into average annual earnings of $80,000 to $160,000 or more), depending on the type of information being sought. However, many of the services and databases used by information brokers charge hourly fees, which must be deducted—along with other operating expenses—from the brokers' profits. Additionally, during the first year or so of acting as an independent information broker, earnings (after expenses) may only run anywhere from $20,000 to $55,000.

Employment Prospects

The continuous and growing demand for information to help determine public policy initiatives and for public records information coupled with the sheer amount of available information help guarantee the need for professional information brokers who are adept at finding data and presenting it in their clients' desired formats. Seasoned researchers/librarians with their research skills and computer technology experience can turn these assets into thriving businesses.

Advancement Prospects

Many information brokers initially work as librarians (particularly reference librarians) or researchers before launching into full-time work as information brokers. They may have spent years perfecting their research expertise within large corporations or research centers. Most Information Brokers start their professional lives by working for information brokerage companies. Eventually, they may leave these firms to establish their own independent public policy or public records consulting businesses.

Education and Training

Most Public Policy and Public Records Information Brokers have master's degrees in either library science (M.L.S.) or in library and information science (M.L.I.S.) as well as some experience working with public records. In addition, many information brokers have advanced degrees in areas related to government or law. Some additional educational background in information brokering, business, marketing, and business planning is necessary if they plan to operate their own consulting firms.

Experience, Skills, and Personality Traits

Both Public Policy and Public Records Information Brokers must have excellent researching abilities, along with strong organizational and computer skills. Since it is necessary for them to be able to explain facts and subject areas in terms that are easily understood by their clients (and easily programmable for computer use), they must have excellent verbal and written communication talents. They need to excel at analyzing problems and questions so they can identify not only the central part of each problem but also be able to use the most likely and time-efficient method to solve the research problem or question.

Public Policy Information Brokers must be able to assess information for accuracy, quality, and utility and be able to organize it into recognizable and useful patterns and associations. They need to know how to sift through scattered collections of facts and data to find and sort needed information into related facts and then use this related material to uncover trends and patterns.

Public Records Information Brokers must develop the ability to be tactful intermediaries between their client(s) and potential sources of information. They need to know how to answer queries, ask effective questions, and elicit information from sources without being threatening in any way.

Information brokers who operate their own independent business must have the ability to handle customers well. Running their enterprises requires a different set of skills from those required for the information profession. They need to be adept at bookkeeping, marketing, advertising, and self-motivation as well as have excellent general office capabilities.

Unions and Associations

Public Policy and Public Records Information Brokers belong to a variety of professional groups that can provide them with educational guidance, support, conferences and meetings with professional colleagues, and information. Organizations of interest include the American Society for Information Science and Technology (ASIS&T), the Association for Information Professionals (AIP), the Association of Independent Information Professionals (AIIP), the Library and Information Technology Association (LITA, a division of the American Library Association), the Public Record Retrievers Network (PRRN), and the Society for Competitor Intelligence Professionals (SCIP). In addition, information on national standards in information resources is available from the National Information Standards Organization (NISO), which is the U.S. nonprofit standards organization that develops, maintains, and publishes technical standards related to bibliographic and library applications. Its Web site is located at http://www.niso.org.

Tips for Entry

1. It is important for you to gain experience and to establish yourself in the profession by working for an employer before setting out on your own. Consider first working for an information brokerage firm. Consult the *Burwell World Directory of Information Brokers* (http://www.burwellinc.com) to locate more than 1,800 information brokerages listed in the directory.

2. After several years of experience, consider setting up your own consulting firm, but first develop a business and marketing plan. During your initial years of operation, be sure you have an alternate means of financial support, as it takes time to make real money, even in this lucrative field.

3. Consider signing up for classes on information brokering, marketing, and business planning to aid you in your (future) business venture. Also, check out continuing education seminars offered by local community colleges or universities.

4. Contact local businesses, law firms, or government agencies, present your résumé, and discuss how your skills may benefit them as your clients. Above all, remember networking, marketing, and contacts are essential to the success of your business.

EDUCATION

DEAN, SCHOOL OF LIBRARY AND INFORMATION SCIENCE

CAREER PROFILE

Duties: Provide academic and administrative leadership; enunciate a persuasive vision of the school's role in library and information science education and research; oversee fund-raising, and develop partnerships within and without the institution; through understanding national trends and issues in library and information science, undertake a national and international role in helping to shape the future of library and information science

Alternate Title(s): None

Salary Range: $75,000 to $160,000 or more

Employment Prospects: Fair

Advancement Prospects: Fair

Prerequisites:

Education or Training—Doctoral degree in library science or library and information science or other doctoral degree appropriate for leadership in library and information science studies; in some cases, commensurate background may be substituted

Experience—Extensive administrative and teaching background necessary; library administrative and budgeting background helpful

CAREER LADDER

Dean, Larger School of Library and Information Science; President, Educational Institution

Dean, School of Library and Information Science

Professor of Library and Information Science

Special Skills and Personality Traits—Capable of a visionary understanding of the roles of information professionals in a technologically and socially changing world; commitment to educational needs of practicing information professionals; excellent time-management and fund-raising talents; good analytical and problem-solving abilities; strong interpersonal and communication skills

Position Description

The Dean, School of Library and Information Science, is the chief academic officer of the institution within the university and is responsible for the faculty and the student body of the school. Deans are expected to pursue standards of excellence for teaching and scholarship that will inspire and lead faculty, students, and staff in their academic pursuits. They motivate and support high levels of faculty performance and promote morale and cohesiveness of both staff and faculty. Deans have the responsibility for expanding, strengthening, and managing the resources of their schools: the faculty and the students, the finances, and the facilities. Along with their curriculum committees, they decide what courses to offer, set class schedules, and develop curricula, ensuring that their schools' programs and research agendas grow and deepen.

Deans express their visions of their schools' roles in library and information science education and research. They are the principal spokespersons for the institution, both internally and externally, and provide the required intellectual leadership and voice for the quickly evolving ideas in which the schools are engaged. In their administering and coordinating of their schools' activities, they also establish links among disciplines within the schools, with other schools and colleges in the universities, and with external colleagues and constituents, thus extending the reach of the schools. They maintain close relations with alumni, professionals in the field of library and information science, and the local communities.

In addition, they are responsible for developing external sources for funding for their schools. They actively engage in fund-raising and grant-seeking activities to support students, faculty, and the schools' programs. Their extensive financial responsibilities include, in addition, management of the institutions' budgets. Deans usually report to the executive vice presidents for academic affairs of the universities and are key members of the universities' leadership teams.

Salaries

Salaries for this position vary significantly depending on the scope of the job responsibilities and the location of the university. In a salary survey report dated October 2007 of the earnings of deans of graduate studies (which includes Deans, School of Library and Information Science), PayScale, Inc., found that median annual salaries ranged from a low of $78,145 to a high of $147,156, depending on years of experience and type of school (two-year or four-year).

Employment Prospects

As there are a limited number of schools of library and information science, jobs for deans of such schools are also limited and are not expected to grow significantly. Job openings will depend on deans retiring or moving into other fields. Most deans have held professorships in the field of library and information science, and the competition for advancement to becoming a dean of the school remains stiff.

Advancement Prospects

Because the Dean is the most senior member of the library and information science school, he or she may find the only way for career progression is to accept a position at a larger, more prestigious university. Some deans may use their administrative talents and seasoning to seek posts as presidents of colleges or universities.

Education and Training

In addition to a doctorate in library and information science (or in a closely related field), deans must have records of academic achievement proportionate to that required of senior-level faculty appointments. Academic credentials include classroom teaching experience and recognized scholarly and professional accomplishments (including being published). In addition, their administrative experience should include management of fiscal and human resources and demonstrated commitment to collaborative leadership that should have been gained at the level of department chair or higher. Many schools look for candidates who have successful records of working with a diversified population and demonstrated commitment to cultural diversity and equal opportunity.

Experience, Skills, and Personality Traits

Deans should provide dynamic and imaginative leadership with an ability to motivate, develop, and direct faculty, staff, and students. They must have thorough understandings of trends in library and information science and be familiar with technological advancements that impinge on the practices, procedures, and policies of libraries in today's world. They must have strong communication, interpersonal, and organizational abilities, be self-confident and persuasive, and be decisive and determined. Their obligation to fundraising and the development of partnerships inside and outside the university is extremely important.

Unions and Associations

Deans of schools of library and information science are usually required to be members of the American Library Association (ALA) and may find it useful to belong to such other organizations as the American Society for Information Science and Technology (ASIS&T), the Association of College and Research Libraries (ACRL), the Council on Library and Information Resources (CLIR), the International Federation of Library Associations and Institutions (IFLA), and the Special Libraries Association (SLA). As educational administrators, they may find it useful to belong to such groups as the American Association of University Administrators (AAUA), the Association of College Administration Professionals (ACAP), and the American Conference of Academic Deans (ACAD).

Tips for Entry

1. As you commence your teaching career in higher education, volunteer to serve on administrative committees in your department, academic unit, or institution as a means of gaining managerial experience and making contact with educational professionals who may prove useful to you in your career.

2. Do not hesitate to use your network of contacts to help you learn about key people, issues, the political climate, and other information regarding the library and information science school in which you are advancing your career.

3. To learn more about the profession of academic deans, visit the Web site of the American Conference of Academic Deans at http://www.acad-edu.org.

PROFESSOR, LIBRARY AND INFORMATION SCIENCE

Duties: Teach courses in library and information science; conduct research and publish research results, articles, books, and so forth

Alternate Title(s): Lecturer, Library and Information Science; Library and Information Science Professor; Library and Information Technology Instructor; Library Technology Instructor

Salary Range: $45,000 to $110,000 or more

Employment Prospects: Fair to good

Advancement Prospects: Fair

Prerequisites:

Education or Training—Both a master's and doctoral degree in library science or library and information science usually required, or another doctoral degree appropriate for information studies curriculum

Experience—Teaching background, particularly in computer and information technology, librarianship, and organization of information; some administrative work helpful; library experience recommended

CAREER LADDER

Assistant or Associate Dean, School of Library and Information Science

↑

Professor of Library and Information Science

↑

Assistant or Associate Professor of Library and Information Science

Special Skills and Personality Traits—Demonstrated knowledge of current and emerging trends and technologies related to library and information services; effective teaching and presentation abilities; excellent computer skills; familiarity with core concepts of librarianship; strong interpersonal, organizational, and written and oral communication talents

Special Requirements—Teaching in state college or university systems may require a state license

Position Description

In general, professors are qualified experts who conduct lectures and seminars in their fields of study, perform advanced research in their fields, publish their findings or author other types of books, provide community service such as advising government and nonprofit organizations, and train young or new academics (usually graduate students). An important part of professorship is the concept of tenure. A tenured professor has a lifetime appointment until retirement, except for dismissal with "due course."

There are three basic levels of professorship in colleges and universities in North America. Assistant professors are entry-level positions, for which they need a doctorate. In some cases, a master's degree may suffice, especially at community colleges. (In community colleges, teaching posts are known as instructors instead of professors.) This position is generally not tenured, although in most educational institutions, the commonly used term *tenure-track position* indicates that

the candidate can become tenured after a probationary period (anywhere from three to seven years). Associate professor is a mid-level post, usually awarded after a substantial publication record (such as a book or book contract, although the requirements vary from institution to institution). Sometimes, though rarely, an individual may be hired at the associate professor level without tenure, usually done as a financial inducement undertaken with the stipulation that the position is tenure-track. At a few large institutions, associate professors are untenured and only rarely promoted to tenure. Full professor is the senior level and is usually tenured (except at some for-profit private educational institutions). The median age of American full professors is currently around 55 years, and very few people attain this position before the age of 40.

Professors, Library and Information Science, are responsible for teaching courses in the field, including library science, cataloging, children's literature, technical services, youth services, school librarianship, and more.

With the increased use of automation in libraries and the introduction of digital technology in library research and collection procedures, the emphasis in many programs of library and information science education has increasingly been on: (1) digital libraries; (2) data curation (the process of identification, verification, and organization) and digital preservation; (3) bibliometrics and infometrics; (4) software engineering; (5) information systems design; (6) user-interface design and usability engineering; (7) information visualization; (8) computational linguistics and natural language processing; (9) information retrieval (including multimedia); (10) grid-based computing and cyber-infrastructure; (11) infomatics in any domain (such as social science, humanities, health and life science, or communications); (12) digital narratives; (13) development and analysis of collaborative and sociotechnical systems; and (14) organizational theory and program evaluation in libraries and related information-based institutions.

Professors prepare course materials such as syllabi, homework assignments, and handouts. They prepare and deliver lectures to undergraduate and/or graduate students on topics such as collection development, archival methods, and indexing and abstracting. They evaluate and grade students' class work, assignments, and papers. Through their teaching aids, they maintain student attendance records, grades, and other required records. They plan, evaluate, and revise curricula course content, and course materials and methods of instruction. They may help to develop school policies. They advise undergraduate and/or graduate students on academic and vocational curricula and on career choices. They conduct research in a chosen particular field of library or information science and publish their findings in professional journals, books, and/or electronic media. Most important, they keep abreast of developments (and the introduction of new technology) in their field by reading current literature, communicating with colleagues, and participating in professional conferences.

Salaries

Salaries for this position vary a great deal depending on the professor's rank and on the size and location of the school or university. According to the 2006–07 National Faculty Salary Survey conducted by the College and University Professional Association of Human Resources (CUPA-HR), median annual salaries for faculty members who taught specific library science courses were as follows: cataloging specialist, $52,108; catalog librarian, $49,382; collection development buyer, $45,195; reference & instruction librarian,

$79,309; reference specialist, $60,583. Faculty members who taught specific librarian courses in computer and information sciences and support services were as follows: cataloging specialist, $51,721; catalog librarian, $49,955; collection development buyer, $47,505; reference & instruction librarian, $91,181; reference specialist, $74,780.

According to the U.S. Department of Labor's Bureau of Labor Statistics in its *Occupational Outlook Handbook, 2007–08 Edition*, median yearly earnings of all postsecondary teachers (which includes Professors of Library and Information Science) were $56,120. The middle 50 percent earned between $39,610 and $80,390. The lowest 10 percent earned less than $27,590 annually, and the highest 10 percent earned more than $113,450.

Many faculty members have significant additional earnings beyond their base salaries—from consulting, teaching additional courses, research, writing for publication, or other employment. Then, too, many college and university faculty members enjoy some unique benefits, including access to campus facilities, tuition waivers for dependents, housing and travel allowances, and paid sabbatical leaves. Instructors in two-year library certificate programs at community colleges tend to earn considerably less than professors in four-year library and information science schools.

Employment Prospects

As the number of schools of library and information science are finite, jobs for professors may not grow significantly. However, they should maintain a steady number of openings as professors retire or move into other fields. Many postsecondary teachers were hired in the late 1960s and the 1970s to teach members of the baby boom generation, and they are expected to retire in growing numbers in the years ahead.

Advancement Prospects

The position of full professor is the most senior faculty post in schools of library and information science. Thus, a professor may advance primarily by accepting a teaching position in a larger, more prestigious university or by moving into a more administrative job, such as assistant or associate dean of the library and information science school, and then on to becoming dean of the school. As such shifting occurs, the probable career advancement of assistant professors and associate professors to tenure-track full professors is enhanced.

Education and Training

Professors at four-year schools of library and information science must have a master's degree in library and information science (M.L.I.S.) and a doctorate in the library and information science, communications, information systems, or closely related fields, as well as records of academic achievement commensurate with such a senior-level faculty appointment. In addition, professors must be able to demonstrate their potential for research and publication as well as their ability to provide high-quality instruction. They need to show clear commitments to collaborative educational leadership and excellence in teaching, research, and professional service.

Special Requirements

Professors teaching in state college or university systems may be required to be licensed by the state.

Experience, Skills, and Personality Traits

Professors must be able to communicate and relate well with students, enjoy working with them, and be able to motivate them. They should have inquiring and analytical minds and a strong desire to pursue and disseminate knowledge. They must have excellent research skills, presentation abilities, and writing talents. They must be self-motivated and have good organizational abilities. They should have good interpersonal and teamwork skills and be able to establish rapport with their colleagues and administrators. Professors at all levels—assistant, associate, and full—must be competent with information and communication technologies applicable to librarianship, with services to multicultural populations, and with interdisciplinary approaches to information problems.

Unions and Associations

Besides membership in the primary associations concerned with library and information science, the Amer-ican Library Association (ALA), the American Society for Information Science and Technology (ASIS&T), and the Special Libraries Association (SLA), Professors of Library Science and Technology should find it useful to belong to one or more educational professional groups. These include the American Association of University Professors (AAUP) and the National Association of Scholars (NAS). Professors in public institutions are also eligible to join the higher education divisions of the American Federation of Teachers (AFT) and the National Education Association (NEA).

Tips for Entry

1. It is highly recommended that doctoral candidates gain practical teaching experience before they earn their doctoral degrees. Obtaining a position as a graduate teaching assistant is a good way to achieve college teaching experience. Some colleges and universities require teaching assistants to attend classes or undertake some training prior to being given responsibility for a course.

2. When looking for teaching posts, examine Web sites for professional associations, as many of them post job announcements. Also visit the Web sites for the Chronicle of Higher Education at http://www.chronicle.com and Higher Education.com at http://www.higheredjobs.com.

3. While completing your education, seek summer jobs or internships that will provide you with experience in information storage and retrieval methodologies, database design and management, information management, developing information technologies, public or technical services, and systems analysis. Experience in the delivery of courses via the Internet would also be valuable.

CHAIR, INFORMATION SCIENCE DEPARTMENT

Position Description

Information science is an interdisciplinary field primarily concerned with the collection, classification, manipulation, storage, retrieval, and dissemination of information. Information science studies the application and use of knowledge in organizations and the interaction between people, organizations, and information systems. Often mistakenly considered to be a branch of computer science, it is instead a broad interdisciplinary field incorporating not only aspects of computer science but also library science, cognitive studies, and social sciences. It focuses on understanding problems from the perspective of the participants involved and the application of information (and other) technologies as needed.

Information science programs at educational institutions examine information systems in their social, cultural, economic, historical, legal, and political contexts. Computer science is an important part of these curricula, but the emphasis stays on information systems and their use rather than on the technologies that underlie them. They cover such topics as data modeling, document management, human-computer interaction, information architecture and ethics, information retrieval procedures, knowledge management, information systems technology, user-centered design, and usability engineering.

Chairs, Information Science Departments, are invariably tenured full professors, which means that they have a lifetime appointment until retirement (except for dismissal with "due course"). There are three basic levels of professorship in colleges and universities in North America. Assistant professors are the entry-level positions, for which they need a Ph.D.'s or other doctorates.

In some instances, a master's degree may suffice, especially at community colleges. (In community colleges, teaching positions are known as instructors instead of professors.) This post is generally not tenured, although in most educational institutions, the term is used for "tenure-track" positions; that is, the candidate can become tenured after a probationary period (anywhere from three to seven years). Associate professor is a mid-level position, usually awarded after a substantial publication record (such as a book or book contract, although the requirements vary from institution to institution). Full professors are the senior positions, and are usually tenured (except at some for-profit private educational institutions). The median age of American full professors is currently around 55 years, and very few people attain this post before the age of 40.

Along with their teaching and research activities, full professors who are chairs (heads) of departments are required to direct faculty meetings of the department's staff in which they discuss and handle relevant matters, such as curriculum, equipment purchases, and hirings. Chairs are also expected to serve on campus academic and administrative advisory committees that deal with institutional policies of their colleges or universities. Chairs, Information Science Departments, are usually charged with leading their educational institutions' effort to build strong research departments and advance their establishments' missions of high-quality, personalized undergraduate and graduate instruction. In some cases, chairs are outstanding scholars in their fields who are appointed as professors to serve as catalysts within the educational institutions to establish specific educational and research programs, such as those fostering interdisciplinary perspectives, or to support the development of advanced technologies and applications and the study of issues of information and computing technology. In addition, many educational institutions look for educators in computer and information science who, besides their educational backgrounds, have experience acting as consultants to commercial organizations, higher education funding councils, database producers, other academic institutions, information brokers, or government departments on such issues as information database design or data protection.

Salaries

According to a December 2007 salary survey conducted by PayScale, Inc., median annual salaries for full professors in postsecondary higher education (which would include Chairs, Information Science Programs) ranged from $49,158 to $93,120, depending on years of experi-

ence and geographic locations of the educational institutions in which they work.

Employment Prospects

Chairs or heads of departments in educational institutions are typically full professors, resident scholars, or scholars brought in from outside the educational institutions. As such, they have had long careers as educators. It may take an assistant professor or associate professor five to seven years to achieve tenure and an additional five to 10 years to achieve full professorship. Thus, the employment possibility of becoming a head (chair) of a department is only fair and is a long-term prospect. However, it is a sign of the career achievement of an individual scholar to attain this post, so the competition for this position can be very strong.

Advancement Prospects

The only real academic career advancement for chairs of departments is to become deans of the schools in which the departments reside. These positions are not readily available and usually occur only when the incumbent moves on to a higher educational post, transfers to another educational institution, or retires altogether. Thus, the chances for career progression at this level are poor to fair and are dependent on events and the reputations and experience of the individuals seeking this advancement.

Education and Training

Full professors (and chairs of departments of computer and information science) are expected to have both a master's degree in library and information science and a doctoral degree (Ph.D.) in computer science, computer engineering, computer information systems, or information technology. Additional doctoral degrees appropriate for information studies curricula are often encouraged.

Special Requirements

Professors teaching in state college and university systems may be required to have a license to teach from the state.

Experience, Skills, and Personality Traits

Even with all their department activities, chairs who teach are expected to communicate and relate well with students, enjoy working with them, and be able to motivate them. They must have inquiring and analytical minds with a strong desire to pursue and disseminate knowledge. Their research skills must be exemplary, and they must be able to teach research methods effectively to students as well as oversee the research strategy goals of the department. They need excellent presentation and writing abilities as well as superior organizational skills. They should have outstanding interpersonal and teamwork skills and be able to establish rapport with their colleagues and administrators.

As chairs of computer and information science departments, they must be fully up to date with the expanding technology in the field and fully competent with information and communication technologies. Above all, they should have strong professional backgrounds with distinguished records of scholarly publications and extramural funding as well as proven track records of innovation, collaboration, stimulation, and leadership in both information education and research.

Unions and Associations

Besides membership in the primary groups concerned with computer and information science, such as the American Society for Information Science and Technology (ASIS&T), the Association for Computing Machinery (ACM), the Computing Research Association (CRA), the Computing Technology Industry Association (CTIA), and the Institute of Electrical and Electronics Engineers (IEEE) Computer Society, Chairs, Information Science Departments, should find it useful to belong to one or more educational professional organizations. These include the American Association of University Professors (AAUP) and the National Association of Scholars (NAS). Full professors in public institutions are also eligible to join the higher-education divisions of the American Federation of Teachers (AFT) and the National Education Association (NEA).

Tips for Entry

1. It is highly recommended that doctoral candidates gain practical teaching experience while they are earning their doctoral degrees. Obtaining a post as a graduate teaching assistant is a good way to gain college teaching experience. Some colleges and universities require teaching assistants to attend classes or take some training prior to being given responsibility for courses.

2. When seeking teaching positions, study Web sites for educational professional associations, as many of them have job announcements. Also visit the Web sites for the Chronicle of Higher Education at http://www.chronicle.com/jobs and Higher Education.com at http://www.highered jobs.com.

3. While completing your education, look for summer jobs or internships that will provide you with practical experience in information storage and retrieval methodologies, database design and management, information management, developing information technologies, public or technical services, and systems analysis.

APPENDIXES

APPENDIX I
EDUCATIONAL INSTITUTIONS

For job candidates entering the fields of library science and information science, a college degree (whether from a two- or four-year program) is generally preferred and often required. Many institutions offer degrees in such relevant majors as artificial intelligence and robotics, computer information sciences—general, information resources management, knowledge management, and library science and statistics. A good place to start looking for such institutions is online at http://edonline.com, at http://degrees.education.yahoo.com/sub2-_and_technology.htm, at http://www.mapping-your-future.org/features/careership, at http://www.jets.org (for careers in technology), or for specific library and information science careers at individual industry professional association Web sites.

The following is a selected list of many of the U.S. four-year colleges and universities that offer undergraduate degrees applicable to the various areas of library science and information science. (Many of these establishments also offer master's and other higher degrees that are *not* detailed herein.)

For the undergraduate schools included in this appendix, the listings below provide addresses, telephone numbers, fax numbers, e-mail addresses, and Web sites. Also provided (in alphabetical order) are each school's majors/specialties allied to the fields of library and information science. For further information about courses offered, admission requirements, and such topics as scholarships, campus housing, and academic calendar, contact the institution(s) of choice. Since the e-mail addresses of college admissions offices frequently change, it is advised to check the institution's Web site. (Increasingly, colleges now provide a link or form on their Web sites for directly contacting school departments.)

For a listing of those institutions offering primarily two-year programs (usually leading to an associate's degree or a specific certificate) dealing with majors appropriate to library and information science, check such directories as *Peterson's Two-Year Colleges* published annually by Thomson Peterson. Most paraprofessional jobs in libraries require an associate's degree, rather than a bachelor's degree.

Most library and many information science positions require, in addition to a bachelor's degree, a master's degree in library science (M.L.S.) or in library and information science (M.L.I.S) from an educational institution accredited by the American Library Association (ALA). For a list of such institutions that offer master's programs in library and information studies, see http://ala.org/ala/accreditation/lisdirb/lis-directory.cfm.

ALABAMA

Alabama A&M University
P.O. Box 908
Normal, AL 35762
Phone: (256) 851-5245
Fax: (256) 851-5249
E-mail: aboyle@asnaam.aamu.edu
http://www.aamu.edu
Computer/information sciences—general.

Alabama State University
915 South Jackson Street
Montgomery, AL 36104
Phone: (334) 229-4291
Fax: (324) 229-4984
E-mail: dlamar@asunet.alasu.edu
http://www.alasu.edu
Information systems.

American Sentinel University
2101 Magnolia Avenue, Suite 200
Birmingham, AL 35205
Phone: (800) 729-2427, ext. 1
Fax: (866) 505-2450
E-mail: webadmissions@
   americansentinel.edu
http://www.americansentinel.edu
Computer/information sciences—general, information systems, information technology, management information systems, systems administration.

Athens State University
300 North Beaty Street
Athens, AL 35611
Phone: (205) 233-8220
Fax: (205) 233-6565
E-mail: At Web site
http://www.athens.edu
Computer/information sciences—general, human resources management, information resources management.

Auburn University—Auburn

202 Mary Martin Hall
Auburn, AL 36849
Phone: (334) 844-4080
Fax: (334) 844-6179
E-mail: admissions@auburn.edu
http://www.auburn.edu
Applied mathematics, computer engineering, computer/information sciences—general, human resources management, software engineering.

Auburn University—Montgomery

P.O. Box 244023
Montgomery, AL 36124
Phone: (334) 244-3611
Fax: (334) 244-3795
E-mail: mmoore@mail.aum.edu
http://www.aum.edu
Applied mathematics, computer engineering, computer engineering technology, human resources management, management information systems, software engineering.

Birmingham-Southern College

900 Arkadelphia Road
Birmingham, AL 35254
Phone: (205) 226-4696
Fax: (205) 226-3074
E-mail: admission@bsc.edu
http://www.bsc.edu
Computer/information sciences—general.

Faulkner University

5345 Atlanta Highway
Montgomery, AL 36109
Phone: (334) 386-7200
Fax: (334) 386-7137
E-mail: admissions@faulkner.edu
http://www.faulkner.edu
Information systems.

Herzing College

280 West Valley Avenue
Birmingham, AL 35209
Phone: (205) 916-2800
Fax: (205) 916-2807

E-mail: info@bhm.herzing.edu
http://www.herzing.edu
Computer/information sciences—general, information systems.

Jacksonville State University

700 Pelham Road North
Jacksonville, AL 36265
Phone: (256) 782-5268
Fax: (256) 782-5953
E-mail: info@jsucc.jsu.edu
http://www.jsu.edu
Computer/information sciences—general.

Miles College

Admissions
5500 Myron Massey Boulevard
Fairfield, AL 35064
Phone: (205) 929-1656
Fax: (205) 929-1627
E-mail: admissions@mail.miles.edu
http://www.miles.edu
Computer/information sciences—general.

Oakwood College

7000 Adventist Boulevard
Huntsville, AL 35896
Phone: (800) 824-5312
Fax: (256) 726-7154
E-mail: admission@oakwood.edu
http://www.oakwood.edu
Applied mathematics, computer/information sciences—general, information systems.

Samford University

800 Lakeshore Drive
Birmingham, AL 35299
Phone: (205) 726-3673
Fax: (205) 726-2171
E-mail: admiss@samford.edu
http://www.samford.edu
Human resources management.

South University

5355 Vaughn Road
Montgomery, AL 36116
Phone: (800) 688-0932
Fax: (334) 395-8859
E-mail: At Web site

http://www.southuniversity.edu
Information technology.

Spring Hill College

4000 Dauphin Street
Mobile, AL 36608
Phone: (251) 380-3030
Fax: (251) 460-2186
E-mail: admit@shc.edu
http://www.shc.edu
Computer/information sciences—general.

Stillman College

P.O. Box 1430
Tuscaloosa, AL 35403
Phone: (800) 841-5722
Fax: NA
E-mail: admissions@stillman.edu
http://www.stillman.edu
Computer/information sciences—general.

Talladega College

627 West Battle Street
Talladega, AL 35160
Phone: (205) 761-6235
Fax: (205) 362-0274
E-mail: admissions@talladega.edu
http://www.talladega.edu
Computer/information sciences—general.

Troy University

111 Adams Administration
Troy, AL 36082
Phone: (334) 670-3179
Fax: (334) 670-3733
E-mail: admit@troy.edu
http://www.troy.edu
Computer/information sciences—general, management information systems.

Tuskegee University

Old Administration Building, Suite 101
Tuskegee, AL 36086
Phone: (334) 727-8500
Fax: (334) 727-5750
E-mail: adm@tuskegee.edu
http://www.tuskegee.edu
Computer/information sciences—general.

University of Alabama—Birmingham

HUC 260
1530 Third Avenue South
Birmingham, AL 35294
Phone: (205) 934-8221
Fax: (205) 975-7114
E-mail: undergradadmit@uab.edu
http://www.uab.edu
Computer/information sciences—general, management information systems.

University of Alabama—Huntsville

301 Sparkman Drive
Huntsville, AL 35899
Phone: (256) 824-6070
Fax: (256) 824-6073
E-mail: admitme@email.uah.edu
http://www.uah.edu
Computer engineering, computer/information sciences—general, management information systems.

University of Mobile

5437 Parkway Drive
Mobile, AL 36663
Phone: (251) 442-2287
Fax: (251) 442-2498
E-mail: adminfo@mail.umobile.edu
http://www.umobile.edu
Computer/information sciences—general.

University of North Alabama

UNA Box 5011
Florence, AL 35632
Phone: (256) 765-4318
Fax: (256) 765-4329
E-mail: admissions@una.edu
http://www.una.edu
Computer/information sciences—general, management information systems.

University of South Alabama

182 Administration Building
Mobile, AL 36688
Phone: (334) 460-6141
Fax: (334) 460-7023

E-mail: admiss@jaguar1.usouthal.edu
http://www.usouthal.edu
Computer/information sciences—general, statistics.

University of West Alabama

Station 4
Livingston, AL 35470
Phone: (888) 636-8000
Fax: (205) 652-3522
E-mail: admissions@uwa.edu
http://www.westal.edu
Management information systems.

ALASKA

Charter College

2221 East Northern Lights Boulevard, Suite 120
Anchorage, AK 99508
Phone: (888) 463-7001
Fax: NA
E-mail: At Web site
http://www.chartercollege.edu
Information systems.

University of Alaska—Anchorage

3211 Providence Drive
Anchorage, AK 99508
Phone: (907) 786-1480
Fax: (907) 786-4888
E-mail: At Web site
http://www.uaa.alaska.edu
Computer/information sciences—general, management information systems.

University of Alaska—Fairbanks

P.O. Box 757480
Fairbanks, AK 99775
Phone: (907) 474-7500
Fax: (907) 474-5379
E-mail: fyapply@uaf.edu
http://www.uaf.edu
Applied mathematics, statistics.

ARIZONA

Arizona State University East

P.O. Box 870112
Tempe, AZ 85387

Phone: (480) 965-7788
Fax: (480) 727-1008
E-mail: Stacie.dana@asu.edu
http://www.east.asu.edu
Applied mathematics, computer engineering, management information systems.

Arizona State University West

P.O. Box 37100
Phoenix, AZ 85069
Phone: (602) 543-813
Fax: (602) 543-8312
E-mail: At Web site
http://www.west.asu.edu
Applied mathematics, management information systems.

Collins College

1140 South Priest Drive
Tempe, AZ 85281
Phone: (480) 966-3000
Fax: (480) 966-2599
E-mail: jen@alcollins.com
http://www.collinscollege.edu
Systems administration.

DeVry University—Phoenix

2149 West Dunlap Avenue
Phoenix, AZ 85201
Phone: (602) 870-9222
Fax: (602) 331-1494
E-mail: admissions@phx.devry.edu
http://www.devry.edu
Computer engineering technology, computer/information sciences—general, human resources management, information systems, management information systems.

Embry-Riddle Aeronautical University—Prescott Campus

3700 Willow Creek Road
Prescott, AZ 86301
Phone: (928) 777-6600
Fax: (928) 777-6606
E-mail: pradmitt@erau.edu
http://www.erau.edu
Computer engineering, software engineering.

Grand Canyon University
3300 West Camelback Road
Phoenix, AZ 85061
Phone: (602) 589-2855
Fax: (602) 589-2580
E-mail: admissions@grand-canyon.
edu
http://www.grand-canyon.edu
Computer/information sciences—
general.

Northcentral University
505 West Whipple Street
Prescott, AZ 86301
Phone: (928) 541-7777
Fax: (928) 541-7817
E-mail: info@ncu.edu
http://www.ncu.edu
Computer/information sciences—
general.

Northern Arizona University
P.O. Box 4080
Flagstaff, AZ 86011
Phone: (926) 523-5511
Fax: (928) 523-0226
E-mail: undergraduate.
admissions@nau.edu
http://www.nau.edu
Computer engineering, computer
engineering technology,
management information
systems.

Prescott College
220 Grove Avenue
Prescott, AZ 86301
Phone: (928) 350-2100
Fax: (928) 776-5242
E-mail: admissions@prescott.edu
http://www.prescott.edu
Computer/information sciences—
general, information systems.

**University of Advancing
Technology**
2625 West Baseline Road
Tempe, AZ 85283
Phone: (602) 383-8228
Fax: (602) 383-8333
E-mail: admissions@uat.edu
http://www.uat.edu
Software engineering.

University of Arizona
P.O. Box 210040
Tucson, AZ 85721
Phone: (520) 621-3237
Fax: (520) 621-9799
E-mail: appinfo@arizona.edu
http://www.arizona.edu
Computer engineering, computer
engineering technology,
human resources management,
management information
systems.

University of Phoenix
Mail Stop AA-K101
4615 East Elwood Street
Phoenix, AZ 85040
Phone: (480) 317-6000
Fax: (480) 594-1758
E-mail: At Web site
http://www.phoenix.edu
Computer/information
sciences—general, management
information systems.

Western International University
9215 North Black Canyon Highway
Phoenix, AZ 85021
Phone: (602) 943-2311
Fax: (602) 371-8637
E-mail: At Web site
http://www.wintu.edu
Computer/information
sciences—general, management
information systems.

ARKANSAS

Arkansas State University
P.O. Box 1630
State University, AR 72467
Phone: (870) 972-3024
Fax: (870) 910-8094
E-mail: admissions@astate.edu
http://www.astate.edu
Computer/information sciences—
general, data processing
technology.

Arkansas Tech University
Doc Bryan #141
Russellville, AR 72801
Phone: (479) 968-0343

Fax: (479) 964-0522
E-mail: tech.enroll@mai.atu.edu
http://www.atu.edu
Computer/information sciences—
general, computer systems
analysis.

Central Baptist College
1501 College Avenue
Conway, AR 72034
Phone: (501) 329-6872
Fax: (501) 329-2941
E-mail: ccalhoun@cbc.edu
http://www.cbc.edu
Data processing technology.

Harding University
P.O. Box 12255
Searcy, AR 72149
Phone: (501) 279-4407
Fax: (501) 279-4865
E-mail: admissions@harding.edu
http://www.harding.edu
Computer engineering, computer/
information sciences—general,
human resources management,
information technology.

Henderson State University
1100 Henderson Street
HSU P.O. Box 7560
Arkadelphia, AR 71999
Phone: (870) 230-5028
Fax: (870) 230-5066
E-mail: hardwrv@hsus.edu
http://www.hsu.edu
Computer/information
sciences—general, management
information systems.

Southern Arkansas University
P.O. Box 9382
Magnolia, AR 71754
Phone: (870) 235-4040
Fax: (870) 235-5072
E-mail: muleriders@saumag.edu
http://www.saumag.edu
Computer/information sciences—
general.

**University of Arkansas—
Fayetteville**
232 Silas Hunt Hall

Fayetteville, AR 72701
Phone: (479) 575-5346
Fax: (479) 575-7515
E-mail: uofa@uark.edu
http://www.uark.edu
Computer engineering, data
processing technology.

University of Arkansas—Fort Smith

5210 Grand Avenue
P.O. Box 3649
Fort Smith, AR 72913
Phone: (888) 512-LION
Fax: NA
E-mail: information@uafortsmith.edu
http://www.uafortsmith.edu
Computer engineering.

University of Arkansas—Little Rock

2801 South University Avenue
Little Rock, AR 72204
Phone: (501) 569-3127
Fax: (501) 569-8915
E-mail: admissions@ualr.edu
http://www.ualr.edu
Applied mathematics, computer
engineering, computer/information sciences—general, information systems, management information systems.

University of Arkansas—Monticello

UAM P.O. Box 3600
Monticello, AR 71656
Phone: (870) 460-1034
Fax: (870) 460-1035
E-mail: whitingm@uamont.edu
http://www.uamont.edu
Computer engineering, data processing technology, management information systems.

University of Arkansas—Pine Bluff

1200 North University Drive, Mail Slot 4981
Pine Bluff, AR 71601
Phone: (870) 575-8000
Fax: (870) 543-8014

E-mail: fulton_E@uapb.edu
http://www.uapb.edu
Applied mathematics, computer
engineering, computer engineering technology, data processing technology.

University of Central Arkansas

201 Donaghey Avenue
Conway, AR 72035
Phone: (501) 450-3128
Fax: (501) 450-5228
E-mail: admissions@mail.uca.edu
http://www.uca.edu
Computer/information sciences—general, data processing technology, human resources management, information systems, management information systems.

Williams Baptist College

P.O. Box 3665
Walnut Ridge, AR 72476
Phone: (870) 886-6741
Fax: (870) 886-3924
E-mail: admissions@wbcoll.edu
http://www.wbcoll.edu
Computer/information sciences—general.

CALIFORNIA

Alliant International University

Admissions Processing Center
10455 Pomerado Road
San Diego, CA 94131
Phone: (866) 825-5426
Fax: (858) 635-4355
E-mail: admissions@alliant.edu
http://www.alliant.edu
Management information systems.

Azusa Pacific University

901 East Alosta Avenue
Azusa, CA 91702
Phone: (626) 812-3016
Fax: (626) 812-3096
E-mail: admissions@apu.edu
http://www.apu.edu
Computer/information sciences—general, information systems, management information systems.

Biola University

13800 Biola Avenue
La Mirada, CA 90639
Phone: (562) 903-4752
Fax: (562) 903-4709
E-mail: admissions@biola.edu
http://www.biola.edu
Management information systems.

California Institute of Technology

Caltech Office of Undergraduate Admissions
Mail Code 1-94
Pasadena, CA 91125
Phone: (626) 395-6341
Fax: (626) 683-3026
E-mail: ugadmissions@caltech.edu
http://www.caltech.edu
Applied mathematics, computer engineering.

California Lutheran University

60 West Olsen Road, 1350
Thousand Oaks, CA 91300
Phone: (805) 493-3135
Fax: (805) 493-3114
E-mail: cluadm@clunet.edu
http://www.clunet.edu
Computer/information sciences—general, information systems.

California Polytechnic State University—San Luis Obispo

Admissions Office
Cal Poly
San Luis Obispo, CA 93407
Phone: (805) 756-2311
Fax: (805) 756-5400
E-mail: admissions@calpoly.edu
http://www.calpoly.edu
Computer engineering, computer/information sciences—general, computer systems analysis, software engineering, statistics.

California State Polytechnic University—Pomona

3801 West Temple Avenue
Pomona, CA 91768
Phone: (909) 468-5020
Fax: (909) 869-5020
E-mail: cppadmit@csupomona.edu

http://www.csu.pomona.edu
Computer engineering, information technology.

California State University— Chico
400 West First Street
Chico, CA 95929
Phone: (530) 898-4428
Fax: (530) 898-6456
E-mail: info@csuchico.edu
http://www.csuchico.edu
Applied mathematics, computer engineering, human resources management, information technology, management information systems, statistics.

California State University— Dominguez Hills
100 East Victoria Street
Carson, CA 90741
Phone: (310) 243-3600
Fax: (310) 516-3609
E-mail: lwise@csudh.edu
http://www.csudh.edu
Computer/information sciences— general, human resources management, management information systems.

California State University— East Bay
25800 Carlos Bee Boulevard
Hayward, CA 94542
Phone: (510) 885-2624
Fax: (510) 885-4059
E-mail: askes@csuhayward.edu
http://www. csuhayward.edu
Applied mathematics, computer/ information sciences—general, human resources management, information systems, management information systems, software engineering, statistics.

California State University— Fresno
5150 North Maple Avenue
M/S JA 57
Fresno, CA 93740
Phone: (559) 278-2261
Fax: (559) 278-4812

E-mail: vivian_franco@csufresno.edu
http://www.csufresno.edu
Computer engineering, computer/ information sciences—general, human resources management, information systems, management information systems.

California State University— Fullerton
800 North State College Boulevard
Fullerton, CA 92834
Phone: (714) 773-2370
Fax: (714) 278-2356
E-mail: admissions@fullerton.edu
http://www.fullerton.edu
Applied mathematics, computer engineering, computer/information sciences—general, information systems, information technology, management information systems, statistics.

California State University— Long Beach
1250 Bellflower Boulevard
Long Beach, CA 90840
Phone: (562) 985-5471
Fax: (562) 985-4973
E-mail: eslb@csulb.edu
http://www.csulb.edu
Applied mathematics, computer engineering, computer/ information sciences—general, human resources management, information systems, statistics.

California State University— Los Angeles
5151 State University Drive
Los Angeles, CA 90032
Phone: (323) 343-3901
Fax: (323) 343-6306
E-mail: admission@calstatela.edu
http://www.calstatela.edu
Computer/information sciences— general, information systems.

California State University— Monterey Bay
100 Campus Center
Seaside, CA 93955
Phone: (831) 582-3000

Fax: (831) 502-3783
E-mail: At Web site
http://www.csumb.edu
Computer/information sciences— general, information systems.

California State University— Northridge
P.O. Box 1286
Northridge, CA 91328
Phone: (818) 677-3773
Fax: (818) 677-4665
E-mail: lorraine.newlon@csun.edu
http://www.csun.edu
Applied mathematics, computer engineering, computer/ information sciences—general, human resources management, management information systems, statistics.

California State University— Sacramento
6000 J Street
Lassen Hall
Sacramento, CA 95819
Phone: (916) 278-3901
Fax: (916) 279-5603
E-mail: admissions@csus.edu
http://www.admissions@csus.edu
Computer engineering, computer/ information sciences—general, human resources management, management information systems.

California State University— San Bernardino
CSUSB-IR, 5500 University Parkway
San Bernardino, CA 92407
Phone: (909) 537-5188
Fax: (909) 537-7034
E-mail: moreinfo@mail.csusb.edu
http://www.csusb.edu
Human resources management, management information systems.

California State University— San Marcos
133 South Twin Oaks Valley Road
San Marcos, CA 92096

Phone: (760) 750-4848
Fax: (760) 750-3248
E-mail: apply@csusm.edu
http://www.csusm.edu
Computer/information sciences—
    general.

**California State University—
    Stanislaus**
801 West Monte Vista Avenue
Turlock, CA 95382
Phone: (209) 667-3070
Fax: (209) 667-3788
E-mail: outreach_help_desk@
    csustan.edu
http://www.csutan.edu
Information technology.

Chapman University
One University Drive
Orange, CA 92866
Phone: (714) 997-6711
Fax: (714) 997-6713
E-mail: admit@chapman.edu
http://www.chapman.edu
Computer/information sciences—
    general.

Cogswell Polytechnical College
1175 Bordeaux Drive
Sunnyvale, CA 94089
Phone: (408) 541-0100
Fax: (408) 747-0764
E-mail: admissions@cogswell.edu
http://www.cogswell.edu
Software engineering.

**Coleman College—San Diego
    Campus**
8888 Balboa Avenue
San Diego, CA 92123
Phone: (858) 499-0202
Fax: (858) 499-0233
E-mail: At Web site
http://www.coleman.edu
Computer engineering, computer
    engineering technology,
    computer/information
    sciences—general.

**Coleman College—San Marcos
    Campus**
1284 West San Marcos Boulevard

San Marcos, CA 92078
Phone: (760) 747-3990
Fax: (760) 752-9808
E-mail: At Web site
http://www.coleman.edu
Computer engineering, computer
    engineering technology.

Concordia University—Irvine
1530 Concordia West
Irvine, CA 92612
Phone: (949) 854-8002
Fax: (949) 854-6894
E-mail: admission@cui.edu
http://www.cui.edu
Information technology.

DeVry University—Fremont
6600 Dumbarton Circle
Fremont, CA 94555
Phone: (510) 574-1200
Fax: (510) 742-0868
E-mail: info@devry.edu
http://www.fre.devry.edu
Computer engineering technology,
    computer systems analysis.

**DeVry University—
    Long Beach**
3880 Kilroy Airport Way
Long Beach, CA 90806
Phone: (562) 427-4162
Fax: (562) 997-5371
E-mail: cblas@socal.devry.edu
http://www.devry.edu
Computer engineering technology,
    computer systems analysis,
    information technology.

DeVry University—Pomona
901 Corporate Center Drive
Pomona, CA 91768
Phone: (909) 622-9800
E-mail: bchung@admin.pom.devry.
    edu
http://www.pom.devry.edu
Computer engineering technology.

DeVry University—West Hills
22801 Roscoe Boulevard
West Hills, CA 91304
Phone: (818) 932-3001
E-mail: admissions@devry.com

http://www.devry.edu
Computer engineering technology.

**Dominican University of
    California**
Office of Admissions
50 Acacia Avenue
San Rafael, CA 94901
Phone: (415) 485-3214
Fax: (415) 485-3214
E-mail: enroll@dominican.edu
http://www.dominican.edu
Human resources management.

Fresno Pacific University
1717 South Chestnut Avenue
Fresno, CA 93702
Phone: (559) 453-2039
Fax: (559) 453-2007
E-mail: ugadmis@fresno.edu
http://www.fresno.edu
Applied mathematics, human
    resources management,
    management information
    systems.

Golden Gate University
536 Mission Street
San Francisco, CA 94105
Phone: (415) 442-7800
Fax: (415) 442-7807
E-mail: info@ggu.edu
http://www.ggu.edu
Human resources management,
    information resources manage-
    ment, information technology.

Harvey Mudd College
301 East Twelfth Street
Claremont, CA 91711
Phone: (909) 621-8011
Fax: (909) 621-8360
E-mail: admission@hmc.edu
http://www.hmc.edu
Applied mathematics, computer/
    information sciences—general.

Holy Names University
3500 Mountain Boulevard
Oakland, CA 94619
Phone: (510) 436-1351
Fax: (510) 436-1325
E-mail: admissions@hnu.edu

http://www.hnu.edu
Human resources management.

Humboldt State University
1 Harpst Street
Arcata, CA 95521
Phone: (707) 826-4402
Fax: (707) 826-6190
E-mail: hsuinfo@humboldt.edu
http://www.humboldt.edu
Computer/information sciences—
general, information systems.

Humphreys College
6650 Inglewood Avenue
Stockton, CA 95207
Phone: (209) 478-0800
Fax: (209) 478-8721
E-mail: slopez@humphreys.edu
http://www.humphreys.edu
Computer/information sciences—
general.

Lincoln University
401 Fifteenth Street
Oakland, CA 94612
Phone: (510) 628-8010
Fax: (510) 628-8012
E-mail: admissions@lincolnuca.edu
http://www.lincolnuca.edu
Computer/information sciences—
general.

Loyola Marymount University
One LMU Drive, Suite 100
Los Angeles, CA 90045
Phone: (310) 338-2750
Fax: (310) 338-2797
E-mail: admissions@lmu.edu
http://www.lmu.edu
Applied mathematics, computer/
information sciences—general.

Master's College and Seminary
21726 Placenta Canyon Road
Santa Clarita, CA 91321
Phone: (661) 259-3540
Fax: (661) 288-1037
E-mail: enrollment@masters.edu
http://www.masters.edu
Applied mathematics, computer/
information sciences—general,
management information
systems.

Mills College
5000 MacArthur Boulevard
Oakland, CA 94613
Phone: (510) 430-2135
Fax: (510) 430-3314
E-mail: admission@mills.edu
http://www.mills.edu
Computer/information sciences—
general.

Mt. Sierra College
101 East Huntington Drive
Monrovia, CA 91016
Phone: (626) 873-2100
Fax: (626) 359-1378
E-mail: At Web site
http://www.mtsierra.edu
Computer/information sciences—
general.

Mount St. Mary's College
12001 Chalon Road
Los Angeles, CA 90049
Phone: (845) 569-3248
Fax: (845) 562-6762
E-mail: mtstmary@msmc.edu
http://www.msmc.edu
Applied mathematics.

National Hispanic University
4271 Story Road
San Jose, CA 95127
Phone: (408) 254-6900
Fax: (408) 254-1369
E-mail: At Web site
http://www.nhu.edu
Computer/information sciences—
general.

National University
11255 North Torrey Pinos Road
La Jolla, CA 92037
Phone: (858) 642-8180
Fax: (858) 642-8710
E-mail: advisor@nu.edu
http://www.nu.edu
Computer/information sciences—
general, human resources man-
agement, information systems.

Northwestern Polytechnic University
47671 Westinghouse Drive
Fremont, CA 94539
Phone: (510) 657-5913
Fax: (510) 657-8975
E-mail: At Web site
http://www.npu.edu
Software engineering.

Notre Dame de Namur University
1500 Ralston Avenue
Belmont, CA 94002
Phone: (650) 508-3600
Fax: (650) 508-3426
E-mail: admiss@ndnu.edu
http://www.ndnu.edu
Computer/information sciences—
general, software engineering.

Occidental College
Office of Admission
1600 Campus Road
Los Angeles, CA 90041
Phone: (323) 259-2700
Fax: (323) 341-4875
E-mail: admission@oxy.edu
http://www.oxy.edu
Cognitive science.

Pacific State University
Admissions Office
1516 South Western Avenue
Los Angeles, CA 90006
Phone: (323) 731-2383
Fax: (323) 731-7276
E-mail: admissions@psuca.edu
http://www.psuca.edu
Computer/information sciences—
general.

Pacific Union College
Enrollment Services
One Angwin Avenue
Angwin, CA 94508
Phone: (800) 862-7080
Fax: (707) 965-6432
E-mail: enroll@puc.edu
http://www.puc.edu
Management information systems.

Point Loma Nazarene University
3900 Lomaland Drive
San Diego, CA 92106

Phone: (619) 849-2273
Fax: (619) 8498-2601
E-mail: admissions@ptloma.edu
http://www.ptloma.edu
Management information systems.

Pomona College
333 North College Way
Claremont, CA 91711
Phone: (909) 621-8134
Fax: (909) 621-8952
E-mail: admissions@pomona.edu
http://www.pomona.edu
Cognitive science.

San Diego State University
5500 Campanile Drive
San Diego, CA 92182
Phone: (619) 594-7800
Fax: (619) 594-1250
E-mail: At Web site
http://www.sdu.edu
Applied mathematics, computer
engineering, computer/
information sciences—general,
information systems, statistics.

San Francisco State University
1600 Holloway Avenue
San Francisco, CA 94132
Phone: (415) 338-6486
Fax: (415) 338-7196
E-mail: ugadmit@sfsu.edu
http://www.sfsu.edu
Applied mathematics, computer/
information sciences—general,
human resources management,
statistics.

San Jose State University
1 Washington Square
San Jose, CA 95112
Phone: (408) 283-7500
Fax: (408) 924-2050
E-mail: contact@sjsu.edu
http://www.sjsu.edu
Applied mathematics, computer
engineering, human resources
management, software
engineering.

Santa Clara University
500 El Camino Real

Santa Clara, CA 95053
Phone: (408) 554-4700
Fax: (408) 554-5255
E-mail: At Web site
http://www.scu.edu
Applied mathematics, computer
engineering, software engineering.

Simpson University
2211 College View Drive
Redding, CA 96003
Phone: (530) 226-4606
Fax: (530) 226-4861
E-mail: admissions@simpson
university.edu
http://www.simpsonuniversity.edu
Management information systems.

Sonoma State University
1801 East Cotati Avenue
Rohnert Park, CA 94928
Phone: (707) 664-2778
Fax: (707) 664-2060
E-mail: admitme@sonoma.edu
http://www.sonoma.edu
Computer engineering.

Stanford University
Undergraduate Admissions
Old Union 232
Stanford, CA 94305
Phone: (650) 723-2091
Fax: (650) 723-6050
E-mail: admissions@stanford.edu
http://www.stanford.edu
Computer/information sciences—
general, statistics.

University of California—Berkeley
110 Sproul Hall
Berkeley, CA 94720
Phone: (510) 642-3175
Fax: (510) 642-7333
E-mail: ouars@uclink.berkeley.edu
http://www.berkeley.edu
Applied mathematics, cognitive
science, statistics.

University of California—Davis
178 Mrak Hall
1 Shields Avenue
Davis, CA 95616

Phone: (530) 752-2971
Fax: (530) 752-1280
E-mail: undergraduateadmissions@
ucdavis.edu
http://www.ucdavis.edu
Computational mathematics,
computer engineering, statistics.

University of California—Irvine
204 Administration Building
Irvine, CA 92697
Phone: (949) 824-6703
Fax: (949) 824-2711
E-mail: admissions@uci.edu
http://www.uci.edu
Computer engineering, computer/
information sciences—general,
information systems.

University of California—Los Angeles
405 Hilgard Avenue
P.O. Box 951436
Los Angeles, CA 90095
Phone: (310) 825-3101
Fax: (310) 206-1206
E-mail: ugadm@saonet.ucla.edu
http://www.ucla.edu
Applied mathematics, cognitive
science, computational mathematics, computer engineering,
computer/information sci-
ences—general, statistics.

University of California—Merced
P.O. Box 2039
Merced, CA 95344
Phone: (866) 270-7301
Fax: NA
E-mail: admissions@ucmerced.edu
http://www.ucmerced.edu
Cognitive science, computer
engineering.

University of California—Riverside
1138 Hinderaker Hall
Riverside, CA 92521
Phone: (909) 787-3411
Fax: (909) 787-6344
E-mail: ugadmiss@pop.ucr.edu

http://www.ucr.edu
Applied mathematics, computer engineering, information systems, statistics.

University of California—San Diego
9500 Gilman Drive, 0021
La Jolla, CA 92093
Phone: (858) 534-4831
Fax: (858) 534-5723
E-mail: admissionsinfo.ucsd.edu
http://www.ucsd.edu
Applied mathematics, cognitive science, computer engineering, computer/information sciences—general, computer systems analysis, information systems.

University of California—Santa Barbara
Office of Admissions
1210 Cheadle Hall
Santa Barbara, CA 93106
Phone: (805) 893-2881
Fax: (805) 893-2676
E-mail: appinfo@sa.ucsb.edu
http://www.ucsb.edu
Computer engineering, computer/information sciences—general, statistics.

University of California—Santa Cruz
Office of Admissions, Cook House
1156 High Street
Santa Cruz, CA 95064
Phone: (831) 459-4008
Fax: (831) 459-4452
E-mail: admissions@ucsc.edu
http://www.admissions.ucsc.edu
Applied mathematics, computer engineering, computer/information sciences—general, computer systems analysis, information systems, management information systems.

University of La Verne
1950 Third Street
La Verne, CA 91750
Phone: (909) 392-2800
Fax: (909) 392-2714
E-mail: admissions@ulv.edu
http://www.ulv.edu
Computer/information sciences—general.

University of Redlands
1200 East Colton Avenue
Redlands, CA 92373
Phone: (909) 335-4074
Fax: (909) 335-4089
E-mail: admissions@redlands.edu
http://www.redlands.edu
Computer/information sciences—general, management information systems.

University of San Francisco
2130 Fulton Street
San Francisco, CA 94117
Phone: (415) 422-6563
Fax: (415) 422-2217
E-mail: admission@usfca.edu
http://www.usfca.edu
Computer/information sciences—general, information systems, management information systems.

University of Southern California
700 Childs Way
Los Angeles, CA 90089
Phone: (213) 740-1111
Fax: (213) 740-6364
E-mail: admitusc@usc.edu
http://www.usc.edu
Computer engineering.

University of the Pacific
3601 Pacific Avenue
Stockton, CA 95211
Phone: (209) 946-2211
Fax: (209) 946-2413
E-mail: admissions@pacific.edu
http://www.pacific.edu
Applied mathematics, computer engineering, computer/information sciences—general, information systems.

Woodbury University
7500 Glenoaks Boulevard
Burbank, CA 91510
Phone: (818) 767-0888
Fax: (818) 767-7520
E-mail: admissions@woodbury.edu
http://www.woodbury.edu
Computer/information sciences—general.

COLORADO

Adams State College
Office of Admissions
Alamosa, CO 81102
Phone: (719) 587-7712
Fax: (719) 587-7522
E-mail: ascadmit@adams.edu
http://www.adams.edu
Computer/information sciences—general, management information systems.

Colorado Christian University
8787 West Alameda Avenue
Lakewood, CO 80226
Phone: (303) 963-3200
Fax: (303) 963-3201
E-mail: ccuadmissions@ccu.edu
http://www.ccu.edu
Computer/information sciences—general, management information systems.

Colorado School of Mines
Weaver Towers, 1811 Elm Street
Golden, CO 80401
Phone: (303) 273-3220
Fax: (303) 273-3509
E-mail: admit@mines.edu
http://www.mines.edu
Applied mathematics, computer/information sciences—general.

Colorado State University—Pueblo
Office of Admissions and Records
2200 Bonforte Boulevard
Pueblo, CO 81001
Phone: (719) 549-2461
Fax: (719) 549-2419
E-mail: info@colostate-pueblo.edu
http://www.colostate-pueblo.edu
Computer engineering, computer/information sciences—general, information systems.

Colorado Technical University
4435 North Chestnut Street
Colorado Springs, CO 80907
Phone: (719) 598-0200
Fax: (719) 598-3740
E-mail: cosadmissions@
   coloradotech.edu
http://www.coloradotech.edu
Computer engineering, computer/
   information sciences—general,
   computer systems analysis,
   human resources management,
   information resources
   management, information
   systems, information technology,
   management information
   systems, software engineering,
   systems administration.

DeVry University—Colorado
   Springs
225 South Union Boulevard
Colorado Springs, CO 80910
Phone: (719) 632-3000
Fax: (719) 632-1909
E-mail: admitcs@cs.devry.edu
http://www.devry.edu
Computer systems analysis.

DeVry University—Greenwood
   Village (Denver South)
6312 South Fiddlers Green Cross,
   Suite 150E
Greenwood Village, CO 80111
Phone: (303) 329-3000
Fax: (303) 329-4486
E-mail: info@devry.edu
http://www.devry.edu
Computer engineering.

DeVry University—Westminster
1870 West 122nd Avenue
Westminster, CO 80234
Phone: (303) 280-7600
Fax: (303) 280-7606
E-mail: denver-admissions@den.
   devry.edu
http://www.devry.edu
Computer engineering technology,
   information systems.

Fort Lewis College
1000 Rim Drive

Durango, CO 91301
Phone: (970) 247-7184
Fax: (970) 247-7179
E-mail: admission@fortlewis.edu
http://www.fortlewis.edu
Applied mathematics, computer/
   information sciences—general,
   information systems, statistics.

Jones International University
9697 East Mineral Avenue
Centennial, CO 90112
Phone: (800) 811-5663
Fax: (303) 799-0966
E-mail: info@jonesinternational.
   edu
http://www.jonesinternational.edu
Computer engineering, systems
   administration.

Mesa State College
P.O. Box 2647
Grand Junction, CO 91502
Phone: (970) 248-1875
Fax: (970) 248-1973
E-mail: admissions@mesastate.edu
http://www.mesastate.edu
Computer/information
   sciences—general, management
   information systems.

Metropolitan State College of
   Denver
Campus Box 16, P.O. Box 173362
Denver, CO 80217
Phone: (303) 556-3058
Fax: (303) 556-6345
E-mail: askmetro@mscd.edu
http://www.mscd.edu
Computer/information sciences—
   general.

National American University
1325 South Colorado Boulevard,
   Suite 100
Denver, CO 80222
Phone: (303) 876-7100
Fax: (303) 876-7105
E-mail: At Web site
http://www.national.edu/
   DenverCampus
Information systems, management
   information systems, systems
   administration.

Regis University
3333 Regis Boulevard, A-12
Denver, CO 80221
Phone: (303) 458-4900
Fax: (303) 964-5534
E-mail: regisadm@regis.edu
http://www.regis.edu
Computer/information sciences—
   general.

Remington College—Colorado
   Springs
6050 Erin Park Drive
Colorado Springs, CO 80918
Phone: (719) 532-1234
Fax: NA
E-mail: At Web site
http://www.remingtoncollege.edu/
   coloradosprings
Systems administration.

United States Air Force
   Academy
HQ USAFA/RRS
2304 Cadet Drive, Suite 2000
USAF Academy, CO 80840
Phone: (719) 333-2520
Fax: (719) 333-3012
E-mail: webmail@usafa.af.mil
http://www.academyadmissions.
   com
Computer engineering.

University of Colorado—
   Boulder
Campus Box 30
Boulder, CO 90309
Phone: (303) 492-6301
Fax: (303) 492-7115
E-mail: apply@colorado.edu
http://www.colorado.edu
Applied mathematics, computer
   engineering, computer/
   information sciences—general,
   human resources management.

University of Colorado—
   Colorado Springs
Admissions Office
P.O. Box 7150
Colorado Springs, CO 80933
Phone: (719) 262-3383

Fax: (719) 262-3116
E-mail: admrec@mail.uccs.edu
http://www.uccs.edu
Computer engineering, human resources management.

University of Colorado— Denver and Health Sciences Center

P.O. Box 173364, Campus Box 167
Denver, CO 80217
Phone: (303) 556-2704
Fax: (303) 556-4838
E-mail: admission@cudenver.edu
http://www.cudenver.edu
Computer/information sciences— general.

University of Denver

University Hall, Room 110
2197 South University Boulevard
Denver, CO 80208
Phone: (303) 871-2036
Fax: (303) 871-3301
E-mail: admission@du.edu
http://www.du.edu
Computer engineering, computer/ information sciences—general.

Western State College of Colorado

600 North Adams Street
Gunnison, CO 81231
Phone: (970) 943-2119
Fax: (970) 943-2212
E-mail: discover@western.edu
http://www.western.edu
Management information systems.

Westwood College of Technology

7350 North Broadway
Denver, CO 80221
Phone: (303) 426-7000
Fax: (303) 426-1832
E-mail: bsimms@westwood.edu
http://www.westwood.edu
Computer/information sciences— general, information systems, management information systems, systems administration.

CONNECTICUT

Albertus Magnus College

700 Prospect Street
New Haven, CT 06511
Phone: (203) 773-8501
Fax: (203) 773-5248
E-mail: admissions@albertus.edu
http://www.albertus.edu
Information systems, management information systems.

Central Connecticut State College

1615 Stanley Street
New Britain, CT 06050
Phone: (860) 832-2278
Fax: (860) 832-2295
E-mail: admissions@ccsu.edu
http://www.ccsu.edu
Computer engineering technology, computer/information sciences—general, management information systems.

Eastern Connecticut State University

83 Windham Street
Willimantic, CT 06226
Phone: (860) 465-5286
Fax: (860) 465-5544
E-mail: admissions@easternct.edu
http://www.easternct.edu
Computer/information sciences—general, management information systems.

Fairfield University

1073 North Benson Road
Fairfield, CT 06824
Phone: (203) 254-4100
Fax: (203) 254-4199
E-mail: admis@mail.fairfield.edu
http://www.fairfield.edu
Computer engineering, computer/ information sciences—general, management information systems.

Post University

P.O. Box 2540
Waterbury, CT 06723
Phone: (203) 596-4520

Fax: (203) 756-5810
E-mail: admissions@post.edu
http://www.post.edu
Computer/information sciences— general.

Quinnipiac University

275 Mount Carmel Avenue
Hamden, CT 06518
Phone: (203) 582-8600
Fax: (203) 582-8906
E-mail: admissions@quinnipiac.edu
http://www.quinnipiac.edu
Computer/information sciences— general, human resources management, management information systems.

Sacred Heart University

5151 Park Avenue
Fairfield, CT 06432
Phone: (203) 371-7880
Fax: (203) 365-7607
E-mail: enroll@sacredheart.edu
http://www.sacredheart.edu
Computer/information sciences— general.

Southern Connecticut State University

SCSU-Admissions House
131 Farmham Avenue
New Haven, CT 06515
Phone: (203) 392-5656
Fax: (203) 392-5727
E-mail: adminfo@scsu.ctstateu.edu
http://www.southernct.edu
Computer/information sciences— general, library science.

Trinity College

300 Summit Street
Hartford, CT 06016
Phone: (860) 297-2180
Fax: (860) 297-2287
E-mail: admissions.office@trincoll. edu
http://www.trincoll.edu
Computer/information sciences— general.

University of Bridgeport

126 Park Avenue

Bridgeport, CT 06604
Phone: (203) 576-4552
Fax: (203) 576-4941
E-mail: admit@bridgeport.edu
http://www.bridgeport.edu
Computer engineering,
  management information
  systems.

University of Connecticut
2131 Hillside Road, Unit 3088
Storrs, CT 06286
Phone: (860) 486-3137
Fax: (860) 486-1476
E-mail: beahusky@uconn.edu
http://www.uconn.edu
Applied mathematics, cognitive
  science, computer engineering,
  computer/information
  sciences—general, management
  information systems, statistics.

University of Hartford
200 Bloomfield Avenue
West Hartford, CT 06117
Phone: (860) 768-4296
Fax: (860) 768-4961
E-mail: admissions@mail.hartford.
  edu
http://www.hartford.edu
Computer engineering, computer
  engineering technology,
  computer/information
  sciences—general, information
  systems, management
  information systems.

University of New Haven
300 Orange Avenue
West Haven, CT 06516
Phone: (203) 932-7319
Fax: (203) 931-6093
E-mail: adminfo@newhaven.edu
http://www.newhaven.edu
Applied mathematics, computer
  engineering, computer/
  information sciences—general,
  information systems.

Wesleyan University
Stewart M. Reid House
70 Wyllys Avenue
Middletown, CT 06459

Phone: (860) 685-3000
Fax: (860) 685-3001
E-mail: admiss@wesleyan.edu
http://www.wesleyan.edu
Computer/information sciences—
  general.

Western Connecticut State University
Undergraduate Admissions Office
181 White Street
Danbury, CT 06810
Phone: (203) 837-9000
Fax: NA
E-mail: At Web site
http://www.wcsu.edu
Computer/information sciences—
  general, management information
  systems.

Yale University
P.O. Box 208234
New Haven, CT 06520
Phone: (203) 432-9316
Fax: (203) 432-9392
E-mail: undergraduate_
  admissions@yale.edu
http://www.yale.edu
Applied mathematics, cognitive
  science, computer/information
  sciences—general.

DELAWARE

Delaware State University
1200 North DuPont Highway
Dover, DE 19901
Phone: (302) 857-6361
Fax: (302) 857-6362
E-mail: admissions@dsu.edu
http://www.dsu/edu
Computer/information sciences—
  general, information systems.

Goldey-Beacom College
4701 Limestone Road
Wilmington, DE 19808
Phone: (302) 998-8814
Fax: (302) 996-5408
E-mail: admissions@gbc.edu
http://www.goldey.gbc.edu
Computer/information
  sciences—general, management
  information systems.

University of Delaware
Admissions Office
116 Hullihen Hall
Newark, DE 19716
Phone: (302) 831-8123
Fax: (302) 931-6095
E-mail: admissions@udel.edu
http://www.udel.edu
Computer engineering, computer/
  information sciences—general,
  statistics.

Wilmington College
320 Dupont Highway
New Castle, DE 19720
Phone: (302) 328-9401
Fax: (302) 328-5902
E-mail: mlee@wilmcoll.edu
http://www.wilmcoll.edu
Computer/information sciences—
  general, computer software
  technology, human resources
  management, information
  resources management.

DISTRICT OF COLUMBIA

American University
4400 Massachusetts Avenue NW
Washington, DC 20016
Phone: (202) 885-6000
Fax: (202) 885-1025
E-mail: afa@american.edu
http://www.american.edu
Applied mathematics, computer/
  information sciences—general,
  management information
  systems, statistics.

Catholic University of America
Office Enrollment Services
Washington, DC 20064
Phone: (202) 319-6305
Fax: (202) 319-6533
E-mail: cua-admissions@cua.edu
http://www.cua.edu
Computer engineering, computer/
  information sciences—general,
  human resources management.

Gallaudet University
800 Florida Avenue NE
Washington, DC 20002

Phone: (202) 651-5750
Fax: (202) 651-5744
E-mail: admissions@gallaudet.edu
http://www.gallaudet.edu
Computer/information sciences—
general, information systems,
management information
systems.

George Washington University
2121 I Street NW, Suite 201
Washington, DC 20052
Phone: (202) 994-6040
Fax: (202) 994-0325
E-mail: gwadm@gwu.edu
http://www.gwu.edu
Applied mathematics, computer
engineering, computer/informa-
tion sciences—general, information systems, management information systems, statistics.

Howard University
2400 Sixth Street NW
Washington, DC 20059
Phone: (202) 806-2700
Fax: (202) 806-4462
E-mail: admission@howard.edu
http://www.howard.edu
Computer engineering, computer
systems analysis, information
systems, management
information systems.

Potomac College
4000 Chesapeake Street NW
Washington, DC 20016
Phone: (202) 686-0876
Fax: (202) 686-0818
E-mail: admissions@potomac.edu
http://www.potomac.edu
Computer/information sciences—
general.

Southeastern University
501 Eye Street SW
Washington, DC 20024
Phone: (202) 265-5343
Fax: (202) 488-8093
E-mail: admissions@admin.seu.edu
http://www.seu.edu
Computer systems analysis, man-
agement information systems.

Strayer University
1025 Fifteenth Street NW
Washington, DC 20005
Phone: (202) 408-2400
Fax: (202) 289-1831
E-mail: Washington@strayer.edu
http://www.strayer.edu
Information systems.

University of the District of Columbia
4200 Connecticut Avenue NW
Washington, DC 20008
Phone: (202) 274-6110
Fax: (202) 274-5552
E-mail: lflannagna@udc.edu
http://www.udc.edu
Computer/information sciences—
general.

FLORIDA

Barry University
11300 North East Second Avenue
Miami Shores, FL 33161
Phone: (305) 899-3100
Fax: (305) 899-2971
E-mail: Des-forms@mail.barry.
edu
http://www.barry.edu
Information systems, management
information systems.

Bethune-Cookman College
640 Dr. Mary McLeod Bethune
Boulevard
Daytona Beach, FL 32114
Phone: (386) 481-2600
Fax: (386) 481-2601
E-mail: admissions@cookman.edu
http://www.bethune.cookman.edu
Computer engineering, information
systems.

DeVry University—Miramar
2300 Southwest 145th Avenue
Miramar, FL 33027
Phone: (954) 499-9700
Fax: (954) 499-9723
E-mail: openhouse@mir.devry.edu
http://www.devry.edu
Computer engineering technology,
information systems.

DeVry University—Orlando
4000 Millenia Boulevard
Orlando, FL 32839
Phone: (407) 370-3131
Fax: (407) 370-3198
E-mail: krochford@orl.devry.edu
http://www.devry.edu
Information systems.

Eckerd College
4200 54th Avenue South
St. Petersburg, FL 33711
Phone: (727) 864-8331
Fax: (727) 866-2304
E-mail: admissions@eckerd.edu
http://www.eckerd.edu
Computer/information sciences—
general.

Embry-Riddle Aeronautical University
600 South Clyde Morris Boulevard
Daytona Beach, FL 32114
Phone: (386) 226-6100
Fax: (386) 226-7070
E-mail: dbadmit@erau.edu
http://www.embryriddle.edu
Computer engineering, computer/
information sciences—general,
software engineering.

Everglades University
5002 T-REX Avenue, Suite 100
Boca Raton, FL 33431
Phone: (888) 772-6077
Fax: (561) 912-1191
E-mail: admissions-boca@
evergladesuniversity.edu
http://www.evergladesuniversity.
edu
Information technology.

Florida A&M University
Suite G-9, Foote-Hilyer
Administration Center
Tallahassee, FL 32307
Phone: (850) 599-3796
Fax: (850) 599-3069
E-mail: adm@famu.edu
http://www.famu.edu
Computer/information sciences—
general.

Florida Atlantic University

777 Glades Road
P.O. Box 3091
Boca Raton, FL 33431
Phone: (561) 297-3040
Fax: (561) 297-3758
E-mail: admisweb@fau.edu
http://www.fau.edu
Computer engineering, computer/
 information sciences—general,
 human resources management,
 management information
 systems.

Florida Gulf Coast University

10501 FGCU Boulevard South
Fort Myers, FL 33965
Phone: (239) 590-7878
Fax: (239) 590-7894
E-mail: admissions@fgcu.edu
http://www.fgcu.edu
Computer/information
 sciences—general, management
 information systems.

Florida Institute of Technology

150 West University Boulevard
Melbourne, FL 32901-6975
Phone: (321) 674-8030
Fax: (321) 723-9468
E-mail: admissions@fit.edu
http://www.fit.edu
Applied mathematics, computer
 engineering, management
 information systems, software
 engineering.

Florida International University

University Park, PC 140
Miami, FL 33119
Phone: (305) 348-2363
Fax: (305) 348-3648
E-mail: admiss@flu.edu
http://www.flu.edu
Applied mathematics, computer
 engineering, computer/
 information sciences—general,
 human resources management,
 information technology,
 management information
 systems, statistics.

Florida Southern College

111 Lake Hollingworth Drive
Lakeland, FL 33801
Phone: (863) 680-4131
Fax: (863) 680-4120
E-mail: fscadm@flsouthern.edu
http://www.flsouthern.edu
Human resources management,
 management information
 systems.

Florida State University

2500 University Center
Tallahassee, FL 32306
Phone: (850) 644-6200
Fax: (850) 644-0197
E-mail: admissions@admin.fsu.edu
http://www.fsu.edu
Applied mathematics,
 computational mathematics,
 computer engineering,
 computer/information
 sciences—general, human
 resources management,
 information systems,
 information technology,
 management information
 systems, software engineering,
 statistics.

Herzing College

1595 South Semoran Boulevard
Winter Park, FL 32792
Phone: (407) 478-0500
Fax: (407) 478-0501
E-mail: info@orl.herzing.edu
http://www.herzing.edu
Information technology.

Jacksonville University

700 Pelham Road North
Jacksonville, FL 36252
Phone: (904) 256-7000
Fax: (904) 256-7012
E-mail: admissions@ju.edu
http://www.jacksonville.edu
Computer/information sciences—
 general.

Jones College

11430 North Kendall Drive, Suite
 200
Kendall Summit

Miami, FL 33176
Phone: (904) 371-1112
Fax: NA
E-mail: At Web site
http://www.jones.edu
Computer/information sciences—
 general.

Lynn University

3601 North Military Trail
Boca Raton, FL 33431
Phone: (561) 237-7000
Fax: (561) 237-7100
E-mail: admission@lynn.edu
http://www.lynn.edu
Management information systems.

Northwood University

2600 North Military Trail
West Palm Beach, FL 33409
Phone: (561) 478-5500
Fax: (561) 640-3328
E-mail: fladmit@northwood.edu
http://www.northwood.edu/fl
Computer/information
 sciences—general, management
 information systems.

Nova Southeastern University

3301 College Avenue
Ft. Lauderdale, FL 33314
Phone: (954) 262-8000
Fax: (954) 262-3811
E-mail: ncsinfo@nova.edu
http://www.nova.edu
Computer/information sciences—
 general.

Palm Beach Atlantic University

P.O. Box 24708
901 South Flagler Drive
West Palm Beach, FL 33416
Phone: (561) 803-2100
Fax: (561) 803-2115
E-mail: admit@pba.edu
http://www.pba.edu
Computer/information sciences—
 general.

Remington College—Largo

8550 Ulmerton Road, Unit 100
Largo, FL 33771
Phone: (800) 560-6192

Fax: NA
E-mail: At Web site
http://www. remingtoncollege.
  edu/largo
Computer/information sciences—
  general, information technology,
  systems administration.

Rollins College
Campus Box 2720
Winter Park, FL 32789
Phone: (407) 646-2161
Fax: (407) 646-1502
E-mail: admission@rollins.edu
http://www.rollins.edu
Computer/information sciences—
  general.

Saint Leo University
Office of Admissions
MC 2008, P.O. Box 6665
Saint Leo, FL 33574
Phone: (352) 588-8283
Fax: (352) 588-8257
E-mail: admission@saintleo.edu
http://www.saintleo.edu
Human resources management,
  management information
  systems.

St. Thomas University
1540 Northwest Thirty-second
  Avenue
Miami, FL 33054
Phone: (305) 628-6546
Fax: (305) 628-6591
E-mail: signup@stu.edu
http://www.stu.edu
Computer/information sciences—
  general.

Schiller International
  University
300 East Bay Drive
Largo, FL 33770
Phone: (800) 336-4133
Fax: (727) 734-0359
E-mail: admissions@schiller.edu
http://www.schiller.edu
Computer/information sciences—
  general, information technology,
  management information
  systems.

South University—West Palm
  Beach Campus
1760 North Congress Avenue
West Palm Beach, FL 33409
Phone: (800) 688-0932
Fax: (561) 697-9944
E-mail: At Web site
http://www.southuniversity.edu
Information systems.

University of Central Florida
P.O. Box 160111
Orlando, FL 32816
Phone: (407) 823-3000
Fax: (407) 823-5625
E-mail: admission@mail.ucf.edu
http://www.ucf.edu
Computer engineering, computer/
  information sciences—general,
  information technology,
  management information
  systems, statistics.

University of Florida
201 Criser Hall, P.O. Box 11400
Gainesville, FL 32611-4000
Phone: (352) 392-1365
Fax: (352) 392-3987
E-mail: At Web site
http://www.ufl.edu
Computer engineering, computer/
  information sciences—general,
  statistics.

University of Miami
P.O. Box 248025
Coral Gables, FL 33124
Phone: (305) 284-4323
Fax: (305) 284-2507
E-mail: admission@miami.edu
http://www.miami.edu/admissions
Applied mathematics, computer
  engineering, human resources
  management, information
  systems.

University of North Florida
4567 St. Johns Bluff Road, South
Jacksonville, FL 32224
Phone: (904) 620-2624
Fax: (904) 620-2414
E-mail: osprey@unf.edu
http://www.unf.edu

Computer/information sciences—
  general, statistics.

University of South Florida—
  St. Petersburg
140 Seventh Avenue South
St. Petersburg, FL 33701
Phone: (727) 553-4USF
Fax: (727) 553-974-2592
E-mail: admissions@stpt.usf.edu
http://www.http.usf.edu
Computer engineering, computer/
  information sciences—general,
  information systems,
  information technology.

University of South Florida—
  Tampa
4202 East Fowler Avenue SVC-1036
Tampa, FL 33620-9951
Phone: (813) 874-3350
Fax: (813) 974-9689
E-mail: jglassma@admin.usf.edu
http://www.usf.edu
Computer engineering, computer/
  information sciences—general,
  information systems,
  information technology,
  management information
  systems.

University of Tampa
401 West Kennedy Boulevard
Tampa, FL 33606
Phone: (813) 253-6211
Fax: (813) 258-7398
E-mail: admissions@ut.edu
http://www.ut.edu
Computer/information sciences—
  general.

University of West Florida
11000 University Parkway
Pensacola, FL 32514
Phone: (850) 474-2230
Fax: (850) 474-3360
E-mail: admissions@uwf.edu
http://uwf.edu
Computer engineering, computer/
  information sciences—general,
  information technology,
  management information
  systems.

Webber International University
P.O. Box 96
Babson Park, FL 33827
Phone: (863) 638-2910
Fax: (863) 638-1591
E-mail: admissions@webber.edu
http://www.webber.edu
Computer/information sciences—general.

GEORGIA

Albany State University
504 College Drive
Albany, GA 31705
Phone: (229) 430-4646
Fax: (229) 430-3936
E-mail: fsuttles@asurams.edu
http://www.asurams.edu
Computer/information sciences—general, management information systems.

Armstrong Atlantic State University
11935 Abercorn Street
Savannah, GA 31419
Phone: (912) 927-5277
Fax: (912) 927-5462
E-mail: adm-info@mail.armstrong.edu
http://www.armstrong.edu
Applied mathematics, computer/information sciences—general, information technology.

Augusta State University
2500 Walton Way
Augusta, GA 3094
Phone: (706) 737-1632
Fax: (706) 667-4355
E-mail: admission@aug.edu
http://www.aug.edu
Computer/information sciences—general, management information systems.

Brewster-Parker College
P.O. Box 2011
Mount Vernon, GA 30445
Phone: (912) 583-3265
Fax: (912) 583-3598

E-mail: admissions@bpc.edu
http://www.bpc.edu
Information systems.

Clark Atlanta University
223 James P. Brawley Drive
Atlanta, GA 30314
Phone: (404) 880-8000
Fax: (404) 880-6174
E-mail: admissions@panthernet.cau.edu
http://www.cau.edu
Computer/information sciences—general.

Clayton College and State University
5900 North Lee Street
Morrow, GA 30206
Phone: (770) 961-3500
Fax: (770) 961-3752
E-mail: ccsu-info@mail.clayton.edu
http://www.clayton.edu
Computer/information sciences—general, computer systems analysis, information systems.

Columbus State University
4225 University Avenue
Columbus, GA 31907
Phone: (866) 264-2035
Fax: NA
E-mail: At Web site
http://www. colstate.edu
Computer/information sciences—general.

Covenant College
14049 Scenic Highway
Lookout Mountain, GA 30750
Phone: (706) 820-2398
Fax: (706) 820-0893
E-mail: as admissions@covenant.edu
http://www.covenant.edu
Computer/information sciences—general.

Dalton State College
650 College Drive
Dalton, GA 30720
Phone: (800) 829-4436
Fax: (706) 272-2530
E-mail: admissions@daltonstate.edu

http://www.daltonstate.edu
Computer/information sciences—general, management information systems.

DeVry University—Alpharetta
2555 Northwinds Parkway
Alpharetta, GA 30005
Phone: (770) 664-9520
Fax: (770) 664-8824
E-mail: info@devry.edu
http://www.devry.edu
Computer engineering technology, human resources management, information systems, management information systems.

DeVry University—Decatur
250 North Arcadia Avenue
Decatur, GA 30030
Phone: (404) 292-2645
Fax: (404) 292-7011
E-mail: dsilva@admin.atl.devry.edu
http://www.atl.devry.edu
Computer engineering technology, human resources management, information systems.

Emmanuel College
P. O. Box 129
Franklin Springs, GA 30639
Phone: (706) 245-7226
Fax: (706) 245-2876
E-mail: admissions@emmanuelcollege.edu
http://www.emmanuelcollege.edu
Computer/information sciences—general.

Fort Valley State University
1005 State University Drive
Fort Valley, GA 31030
Phone: (912) 825-6307
Fax: (912) 875-6394
E-mail: fordd@fvsu.edu
http://www. www.fvsu.edu
Computer/information sciences—general, information systems.

Georgia College & State University
Campus Box 23

Milledgeville, GA 31061
Phone: (478) 445-5004
Fax: (478) 445-1914
E-mail: gcsu@mail.gcsu.edu
http://www.gcsu.edu
Computer/information sciences—
general.

Georgia Institute of Technology
219 Uncle Heine Way
Atlanta, GA 30332
Phone: (404) 894-4154
Fax: (404) 894-9511
E-mail: admissions@gatech.edu
http://www.gatech.edu
Applied mathematics, computer
engineering, computer/
information sciences—general.

Georgia Southern University
P.O. Box 8024
Statesboro, GA 30460
Phone: (912) 681-5391
Fax: (912) 486-7240
E-mail: admissions@
georgiasouthern.edu
http://www.georgiasouthern.edu
Computer/information
sciences—general, management
information systems.

Georgia Southwestern State University
800 Wheatley Street
Americus, GA 31709
Phone: (912) 928-1273
Fax: (912) 931-2983
E-mail: gswapps@canes.gsw.edu
http://www.gsw.edu
Computer engineering technology,
computer/information
sciences—general, human
resources management.

Georgia State University
P.O. Box 4009
Atlanta, GA 30302
Phone: (404) 651-2365
Fax: (404) 651-4811
E-mail: admissions@gsu.edu
http://www.gsu.edu
Applied mathematics, computer/
information sciences—general.

Kennesaw State University
1000 Chastain Road, Campus Box
0115
Kennesaw, GA 30144
Phone: (770) 423-6000
Fax: (770) 423-6541
E-mail: ksuadmit@kennesaw.edu
http://www.kennesaw.edu
Computer/information sciences—
general, information systems.

LaGrange College
Office of Admission
601 Broad Street
LaGrange, GA 30240
Phone: (706) 880-8005
Fax: (706) 880-8010
E-mail: lgcadmis@lagrange.edu
http://www.lagrange.edu
Computer/information sciences—
general.

Life University
1269 Barclay Circle
Marietta, GA 30060
Phone: (770) 426-2884
Fax: (770) 426-9886
E-mail: admission@life.edu
http://www.life.edu
Information systems.

Macon State College
100 College Station Drive
Macon, GA 31206
Phone: (478) 471-2700
Fax: NA
E-mail: At Web site
http://www.maconstate.edu
Information systems.

Mercer University—Macon
Admissions Office
1400 Coleman Avenue
Macon, GA 31207
Phone: (478) 301-2650
Fax: (478) 301-2828
E-mail: admissions@mercer.edu
http://www.mercer.edu
Information systems.

Morehouse College
830 Westview Drive SW
Atlanta, GA 30314

Phone: (404) 215-2632
Fax: (404) 524-5635
E-mail: janderso@morehouse.edu
http://www.morehouse.edu
Computer/information sciences—
general.

North Georgia College & State University
Office of Undergraduate
Admissions
82 College Circle
Dahlonega, GA 30597
Phone: (706) 864-1800
Fax: (706) 864-1478
E-mail: admissions@ngcsu.edu
http://www.ngcsu.edu
Computer/information sciences—
general.

Paine College
1235 Fifteenth Street
Augusta, GA 30901
Phone: (800) 476-7703
Fax: (706) 821-8691
E-mail: simpkins@mail.paine.edu
http://www.paine.edu
Management information systems.

Reinhardt College
7300 Reinhardt College Circle
Waleska, GA 30183
Phone: (770) 720-5526
Fax: (770) 720-5899
E-mail: admissions@reinhardt.edu
http://www.reinhardt.edu
Information systems.

Savannah State University
College Station, P.O. Box 20209
Savannah, GA 31404
Phone: (912) 356-2181
Fax: (912) 356-2256
E-mail: SSUAdmission@savstate.
edu
http://www.savstate.edu
Computer/information sciences—
general, information systems.

Shorter College
315 Shorter Avenue, Box 1
Rome, GA 30165
Phone: (706) 233-7319

Fax: (706) 233-7224
E-mail: admissions@shorter.edu
http://www.shorter.edu
Computer/information sciences—
general.

Southern Polytechnic State University

1100 South Marietta Parkway
Marietta, GA 30060
Phone: (678) 915-4188
Fax: (678) 915-7292
E-mail: admissions@spsu.edu
http://www.spsu.edu
Computer engineering technology,
information technology,
software engineering.

Spelman College

350 Spelman Lane SW
Atlanta, GA 30314
Phone: (404) 270-5193
Fax: (404) 270-5201
E-mail: admiss@spelman.edu
http://www.spelman.edu
Computer/information sciences—
general.

Thomas University

1501 Millpond Road
Thomasville, GA 31792
Phone: (912) 227-6934
Fax: (912) 226-1653
E-mail: gferrell@thomasu.edu
http://www.thomasu.edu
Management information systems.

University of Georgia

Terrell Hall
Athens, GA 30602
Phone: (706) 542-8776
Fax: (706) 542-1466
E-mail: undergrad@admissions.
uga.edu
http://www.uga.edu
Computer engineering,
management information
systems, statistics.

University of West Georgia

1601 Maple Street
Carrollton, GA 30118
Phone: (678) 839-4000

Fax: (678) 839-4747
E-mail: admiss@westga.edu
http://www.westga.edu
Computer/information
sciences—general, management
information systems.

Valdosta State University

1500 North Patterson Street
Valdosta, GA 31698
Phone: (229) 333-5791
Fax: (229) 333-5482
E-mail: admissions@valdosta.edu
http://www.valdosta.edu
Applied mathematics, computer/
information sciences—general.

Wesleyan College

4760 Forsyth Road
Macon, GA 31201
Phone: (478) 477-1110
Fax: (478) 477-4030
E-mail: admissions@
wesleyancollege.edu
http://www.wesleyancollege.edu
Computer/information sciences—
general.

HAWAII

Brigham Young University— Hawaii

BYU-Hawaii #1973
55-220 Kulanui Street
Laie, HI 96762
Phone: (808) 293-3738
Fax: (808) 293-3457
E-mail: admissions@byuh.edu
http://www.byuh.edu
Information systems.

Chaminade University of Honolulu

3140 Waialae Avenue
Honolulu, HI 96816
Phone: (808) 735-4735
Fax: (808) 739-4647
E-mail: admissions@chaminade.
edu
http://www.chaminade.edu
Computer/information sciences—
general.

Hawaii Pacific University

1164 Bishop Street
Honolulu, HI 96813
Phone: (808) 544-0238
Fax: (808) 544-1136
E-mail: admissions@hpu.edu
http://www.hpu.edu
Applied mathematics, computer/
information sciences—general,
human resources management,
management information
systems.

University of Hawaii—Hilo

200 West Kawili Street
Hilo, HI 96720
Phone: (808) 974-7414
Fax: (808) 933-0861
E-mail: uhhadm@hawaii.edu
http://www.uhh.hawaii.edu
Computer/information sciences—
general.

University of Hawaii—Manoa

2600 Campus Road, QLCSS Room
001
Honolulu, HI 96822
Phone: (808) 956-8975
Fax: (808) 956-4148
E-mail: ar-info@hawaii.edu
http://www.uhm.hawaii.edu
Computer/information sciences—
general, human resources
management, management
information systems.

IDAHO

Albertson College of Idaho

2112 Cleveland Boulevard
Caldwell, ID 83605
Phone: (208) 459-5305
Fax: (208) 459-5116
E-mail: admission@albertson.edu
http://www.albertson.edu
Applied mathematics.

Boise State University

1910 University Drive
Boise, ID 83725
Phone: (208) 426-1156
Fax: (208) 426-3765
E-mail: bsuinfo@boisestate.edu

http://www.boisestate.edu
Applied mathematics, human resources management, information systems, management information systems.

Brigham Young University— Idaho
Admissions Office
KIM 120
Rexburg, ID 83460
Phone: (208) 496-1020
Fax: (208) 496-1220
E-mail: admissions@byui.edu
http://www.byui.edu
Computer engineering, computer/ information sciences—general.

Idaho State University
Admissions Office
Campus P.O. Box 8270
Pocatello, ID 93208
Phone: (208) 282-2475
Fax: (208) 282-4231
E-mail: info@isu.edu
http://www.isu.edu
Computer/information sciences— general, human resources management, information systems.

Northwest Nazarene University
623 Holly Street
Nampa, ID 83686
Phone: (208) 467-8000
Fax: (208) 467-8645
E-mail: admissions@nnu.edu
http://www.nnu.edu
Computer/information sciences—general, management information systems.

University of Idaho
UI Admissions Office
P.O. Box 44264
Moscow, ID 83844
Phone: (308) 885-6326
Fax: (308) 885-9119
E-mail: admappl@uidaho.edu
http://www.uidaho.edu
Applied mathematics, computer engineering, computer/

information sciences—general, human resources management, management information systems.

ILLINOIS

Augustana College
639 Thirty-eighth Street
Rock Island, IL 61201
Phone: (309) 794-7341
Fax: (309) 794-7422
E-mail: admissions@augustana. edu
http://www.augustana.edu
Management information systems.

Aurora University
347 South Gladstone Avenue
Aurora, IL 60506
Phone: (630) 844-5533
Fax: (630) 844-5535
E-mail: admission@aurora.edu
http://www.aurora.edu
Computer/information sciences—general, management information systems.

Benedictine University
5700 College Road
Lisle, IL 60532
Phone: (630) 829-6300
Fax: (630) 829-6301
E-mail: admissions@ben.edu
http://www.ben.edu
Information systems.

Blackburn College
700 College Avenue
Carlinville, IL 62626
Phone: (217) 854-3231
Fax: (217) 854-3713
E-mail: At Web site
http://www.blackburn.edu
Computer/information sciences—general, management information systems.

Bradley University
1501 West Bradley Avenue
Peoria, IL 61625
Phone: (309) 677-1000
Fax: (309) 677-2797

E-mail: admissions@bradley.edu
http://www.bradley.edu
Computer engineering, human resources management, information systems, management information systems.

Chicago State University
9501 South Street King Drive, ADM-200
Chicago, IL 60628
Phone: (773) 995-2513
Fax: (773) 995-3820
E-mail: ug-admissions@csu.edu
http://www.csu.edu
Computer/information sciences—general, information systems, management information systems.

Concordia University
7400 Augusta Street
River Forest, IL 60305
Phone: (708) 209-3100
Fax: (708) 209-3473
E-mail: crfadmis@curf.edu
http://www.curf.edu
Computer/information sciences—general.

DePaul University
1 East Jackson Boulevard
Chicago, IL 60604
Phone: (312) 362-8300
Fax: (312) 362-5749
E-mail: admitdpu@depaul.edu
http://www.depaul.edu
Computer/information sciences—general, human resources management, information systems.

DeVry University—Addison
1221 North Swift Road
Addison, IL 60101
Phone: (630) 953-2000
Fax: (630) 953-1236
E-mail: info@devry.edu
http://www.devry.edu
Computer engineering technology, information systems, information technology.

DeVry University—Chicago

3300 North Cambell Avenue
Chicago, IL 60618
Phone: (773) 697-2155
Fax: (773) 697-2710
E-mail: keaster@chi.devry.edu
http://www.devry.edu
Computer engineering technology,
information systems,
information technology.

DeVry University—Tinley Park

18624 West Creek Drive
Tinley Park, IL 60477
Phone: (708) 342-3100
Fax: (708) 342-3505
E-mail: imccauley@tp.devry.edu
http://www.tp.devry.edu
Computer engineering technology,
human resources management,
information systems,
management information
systems.

Dominican University

7900 West Division
River Forest, IL 60305
Phone: (708) 524-6800
Fax: (708) 524-5990
E-mail: domadmis@dom.edu
http://www.dom.edu
Computer engineering, computer/
information sciences—general,
information systems.

Eastern Illinois University

600 Lincoln Avenue
Charleston, IL 61920
Phone: (217) 581-2223
Fax: (217) 581-7060
E-mail: cdadmit@eiu.edu
http://www.eiu.edu
Management information systems.

East-West University

816 South Michigan Avenue
Chicago, IL 60605
Phone: (312) 939-0111
Fax: (312) 939-0083
E-mail: admissions@eastwest.edu
http://www.eastwest.edu
Computer/information sciences—
general.

Elmhurst College

190 South Prospect Avenue
Elmhurst, IL 60126
Phone: (630) 617-3400
Fax: (630) 617-5501
E-mail: admit@elmhurst.edu
http://www.elmhurst.edu
Information systems.

Eureka College

300 East College Avenue
Eureka, IL 61530
Phone: (309) 467-6350
Fax: (309) 467-6576
E-mail: admissions@eureka.edu
http://www.eureka.edu
Computer/information sciences—
general, management information
systems.

Governors State University

1 University Parkway
University Park, IL 60466
Phone: (708) 534-4490
Fax: (708) 534-1640
E-mail: gcunow@govst.edu
http://www.govst.edu
Computer/information sciences—
general, human resources
management, management
information systems.

Greenville College

315 East College Avenue
Greenville, IL 62246
Phone: (618) 664-7100
Fax: (618) 664-9841
E-mail: admissions@greenville.
edu
http://www.greenville.edu
Management information systems.

Illinois College

1101 West College
Jacksonville, IL 62650
Phone: (217) 245-3030
Fax: (217) 245-3034
E-mail: admissions@hilltop.ic.edu
http://www.ic.edu
Computer/information sciences—
general, management information
systems.

Illinois Institute of Technology

10 West Thirty-third Street
Chicago, IL 60616
Phone: (312) 567-3025
Fax: (312) 567-6939
E-mail: admission@iit.edu
http://www.iit.edu
Computer engineering.

Illinois Wesleyan College

P.O. Box 2900
Bloomington, IL 61702
Phone: (309) 556-3031
Fax: (309) 556-3820
E-mail: iwuadmit@iwu.edu
http://www.iwu.edu
Computer/information sciences—
general.

Judson College

1151 North State Street
Elgin, IL 60123
Phone: (847) 628-2510
Fax: (847) 628-2526
E-mail: admission@judsoncollege.
edu
http://www.judsoncollege.edu
Management information systems.

Knox College

Box K-148
Galesburg, IL 61401
Phone: (309) 341-7100
Fax: (309) 341-7070
E-mail: admission@knox.edu
http://www.knox.edu
Applied mathematics.

Lewis University

One University Parkway
P.O. Box 297
Romeoville, IL 60446
Phone: (815) 836-5250
Fax: (815) 836-5002
E-mail: admissions@lewisu.edu
http://www.lewisu.edu
Computer/information sciences—
general, human resources
management, information sys-
tems, management information
systems.

Loyola University—Chicago

820 North Michigan Avenue

Chicago, IL 60611
Phone: (312) 915-6500
Fax: (312) 915-7216
E-mail: admission@luc.edu
http://www.luc.edu
Computer/information sciences—
general, human resources
management, management
information systems, statistics.

MacMurray College
447 East College Avenue
Jacksonville, IL 62650
Phone: (217) 479-7056
Fax: (217) 291-0702
E-mail: admissions@mac.edu
http://www.mac.edu
Computer/information
sciences—general, management
information systems.

McKendree College
701 College Road
Lebanon, IL 62254
Phone: (618) 537-6831
Fax: (618) 537-6496
E-mail: inquiry@mckendree.edu
http://www.mckendree.edu
Computer/information sciences—
general, information systems,
information technology.

Midstate College
411 West Northmoor Road
Peoria, IL 61614
Phone: (800) 251-4299
Fax: NA
E-mail: midstate@midstate.edu
http://www.midstate.edu
Information systems.

Millikin University
1184 West Main Street
Decatur, IL 62522
Phone: (217) 424-6210
Fax: (217) 425-4669
E-mail: admis@mail.millikin.edu
http://www.millikin.edu
Applied mathematics, human
resources management,
management information
systems.

Monmouth College
700 East Broadway
Monmouth, IL 61462
Phone: (309) 457-2131
Fax: (309) 457-2141
E-mail: admit@monm.edu
http://www.monm.edu
Computer/information
sciences—general, management
information systems.

National-Louis University
2840 Sheridan Road
Evanston, IL 60201
Phone: (847) 465-0575
Fax: NA
E-mail: ninuinfo@wheeling1.nl.edu
http://www.nl.edu
Applied mathematics, information
systems.

North Central College
30 North Brainard Street
P.O. Box 3063
Naperville, IL 60506
Phone: (630) 637-5800
Fax: (630) 637-5819
E-mail: ncadm@noctrl.edu
http://www.northcentralcollege.edu
Applied mathematics, computer/
information sciences—general,
human resources management,
management information
systems.

Northeastern Illinois
University
5500 North St. Louis Avenue
Chicago, IL 60625
Phone: (773) 442-4000
Fax: (773) 442-4020
E-mail: admrec@neiu.edu
http://www.neiu.edu
Applied mathematics.

Northern Illinois University
Office of Admissions
Williston Hall 1010, NIU
DeKalb, IL 60115
Phone: (815) 753-0446
Fax: (815) 753-1783
E-mail: admissions-info@niu.edu

http://www.reg.niu.edu
Applied mathematics, computational
mathematics, computer/
information sciences—general.

North Park University
3225 West Foster Avenue
Chicago, IL 60625
Phone: (773) 244-5500
Fax: (773) 244-4953
E-mail: admission@northpark.edu
http://www.northpark.edu
Applied mathematics, computer/
information sciences—general.

Northwestern University
P.O. Box 3060
1801 Hinman Avenue
Evanston, IL 60208
Phone: (847) 491-7271
Fax: (847) 491-5565
E-mail: ug-admission@
northwestern.edu
http://www.northwestern.edu
Applied mathematics, computer
engineering, information
systems, statistics.

Olivet Nazarene University
1 University Avenue
Bourbonnais, IL 60914
Phone: (815) 939-5603
Fax: (815) 935-4998
E-mail: admissions@olivet.edu
http://www.olivet.edu
Computer/information sciences—
general, information systems.

Principia College
1 Maybeck Place
Elsah, IL 62028
Phone: (618) 374-5181
Fax: (618) 374-4000
E-mail: collegeadmissions@prin.
edu
http://www.prin.edu/college
Computer/information sciences—
general.

Quincy University
1800 College Avenue
Quincy, IL 62301
Phone: (217) 228-5215

Fax: (217) 228-5479
E-mail: admissions@quincy.edu
http://www.quincy.edu
Information systems.

Robert Morris College
401 South Street
Chicago, IL 60605
Phone: (800) 762-5960
Fax: (312) 935-6819
E-mail: enroll@robertmorris.edu
http://www.robertmorris.edu
Information technology.

Rockford College
Office of Undergraduate Admissions
5050 East State Street
Rockford, IL 61108
Phone: (815) 226-4050
Fax: (815) 226-2282
E-mail: admissions@rockford.edu
http://www.rockford.edu
Computer/information science—
    general, human resources
    management, information
    systems, management
    information systems.

Roosevelt University
430 South Michigan Avenue
Chicago, IL 60605
Phone: (312) 341-3515
Fax: (312) 341-3523
E-mail: applyRU@roosevelt.edu
http://www.roosevelt.edu
Computer/information science—
    general, human resources
    management, information
    systems, management
    information systems.

Saint Xavier University
3700 West 103rd Street
Chicago, IL 60655
Phone: (773) 298-3050
Fax: (773) 298-3076
E-mail: admissions@sxu.edu
http://www.sxu.edu
Computer/information sciences—
    general.

Southern Illinois University—
    Carbondale
Admissions & Records, MC 4710

Carbondale, IL 62901
Phone: (618) 453-4405
Fax: (618) 453-3250
E-mail: joinsiuc@siuc.edu
http://www.siuc.edu
Computer engineering, information
    systems.

Southern Illinois University—
    Edwardsville
P.O. Box 1600
Edwardsville, IL 62026
Phone: (618) 650-3705
Fax: (618) 650-5013
E-mail: admis@siue.edu
http://www.siue.edu
Computer/information
    sciences—general, management
    information systems.

Trinity Christian College
6601 West College Drive
Palos Heights, IL 60463
Phone: (708) 239-4708
Fax: (708) 239-4826
E-mail: admissions@trnty.edu
http://www.trnty.edu
Information systems, management
    information systems.

Trinity International University
2065 Half Day Road
Deerfield, IL 60015
Phone: (847) 317-7000
Fax: (847) 317-8097
E-mail: tcadmissions@tiu.edu
http://www.tiu.edu
Human resources management.

University of Chicago
1116 East Fifty-ninth Street
Chicago, IL 60637
Phone: (773) 702-8650
Fax: (773) 702-4199
E-mail: toneill@uchicago.edu
http://www.uchicago.edu
Applied mathematics, computer/
    information sciences—general,
    statistics.

University of Illinois—Chicago
P.O. Box 5220
Chicago, IL 60680

Phone: (312) 996-4350
Fax: (312) 413-7628
E-mail: uicAdmit@uic.edu
http://www.uic.edu
Computer engineering, computer/
    information sciences—general,
    management information
    systems, statistics.

University of Illinois—
    Urbana-Champaign
901 West Illinois Street
Urbana, IL 61801
Phone: (217) 333-0302
Fax: (217) 333-9758
E-mail: admissions@oar.uiuc.edu
http://www.uiuc.edu
Computational mathematics,
    computer engineering,
    computer/information
    sciences—general, human
    resources management,
    management information
    systems, statistics.

University of Saint Francis
500 Wilcox Street
Joliet, IL 60435
Phone: (815) 740-5037
Fax: (815) 740-5032
E-mail: admissions@stfrancis.edu
http://www.stfrancis@edu
Human resources management,
    information technology.

Western Illinois University
1 University Circle
115 Sherman Hall
Macomb, IL 61455
Phone: (309) 298-3157
Fax: (309) 298-3111
E-mail: wiuadm@wiu.edu
http://www.wiu.edu
Computer/information sciences—
    general, human resources
    management, management
    information systems.

Westwood College of
    Technology—O'Hare
8501 West Higgins Road
Chicago, IL 60631
Phone: (773) 380-6801

Fax: NA
E-mail: At Web site
http://www.westwood.edu
Computer/information sciences—
general.

INDIANA

Anderson University
1100 East Fifth Street
Anderson, IN 46012
Phone: (765) 641-4080
Fax: (765) 641-4091
E-mail: info@anderson.edu
http://www.anderson.edu
Information systems.

Ball State University
Office of Admissions
2000 West University Avenue
Muncie, IN 47306
Phone: (765) 285-8300
Fax: (765) 285-1632
E-mail: askus@bsu.edu
http://www.bsu.edu
Computer/information sciences—
general, library science.

Bethel College
1001 West McKinley Avenue
Mishawaka, IN 46545
Phone: (574) 257-3339
Fax: (574) 257-3335
E-mail: admissions@bethelcollege.
edu
http://www.bethelcollege.edu
Human resources management,
information systems.

Butler University
4600 Sunset Avenue
Indianapolis, IN 46208
Phone: (317) 940-8100
Fax: (317) 940-8150
E-mail: admission@butler.edu
http://www.butler.edu
Computer/information sciences—
general.

Calumet College of Saint
Joseph
2400 New York Avenue
Whiting, IN 46394

Phone: (219) 473-4215
Fax: (219) 473-4359
E-mail: admissions@ccsj.edu
http://www.ccsj.edu
Computer/information sciences—
general.

Earlham College
801 National Road West
Richmond, IN 47374
Phone: (765) 983-1600
Fax: (765) 983-1560
E-mail: admission@earlham.edu
http://www.earlham.edu
Computer/information sciences—
general.

Franklin College
101 Branigin Boulevard
Franklin, IN 46131
Phone: (317) 738-8062
Fax: (317) 738-8274
E-mail: admissions@
franklincollege.edu
http://www.franklincollege.edu
Computer/information sciences—
general.

Goshen College
1700 South Main Street
Goshen, IN 46526
Phone: (574) 535-7535
Fax: (574) 535-7609
E-mail: admissions@goshen.edu
http://www.goshen.edu
Applied mathematics, computer/
information sciences—general,
information systems.

Grace College and Seminary
200 Seminary Drive
Winona Lake, IN 46590
Phone: (800) 544-7223
Fax: (574) 372-5120
E-mail: enroll@grace.edu
http://www.grace.edu
Information technology,
management information
systems.

Hanover College
P.O. Box 108
Hanover, IN 47243

Phone: (812) 866-7021
Fax: (812) 866-7098
E-mail: admission@hanover.edu
http://www.hanover.edu
Computer/information sciences—
general.

Indiana Institute of Technology
1600 East Washington Boulevard
Fort Wayne, IN 46803
Phone: (260) 422-5561
Fax: (260) 422-7696
E-mail: admissions@indtech.edu
http://www.indtech.edu
Computer engineering, computer/
information sciences—general,
human resources management,
information systems, management information systems.

Indiana State University
Office of Admissions
Trey Hall 134
Terre Haute, IN 47809
Phone: (812) 237-2121
Fax: (812) 237-8023
E-mail: admissions@indstate.edu
http://www.indstate.edu
Computer engineering technology,
computer/information
sciences—general, human
resources management,
information technology.

Indiana University—
Bloomington
300 North Jordan Avenue
Bloomington, IN 47405
Phone: (812) 855-0661
Fax: (812) 855-5102
E-mail: iuadmit@indiana.edu
http://www.indiana.edu
Computer/information sciences—
general.

Indiana University—East
2325 Chester Boulevard, WZ 116
Richmond, IN 47374
Phone: (765) 973-8208
Fax: (765) 973-8288
E-mail: eaadmit@indiana.edu
http://www.indiana.edu
Management information systems.

Indiana University—Kokomo
Office of Admissions
P.O. Box 9003, KC 230A
Kokomo, IN 46904
Phone: (765) 455-9217
Fax: (765) 455-9537
E-mail: iuadmis@iuk.edu
http://www.iuk.edu
Computer/information sciences—general, data processing technology.

Indiana University—Purdue University Fort Wayne
2101 East Coliseum Boulevard
Fort Wayne, IN 46805
Phone: (260) 481-6812
Fax: (260) 481-6880
E-mail: ipfwadms@ipfw.edu
http://www.ipfw.edu
Computational mathematics, computer engineering, computer engineering technology, human resources management, information systems, management information systems, statistics.

Indiana University—Purdue University Indianapolis
425 North University Boulevard
Cavanaugh Hall, Room 129
Indianapolis, IN 46202
Phone: (317) 274-4591
Fax: (317) 278-1862
E-mail: apply@iupui.edu
http://www.iu.edu
Computer engineering, computer engineering technology, computer/information sciences—general, computer software technology, systems administration.

Indiana University South Bend
1700 Mishawaka Avenue
P.O. Box 7111, A169
South Bend, IN 46634
Phone: (574) 237-4840
Fax: (574) 237-4834
E-mail: admission@iusb.edu
http://www.iusb.edu
Applied mathematics, computer/information sciences—general.

Indiana University Southeast
4201 Grant Line Road, UC-100
New Albany, IN 47150
Phone: (812) 941-2212
Fax: (812) 941-2595
E-mail: admissions@ius.edu
http://www.ius.edu
Computer/information sciences—general.

Indiana Wesleyan University
4201 South Washington Street
Marion, IN 46953
Phone: (765) 677-2138
Fax: (317) 677-2333
E-mail: admissions@indwes.edu
http://www.indwes.edu
Computer/information sciences—general, management information systems.

Manchester College
604 College Avenue North
Manchester, IN 46962
Phone: (260) 982-5055
Fax: (260) 982-5239
E-mail: admitinfo@manchester.edu
http://www.manchester.edu
Computer/information sciences—general.

Marian College
3200 Cold Spring Road
Indianapolis, IN 46222
Phone: (317) 955-6300
Fax: (317) 955-6401
E-mail: admit@marian.edu
http://www.marian.edu
Management information systems.

Oakland City University
143 North Lucretia Street
Oakland City, IN 47660
Phone: (812) 749-4781
Fax: (812) 749-1233
E-mail: ocuadmit@oak.edu
http://www.oak.edu
Applied mathematics, computer engineering, computer/information sciences—general, human resources management, management information systems.

Purdue University—Calumet
Office of Admissions
2200 169th Street
Hammond, IN 46323
Phone: (219) 989-2213
Fax: (219) 989-2775
E-mail: adms@calumet.purdue.edu
http://www.calumet.purdue.edu
Applied mathematics, computer engineering, computer/information sciences—general, human resources management, information systems, software engineering, statistics.

Purdue University—North Central Campus
1401 South U.S. Highway 421
Westville, IN 46391
Phone: (219) 785-5458
Fax: (219) 785-5538
E-mail: admissions@purduenc.edu
http://www.pnc.edu
Computer engineering, computer/information sciences—general, human resources management, statistics.

Purdue University—West Lafayette
1080 Schleman Hall
West Lafayette, IN 47907
Phone: (765) 494-1776
Fax: (765) 494-0544
E-mail: admissions@purdue.edu
http://www.purdue.edu
Computer engineering, computer/information sciences—general, statistics.

Rose-Hulman Institute of Technology
5500 Wabash Avenue
Terre Haute, IN 47803
Phone: (812) 877-8213
Fax: (812) 877-8941
E-mail: admis.ofc@rose-hulman.edu
http://www.rose-hulman.edu
Computer engineering, software engineering.

Saint Joseph's College
P.O. Box 890

Rensselaer, IN 47978
Phone: (219) 866-6170
Fax: (219) 866-6122
E-mail: admissions@saintjoe.edu
http://www.saintjoe.edu
Computer/information
sciences—general, management
information systems.

Saint Mary-of-the-Woods College

Office of Admissions
Guerin Hall
Saint Mary-of-the-Woods, IN 47876
Phone: (812) 535-5106
Fax: (812) 535-4900
E-mail: smwcadms@smwc.edu
http://www.smwc.edu
Computer/information sciences—
general, human resources
management, information
technology, management
information systems.

Saint Mary's College

Admission Office
Notre Dame, IN 46556
Phone: (574) 284-4587
Fax: (574) 284-4841
E-mail: admission@saintmarys.edu
http://www.saintmarys.edu
Applied mathematics, management
information systems, statistics.

Taylor University—Fort Wayne Campus

1025 West Rudisill Boulevard
Fort Wayne, IN 46807
Phone: (800) 233.3922
Fax: (260) 744-8660
E-mail: admissions_f@tayloru.edu
http://www.tayloru.edu/fw
Computer engineering, computer/
information sciences—general.

Taylor University—Upland

236 West Reade Avenue
Upland, IN 46989
Phone: (765) 998-5134
Fax: (765) 998-4925
E-mail: admissions_U@tayloru.edu
http://www.tayloru.edu
Computer engineering.

Tri-State University

1 University Avenue
Angola, IN 46703
Phone: (260) 665-4132
Fax: (260) 665-4578
E-mail: admit@tristate.edu
http://www.tristate.edu
Computer/information
sciences—general, management
information systems.

University of Evansville

1800 Lincoln Avenue
Evansville, IN 47722
Phone: (812) 479-2468
Fax: (812) 474-4076
E-mail: admission@evansville.edu
http://www.evansville.edu
Cognitive science, computer
engineering, computer/
information sciences—general,
information systems.

University of Indianapolis

1400 East Hanna Avenue
Indianapolis, IN 46227
Phone: (317) 788-3216
Fax: (317) 788-3300
E-mail: admissions@uindy.edu
http://www.indy.edu
Computer/information
sciences—general, management
information systems.

University of Notre Dame

230 Main Building
Notre Dame, IN 46556
Phone: (574) 631-7505
Fax: (574) 631-8865
E-mail: admissio.1@nd.edu
http://www.nd.edu
Computer engineering, computer/
information sciences—general,
management information
systems.

University of Saint Francis

2701 Spring Street
Fort Wayne, IN 46808
Phone: (260) 434-3279
Fax: (260) 434-7590
E-mail: admis@sf.edu
http://www.sf.edu

Human resources management.

University of Southern Indiana

8600 University Boulevard
Evansville, IN 47712
Phone: (812) 464-1765
Fax: (812) 465-7154
E-mail: enroll@usi.edu
http://www.usi.edu
Computer/information sciences—
general, data processing
technology.

Valparaiso University

Office of Admissions, Kretzman
Hall
1700 Chapel Drive
Valparaiso, IN 46383-4520
Phone: (219) 464-5011
Fax: (219) 464-6898
E-mail: undergrad.admissions@
valpo.edu
http://www.valpo.edu
Computer engineering.

IOWA

Ashford University

400 North Bluff Boulevard
Clinton, IA 52732
Phone: (866) 711-1700
Fax: NA
E-mail: At Web site
http://www.ashford.edu
Computer/information sciences—
general, human resources
management.

Briar Cliff University

Admissions Office
P.O. Box 100
Sioux City, IA 51104
Phone: (712) 279-5200
Fax: (712) 279-1632
E-mail: admissions@briarcliff.edu
http://www.briarcliff.edu
Computer/information sciences—
general, human resources
management, management
information systems.

Buena Vista University

610 West Fourth Street

Storm Lake, IA 50588
Phone: (712) 749-2235
Fax: (712) 749-1459
E-mail: admissions@bvu.edu
http://www.bvu.edu
Management information systems.

Central College

812 University Street
Pella. IA 50219
Phone: (877) 462-3687
Fax: (641) 628-5316
E-mail: admission@central.edu
http://www.central.edu
Computer/information sciences—
general, information systems.

Clarke College

1550 Clarke Drive
Dubuque, IA 52001
Phone: (563) 588-6316
Fax: (563) 588-6789
E-mail: admissions@clarke.edu
http://www.clarke.edu
Computer/information
sciences—general, management
information systems.

Dordt College

498 Fourth Avenue NE
Sioux Center, IA 51250
Phone: (712) 722-6080
Fax: (712) 722-1987
E-mail: admissions@dordt.edu
http://www.dordt.edu
Computer engineering, computer/
information sciences—general,
information resources
management, information
systems, systems administration.

Drake University

2507 University Avenue
Des Moines, IA 50311
Phone: (515) 271-3181
Fax: (515) 271-2831
E-mail: admission@drake.edu
http://www.choose.drake.edu
Computer/information sciences—
general, information technology,
management information
systems.

Emmaus Bible College

2570 Asbury Road
Dubuque, IA 5200
Phone: (563) 588-8000
Fax: (563) 588-1216
E-mail: info@emmaus.edu
http://www.emmaus.edu
Computer/information sciences—
general.

Graceland University

1 University Place
Lamoni, IA 50140
Phone: (641) 784-5196
Fax: (641) 784-5480
E-mail: admissions@graceland.
edu
http://www.graceland.edu
Computer engineering, computer/
information sciences—general,
information systems.

Grand View College

1200 Grandview Avenue
Des Moines, IA 50316
Phone: (515) 263-2810
Fax: (515) 263-2974
E-mail: admiss@gvc.edu
http://www.gvc.edu
Applied mathematics.

Iowa State University

100 Alumni Hall
Ames, IA 50011
Phone: (515) 294-5836
Fax: (515) 294-2592
E-mail: admissions@iastate.edu
http://www.iastate.edu
Computer engineering, computer/
information sciences—general,
management information
systems, statistics.

Iowa Wesleyan College

601 North Main Street
Mt. Pleasant, IA 52641
Phone: (319) 385-6231
Fax: (319) 385-6296
E-mail: admitrwl@iwc.edu
http://www.iwc.edu
Computer/information sciences—
general, library science.

Kaplan University

1801 East Kimberly Road, Suite 1
Davenport, IA 52807
Phone: (563) 355-3500
Fax: NA
E-mail: At Web site
http://www.kucampus.edu
Management information systems.

Loras College

1450 Alta Vista Street
Dubuque, IA 52004
Phone: (800) 245-6727
Fax: (563) 588-7119
E-mail: admissions@loras.edu
http://www.loras.edu
Human resources management,
management information
systems.

Luther College

700 College Drive
Decorah, IA 52101
Phone: (563) 387-1287
Fax: (563) 387-3159
E-mail: admissions@luther.edu
http://www.luther.edu
Management information systems,
statistics.

Morningside College

1501 Morningside Avenue
Sioux City, IA 51106
Phone: (712) 274-5111
Fax: (712) 274-5101
E-mail: mscadm@morningside.edu
http://www.morningside.edu
Human resources management.

Mount Mercy College

1330 Elmhurt Drive NE
Cedar Rapids, IA 52042
Phone: (319) 368-6460
Fax: (319) 363-5270
E-mail: admission@mtmercy.edu
http://www.mtmercy.edu
Computer/information sciences—
general.

Northwestern College

101 Seventh Street SW
Orange City, IA 51041
Phone: (712) 707-7130

Fax: (712) 707-7164
E-mail: admissions@nwciowa.edu
http://www.nwciowa.edu
Computer/information sciences—
general.

Saint Ambrose University

518 West Locust Street
Davenport, IA 52803
Phone: (563) 444-6300
Fax: (563) 333-6297
E-mail: admit@sau.edu
http://www.sau.edu
Computer/information sciences—
general, computer systems
analysis, information systems.

Simpson College

701 North C Street
Indianola, IA 50125
Phone: (515) 961-1624
Fax: (515) 961-1870
E-mail: admiss@simpson.edu
http://www.simpson.edu
Information systems.

University of Dubuque

2000 University Avenue
Dubuque, IA 52001
Phone: (319) 589-3200
Fax: (319) 589-3690
E-mail: admssns@dbq.edu
http://www.dbq.edu
Computer/information sciences—
general.

University of Iowa

107 Calvin Hall
Iowa City, IA 52242
Phone: (319) 335-3847
Fax: (319) 335-1535
E-mail: admissions@uiowa.edu
http://www.uiowa.edu
Applied mathematics, computer
engineering, computer/
information sciences—general,
human resources management,
management information
systems.

University of Northern Iowa

1227 West Twenty-seventh Street
Cedar Falls, IA 50614

Phone: (319) 273-2281
Fax: (319) 273-2885
E-mail: admissions@uni.edu
http://www.uni.edu
Applied mathematics, computer/
information sciences—general,
management information
systems.

Upper Iowa University

Parker Fox Hall, Box 1959
Fayette, IA 52142
Phone: (800) 553-4150
Fax: (319) 425-5277
E-mail: admission@uiu.edu
http://www.uiu.edu
Management information systems.

Waldorf College

106 South Sixth Street
Forest City, IA 50436
Phone: (641) 585-8112
Fax: (641) 585-8125
E-mail: admissions@waldorf.edu
http://www.waldorf.edu
Computer/information sciences—
general, information systems.

Wartburg College

100 Wartburg Boulevard, P.O. Box
1003
Waverly, IA 50677
Phone: (319) 352-8264
Fax: (319) 352-8579
E-mail: admission@wartburg.edu
http://www.wartburg.edu
Computer/information sciences—
general, information systems.

William Penn University

201 Trueblood Avenue
Oskaloosa, IA 52577
Phone: (641) 673-1012
Fax: (641) 673-2113
E-mail: admissions@wmpenn.edu
http://www.wmpenn.edu
Computer/information sciences—
general.

KANSAS

Baker University College of Arts and Sciences

P.O. Box 65
Baldwin City, KS 66006
Phone: (785) 594-8307
Fax: (785) 594-8372
E-mail: admissions@bakeru.edu
http://www.bakeru.edu
Information systems.

Emporia State University

1200 Commercial Street
Emporia, KS 66801
Phone: (620) 341-5465
Fax: (620) 341-6599
E-mail: goto@emporia.edu
http://www.emporia.edu
Computer/information sciences—
general, information systems.

Fort Hays State University

600 Park Street
Hays, KS 67601
Phone: (785) 628-5666
Fax: (785) 628-4187
E-mail: tigers@fhsu.edu
http://www.fhsu.edu
Computer/information sciences—
general.

Friends University

2100 University Street
Wichita, KS 67213
Phone: (316) 295-5100
Fax: (316) 295-5101
E-mail: learn@friends.edu
http://www.friends.edu
Computer/information sciences—
general, human resources
management, management
information systems.

Kansas State University

119 Anderson Hall
Manhattan, KS 66506
Phone: (785) 532-6250
Fax: (785) 532-6393
E-mail: kstate@ksu.edu
http://www.consider.k-state.edu

Computer engineering, computer/
information sciences—general,
information systems, statistics.

Kansas Wesleyan University
100 East Claflin Avenue
Salina, KS 67401
Phone: (785) 827-5541
Fax: (785) 827-0927
E-mail: admissions@kwu.edu
http://www.kwu.edu
Computer/information sciences—
general.

MidAmerica Nazarene University
2030 College Way
Olathe, KS 66062
Phone: (913) 791-3380
Fax: (913) 791-3481
E-mail: admissions@mnu.edu
http://www.mnu.edu
Computer/information sciences—
general, human resources
management, information
systems.

Newman University
3100 McCormick Avenue
Wichita, KS 67213
Phone: (316) 942-4291
Fax: (316) 942-4483
E-mail: admissions@newmanu.edu
http://www.newmanu.edu
Information systems, management
information systems.

Ottawa University
1001 South Cedar Street, Suite 17
Ottawa, KS 66067
Phone: (785) 242-5200
Fax: (785) 229-1008
E-mail: admiss@ottawa.edu
http://www.ottawa.edu
Information technology, manage-
ment information systems.

Pittsburg State University
1701 South Broadway
Pittsburg, KS 66762
Phone: (620) 235-4251
Fax: (620) 235-6003
E-mail: psuadmit@pittstate.edu

http://www.pittstate.edu
Information technology.

Southwestern College
100 College Street
Winfield, KS 67156
Phone: (620) 229-6236
Fax: (620) 229-6344
E-mail: scadmit@sckans.edu
http://www.sckans.edu
Human resources management,
management information
systems, software engineering.

Sterling College
125 West Cooper Street
Sterling, KS 67579
Phone: (620) 278-4275
Fax: (620) 278-4416
E-mail: admissions@sterling.edu
http://www.sterling.edu
Computer/information sciences—
general.

Tabor College
400 South Jefferson Street
Hillsboro, KS 67063
Phone: (620) 947-3121
Fax: (620) 947-6276
E-mail: admissions@tabor.edu
http://www.tabor.edu
Systems administration.

University of Kansas
Office of Admissions and
Scholarships
1502 Iowa Street
Lawrence, KS 66045
Phone: (785) 864-3911
Fax: (785) 864-5017
E-mail: adm@ku.edu
http://www.ku.edu
Computer engineering, computer/
information sciences—general.

University of Saint Mary
4100 South Fourth Street Trafficway
Leavenworth, KS 66048
Phone: (913) 758-6118
Fax: (913) 758-6140
E-mail: admiss@stmary.edu
http://www.stmary.edu
Information technology.

Washburn University
1700 Southwest College Avenue
Topeka, KS 66621
Phone: (785) 231-1030
Fax: (785) 296-7933
E-mail: zzdpadm@washburn.edu
http://www.washburn.edu
Computer/information sciences—
general, computer systems
analysis.

Wichita State University
1845 Fairmount Street
Wichita, KS 67260
Phone: (316) 978-3085
Fax: (316) 978-3174
E-mail: admissions@wichita.edu
http://www.wichita.edu
Computer engineering, computer/
information sciences—general,
human resources management,
management information
systems.

KENTUCKY

Asbury College
1 Macklem Drive
Wilmore, KY 403390
Phone: (859) 858-3511
Fax: (859) 858-3921
E-mail: admissions@asbury.edu
http://www.asbury.edu
Computational mathematics.

Bellarmine University
2001 Newburg Road
Louisville, KY 4025
Phone: (502) 452-8131
Fax: (502) 452-8002
E-mail: admissions@bellarmine.
edu
http://www.bellarmine.edu
Computer engineering,
computer/information
sciences—general.

Brescia University
717 Frederica Street
Owensboro, KY 42301
Phone: (270) 686-4241
Fax: (270) 686-4314
E-mail: admissions@brescia.edu

http://www.brescia.edu
Applied mathematics, computer/
information sciences—general.

Campbellsville University

1 University Drive
Campbellsville, KY 42718
Phone: (270) 789-5220
Fax: (270) 789-5071
E-mail: admissions@campbellsville.
edu
http://www.campbellsville.edu
Computer/information sciences—
general.

Eastern Kentucky University

521 Lancaster Avenue
Richmond, KY 40475
Phone: (859) 622-2106
Fax: (859) 622-8024
E-mail: stephen.byn@eku.edu
http://www.eku.edu
Computer/information
sciences—general, management
information systems, statistics.

Georgetown College

400 East College Street
Georgetown, KY 40324
Phone: (502) 863-8009
Fax: (502) 868-7793
E-mail: admissions@georgetown
college.edu
http://www.georgetowncollege.edu
Computer/information sciences—
general.

Kentucky State University

400 East Main Street, 3rd floor
Frankfort, KY 40601
Phone: (502) 597-6813
Fax: (502) 597-5814
E-mail: jburrell@gwmail.kysu.edu
http://www.kysu.edu
Computer/information sciences—
general.

Kentucky Wesleyan College

3000 Frederica Street
P.O. Box 1039
Owensboro, KY 42302
Phone: (270) 852-3120
Fax: (270) 852-3133

E-mail: admitme@kwc.edu
http://www.kwc.edu
Computer/information sciences—
general.

Midway College

512 East Stephen Street
Midway, KY 40347
Phone: (859) 846-5346
Fax: (859) 846-5787
E-mail: admissions@midway.edu
http://www.midway.edu
Computer/information sciences—
general.

Morehead State University

Admissions Center
Morehead, KY 40351
Phone: (606) 783-2000
Fax: (606) 783-5038
E-mail: admissions@morehead-
st.edu
http://www.moreheadstate.edu
Computer/information
sciences—general, management
information systems.

Murray State University

P.O. Box 9
Murray, KY 42071
Phone: (270) 762-3741
Fax: (270) 762-3780
E-mail: admissions@murraystate.edu
http://www.murraystate.edu
Computer/information
sciences—general, management
information systems.

Northern Kentucky University

Administrative Center 400
Nunn Drive
Highland Heights, KY 41099
Phone: (859) 572-5220
Fax: (859) 572-6665
E-mail: admitnku@nku.edu
http://www.nku.edu
Computer/information sciences—
general, information technology,
management information
systems.

Pikeville College

Admissions Office

147 Sycamore Street
Pikeville, KY 41501
Phone: (606) 218-5251
Fax: (606) 218-5255
E-mail: wewantyou@pc.edu
http://www.pc.edu
Computer/information sciences—
general.

Sullivan University

3101 Bardstown Road
Louisville, KY 40205
Phone: (800) 844-1354
Fax: NA
E-mail: At Web site
http://www.sullivan.edu
Computer/information sciences—
general.

Thomas More College

333 Thomas More Parkway
Crestview Hill, KY 40107
Phone: (859) 344-3332
Fax: (859) 344-3444
E-mail: admissions@thomasmore.
edu
http://www.thomasmore.edu
Computer/information sciences—
general.

Transylvania University

300 North Broadway
Lexington, KY 40508
Phone: (859) 233-8242
Fax: (859) 233-8797
E-mail: admissions@transy.edu
http://www.transy.edu
Computer/information sciences—
general.

University of Kentucky

100 Funkhuser Building
Lexington, KY 40506
Phone: (859) 257-2000
Fax: (859) 257-3823
E-mail: admission@uky.edu
http://www.uky.edu
Computer/information sciences—
general, statistics.

University of Louisville

Admissions Office

Louisville, KY 40292
Phone: (502) 852-6531
Fax: (502) 852-4776
E-mail: admitme@louisville.edu
http://www.louisville.edu
Applied mathematics, computer
  engineering, management
  information systems.

University of the Cumberlands

6178 College Station Drive
Williamsburg, KY 40769
Phone: (606) 539-4241
Fax: (606) 539-4303
E-mail: admiss@ucumberlands.
  edu
http://www.ucumberlands.edu
Computer/information sciences—
  general.

Western Kentucky University

Potter Hall 117
1 Big Red Way
Bowling Green, KY 42101
Phone: (270) 745-2551
Fax: (270) 745-6133
E-mail: admission@wku.edu
http://www.wku.edu
Computer/information sciences—
  general, management
  information systems.

LOUISIANA

Grambling State University

P.O. Box 864
Grambling, LA 71245
Phone: (318) 274-6423
Fax: (318) 274-3292
E-mail: taylorn@gram.edu
http://www.gram.edu
Information systems.

Grantham University

34641 Grantham College Road
Slidell, LA 70460
Phone: (985) 649-4191
Fax: (985) 649-4183
E-mail: admissions@grantham.edu
http://www.grantham.edu
Computer software technology.

Louisiana State University— Baton Rouge

110 Thomas Boyd Hall
Baton Rouge, LA 70803
Phone: (225) 578-1175
Fax: (225) 578-4433
E-mail: admissions@lsu.edu
http://www.lsu.edu
Computer engineering.

Louisiana State University— Shreveport

1 University Place
Shreveport, LA 71115
Phone: (318) 797-5061
Fax: (318) 797-5204
E-mail: admissions@pilot.lsus.edu
http://www.lsus.edu
Computer engineering.

Louisiana Tech University

P.O. Box 3178
Ruston, LA 71272
Phone: (318) 257-3036
Fax: (318) 257-2499
E-mail: bulldog@latech.edu
http://www.latech.edu
Management information systems.

Loyola University—New Orleans

6363 St. Charles Avenue, Box 18
New Orleans, LA 70119
Phone: (504) 865-3240
Fax: (504) 865-3383
E-mail: admit@loyno.edu
http://www.loyno.edu
Computer/information sciences—
  general, information systems.

Nicholls State University

P.O. Box 2004
Thibodaux, LA 70310
Phone: (985) 448-4507
Fax: (985) 448-4929
E-mail: nicholls@nicholls.edu
http://www.nicholls.edu
Management information systems.

Southern University—New Orleans

6801 Press Drive
New Orleans, LA 70126

Phone: (504) 286-5314
Fax: NA
E-mail: At Web site
http://www.suno.edu
Computer/information sciences—
  general, computer systems
  analysis.

Southern University— Shreveport

3050 Martin Luther King Jr. Drive
Shreveport, LA 71107
Phone: (318) 674-3342
Fax: (318) 674-3338
E-mail: admissions@susla.edu
http://www.susla.edu
Computer/information sciences—
  general.

Tulane University

6823 St. Charles Avenue
New Orleans, LA 70118
Phone: (504) 865-5731
Fax: (504) 862-8715
E-mail: undergrad.admission@
  tulane.edu
http://www.tulane.edu
Management information systems.

University of Louisiana— Lafayette

P.O. Drawer 41210
Lafayette, LA 70504
Phone: (337) 482-6457
Fax: (337) 482-6195
E-mail: admissions@louisiana.edu
http://www.louisiana.edu
Computer engineering,
  management information
  systems.

University of Louisiana— Monroe

700 University Avenue
Monroe, LA 71209
Phone: (318) 342-5252
Fax: (318) 342-5274
E-mail: rehood@ulm.edu
http://www.ulm.edu
Computer engineering,
  management information
  systems.

University of New Orleans

Admissions Office
AD-103 Lakefront
New Orleans, LA 70148
Phone: (504) 280-6595
Fax: (504) 280-5522
E-mail: admissions@uno.edu
http://www.uno.edu
Management information systems.

Xavier University of Louisiana

One Drexel Drive
Attn: Admissions Office
New Orleans, LA 70125
Phone: (504) 483-7388
Fax: (504) 485-7941
E-mail: apply@xula.edu
http://www.xula.edu
Computer engineering, computer/
    information sciences—general,
    statistics.

MAINE

Husson College

One College Circle
Bangor, ME 04401
Phone: (207) 941-7100
Fax: (207) 941-7935
E-mail: admit@husson.edu
http://www.husson.edu
Computer systems analysis, man-
    agement information systems.

Saint Joseph's College of Maine

278 Whites Bridge Road
Standish, ME 04084
Phone: (207) 893-7746
Fax: (207) 893-7862
E-mail: admission@sjcme.edu
http://www.sjcme.edu
Computer/information sciences—
    general.

Thomas College

180 West River Road
Waterville, ME 04901
Phone: (207) 859-1101
Fax: (207) 859-1114
E-mail: admiss@thomas.edu
http://www.thomas.edu
Computer/information sciences—
    general, human resources

management, information
    systems, management
    information systems, software
    engineering.

University of Maine—Augusta

46 University Drive
Augusta, ME 04330
Phone: (207) 621-3185
Fax: (207) 621-3116
E-mail: umaar@maine.edu
http://www.uma.maine.edu
Computer engineering, computer/
    information sciences—general,
    library science.

University of Maine—Farmington

246 Main Street
Farmington, ME 04938
Phone: (207) 778-7050
Fax: (207) 778-8182
E-mail: umfadmit@maine.edu
http://www.umf.maine.edu
Computer engineering, computer/
    information sciences—general.

University of Maine—Fort Kent

23 University Drive
Fort Kent, ME 04743
Phone: (207) 834-7500
Fax: (207) 834-7609
E-mail: umfkadm@maine.edu
http://www.umfk.maine.edu
Computer engineering, computer/
    information sciences—general,
    information technology, man-
    agement information systems.

University of Maine—Orono

5713 Chadbourne Hall
Orono, ME 04469
Phone: (207) 581-1561
Fax: (207) 581-1213
E-mail: um-admit@maine.edu
http://www.maine.edu
Computer engineering, computer/
    information sciences—general.

University of Maine—Presque Isle

Office of Admissions
181 Main Street

Presque Isle, ME 04769
Phone: (207) 768-9532
Fax: (207) 768-9777
E-mail: adventure@umpi.maine.edu
http://www.umpi.maine.edu
Computer engineering, computer/
    information sciences—general.

University of Southern Maine

37 College Avenue
Gorham, ME 04038
Phone: (207) 780-5670
Fax: (207) 780-5640
E-mail: usmadm@usm.maine.edu
http://usm.maine.edu
Computer/information
    sciences—general, management
    information systems.

MARYLAND

Bowie State University

14000 Jericho Park Road
Henry Administration Building
Bowie, MD 20715
Phone: (301) 860-3415
Fax: (301) 860-3438
E-mail: schanaiwa@bowiestate.edu
http://www.bowiestate.edu
Computer/information
    sciences—general, management
    information systems.

Capitol College

11301 Springfield Road
Laurel, MD 20708
Phone: (800) 950-1992
Fax: (301) 953-1442
E-mail: admissions@capitol-college.
    edu
http://www.capitol-college.edu
Computer engineering, software
    engineering.

Columbia Union College

7600 Flower Avenue
Takoma Park, MD 20912
Phone: (301) 891-4080
Fax: (301) 891-4230
E-mail: enroll@cuc.edu
http://www.cuc.edu
Computer/information sciences—
    general, information systems.

Coppin State University
2500 West North Avenue
Baltimore, MD 21216
Phone: (410) 951-3600
Fax: (410) 523-7351
E-mail: admissions@coppin.edu
http://www.coppin.edu
Human resources management.

DeVry University—Bethesda
4550 Montgomery Avenue, Suite
    100
North Bethesda, MD 20814
Phone: (301) 652-8477
Fax: (301) 652-8577
E-mail: bethesda@keller.edu
http://www.devry.edu
Computer/information sciences—
    general.

Hood College
401 Rosemont Avenue
Frederick, MD 21701
Phone: (301) 696-3400
Fax: (301) 696-3819
E-mail: admissions@hood.edu
http://www.hood.edu
Information systems.

Johns Hopkins University
3400 North Charles Street
140 Garland Hall
Baltimore, MD 21218
Phone: (410) 516-8171
Fax: (410) 516-6025
E-mail: gotojhu@jhu.edu
http://www.jhu.edu
Cognitive science, computer
    engineering, computer/
    information sciences—general.

Loyola College in Maryland
4501 North Charles Street
Baltimore, MD 21210
Phone: (800) 221-9107
Fax: (410) 617-2176
E-mail: admissions@loyola.edu
http://www.loyola.edu
Applied mathematics, computer/
    information sciences—general.

McDaniel College
2 College Hill

Westminster, MD 21157
Phone: (410) 857-2230
Fax: (410) 857-2757
E-mail: admissions@mcdaniel.edu
http://www.mcdaniel.edu
Computer/information sciences—
    general.

Morgan State University
1700 East Cold Spring Lane
Baltimore, MD 21251
Phone: (800) 332-6674
Fax: (410) 319-3684
E-mail: tjenness@moac.morgan.edu
http://www.morgan.edu
Computer/information sciences—
    general, information systems.

Mount St. Mary's University
16300 Old Emmitsburg Road
Emmitsburg, MD 21727
Phone: (301) 447-5214
Fax: (301) 447-5860
E-mail: admissions@msmary.edu
http://www.msmary.edu
Computer/information sciences—
    general, information resources
    management.

St. Mary's College of Maryland
Admissions Office
18952 East Fisher Road
St. Mary's City, MD 20686
Phone: (240) 895-5000
Fax: (240) 895-5001
E-mail: admissions@smcm.edu
http://www.smcm.edu
Computer/information sciences—
    general.

Salisbury University
Admissions Office
1101 Camden Avenue
Salisbury, MD 21801
Phone: (410) 543-6161
Fax: (410) 546-6016
E-mail: admissions@salisbury.edu
http://www.salisbury.edu
Management information systems.

Sojourner-Douglass College
200 North Central Avenue
Baltimore, MD 21202

Phone: (800) 732-2630
Fax: NA
E-mail: At Web site
http://www.sdc.edu
Management information systems.

Towson University
8000 York Road
Towson, MD 21252
Phone: (410) 704-2113
Fax: (410) 704-3030
E-mail: admissions@towson.edu
http://www.towson.edu
Computer/information sciences—
    general.

United States Naval Academy
117 Decatur Road
Annapolis, MD 21402
Phone: (410) 293-4361
Fax: (410) 295-1815
E-mail: webmail@usna.com
http://www.usna.edu
Computer/information sciences—
    general, information technology.

University of Baltimore
1420 North Charles Street
Baltimore, MD 21201
Phone: (410) 837-4777
Fax: (410) 837-4793
E-mail: admissions@ubmail.ubalt.
    edu
http://www.ubalt.edu
Human resources management,
    management information
    systems.

**University of Maryland—
    Baltimore County**
1000 Hilltop Circle
Baltimore, MD 21250
Phone: (410) 455-2291
Fax: (410) 455-1094
E-mail: admissions@umbc.edu
http://www.umbc.edu
Computer engineering, computer/
    information sciences—general,
    information systems, statistics.

**University of Maryland—
    College Park**
Mitchell Building

College Park, MD 20742
Phone: (301) 314-8385
Fax: (301) 314-9693
E-mail: um-admit@uga.umd.edu
http://www.umd.edu
Computer engineering, computer/
   information sciences—general,
   human resources management,
   information systems.

University of Maryland— Eastern Shore

Office of Admissions
Backbone Road
Princess Anne, MD 21853
Phone: (410) 651-6410
Fax: (410) 651-7922
E-mail: ccmills@mail.umes.edu
http://www.umes.edu
Computer/information sciences—
   general.

University of Maryland— University College

3501 University Boulevard East
Adelphi, MD 20783
Phone: (301) 985-7000
Fax: (301) 985-7364
E-mail: umucinfo@nova.umuc.edu
http://www.umuc.edu
Computer/information sciences—
   general, information systems,
   management information
   systems.

Villa Julia College

1525 Greenspring Valley Road
Stevenson, MD 21153
Phone: (410) 486-7001
Fax: (410) 602-6600
E-mail: admissions@vjc.edu
http://www.vjc.edu
Computer/information sciences—
   general, information systems.

MASSACHUSETTS

American International College

1000 State Street
Springfield, MA 01109
Phone: (413) 205-3201
Fax: (413) 205-3051

E-mail: inquiry@aic.edu
http://www.aic.edu
Human resources management,
   information systems,
   management information
   systems.

Anna Marie College

50 Sunset Lane, Box O
Paxton, MA 01612
Phone: (508) 849-3260
Fax: (508) 849-3362
E-mail: admission@annamaria.edu
http://www.annamaria.edu
Computer/information
   sciences—general, management
   information systems.

Assumption College

500 Salisbury Street
Worcester, MA 01609
Phone: (508) 767-7285
Fax: (508) 799-4412
E-mail: admiss@assumption.edu
http://www.assumption.edu
Computer/information sciences—
   general.

Atlantic Union College

338 Main Street
South Lancaster, MA 01561
Phone: (978) 368-2235
Fax: (978) 368-2517
E-mail: At Web site
http://www.auc.edu
Computer/information sciences—
   general.

Babson College

Lunder Hall
Babson Park, MA 02457
Phone: (781) 239-5522
Fax: (781) 239-4135
E-mail: ugradadmission@babson.
   edu
http://www.babson.edu
Computer/information sciences—
   general, information systems,
   management information
   systems.

Becker College

61 Sever Street

Worcester, MA 01609
Phone: (508) 791-9241
Fax: (508) 890-1500
E-mail: admissions@beckercollege.
   edu
http://www.beckercollege.edu
Human resources management.

Bentley College

175 Forest Street
Waltham, MA 02452
Phone: (781) 891-2244
Fax: (781) 891-3414
E-mail: ugadmission@bentley.edu
http://www.bentley.edu
Computer/information sciences—
   general.

Boston College

140 Commonwealth Avenue,
   Devlin Hall 208
Chestnut Hill, MA 02467
Phone: (617) 552-3100
Fax: (617) 552-0798
E-mail: ugadmis@bc.edu
http://www.bc.edu
Computer/information sciences—
   general, human resources
   management, information
   systems, management
   information systems.

Boston University

121 Bay State Road
Boston, MA 02215
Phone: (617) 353-2300
Fax: (617) 353-9695
E-mail: admissions@bu.edu
http://www.bu.edu
Computer engineering, computer/
   information sciences—general,
   management information
   systems.

Brandeis University

415 South Street, MS003
Waltham, MA 02454
Phone: (781) 736-3500
Fax: (781) 736-3536
E-mail: admissions@brandeis.edu
http://www.brandeis.edu
Computer/information sciences—
   general.

Bridgewater State College
Gates House
Bridgewater, MA 02325
Phone: (508) 531-1237
Fax: (508) 531-1746
E-mail: admission@bridgew.edu
http://www.bridgew.edu
Management information systems.

Clark University
950 Main Street
Worcester, MA 01610
Phone: (508) 793-7431
Fax: (508) 793-8821
E-mail: admissions@clarku.edu
http://www.clarku.edu
Computer/information sciences—
  general.

College of the Holy Cross
Admissions Office
1 College Street
Worcester, MA 01610
Phone: (508) 793-2443
Fax: (508) 793-3888
E-mail: admissions@holycross.edu
http://www.holycross.edu
Computer/information sciences—
  general.

Curry College
1071 Blue Hill Avenue
Milton, MA 02186
Phone: (617) 333-2210
Fax: (617) 333-2114
E-mail: curryadm@curry.edu
http://www.curry.edu
Computer/information sciences—
  general.

Eastern Nazarene College
23 East Elm Avenue
Quincy, MA 02170
Phone: (617) 745-3000
Fax: (617) 745-3490
E-mail: admissions@enc.edu
http://www.enc.edu
Computer engineering.

Elms College
291 Springfield Street
Chicopee, MA 01013
Phone: (413) 592-3189

Fax: (413) 594-2781
E-mail: admissions@elms.edu
http://www.elms.edu
Computer/information sciences—
  general.

Endicott College
376 Hale Street
Beverly, MA 01915
Phone: (978) 921-1000
Fax: (978) 232-2520
E-mail: admission@endicott.edu
http://www.endicott.edu
Computer/information sciences—
  general.

Fisher College
118 Beacon Street
Boston, MA 02116
Phone: (866) 266-6007
Fax: (617) 236-5473
E-mail: admissions@fisher.edu
http://www.fisher.edu
Human resources management.

Fitchburg State College
160 Pearl Street
Fitchburg, MA 01420
Phone: (978) 665-3144
Fax: (978) 665-4540
E-mail: admissions@fsc.edu
http://www.fsc.edu
Computer/information sciences—
  general.

Framingham State College
P.O. Box 9101
100 State Street
Framingham, MA 01701
Phone: (508) 626-4500
Fax: (508) 626-4017
E-mail: admiss@frc.mass.edu
http://www.framingham.edu
Computer/information sciences—
  general.

Hampshire College
Admissions Office
893 West Street
Amherst, MA 01002
Phone: (413) 559-5471
Fax: (413) 559-5631
E-mail: admissions@hampshire.edu

http://www.hampshire.edu
Computer/information sciences—
  general.

Harvard College
Byerly Hall
8 Garden Street
Cambridge, MA 02138
Phone: (617) 495-1551
Fax: (617) 495-8821
E-mail: college@fas.harvard.edu
http://www.fas.harvard.edu
Applied mathematics, statistics.

Lasell College
Office of Undergraduate
  Admissions
1844 Commonwealth Avenue
Newton, MA 02466
Phone: (617) 243-2225
Fax: (617) 243-2380
E-mail: info@lasell.edu
http://www.lasell.edu
Computer/information
  sciences—general, management
  information systems.

**Massachusetts College of
  Liberal Arts**
375 Church Street
North Adams, MA 01247
Phone: (413) 662-5410
Fax: (413) 662-5179
E-mail: admissions@mcla.edu
http://www.mcla.edu
Computer/information sciences—
  general, information systems.

Merrimack College
Office of Admissions
Austin Hall
North Andover, MA 01845
Phone: (978) 837-5100
Fax: (978) 837-5133
E-mail: admission@merrimack.
  edu
http://www.merrimack.edu
Computer engineering.

Mount Holyoke College
Office of Admissions
Newhall Center
South Hadley, MA 010175

Phone: (413) 538-2023
Fax: (413) 538-2409
E-mail: admission@mtholyoke.edu
http://www.mtholyoke.edu
Statistics.

Newbury College
129 Fisher Avenue
Brookline, MA 02445
Phone: (617) 730-7076
Fax: (617) 731-9618
E-mail: brookline@newbury.edu
http://www.newbury.edu
Computer/information sciences—
general.

Nichols College
P.O. Box 5000, 124 Center Road
Dudley, MA 01571
Phone: (508) 213-2203
Fax: (508) 943-9885
E-mail: admissions@nichols.edu
http://www.nichols.edu
Computer systems analysis,
human resources management,
management information
systems.

Northeastern University
260 Huntington Avenue, 150
Richards Hall
Boston, MA 02115
Phone: (617) 373-2200
Fax: (617) 373-8780
E-mail: admissions@neu.edu
http://www.neu.edu
Computer engineering, computer
engineering technology,
computer/information
sciences—general, human
resources management,
management information
systems.

Regis College
235 Wellesley Street
Weston, MA 02493
Phone: (781) 768-7100
Fax: (781) 768-7071
E-mail: admission@regiscollege.edu
http://www.regiscollege.edu
Computer/information sciences—
general, information systems.

Salem State College
352 Lafayette Street
Salem, MA 019780
Phone: (978) 542-6200
Fax: (978) 542-6893
E-mail: admissions@salemstate.edu
http://www.salemstate.edu
Computer/information sciences—
general, human resources
management, management
information systems.

Simmons College
300 The Fenway
Boston, MA 02115
Phone: (617) 521-2051
Fax: (617) 521-3190
E-mail: ugadm@simmons.edu
http://www.simmons.edu
Computer/information
sciences—general, management
information systems.

Simon's Rock College of Bard
84 Alford Road
Great Barrington, MA 01230
Phone: (413) 528-7312
Fax: (413) 528-7334
E-mail: admit@simons-rock.edu
http://www.simons-rock.edu
Cognitive science, statistics.

Smith College
17 College Lane
Northampton, MA 01063
Phone: (413) 585-2500
Fax: (413) 585-2527
E-mail: admission@smith.edu
http://www.smith.edu
Computer engineering.

Springfield College
263 Alden Street
Springfield, MA 01109
Phone: (413) 748-3136
Fax: (413) 748-3694
E-mail: admissions@spfldcol.edu
http://www.spfldcol.edu
Computer/information sciences—
general, information systems.

Suffolk University
8 Ashburton Place

Boston, MA 02108
Phone: (617) 573-8460
Fax: (617) 742-4291
E-mail: admission@suffolk.edu
http://www.suffolk.edu
Computer engineering, computer/
information sciences—general,
information systems, management information systems.

Tufts University
Bendetson Hall
Medford, MA 02156
Phone: (617) 627-3170
Fax: (617) 627-3860
E-mail: inquiry@ase.tufts.edu
http://www.tufts.edu
Computer engineering, computer/
information sciences—general,
information systems.

University of Massachusetts— Amherst
University Admissions Center
Amherst, MA 01003
Phone: (413) 545-0222
Fax: (413) 545-4312
E-mail: mail@admissions.umass.edu
http://www.umass.edu
Computer engineering.

University of Massachusetts— Boston
100 Morrissey Boulevard
Boston, MA 02125
Phone: (617) 287-6000
Fax: (617) 287-5999
E-mail: undergrad@umb.edu
http://www.umb.edu
Computer/information sciences—
general.

University of Massachusetts— Dartmouth
285 Old Westport Road
North Dartmouth, MA 02747
Phone: (508) 999-9605
Fax: (508) 999-8755
E-mail: admissions@umassd.edu
http://www.umassd.edu
Computer engineering, computer/
information sciences—general,
management information
systems.

University of Massachusetts—Lowell
Office of Undergrad Admissions
883 Broadway Street, Room 110
Lowell, MA 01854
Phone: (978) 934-3931
Fax: (978) 934-3086
E-mail: admissions@uml.edu
http://www.uml.edu
Applied mathematics, information systems.

Wellesley College
Board of Admissions
106 Central Street
Wellesley, MA 02481
Phone: (781) 283-2270
Fax: (781) 283-3678
E-mail: admission@wellesley.edu
http://www.wellesley.edu
Computer/information sciences—general.

Wentworth Institute of Technology
555 Huntington Avenue
Boston, MA 02115
Phone: (800) 556-0610
Fax: (617) 989-4591
E-mail: admissions@wit.edu
http://www.wit.edu
Computer engineering technology, computer/information sciences—general, information systems.

Western New England College
Admissions Office
1215 Wilbraham Road
Springfield, MA 01119
Phone: (413) 782-1321
Fax: (413) 782-1777
E-mail: ugradmis@wnec.edu
http://www.wnec.edu
Management information systems.

Westfield State College
577 Western Avenue
Westfield, MA 01086
Phone: (413) 572-5218
Fax: (413) 572-0520
E-mail: admission@wsc.mass.edu
http://www.wsc.mass.edu
Information systems.

Wheaton College
Office of Admissions
Norton, MA 02766
Phone: (508) 286-8251
Fax: (508) 286-8271
E-mail: admission@wheatoncollege.edu
http://www.wheatoncollege.edu
Computer/information sciences—general.

Worcester Polytechnic Institute
100 Institute Road
Worcester, MA 01609
Phone: (508) 831-5286
Fax: (508) 831-5875
E-mail: admissions@wpi.edu
http://www.wpi.edu
Applied mathematics, management information systems.

Worcester State College
Department of Admissions
486 Chandler Street
Worcester, MA 01602
Phone: (508) 929-8040
Fax: (508) 929-8183
E-mail: admissions@worcester.edu
http://www.worcester.edu
Computer/information sciences—general.

MICHIGAN

Albion College
611 East Porter Street
Albion, MI 49224
Phone: (517) 629-0321
Fax: (517) 629-0569
E-mail: admissions@albion.edu
http://www.albion.edu
Computer/information sciences—general.

Andrews University
Office of Admissions
Berien Springs, MI 49104
Phone: (800) 253-2874
Fax: (616) 471-3228
E-mail: enroll@andrews.edu
http://www.andrews.edu
Computer/information sciences—general, information systems.

Aquinas College
1607 Robinson Road SE
Grand Rapids, MI 49506
Phone: (616) 632-2900
Fax: (616) 732-4469
E-mail: admissions@aquinas.edu
http://www.aquinas.edu
Computer/information sciences—general.

Baker College of Cadillac
9600 East 13th Street
Cadillac, MI 49601
Phone: (888) 313-3463
Fax: (231) 775-8505
E-mail: adm-ca@baker.edu
http://www.baker.edu
Human resources management.

Baker College of Clinton Township
34950 Little Mack Avenue
Clinton Township, MI 48035
Phone: (888) 272-2842
Fax: (586) 791-6611
E-mail: At Web site
http://www.baker.edu
Computer/information sciences—general, human resources management.

Baker College of Flint
1050 West Bristol Road
Flint, MI 48507-5508
Phone: (800) 964-4299
Fax: (810) 766-4293
E-mail: adm-fl@baker.edu
http://www.baker.edu
Computer/information sciences—general, management information systems.

Baker College of Muskegon
1903 Marquette Avenue
Muskegon, MI 49442
Phone: (231) 777-5200
Fax: (231) 777-5201
E-mail: kathy.jacobson@baker.edu
http://www.baker.edu
Computer/information sciences—general, computer systems analysis, human resources management, information systems.

Baker College of Owosso

1020 South Washington Street
Owosso, MI 48867
Phone: (989) 729-3350
Fax: (989) 723-3355
E-mail: mike.konopacke.@baker.
edu
http://www.baker.edu
Computer/information sciences—
general, human resources
management, management
information systems.

Baker College of Port Huron

3403 Lapeer Road
Port Huron, MI 48060
Phone: (810) 985-7000
Fax: (810) 985-7066
E-mail: kenny_d@porthuron.baker.
edu
http://www.baker.edu
Computer/information sciences—
general, human resources
management, information
systems, management
information systems.

Calvin College

3201 Burton Street SE
Grand Rapids, MI 49546
Phone: (616) 526-6106
Fax: (616) 526-6777
E-mail: admissions@calvin.edu
http://www.calvin.edu
Computer/information sciences—
general, information systems,
management information
systems.

Central Michigan University

205 Warriner Hall
Mount Pleasant, MI 48859
Phone: (989) 774-3076
Fax: (989) 774-7267
E-mail: cmuadmit@cmich.edu
http://www.cmich.edu
Computer engineering technology,
computer/information
sciences—general, human
resources management,
information systems,
management information
systems, statistics.

Cleary University

3750 Cleary Drive
Howell, MI 48843
Phone: (517) 548-3670
Fax: (517) 552-7805
E-mail: admissions@cleary.edu
http://www.cleary.edu
Human resources management,
management information
systems.

Concordia University

4090 Geddes Road
Ann Arbor, MI 48105
Phone: (888) 734-4237
Fax: NA
E-mail: admissions@cuaa.edu
http://www.cuaa.edu
Computer/information sciences—
general.

Cornerstone University

1001 East Beltline Avenue NE
Grand Rapids, MI 49525
Phone: (616) 222-1418
Fax: (616) 222-1418
E-mail: admissions@cornerstone.edu
http://www.cornerstone.edu
Computer/information sciences—
general, information systems,
management information
systems.

Eastern Michigan University

400 Pierce Hall
Ypsilanti, MI 48197
Phone: (734) 487-3060
Fax: (734) 487-1484
E-mail: admissions@emich.edu
http://www.emich.edu
Computer engineering, computer/
information sciences—general,
information systems, statistics.

Ferris State University

1201 South State Street
Center for Student Services
Big Rapids, MI 49307
Phone: (231) 591-2100
Fax: (231) 591-3944
E-mail: admissions@ferris.edu
http://www.ferris.edu
Applied mathematics, human
resources management, statistics.

Grace Bible College

1011 Aldon Street SW
Grand Rapids, MI 49509
Phone: (616) 538-2330
Fax: (616) 538-0599
E-mail: At Web site
http://www.gbcol.edu
Computer/information sciences—
general, information technology.

Grand Valley State University

1 Campus Drive
Allendale, MI 49401
Phone: (616) 331-5000
Fax: (616) 331-2000
E-mail: go@gvsu@gvsu.edu
http://www.gvsu.edu
Computer/information sciences—
general, human resources
management, information
systems, statistics.

Hillsdale College

33 East College Street
Hillsdale, MI 49242
Phone: (517) 607-2327
Fax: (517) 607-2223
E-mail: admissions@hillsdale.edu
http://www.hillsdale.edu
Computational mathematics.

Hope College

69 East Tenth Street, P.O. Box 9000
Holland, MI 49422
Phone: (616) 395-7850
Fax: (616) 395-7130
E-mail: admissions@hope.edu
http://www.hope.edu
Computer/information sciences—
general.

Kalamazoo College

1200 Academy Street
Kalamazoo, MI 49006
Phone: (616) 337-7166
Fax: (616) 337-7390
E-mail: admission@kzoo.edu
http://www.kzoo.edu
Computer/information sciences—
general.

Kettering University

1700 West Third Avenue

Flint, MI 48504
Phone: (810) 762-7865
Fax: (810) 762-9837
E-mail: admissions@kettering.edu
http://www.kettering.edu
Applied mathematics,
computational mathematics,
computer engineering,
management information
systems, statistics.

Kuyper College
3333 East Beltline NE
Grand Rapids, MI 49525
Phone: (616) 222-3000
Fax: NA
E-mail: admissions@kuyper.edu
http://www.kuyper.edu
Computer/information sciences—
general.

Lake Superior State University
650 West Easterday Avenue
Sault Ste. Marie, MI 49783
Phone: (906) 635-2231
Fax: (906) 635-6669
E-mail: admissions@lssu.edu
http://www.lssu.edu
Computer engineering.

Lawrence Technological University
21000 West Ten Mile Road
Southfield, MI 48075
Phone: (248) 204-3160
Fax: (248) 204-3188
E-mail: admissions@ltu.edu
http://www.ltu.edu
Computer engineering, information
technology.

Madonna University
36600 Schoolcraft Road
Livonia, MI 48150
Phone: (734) 432-5339
Fax: (734) 432-5393
E-mail: muinfo@smtp.munet.edu
http://www.munet.edu
Computer/information sciences—
general, human resources
management, management
information systems.

Marygrove College
8425 West McNichols Road
Detroit, MI 48221
Phone: (313) 927-1240
Fax: (313) 927-1345
E-mail: info@marygrove.edu
http://www.marygrove.edu
Computer/information sciences—
general.

Michigan State University
250 Administration Building
East Lansing, MI 48824-1046
Phone: (517) 355-8332
Fax: (517) 353-1647
E-mail: adis@msu.edu
http://www.msu.edu
Applied mathematics, computational mathematics, computer
engineering, computer/informa-
tion sciences—general, human
resources management, information systems, statistics.

Michigan Technological University
1400 Townsend Drive
Houghton, MI 49931
Phone: (906) 487-2335
Fax: (906) 487-2125
E-mail: mtu4u@mtu.edu
http://www.mtu.edu
Computer engineering, computer/
information sciences—general,
software engineering, system
administration.

Northern Michigan University
1401 Presque Isle Avenue
304 Cohodas
Marquette, MI 49855
Phone: (906) 227-2650
Fax: (906) 227-1747
E-mail: admiss@nmu.edu
http://www.nmu.edu
Applied mathematics, computer/
information sciences—general,
management information
systems.

Northwood University
4000 Whiting Drive
Midland, MI 48640
Phone: (989) 837-4273
Fax: (989) 837-4490
E-mail: admissions@northwood.edu
http://www.northwood.edu
Computer/information
sciences—general, management
information systems.

Oakland University
Office of Admissions
101 North Foundation Hall
Rochester, MI 48309
Phone: (248) 370-3360
Fax: (248) 370-4462
E-mail: ouinfo@oakland.edu
http://www.oakland.edu
Computer engineering, computer/
information sciences—general,
management information
systems, statistics.

Rochester College
800 West Avon Road
Rochester Hills, MI 48307
Phone: (248) 218-2031
Fax: (248) 218-2035
E-mail: admissions@rc.edu
http://www.rc.edu
Computer/information
sciences—general, management
information systems.

Saginaw Valley State University
7400 Bay Road
University Center, MI 48710
Phone: (989) 964-4200
Fax: (989) 790-0180
E-mail: admissions@svsu.edu
http://www.svsu.edu
Applied mathematics, computer/
information sciences—general,
computer systems analysis.

Siena Heights University
1247 East Siena Heights Drive
Adrian, MI 49221
Phone: (517) 263-0731
Fax: (517) 264-7704
E-mail: admissions@alpha.sienahts.
edu
http://www.sienahts.edu
Computer/information sciences—
general.

Southwest Michigan College

2229 U.S. 12 East
Niles, MI 49120
Phone: (800) 456-8675
Fax: NA
E-mail: info@swmich.edu
http://www.swmich.edu
Computer/information sciences—
general.

Spring Arbor University

106 East Main Street
Spring Arbor, MI 49283
Phone: (517) 750-6458
Fax: (517) 750-6458
E-mail: admissions@admin.arbor.
edu
http://www.arbor.edu
Management information systems.

University of Detroit—Mercy

P.O. Box 19900
Detroit, MI 48219
Phone: (313) 993-1245
Fax: (313) 993-3326
E-mail: admissions@udmercy.edu
http://www.udmercy.edu
Applied mathematics, computer
engineering, computer/
information sciences—general,
computer systems analysis.

University of Michigan—Ann Arbor

1220 Student Activities Building
Ann Arbor, MI 48109
Phone: (734) 764-7433
Fax: (734) 936-0740
E-mail: ugadmiss@umich.edu
http://www.umich.edu
Applied mathematics, computer/
information sciences—general,
statistics.

University of Michigan—Dearborn

4901 Evergreen Road
Dearborn, MI 48128
Phone: (313) 593-5100
Fax: (313) 436-9167
E-mail: admissions@umd.umich.
edu

http://www.umd.umich.edu
Applied mathematics, computer
engineering, computer/
information sciences—general,
statistics.

University of Michigan—Flint

303 East Kearsley Street
245 UPAV
Flint, MI 48502
Phone: (810) 762-3300
Fax: (810) 762-3272
E-mail: admissions@umflint.edu
http://www.umflint.edu
Applied mathematics, computer/
information sciences—general,
information systems, statistics.

Wayne State University

656 West Kirby Street
Detroit, MI 48202
Phone: (313) 577-3577
Fax: (313) 577-7536
E-mail: admissions@wayne.edu
http://www.wayne.edu
Computer/information sciences—
general, information systems,
management information
systems.

Western Michigan University

1903 West Michigan Avenue
Kalamazoo, MI 49008
Phone: (269) 387-2000
Fax: (269) 387-2096
E-mail: ask-wmu@umich.edu
http://www.wmich.edu
Applied mathematics, computer
engineering, computer/
information sciences—general,
human resources management,
information resources
management, statistics.

MINNESOTA

Academy College

1101 East Seventy-eighth Street,
Suite 100
Bloomington, MN 55420
Phone: (800) 292-9149
Fax: (952) 851-0094
E-mail: At Web site

http://www.academycollege.edu
Computer/information sciences—
general.

Augsburg College

2211 Riverside Avenue South
Minneapolis, MN 55454
Phone: (612) 330-1001
Fax: (612) 330-1590
E-mail: admissions@augsburg.edu
http://www.augsburg.edu
Management information systems.

Bemidji State University

1500 Birchmont Drive NE, Deputy
Hall
Bemidji, MN 56601
Phone: (218) 755-2040
Fax: (218) 755-2074
E-mail: admissions@bemidjistate.
edu
http://www.bemidjistate.edu
Computer/information sciences—
general.

Bethel University

Office of Admissions-CAS
3900 Bethel Drive
Saint Paul, MN 55112
Phone: (651) 638-6242
Fax: (651) 635-1490
E-mail: buadmissions-cas@bethel.
edu
http://www.bethel.edu
Computer/information sciences—
general.

Brown College

1440 Northland Drive
Mendota Heights, MN 55120
Phone: (888) 574-3777
Fax: NA
E-mail: At Web site
http://www.browncollege.com
Information technology.

Capella University

222 South Ninth Street, 20th floor
Minneapolis, MN 55402
Phone: (888) 227-3552
Fax: (612) 339-8022
E-mail: info@capella.edu

http://www.capella.edu
Computer/information sciences—
general, human resources
management, information
systems, information
technology.

College of St. Catherine

Office of Admission, #F-02
2004 Randolph Avenue
St. Paul, MN 55105
Phone: (800)-656-5283
Fax: NA
E-mail: admissions@stkate.edu
http://www.stkate.edu
Computer/information sciences—
general, information systems,
library science, management
information systems.

College of St. Scholastica

1200 Kenwood Avenue
Duluth, MN 55811
Phone: (218) 723-6000
Fax: (218) 723-5991
E-mail: admissions@css.edu
http://www.css.edu
Computer/information sciences—
general.

Concordia College—Moorhead

901 Eighth Street South
Moorhead, MN 56562
Phone: (218) 299-3004
Fax: (218) 299-4720
E-mail: admissions@cord.edu
http://www.goconcordia.com
Applied mathematics.

Concordia University—St. Paul

275 Syndicate Street North
Saint Paul, MN 55104
Phone: (651) 641-8230
Fax: (651) 603-6320
E-mail: admiss@csp.edu
http://www.csp.edu
Management information systems.

Crown College

8700 College View Drive
St. Bonifacius, MN 55375
Phone: (952) 446-4142
Fax: (952) 446-4149

E-mail: info@crown.edu
http://www.crown.edu
Computer/information sciences—
general, information technology.

Globe University

8089 Globe Drive
Woodbury, MN 55125
Phone: (651) 730-5100
Fax: (651) 730-5151
E-mail: At Web site
http://www.msbcollege.edu
Computer/information sciences—
general, information technology,
system administration.

Gustavus Adolphus College

800 West College Avenue
Saint Peter, MN 56082
Phone: (507) 933-7676
Fax: (507) 933-7474
E-mail: admission@gustavus.edu
http://www.gustavus.edu
Computer/information sciences—
general.

Macalester College

1600 Grand Avenue
St. Paul, MN 55105
Phone: (651) 696-6357
Fax: (651) 696-6724
E-mail: admissions@macalester.edu
http://www.macalester.edu
Computer/information sciences—
general.

Metropolitan State University

1501 Hennepin Avenue
Minneapolis, MN 55403
Phone: (612) 659-6000
Fax: NA
E-mail: At Web site
http://www.metrostate.edu
Applied mathematics, computer
systems analysis, human
resources management,
information systems,
management information
systems.

Minnesota State University— Mankato

Mankato, TC 122

Mankato, MN 56001
Phone: (507) 389-1822
Fax: (507) 389-1511
E-mail: admissions@mnsu.edu
http://www.mnsu.edu
Computer engineering, computer
engineering technology,
computer/information
sciences—general, human
resources management,
information systems,
management information
systems.

Minnesota State University— Moorhead

Owens Hall
Moorhead, MN 56563
Phone: (218) 477-2161
Fax: (218) 477-4374
E-mail: dragon@mnstate.edu
http://www.mnstate.edu
Computer/information
sciences—general, management
information systems.

National American University

1550 West Highway 36
Roseville, MN 55113
Phone: (651) 855-6300
Fax: (651) 644-0690
E-mail: At Web site
http://www.national.edu
Computer/information
sciences—general, management
information systems.

Saint Cloud State University

720 South Fourth Avenue
Saint Cloud, MN 56301
Phone: (320) 308-2244
Fax: (320) 308-2243
E-mail: scsu4u@stcloudstate.edu
http://www.stcoudstate.edu
Computer engineering, computer/
information sciences—general,
human resources management,
library science, statistics.

Saint Mary's University of Minnesota

700 Terrace Heights #2
Winona, MN 55987

Phone: (507) 457-1600
Fax: (507) 457-1722
E-mail: admissions@smumn.edu
http://www.smumn.edu
Human resources management, information systems.

Southwest Minnesota State University

Admissions Office
1501 State Street
Marshall, MN 56258
Phone: (800) 642-0684
Fax: (507) 537-7154
E-mail: shearerr@southwest.msus. edu
http://www.southwest.msus.edu
Computer/information sciences— general.

University of Minnesota— Crookston

170 Owen Hall
2900 University Avenue
Crookston, MN 56716
Phone: (218) 281-8569
Fax: (218) 281-8575
E-mail: info@umcrookston.edu
http://www.umcrookston.edu
Information resources management, information systems, management information systems, systems administration.

University of Minnesota— Duluth

23 Solon Campus Center
1117 University Drive
Duluth, MN 55812
Phone: (218) 726-7171
Fax: (218) 726-7040
E-mail: undadmis@d.umn.edu
http://www.d.umn.edu
Computer engineering, statistics.

University of Minnesota— Morris

600 East Fourth Street
Morris, MN 56267
Phone: (320) 589-6035
Fax: (320) 589-1673
E-mail: admissions@morris.umn. edu

http://www.morris.umn.edu
Statistics.

University of Minnesota—Twin Cities

240 Williamson Hall
231 Pillsbury Drive SE
Minneapolis, MN 55455
Phone: (612) 625-2008
Fax: (612) 626-1693
E-mail: admissions@tc.umn.edu
http://www1.umn.edu/twincities
Computer engineering, human resources management, management information systems, statistics.

University of Saint Thomas

2115 Summit Avenue, Mail #32-F1
St. Paul, MN 55105
Phone: (651) 962-6150
Fax: (651) 962-6160
E-mail: admissions@stthomas.edu
http://www.stthomas.edu
Computer/information sciences— general.

Winona State University

Office of Admissions
P.O. Box 5838
Winona. MN 55987
Phone: (507) 457-5100
Fax: (507) 457-5620
E-mail: admissions@winona.edu
http://www.winona.edu
Applied mathematics, computer/ information sciences—general, computer systems analysis, data processing technology, human resources management, information systems, information technology, management information systems, statistics.

MISSISSIPPI

Alcorn State University

1000 ASU Drive #300
Alcorn State, MS 39096
Phone: (601) 877-6147
Fax: (601) 977-6347

E-mail: ebarnes@alcorn.edu
http://www.alcorn.edu
Computer/information sciences— general.

Belhaven College

15600 Peachtree Street, Box 153
Jackson, MS 39202
Phone: (601) 968-5940
Fax: (601) 968-8946
E-mail: admission@belhaven.edu
http://www.belhaven.edu
Information systems.

Delta State University

Highway 8 West
Cleveland, MS 38733
Phone: (662) 846-4018
Fax: (662) 846-4683
E-mail: dheslep@deltastate.edu
http://www.deltastate.edu
Management information systems.

Jackson State University

1400 Lynch Street
P.O. Box 17330
Jackson, MS 39217
Phone: (601) 979-2100
Fax: (601) 979-3445
E-mail: schatman@ccaix.jsums.edu
http://www.jsums.edu
Computer engineering, computer/ information sciences—general.

Mississippi College

P.O. Box 4026
Clinton, MS 39058
Phone: (601) 925-3800
Fax: (601) 925-3950
E-mail: enrollment-services@ mc.edu
http://www.mc.edu
Computer/information sciences— general.

Mississippi State University

P.O. Box 6305
Mississippi State, MS 39762
Phone: (662) 325-2224
Fax: (662) 325-7360
E-mail: admit@admissions.msstate. edu

http://www.msstate.edu
Computer engineering, computer/
  information sciences—general,
  management information
  systems, software engineering.

University of Mississippi

145 Martindale
University, MS 38677
Phone: (662) 915-7226
Fax: (662) 915-5869
E-mail: admissions@olemiss.edu
http://www.olemiss.edu
Computer/information
  sciences—general, management
  information systems.

University of Southern Mississippi

P.O. Box 5166
Southern Station
Hattiesburg, MS 38406
Phone: (601) 266-5000
Fax: (601) 266-5148
E-mail: admissions@usm.edu
http://www.usm.edu
Computer/information sciences—
  general, data processing
  technology, human resources
  management, library science,
  management information
  systems.

MISSOURI

Avila University

11901 Wornall Road
Kansas City, MO 64145
Phone: (816) 942-8400
Fax: (816) 942-3362
E-mail: admissions@mail.avila.edu
http://www.avila.edu
Computer/information sciences—
  general.

Central Methodist College

411 CMC Square
Fayette, MO 65248
Phone: (660) 248-6251
Fax: (660) 248-1872
E-mail: admissions@cmc.edu
http://www.cmc.edu
Management information systems.

Central Missouri State University

Office of Admissions
WDE 1401
Warrensburg, MO 64093
Phone: (660) 543-4290
Fax: (660) 543-8517
E-mail: admit@cmsuvmb.cmsu.
  edu
http://www.cmsu.edu
Computer/information sciences—
  general, data processing
  technology, human resources
  management, management
  information systems.

College of the Ozarks

Office of Admissions
P.O. Box 17
Point Lookout, MO 65726
Phone: (417) 334-6411
Fax: (417) 335-2618
E-mail: admiss4@cofo.edu
http://www.cofo.edu
Computer/information sciences—
  general.

Columbia College

1001 Rogers Street
Columbia, MO 65216
Phone: (573) 875-7352
Fax: (573) 875-7506
E-mail: admissions@ccis.edu
http://www.ccis.edu
Computer/information sciences—
  general.

Culver-Stockton College

One College Hill
Canton, MO 63435
Phone: (573) 288-6331
Fax: (573) 288-6618
E-mail: enrollment@culver.edu
http://www.culver.edu
Management information systems.

DeVry University—Kansas City

11224 Homes Street
Kansas City, MO 64131
Phone: (816) 941-2810
Fax: (816) 941-0896
E-mail: ssmeed@kc.devry.edu

http://www.devry.edu
Computer engineering technology,
  computer/information
  sciences—general.

Drury University

900 North Benton Avenue
Springfield, MO 65802
Phone: (417) 873-7205
Fax: (417) 866-3873
E-mail: druryead@drury.edu
http://www.drury.edu
Computer/information sciences—
  general, information systems,
  management information
  systems.

Evangel University

111 North Glenstone Avenue
Springfield, MO 65802
Phone: (417) 865-2811
Fax: (417) 520-0545
E-mail: admissions@evangel.edu
http://www.evangel.edu
Computer/information sciences—
  general.

Fontbonne University

6800 Wydown Boulevard
St. Louis, MO 63105
Phone: (314) 889-1478
Fax: (314) 889-1451
E-mail: fcadmis@fontbonne.edu
http://www.fontbonne.edu
Computer/information sciences—
  general.

Grantham University

7200 Northwest 86th Street
Kansas City, MO 64153
Phone: (800) 955-2527
Fax: (816) 595-5757
E-mail: admissions@grantham.edu
http://www.grantham.edu
Computer engineering, computer
  engineering technology,
  computer/information
  sciences—general, computer
  systems analysis, data processing
  technology, information
  systems, management
  information systems, software
  engineering.

Hannibal-LaGrange College

2800 Palmyra Road
Hannibal, MO 63401
Phone: (573) 221-3113
Fax: (573) 221-6594
E-mail: admission@hlg.edu
http://www.hlg.edu
Computer/information sciences—
general.

Harris-Stowe State University

3026 Laclede Avenue
St. Louis, MO 63103
Phone: (314) 340-3366
Fax: (314) 340-3322
E-mail: At Web site
http://www.hssu.edu
Computer/information sciences—
general, information systems.

Lincoln University

Admissions Office, P.O. Box 29
Jefferson City, MO 65102
Phone: (573) 681-5599
Fax: (573) 681-5889
E-mail: enroll@lincolnu.edu
http://www.lincolnu.edu
Information systems.

Lindenwood University

309 South Kingshighway
St. Charles, MO 63301
Phone: (314) 949-4949
Fax: (314) 949-4989
E-mail: admissions@lindenwood.
edu
http://www.lindenwood.edu
Computer/information sciences—
general, human resources
management, information
technology, management
information systems.

Maryville University of Saint Louis

13550 Conway Road
St. Louis, MO 63141
Phone: (314) 529-9350
Fax: (314) 529-9927
E-mail: admissions@maryville.edu
http://www.maryville.edu
Applied mathematics, management
information systems.

Missouri Baptist University

One College Park Drive
St. Louis, MO 63141
Phone: (314) 434-1115
Fax: (314) 434-7496
E-mail: admissions@mobap.edu
http://www.mobap.edu
Computer/information sciences—
general.

Missouri Southern State University

3950 East Newman Road
Joplin, MO 64801
Phone: (417) 625-9378
Fax: (417) 659-4429
E-mail: admissions@mssu.edu
http://www.mssu.edu
Computer/information sciences—
general, information systems.

Missouri State University

901 South National Avenue
Springfield, MO 65897
Phone: (800) 492-7900
Fax: (417) 836-6334
E-mail: info@missouristate.edu
http://www.missouristate.edu
Computational mathematics,
computer/information
sciences—general.

Missouri Technical School

1167 Corporate Lake Drive
St. Louis, MO 63132
Phone: (800) 960-TECH
Fax: NA
E-mail: At Web site
http://www.motech.edu
Computer engineering, computer
systems analysis, software
engineering.

Missouri Valley College

500 East College Street
Marshall, MO 65340
Phone: (660) 831-4114
Fax: (660) 831-4233
E-mail: admissions@moval.edu
http://www.moval.edu
Computer/information sciences—
general.

Missouri Western State University

4525 Downs Drive
Saint Joseph, MO 64507
Phone: (816) 271-4266
Fax: (816) 271-5833
E-mail: admissn@mwsc.edu
http://www.mwsc.edu
Computer engineering technology,
computer/information
sciences—general, information
systems.

National American University

3620 Arrowhead Avenue
Independence, MO 64057
Phone: (816) 353-4554
Fax: (816) 412-7705
E-mail: At Web site
http://www.national.edu
Management information systems.

Northwest Missouri State University

800 University Drive
Maryville, MO 64468
Phone: (800) 633-1175
Fax: (660) 562-1121
E-mail: admissions@nwmissouri.
edu
http://www.nwmissouri.edu
Computer/information sciences—
general, human resources
management, information
systems.

Park University

8700 River Park Drive, Campus
Box 1
Parkville, MO 64152
Phone: (816) 741-2000
Fax: (816) 741-4462
E-mail: admissions@mail.park.edu
http://www.park.edu
Computer/information
sciences—general, management
information systems, statistics.

Rockhurst University

1100 Rockhurst Road
Kansas City, MO 64110
Phone: (816) 501-4100
Fax: (816) 501-4241

E-mail: admission@rockhurst.edu
http://www.rockhurst.edu
Computer/information sciences—
general, computer systems
analysis, information systems.

St. Louis University

221 North Grand Boulevard
St. Louis, MO 63103
Phone: (314) 977-2500
Fax: (314) 977-7136
E-mail: admitme@slu.edu
http://www.slu.edu
Applied mathematics, computer/
information sciences—general,
human resources management,
information technology,
management information
systems.

Southwest Baptist University

160 University Avenue
Bolivar, MO 65613
Phone: (417) 328-1810
Fax: (417) 328-1808
E-mail: admitme@sbuniv.edu
http://www.sbuniv.edu
Computer/information sciences—
general.

Truman State University

McClain Hall 205
100 East Normal Street
Kirksville, MO 63501
Phone: (660) 785-4114
Fax: (660) 785-7456
E-mail: admissions@truman.edu
http://www.truman.edu
Applied mathematics, computer/
information sciences—general.

University of Missouri—Columbia

230 Jesse Hall
Columbia, MO 65211
Phone: (573) 882-7786
Fax: (573) 882-7887
E-mail: admissions@missouri.edu
http://www.missouri.edu
Computer engineering, computer/
information sciences—general,
statistics.

University of Missouri—Kansas City

5100 Rockhill Road, 101 AC
Kansas City, MO 64114
Phone: (816) 235-1111
Fax: (816) 235-5544
E-mail: admit@umkc.edu
http://www.umkc.edu
Computer/information sciences—
general, information systems,
statistics.

University of Missouri—Rolla

106 Parker Hall
Rolla, MO 65409
Phone: (573) 341-4165
Fax: (573) 341-4082
E-mail: admissions@umr.edu
http://www.umr.edu
Applied mathematics, computer
engineering, computer/
information sciences—general,
information systems,
information technology,
management information
systems.

University of Missouri—Saint Louis

351 Millennium Student Center
9001 Natural Bridge Road
St. Louis, MO 63121
Phone: (314) 516-8675
Fax: (314) 516-5310
E-mail: admissions@umsl.edu
http://www.umsl.edu
Applied mathematics, computer/
information sciences—general,
management information
systems.

Washington University in St. Louis

Campus Box 1089
One Brookings Drive
St. Louis, MO 63130
Phone: (314) 935-6000
Fax: (314) 935-4290
E-mail: admissions@wustl.edu
http://www.wustl.edu
Applied mathematics, computer
engineering, computer/
information sciences—general,

data processing technology,
human resources management,
statistics.

Westminster College

501 Westminster Avenue
Fulton, MO 65251
Phone: (573) 592-5251
Fax: (573) 592-5255
E-mail: admissions@westminster-
mo.edu
http://www.westminster-mo/edu
Computer/information
sciences—general, management
information systems.

William Jewell College

500 College Hill
Liberty, MO 64068
Phone: (816) 781-7700
Fax: (816) 415-5040
E-mail: admission@william.jewell.
edu
http://www.jewell.edu
Computer/information sciences—
general, information systems.

William Woods University

One University Avenue
Fulton, MO 65251
Phone: (573) 592-4221
Fax: (573) 592-1146
E-mail: admissions@williamwoods.
edu
http://www.williamwoods.edu
Computer/information
sciences—general, management
information systems.

MONTANA

Carroll College

1601 North Benton Avenue
Helena, MT 59625
Phone: (406) 447-4384
Fax: (406) 447-4533
E-mail: enroll@carroll.edu
http://www.carroll.edu
Software engineering.

Montana State University—Bozeman

New Student Services

P.O. Box 172190
Bozeman, MT 59717
Phone: (406) 994-2452
Fax: (406) 994-1923
E-mail: admissions@montana.edu
http://www.montana.edu
Computer engineering.

Montana Tech of the University of Montana
1300 West Park Street
Butte, MT 59701
Phone: (406) 496-4178
Fax: (406) 496-4710
E-mail: admissions@mtech.edu
http://www.mtech.edu
Applied mathematics, computer engineering, computer/information sciences—general, computer systems analysis, information systems, software engineering, statistics.

Rocky Mountain College
1511 Poly Drive
Billings, MT 59102
Phone: (406) 657-1026
Fax: (406) 657-1189
E-mail: admissions@rocky.edu
http://www.rocky.edu
Information technology.

Salish-Kootenai College
Attn: Jackie Moran
P.O. Box 117
Pablo, MT 59855
Phone: (406) 275-4866
Fax: (406) 275-4810
E-mail: jacie_moran@skc.edu
http://www.skc.edu
Computer/information sciences—general.

University of Great Falls
1301 20th Street South
Great Falls, MT 59405
Phone: (406) 791-5200
Fax: (406) 791-5209
E-mail: enroll@ugf.edu
http://www.ugf.edu
Computer systems analysis, data processing technology, systems administration.

University of Montana—Missoula
103 Lodge Building
Missoula, MT 59812
Phone: (406) 243-62667
Fax: (406) 243-5711
E-mail: admiss@selway.umt.edu
http://www.umt.edu
Management information systems.

University of Montana—Western
710 South Atlantic
Dillon, MT 59725
Phone: (406) 683-7331
Fax: (406) 683-7493
E-mail: admissions@umwestern.edu
http://www.umwestern.edu
Applied mathematics.

NEBRASKA

Bellevue University
1000 Galvin Road South
Bellevue, NE 68005
Phone: (402) 293-2000
Fax: (402) 293-3730
E-mail: info@bellevue.edu
http://www.bellevue.edu
Computer/information sciences—general, human resources management, information systems, information technology, management information systems.

Chadron State College
1000 Main Street
Chadron, NE 69337
Phone: (308) 432-6263
Fax: (308) 432-6229
E-mail: inquire@csc.edu
http://www.csc.edu
Information systems, library science, management information systems.

College of Saint Mary
7000 Mercy Road
Omaha, NE 68106
Phone: (402) 399-2405
Fax: (402) 399-2412

E-mail: enroll@csm.edu
http://www.csm.edu
Computer/information sciences—general.

Concordia University
800 North Columbia Avenue
Seward, NE 68434
Phone: (800) 535-5494
Fax: (402) 643-4073
E-mail: admiss@cune.edu
http://www.cune.edu
Management information systems.

Creighton University
2500 California Plaza
Omaha, NE 68178
Phone: (402) 280-2703
Fax: (402) 280-2685
E-mail: admissions@creighton.edu
http://www.creighton.edu
Applied mathematics, management information systems.

Doane College
1014 Boswell Avenue
Crete, NE 68333
Phone: (402) 826-8222
Fax: (402) 826-8600
E-mail: admissions@doane.edu
http://www.doane.edu
Computer/information sciences—general, information systems.

Hastings College
710 North Turner Avenue
Hastings, NE 68901
Phone: (402) 461-7403
Fax: (402) 461-7490
E-mail: mmolliconi@hastings.edu
http://www.hastings.edu
Computer/information sciences—general, human resources management.

Midland Lutheran College
900 North Clarkson Street
Fremont, NE 68025
Phone: (402) 721-5487
Fax: (402) 721-0250
E-mail: admissions@admin.mlc.edu

http://www.mlc.edu
Computer/information
sciences—general, management
information systems.

Nebraska Wesleyan University
Admissions Office
5000 Saint Paul Avenue
Lincoln, NE 68504
Phone: (402) 465-2218
Fax: (402) 465-2177
E-mail: admissions@nebrwesleyan.
edu
http://www.nebrwesleyan.edu
Information systems.

Peru State College
P.O. Box 10
Peru, NE 68421
Phone: (402) 872-2221
Fax: (402) 872-2296
E-mail: admissions@oakmail.peru.
edu
http://www.peru.edu
Computer/information sciences—
general.

Union College
3800 South Forty-eighth Street
Lincoln, NE 68506
Phone: (402) 486-2504
Fax: (402) 486-2566
E-mail: ucenroll@ucollege.edu
http://www.ucollege.edu
Computer systems analysis,
information systems.

University of Nebraska—
   Kearney
905 West Twenty-fifth Street
Kearney, NE 68849
Phone: (800) 532-7639
Fax: (308) 865-7639
E-mail: admissionsug@unk.edu
http://www.unk.edu
Computer/information sciences—
general, statistics.

University of Nebraska—
   Lincoln
1410 Q Street
Lincoln, NE 68588
Phone: (402) 472-2023

Fax: (402) 472-0670
E-mail: nuhusker@unl.edu
http://www.unl.edu
Computer engineering, computer/
information sciences—general.

University of Nebraska—Omaha
Office of Admissions
6001 Dodge Street, EAB Room 103
Omaha, NE 68182
Phone: (402) 554-2393
Fax: (402) 554-3472
E-mail: unoadm@unomaha.edu
http://www.unomaha.edu
Computer engineering, library
science, management
information systems.

Wayne State College
1111 Main Street
Wayne, NE 68787
Phone: (402) 375-7234
Fax: (402) 375-7204
E-mail: admit1@wsc.edu
http://www.wsc.edu
Computer/information sciences—
general, information systems.

York College
1125 East Eighth Street
York, NE 68467
Phone: (800) 950-9675
Fax: (402) 363-5623
E-mail: enroll@york.edu
http://www.york.edu
Human resources management.

NEVADA

Sierra Nevada College
999 Tahoe Boulevard
Incline Village, NV 89451
Phone: (775) 831-1314
Fax: (775) 831-1347
E-mail: admissions@sierranevada.
edu
http://www.sierranevada.edu
Computer/information sciences—
general.

University of Nevada—Las Vegas
4505 Maryland Parkway
P.O. Box 451021
Las Vegas, NV 89154

Phone: (702) 774-8658
Fax: (702) 774-8008
E-mail: undergraduate.recruitment
@ccmail.nevada.edu
http://www.unlv.edu
Applied mathematics, computer
engineering, human resources
management, management
information systems, software
engineering.

University of Nevada—Reno
1664 North Virginia Street
Reno, NV 89557
Phone: (775) 784-4700
Fax: (775) 784-4283
E-mail: asknevada@unr.edu
http://www.unr.edu
Computer/information sciences—
general, information technology,
management information
systems.

NEW HAMPSHIRE

Daniel Webster College
20 University Drive
Nashua, NH 03063
Phone: (603) 577-6600
Fax: (603) 577-6001
E-mail: admissions@dwc.edu
http://www.dwc.edu
Computer/information sciences—
general, information systems,
management information
systems.

Franklin Pierce College
Admissions Office
P.O. Box 60
20 College Road
Rindge, NH 03461
Phone: (603) 899-4050
Fax: (603) 889-4394
E-mail: admissions@fpc.edu
http://www.fpc.edu
Computer/information sciences—
general, information systems,
management information
systems.

Granite State College
8 Old Suncook Road
Concord, NH 03301

Phone: (888) 228-3000
Fax: (603) 513-1389
E-mail: ask.granite@granite.edu
http://www.granite.edu
Computer/information sciences—
general.

Keene State College
229 Main Street
Keene, NH 03435
Phone: (603) 358-2276
Fax: (603) 358-2767
E-mail: admissions@keene.edu
http://www.keene.edu
Applied mathematics, computer/
information sciences—general.

New England College
26 Bridge Street
Henniker, NH 03242
Phone: (603) 428-2223
Fax: (603) 428-3155
E-mail: admission@nec.edu
http://www.nec.edu
Computer/information sciences—
general, human resources
management, management
information systems.

Rivier College
420 South Main Street
Nashua, NH 02060
Phone: (603) 897-8219
Fax: (603) 891-1799
E-mail: rivadmit@rivier.edu
http://www.rivier.edu
Management information systems.

Southern New Hampshire University
2500 North River Road
Manchester, NH 03108
Phone: (603) 645-9611
Fax: (603) 645-9693
E-mail: admission@snhu.edu
http://www.snhu.edu
Management information systems.

University of New Hampshire—Durham
4 Garrison Avenue
Durham, NH 03024
Phone: (603) 862-1360

Fax: (603) 862-0077
E-mail: admissions@unh.edu
http://www.unh.edu
Applied mathematics, computer
engineering, computer/
information sciences—general.

University of New Hampshire—Manchester
400 Commercial Street
Manchester, NH 03101
Phone: (603) 629-4150
Fax: (603) 629-2745
E-mail: unhm.admissions@unh.edu
http://www.unh.edu/unhm
Applied mathematics, computer
engineering, computer/
information sciences—general.

NEW JERSEY

Bloomfield College
1 Park Place
Bloomfield, NJ 07003
Phone: (973) 748-9000
Fax: (973) 748-0916
E-mail: admission@bloomfield.edu
http://www.bloomfield.edu
Applied mathematics, computer/
information sciences—general,
human resources management.

Centenary College
400 Jefferson Street
Hackettstown, NJ 07840
Phone: (800) 236-8679
Fax: (908) 852-3454
E-mail: admissions@
centenarycollege.edu
http://www.centenarycollege.edu
Computer/information sciences—
general.

The College of New Jersey
P.O. Box 7718
Ewing, NJ 08628
Phone: (609) 771-2131
Fax: (609) 637-5174
E-mail: admiss@vm.tcnj.edu
http://www.tcnj.edu
Computer engineering, computer/
information sciences—general,
statistics.

College of Saint Elizabeth
Admissions Office
2 Convent Road
Morristown, NJ 07960
Phone: (973) 290-4700
Fax: (973) 290-4710
E-mail: apply@cse.edu
http://www.cse.edu
Computer/information sciences—
general.

DeVry University—North Brunswick
630 U.S. Highway One
North Brunswick, NJ 08902
Phone: (732) 729-3532
Fax: (732) 435-4850
E-mail: admissions@devry.edu
http://www.devry.edu
Computer systems analysis.

Fairleigh Dickinson University—College at Florham
285 Madison Avenue
Madison, NJ 07940
Phone: (800) 0339-8803
Fax: (973) 443-8088
E-mail: globaleducation@fdu.edu
http://www.fdu.edu
Computer/information sciences—
general, information technology.

Fairleigh Dickinson University—Metropolitan Campus
1000 River Road
Teaneck, NJ 07666
Phone: (201) 692-2553
Fax: (201) 692-7319
E-mail: globaleducation@fdu.edu
http://www.fdu.edu
Computer/information sciences—
general.

Felician College
262 South Main Street
Lodi, NJ 7644
Phone: (201) 559-6131
Fax: (201) 559-6138
E-mail: admissions@inet.felician.
edu
http://www.felician.edu
Computer/information sciences—
general.

Georgian Court University

900 Lakewood Avenue
Lakewood, NJ 08701
Phone: (732) 364-2200
Fax: (732) 987-2200
E-mail: admissions@georgian.edu
http://www.georgian.edu
Computer/information sciences—
general.

Kean University

P.O. Box 411
Union, NJ 07083
Phone: (908) 737-7100
Fax: (908) 737-7105
E-mail: admitme@kean.edu
http://www.kean.edu
Computer/information sciences—
general.

Monmouth University

Admissions
400 Cedar Avenue West
Long Branch, NJ 07764
Phone: (732) 571-3456
Fax: (732) 263-5166
E-mail: admission@monmouth.
edu
http://www.monmouth.edu
Computer/information sciences—
general, software engineering.

Montclair State University

1 Normal Avenue
Montclair, NJ 07043
Phone: (973) 655-4444
Fax: (973) 655-7700
E-mail: undergraduate.
admissions@montclair.edu
http://www.montclair.edu
Computer/information sciences—
general.

New Jersey City University

2039 Kennedy Boulevard
Jersey City, NJ 07305
Phone: (888) 441-6528
Fax: (201) 200-2044
E-mail: admissions@njcu.edu
http://www.njcu.edu
Computer/information sciences—
general.

New Jersey Institute of Technology

University Heights
Newark, NJ 07102
Phone: (973) 596-3300
Fax: (973) 596-3461
E-mail: admissions@njit.edu
http://www.njit.edu
Applied mathematics, computer
engineering, computer/
information sciences—general,
information systems,
information technology.

Princeton University

P.O. Box 430, Admissions Office
Princeton, NJ 08544
Phone: (609) 258-3060
Fax: (609) 258-6743
E-mail: uaoffice@princeton.edu
http://www.princeton.edu
Computer engineering.

Ramapo College of New Jersey

505 Ramapo Valley Road
Mahwah, NJ 07430
Phone: (201) 684-7300
Fax: (201) 684-7964
E-mail: admissions@ramapo.edu
http://www.ramapo.edu
Computer/information sciences—
general, information systems.

Richard Stockton College of New Jersey

Jim Leeds Road, P.O. Box 195
Pomona, NJ 08240
Phone: (609) 652-4261
Fax: (609) 748-5541
E-mail: admissions@stockton.edu
http://www.stockton.edu
Information systems.

Rider University

2083 Lawrenceville Road
Lawrenceville, NJ 08648
Phone: (609) 896-5042
Fax: (609) 895-6645
E-mail: admissions@rider.edu
http://www.rider.edu
Computer/information sciences—
general, human resources
management.

Rowan University

201 Mullica Hill Road
Glassboro, NJ 08028
Phone: (856) 256-4200
Fax: (856) 256-4430
E-mail: admissions@rowan.edu
http://www.rowan.edu
Computer/information sciences—
general, data processing
technology, human resources
management, management
information systems.

Rutgers, The State University of New Jersey—Newark

249 University Avenue
Newark, NJ 07102
Phone: (973) 353-5205
Fax: (973) 353-1440
E-mail: newarkadmission@ugadm.
rutgers.edu
http://www.rutgers.edu
Applied mathematics, information
systems.

Rutgers, The State University of New Jersey—New Brunswick/Piscataway

65 Davidson Road
Piscataway, NJ 08854
Phone: (732) 932-4636
Fax: (732) 445-0237
E-mail: admissions@ugadm.
rutgers.edu
http://www.rutgers.edu
Management information systems,
statistics.

Saint Peter's College

2641 Kennedy Boulevard
Jersey City, NJ 07306
Phone: (201) 915-9213
Fax: (201) 432-5860
E-mail: admissions@spc.edu
http://www.spc.edu
Computer/information sciences—
general, information systems,
management information
systems.

Seton Hall University

Enrollment Services
400 South Orange Avenue

South Orange, NJ 07079
Phone: (973) 761-9332
Fax: (973) 275-2040
E-mail: thehall@shu.edu
http://www.shu.edu
Computer/information sciences—general, management information systems.

Stevens Institute of Technology
Castle Point on Hudson
Hoboken, NJ 07030
Phone: (201) 216-5194
Fax: (201) 216-8348
E-mail: admissions@stevens.edu
http://www.stevens.edu
Applied mathematics, computer engineering, computer/information sciences—general, management information systems.

Thomas Edison State College
101 West State Street
Trenton, NJ 08608
Phone: (609) 984-1150
Fax: (609) 984-8447
E-mail: info@tesc.edu
http://www.tesc.edu
Human resources management.

William Paterson University of New Jersey
Admissions Hall
300 Pompton Road
Wayne, NJ 07470
Phone: (973) 720-2125
Fax: (973) 720-2910
E-mail: admissions@wpunj.edu
http://www.wpunj.edu
Computer/information sciences—general.

NEW MEXICO

College of Santa Fe
1600 St. Michaels Drive
Santa Fe, NM 87505
Phone: (505) 473-6133
Fax: (505) 473-6127
E-mail: admissions@csf.edu
http://www.csf.edu
Information technology, management information systems.

College of the Southwest
6610 Lovington Highway
Hobbs, NM 88240
Phone: (505) 392-6563
Fax: (505) 392-6006
E-mail: admissions@csw.edu
http://www.csw.edu
Management information systems.

Eastern New Mexico University
Station #7, ENMU
Portales, NM 88130
Phone: (505) 562-2178
Fax: (505) 562-2118
E-mail: admissions@enmu.edu
http://www.enmu.edu
Computer/information sciences—general, human resources management, management information systems.

National American University
4775 Indian School Road NE, Suite 200
Albuquerque, NM 87110
Phone: (505) 348-3700
Fax: (505) 348-3705
E-mail: At Web site
http://www.national.edu
Management information systems.

New Mexico Highlands University
NMHU Office of Student Recruitment
P.O. Box 900
Las Vegas, NM 87701
Phone: (505) 454-3593
Fax: (505) 454-3511
E-mail: recruitment@nmhu.edu
http://www.nmhu.edu
Computer/information sciences—general, information systems, management information systems.

New Mexico Institute of Mining and Technology
Campus Station
801 Leroy Place
Socorro, NM 87801

Phone: (505) 835-5424
Fax: (505) 835-5989
E-mail: admission@admin.nmt.edu
http://www.nmt.edu
Applied mathematics, computer/information sciences—general, information technology.

New Mexico State University
P.O. Box 30001, MSC 3A
Las Cruces, NM 88003
Phone: (505) 646-3121
Fax: (505) 646-6330
E-mail: admissions@nmsu.edu
http://www.nmsu.edu
Computer/information sciences—general, information technology.

University of New Mexico
Office of Admissions
Student Services Center 150
Albuquerque, NM 87131
Phone: (505) 277-2446
Fax: (505) 277-6686
E-mail: apply@unm.edu
http://www.unm.edu
Computer engineering, computer/information sciences—general, statistics.

Western New Mexico University
P.O. Box 680
Silver City, NM 88061
Phone: (800) 872-9688
Fax: (575) 538-6127
E-mail: terrazast@wnmu.edu
http://www.wnmu.edu
Computer/information sciences—general.

NEW YORK

Adelphi University
Levermore Hall 114
1 South Avenue
Garden City, NY 11530
Phone: (516) 877-3050
Fax: (516) 877-3039
E-mail: admissions@adelphi.edu
http://www.adelphi.edu
Computer/information sciences—general, information systems.

Barnard College
3090 Broadway
New York, NY 10027
Phone: (212) 854-2014
Fax: (212) 854-6220
E-mail: admissions@barnard.edu
http://www.barnard.edu
Applied mathematics, computer/
information sciences—general,
statistics.

Canisius College
2001 Main Street
Buffalo, NY 14208
Phone: (716) 888-2200
Fax: (716) 888-3230
E-mail: inquiry@canisius.edu
http://www.canisius.edu
Management information systems.

**City University of New York—
Baruch College**
Undergraduate Admissions
1 Bernard Baruch Way
P.O. Box H-0720
New York, NY 10010
Phone: (646) 312-1400
Fax: (646) 312-1361
E-mail: admissions@baruch.cuny.
edu
http://www.baruch.cuny.edu
Computer/information sciences—
general, human resources
management, information
systems, management
information systems, statistics.

**City University of New York—
Brooklyn College**
3000 Bedford Avenue
Brooklyn, NY 11210
Phone: (718) 951-5001
Fax: (718) 951-4506
E-mail: adminqry@brooklyn.cuny.
edu
http://www.brooklyn.cuny.edu
Computational mathematics,
computer/information
sciences—general.

**City University of New York—
City College**
Convent Avenue at 138th Street

New York, NY 10031
Phone: (212) 650-6977
Fax: (212) 650-6417
E-mail: admissions@ccny.cuny.edu
http://www.ccny.cuny.edu
Computer engineering.

**City University of New York—
College of Staten Island**
2800 Victory Boulevard, Bldg. 2A,
Room 104
Staten Island, NY 10314
Phone: (718) 982-2010
Fax: (718) 982-2500
E-mail: recruitment@postbox.csi.
cuny.edu
http://www.csi.cuny.edu
Computer/information sciences—
general, information systems.

**City University of New York—
Hunter College**
695 Park Avenue
New York, NY 10021
Phone: (212) 772-4490
Fax: (212) 650-3336
E-mail: admissions@hunter.cuny.
edu
http://www.hunter.cuny.edu
Computer/information sciences—
general, statistics.

**City University of New York—
Lehman College**
350 Bedford Park Boulevard West
Bronx, NY 10468
Phone: (718) 960-8000
Fax: (718) 960-8712
E-mail: wilkes@alpha.lehman.cuny.
edu
http://www.lehman.cuny.edu
Computer/information sciences—
general, information systems.

**City University of New York—
Medgar Evers College**
1650 Bedford Avenue
Brooklyn, NY 11225
Phone: (718) 270-6023
Fax: (718) 270-6188
E-mail: enroll@mec.cuny.edu
http://www.mec.cuny.edu
Information systems.

**City University of New York—
New York City College of
Technology**
300 Jay Street, NG17
Brooklyn, NY 11201
Phone: (718) 260-5500
Fax: (718) 260-5504
E-mail: admissions@citytech.cuny.
edu
http://www.citytech.cuny.edu
Applied mathematics, computer/
information sciences—general.

**City University of New York—
York College**
94-20 Guy R. Brewer Boulevard
Jamaica, NY 11451
Phone: (718) 262-2165
Fax: (718) 262-2601
E-mail: admissions@york.cuny.edu
http://www.york.cuny.edu
Management information systems.

Clarkson University
P.O. Box 5605
Potsdam, NY 13699
Phone: (315) 268-6479
Fax: (315) 268-7647
E-mail: admission@clarkson.edu
http://www.clarkson.edu
Applied mathematics, computer
engineering, computer/
information sciences—general,
information resources
management, management
information systems, software
engineering, statistics.

Colgate University
13 Oak Drive
Hamilton, NY 13346
Phone: (315) 228-7401
Fax: (315) 228-7544
E-mail: admission@mail.colgate.
edu
http://www.colgate.edu
Computer/information sciences—
general.

College of Mount St. Vincent
6301 Riverdale Avenue
Riverdale, NY 10471
Phone: (718) 405-3267

Fax: (718) 549-7945
E-mail: admissns@
mountsaintvincent.edu
http://www.mountsaintvincent.edu
Computer/information sciences—
general.

College of Saint Rose

432 Western Avenue
Albany, NY 12203
Phone: (518) 454-5150
Fax: (518) 454-2013
E-mail: admit@mail.strose.edu
http://www.strose.edu
Computer/information sciences—
general.

Columbia University—Columbia College

212 Hamilton Hall, MC 2807
1130 Amsterdam Avenue
New York, NY 10027
Phone: (212) 854-2521
Fax: (212) 894-1209
E-mail: At Web site
http://www.college.columbia.edu
Applied mathematics, statistics.

Columbia University—School of Engineering and Applied Science

212 Hamilton Hall, MC 2807
1130 Amsterdam Avenue
New York, NY 10027
Phone: (212) 854-2521
Fax: (212) 894-1209
E-mail: ugrad-ask@columbia.edu
http://www.engineeering.columbia.
edu
Applied mathematics, computer
engineering.

Columbia University—School of General Studies

408 Lewisohn Hall, Mail Code 4101
2970 Broadway
New York, NY 10027
Phone: (800) 895-1169
Fax: (212) 854-6316
E-mail: gs-admit@columbia.edu
http://www.gs.columbia.edu
Applied mathematics, computer/
information sciences—general,
statistics.

Cornell University

Undergraduate Admissions
410 Thurston Avenue
Ithaca, NY 14850
Phone: (607) 255-5241
Fax: (607) 255-0659
E-mail: admissions@cornell.edu
http://www.cornell.edu
Applied mathematics, computer/
information sciences—general,
human resources management,
statistics.

DeVry Institute of Technology

3020 Thomson Avenue
Long Island City, NY 11101
Phone: (718) 472-2728
Fax: (718) 361-0004
E-mail: leads@ny.devry.edu
http://www.devry.edu
Computer engineering technology,
information technology.

Dominican College

470 Western Highway
Orangeburg, NY 10962
Phone: (866) 432-4636
Fax: (845) 365-3150
E-mail: admissions@dc.edu
http://www.dc.edu
Computer/information sciences—
general, human resources
management, management
information systems.

Dowling College

Idle Hour Boulevard
Oakdale, NY 11769
Phone: (800) 369-5464
Fax: (631) 563-3827
E-mail: admissions@dowling.edu
http://www.dowling.edu
Computer/information sciences—
general, management informa-
tion systems.

D'Youville College

One D'Youville Square
320 Porter Avenue
Buffalo, NY 14201
Phone: (716) 829-7600
Fax: (716) 829-7790
E-mail: admiss@dyc.edu

http://www.dyc.edu
Information technology.

Elmira College

1 Park Place
Elmira, NY 14901
Phone: (607) 735-1724
Fax: (607) 735-1718
E-mail: admissions@elmira.edu
http://www.elmira.edu
Management information systems.

Excelsior College

7 Columbia Circle
Albany, NY 12203
Phone: (518) 464-8500
Fax: (518) 464-8777
E-mail: admissions@excelsior.edu
http://www.excelsior.edu
Computer/information sciences—
general, human resources
management, information systems, management information
systems.

Fordham University

441 East Fordham Road
Duane Library
New York, NY 10458
Phone: (718) 817-4000
Fax: (718) 367-9404
E-mail: enroll@fordham.edu
http://www.fordham.edu
Computer/information sciences—
general, management information
systems.

Globe Institute of Technology

291 Broadway
New York, NY 10007
Phone: (212) 349-4330
Fax: (212) 227-5820
E-mail: admissions@globe.edu
http://www.globe.edu
Artificial intelligence/robotics, com-
puter/information sciences—
general, computer systems
analysis, information technology,
management information systems, systems administration.

Hamilton College

Office of Admissions

198 College Hill Road
Clinton, NY 13323
Phone: (315) 859-4421
Fax: (315) 859-4457
E-mail: admission@hamilton.edu
http://www.hamilton.edu
Computer/information sciences—
  general.

Hartwick College

P.O. Box 4020
Oneonta, NY 13820
Phone: (607) 431-4154
Fax: (607) 431-4102
E-mail: admissions@hartwick.edu
http://www.hartwick.edu
Computer/information sciences—
  general, information systems.

Hobart and William Smith College

629 South Main Street
Geneva, NY 14456
Phone: (315) 781-3472
Fax: (315) 781-3471
E-mail: admissions@hws.edu
http://www.hws.edu
Computer/information sciences—
  general.

Hofstra University

Admission Center
Bernon Hall
1000 Fulton Avenue
Hempstead, NY 11549
Phone: (516) 463-6700
Fax: (516) 463-5100
E-mail: admitme@hofstra.edu
http://www.hofstra.edu
Applied mathematics, computer
  engineering, management
  information systems.

Houghton College

P.O. Box 128
Houghton, NY 14744
Phone: (800) 777-2556
Fax: NA
E-mail: admission@houghton.
  edu
http://www. houghton.edu
  Information technology.

Iona College

715 North Avenue
New Rochelle, NY 10801
Phone: (914) 633-2502
Fax: (914) 633-2642
E-mail: icad@iona.edu
http://www.iona.edu
Applied mathematics, management
  information systems.

Ithaca College

100 Job Hall
Ithaca, NY 14850
Phone: (607) 274-3124
Fax: (607) 274-1900
E-mail: admission@ithaca.edu
http://www.ithaca.edu
Computer/information sciences—
  general, information technology.

Le Moyne College

1419 Salt Springs Road
Syracuse, NY 13214
Phone: (315) 445-4300
Fax: (315) 445-4711
E-mail: admission@lemoyne.edu
http://www.lemoyne.edu
Human resources management,
  management information
  systems.

Long Island University— Brooklyn Campus

1 University Plaza
Brooklyn, NY 11201
Phone: (800) 548-7526
Fax: (718) 797-2399
E-mail: admissions@brooklyn.liu.
  edu
http://www.liunet.edu
Computer/information sciences—
  general.

Long Island University—C. W. Post Campus

720 Northern Boulevard
Brookville, NY 11548
Phone: (516) 299-2900
Fax: (516) 299-2137
E-mail: enroll@cwpost.liu.edu
http://www.liu.edu
Applied mathematics, information
  systems, information technology.

Manhattan College

Manhattan College Parkway
Riverdale, NY 10471
Phone: (718) 862-7200
Fax: (718) 862-8019
E-mail: admit@manhattan.edu
http://www.manhattan.edu
Computer/information sciences—
  general, information systems,
  management information
  systems.

Marist College

3399 North Road
Poughkeepsie, NY 12601
Phone: (845) 575-3226
Fax: (845) 575-3215
E-mail: admissions@marist.edu
http://www.marist.edu
Computational mathematics,
  computer/information
  sciences—general, information
  systems, information
  technology.

Medaille College

18 Agassiz Circle
Buffalo, NY 14214
Phone: (716) 884-3281
Fax: (716) 884-0291
E-mail: jmatheny@medaille.edu
http://www.medaille.edu
Computer/information sciences—
  general.

Mercy College

555 Broadway
Dobbs Ferry, NY 10522
Phone: (914) 674-7324
Fax: (914) 674-7382
E-mail: admissions@mercy.edu
http://www.mercy.edu
Computer/information sciences—
  general, information systems.

Molloy College

1000 Hempstead Avenue
Rockville Centre, NY 11570
Phone: (516) 678-5000
Fax: (516) 256-2247
E-mail: admissions@molloy.edu
http://www.molloy.edu
Information systems.

Monroe College
2501 Jerome Avenue
Bronx, NY 10468
Phone: (718) 933-6700
Fax: (718) 364-3552
E-mail: ejerome@monroecollege.edu
http://www.monroecollege.edu
Computer/information sciences—
general.

Mount Saint Mary College
330 Powell Avenue
Newburgh, NY 12550
Phone: (845) 569-3248
Fax: (845) 562-6762
E-mail: mtstmary@msmc.edu
http://www.msmc.edu
Computer/information sciences—
general, information technology.

Nazareth College of Rochester
4245 East Avenue
Rochester, NY 14618
Phone: (585) 389-2860
Fax: (585) 389-2826
E-mail: admissions@naz.edu
http://www.naz.edu
Information systems.

**New York Institute of
Technology**
P.O. Box 8000
Northern Boulevard
Old Westbury, NY 11568
Phone: (516) 686-7520
Fax: (516) 686-7613
E-mail: admissions@nyit.edu
http://www.nyit.edu
Computer engineering, computer/
information sciences—general,
human resources management,
management information
systems.

New York University
22 Washington Square North
New York, NY 10011
Phone: (212) 998-4500
Fax: (212) 995-4902
E-mail: admissions@nyu.edu
http://www.nyu.edu
Applied mathematics, computer/
information sciences—general,
statistics.

Niagara University
Bailo Hall, P.O. Box 2011
Niagara University, NY 24109
Phone: (716) 286-8700
Fax: (716) 286-8710
E-mail: admissions@niagara.edu
http://www.niagara.edu
Computer/information sciences—
general, human resources
management, information
systems.

Nyack College
1 South Boulevard
Nyack, NY 10960
Phone: (845) 358-1710
Fax: (845) 358-3047
E-mail: enroll@nyackcollege.edu
http://www.nyackcollege.edu
Computer/information sciences—
general.

Pace University
1 Pace Plaza
New York, NY 10038
Phone: (212) 346-1323
Fax: (212) 346-1040
E-mail: infoctr@pace.edu
http://www.pace.edu
Computer/information sciences—
general, computer systems
analysis, human resources
management, information
systems.

Polytechnic University
6 Metrotech Center
Brooklyn, NY 11201
Phone: (718) 260-3100
Fax: (718) 260-3446
E-mail: admitme@poly.edu
http://www.poly.edu
Computer engineering, computer/
information sciences—general,
management information
systems.

**Rensselaer Polytechnic
Institute**
110 Eighth Street
Troy, NY 12180
Phone: (518) 276-6216
Fax: (518) 276-4072

E-mail: At Web site
http://www.rpi.edu
Computer engineering, computer/
information sciences—general.

Roberts Wesleyan College
2301 Westside Drive
Rochester, NY 14624
Phone: (585) 594-6400
Fax: (585) 594-6371
E-mail: admissions@roberts.edu
http://www.roberts.edu
Computer/information sciences—
general, human resources
management.

**Rochester Institute of
Technology**
60 Lomb Memorial Drive
Rochester, NY 14623
Phone: (585) 475-6631
Fax: (585) 475-7424
E-mail: admissions@rit.edu
http://www.rit.edu
Applied mathematics, computational mathematics, computer
engineering, computer engineering technology, computer/
information sciences—general,
computer systems analysis,
information technology, management information systems,
software engineering, statistics,
systems administration.

Russell Sage College
Office of Admissions
45 Ferry Street
Troy, NY 12180
Phone: (518) 244-2217
Fax: (518) 244-6880
E-mail: rscadm@sage.edu
http://www.sage.edu
Computer/information sciences—
general.

Sage College of Albany
140 New Scotland Avenue
Albany, NY 12208
Phone: (518) 244-2000
Fax: NA
E-mail: At Web site
http://www.sage.edu
Systems administration.

St. Bonaventure University
P.O. Box D
St. Bonaventure, NY 14778
Phone: (716) 375-2400
Fax: (716) 375-4005
E-mail: admissions@sbu.edu
http://www.sbu.edu
Computer/information
   sciences—general, management
   information systems.

Saint Francis College
180 Remsen Street
Brooklyn Heights, NY 11201
Phone: (718) 489-5200
Fax: (718) 802-0453
E-mail: admissions@
   stfranciscollege.edu
http://www.stfranciscollege.edu
Information technology.

Saint John Fisher College
3690 East Avenue
Rochester, NY 14618
Phone: (585) 385-8064
Fax: (585) 385-8386
E-mail: admissions@sjfc.edu
http://www.sjfc.edu
Computer/information sciences—
   general, human resources
   management, management
   information systems.

St. John's University
8000 Utopia Parkway
Jamaica, NY 11439
Phone: (718) 990-2000
Fax: (718) 990-5728
E-mail: admissions@stjohns.edu
http://www.stjohns.edu
Computer/information
   sciences—general, management
   information systems.

St. Joseph's College
245 Clinton Avenue
Brooklyn, NY 11205
Phone: (718) 636-6868
Fax: (718) 636-8303
E-mail: brooklynas@sjcny.edu
http://www.sjcny.edu
Human resources management,
   information technology.

Saint Thomas Aquinas College
125 Route 340
Sparkill, NY 10976
Phone: (845) 398-4100
Fax: (845) 398-4224
E-mail: admissions@stac.edu
http://www.stac.edu
Applied mathematics, computer/
   information sciences—general.

Siena College
515 Loudon Road
Loudonville, NY 12211
Phone: (518) 783-2423
Fax: (518) 783-2436
E-mail: admit@siena.edu
http://www.siena.edu
Applied mathematics, computer/
   information sciences—general.

Skidmore College
815 North Broadway
Saratoga Springs, NY 12866
Phone: (518) 580-5570
Fax: (518) 580-5584
E-mail: admissions@skidmore.
   edu
http://www.skidmore.edu
Computer/information sciences—
   general.

State University of New York at Albany
Office of Undergraduate
   Admissions
1400 Washington Avenue
Albany, NY 12222
Phone: (518) 442-5435
Fax: (518) 442-5383
E-mail: ugadmissions@albany.edu
http://www.albany.edu
Applied mathematics, computer/
   information sciences—general,
   information systems.

State University of New York at Binghamton
P.O. Box 6001
Binghamton, NY 13902
Phone: (607) 777-2171
Fax: (607) 777-4445
E-mail: admit@binghamton.edu

http://www.binghamton.edu
Computer engineering, computer/
   information sciences—general.

State University of New York at Brockport
350 New Campus Drive
Brockport, NY 14420
Phone: (585) 395-2751
Fax: (585) 395-5452
E-mail: admit@brockport.edu
http://www.brockport.edu
Computer/information sciences—
   general.

State University of New York at Farmingdale
2350 Broadhollow Road
Farmingdale, NY 11735
Phone: (631) 420-2000
Fax: (631) 420-2633
E-mail: admissions@farmingdale.
   edu
http://www.farmingdale.edu
Applied mathematics, computer
   engineering technology.

State University of New York at Fredonia
178 Central Avenue
Fredonia, NY 14063
Phone: (716) 673-3251
Fax: (716) 673-3249
E-mail: admissions.office@
   fredonia.edu
http://www.fredonia.edu
Computer/information
   sciences—general, management
   information systems.

State University of New York at Geneseo
1 College Circle
Geneseo, NY 14454
Phone: (716) 245-5571
Fax: (716) 245-5550
E-mail: admissions@geneseo.edu
http://www.geneseo.edu
Computer/information sciences—
   general.

State University of New York at New Paltz
75 South Manheim Boulevard,
   Suite 1

New Paltz, NY 12561
Phone: (845) 257-3200
Fax: (845) 257-3209
E-mail: admissions@newpaltz.edu
http://www.newpaltz.edu
Computer engineering.

State University of New York at Oswego

211 Culkin Hall
Oswego, NY 13126
Phone: (315) 312-2250
Fax: (315) 312-3260
E-mail: admiss@oswego.edu
http://www.oswego.edu
Applied mathematics, cognitive science, human resources management.

State University of New York at Plattsburgh

1001 Kehoe Building
Plattsburgh, NY 12091
Phone: (518) 564-2040
Fax: (518) 564-2045
E-mail: admissions@plattsburgh. edu
http://www.plattsburgh.edu
Computer/information sciences— general.

State University of New York at Potsdam

44 Pierrepont Avenue
Potsdam, NY 13676
Phone: (315) 267-2180
Fax: (315) 267-2163
E-mail: admissions@potsdam.edu
http://www.potsdam.edu
Computer/information sciences— general.

State University of New York College at Old Westbury

P.O. Box 210
Old Westbury, NY 11568
Phone: (516) 876-3000
Fax: (516) 876-3307
E-mail: enroll@oldwestbury.edu
http://www.oldwestbury.edu
Computer/information sciences— general, information systems.

State University of New York College at Oneonta

Alumni Hall 116
State University College
Oneonta, NY 13820
Phone: (607) 436-2524
Fax: (607) 436-3074
E-mail: admissions@oneonta.edu
http://www.oneonta.edu
Statistics.

State University of New York College—Buffalo State College

1300 Elmwood Avenue
Buffalo, NY 14222
Phone: (716) 878-4017
Fax: (716) 878-6100
E-mail: admissions@buffalostate.edu
http://www.buffalostate.edu
Computer engineering, computer/ information sciences—general, information systems.

State University of New York College of Agriculture and Technology at Cobleskill

Office of Admissions
Cobleskill, NY 12043
Phone: (518) 255-5525
Fax: (518) 255-6769
E-mail: admissions@cobleskill.edu
http://www.cobleskill.edu
Information technology.

State University of New York College of Agriculture and Technology at Morrisville

P.O. Box 901
Morrisville, NY 13408
Phone: (800) 258-0111
Fax: (315) 684-6427
E-mail: admissions@morrisville.edu
http://www.morrisville.edu
Systems administration.

State University of New York College of Technology at Alfred

Huntington Administration Building
Alfred, NY 14802
Phone: (800) 425-3733
Fax: (607) 587-4299

E-mail: admissions@alfredstate.edu
http://www.alfredstate.edu
Computer/information sciences— general.

State University of New York College of Technology at Canton

34 Cornell Drive
Canton, NY 13617
Phone: (800) 388-7123
Fax: NA
E-mail: admissions@canton.edu
http://www.canton.edu
Computer/information sciences— general.

State University of New York— Institute of Technology at Utica/Rome

P.O. Box 3050
Utica, NY 13504
Phone: (315) 792-7500
Fax: (315) 792-7837
E-mail: admissions@sunyit.edu
http://www.sunyit.edu
Applied mathematics, computer engineering technology, computer/information sciences— general, information systems.

Syracuse University

Office of Admissions
200 Crouse-Hinds Hall
Syracuse, NY 13244
Phone: (315) 443-3611
Fax: (315) 443-4226
E-mail: orange@syr.edu
http://www.syracuse.edu
Computer engineering, computer/ information sciences—general, information systems, information technology.

Touro College

1602 Avenue J
Brooklyn, NY 14230
Phone: (718) 252-7800
Fax: (718) 253-6479
E-mail: lasAdmit@touro.edu
http://www.touro.edu
Computer/information sciences—general, management information systems.

Union College
Grant Hall, Union College
Schenectady, NY 12308
Phone: (518) 388-6112
Fax: (518) 388-6986
E-mail: admissions@union.edu
http://www.union.edu
Computer/information sciences—
general.

**United States Military
Academy**
646 Swift Road
West Point, NY 10996
Phone: (845) 938-4041
Fax: (845) 938-3021
E-mail: admissions@usma.edu
http://www.usma.edu
Computer engineering, information
systems.

University of Rochester
300 Wilson Boulevard
P.O. Box 270251
Rochester, NY 14627
Phone: (585) 275-3221
Fax: (585) 461-4595
E-mail: admit@admissions.
rochester.edu
http://www.rochester.edu
Computer/information sciences—
general, statistics.

Utica College
1600 Burnside Road
Utica, NY 13052
Phone: (315) 792-3006
Fax: (315) 792-3003
E-mail: admiss@utica.edu
http://www.utica.edu
Applied mathematics, computer/
information sciences—general.

Vassar College
124 Raymond Avenue
Poughkeepsie, NY 12604
Phone: (845) 437-7300
Fax: (845) 437-7063
E-mail: admissions@vassar.edu
http://www.vassar.edu
Cognitive science, computer/
information sciences—general.

Yeshiva University
500 West 18th Street
New York, NY 10033
Phone: (212) 960-5277
Fax: (212) 960-0866
E-mail: yuadmitt@yu.edu
http://www.yu.edu
Computer/information sciences—
general.

NORTH CAROLINA

Appalachian State University
Office of Admissions
P.O. Box 32004
Boone, NC 28608
Phone: (828) 262-2120
Fax: (828) 262-3296
E-mail: admissions@appstate.edu
http://www.appstate.edu
Management information systems,
statistics.

Barton College
P.O. Box 5000
Wilson, NC 27893
Phone: (252) 399-6317
Fax: (252) 399-6572
E-mail: enroll@barton.edu
http://www.barton.edu
Computer/information sciences—
general, human resources
management.

Bennett College for Women
900 East Washington Street
Greensboro, NC 27401
Phone: (336) 370-8624
Fax: (336) 370-8653
E-mail: admiss@bennett.edu
http://www.bennett.edu
Computer/information sciences—
general.

Campbell University
P.O. Box 546
Buies Creek, NC 27506
Phone: (910) 893-1320
Fax: (910) 893-1288
E-mail: adm@mailcenter.campbell.
edu
http://www.campbell.edu
Information systems, management
information systems.

Catawba College
2300 West Innes Street
Salisbury, NC 28144
Phone: (704) 637-4402
Fax: (704) 637-4222
E-mail: admission@catawba.edu
http://www.catawba
Computer/information sciences—
general.

Chowan College
One University Place
Murfreesboro, NC 27855
Phone: (252) 398-1236
Fax: (252) 398-1190
E-mail: admissions@chowan.edu
http://www.chowan.edu
Information resources management.

DeVry University—Charlotte
4521 Sharon Road, Suite 145
Charlotte, NC 28211
Phone: (704) 362-2345
Fax: (704) 362-2668
E-mail: At Web site
http://www.devry.edu
Computer/information sciences—
general.

Duke University
2138 Campus Drive
Durham, NC 27708
Phone: (919) 684-3214
Fax: (919) 681-8941
E-mail: undergrad.admissions@
duke.edu
http://www.duke.edu
Computer/information sciences—
general.

East Carolina University
Office of Undergraduate
Admissions
106 Whichard Building
Greenville, NC 27858
Phone: (252) 328-6640
Fax: (252) 328-6945
E-mail: admis@mail.ecu.edu
http://www.ecu.edu
Computer engineering technology,
information technology,
management information
systems.

Elon University

2700 Campus Box
Elon, NC 27244
Phone: (336) 278-3566
Fax: (336) 278-7699
E-mail: admissions@elon.edu
http://www.elon.edu
Computer engineering, computer/
    information sciences—general,
    information systems.

Fayetteville State University

Newbold Station
Fayetteville, NC 28301
Phone: (910) 672-1371
Fax: (910) 672-1414
E-mail: admissions@uncfsu.edu
http://www.uncfsu.edu
Computer/information sciences—
    general.

Gardner-Webb University

P.O. Box 817
Boiling Springs, NC 28017
Phone: (704) 406-4498
Fax: (704) 406-4488
E-mail: admissions@gardner-webb.
    edu
http://www.gardner-webb.edu
Computer/information sciences—
    general, management information
    systems.

Guilford College

5800 West Friendly Avenue
Greensboro, NC 27410
Phone: (336) 316-2100
Fax: (336) 316-2954
E-mail: admission@guilford.edu
http://www.guilford.edu
Computer/information sciences—
    general, information systems.

High Point University

University Station 3598
High Point, NC 27262
Phone: (336) 841-9216
Fax: (336) 888-6382
E-mail: admiss@highpoint.edu
http://www.highpoint.edu
Computer/information sciences—
    general, human resources
    management, management
    information systems.

Johnson C. Smith University

100 Beatties Ford Road
Charlotte, NC 28216
Phone: (704) 378-1011
Fax: (704) 378-01242
E-mail: admissions@jcsu.edu
http://www.jcsu.edu
Applied mathematics, computer
    engineering, computer/
    information sciences—general,
    information technology.

Lees-McRae College

Admissions Officer
P.O. Box 128
Banner Elk, NC 28604
Phone: (828) 898-8723
Fax: (828) 898-8707
E-mail: admissions@lmc.edu
http://www.lmc.edu
Information systems.

Lenoir-Rhyme College

Admissions Office
LRC Box 7227
Hickory, NC 28603
Phone: (828) 328-7300
Fax: (828) 328-7378
E-mail: admission@lrc.edu
http://www.lrc.edu
Computer/information sciences—
    general, information systems,
    management information
    systems.

Livingstone College

701 West Monroe Street
Salisbury, NC 28144
Phone: (704) 216-6001
Fax: (704) 216-6215
E-mail: admissions@livingstone.edu
http://www.livingstone.edu
Computer/information sciences—
    general.

Meredith College

3800 Hillsborough Street
Raleigh, NC 27607
Phone: (919) 760-8581
Fax: (919) 760-2348
E-mail: admissions@meredith.edu
http://www.meredith.edu
Computer/information sciences—
    general.

Methodist College

5400 Ramsey Street
Fayetteville, NC 28311
Phone: (910) 630-7027
Fax: (910) 630-7285
E-mail: admissions@methodist.edu
http://www.methodist.edu
Communications technology,
    management information
    systems.

Montreat College

310 Gaither Circle
Montreat, NC 28757
Phone: (828) 669-8011
Fax: (828) 669-0120
E-mail: admissions@montreat.edu
http://www.montreat.edu
Computer/information sciences—
    general.

Mount Olive College

634 Henderson Street
Mount Olive, NC 28365
Phone: (919) 658-7164
Fax: (919) 658-7180
E-mail: admissions@moc.edu
http://www.moc.edu
Computer/information sciences—
    general, human resources
    management, management
    information systems.

North Carolina A&T University

1601 East Market Street
Greensboro, NC 27411
Phone: (336) 334-7946
Fax: (336) 334-7478
E-mail: uadmit@ncat.edu
http://www.ncat.edu
Computer/information sciences—
    general.

North Carolina Central University

Fayetteville Street
Durham, NC 27707
Phone: (919) 560-6298
Fax: (919) 530-7625
E-mail: ebridges@wpo.nccu.edu
http://www.nccu.edu
Information systems.

North Carolina State University
P.O. Box 7103
Raleigh, NC 27695
Phone: (919) 515-2434
Fax: (919) 515-5039
E-mail: undergrad_admissions@
  ncsu.edu
http://www.ncsu.edu
Applied mathematics, computer
  engineering, statistics.

Peace College
15 East Peace Street
Raleigh, NC 27604
Phone: (800) 732-2306
Fax: (919) 508-2306
E-mail: mmcleery@peace.edu
http://www.peace.edu
Human resources management.

Pfeiffer College
P.O. Box 960
Misenheimer, NC 28109
Phone: (800) 338-2060
Fax: (704) 463-1363
E-mail: admissions@pfeiffer.edu
http://www.pfeiffer.edu
Computer/information sciences—
  general.

**Queens University of
  Charlotte**
1900 Selwyn Avenue
Charlotte, NC 28274
Phone: (704) 337-2212
Fax: (704) 337-2403
E-mail: admissions@queens.edu
http://www.queens.edu
Information systems, management
  information systems.

Saint Augustine's College
1315 Oakwood Avenue
Raleigh, NC 27610
Phone: (919) 516-4016
Fax: (919) 516-5805
E-mail: admissions@st-aug.edu
http://www.st-aug.edu
Computer/information sciences—
  general.

Shaw University
118 East South Street

Raleigh, NC 27601
Phone: (919) 546-8275
Fax: (919) 546-8271
E-mail: admission@shawu.edu
http://www.shawu.edu
Computer/information sciences—
  general.

**University of North Carolina—
  Chapel Hill**
Office of Undergraduate
  Admissions
Jackson Hall 153A
Campus P.O. Box 2220
Chapel Hill, NC 27599
Phone: (919) 966-3621
Fax: (919) 962-3045
E-mail: uadm@email.unc.edu
http://www.unc.edu
Applied mathematics, information
  systems.

**University of North Carolina—
  Charlotte**
9201 University City Boulevard
Charlotte, NC 28223
Phone: (704) 687-2213
Fax: (704) 687-6483
E-mail: uncadm@email.uncc.edu
http://www.uncc.edu
Computer engineering,
  management information
  systems.

**University of North Carolina—
  Wilmington**
601 South College Road
Wilmington, NC 28403
Phone: (910) 962-3243
Fax: (910) 962-3038
E-mail: admissions@uncw.edu
http://www.uncw.edu
Management information systems.

Western Carolina University
232 HFR Administration
Cullowhee, NC 28723
Phone: (828) 227-7317
Fax: (828) 227-7319
E-mail: cauley@email.wcu.edu
http://www.wcu.edu
Management information systems.

Winston-Salem State University
601 Martin Luther King Jr. Drive
Winston-Salem, NC 27100
Phone: (336) 750-2070
Fax: (336) 750-2079
E-mail: admissions@wssu.edu
http://www.wssu.edu
Information technology.

NORTH DAKOTA

Dickinson State University
Office of Enrollment Services, Box
  173
Dickinson, ND 58601
Phone: (701) 483-2175
Fax: (701) 483-2409
E-mail: dsu.hawks@dsu.nodak.edu
http://www.dickinsonstate.com
Management information systems.

Jamestown College
6081 College Lane
Jamestown, ND 58405
Phone: (701) 252-3467
Fax: (701) 253-4318
E-mail: admissions@jc.edu
http://www.jc.edu
Applied mathematics, management
  information systems.

Mayville State University
330 Third Street NE
Mayville, ND 58257
Phone: (701) 788-4842
Fax: (701) 788-4748
E-mail: admit@mayvillestate.edu
http://www.mayvillestate.edu
Computer/information sciences—
  general.

Minot State University—Minot
500 University Avenue
West Minot, ND 58707
Phone: (701) 858-3350
Fax: (701) 858-3386
E-mail: msu@minotstateu.edu
http://www.minotstateu.edu
Computer/information sciences—
  general.

North Dakota State University
P.O. Box 5454

Fargo, ND 58105
Phone: (701) 231-8643
Fax: (701) 231-8802
E-mail: ndsu.admission@ndsu.
nodak.edu
http://www.ndsu.edu
Management information systems.

University of Mary
7500 University Drive
Bismarck, ND 58504
Phone: (701) 255-7500
Fax: (701) 255-7687
E-mail: suerood@umary.edu
http://www.umary.edu
Information systems.

University of North Dakota
Enrollment Services
Carnegie Building
Box 8135
Grand Forks, ND 58202
Phone: (800) CALL-UND
Fax: (701) 777-2696
E-mail: enrollment_services@mail.
und.nodak.edu
http://www.und.edu
Computer/information
sciences—general, management
information systems.

Valley City State University
101 College Street SW
Valley City, ND 58072
Phone: (701) 845-7101
Fax: (701) 845-7299
E-mail: enrollment.services@vcsu.
edu
http://www.vcsu.edu
Computer/information sciences—
general, human resources
management.

OHIO

Ashland University
401 College Avenue
Ashland, OH 44805
Phone: (419) 289-5052
Fax: (419) 289-5999
E-mail: enrollme@ashland.edu
http://www.ashland.edu
Management information systems.

Baldwin-Wallace College
275 Eastland Road
Berea, OH 44017
Phone: (440) 826-2222
Fax: (440) 826-3830
E-mail: admission@bw.edu
http://www.bw.edu
Computer systems analysis, human
resources management.

Bluffton University
Office of Admissions
1 University Drive
Bluffton, OH 45817
Phone: (419) 358-3257
Fax: (419) 358-3232
E-mail: admissions@bluffton.edu
http://www.bluffton.edu
Information systems, information
technology, management
information systems.

Bowling Green State University
110 McFall Center
Bowling Green, OH 43403
Phone: (419) 372-2478
Fax: (419) 372-6955
E-mail: admissions@bgnet.bgsu.
edu
http://www.bgsu.edu
Applied mathematics, computer/
information sciences—general,
human resources management,
management information
systems, statistics.

Capital University
2199 East Main Street
Columbus, OH 43209
Phone: (614) 236-6101
Fax: (614) 236-6926
E-mail: admissions@capital.edu
http://www.capital.edu
Computer/information sciences—
general.

Case Western Reserve University
103 Tomlinson Hall
10900 Euclid Avenue
Cleveland, OH 44106
Phone: (216) 368-4450
Fax: (216) 368-5111

E-mail: admission@case.edu
http://www.case.edu
Applied mathematics, cognitive
science, computer engineering,
computer/information
sciences—general, statistics.

Cedarville University
251 North Main Street
Cedarville, OH 45314
Phone: (937) 766-7700
Fax: (937) 766-7575
E-mail: admissions@cedarville.edu
http://www.cedarville.edu
Computer/information
sciences—general, management
information systems.

Cincinnati Christian University
2700 Glenway Avenue
Cincinnati, OH 45204
Phone: (800) 949-4338
Fax: (513) 244-8140
E-mail: At Web site
http://www. ccuniversity.edu
Data processing technology,
information technology.

Cleveland State University
East 24 and Euclid Avenue
Cleveland, OH 44114
Phone: (216) 687-2100
Fax: (216) 687-9210
E-mail: admissions@csuohio.edu
http://www.csuohio.edu
Computer/information
sciences—general, management
information systems.

College of Mount Saint Joseph
5701 Delhi Road
Cincinnati, OH 45233
Phone: (513) 244-4531
Fax: (513) 244-4629
E-mail: peggy_minnich@mail.msj.
edu
http://www.msj.edu
Computer/information sciences—
general.

The College of Wooster
847 College Avenue
Wooster, OH 44091

Phone: (330) 263-2322
Fax: (330) 263-2621
E-mail: admissions@wooster.edu
http://www.wooster.edu
Computer/information sciences—
    general.

Defiance College
701 North Clinton Street
Defiance, OH 43612
Phone: (419) 783-2359
Fax: (419) 783-2468
E-mail: admissions@defiance.edu
http://www.defiance.edu
Computer/information sciences—
    general, human resources
    management, management
    information systems.

Denison University
P.O. Box H
Granville, OH 43023
Phone: (740) 587-6276
Fax: (740) 587-6306
E-mail: admissions@denison.edu
http://www.denison.edu
Computer/information sciences—
    general.

DeVry University—Columbus
1350 Alum Creek Drive
Columbus, OH 43209
Phone: (614) 253-1525
Fax: (614) 253-0843
E-mail: admissions@devry.edu
http://www.devry.edu
Computer engineering technology,
    human resources management,
    information systems,
    management information
    systems.

Franciscan University of
Steubenville
1235 University Boulevard
Steubenville, OH 43952
Phone: (740) 283-6226
Fax: (740) 284-5456
E-mail: admissions@franciscan.edu
http://www.franciscan.edu
Computer/information sciences—
    general.

Franklin University
201 South Grant Avenue
Columbus, OH 43215
Phone: (614) 797-4700
Fax: (614) 224-8027
E-mail: info@franklin.edu
http://www.franklin.edu
Computer/information sciences—
    general, human resources
    management, management
    information systems.

Heidelberg College
310 East Market Street
Tiffin, OH 44883
Phone: (419) 448-2330
Fax: (419) 448-2334
E-mail: adminfo@heidelberg.edu
http://www.heidelberg.edu
Computer/information sciences—
    general.

Hiram College
P.O. Box 96
Hiram, OH 44234
Phone: (330) 569-5169
Fax: (330) 569-5944
E-mail: admission@hiram.edu
http://www.hiram.edu
Computer/information sciences—
    general.

John Carroll University
20700 North Park Boulevard
University Heights, OH 44118
Phone: (216) 397-4294
Fax: (216) 397-3098
E-mail: admission@jcu.edu
http://www.jcu.edu
Computer/information sciences—
    general.

Kent State University
161 Michael Schwartz
Kent, OH 44242
Phone: (330) 672-2444
Fax: (330) 672-2499
E-mail: kentadm@admissions.kent.
    edu
http://www.kent.edu
Applied mathematics, computer
    systems analysis, management
    information systems.

Lourdes College
6832 Convent Road
Sylvania, OH 43560
Phone: (419) 885-5291
Fax: (419) 882-3987
E-mail: lcadmits@lourdes.edu
http://www.lourdes.edu
Human resources management.

Marietta College
215 Fifth Street
Marietta, OH 45750
Phone: (740) 376-4600
Fax: (740) 376-8888
E-mail: admit@marietta.edu
http://www.marietta.edu
Computer/information sciences—
    general, human resources
    management, information
    systems, management
    information systems.

Miami University—Oxford
Campus
301 South Campus Avenue
Oxford, OH 45056
Phone: (513) 529-2531
Fax: (513) 529-1550
E-mail: admissions@muohio.edu
http://www.muohio.edu
Computer engineering, computer
    systems analysis, human
    resources management,
    management information
    systems, statistics.

Mount Union College
1972 Clark Avenue
Alliance, OH 44601
Phone: (800) 334-6682
Fax: (330) 823-3457
E-mail: admissn@muc.edu
http://www.muc.edu
Computer/information sciences—
    general.

Mount Vernon Nazarene
University
800 Martinsburg Road
Mount Vernon, OH 43050
Phone: (740) 392-6868
Fax: (740) 393-0511
E-mail: admissions@mvnu.edu

http://www.mvnu.edu
Computer/information sciences—
general, management information
systems.

Oberlin College
101 North Professor Street
Oberlin, OH 44074
Phone: (440) 775-8411
Fax: (440) 775-6905
E-mail: college.admissions@oberlin.
edu
http://www.oberlin.edu
Computer/information sciences—
general.

Ohio Dominican University
1216 Sunbury Road
Columbus, OH 42319
Phone: (614) 251-4500
Fax: (614) 251-0156
E-mail: admissions@ohiodominican.
edu
http://www.ohiodominican.edu
Information systems, management
information systems.

Ohio Northern University
525 South Main Street
Ada, OH 45810
Phone: (419) 772-2260
Fax: (419) 772-2313
E-mail: admissions-ug@onu.edu
http://www.onu.edu
Statistics.

Ohio State University—
Columbus
Third Floor Lincoln Tower
1800 Cannon Drive
Columbus, OH 43210
Phone: (614) 292-3980
Fax: (614) 292-4818
E-mail: askabuckeye@osu.edu
http://www.osu.edu
Computer engineering, computer/
information sciences—general,
human resources management,
information systems, management information systems.

Ohio University—Athens
120 Chubb Hall

Athens, OH 45701
Phone: (740) 593-4100
Fax: (740) 593-0560
E-mail: admissions.freshmen@
ohiou.edu
http://www.ohiou.edu
Applied mathematics, computer/
information sciences—general,
human resources management,
information technology.

Ohio University—Chillicothe
Campus
101 University Drive
Chillicothe, OH 45601
Phone: (740) 774-7200
Fax: NA
E-mail: At Web site
http://www.chillicothe.ohiou.edu
Applied mathematics, computer/
information sciences—general,
human resources management,
information technology.

Ohio University—Southern
Office of Enrollment Services
1804 Liberty Avenue
Ironton, OH 45638
Phone: (740) 533-4600
Fax: (740) 533-4632
E-mail: askousc.@mail_southern.
ohiou.edu
http://www.southern.ohiou.edu
Applied mathematics, computer/
information sciences—general,
human resources management,
information technology.

Ohio University—Zanesville
Office of Admissions
1425 Newark Road
Zanesville, OH 43701
Phone: (740) 588-1439
Fax: (740) 588-1444
E-mail: tumbling@ohiou.edu
http://www.zanesville.ohiou.edu
Applied mathematics, computer/
information sciences—general,
human resources management,
information technology.

Ohio Wesleyan University
Admissions Office

61 South Sandusky Street
Delaware, OH 43015
Phone: (740) 368-3020
Fax: (740) 368-3314
E-mail: owuadmit@owu.edu
http://www.owu.edu
Computer/information sciences—
general, statistics.

Shawnee State University
940 Second Street
Portsmouth, OH 45662
Phone: (740) 351-4SSU
Fax: (740) 351-3111
E-mail: to_ssu@shawnee.edu
http://www.shawnee.edu
Computer engineering technology,
management information
systems.

Tiffin University
155 Miami Street
Tiffin, OH 44883
Phone: (419) 448-3423
Fax: (419) 443-5006
E-mail: admiss@tiffin.edu
http://www.tiffin.edu
Human resources management,
information systems.

Union Institute & University
440 East McMillan Street
Cincinnati, OH 45206
Phone: (513) 861-6400
Fax: (513) 861-3238
E-mail: admissions@tui.edu
http://www.tui.edu
Computer/information sciences—
general, information systems,
management information
systems.

University of Akron
381 Butchel Common
Akron, OH 44325
Phone: (330) 972-7100
Fax: (330) 972-7022
E-mail: admissions@uakron.edu
http://www.uakron.edu
Computer engineering, computer/
information sciences—general,
computer systems analysis,
human resources management,
management information systems, statistics.

University of Cincinnati

P.O. Box 210091
Cincinnati, OH 45221
Phone: (513) 556-1100
Fax: (513) 556-1105
E-mail: admissions@uc.edu
http://www.uc.edu
Computer engineering, computer/
information sciences—general,
management information
systems.

University of Dayton

300 College Park
Dayton, OH 45469
Phone: (937) 229-4411
Fax: (937) 229-4729
E-mail: admission@udayton.edu
http://www.udayton.edu
Computer engineering, computer
engineering technology,
computer/information
sciences—general, management
information systems.

The University of Findlay

1000 North Main Street
Findlay, OH 45840
Phone: (419) 424-4732
Fax: (419) 434-4898
E-mail: admissions@findlay.edu
http://www.findlay.edu
Computer/information sciences—
general, computer systems
analysis, human resources
management.

University of Rio Grande

218 North College Avenue,
Admissions
Rio Grande, OH 45774
Phone: (740) 245-7206
Fax: (740) 245-7260
E-mail: mabell@urgrgcc.edu
http://www.urgrgcc.edu
Computer/information sciences—
general, human resources
management.

University of Toledo

2801 West Bancroft Street
Toledo, OH 43606
Phone: (419) 530-8700

Fax: (419) 530-5713
E-mail: enroll@utnet.utoledo.edu
http://www.utoledo.edu
Computer engineering, human
resources management,
information systems,
management information
systems.

Urbana University

579 College Way
Urbana, OH 43076
Phone: (937) 484-1356
Fax: (937) 484-1389
E-mail: admiss@urbana.edu
http://www.urbana.edu
Human resources management,
information systems.

Ursuline College

2550 Lander Road
Pepper Pike, OH 44124
Phone: (440) 449-4203
Fax: (440) 684-6138
E-mail: admission@ursuline.edu
http://www.ursuline.edu
Management information systems.

Walsh University

2020 East Maple Street
North Canton, OH 44720
Phone: (800) 362-9846
Fax: (330) 490-7165
E-mail: admissions@walsh.edu
http://www.walsh.edu
Computer/information
sciences—general, management
information systems.

Wilmington College

Pyle Center, Box 1325
251 Ludovic Street
Wilmington, OH 45117
Phone: (937) 382-6661
Fax: (937) 382-7077
E-mail: admission@wilmington.edu
http://www.wilmington.edu
Computer/information sciences—
general.

Wright State University

3640 Colonel Glenn Highway
Dayton, OH 54435

Phone: (937) 775-5700
Fax: (937) 775-5795
E-mail: admissions@wright.edu
http://www.wright.edu
Applied mathematics, computer
engineering, computer/
information sciences—general,
human resources management,
information systems,
management information
systems, statistics.

Xavier University

3800 Victory Parkway
Cincinnati, OH 45207
Phone: (513) 745-3301
Fax: (513) 745-4319
E-mail: xuadmit@xavier.edu
http://www.xavier.edu
Human resources management,
management information
systems.

Youngstown State University

One University Plaza
Youngstown, OH 44555
Phone: (330) 941-2000
Fax: (330) 941-3674
E-mail: enroll@ysu.edu
http://www.ysu.edu
Computer engineering, computer/
information sciences—general,
human resources management,
information systems,
information technology,
management information
systems.

OKLAHOMA

Cameron University

2800 West Gore Boulevard
Lawton, OK 73505
Phone: (580) 581-2230
Fax: (580) 581-5514
E-mail: admiss@cua.cameron.edu
http://www.cameron.edu
Computer/information sciences—
general.

East Central University

Office of Admissions & Records
1100 E 14 PMB J8

Ada, OK 74820
Phone: (580) 332-8000
Fax: (580) 436-5495
E-mail: pdenny@mailclerk.ecok.edu
http://www.ecok.edu
Applied mathematics, computer/
  information sciences—general.

Mid-America Christian University
3500 Southwest 119th Street
Oklahoma City, OK 73170
Phone: (405) 691-3188
Fax: (405) 692-3165
E-mail: info@macu.edu
http://www.macu.edu
Management information systems.

Northeastern State University
Office of Admissions and Records
600 North Grand Avenue
Tahlequah. OK 74464
Phone: (918) 456-5511
Fax: (918) 458-2342
E-mail: nsuadmis@cherkoee.nsuok.
  edu
http://www.nsuok.edu
Human resources management,
  management information
  systems.

Northwestern Oklahoma State University
709 Oklahoma Boulevard
Alva, OK 73717
Phone: (580) 327-8545
Fax: (580) 327-1881
E-mail: At Web site
http://www.nwosu.edu
Computer/information sciences—
  general, information systems.

Oklahoma Baptist University
500 West University
Shawnee, OK 74804
Phone: (800) 654-3285
Fax: (405) 521-5264
E-mail: At Website
http://www.okbu.edu
Computer/information sciences—
  general, computer systems analysis, information systems, management information systems.

Oklahoma Christian University
P.O. Box 11000
Oklahoma City, OK 73136
Phone: (405) 425-5050
Fax: (405) 425-5269
E-mail: info@oc.edu
http://www.oc.edu
Computer engineering, computer/
  information sciences—general,
  information systems.

Oklahoma City University
2501 North Blackwelder Avenue
Oklahoma City, OK 73106
Phone: (405) 521-5050
Fax: (405) 521-5264
E-mail: uadmission@okcu.edu
http://www.okcu.edu
Computer/information sciences—
  general.

Oklahoma Panhandle State University
P.O. Box 430
Goodwell, OK 73939
Phone: (580) 349-1312
Fax: (580) 349-2302
E-mail: opsu@opsu.edu
http://www.opsu.edu
Computer/information sciences—
  general, information systems.

Oklahoma State University
323 Student Union
Stillwater, OK 74078
Phone: (405) 744-6858
Fax: (405) 744-5285
E-mail: admit@okstate.edu
http://www.okstate.edu
Computer/information sciences—
  general, management information
  systems, statistics.

Oklahoma Wesleyan University
2201 Silver Lake Road
Bartlesville, OK 74006
Phone: (918) 335-6219
Fax: (918) 335-6229
E-mail: admissions@okwu.edu
http://www.okwu.edu
Computer/information sciences—
  general.

Oral Roberts University
7777 South Lewis Avenue
Tulsa, OK 74171
Phone: (918) 495-0518
Fax: (918) 495-6222
E-mail: admissions@oru.edu
http://www.oru.edu
Computer engineering, computer/
  information sciences—general,
  management information
  systems.

Southeastern Oklahoma State University
1405 North Fourth Avenue, PMB
  4225
Durant, OK 74701
Phone: (580) 745-2060
Fax: (580) 745-7502
E-mail: admissions@sosu.edu
http://www.sosu.edu
Computer/information sciences—
  general, information systems.

Southwestern Oklahoma State University
100 Campus Drive
Weatherford, OK 73096
Phone: (580) 774-3795
Fax: (580) 774-2795
E-mail: admissions@swosu.edu
http://www.swosu.edu
Human resources management,
  information systems, manage-
  ment information systems.

University of Central Oklahoma
100 North University Drive
Edmond, OK 73034
Phone: (405) 974-2338
Fax: (405) 341-4964
E-mail: admituco@ucok.edu
http://www.ucok.edu
Applied mathematics, computer/
  information sciences—general,
  human resources management,
  information technology, management information systems,
  statistics.

University of Oklahoma
1000 Asp Avenue
Norman, OK 73019

Phone: (405) 325-2252
Fax: (405) 325-7124
E-mail: admrec@ou.edu
http://www.ou.edu
Computer engineering.

University of Tulsa

500 South College Avenue
Tulsa, OK 741045
Phone: (918) 631-2307
Fax: (918) 631-5003
E-mail: admission@utulsa.edu
http://www.utulsa.edu
Applied mathematics, computer/
information sciences—general,
information technology, man-
agement information systems.

OREGON

Corban College

5000 Deer Park Drive SE
Salem, OR 97317
Phone: (503) 375-7005
Fax: (503) 585-4316
E-mail: admissions@corban.edu
http://www.corban.edu
Management information systems.

DeVry University—Portland

Peterkort Center II
9755 Southwest Barnes Road, Suite
150
Portland, OR 97225
Phone: (503) 296-7468
Fax: (503) 296-6114
E-mail: admissions@devry.edu
http://www.devry.edu
Computer/information sciences—
general.

Eastern Oregon University

1 University Boulevard
LaGrande, OR 97850
Phone: (541) 962-3393
Fax: (541) 962-3418
E-mail: admissions@eou.edu
http://www.eou.edu
Computer/information sciences—
general.

George Fox University

414 North Meridian Street

Newberg, OR 97132
Phone: (503) 554-2240
Fax: (503) 554-3110
E-mail: admissions@georgefox.edu
http://www.georgefox.edu
Computer/information sciences—
general, human resources
management, information
systems, management
information systems.

Northwest Christian College

828 East 11th Avenue
Eugene, OR 97401
Phone: (541) 684-7201
Fax: (541) 628-7317
E-mail: admissions@nwcc.edu
http://www.nwcc.edu
Computer/information
sciences—general, management
information systems.

Oregon Institute of Technology

3201 Campus Drive
Klamath Falls, OR 97601
Phone: (541) 885-1150
Fax: (541) 885-1115
E-mail: oit@oit.edu
http://www.oit.edu
Computer software technology,
information systems,
management information
systems.

Oregon State University

104 Kerr Administration Building
Corvallis, OR 97331
Phone: (541) 737-4411
Fax: (541) 737-2482
E-mail: osuadit@orst.edu
http://www.oregonstate.edu
Computer engineering, computer/
information sciences—general.

Pacific University

2043 College Way
Forest Grove, OR 97116
Phone: (503) 352-2218
Fax: (503) 352-2975
E-mail: admissions@pacificu.edu
http://www.pacificu.edu
Computer/information sciences—
general.

Pioneer Pacific College

27501 Southwest Parkway Avenue
Wilsonville, OR 97070
Phone: (503) 682-3903
Fax: NA
E-mail: At Web site
http://www.pioneerpacificcollege.edu
Information technology.

Portland State University

P.O. Box 751
Portland, OR 97207
Phone: (503) 725-3511
Fax: (503) 725-5525
E-mail: admissions@pdx.edu
http://www.pdx.edu
Computer engineering, human
resources management, manage-
ment information systems.

University of Oregon

1217 University of Oregon
Eugene, OR 97403
Phone: (541) 346-3201
Fax: (541) 346-5815
E-mail: uoadmit@oregon.uoregon.
edu
http://www.uoregon.edu
Computer/information sciences—
general.

University of Portland

5000 North Willamette Boulevard
Portland, OR 97203
Phone: (503) 943-7147
Fax: (503) 283-7315
E-mail: admission@up.edu
http://www.up.edu
Computer engineering.

Western Oregon University

345 North Monmouth Avenue
Monmouth, OR 97361
Phone: (503) 838-8211
Fax: (503) 838-8067
E-mail: wolfgram@wou.edu
http://www.wou.edu
Computer/information sciences—
general.

Willamette University

900 State Street
Salem, OR 97301
Phone: (503) 370-6303

Fax: (503) 375-5363
E-mail: libarts@willamette.edu
http://www.willamette.edu
Computer/information sciences—
general.

PENNSYLVANIA

Albright College
P.O. Box 15234
13th and Bern Streets
Reading, PA 19612
Phone: (610) 921-7512
Fax: (610) 921-7294
E-mail: admissions@albright.edu
http://www.albright.edu
Computer/information sciences—
general, information systems.

Allegheny College
Office of Admissions
Meadville, PA 16335
Phone: (814) 332-4351
Fax: (814) 337-0431
E-mail: admissions@allegheny.edu
http://www.allegheny.edu
Software engineering.

Alvernia College
400 South Bernardine Street
Reading, PA 19607
Phone: (610) 796-8220
Fax: (610) 796-8336
E-mail: admissions@alvernia.edu
http://www.alvernia.edu
Computer/information sciences—
general, human resources
management.

Arcadia University
450 South Easton Road
Glenside, PA 19038
Phone: (215) 572-2910
Fax: (215) 572-4049
E-mail: admiss@arcadia.edu
http://www.arcadia.edu
Computer/information sciences—
general, human resources
management, management
information systems.

Bloomsburg University of Pennsylvania
104 Student Services Center
400 East Second Street
Bloomsburg, PA 17815
Phone: (570) 389-4316
Fax: (570) 389-4741
E-mail: buadmiss@bloomu.edu
http://www.bloomu.edu
Computer/information sciences—
general.

Bucknell University
Freas Hall
Bucknell University
Lewisburg, PA 17837
Phone: (570) 577-1101
Fax: (570) 577-3538
E-mail: admissions@bucknell.edu
http://www.bucknell.edu
Computer engineering, computer/
information sciences—general.

Cabrini College
610 King of Prussia Road
Radnor, PA 19087
Phone: (610) 902-8552
Fax: (610) 902-8552
E-mail: admit@cabrini.edu
http://www.cabrini.edu
Computer/information sciences—
general, human resources
management, management
information systems.

California University of Pennsylvania
250 University Avenue
California, PA 15419
Phone: (724) 938-4404
Fax: (724) 938-4564
E-mail: inquiry@cup.edu
http://www.cup.edu
Computer engineering technology,
computer/information
sciences—general.

Carlow University
3333 Fifth Avenue
Pittsburgh, PA 15213
Phone: (412) 578-6059
Fax: (412) 578-6668
E-mail: admissions@carlow.edu
http://www.carlow.edu
Human resources management,
information systems, manage-
ment information systems.

Carnegie Mellon University
5000 Forbes Avenue
Pittsburgh, PA 15213
Phone: (412) 268-2082
Fax: (412) 268-7838
E-mail: undergraduateadmissions@
andrew.cmu.edu
http://www.cmu.edu
Applied mathematics, cognitive
science, computational
mathematics, information
systems, statistics.

Cedar Crest College
100 College Drive
Allentown, PA 18104
Phone: (610) 740-3780
Fax: (610) 606-4647
E-mail: cccadmis@cedarcrest.edu
http://www.cedarcrest.edu
Computer/information sciences—
general, information systems.

Chestnut Hill College
9601 Germantown Avenue
Philadelphia, PA 19118
Phone: (215) 248-7001
Fax: (215) 248-7082
E-mail: chcapply@chc.edu
http://www.chc.edu
Computer/information sciences—
general, human resources
management.

Cheyney University of Pennsylvania
Cheyney and Creek Roads
Cheyney, PA 19319
Phone: (610) 399-2275
Fax: (610) 399-2099
E-mail: jbrowne@cheyney.edu
http://www.cheyney.edu
Computer/information sciences—
general.

Clarion University of Pennsylvania
Admissions Office
840 Wood Street
Clarion, PA 16214
Phone: (814) 393-2306
Fax: (814) 393-2030
E-mail: admissions@clarion.edu

http://www.clarion.edu
Information systems, library
   science.

College Misericordia

301 Lake Street
Dallas, PA 18612
Phone: (866) 262-6363
Fax: NA
E-mail: info@misericordia.edu
http://www.misericordia.edu
Information technology,
   management information
   systems.

Delaware Valley College

700 East Butler Avenue
Doylestown, PA 18901
Phone: (215) 489-2211
Fax: (215) 230-2968
E-mail: admitme@devalcol.edu
http://www.devalcol.edu
Computer/information
   sciences—general, management
   information systems.

DeSales University

2755 Station Avenue
Center Valley, PA 18034
Phone: (610) 282-4443
Fax: (610) 282-0131
E-mail: admiss@desales.edu
http://www.desales.edu
Human resources management,
   management information
   systems.

DeVry University—Ft. Washington

1140 Virginia Drive
Ft. Washington, PA 19034
Phone: (866) 338-7934
Fax: NA
E-mail: info.devry.edu
http://www.devry.edu
Computer engineering technology,
   computer systems analysis.

Dickinson College

P.O. Box 1773
Carlisle, PA 17013
Phone: (717) 245-1231
Fax: (717) 245-1443

E-mail: admit@dickinson.edu
http://www.dickinson.edu
Computer/information sciences—
   general.

Drexel University

3141 Chestnut Street
Philadelphia, PA 19104
Phone: (215) 895-2400
Fax: (215) 895-5939
E-mail: enroll@drexel.edu
http://www.drexel.edu
Computer engineering, computer
   systems analysis, human
   resources management,
   information systems,
   management information
   systems.

Duquesne University

600 Forbes Avenue
Pittsburgh, PA 15282
Phone: (412) 396-5000
Fax: (412) 396-5644
E-mail: admissions@duq.edu
http://www.duq.edu
Management information systems.

Eastern University

1300 Eagle Road
St. Davids, PA 19087
Phone: (610) 341-5967
Fax: (610) 341-1723
E-mail: ugadm@eastern.edu
http://www.eastern.edu
Management information systems.

East Stroudsburg University of Pennsylvania

200 Prospect Street
East Stroudsburg, PA 18301
Phone: (570) 422-3542
Fax: (570) 422-3933
E-mail: undergrads@po-box.esu.
   edu
http://www.esu.edu
Computer/information sciences—
   general.

Edinboro University of Pennsylvania

Biggers House
Edinboro, PA 16444

Phone: (814) 732-2761
Fax: (814) 732-2420
E-mail: eup_admissions@edinboro.
   edu
http://www.edinboro.edu
Computer/information sciences—
   general.

Elizabethtown College

Leffler House
One Alpha Drive
Elizabethtown, PA 17022
Phone: (717) 361-1400
Fax: (717) 361-1365
E-mail: admissions@etown.edu
http://www.etown.edu
Applied mathematics, computer
   engineering, computer/informa-
   tion sciences—general, infor-
   mation systems, management
   information systems.

Gannon University

University Square
Erie, PA 16541
Phone: (814) 871-7240
Fax: (814) 871-5803
E-mail: admissions@gannon.edu
http://www.gannon.edu
Computer/information
   sciences—general, management
   information systems.

Geneva College

3200 College Avenue
Beaver Falls, PA 15010
Phone: (724) 847-6500
Fax: (724) 847-6776
E-mail: admissions@geneva.edu
http://www.geneva.edu
Applied mathematics, computer/
   information sciences—general,
   human resources management.

Gettysburg College

300 North Washington Street
Gettysburg, PA 17325
Phone: (717) 337-6100
Fax: (717) 337-6145
E-mail: admiss@gettysburg.edu
http://www.gettysburg.edu
Computer engineering, computer/
   information sciences—general.

Grove City College
100 Campus Drive
Grove City, PA 16127
Phone: (724) 458-2100
Fax: (724) 458-3395
E-mail: admissions@gcc.edu
http://www.gcc.edu
Computer/information sciences—
general, computer systems
analysis.

Gwynedd-Mercy College
1325 Sumneytown Pike
P.O. Box 901
Gwynedd Valley, PA 19437
Phone: (215) 641-5510
Fax: (215) 641-5556
E-mail: admissions@gmc.edu
http://www.gmc.edu
Computer/information sciences—
general.

Haverford College
370 West Lancaster Avenue
Haverford, PA 19041
Phone: (610) 896-1350
Fax: (610) 896-1338
E-mail: admitme@haverford.edu
http://www.haverford.edu
Computer/information sciences—
general.

Holy Family University
Grant and Frankford Avenue
Philadelphia, PA 19114
Phone: (215) 637-3050
Fax: (215) 281-1022
E-mail: undergrad@hfu.edu
http://www.holyfamily.edu
Computer/information sciences—
general, human resources
management.

Immaculata University
1145 King Road
P.O. Box 642
Immaculata, PA 19345
Phone: (610) 647-4400
Fax: (610) 647-0836
E-mail: admiss@immaculata.edu
http://www.immaculata.edu
Human resources management,
information systems.

**Indiana University of
Pennsylvania**
216 Pratt Hall
Indiana, PA 15075
Phone: (724) 357-2230
Fax: (724) 357-6281
E-mail: admissions-inquiry@iup.edu
http://www.iup.edu
Applied mathematics, computer/
information sciences—general,
human resources management,
management information
systems.

Juniata College
1700 Moore Street
Huntington, PA 16652
Phone: (814) 641-3420
Fax: (814) 641-3100
E-mail: admissions@juniata.edu
http://www.juniata.edu
Computer/information sciences—
general, human resources
management, information
resources management.

Keystone College
1 College Green
La Plume, PA 18440
Phone: (570) 945-8111
Fax: (570) 945-7916
E-mail: admissions@keystone.edu
http://www.keystone.edu
Computer/information sciences—
general, computer systems analysis, information systems, information technology, management
information systems.

King's College
133 North River Street
Wilkes-Barre, PA 18711
Phone: (570) 208-5858
Fax: (570) 208-5971
E-mail: admissions@kings.edu
http://www.kings.edu
Computer/information sciences—
general, human resources
management.

**Kutztown University of
Pennsylvania**
Admission Office

P.O. Box 730
Kutztown, PA 19530
Phone: (610) 683-4060
Fax: (610) 683-1375
E-mail: admission@kutztown.edu
http://www.kutztown.edu
Human resources management,
information technology, library
science.

Lafayette College
118 Markle Hall
Easton, PA 18042
Phone: (610) 330-5100
Fax: (610) 330-5355
E-mail: admissions@lafayette.edu
http://www.lafayette.edu
Computer/information sciences—
general.

La Roche College
9000 Babcock Boulevard
Pittsburgh, PA 15237
Phone: (412) 536-1271
Fax: (412) 536-1048
E-mail: admissions@laroche.edu
http://www.laroche.edu
Computer/information sciences—
general, information technology.

La Salle University
1900 West Olney Avenue
Philadelphia, PA 19141
Phone: (215) 951-1500
Fax: (215) 951-1656
E-mail: admiss@lasalle.edu
http://www.lasalle.edu
Applied mathematics, computer/
information sciences—general,
human resources management,
information systems,
information technology,
statistics.

Lehigh University
27 Memorial Drive West
Bethlehem, PA 18015
Phone: (610) 758-3000
Fax: (610) 758-4361
E-mail: admissions@lehigh.edu
http://www.lehigh.edu
Computer engineering, information
systems, statistics.

Lincoln University
1570 Baltimore Pike, P.O. Box 179
Lincoln University, PA 19352
Phone: (610) 932-8300
Fax: (610) 932-1209
E-mail: admiss@lincoln.edu
http://www.lincoln.edu
Human resources management.

Lock Haven University of Pennsylvania
Lock Haven University
Akeley Hall
Lock Haven, PA 17745
Phone: (570) 893-2027
Fax: (570) 893-2201
E-mail: admissions@lhup.edu
http://www.lhup.edu
Computer/information sciences—
general, library science.

Lycoming College
700 College Place, Box 164
Williamsport, PA 17701
Phone: (570) 321-4026
Fax: (570) 321-4317
E-mail: At Web site
http://www.lycoming.edu
Computer/information sciences—
general.

Mansfield University of Pennsylvania
Office of Admissions, Alumni Hall
Mansfield, PA 16933
Phone: (570) 662-4243
Fax: (570) 662-4121
E-mail: admissions@mansfield.edu
http://www.mansfield.edu
Computer/information sciences—
general, human resources
management, information
systems.

Marywood University
2300 Adams Avenue
Scranton, PA 18509
Phone: (570) 348-6234
Fax: (570) 961-4763
E-mail: ugadm@ac.marywood.edu
http://www.marywood.edu
Computer/information sciences—
general.

Mercyhurst College
Admissions
501 East 38th Street
Erie, PA 16546
Phone: (800) 825-1926
Fax: (814) 824-2071
E-mail: admug@mercyhurst.edu
http://www.mercyhurst.edu
Computer/information sciences—
general.

Messiah College
P.O. Box 3005
1 College Avenue
Grantham, PA 17027
Phone: (717) 691-6000
Fax: (717) 796-5374
E-mail: admiss@messiah.edu
http://www.messiah.edu
Human resources management,
information systems.

Millersville University of Pennsylvania
P.O. Box 1002
Millersville, PA 17551
Phone: (717) 872-3371
Fax: (717) 871-2147
E-mail: admissions@millersville.edu
http://www.millersville.edu
Computer/information sciences—
general.

Mount Aloysius College
7373 Admiral Peary Highway
Cresson, PA 16630
Phone: (814) 886-6383
Fax: (814) 886-6441
E-mail: admissions@mtaloy.edu
http://www.mtaloy.edu
Computer/information sciences—
general, information technology.

Muhlenberg College
2400 West Chew Street
Allentown, PA 18104
Phone: (484) 664-3200
Fax: (484) 664-3234
E-mail: admission@muhlenberg.edu
http://www.muhlenberg.edu
Computer/information sciences—
general, management information
systems.

Peirce College
1420 Pine Street
Philadelphia, PA 19102
Phone: (888) GO-PEIRCE ext. 9214
Fax: (215) 546-5996
E-mail: At Web site
http://www.peirce.edu
Information systems.

Pennsylvania College of Technology
One College Avenue
Williamsport, PA 17701
Phone: (800) 367-9222
Fax: (570) 321-5551
E-mail: admissions@pct.edu
http://www.pct.edu
Computer systems analysis.

Pennsylvania State University— Abington
106 Sutherland
Abington, PA 19001
Phone: (215) 881-7600
Fax: (215) 881-7317
E-mail: abingtonadmissions@psu.edu
http://www.abington.psu.edu
Computer engineering, information
systems, management
information systems, statistics.

Pennsylvania State University— Altoona
Office of Admissions
E108 Raymond Smith Building
Altoona, PA 16601
Phone: (800) 848-9843
Fax: (814) 949-5564
E-mail: aaadmit@psu.edu
http://www.aa.psu.edu
Computer engineering, information
systems, management
information systems, statistics.

Pennsylvania State University— Beaver
100 University Drive
Monaca, PA 15061
Phone: (724) 773-3800
Fax: (724) 773-3658
E-mail: br-admissions@psu.edu
http://www.br.psu.edu
Computer engineering, manage-
ment information systems.

Pennsylvania State University—Berks

14 Perkins Student Center
Reading, PA 19610
Phone: (610) 396-6060
Fax: (610) 396-6077
E-mail: admissions@psu.edu
http://www.bk.psu.edu
Computer engineering, information systems, management information systems, statistics.

Pennsylvania State University—Delaware County

25 Yearsley Mill Road
Media, PA 19083
Phone: (610) 892-1200
Fax: (610) 892-1357
E-mail: admissions-delco@psu.edu
http://www.de.psu.edu
Computer engineering, information systems, information technology, management information systems, statistics.

Pennsylvania State University—Dubois

108 Hiller
Dubois, PA 15801
Phone: (814) 375-4720
Fax: (814) 375-4784
E-mail: mabl@psu.edu
http://www.ds.psu.edu
Computer engineering, information systems, management information systems, statistics.

Pennsylvania State University—Erie, The Behrend College

5091 Station Road
Erie, PA 16563
Phone: (814) 898-6100
Fax: (814) 898-6044
E-mail: behrend.admissions@psu.edu
http://www.pserie.psu.edu
Computer engineering, information systems, management information systems, statistics.

Pennsylvania State University—Fayette

P.O. Box 519
Route 119 North

108 Williams Building
Uniontown, PA 15041
Phone: (724) 430-4130
Fax: (724) 430-4175
E-mail: feadm@psu.edu
http://www.fe.psu.edu
Computer engineering, information systems, management information systems, statistics.

Pennsylvania State University—Harrisburg

Swatapa Building
777 West Harrisburg Pike
Middletown, PA 17057
Phone: (717) 948-6250
Fax: (717) 948-6325
E-mail: hbgadmit@psu.edu
http://www.hbg.psu.edu
Applied mathematics, computer engineering, information systems, management information systems, statistics.

Pennsylvania State University—Hazelton

110 Administrative Building
76 University Drive
Hazelton, PA 18202
Phone: (570) 450-3142
Fax: (570) 450-3182
E-mail: admissions-hn@psu.edu
http://www.hn.psu.edu
Computer engineering, information systems, management information systems, statistics.

Pennsylvania State University—Lehigh Valley

8380 Mohr Lane
Academic Building
Fogelsville, PA 19051
Phone: (610) 285-5035
Fax: (610) 285-5220
E-mail: admissions-lv@psu.edu
http://www.lv.psu.edu
Computer engineering, information systems, management information systems, statistics.

Pennsylvania State University—McKeesport

100 Frable Building

4000 University Drive
McKeesport, PA 15132
Phone: (412) 675-9010
Fax: (412) 675-9056
E-mail: psumk@psu.edu
http://www.mk.psu.edu
Computer engineering, information systems, management information systems, statistics.

Pennsylvania State University—Mont Alto

1 Campus Drive
Mont Alto, PA 17237
Phone: (717) 749-6130
Fax: (717) 749-6132
E-mail: psuma@psu.edu
http://www.ma.psu.edu
Computer engineering, information systems, management information systems, statistics.

Pennsylvania State University—New Kensington

3550 Seventh Street Road, Route 780
Upper Barrell, PA 15068
Phone: (724) 334-5466
Fax: (724) 334-6111
E-mail: nkadmissions@psu.edu
http://www.nk.psu.edu
Computer engineering, information systems, management information systems, statistics.

Pennsylvania State University—Schuylkill—Capital College

200 University Drive
A102 Administrative Building
Schuylkill Haven, PA 17072
Phone: (570) 385-6252
Fax: (570) 385-6272
E-mail: sl-admissions@psu.edu
http://www.sl.psu.edu
Computer engineering, computer/information sciences—general, information systems, management information systems, statistics.

Pennsylvania State University—Shenango

147 Shenango Avenue

Sharon, PA 16146
Phone: (724) 983-2803
Fax: (724) 983-2820
E-mail: psushenango@psu.edu
http://www.shenango.psu.edu
Computer engineering, information
 systems, management
 information systems, statistics.

Pennsylvania State University—
 University Park

201 Shields Building
P.O. Box 3000
University Park, PA 16802
Phone: (814) 865-5471
Fax: (814) 863-7590
E-mail: admissions@psu.edu
http://www.psu.edu
Computer engineering, computer/
 information sciences—general,
 information systems,
 information technology,
 management information
 systems, statistics.

Pennsylvania State University—
 Wilkes-Barre

P.O. Box PSU
Lehman, PA 18627
Phone: (570) 675-9238
Fax: (570) 675-9113
E-mail: wbadmissions@psu.edu
http://www.psu.edu
Computer engineering, information
 systems, information
 technology, management
 information systems, statistics.

Pennsylvania State University—
 Worthington Scranton

120 Ridge View Drive
Dunmore, PA 18512
Phone: (570) 963-2500
Fax: (570) 963-2524
E-mail: wsadmissions@psu.edu
http://www.sn.psu.edu
Computer engineering, information
 systems, management
 information systems.

Pennsylvania State University—
 York

1031 Edgecomb Avenue

York, PA 17403
Phone: (717) 771-4040
Fax: (717) 771-4005
E-mail: ykadmisson@psu.edu
http://www.yk.psu.edu
Computer engineering, information
 systems, management
 information systems.

Point Park University

201 Wood Street
Pittsburgh, PA 15222
Phone: (412) 392-3430
Fax: (412) 391-1980
E-mail: enroll@ppc.edu
http://www.ppc.edu
Human resources management,
 information technology.

Robert Morris University

6001 University Boulevard
Moon Township, PA 15108
Phone: (412) 262-8206
Fax: (412) 299-2425
E-mail: enrollmentoffice@rmu.edu
http://www.rmu.edu
Applied mathematics, human
 resources management,
 information systems, software
 engineering.

Rosemont College

1400 Montgomery Avenue
Rosemont, PA 19010
Phone: (610) 526-2966
Fax: (610) 520-4399
E-mail: admissions@rosemont.edu
http://www.rosemont.edu
Human resources management.

Saint Francis University

P.O. Box 600
Loretto, PA 15940
Phone: (814) 472-3000
Fax: (814) 472-3335
E-mail: admissions@francis.edu
http://www.francis.edu
Computer/information sciences—
 general, information systems.

Saint Joseph's University

5600 City Avenue
Philadelphia, PA 19131
Phone: (610) 660-1300

Fax: (610) 660-1314
E-mail: admit@sju.edu
http://www.sju.edu
Computer/information sciences—
 general, information systems.

Saint Vincent College

3000 Fraser Purchase Road
Latrobe, PA 10650
Phone: (724) 537-4540
Fax: (724) 532-5069
E-mail: admission@stvincent.edu
http://www.stvincent.edu
Computer/information sciences—
 general.

Seton Hill University

1 Seton Hill Drive
Greensburg, PA 15601
Phone: (724) 838-4255
Fax: (724) 830-1294
E-mail: admit@setonhill.edu
http://www.setonhill.edu
Human resources management.

Shippensburg University of
 Pennsylvania

Old Main 105
1871 Old Main Drive
Shippensburg, PA 17257
Phone: (717) 477-1231
Fax: (717) 477-4016
E-mail: admiss@ship.edu
http://www.ship.edu
Computer/information sciences—
 general, computer systems
 analysis.

Slippery Rock University of
 Pennsylvania

Office of Admissions
146 North Hall Welcome Center
Slippery Rock, PA 16057
Phone: (724) 738-2015
Fax: (724) 738-2913
E-mail: apply@sru.edu
http://www.sru.edu
Information technology.

Susquehanna University

514 University Avenue
Susquehanna, PA 17870
Phone: (570) 372-4260

Fax: (570) 372-2722
E-mail: suadmiss@susque.edu
http://www.susque.edu
Human resources management, information systems.

Swarthmore College

500 College Avenue
Swarthmore, PA 19081
Phone: (610) 328-8300
Fax: (610) 328-8580
E-mail: admissions@swarthmore. edu
http://www.swarthmore.edu
Computer/information sciences— general.

Temple University

1801 North Broad Street
Philadelphia, PA 19122
Phone: (215) 204-7200
Fax: (215) 204-5694
E-mail: tuadm@mail.temple.edu
http://www.temple.edu
Computer/information sciences— general, information technology.

Thiel College

75 College Avenue
Greenville, PA 16125
Phone: (724) 589-2345
Fax: (724) 589-2013
E-mail: admission@thiel.edu
http://www.thiel.edu
Computer/information sciences— general, information systems.

University of Pennsylvania

1 College Hall
Philadelphia, PA 19104
Phone: (215) 898-7507
Fax: (215) 898-9670
E-mail: info@admissions.ugao. upenn.edu
http://www.upenn.edu
Cognitive science, computer engineering, computer/information sciences—general, human resources management, statistics.

University of Pittsburgh— Bradford

Office of Admissions—Hanley Library

300 Campus Drive
Bradford, PA 16701
Phone: (814) 362-7555
Fax: (814) 362-7578
E-mail: admissions@www.upb.pitt. edu
http://www.upb.pitt.edu
Applied mathematics, computer engineering.

University of Pittsburgh— Greensburg

1150 Mouth Pleasant Road
Greensburg, PA 15601
Phone: (724) 836-9880
Fax: (724) 836-7160
E-mail: upgadmit@pitt.edu
http://www.upg.pitt.edu
Applied mathematics, computer engineering, information systems, statistics.

University of Pittsburgh— Johnstown

157 Blackington Hall
450 Schoolhouse Road
Johnstown, PA 15904
Phone: (814) 269-7050
Fax: (814) 269-7044
E-mail: upjadmit@pitt.edu
http://www.upj.pitt.edu
Computer engineering, computer/ information sciences—general, information systems.

University of Pittsburgh— Pittsburgh

4227 Fifth Avenue
First Floor Alumni Hall
Pittsburgh, PA 15260
Phone: (412) 624-7488
Fax: (412) 648-8815
E-mail: oafa@pitt.edu
http://www.pitt.edu
Applied mathematics, computer engineering, information systems.

The University of Scranton

800 Linden Street
Scranton, PA 18501
Phone: (570) 941-7540
Fax: (570) 941-5928
E-mail: admissions@scranton.edu

http://www.scranton.edu
Human resources management, information systems.

University of the Sciences in Philadelphia

Admissions Office
600 South 43rd Street
Philadelphia, PA 19104
Phone: (215) 596-8810
Fax: (215) 596-8821
E-mail: admit@usip.edu
http://www.usip.edu
Computer/information sciences— general.

Villanova University

800 Lancaster Avenue
Villanova, PA 19085
Phone: (610) 519-4000
Fax: (610) 519-6450
E-mail: gotovu@villanova.edu
http://www.villanova.edu
Computer/information sciences— general, human resources management, information systems, management information systems.

Washington and Jefferson College

60 South Lincoln Street
Washington, PA 15301
Phone: (724) 223-6025
Fax: (724) 223-6534
E-mail: admission@washjeff.edu
http://www.washjeff.edu
Information technology.

Waynesburg College

51 West College Street
Waynesburg, PA 15370
Phone: (724) 852-3248
Fax: (724) 627-8124
E-mail: admissions@waynesburg.edu
http://www.waynesburg.edu
Computer/information sciences— general, information technology.

West Chester University of Pennsylvania

Messikomer Hall
100 West Rosedale Avenue

West Chester, PA 19383
Phone: (610) 436-3411
Fax: (610) 436-2907
E-mail: ugadmiss@wcupa.edu
http://www.wcupa.edu
Computer/information sciences—
general.

Westminster College

319 South Market Street
New Wilmington, PA 16172
Phone: (724) 946-7100
Fax: (724) 946-7171
E-mail: admis@westminster.edu
http://www.westminster.edu
Computer/information sciences—
general.

Widener University

One University Place
Chester, PA 19013
Phone: (610) 499-4126
Fax: (610) 499-4676
E-mail: admissions.office@widener.
edu
http://www.widener.edu
Computer/information sciences—
general, human resources
management, information systems, management information
systems.

Wilkes University

84 West South Street
Wilkes-Barre, PA 18766
Phone: (570) 408-4400
Fax: (570) 408-4904
E-mail: admissions@wilkes.edu
http://www.wilkes.edu
Computer/information sciences—
general, information systems.

Wilson College

1015 Philadelphia Avenue
Chambersburg, PA 17201
Phone: (717) 262-2002
Fax: (717) 262-1546
E-mail: admissions@wilson.edu
http://www.wilson.edu
Management information systems.

York College of Pennsylvania

Country Club Road

York, PA 17405
Phone: (800) 455-8018
Fax: (717) 849-1607
E-mail: admissions@ycp.edu
http://www.ycp.edu
Computer engineering, computer/
information sciences—general,
information systems, knowledge
management.

RHODE ISLAND

Brown University

P.O. Box 1876
45 Prospect Street
Providence, RI 02912
Phone: (401) 863-2378
Fax: (401) 863-9300
E-mail: admission_undergraduate@
brown.edu
http://www.brown.edu
Applied mathematics, cognitive
science, computer engineering,
statistics.

Bryant University

1150 Douglas Pike, Suite 2
Smithfield, RI 02917
Phone: (401) 232-6100
Fax: (401) 232-6741
E-mail: admission@bryant.edu
http://www.bryant.edu
Computer/information sciences—
general, information
technology.

Johnson & Wales University— Providence

8 Abbott Park Place
Providence, RI 02903
Phone: (401) 598-2310
Fax: (401) 598-2948
E-mail: admissions@jwu.edu
http://www.jwu.edu
Information systems.

New England Institute of Technology

2500 Post Road
Warwick, RI 02886
Phone: (800) 736-7744
Fax: NA
E-mail: At Web site

http://www.neit.edu
Computer/information sciences—
general, computer systems
analysis, information
technology.

Rhode Island College

Office of Undergraduate
Admissions
600 Mount Pleasant Avenue
Providence, RI 02908
Phone: (401) 456-8234
Fax: (401) 456-8817
E-mail: admissions@ric.edu
http://www.ric.edu
Computer/information sciences—
general, human resources
management, management
information systems.

Roger Williams University

One Old Ferry Road
Bristol, RI 02809
Phone: (401) 254-3500
Fax: (401) 254-3557
E-mail: admit@rwu.edu
http://www.rwu.edu
Computer engineering, computer/
information sciences—general,
management information
systems.

Salve Regina University

100 Ochre Point Avenue
Newport, RI 02840
Phone: (401) 341-2908
Fax: (401) 848-2823
E-mail: sruadmis@salve.edu
http://www.salve.edu
Information systems.

University of Rhode Island

Undergraduate Admissions Office
14 Upper College Road
Kingston, RI 02881
Phone: (401) 874-7100
Fax: (401) 874-5523
E-mail: uriadmit@etal.uri.edu
http://www.uri.edu
Computer engineering, computer/
information sciences—general,
management information
systems.

SOUTH CAROLINA

Anderson University
316 Boulevard
Anderson, SC 29621
Phone: (864) 231-5607
Fax: (864) 231-2033
E-mail: admissions@ac.edu
http://www.ac.edu
Computer/information sciences—
general, human resources
management, management
information systems.

Benedict College
Harden and Blanding Streets
Columbia, SC 29204
Phone: (803) 253-5143
Fax: (803) 253-5167
E-mail: admission@benedict.edu
http://www.benedict.edu
Computer/information sciences—
general.

Charleston Southern University
Enrollment Services
P.O. Box 118087
Charleston, SC 29433
Phone: (843) 863-7050
Fax: (843) 863-7070
E-mail: enropll@csuniv.edu
http://www.charlestonsouthern.edu
Applied mathematics, information
systems, management
information systems.

The Citadel
171 Moultrie Street
Charleston, SC 29409
Phone: (843) 953-5230
Fax: (843) 953-7036
E-mail: admissions@citadel.edu
http://www.citadel.edu
Computer/information sciences—
general.

Claflin University
400 Magnolia Street
Orangeburg, SC 29115
Phone: (803) 535-5340
Fax: (803) 535-5387
E-mail: mzeigler@claflin.edu
http://www.claflin.edu
Management information systems,
software engineering.

Clemson University
106 Sikes Hall, Box 345124
Clemson, SC 219634
Phone: (864) 656-2987
Fax: (864) 656-2464
E-mail: cuadmissions@clemson.
edu
http://www.clemson.edu
Computer engineering, computer/
information sciences—general,
information systems.

Coastal Carolina University
P.O. Box 261954
Conway, SC 29528
Phone: (843) 349-2026
Fax: (843) 349-2127
E-mail: admissions@coastal.edu
http://www.coastal.edu
Applied mathematics, computer/
information sciences—general.

College of Charleston
66 George Street
Charleston, SC 29424
Phone: (843) 953-5670
Fax: (843) 953-6322
E-mail: admissions@cofc.edu
http://www.cofc.edu
Information systems.

Converse College
580 East Main Street
Spartanburg, SC 29302
Phone: (864) 596-9040
Fax: (864) 596-9225
E-mail: admissions@converse.edu
http://www.converse.edu
Computer/information sciences—
general.

Francis Marion University
Office of Admissions
P.O. Box 100547
Florence, SC 29501
Phone: (843) 661-1231
Fax: (843) 661-4635
E-mail: admissions@marion.edu
http://www.marion.edu
Computer/information
sciences—general, management
information systems.

Furman University
3300 Poinsett Highway
Greenville, SC 29613
Phone: (864) 294-2034
Fax: (864) 294-3127
E-mail: admissions@furman.edu
http://www.furman.edu
Management information systems.

Lander University
320 Stanley Avenue
Greenwood, SC 29649
Phone: (864) 388-8307
Fax: (864) 388-8125
E-mail: admissions@lander.edu
http://www.lander.edu
Computer/information sciences—
general.

Limestone College
1115 College Drive
Gaffney, SC 29340
Phone: (864) 488-4549
Fax: (864) 487-8706
E-mail: admiss@limestone.edu
http://www.limestone.edu
Systems administration.

South Carolina State University
300 College Street NE
Orangeburg, SC 29117
Phone: (800) 260-5956
Fax: (803) 536-8990
E-mail: admissions@scsu.edu
http://www.scsu.edu
Computer/information sciences—
general.

Southern Wesleyan University
907 Wesleyan Drive
P.O. Box 1020
Central, SC 29630
Phone: (864) 644-5550
Fax: (864) 644-5972
E-mail: admissions@swu.edu
http://www.swu.edu
Human resources management,
information technology.

University of South Carolina—
Aiken
471 University Parkway
Aiken, SC 29801

Phone: (803) 641-3366
Fax: (803) 641-3727
E-mail: admit@sc.edu
http://www.usca.edu
Applied mathematics, computer
    engineering, statistics.

University of South Carolina—Columbia

Office of Undergraduate Admissions
Columbia, SC 29208
Phone: (803) 777-7000
Fax: (803) 777-0101
E-mail: admissions-ugrad@sc.edu
http://www.sc.edu
Computer engineering, statistics.

University of South Carolina—Upstate

800 University Way
Spartanburg, SC 29303
Phone: (864) 503-5246
Fax: (864) 503-5727
E-mail: dstewart@uscs.edu
http://www.uscs.edu
Applied mathematics, computer
    engineering, computer/
    information sciences—general,
    information systems, statistics.

Voorhees College

P.O. Box 678
Denmark, SC 29042
Phone: (803) 703-7111
Fax: (803) 793-1117
E-mail: white@vooorhees.edu
http://www.voorhees.edu
Computer/information sciences—
    general, management information
    systems.

Winthrop University

701 Oakland Avenue
Rock Hill, SC 29733
Phone: (803) 323-2137
Fax: (803) 323-2137
E-mail: admissions@winthrop.edu
http://www.winthrop.edu
Computer/information sciences—
    general.

Wofford College

429 North Church Street

Spartanburg, SC 29303
Phone: (864) 597-4130
Fax: (864) 597-4147
E-mail: admission@wofford.edu
http://www.wofford.edu
Computer/information sciences—
    general.

SOUTH DAKOTA

Black Hills State University

1200 University Street, Unit 9502
Spearfish, SD 57799
Phone: (605) 642-6343
Fax: (605) 642-6254
E-mail: admissions@bhsu.edu
http://www.bhsu.edu
Human resources management.

Dakota State University

Enrollment Services
820 North Washington Avenue
Madison, SD 57042
Phone: (605) 256-5139
Fax: (605) 256-5020
E-mail: yourfuture@dsu.edu
http://www.dsu.edu
Computer/information sciences—
    general, information systems.

Mount Mary College

1105 West Eighth Street
Yankton, SD 57078
Phone: (605) 668-1545
Fax: (605) 668-1607
E-mail: mmcadmit@mtmc.edu
http://www.mtmc.edu
Information technology.

Northern State University

1200 South Jay Street
Aberdeen, SD 57401
Phone: (605) 626-2544
Fax: (605) 626-2431
E-mail: admissions@northern.edu
http://www.northern.edu
Computer/information sciences—
    general.

South Dakota School of Mines and Technology

501 East Saint Joseph Street
Rapid City, SD 57701

Phone: (605) 394-2414
Fax: (605) 394-6131
E-mail: admissions@sdsmt.edu
http://www.sdsmt.edu
Computer engineering.

South Dakota State University

P.O. Box 2201
Brookings, SD 57007
Phone: (605) 688-4121
Fax: (605) 688-6891
E-mail: admissions@sdstate.edu
http://www.sdstate.edu
Computer/information sciences—
    general, software engineering.

University of Sioux Falls

1101 West Twenty-second Street
Sioux Falls, SD 57105
Phone: (605) 331-6600
Fax: (605) 331-6615
E-mail: admissions@usiouxfalls.edu
http://www.usiouxfalls.edu
Applied mathematics, computer/
    information sciences—general.

The University of South Dakota

414 East Clark Street
Vermillion, SD 57069
Phone: (605) 677-5434
Fax: (605) 677-6323
E-mail: admiss@usd.edu
http://www.usd.edu
Computer/information sciences—
    general.

TENNESSEE

Aquinas College

4210 Harding Road
Nashville, TN 37205
Phone: (615) 297-7545
Fax: (615) 297-7970
E-mail: info@aquinascollege.edu
http://www.aquinascollege.edu
Management information systems.

Austin Peay State University

P.O. Box 4548
Clarksville, TN 37044
Phone: (931) 221-7661
Fax: (931) 221-6168
E-mail: admissions@apsu.edu

http://www.apsu.edu
Computer/information sciences—
    general.

Belmont University
1900 Belmont Boulevard
Nashville, TN 37212
Phone: (615) 460-6785
Fax: (615) 460-5434
E-mail: buadmission@mail.
    belmont.edu
http://www.belmont.edu
Information systems, management
    information systems.

Bethel College
325 Cherry Avenue
McKenzie, TN 38201
Phone: (731) 352-4030
Fax: (731) 352-4069
E-mail: admissons@bethel-college.
    edu
http://www.bethel-college.edu
Applied mathematics, computer/
    information sciences—general.

Bryan College
P.O. Box 7000
Dayton, TN 37321
Phone: (423) 775-2041
Fax: (423) 775-7199
E-mail: admissbryan.edu
http://www.bryan.edu
Management information systems.

Carson-Newman College
1646 Russell Avenue
Jefferson City, TN 37760
Phone: (865) 471-3223
Fax: (865) 471-3502
E-mail: admitme@cn.edu
http://www.cn.edu
Computer/information sciences—
    general.

Christian Brothers University
Admissions
P.O. Box T-6
650 East Parkway South
Memphis, TN 38104
Phone: (901) 321-3205
Fax: (901) 321-3202
E-mail: admissions@chu.edu

http://www.chu.edu
Computer engineering.

Crichton College
255 North Highland Street
Memphis, TN 38111
Phone: (901) 320-9797
Fax: (901) 320-9791
E-mail: info@crichton.edu
http://www.crichton.edu
Management information systems.

East Tennessee State University
P.O. Box 70731
Johnson City, TN 37614
Phone: (423) 439-4213
Fax: (423) 439-4630
E-mail: go2etsu@etsu.edu
http://www.etsu.edu
Computer/information sciences—
    general.

Freed-Hardeman University
158 East Main Street
Henderson, TN 38340
Phone: (731) 989-6651
Fax: (731) 989-6047
E-mail: admissions@fhu.edu
http://www.fhu.edu
Computer/information sciences—
    general, human resources
    management, management
    information systems.

Lambuth University
705 Lambuth Boulevard
Jackson, TN 38301
Phone: (731) 425-3223
Fax: (731) 425-3496
E-mail: admit@lambuth.edu
http://www.lambuth.edu
Computer/information
    sciences—general, management
    information systems.

Lee University
P.O. Box 3450
Cleveland, TN 37320
Phone: (423) 614-8500
Fax: (423) 614-8533
E-mail: admissions@leeuniversity.
    edu
http://www.leeuniversity.edu
Information systems.

Lincoln Memorial University
Cumberland Gap Parkway
Harrogate, TN 37752
Phone: (423) 869-6280
Fax: (423) 869-6250
E-mail: At Web site
http://www.lmunet.edu
Computer/information sciences—
    general.

Lipscomb University
One University Park Drive
Nashville, TN 37204
Phone: (800) 333-4358
Fax: (615) 269-1804
E-mail: admissions@lipscomb.edu
http://www.lipscomb.edu
Human resources management,
    information technology.

Maryville College
502 East Lamar Alexander Parkway
Maryville, TN 37804
Phone: (865) 981-8092
Fax: (865) 981-8005
E-mail: admissions@
    maryvillecollege.edu
http://www.maryvillecollege.edu
Computer/information sciences—
    general.

Middle Tennessee State University
Office of Admissions
1301 East Main Street
Murfreesboro, TN 37132
Phone: (800) 433-6878
Fax: (615) 898-5478
E-mail: admissions@mtsu.edu
http://www.mtsu.edu
Computer/information
    sciences—general, management
    information systems.

Milligan College
P.O. Box 210
Milligan College, TN 37682
Phone: (423) 461-8730
Fax: (423) 461-8982
E-mail: admissions@milligan.edu
http://www.milligan.edu
Computer/information sciences—
    general.

Southern Adventist University
P.O. Box 370
Collegedale, TN 37315
Phone: (423) 238-2844
Fax: (423) 238-3005
E-mail: admissions@southern.edu
http://www.southern.edu
Management information systems, system administration.

Tennessee State University
P.O. Box 5006
Cookeville, TN 38505
Phone: (931) 372-3888
Fax: (931) 372-6250
E-mail: jcade@tnstate.edu
http://www.tnstate.edu
Computer/information sciences—general.

Tennessee Technological University
P.O. Box 5006
Cookeville, TN 38505
Phone: (931) 372-3888
Fax: (931) 372-6250
E-mail: admissions@tntech.edu
http://www.tntech.edu
Computer engineering, computer/information sciences—general.

Tennessee Wesleyan College
P.O. Box 40
Athens, TN 37371
Phone: (423) 745-7504
Fax: (423) 745-9335
E-mail: twilliams.twcnet.edu
http://www.twcnet.edu
Computer/information sciences—general, human resources management.

Trevecca Nazarene University
333 Murfreesboro Road
Nashville, TN 37210
Phone: (888) 210-4868
Fax: (615) 248-7406
E-mail: At Web site
http://www.trevecca.edu
Management information systems.

Union University
1050 Union University Drive
Jackson, TN 38305
Phone: (731) 661-5000
Fax: (731) 661-5017
E-mail: cgriffin@uu.edu
http://www.uu.edu
Computer/information sciences—general.

University of Memphis
229 Administration Building
Memphis, TN 38152
Phone: (901) 678-2111
Fax: (901) 678-3053
E-mail: recruitment@memphis.edu
http://www.memphis.edu
Computer engineering, computer engineering technology, management information systems.

University of Tennessee—Chattanooga
615 McCallie Avenue
131 Hooper Hall
Chattanooga, TN 37403
Phone: (423) 425-4662
Fax: (423) 425-4157
E-mail: yancy-freeman@utc.edu
http://www.utc.edu
Applied mathematics, computer/information sciences—general.

University of Tennessee—Knoxville
320 Science Building
Circle Park Drive
Knoxville, TN 37996
Phone: (865) 974-2184
Fax: (865) 974-6341
E-mail: admissions@utk.edu
http://www.utk.edu
Computer/information sciences—general.

University of Tennessee—Martin
200 Hall-Moody Administrative Building
Martin, TN 38238
Phone: (731) 881-7020
Fax: (731) 881-7029
E-mail: admitme@utm.edu
http://www.utm.edu
Management information systems.

University of the South
735 University Avenue
Sewanee, TN 37383
Phone: (800) 522-2234
Fax: (931) 598-1145
E-mail: admiss@sewanee.edu
http://www.admission.sewanee.edu
Computer/information sciences—general.

Vanderbilt University
2305 West End Avenue
Nashville, TN 37203
Phone: (615) 322-2561
Fax: (615) 343-7765
E-mail: admissions@vanderbilt.edu
http://www.vanderbilt.edu
Computer engineering, computer/information sciences—general, human resources management.

TEXAS

Angelo State University
2601 West Avenue
San Angelo, TX 76909
Phone: (325) 942-2041
Fax: (325) 942-2078
E-mail: admissions@angelo.edu
http://www.angelo.edu
Computer/information sciences—general.

Baylor University
P.O. Box 97056
Waco, TX 76798
Phone: (254) 710-3435
Fax: (254) 710-3436
E-mail: admissions_serv_office@baylor.edu
http://www.baylor.edu
Applied mathematics, human resources management, management information systems, statistics.

Dallas Baptist University
3000 Mountain Creek Parkway
Dallas, TX 75211
Phone: (214) 333-5360
Fax: (214) 333-5447
E-mail: admiss@dbu.edu

http://www.dbu.edu
Computer/information
sciences—general, management
information systems.

DeVry University—Irving
4800 Regent Boulevard
Irving, TX 75063
Phone: (972) 929-5777
Fax: (972) 929-2860
E-mail: cwilliams@mail.dal.devry.
edu
http://www.devry.edu
Computer engineering technology,
computer systems analysis,
information technology.

East Texas Baptist University
1209 North Grove Street
Marshall, TX 75670
Phone: (903) 923-2000
Fax: (903) 923-2001
E-mail: admissions@etbu.edu
http://www.etbu.edu
Computer/information
sciences—general, management
information systems.

Houston Baptist University
7502 Fondren Road
Houston, TX 77074
Phone: (281) 649-3211
Fax: (281) 649-3217
E-mail: unadm@hbu.edu
http://www.hbu.edu
Information resources management,
management information
systems.

Howard Payne University
Howard Payne Station
Brownwood, TX 76801
Phone: (325) 649-8027
Fax: (325) 649-8901
E-mail: enroll@hputx.edu
http://www.hputx.edu
Information systems.

Huston-Tillotson University
900 Chicon Street
Austin, TX 8702
Phone: (512) 505-3028

Fax: (512) 505-3192
E-mail: thshakir@htu.edu
http://www.htu.edu
Computer/information sciences—
general.

Jarvis Christian College
P.O. Box 1470
Hawkins, TX 75765
Phone: (903) 769-5730
Fax: (903) 769-1282
E-mail: felecia_tyiska@jarvis.edu
http://www.jarvis.edu
Computer/information sciences—
general.

Lamar University
P.O. Box 10009
Beaumont, TX 77710
Phone: (409) 880-8888
Fax: (409) 880-8463
E-mail: admissions@hal.lamar.edu
http://www.lamar.edu
Applied mathematics, computer/
information sciences—general,
human resources management,
management information
systems.

LeTourneau University
P.O. Box 7001
Longview, TX 75607
Phone: (903) 233-3400
Fax: (903) 233-3411
E-mail: admissions@letu.edu
http://www.letu.edu
Computer engineering, computer
engineering technology,
computer/information
sciences—general, human
resources management,
information systems,
management information
systems.

Lubbock Christian University
5601 19th Street
Lubbock, TX 79407
Phone: (800) 720-7151
Fax: (806) 720-7162
E-mail: admissions@lcu.edu
http://www.lcu.edu
Management information systems.

McMurry University
South 14th and Sayles Boulevard
Abilene, TX 79697
Phone: (915) 793-4700
Fax: (915) 793-4718
E-mail: admissions@mcm.edu
http://www.mcm.edu
Computer/information sciences—
general, information systems,
management information
systems.

Midwestern State University
3410 Taft Boulevard
Wichita Falls, TX 76308
Phone: (940) 397-4334
Fax: (940) 397-4672
E-mail: admissions@mwsu.edu
http://www.mwsu.edu
Computer/information
sciences—general, management
information systems.

Northwood University—Texas Campus
1114 West FM 1382
Cedar Hill, TX 75104
Phone: (800) 927-9663
Fax: (972) 291-3824
E-mail: txadmit@northwood.edu
http://www.northwood.edu/tx
Computer/information
sciences—general, management
information systems.

Our Lady of the Lake University of San Antonio
Admissions Office
411 South West 24th Street
San Antonio, TX 78207
Phone: (210) 434-6711
Fax: (210) 431-4036
E-mail: admission@lake.ollusa.edu
http://www.ollusa.edu
Computer/information sciences—
general, human resources
management, management
information systems.

Paul Quinn College
3837 Simpson Stuart Road
Dallas, TX 75241
Phone: (214) 376-1000
Fax: NA

E-mail: admissions@pqc.edu
http://www.pqc.edu
Computer/information sciences—
general.

Prairie View A&M University

P.O. Box 3089
University Drive
Prairie View, TX 77446
Phone: (936) 857-2626
Fax: (936) 857-2699
E-mail: admissions@pvamu.edu
http://www.pvamu.edu
Computer engineering, computer
engineering technology, computer/
information sciences—general,
management information
systems.

Rice University

P.O. Box 1892
Houston, TX 77251
Phone: (713) 348-7423
Fax: (713) 348-5952
E-mail: admission@rice.edu
http://www.rice.edu
Applied mathematics, cognitive
science, computer engineering,
statistics.

St. Edward's University

3001 South Congress Avenue
Austin, TX 78704
Phone: (512) 448-8400
Fax: (512)464-8877
E-mail: seu.admit@admin.
stedwards.edu
http://www.stedwards.edu
Computer/information sciences—
general.

St. Mary's University

One Camino Santa Maria
San Antonio, TX 78228
Phone: (210) 436-3126
Fax: (210) 431-6742
E-mail: uadm@stmarytx.edu
http://www.stmarytx.edu
Computer engineering, computer/
information sciences—general,
human resources management.

Sam Houston State University

P.O. Box 2418, SHSU

Huntsville, TX 77341
Phone: (936) 294-1828
Fax: (936) 294-3758
E-mail: admissions@shsu.edu
http://www.shsu.edu
Computer/information sciences—
general, human resources
management.

Schreiner University

2100 Memorial Boulevard
Kenville, TX 78028
Phone: (830) 792-7217
Fax: (830) 792-7226
E-mail: admissions@schreiner.edu
http://www.schreiner.edu
Management information systems.

Southern Methodist University

P.O. Box 750296
Dallas, TX 75275
Phone: (214) 768-2058
Fax: (214) 768-2507
E-mail: enroll_serv@mail.smu.edu
http://www.smu.edu
Computer engineering, manage-
ment information systems,
statistics.

Southwestern Adventist University

P.O. Box 567
Keene, TX 76059
Phone: (800) 433-2240
Fax: (817) 645-3921
E-mail: illingworth@swac.edu
http://www.swac.edu
Applied mathematics, computer/
information sciences—general,
management information
systems.

Stephen F. Austin State University

P.O. Box 13051, SFA Station
Nacogdoches, TX 75962
Phone: (936) 468-2504
Fax: (936) 468-3849
E-mail: admissions@sfasu.edu
http://www.sfasu.edu
Computer/information sciences—
general, data processing
technology.

Sul Ross State University

P.O. Box C-2
Alpine, TX 79832
Phone: (915) 837-8050
Fax: (915) 837-8431
E-mail: admissions@sulross.edu
http://www.sulross.edu
Computer/information sciences—
general.

Tarleton State University

P.O. Box T-0030
Tarleton Station
Stephenville, TX 76402
Phone: (254) 968-9125
Fax: (254) 968-9951
E-mail: uadm@tarleton.edu
http://www.tarleton.edu
Computer/information sciences—
general, human resources
management, management
information systems.

Texas A&M University— Commerce

P.O. Box 3011
Commerce, TX 75429
Phone: (903) 886-5106
Fax: (903) 886-5888
E-mail: admissions@tamu-
commerce.edu
http://www.tamu-commerce.edu
Applied mathematics, computer
engineering, computer/
information sciences—general,
human resources management,
information systems, library
science, management
information systems.

Texas A&M University— Corpus Christi

6300 Ocean Drive
Corpus Christi, TX 78412
Phone: (361) 825-2624
Fax: (361) 825-5887
E-mail: judith.perales@mail.
tamucc.edu
http://www.tamucc.edu
Applied mathematics, computer
engineering, computer/
information sciences—general.

Texas A&M University— Galveston

Admissions Office
P. O. Box 1675
Galveston, TX 77553
Phone: (409) 740-4414
Fax: (409) 740-4731
E-mail: seaaggie@tamug.edu
http://www.tamug.edu
Applied mathematics, computer engineering, computer/ information sciences—general.

Texas A&M University— Kingsville

700 University Boulevard, MSC 128
Kingsville, TX 78363
Phone: (361) 593-2315
Fax: (361) 593-2195
E-mail: ksossrx@tamuk.edu
http://www.tamuk.edu
Applied mathematics, computer engineering, computer/information sciences—general, management information systems.

Texas A&M University— Texarkana

P.O. Box 5518
Texarkana, TX 75505
Phone: (903) 223-3069
Fax: (903) 223-3140
E-mail: admissions@tamut.edu
http://www.tamut.edu
Human resources management, management information systems.

Texas Christian University

Office of Admissions
TCU, P.O. Box 297013
Fort Worth, TX 76129
Phone: (817) 257-7490
Fax: (817) 257-7268
E-mail: frogmail@tcu.edu
http://www.tcu.edu
Computer/information sciences— general.

Texas Lutheran University

1000 West Court Street
Seguin, TX 78155
Phone: (830) 372-8050
Fax: (830) 372-8096
E-mail: admissions@tlu.edu
http://www.tlu.edu
Information systems.

Texas Southern University

3100 Cleburne Street
Houston, TX 77004
Phone: (713) 313-7420
Fax: (713) 313-4317
E-mail: admissions@tsu.edu
http://www.tsu.edu
Computer/information sciences— general.

Texas State University—San Marcos

429 North Guadalupe Street
San Marcos, TX 78666
Phone: (512) 245-2364
Fax: (512) 245-9020
E-mail: admissions@txstate.edu
http://www.txstate.edu
Applied mathematics, computer/ information sciences—general, data processing technology, management information systems.

Texas Tech University

P.O. Box 45005
Lubbock, TX 79409
Phone: (806) 742-1480
Fax: (806) 742-0062
E-mail: admissions@ttu.edu
http://www.ttu.edu
Computer engineering, computer/ information sciences—general, management information systems.

Texas Wesleyan University

1201 Wesleyan Street
Fort Worth, TX 76105
Phone: (817) 531-4422
Fax: (817) 531-7515
E-mail: info@txwesleyan.edu
http://www.txwesleyan.edu
Computer/information sciences— general, information systems.

Trinity University

One Trinity Place
San Antonio, TX 78212
Phone: (210) 999-7207
Fax: (210) 999-8164
E-mail: admissions@trinity.edu
http://www.trinity.edu
Computer/information sciences— general.

University of Houston—Clear Lake

2700 Bay Area Boulevard
Houston, TX 77058
Phone: (281) 283-7600
Fax: (281) 283-2530
E-mail: admissions@cl.uh.edu
http://www.uhcl.edu
Computer engineering, computer/ information sciences—general, computer systems analysis, information systems.

University of Houston— Downtown

Admission Office
One Main Street
Houston, TX 77002
Phone: (713) 221-8522
Fax: (713) 221-8157
E-mail: uhdadmit@dt.uh.edu
http://www.uhd.edu
Applied mathematics, computer engineering, computer engineering technology, computer/ information sciences—general, computer systems analysis, information systems, management information systems.

University of Houston— Houston

Office of Admissions
122 East Cullen Building
Houston, TX 77204
Phone: (713) 743-1010
Fax: (713) 743-9633
E-mail: admissions@uh.edu
http://www.uh.edu
Applied mathematics, computer engineering, computer/information sciences—general, computer systems analysis, information systems, management information systems.

University of Houston—Victoria Campus
Enrollment Management Office, UHV
Victoria, TX 77901
Phone: (361) 788-6222
Fax: (361) 572-9377
E-mail: urbanom@jade.vic.uh.edu
http://www.vic.uh.edu
Applied mathematics, computer engineering, computer/information sciences—general, computer systems analysis, information systems.

University of Mary Hardin—Baylor
UMHB Box 8004
900 College Street
Belton, TX 76513
Phone: (254) 295-4520
Fax: (254) 295-5049
E-mail: admission@umhb.edu
http://www.umhb.edu
Computer/information sciences—general, information systems, management information systems.

University of North Texas
P.O. Box 311277
Denton, TX 76203
Phone: (940) 565-2681
Fax: (940) 565-2408
E-mail: undergrad@unt.edu
http://www.unt.edu
Computer/information sciences—general, human resources management, library science, management information systems.

University of St. Thomas
3800 Montrose Boulevard
Houston, TX 77006
Phone: (800) 856-8565
Fax: NA
E-mail: admissions@stthom.edu
http://www.stthom.edu
Management information systems.

University of Texas—Arlington
Office of Admissions

P.O. Box 19111
Arlington, TX 76019
Phone: (817) 272-6287
Fax: (817) 272-3435
E-mail: admissions@uta.edu
http://www.uta.edu
Computer engineering, management information systems, software engineering.

University of Texas—Austin
P.O. Box 8058
Austin, TX 78713
Phone: (512) 475-7440
Fax: (512) 475-7475
E-mail: frmn@uts.cc.utexas.edu
http://www.utexas.edu
Computer/information sciences—general, management information systems.

University of Texas—Brownsville
80 Fort Brown Street
Brownsville, TX 78520
Phone: (956) 544-8295
Fax: (956) 983-7810
E-mail: admissions@utb.edu
http://www.utb.edu
Computer/information sciences—general, information systems.

University of Texas—Dallas
P.O. Box 830688, MC 11
Richardson, TX 75083
Phone: (972) 883-2342
Fax: (972) 883-6803
E-mail: admissions-status@utdallas.edu
http://www.utdallas.edu
Applied mathematics, computer engineering, computer/information sciences—general, statistics.

University of Texas—El Paso
500 West University Avenue
El Paso, TX 79968
Phone: (915) 747-5576
Fax: (915) 747-8893
E-mail: admission@utep.edu
http://www.utep.edu
Applied mathematics, computer engineering, computer/

information sciences—general, management information systems, statistics.

University of Texas of the Permian Basin
4901 East University Boulevard
Odessa, TX 79762
Phone: (915) 552-2605
Fax: (915) 552-3605
E-mail: admissions@utpb.edu
http://www.utpb.edu
Computer/information sciences—general, information systems.

University of Texas—Pan American
Office of Admissions and Records
1201 West University Drive
Edinburgh, TX 78541
Phone: (956) 381-2201
Fax: (956) 381-2212
E-mail: admissions@panam.edu
http://www.panam.edu
Computer/information sciences—general, management information systems.

University of Texas—San Antonio
6900 North Loop 1604 West
San Antonio, TX 78249
Phone: (210) 458-4530
Fax: (210) 458-7716
E-mail: prospects@utsa.edu
http://www.utsa.edu
Computer engineering, computer/information sciences—general, management information systems, statistics.

University of Texas—Tyler
3900 University Boulevard
Tyler, TX 75799
Phone: (903) 566-7202
Fax: (903) 566-7068
E-mail: info@uttyler.edu
http://www.uttyler.edu
Computer/information sciences—general.

University of the Incarnate Word
4301 Broadway, Box 285

San Antonio, TX 78209
Phone: (210) 829-6005
Fax: (210) 829-3921
E-mail: admis@universe.uiwtx.edu
http://www.uiw.edu
Human resources management, information technology.

West Texas A&M University
P.O. Box 60907
Canyon, TX 79016
Phone: (806) 651-2020
Fax: (806) 651-5268
E-mail: admissions@mail.wtamu.edu
http://www.wtamu.edu
Computer/information sciences—general, management information systems.

UTAH

Brigham Young University
A-153 ASB
Provo, UT 84602
Phone: (801) 422-2507
Fax: (801) 422-0005
E-mail: admissions@byu.edu
http://www.byu.edu
Computer engineering, information resources management, information technology, management information systems, statistics.

Dixie State College of Utah
225 South 700 East
St. George, UT 84770
Phone: (435) 652-7500
Fax: NA
E-mail: At Web site
http://new.dixie.edu
Data processing technology.

Southern Utah University
Admissions Office
351 West Center
Cedar City, UT 84720
Phone: (435) 586-7740
Fax: (435) 865-8223
E-mail: adminfo@suu.edu
http://www.suu.edu
Information systems, management information systems, statistics.

Stevens-Henager College
383 West Vine Street
Murray, UT 84123
Phone: (800) 622-2640
Fax: NA
E-mail: At Web site
http://www.stevenshenager.edu
Computer/information sciences—general.

University of Utah
210 South 1460 East, Room 250 South
Salt Lake City, UT 84112
Phone: (801) 581-7281
Fax: (801) 585-7864
E-mail: admiss@sa.utah.edu
http://www.utah.edu
Computer engineering, management information systems.

Utah State University
0160 Old Main Hill
Logan, UT 84322
Phone: (435) 797-1079
Fax: (435) 797-3708
E-mail: admit@cc.usu.edu
http://www.usu.ed
Computer engineering, computer/information sciences—general, human resources management, information systems, statistics.

Utah Valley State College
800 West University Parkway
Orem, UT 84058
Phone: (801) 863-INFO
Fax: (801) 863-7305
E-mail: uvstart@uvsc.edu
http://www.uvsc.edu
Data processing technology.

Weber State University
1137 University Circle
Ogden, UT 84408
Phone: (801) 626-6744
Fax: (801) 626-6747
E-mail: admissions@weber.edu
http://www.weber.edu
Applied mathematics, computer/information sciences—general, human resources management, information systems, management information systems.

Castleton State College
Office of Admissions
Castleton, VT 05735
Phone: (802) 468-1213
Fax: (802) 468-1476
E-mail: info@castleton.edu
http://www.castleton.edu
Computer/information sciences—general, statistics.

Champlain College
163 South Willard Street
P.O. Box 670
Burlington, VT 05402
Phone: (802) 860-2727
Fax: (802) 860-2767
E-mail: admission@champlain.edu
http://www.champlain.edu
Computer/information sciences—general, computer systems analysis, human resources management, information systems, software engineering.

Lyndon State College
1001 College Road
Lyndonville, VT 05851
Phone: (802) 626-6200
Fax: (802) 626-6335
E-mail: admissions@lyndonstate.edu
http://www.lyndonstate.edu
Computer/information sciences—general.

Marlboro College
P.O. Box A, South Road
Marlboro, VT 05344
Phone: (802) 258-9236
Fax: (802) 451-7555
E-mail: admissions@marlboro.edu
http://www.marlboro.edu
Computer/information sciences—general.

Norwich University
Admissions Office
158 Harmon Drive
Northfield, VT 05663
Phone: (802) 485-2001
Fax: (802) 485-2032
E-mail: nuadm@norwich.edu

http://www.norwich.edu
Computer/information sciences—
    general.

Saint Michael's College
1 Winooski Park
Colchester, VT 05439
Phone: (802) 654-3000
Fax: (802) 654-2906
E-mail: admission@smcvt.edu
http://www.smcvt.edu
Information systems.

University of Vermont
Admissions Office
194 South Prospect Street
Burlington, VT 05401
Phone: (802) 656-3370
Fax: (802) 656-8611
E-mail: admissions@uvm.edu
http://www.uvm.edu
Computer/information sciences—
    general, information systems,
    statistics.

Vermont Technical College
P.O. Box 500
Randolph Center, VT 05061
Phone: (800) 442-8821
Fax: NA
E-mail: At Web site
http://www.vtc.edu
Computer engineering, computer/
    information sciences—general,
    information technology,
    software engineering, systems
    administration.

VIRGINIA

Averett University
420 West Main Street
Danville, VA 24541
Phone: (434) 791-4996
Fax: (434) 797-2784
E-mail: admit@averett.edu
http://www.averett.edu
Information systems.

Bluefield College
3000 College Drive
Bluefield, VA 24605
Phone: (540) 326-4214

Fax: (540) 326-4288
E-mail: bluefield@bluefield.edu
http://www.bluefield.edu
Computer/information sciences—
    general.

Bridgewater College
402 East College Street
Bridgewater, VA 22812
Phone: (540) 828-5375
Fax: (540) 828-5481
E-mail: admissions@bridgewater.edu
http://www.bridgewater.edu
Management information systems.

Christopher Newport University
1 University Place
Newport News, VA 23606
Phone: (757) 594-7015
Fax: (757) 594-7333
E-mail: admit@cnu.edu
http://www.cnu.edu
Computer engineering, computer/
    information sciences—general.

DeVry University—Arlington
2450 Crystal Drive
Arlington, VA 22202
Phone: (703) 414-4100
Fax: (703) 414-4040
E-mail: admissions@devry.edu
http://www.devry.edu
Information systems.

Eastern Mennonite University
1200 Park Road
Harrisonburg, VA 22802
Phone: (540) 432-4118
Fax: (540) 432-4444
E-mail: admiss@emu.edu
http://www.emu.edu
Computer systems analysis.

ECPI College of Technology
5555 Greenwich Road
Virginia Beach, VA 23462
Phone: (866) 499-0336
Fax: NA
E-mail: At Web site
http://www.ecpi.edu/campus/
    virginia_beach_va
Computer/information sciences—
    general.

Emory and Henry College
P.O. Box 947
Emory, VA 24327
Phone: (800) 848-5493
Fax: (276) 944-6935
E-mail: ehadmiss@ehc.edu
http://www.ehc.edu
Computer/information sciences—
    general.

Ferrum College
P.O. Box 1000
Ferrum, VA 24088
Phone: (540) 365-4290
Fax: (540) 365-4366
E-mail: admissions@ferrum.edu
http://www.ferrum.edu
Information systems.

George Mason University
Undergraduate Admissions Office
400 University Drive, MSN 3A4
Fairfax, VA 22030
Phone: (703) 993-2400
Fax: (703) 993-2392
E-mail: admissions@gmu.edu
http://www.gmu.edu
Computer/information sciences—
    general.

Hampden-Sydney College
P.O. Box 667
Hampden-Sydney, VA 23943
Phone: (434) 223-6120
Fax: (434) 223-6346
E-mail: hsapp@hsc.edu
http://www.hsc.edu
Applied mathematics.

Hampton University
Office of Admissions
Hampton, VA 23668
Phone: (757) 727-5328
Fax: (757) 727-5095
E-mail: admissions@hamptonu.edu
http://www.hamptonu.edu
Computer engineering, computer/
    information sciences—general,
    management information
    systems.

James Madison University
Sonner Hall, MSC 0101

Harrisonburg, VA 22807
Phone: (540) 568-5681
Fax: (540) 568-3332
E-mail: gotojmu@jmu.edu
http://www.jmu.edu
Computer/information sciences—
general, information systems.

Liberty University
1971 University Boulevard
Lynchburg, VA 24502
Phone: (434) 582-5985
Fax: (800) 542-2311
E-mail: admissions@liberty.edu
http://www.liberty.edu
Computer/information
sciences—general, management
information systems.

Longwood University
Admissions Office
201 High Street
Farmville, VA 23909
Phone: (434) 395-2060
Fax: (434) 395-2332
E-mail: admissions@longwood.
edu
http://www.longwood.edu
Computer/information
sciences—general, management
information systems.

Mary Baldwin College
P.O. Box 1500
Staunton, VA 24402
Phone: (540) 887-7019
Fax: (540) 887-7279
E-mail: admit@mbc.edu
http://www.mbc.edu
Applied mathematics, computer/
information sciences—general,
information systems.

Marymount University
2807 North Glebe Road
Arlington, VA 22207
Phone: (703) 284-1500
Fax: (703) 522-0349
E-mail: admissions@marymount.
edu
http://www.marymount.edu
Computer/information sciences—
general, information systems.

Norfolk State University
700 Park Avenue
Norfolk, VA 23504
Phone: (757) 823-8396
Fax: (757) 823-2078
E-mail: admissions@nsu.edu
http://www.nsu.edu
Computer engineering technology,
computer/information
sciences—general.

Old Dominion University
108 Rollins Hall
5215 Hampton Boulevard
Norfolk, VA 23529
Phone: (757) 683-3685
Fax: (757) 683-3255
E-mail: admit@odu.edu
http://www.odu.edu
Computer engineering, computer
engineering technology,
computer/information
sciences—general, management
information systems.

Potomac College
1029 Herndon Parkway
Herndon, VA 20170
Phone: (703) 709-5875
Fax: (703) 709-8972
E-mail: admissions.potomac@
gmail.com
http://www.potomac.edu
Computer/information sciences—
general, information technology.

Radford University
P.O. Box 6903
RU Station
Radford, VA 24142
Phone: (540) 831-5371
Fax: (540) 831-5038
E-mail: ruadmiss@radford.edu
http://www.radford.edu
Information systems, management
information systems.

Randolph-Macon College
P.O. Box 5005
Ashland, VA 23005
Phone: (804) 752-7305
Fax: (804) 752-4707
E-mail: admissions@rmc.edu

http://www.rmc.edu
Computer/information sciences—
general.

Roanoke College
221 College Lane
Salem, VA 24153
Phone: (540) 375-2270
Fax: (540) 375-2267
E-mail: admissions@roanoke.edu
http://www.roanoke.edu
Computer/information sciences—
general, information systems.

Saint Paul's College
115 College Drive
Lawrenceville, VA 23868
Phone: (434) 848-1856
Fax: (434) 848-6407
E-mail: admissions@saintpauls.edu
http://www.saintpauls.edu
Computer/information
sciences—general, management
information systems.

University of Northern Virginia
10021 Balls Ford Road
Manassas, VA 20109
Phone: (703) 392-0771
Fax: (703) 392- 0756
E-mail: At Web site
http://www.unva.edu
Computer/information sciences—
general, information technology.

University of Virginia
Office of Admissions
P.O. Box 400160
Charlottesville, VA 22906
Phone: (434) 982-3200
Fax: (434) 924-3587
E-mail: undergradadmission@
virginia.edu
http://www.virginia.edu
Applied mathematics, computer
engineering, computer/
information sciences—general.

**University of Virginia's
College—Wise**
1 College Avenue
Wise, VA 24293
Phone: (276) 328-0102

Fax: (276) 328-0251
E-mail: admissions@uvwise.edu
http://www.uvwise.edu
Management information systems.

Virginia Commonwealth University

821 West Franklin Street
P.O. Box 842526
Richmond, VA 23284
Phone: (804) 828-1222
Fax: (804) 828-1899
E-mail: vcuinfo@vcu.edu
http://www.vcu.edu
Computer engineering, computer/
information sciences—general,
information systems.

Virginia Intermont College

1013 Moore Street
Bristol, VA 24201
Phone: (276) 466-7856
Fax: (276) 466-7855
E-mail: viadmit@vic.edu
http://www.vic.edu
Computer/information sciences—
general.

Virginia Polytechnic Institute and State University

201 Burruss Hall
Blacksburg, VA 24061
Phone: (540) 231-6267
Fax: NA
E-mail: vtadmiss@vt.edu
http://www.vt.edu
Computer engineering, computer/
information sciences—general.

Virginia State University

One Hayden Street
P.O. Box 9018
Petersburg, VA 23806
Phone: (804) 524-5902
Fax: (804) 524-5056
E-mail: admiss@vsu.edu
http://www.vsu.edu
Computer engineering, information
technology.

Virginia Union University

Undergraduate Office of
Admissions
1500 North Lombardy Street

Richmond, VA 23220
Phone: (800) 368-3227
Fax: (804) 342-3511
E-mail: admission@vuu.edu
http://www.vuu.edu
Computer/information sciences—
general.

Washington and Lee University

204 West Washington Street
Lexington, VA 24450
Phone: (540) 458-8710
Fax: (540) 458-8062
E-mail: admissions@wlu.edu
http://www.wlu.edu
Computer/information sciences—
general.

WASHINGTON

Central Washington University

Admissions Office
400 East Eighth Avenue
Ellensburg, WA 98926
Phone: (509) 963-1211
Fax: (509) 963-3022
E-mail: cwuadmis@cwu.edu
http://www.cwu.edu
Computer/information sciences—
general.

DeVry University—Seattle

3600 South 344th Way
Federal Way, WA 98001
Phone: (253) 943-2800
Fax: (253) 943-3291
E-mail: admissions@sea.devry.edu
http://www.devry.edu
Computer engineering technology,
computer systems analysis,
information technology.

Eastern Washington University

526 Fifth Street
Cheney, WA 99004
Phone: (509) 359-2397
Fax: (509) 359-6692
E-mail: admissions@mail.ewu.edu
http://www.ewu.edu
Computer engineering, human
resources management, infor-
mation systems, management
information systems.

The Evergreen State College

2700 Evergreen Parkway NW
Office of Admissions
Olympia, WA 98505
Phone: (360) 867-6170
Fax: (360) 867-6576
E-mail: admissions@evergreen.edu
http://www.evergreen.edu
Computer/information sciences—
general.

Gonzaga University

502 East Boone Avenue
Spokane, WA 99258
Phone: (509) 323-6572
Fax: (509) 324-5780
E-mail: admissions@gonzaga.edu
http://www.gonzaga.edu
Computer engineering,
management information
systems.

Heritage University

3240 Fort Road
Toppenish, WA 98948
Phone: (509) 865-8508
Fax: (509) 865-8659
E-mail: 3w_admissions@heritage.
edu
http://www.heritage.edu
Computer/information sciences—
general, human resources
management.

Pacific Lutheran University

Office of Admissions
12180 Park Street South
Tacoma, WA 98447
Phone: (253) 535-7151
Fax: (253) 536-5136
E-mail: admissions@plu.edu
http://www.plu.edu
Computer engineering.

Saint Martin's University

5300 Pacific Avenue SE
Lacey, WA 98503
Phone: (360) 438-4311
Fax: (360) 412-6189
E-mail: admissions@stmartin.edu
http://www.stmartin.edu
Computer/information sciences—
general.

Seattle Pacific University

3307 Third Avenue West
Seattle, WA 98119
Phone: (206) 281-2021
Fax: (206) 281-2669
E-mail: admissions@spu.edu
http://www.spu.edu
Computational mathematics, computer/information sciences—general.

University of Puget Sound

1500 North Warner Street
Tacoma, WA 98416
Phone: (253) 879-3211
Fax: (253) 879-3993
E-mail: admission@ups.edu
http://www.ups.edu
Computer/information sciences—general.

University of Washington

1410 Northeast Campus Parkway
320 Schmitz, P.O. Box 355840
Seattle, WA 98195
Phone: (206) 543-9686
Fax: (206) 685-3655
E-mail: askuwadm@u.washington.edu
http://www.washington.edu
Applied mathematics, computer engineering, computer/information sciences—general, human resources management, information systems, information technology, management information systems.

Walla Walla College

Office of Admissions
204 South College Avenue
College Place, WA 99324
Phone: (509) 527-2327
Fax: (509) 527-2397
E-mail: info@wwc.edu
http://www.wwc.edu
Computer engineering, computer/information sciences—general, human resources management, information systems.

Washington State University

370 Lighty Student Services
Pullman, WA 99164
Phone: (509) 335-5586
Fax: (509) 335-4902
E-mail: admiss2@wsu.edu
http://www.wsu.edu
Applied mathematics, computer engineering, computer/information sciences—general, human resources management, management information systems.

Western Washington University

Mail Stop 9009
Bellingham, WA 98225
Phone: (360) 650-3440
Fax: (360) 650-7369
E-mail: admit@cc.wwu.edu
http://www.wwu.edu
Applied mathematics, computer/information sciences—general, human resources management, management information systems.

Whitworth College

300 West Hawthorne Road
Spokane, WA 99251
Phone: (509) 777-4786
Fax: (509) 777-3758
E-mail: admission@whitworth.edu
http://www.whitworth.edu
Applied mathematics, computer/information sciences—general.

WEST VIRGINIA

Alderson-Broddus College

P.O. Box 2003
Philippi, WV 26416
Phone: (800) 263-1549
Fax: (304) 457-6239
E-mail: admissions@ab.edu
http://www.ab.edu
Applied mathematics, management information systems.

Bethany College

Office of Admissions
Bethany, WV 26032
Phone: (304) 829-7611
Fax: (304) 829-7142
E-mail: admission@bethanywv.edu
http://www.bethanywv.edu
Computer/information sciences—general.

Bluefield State College

219 Rock Street
Bluefield, WV 24701
Phone: (304) 327-4065
Fax: (304) 325-7747
E-mail: bscadmit@bluefieldstate.edu
http://www.bluefieldstate.edu
Computer/information sciences—general.

Concord University—Athens

1000 Vermillion Street
P.O. Box 1000
Athens, WV 24712
Phone: (304) 384-5248
Fax: (304) 384-9044
E-mail: admissions@concord.edu
http://www.concord.edu
Computer/information sciences—general, human resources management, library science.

Marshall University

1 John Marshall Drive
Huntington, WV 35755
Phone: (304) 696-3160
Fax: (304) 696-3135
E-mail: admissions@marshall.edu
http://www.marshall.edu
Computer engineering technology, computer/information sciences—general.

Mountain State University

609 South Kanawha Street
Beckley, WV 25801
Phone: (304) 929-1433
Fax: (304) 253-3463
E-mail: gomsu@mountainstate.edu
http://www.mountainstate.edu
Human resources management, information systems, library science.

Ohio Valley University

1 Campus View Drive
Vienna, WV 26105
Phone: (304) 865-6200
Fax: (304) 865-6001

E-mail: admissions@ovu.edu
http://www.ovu.edu
Human resources management,
   information technology.

Salem International University
223 West Main Street
Salem, WV 26426
Phone: (304) 782-5336
Fax: (304) 782-5592
E-mail: admissions@salemiu.edu
http://www.salemiu.edu
Computer/information sciences—
   general.

Shepherd University
Office of Admissions
P.O. Box 3210
Shepherdstown, WV 25443
Phone: (304) 876-5212
Fax: (304) 876-5165
E-mail: admoff@shepherd.edu
http://www.shepherd.edu
Computer/information sciences—
   general.

University of Charleston
2300 MacCorkle Avenue SE
Charleston, WV 25304
Phone: (304) 357-4750
Fax: (304) 357-4781
E-mail: admissions@uchaswv.edu
http://www.uchaswv.edu
Computer/information sciences—
   general, information technology.

West Liberty State College
P.O. Box 295
West Liberty, WV 26074
Phone: (304) 336-8076
Fax: (304) 336-8403
E-mail: wladmsn1@westliberty.edu
http://www.westliberty.edu
Information systems.

West Virginia State University
P.O. Box 1000
Institute, WV 25112
Phone: (800) 987-2112
Fax: NA
E-mail: At Web site
http://www.wvstateu.edu
Applied mathematics.

West Virginia University
Admissions Office
P.O. Box 6009
Morgantown. WV 26506
Phone: (304) 293-2121
Fax: (304) 293-3080
E-mail: wvuadmissions@arc.wvu.
   edu
http://www.wvu.edu
Management information systems.

West Virginia University
Institute of Technology
Box 10, Old Main
Montgomery, WV 25136
Phone: (304) 442-3167
Fax: (304) 442-3097
E-mail: admissions@wvutech.edu
http://www.wvutech.edu
Computer/information sciences—
   general.

West Virginia Wesleyan College
59 College Avenue
Buckhannon, WV 26201
Phone: (304) 473-8510
Fax: (304) 473-8108
E-mail: admission@wvwc.edu
http://www.wvwc.edu
Computer/information sciences—
   general, information systems.

WISCONSIN

Alverno College
3400 South 43rd Street
P.O. Box 343922
Milwaukee, WI 53234
Phone: (414) 382-6100
Fax: (414) 382-6354
E-mail: admissions@alverno.edu
http://www.alverno.edu
Computer/information sciences—
   general.

Cardinal Stritch University
6801 North Yates Road, Box 237
Milwaukee, WI 53217
Phone: (414) 410-4040
Fax: (414) 410-4058
E-mail: admityou@stritch.edu
http://www.stritch.edu
Management information systems.

Carroll College
100 North East Avenue
Waukesha, WI 53186
Phone: (262) 524-7220
Fax: (262) 951-3037
E-mail: ccinfo@ccadmin.cc.edu
http://www.cc.edu
Applied mathematics, computer/
   information sciences—general,
   human resources management,
   information systems,
   management information
   systems, software engineering.

Carthage College
2001 Alford Park Drive
Kenosha, WI 53140
Phone: (262) 551-6000
Fax: (262) 551-5762
E-mail: admissions@carthage.edu
http://www.carthage.edu
Information technology.

Concordia University—
Wisconsin
12800 North Lakeshore Drive
Mequon, WI 53097
Phone: (262) 243-5700
Fax: (262) 243-4545
E-mail: admission@cuw.edu
http://www.cuw.edu
Computer/information sciences—
   general.

DeVry University—Milwaukee
100 East Wisconsin Avenue, Suite
   2550
Milwaukee, WI 53202
Phone: (414) 278-7677
Fax: (414) 278-0137
E-mail: ejohnson@keller.edu
http://www.devry.edu
Computer/information sciences—
   general.

Edgewood College
1000 Edgewood College Drive
Madison, WI 53711
Phone: (608) 663-2294
Fax: (608) 663-3291
E-mail: admissions@edgewood.
   edu

http://www.edgewood.edu
Computer/information sciences—
general, information systems,
management information
systems.

Lawrence University
P.O. Box 599
Appleton, WI 54912
Phone: (920) 832-6500
Fax: (920) 832-6782
E-mail: excel@lawrence.edu
http://www.lawrence.edu
Cognitive science, computer/
information sciences—general,
management information
systems.

Maranatha Baptist Bible College
745 West Main Street
Watertown, WI 53094
Phone: (800) 622-2947
Fax: (920) 261-9109
E-mail: At Web site
http://www.mbbc.edu
Management information systems.

Marian College of Fond Du Lac
45 South National Avenue
Fond du Lac, WI 54935
Phone: (920) 923-7650
Fax: (920) 923-8755
E-mail: admissions@mariancollege.
edu
http://www.mariancollege.edu
Information technology.

Marquette University
P.O. Box 1881
Milwaukee, WI 53201
Phone: (414) 288-7302
Fax: (414) 288-3764
E-mail: admissions@marquette.edu
http://www.marquette.edu
Computational mathematics,
computer engineering,
management information
systems, statistics.

Milwaukee School of Engineering
1025 North Broadway

Milwaukee, WI 53202
Phone: (414) 277-6763
Fax: (414) 277-7475
E-mail: explore@msoe.edu
http://www.msoe.edu
Computer engineering, software
engineering.

Northland College
1411 Ellis Avenue
Ashland, WI 54806
Phone: (715) 682-1224
Fax: (715) 682-1258
E-mail: admit@northland.edu
http://www.northland.edu
Computer/information sciences—
general, information systems.

St. Norbert College
100 Grant Street
De Pere, WI 54115
Phone: (920) 403-3005
Fax: (920) 403-4072
E-mail: admit@snc.edu
http://www.snc.edu
Computer/information sciences—
general.

Silver Lake College
2406 South Alverno Road
Manitowoc, WI 54220
Phone: (920) 686-6175
Fax: (920) 684-7082
E-mail: admisc@silver.sl.edu
http://www.sl.edu
Human resources management,
information systems.

University of Wisconsin—Eau Claire
105 Garfield Avenue
Eau Claire, WI 54701
Phone: (715) 836-5415
Fax: (715) 836-2409
E-mail: admissions@uwec.edu
http://www.uwec.edu
Computer/information sciences—
general, information resources
management.

University of Wisconsin—Green Bay
2420 Nicolet Drive

Green Bay, WI 53411
Phone: (920) 465-2111
Fax: (920) 465-5754
E-mail: uwgb@uwgb.edu
http://www.uwgb.edu
Information systems.

University of Wisconsin—La Crosse
1725 State Street
La Crosse, WI 54601
Phone: (608) 785-8939
Fax: (608) 785-8940
E-mail: admissions@uwlax.edu
http://www.uwlax.edu
Computer/information
sciences—general, management
information systems.

University of Wisconsin—Madison
Red Gym and Armory
716 Langdon Street
Madison, WI 53706
Phone: (608) 262-3961
Fax: (608) 262-7706
E-mail: onwisconsin@admissions.
wisc.edu
http://www.wisc.edu
Applied mathematics, computer
engineering, computer/
information sciences—general,
management information
systems, statistics.

University of Wisconsin—Milwaukee
P.O. Box 749
Milwaukee, WI 53201
Phone: (414) 229-3800
Fax: (414) 229-6940
E-mail: uwmlook@uwm.edu
http://www.uwm.edu
Applied mathematics, human
resources management,
management information
systems.

University of Wisconsin—Oshkosh
Dempsey Hall 135
800 Algoma Boulevard
Oshkosh, WI 54901

Phone: (920) 424-0202
Fax: (920) 424-1098
E-mail: oshadmuw@uwosh.edu
http://www.uwosh.edu
Human resources management, management information systems.

University of Wisconsin— Parkside

P.O. Box 2000
Kenosha, WI 53141
Phone: (262) 595-2355
Fax: (262) 595-2008
E-mail: matthew.jensen@uwp.edu
http://www.uwp.edu
Human resources management, management information systems,

University of Wisconsin— Platteville

1 University Plaza
Platteville, WI 53818
Phone: (608) 342-1125
Fax: (608) 342-1122
E-mail: schumacr@uwplatt.edu
http://www.uwplatt.edu
Human resources management.

University of Wisconsin—River Falls

410 South Third Street
112 South Hall
River Falls, WI 54022
Phone: (715) 425-3500

Fax: (715) 425-0676
E-mail: admit@uwrf.edu
http://www.uwrf.edu
Computer/information sciences— general.

University of Wisconsin— Stevens Point

Student Services Center
Stevens Point, WI 54481
Phone: (715) 346-2441
Fax: (715) 346-3957
E-mail: admiss@uwsp.edu
http://www.uwsp.edu
Computer/information sciences— general.

University of Wisconsin—Stout

Admissions, UW—Stout
Menomonie, WI 54751
Phone: (715) 232-1411
Fax: (715) 232-1667
E-mail: admissions@uwstout.edu
http://www.uwstout.edu
Applied mathematics.

University of Wisconsin— Superior

Belknap and Catlin
P.O. Box 2000
Superior, WI 54880
Phone: (715) 394-8230
Fax: (715) 394-8107
E-mail: admissions@uwsuper.edu
http://www.uwsuper.edu
Management information systems.

University of Wisconsin— Whitewater

800 West Main Street
Baker Hall
Whitewater, WI 53190
Phone: (414) 472-1234
Fax: (414) 472-1515
E-mail: uwwadmit@uww.edu
http://www.uww.edu
Computer/information sciences— general, computer systems analysis, human resources management, information technology.

Viterbo University

900 Viterbo Drive
La Crosse, WI 54601
Phone: (608) 796-3010
Fax: (608) 796-3020
E-mail: admission@viterbo.edu
http://www.viterbo.edu
Management information systems.

WYOMING

University of Wyoming

Admissions Office
P.O. Box 3435
Laramie, WY 82071
Phone: (307) 766-5160
Fax: (307) 766-4042
E-mail: why-wyo@uwyo.edu
http://www.uwyo.edu
Computer engineering, management information systems, statistics.

APPENDIX II
PERIODICALS, DIRECTORIES, AND ANNUALS

Most professional associations and organizations related to library and information science publish their own journals and newsletters (as well as other publications), some of which are indicated below. Check the Web sites of associations (particularly that of the American Library Association) and organizations of interest for the availability of all such publications. For a selected list of e-mail newsletters and blogs, consult Appendix IV, Useful Web Sites.

Available in print only *
Available in print and online **
Available online only ***

A. DIRECTORIES AND ANNUALS

American Library Directory (ALD) **
R. R. Bowker Company
121 Chanlon Road
New Providence, NJ 07974
Phone: (888) 269-5372
Fax: (908) 665-3528
E-mail: info@bowker.com
http://www.bowker.com
Available in online format from:
Information Today, Inc.
143 Old Marlton Pike
Medford, NJ 08055
Phone: (609) 654-6266
Fax: (609) 654-4309
E-mail: custserv@infotoday.com
http://www.infotoday.com
  A serial published annually that provides directory information (name, location, phone and fax number[s], department heads, budget, collection size, special collections, electronic resources, network participation, etc.) for more than 30,000 academic, public, research, county, provincial, regional, medical, law, and other special libraries in the United States, Canada, and Mexico. It also includes separate sections that list library networks and consortia, library systems, libraries for persons with special needs, and state and federal library agencies.

ARIST—The Annual Review of Information
  Science and Technology *
(Published by the American Society for Information
  Science and Technology [ASIS&T])
Available from:
Information Today, Inc.

143 Old Marlton Pike
Medford, NJ 08055
Phone: (609) 654-6266
Fax: (609) 654-4309
E-mail: custserv@infotoday.com
http://www.infotoday.com
  An annual survey of the landscape of information science and technology, providing the reader with an analytical, authoritative, and accessible overview of recent trends and significant developments.

The Bowker Annual Library and Book Trade
  Almanac 2008 *
(Published by the R. R. Bowker Company)
Available from:
Information Today, Inc.
143 Old Marlton Pike
Medford, NJ 08055
Phone: (609) 654-6266
Fax: (609) 654-4309
E-mail: custserv@infotoday.com
http://www.infotoday.com
  This reference serial, published annually, is a compilation of practical information and informed analysis of topics and issues of interest to the library, information, and book trade community.

Libweb ***
http://lists.webjunction.org/libweb
  A comprehensive worldwide directory of Web home pages for all types of libraries updated daily by Thomas Dowling of OhioLINK.
E-mail: tdowling@ohiolink.edu

Literary Market Place (LMP) 2008 **
(Published by the R. R. Bowker Company)
Available from:
Information Today, Inc.
143 Old Marlton Pike
Medford, NJ 08055
Phone: (609) 654-6266
Fax: (609) 654-4309
E-mail: custserv@infotoday.com
http://www.infotoday.com

Published annually, *LMP* is a directory of the book publishing industry in the United States and Canada containing an alphabetic list of U.S. publishers indexed by subject, type of publication, and geographically by state as well as Canadian publishers, small presses, editorial services, literary agents, book trade associations, writers' conferences and workshops, literary awards and prizes, and fellowships and grants.

The Serials Directory **
EBSCO Publishing
10 Estes Street
Ipswich, MA 01938
Phone: (800) 653-2726
Fax: (978) 356-6565
E-mail: information@ebscohost.com
http://www.ebscohost.com

Issued annually, this directory provides bibliographic information and pricing for a classified list of more than 140,000 serials currently published in the United States and internationally.

Ulrich's International Periodicals Directory **
R. R. Bowker Company
630 Central Avenue
New Providence, NJ 07974
Phone: (888) 269-5372
Fax: (908) 665-3528
E-mail: info@bowker.com
http://www.bowker.com
http://www.ulrichsweb.com

This annual reference serial provides bibliographic information and pricing for a classified list of more than 164,000 regularly and irregularly issued periodicals currently published in the United States and internationally, including titles available electronically.

B. PERIODICALS

Against the Grain (ATG) **
c/o Katina Strauch
MSC 98
The Citadel
Charleston, SC 29409
Phone: (843) 509-2848
Fax: (843) 805-7918
E-mail: kstrauch@comcast.net
http://www.against-the-grain.com

American Libraries **
American Library Association
(ALA)
50 East Huron Street
Chicago, IL 60611
Phone: (800) 545-2433, ext. 4216
Fax: (312) 440-0901
E-mail: americanlibraries@ala.org
http://www.ala.org/ala

Book Links Magazine **
American Library Association
50 East Huron Street
Chicago, IL 60611
Phone: (800) 545-2433
Fax: NA

E-mail: booklinks@ala.org
http://www.ala.org/ala/booklinks

Booklist **
(Published by the American Library
Association)
P.O. Box 607
Mount Morris, IL 61054
Phone: (888) 359-0949
Fax: NA
E-mail: At Web site
http://www.ala.org/ala/booklist

**Bookwire: The Book Industry
Online Resource** ***
R. R. Bowker Company
630 Central Avenue
New Providence, NJ 07974
Phone: (888) 269-5372
Fax: (908) 665-3528
E-mail: At Web site
http://www.bookwire.com

**The Bulletin of the Center for
Children's Books (BCCB)** **
Johns Hopkins University Press

2715 North Charles Street
Baltimore, MD 21218
Phone: (800) 548-1784
Fax: (410) 516-6968
E-mail: jlorder@jhupress.jhu.edu
http://www.press.jhu.edu/journals

**CHOICE: Current Reviews for
Academic Libraries** **
(Published by the Association of
College and Research Libraries)
Available from:
P.O. Box 141
Annapolis Junction, MD 20701
Phone: (240) 646-7027
Fax: (301) 206-9789
E-mail: choicesubscriptions@
brightkey.net
http://www.ala.org/ala/acrl/
acrlpubs/choice/home.cfm

Computers in Libraries **
Information Today, Inc.
143 Old Marlton Pike
Medford, NJ 08055
Phone: (609) 654-6466

Fax: (609) 654-4309
E-mail: custserv@infotoday.com
http://www.infotoday.com

Information Management Journal **

Association of Records Managers
and Administrators (ARMA)
International
13725 West 109th Street, Suite 101
Lenexa, KS 66215
Phone: (800) 422-2762
Fax: (913) 341-3742
E-mail: hq@arma.org
http://www.arma.org

Information Processing and Management: An International Journal **

Elsevier, Ltd.
The Boulevard
Langford Lane
Kidlington Oxford OX5 1GB
United Kingdom
Phone: +44 1865 843000
Fax: +44 1865 843010
E-mail: v.wetherell@elsevier.co.uk
http://www.elsevier.co.uk

Information Today Magazine **

Information Today, Inc.
143 Old Marlton Pike
Medford, NJ 08055
Phone: (609) 654-6466
Fax: (609) 654-4309
E-mail: custserv@infotoday.com
http://www.infotoday.com

Journal of Information Science **

Sage Publications USA
2455 Teller Road
Thousand Oaks, CA 91320
Phone: (805) 499-0721
Fax: NA
E-mail: info@sagepub.com
http://www.sagepub.com

Journal of the American Society for Information Science and Technology **

American Society for Information
Science and Technology (ASIS&T)
1320 Fenwick Lane, Suite 510

Silver Spring, MD 20910
Phone: (301) 495-0900
Fax: (301) 495-0810
E-mail: At Web site
http://www.asis.org

Knowledge Organization: An International Journal *

(Published by the International
Society for Knowledge
Organization [ISKO])
Available from:
Ergon Verlag
Grombühlstrasse 7
97080 Würzburg
Germany
Phone: +49 (0) 931-280084
Fax: +49 (0) 931-282872
E-mail: isko@iz-soz.de
http://www.isko.org/ko.html

Library and Information Science Research: An International Journal **

Elsevier, Ltd.
The Boulevard
Langford Lane
Kidlington Oxford OX5 1GB
United Kingdom
Phone: +44 1865 843000
Fax: +44 1865 843010
E-mail: v.wetherell@elsevier.co.uk
http://www.elsevier.co.uk

Library Journal **

(Published by R. R. Bowker Company)
Available from:
Reed Business Information
360 Park Avenue South
New York, NY 10010
Phone: (646) 746-6819
Fax: (646) 746-6734
E-mail: ljinfo@reedbusiness.com
http://www.libraryjournal.com

The Library Quarterly *

University of Chicago Press
Journals Division
1427 East 60th Street
Chicago, IL 60637
Phone: (773) 702-7600
Fax: (773) 702-0694

E-mail: query@journals.uchicago.
edu
http://www.journals.uchicago.edu

LIS Journal **

International Federation of Library
Associations and Institutions
(IFLA)
P.O. Box 95312
2509 CH The Hague
Netherlands
Phone: +31 70 3140884
Fax: +31 70 3834827
E-mail: IFLA@iflac.org
http://www.ifla.org

New Library World *

Emerald Group Publishing, Ltd.
Howard House
Wagon Lane
Bingley BD16 1WA
United Kingdom
Phone: +44 (0) 1274 777700
Fax: +44 (0) 1274 785201
E-mail: emerald@emeraldinsight.
com
http://www.emaraldinsight.com

ONLINE **

Information Today, Inc.
143 Old Marlton Pike
Medford, NJ 08055
Phone: (609) 654-6466
Fax: (609) 654-4309
E-mail: custserv@infotoday.com
http://www.infotoday.com

Public Libraries Magazine *

Public Library Association (PLA)
American Library Association
50 East Huron Street
Chicago, IL 60611
Phone: (800) 545-2433, ext 5752
Fax: (312) 280-5029
E-mail: pla@ala.org
http://www.ala.org/pla

Public Library Quarterly *

(Published by Haworth Press, Inc.)
Available from:
Taylor & Francis Group, LLC
325 Chestnut Street, Suite 800
Philadelphia, PA 19106

Phone: (800) 354-1420
Fax: (215) 625-2940
E-mail: At Web site
http://www.taylorandfrancis.com

Publishers Weekly **
(Published by R. R. Bowker Company)
Available from:
Reed Business Information

360 Park Avenue South
New York, NY 10010
Phone: (646) 746-6758
Fax: (646) 746-6631
E-mail: pwinfo@reedbusiness.com
http://www.publishersweekly.com

School Library Journal **
(Published by R. R. Bowker Company)

Available from:
Reed Business Information
360 Park Avenue South
New York, NY 10010
Phone: (646) 746-6758
Fax: (646) 746-6631
E-mail: sljinfo@reedbusiness.com
http://www.schoollibraryjournal.
com

APPENDIX III
PROFESSIONAL, INDUSTRY, AND TRADE ASSOCIATIONS, UNIONS, GUILDS, AND GOVERNMENT AGENCIES

Since many of these organizations operate on limited budgets, be sure to enclose a self-addressed, stamped envelope when querying any of them for data not available online. Not all of these groups maintain full-time offices, so some cannot be reached via phone, fax, or e-mail. In addition, contact information for some of these organizations may change when a new president or director is selected.

Besides the federal libraries listed below, many federal government agencies and departments have their own libraries. In addition, most states have their own state libraries. Contact information is frequently available at the Web site for the agency, federal department, or state government.

A. PROFESSIONAL, INDUSTRY, AND TRADE ASSOCIATIONS

American Association for Artificial Intelligence (AAAI)
445 Burgess Drive, Suite 100
Menlo Park, CA 94025
Phone: (650) 328-3123
Fax: (650) 321-4457
E-mail: info@aaai.org
http://www.aaai.org

American Association of Law Libraries (AALL)
53 West Jackson Boulevard, Suite 940
Chicago, IL 60604
Phone: (312) 939-4764
Fax: (312) 431-1097
E-mail: At Web site
http://www.aallnet.org

American Association of School Librarians (AASL)
American Library Association
50 East Huron Street
Chicago, IL 60611
Phone: (800) 545-2433, ext 4382
Fax: (312) 664-7459
E-mail: aasl@ala.org
http://www.ala.org/aasl

American Indian Library Association (AILA)
c/o Rhonda Harris Taylor
University of Oklahoma
School of Library and Information Science
401 West Brook Street, Room 120
Norman, OK 73109
Phone: (405) 375-3921
Fax: (405) 325-7648
E-mail: At Web site
http://www.ailanet.org

American Institute for Conservation of Historic and Artistic Works (AIC)
1156 15th Street NW, Suite 320
Washington, DC 20005
Phone: (202) 452-9245
Fax: (202) 452-9328
E-mail: info@aic-faic.org
http://www.aic.stanford.edu

American Library Association (ALA)
50 East Huron Street
Chicago, IL 60611
Phone: (800) 545-2433
Fax: (312) 440-9374

E-mail: library@ala.org
http://www.ala.org

American Medical Informatics Association (AMIA)
4915 St. Elmo Avenue, Suite 401
Bethesda, MD 20814
Phone: (301) 657-1291
Fax: (301) 657-1296
E-mail: mail@amia.org
http://www.amia.org

American National Standards Institute (ANSI)
1819 L Street NW, 6th floor
Washington, DC 20036
Phone: (202) 293-8020
Fax: (202) 293-9287
E-mail: info@ansi.org
http://www.ansi.org

American Society for Indexing (ASI)
10200 West 44th Avenue, Suite 304
Wheat Ridge, CO 80033
Phone: (303) 463-2887
Fax: (303) 422-8894
E-mail: info@asindexing.org
http://www.asindexing.org

American Society for Information Science and Technology (ASIS&T)
1320 Fenwick Lane, Suite 510
Silver Spring, MD 20910
Phone: (301) 495-0900
Fax: (301) 495-0810
E-mail: asis@asis.org
http://www.asis.org

American Theological Library Association (ATLA)
300 South Wacker Drive, Suite 2100
Chicago, IL 60606
Phone: (888) 665-2852
Fax: (312) 454-5505
E-mail: atla@atla.com
http://www.atla.com

Archivists and Librarians in the History of the Health Sciences (ALHHS)
Louise M. Darling Biomedical Library
University of California, Los Angeles
UCLA12-077 CHS, Box 951798
Los Angeles, CA 90095
Phone: (310) 825-6940
Fax: (310) 875-0465
E-mail: At Web site
http://www.alhhs.org

Art Libraries Society of North America (ARLIS/NA)
232-329 March Road, Box 11
Ottawa, ON K2K 2E1
Canada
Phone: (800) 817-0621
Fax: (613) 599-7027
E-mail: info@arlisna.org
http://www.arlisna.org

Asian/Pacific American Librarians Association (APALA)
3735 Palomar Centre, Suite 150, PMB 26
Lexington, KY 40513
Phone: (859) 257-5679
Fax: NA
E-mail: At Web site
http://www.apalaweb.org

Association for Computational Linguistics (ACL)
209 North Eighth Street
East Stroudsberg, PA 18360
Phone: (570) 476-8006
Fax: (570) 476-0860
E-mail: At Web site
http://www.aclweb.org

Association for Computing Machinery (ACM)
One Astor Plaza, 17th floor
New York, NY 10036
Phone: (800) 342-6626
Fax: NA
E-mail: acmhelp@acm.org
http://www.acm.org

Association for Educational Communications and Technology (AECT)
1800 North Stonelake Drive, Suite 2
Bloomington, IN 47404
Phone: (877) 677-2328
Fax: (812) 335-7675
E-mail: aect@aect.org
http://www.aect.org

Association for Information and Image Management (AIIM)
1100 Wayne Avenue, Suite 1100
Silver Spring, MD 20910
Phone: (800) 477-2446
Fax: (301) 587-2711
E-mail: aiim@aiim.org
http://www.aiim.org

Association for Information Systems (AIS)
P.O. Box 2712
Atlanta, GA 30301
Phone: (404) 413-7444
Fax: (404) 413-7443
E-mail: office@aisnet.org
http://home.aisnet.org

Association for Library and Information Science Education (ALISE)
62 East Wacker Drive, Suite 1900
Chicago, IL 60601
Phone: (312) 795-0996

Fax: (312) 419-8950
E-mail: contact@alise.org
http://www.alise.org

Association for Library Collections and Technical Services (ALCTS)
American Library Association
50 East Huron Street
Chicago, IL 60611
Phone: (800) 545-2433, ext 5038
Fax: (312) 280-5033
E-mail: alcts@ala.org
http://www.ala.org/alcts

Association for Library Services to Children (ALSC)
American Library Association
50 East Huron Street
Chicago, IL 60611
Phone: (800) 545-2433, ext 2163
Fax: (312) 280-5271
E-mail: alsc@ala.org
http://www.ala.org/alsc

Association for Library Trustees and Advocates (ALTA)
American Library Association
50 East Huron Street
Chicago, IL 60611
Phone: (800) 545-2433, ext 2161
Fax: NA
E-mail: alta@ala.org
http://www.ala.org/alta

Association for the Management of Information Technology in Higher Education
(CAUSE)
4840 Pearl East Circle, Suite 302E
Boulder, CO 80301
Phone: (303) 449-4430
Fax: NA
E-mail: info@cni.org
http://www.cni.org/docs/CAUSE.html

Association of Academic Health Sciences Libraries (AAHSL)
2150 North 107th Street, Suite 205

Seattle, WA 98133
Phone: (206) 367-8704
Fax: NA
E-mail: aahsl@sbims.com
http://www.aahsl.org

Association of Bookmobile and Outreach Services (ABOS)

c/o Theresa Gemmer, President
Everett Public Library
2702 Hoyt Avenue
Everett, WA 98201
Phone: (425) 257-7645
Fax: NA
E-mail: theresaanne@msn.com
http://www.abos-outreach.org

Association of Christian Librarians (ACL)

P.O. Box 4
Cedarville, OH 45314
Phone: (937) 766-2255
Fax: (937) 766-5499
E-mail: info@acl.org
http://www.acl.org

Association of College and Research Libraries (ACRL)

American Library Association
50 East Huron Street
Chicago, IL 60611
Phone: (800) 545-2433, ext 2523
Fax: (312) 280-2520
E-mail: acrl@ala.org
http://www.ala.org/acrl

Association of Computer Support Specialists (ACSS)

c/o Edward J. Weisberg, President
333 Mamaroneck Avenue, Suite 129
White Plains, NY 10605
Phone: (917) 438-0865
Fax: (914) 713-7227
E-mail: At Web site
http://www.acss.org

Association of Independent Information Professionals (AIIP)

8550 United Plaza Boulevard, Suite 101
Baton Rouge, LA 70809
Phone: (225) 408-4400

Fax: (225) 408-4422
E-mail: info@aiip.org
http://www.aiip.org

Association of Information and Dissemination Centers (ASIDIC)

P.O. Box 3212
Maple Glen, PA 19002
Phone: (215) 654-9129
Fax: (215) 654-9129
E-mail: At Web site
http://www.asidic.org

Association of Information System Professionals (AISP)

c/o University of Wisconsin—Madison
School of Business
4267 Grainger Hall
Madison, WI 53706
Phone: (608) 263-2538
Fax: NA
E-mail: aisp@bus.wisc.edu
http://www.aisp.bus.wisc.edu

Association of Information Technology Professionals (AITP)

401 North Michigan Avenue, Suite 2400
Chicago, IL 60611
Phone: (800) 244-9371
Fax: (312) 673-6659
E-mail: aitp_hq@aitp.org
http://www.aitp.org

Association of Jewish Libraries (AJL)

P.O. Box 1118
Teaneck, NJ 07666
Phone: (212) 725-5359
Fax: NA
E-mail: ajlibs@osu.edu
http://www.jewishlibraries.org

Association of Mental Health Libraries (MHLIB)

c/o Stuart Moss
Nathan Kline Institute for Psychiatric Research
140 Old Orangeburg Road
Orangeburg, NY 10962

Phone: (845) 398-6576
Fax: (845) 398-5551
E-mail: moss@nki.rfmb.org
http://www.mhlib.org

Association of Moving Image Archivists (AMIA)

1313 North Vine Street
Hollywood, CA 90028
Phone: (323) 463-1500
Fax: (323) 463-1506
E-mail: AMIA@amianet.org
http://www.amianet.org

Association of Records Managers and Administrators (ARMA) International

13725 West 109th Street, Suite 101
Lenexa, KS 66215
Phone: (800) 422-2762
Fax: (913) 341-3742
E-mail: hq@arma.org
http://www.arma.org

Association of Research Libraries (ARL)

21 Dupont Circle, Suite 800
Washington, DC 20036
Phone: (202) 296-2296
Fax: (202) 872-0884
E-mail: arlhq@arl.org
http://www.arl.org

Association of Specialized and Cooperative Library Agencies (ASCLA)

American Library Association
50 East Huron Street
Chicago, IL 60611
Phone: (800) 545-2433, ext 4398
Fax: (312) 280-5273
E-mail: ascla@ala.org
http://www.ala.org/ascla

Bibliographical Center for Research (BCR)

14394 East Evans Avenue
Aurora, CO 80014
Phone: (800) 397-1552
Fax: (303) 751-9787
E-mail: info@bcr.org
http://www.bcr.org

Bibliographical Society of America (BSA)
P.O. Box 1537
Lenox Hill Station
New York, NY 10021
Phone: (212) 452-2710
Fax: NA
E-mail: bsa@bibsocamer.org
http://www.bibsocamer.org

California Digital Library (CDL)
University of California
Office of the President
415 20th Street, 4th floor
Oakland, CA 94612
Phone: (510) 987-0555
Fax: (510) 893-5212
E-mail: cdl@www.cdlib.org
http://www.cdlib.org

Career Resource Managers Association (CRMA)
c/o Lisa Morency
Career Services Office
Salem State College
352 Lafayette Street
Salem, MA 01970
Phone: (617) 499-6950
Fax: NA
E-mail: At Web site
http://www.crmaonline.org

Catholic Library Association (CLA)
100 North Street, Suite 224
Pittsfield, MA 01201
Phone: (413) 443-2252
Fax: (413) 442-2252
E-mail: At Web site
http://www.cathla.org

Center for Research Libraries (CRL)
6050 South Kenwood Avenue
Chicago, IL 60637
Phone: (800) 621-6044
Fax: (773) 955-4339
E-mail: At Web site
http://www.crl.edu

Chief Officers of State Library Agencies (COSLA)
167 West Main Street, Suite 600

Lexington, KY 40507
Phone: (859) 514-9151
Fax: (859) 514-9166
E-mail: ttucker@AMRms.com
http://www.cosla.org

Chinese American Librarians Association (CALA)
c/o Sally C. Tseng
P.O. Box 4992
Irvine, CA 92616
Phone: (949) 552-5615
Fax: (949) 857-1988
E-mail: sctseng888@yahoo.com
http://www.ala.org/cala

Church and Synagogue Library Association (CSLA)
2920 Southwest Dolph Court, Suite 3A
Portland, OR 97219
Phone: (800) 542-2752
Fax: (503) 977-3734
E-mail: csla@worldaccessnet.com
http://www.cslainfo.org

Classification Society (CSNA)
c/o Professor Stanley L. Sclove
IDS Dept. (MC 294)
University of Illinois at Chicago
601 South Morgan Street
Chicago, IL 60607
Phone: (312) 996-2681
Fax: (312) 413-0385
E-mail: At Web site
http://www.classification-society.org

Coalition for Networked Information (CNI)
21 Dupont Circle, Suite 800
Washington, DC 20036
Phone: (202) 296-5098
Fax: (202) 872-0884
E-mail: info@cni.org
http://www.cni.org

Cognitive Science Society, Inc. (CSS)
10200 West 44th Avenue, Suite 304
Wheat Ridge, CO 80033
Phone: (303) 327-7547
Fax: (303) 422-8894

E-mail: At Web site
http://cognitivesciencesociety.org

College Center of Library Automation (CCLA)
1753 West Paul Dirac Drive
Tallahassee, FL 32310
Phone: (850) 922-6044
Fax: (850) 922-4869
E-mail: At Web site
http://www.cclaflorida.org

Computing Research Association (CRA)
1100 17th Street NW, Suite 507
Washington, DC 20036
Phone: (202) 234-2111
Fax: (202) 667-1066
E-mail: info@cra.org
http://www.cra.org

Congregational Library Associations (CLA)
c/o Ellen Bosman
New Mexico State University Library
P.O. Box 30001
Las Cruces, NM 88003
Phone: (505) 646-0111
Fax: NA
E-mail: ebosman@nmsu.edu
http://web.nmsu.edu

Council on Library and Information Resources (CLIR)
1755 Massachusetts Avenue NW, Suite 500
Washington, DC 20036
Phone: (202) 939-4750
Fax: (202) 939-4765
E-mail: At Web site
http://www.clir.org

Council on Library/Media Technicians (COLT)
P.O. Box 951
Oxon Hill, MD 20750
Phone: (202) 231-3836
Fax: (202) 231-3838
E-mail: jmhite0@dia.mil
http://colt.ucr.edu

Educause
1150 18th Street NW, Suite 1010
Washington, DC 20036
Phone: (202) 872-4200
Fax: (202) 872-4318
E-mail: info@educause.edu
http://www.educause.edu

Foundation for Information Technology Education
500 North Michigan Avenue, Suite 300
Chicago, IL 60611
Phone: NA
Fax: NA
E-mail: kjetton@satx.rr.com
http://www.edfoundation.org

Friends of Libraries U.S.A. (FOLUSA)
1420 Walnut Street, Suite 450
Philadelphia, PA 19102
Phone: (800) 436-5872
Fax: NA
E-mail: friends@folusa.org
http://www.folusa.org

Information Systems Audit and Control Association (ISACA)
3701 Algonquin Road, Suite 1010
Rolling Meadows, IL 60008
Phone: (847) 253-1545
Fax: (847) 253-1443
E-mail: membership@isaca.org
http://www.isaca.org

Information Systems Security Association (ISSA)
9220 Southwest Barbour Boulevard, Suite 119-333
Portland, OR 97219
Phone: (866) 349-5818
Fax: (206) 299-3366
E-mail: At Web site
http://www.issa.org

Information Technology Association of America (ITAA)
1401 Wilson Boulevard, Suite 1100
Arlington, VA 22209
Phone: (703) 522-5055

Fax: (703) 525-2279
E-mail: info@itaa.org
http://www.itaa.org

Institute for Certification of Computing Professionals (ICCP)
2350 East Devon Avenue, Suite 115
Des Plaines, IL 60018
Phone: (800) 843-8227
Fax: NA
E-mail: office@iccp.org
http://www.iccp.org

Institute for Operations Research and Management Sciences (INFORMS)
7240 Parkway Drive, Suite 310
Hanover, MD 21076
Phone: (800) 446-3676
Fax: (445) 757-3515
E-mail: informs@informs.org
http://www.informs.org

Institute of Electrical and Electronics Engineers (IEEE) Computer Society
1828 L Street NW, Suite 1202
Washington, DC 20036
Phone: (202) 371-0101
Fax: (202) 728-9614
E-mail: membership@computer.org
http://www.computer.org

International Association for Computer Information Systems (IACIS)
c/o G. Daryl Nord
Spears School of Business
Oklahoma State University
Stillwater, OK 74048
Phone: NA
Fax: NA
E-mail: DNord@OKState.edu
http://www.iacis.org

International Federation for Information Processing (IFIP)
Hofstrasse 3
A-2361 Laxenburg
Austria
Phone: + 43 2236 73616

Fax: +43 2236 73616 9
E-mail: ifip@ifip.org
http://www.ifip.org

International Federation of Library Associations and Institutions (IFLA)
P.O. Box 95312
2509 CH The Hague
Netherlands
Phone: +31 70 3140884
Fax: +31 70 3834827
E-mail: IFLA@ifla.org
http://www.ifla.org

International Organization for Standardization (ISO)
1, ch. De la Voie-Creuse
Case postale 56
Ch-1211 Geneva 20
Switzerland
Phone: + 41 22 749 01 11
Fax: + 41 22 733 34 30
E-mail: At Web site
http://www.iso.org

International Society for Knowledge Organization (ISKO)
c/o Maria J. López-Huertas
Facultad Biblioteconomía y Documentación
Universidad de Granada
Campus Universitario de la Cartuja
18071 Granada
España
Phone: NA
Fax: NA
E-mail: njlopez@ugr.es
http://www.idko.org/ko.html

Libraries for the Future (LFF)
27 Union Square West, Suite 204
New York, NY 10003
Phone: (646) 336-6236
Fax: (646) 336-6318
E-mail: info@lff.org
http://www.lff.org

Library Administration and Management Association (LAMA)
American Library Association

50 East Huron Street
Chicago, IL 60611
Phone: (800) 545-2433, ext 5032
Fax: (312) 280-5033
E-mail: lama@ala.org
http://www.ala.org/lama

Library and Information Technology Association (LITA)

American Library Association
50 East Huron Street
Chicago, IL 60611
Phone: (800) 545-2433, ext 4270
Fax: (312) 280-3257
E-mail: lita@ala.org
lillp://www.ala.org/lita

Library Support Staff Interests Round Table (LSSIRT)

American Library Association
50 East Huron Street
Chicago, IL 60611
Phone: (800) 545-2433, ext 9
Fax: (312) 944-2641
E-mail: At Web site
http://www.ala.org/lssirt

Medical Library Association (MLA)

65 East Wacker Place, Suite 1900
Chicago, IL 60601
Phone: (312) 419-9094
Fax: (312) 419-8950
E-mail: info@mlahq.org
http://www.mlanet.org

Medical Records Institute (MRI)

425 Boylston Street
Boston, MA 02116
Phone: (617) 964-3923
Fax: (617) 964-3926
E-mail: At Web site
http://www.medrecinst.com

MINITEX Library Information Network

University of Minnesota
15 Andersen Library
222 21st Avenue South
Minneapolis, MN 55455
Phone: (800) 462-5348
Fax: (612) 624-4508

E-mail: At Web site
http://www.minitex.umn.edu

Modern Language Association (MLA)

26 Broadway, 3rd floor
New York, NY 10004
Phone: (646) 576-5000
Fax: (646) 458-0030
E-mail: membership@mla.org
http://www.mla.org

Music Library Association (MLA)

8551 Research Way, Suite 180
Middleton, WI 53562
Phone: (608) 836 5825
Fax: (608) 831-8200
E-mail: mla@areditions.com
http://www.musiclibraryassoc.org

National Association of Government Archives and Records Administrators (NAGARA)

90 State Street, Suite 1009
Albany, NY 12207
Phone: (518) 463-8644
Fax: (518) 463-8656
E-mail: nagara@caphill.com
http://www.nagara.org

National Association to Promote Library and Information Services to Latinos and the Spanish-Speaking (REFORMA)

c/o Sandra Rios Balderrama
P.O. Box 25963
Scottsdale, AZ 85255
Phone: (480) 471-7452
Fax: NA
E-mail: REFORMAoffice@
riosbalderrama.com
http://www.reforma.org

National Church Library Association (NCLA)

275 South Third Street, Suite 101-A
Stillwater, MN 55082
Phone: (651) 430-0770
Fax: NA
E-mail: info@churchlibraries.org
http://www.churchlibraries.org

National Federation of Advanced Information Services (NFAIS)

1518 Walnut Street, Suite 1004
Philadelphia, PA 19102
Phone: (215) 893-1561
Fax: (215) 893-1564
E-mail: NFAIS@nfais.org
http://www.nfais.org

National Information Standards Organization (NISO)

One North Charles Street, Suite 1905
Bethesda. MD 21201
Phone: (866) 957-1593
Fax: (410) 685-5278
E-mail: At Web site
http://www.niso.org

National Workforce Center for Emerging Technologies (NWCET)

Bellevue Community College
3000 Lauderholm Circle SE, N258
Bellevue, WA 98007
Phone: (425) 564-4229
Fax: (425) 564-6193
E-mail: mmajury@bcc.ctc.edu
http://www.nwcet.org

Nelinet, Inc.

153 Cordaville Road
Southborough, MA 01772
Phone: (800) 635-4638
Fax: (508) 460-9455
E-mail: abell@nelinet.net
http://www.nelinet.net

Online Computer Library Center (OCLC)

6565 Kilgaur Place
Dublin, OH 43017
Phone: (800) 848-5878
Fax: (614) 764-6096
E-mail: oclc@oclc.org
http://www.oclc.org

Public Library Association (PLA)

American Library Association
50 East Huron Street
Chicago, IL 60611
Phone: (800) 545-2433, ext 5752

Fax: (312) 280-5029
E-mail: pla@ala.org
http://www.ala.org/pla

Reference and User Services Association (RUSA)

American Library Association
50 East Huron Street
Chicago, IL 60611
Phone: (800) 545-2433, ext 4398
Fax: (312) 280-5273
E-mail: rusa@ala.org
http://www.ala.org/rusa

Research Libraries Group (RLG)

Now joined with Online Computer
Library Center (OCLC)

Society for Human Resources Management (SHRM)

1800 Duke Street
Alexandria, VA 22314
Phone: (800) 283-7476
Fax: (703) 535-6490
E-mail: info@shrm.org
http://www.shrm.org

Society for Information Management (SIM)

401 North Michigan Avenue
Chicago, IL 60611
Phone: (800) 387-9746
Fax: NA
E-mail: info@simnet.org
http://www.simnet.org

Society for Technical Communication (STC)

901 North Stuart Street, Suite 904
Arlington, VA 22203
Phone: (703) 572-4114
Fax: (703) 522-2075
E-mail: stc@stc.org
http://www.stc.org

Society of American Archivists (SAA)

17 North State Street, Suite 1425
Chicago, IL 60602
Phone: (866) 722-7858
Fax: (312) 606-0728
E-mail: servicecenter@archivists.org
http://www.archivists.org

Society of Competitive Intelligence Professionals (SCIP)

1700 Diagonal Road, Suite 600
Alexandria, VA 22314
Phone: (703) 739-0696
Fax: (703) 739-2524
E-mail: info@scip.org
http://www.scip.org

Software and Information Industry Association (SIIA)

1090 Vermont Avenue NW, 6th floor
Washington, DC 20005
Phone: (202) 289-7442
Fax: (202) 289-7097
E-mail: At Web site
http://www.siia.net

Software Engineering Institute (SEI)

4500 Fifth Avenue
Pittsburgh, PA 15213
Phone: (412) 268-5800
Fax: (412) 268-6257
E-mail: customer-relations@sei.
cmu.edu
http://www.sei.cmu.edu

Special Libraries Association (SLA)

331 South Patrick Street
Alexandria, VA 22314
Phone: (703) 647-4900
Fax: (703) 647-4901
E-mail: At Web site
http://www.sla.org

Special Libraries Association Legal Division (SLA Legal Division)

c/o Nola Vanhoy
Director of Practice Innovation
Alston and Bird, LLP
1201 West Peachtree Street
Atlanta, GA 30309
Phone: (404) 881-4903
Fax: (404) 253-8443
E-mail: nola.vanhoy@alston.com
http://units.sla.org/division/dleg

Substance Abuse Librarians and Information Specialists (SALIS)

P.O. Box 9513

Berkeley, CA 94709
Phone: (510) 769-1831
Fax: (510) 865-2467
E-mail: salis@salis.org
http://salis.org

Theatre Library Association (TLA)

c/o The New York Public Library
for the Performing Arts
40 Lincoln Center Plaza
New York, NY 10023
Phone: NA
Fax: NA
E-mail: dnochimson100@qc.cuny.
edu
http://tla.library.unt.edu

Triangle Research Library Network (TRLN)

CB#3940 Wilson Library, Suite 712
Chapel Hill, NC 27514
Phone: (919) 962-8022
Fax: (919) 962-4452
E-mail: mona_couts@unc.edu
http://www.trln.org

Urban and Regional Information Systems Association (URISA)

1460 Renaissance Drive, Suite 305
Park Ridge, IL 60068
Phone: (847) 824-6300
Fax: (847) 824-6363
E-mail: At Web site
http://www.urisa.org

Urban Libraries Council (ULC)

125 South Wacker Drive, Suite 1050
Chicago, IL 60606
Phone: (312) 676-0999
Fax: (312) 676-0950
E-mail: info@urbanlibraries.org
http://www.urbanlibraries.org

Young Adult Library Services Association (YALSA)

American Library Association
50 East Huron Street
Chicago, IL 60611
Phone: (800) 545-2433 ext. 4390
Fax: (312) 280-5276
E-mail: yalsa@ala.org
http://www.ala.org/yalsa

B. UNIONS, GUILDS, AND GOVERNMENT AGENCIES AND LIBRARIES

American Federation of Teachers (AFT)
555 New Jersey Avenue NW
Washington, DC 20001
Phone: (202) 879-4400
Fax: NA
E-mail: At Web site
http://www.aft.org

Communications Workers of America (CWA)
501 Third Street NW
Washington, DC 20001
Phone: (202) 434-1100
Fax: (202) 434-1271
E-mail: cwaweb@cwa-union.org
http://www.cwa-union.org

Institute of Museum and Library Services (IMLS)
Office of Library Services
1800 M Street NW, 9th floor
Washington, DC 20036
Phone: (202) 653-4657
Fax: (202) 653-4600
E-mail: imlsinfo@imls.gov
http://www.imls.gov

Library of Congress (LC)
101 Independence Avenue SE
Washington, DC 20540
Phone: (202) 707-5000
Fax: NA
E-mail: At Web site
http://www.loc.gov

National Agricultural Library (NAL)
Abraham Lincoln Building
10301 Baltimore Avenue

Beltsville, MD 20705
Phone: (301) 504-5755
Fax: NA
E-mail: At Web site
http://www.nalusda.gov

National Archives and Records Administration (NARA)
8601 Adelphi Road
College Park, MD 20740
Phone: (866) 272-6272
Fax: (301) 837-0483
E-mail: At Web site
http://www.archives.gov

National Center for Education Statistics (NCES)
U.S. Department of Education
1990 K Street NW
Washington, DC 20006
Phone: (202) 502-7300
Fax: NA
E-mail: At Web site
http://nces.ed.gov

National Commission on Libraries and Information Science (NCLIS)
1800 M Street NW
Suite 350 North Tower
Washington, DC 20036
Phone: (202) 606-9200
Fax: (202) 606-9203
E-mail: info@nclis.gov
http://www.nclis.gov

National Education Association (NEA)
1201 16th Street NW
Washington, DC 20036

Phone: (202) 833-4000
Fax: (202) 822-7974
E-mail: At Web site
http://www.nea.org

National Library of Education (NLE)
400 Maryland Avenue SW
Washington, DC 20202
Phone: (800) 424-1616
Fax: (202) 401-0547
E-mail: library@ed.gov
http://ies.ed.gov/ncee/projects/nat_ed_library.asp

National Library of Medicine (NLM)
8600 Rockville Pike
Bethesda, MD 20894
Phone: (888) 346-3656
Fax: (301) 402-1384
E-mail: custserv@nlm.nih.gov
http://www.nlm.nih.gov

United Automobile, Aerospace and Agricultural Implement Workers of America International Union (United Auto Workers) (UAW)
Solidarity House
8000 East Jefferson Avenue
Detroit, MI 48214
Phone: (313) 926-5000
Fax: NA
E-mail: At Web site
http://www.uaw.org

APPENDIX IV
USEFUL WEB SITES FOR LIBRARY AND INFORMATION SCIENCE

For anyone involved in any aspect of library and information science as a vocation, the Internet has become an increasingly valuable resource in today's high-tech electronic age. The following are a *selection* of useful Web sites to help in your industry research, such as job searching, career research, and networking. Most libraries have their own Web sites that often include help pages and useful research/reference/library and information science links, and they are *not* included herein. (Web sites that do *not* have self-explanatory names are annotated with a brief explanation situated between the site name and its URL.)

These URLs may well be ones you wish to bookmark and/or list in your favorites folder. In addition, by using one or more of the search engines listed below—or using one of your own preferred search engines—you can fairly easily lay the foundation for researching almost any organization, individual, topic, or blog. Naturally, the information offered on any Web site is only as good as the source itself; readers should evalu-

ate sites for their track record of providing consistently reliable data. As has always been true, the Internet is in a constant state of flux. Even well-established Web sites often change their Web address. Typically, if you click on a link that has recently changed its URL, you will be switched automatically to its new Web address (which you can then bookmark and/or list in your favorites). If your link proves to be cold or dead, use a search engine to provide hits for the Web site in question. Usually this step will lead you to the new home page of the desired site. (As always, when using a search engine, if your query is more than one word, place the name/term in quotes to narrow and target the search.)

While the Internet and e-mail are great tools to employ in starting and furthering your career in library and information science, do not ignore traditional person-to-person contact with colleagues, mentors, family, friends, and others within your support network. They are equally vital in keeping you on track in your work and life.

A. SEARCH ENGINES

HOW TO USE SEARCH ENGINES

Bare Bones 101
http://www.sc.edu/beaufort/library/pages/bones/bones.shtml

Organic SEO Wiki
http://www.organicseo.org

Search.com
http://www.search.com

SearchEngineWatch
http://searchenginewatch.com

Spider's Apprentice
http://www.monash.com/spidap4.html

WebRef
http://webreference.com/content/search

SEARCH ENGINES (BY COUNTRY)
http://www.philb.com/countryse.htm

SEARCH ENGINES (GENERAL)

Alltheweb
http://alltheweb.com

Alta Vista
http://www.altavista.com

A9
http://a9.com

Answers.com
http://www.answers.com

AOL
http://www.aol.com

Ask.com
http://www.ask.com

AT1
http://www.at1.com

Blogs—Search Engines

An increasingly important venue for industry news and trends; note that many general search engines now provide a subcategory targeted for locating blogs by subject matter.

Blogdigger
http://www.blogdigger.com

Blogflux
http://dir.blogflux.com

Bloggernity
http://www.bloggernity.com

Bloglines
http://www.bloglines.com

BlogPulse
http://www.blogpulse.com

BlogSearchEngine
http://www.blogsearchengine.com

Bloogz: World Wide Blog
http://www.bloogz.com

Daypop
http://www.daypop.com

Feedster
http://www.feedster.com

Gigablast
http://www.gigablast.com

Google Blog Search
http://blogsearch.google.com

Icerocket.com
http://blogs.icerocket.com

LS Blog
http://www.lsblogs.com

QuackTrack
http://quacktrack.com

Technorati
http://www.technorati.com

Yahoo Blog Search
http://ysearchblog.com

Clusty
http://clusty.com

Copernic
Free and paid versions of special downloadable software available at site; generally does not work with Macintosh systems.
http://copernic.com

CrossEngine
http://www.crossengine.com

Ditto
http://www.ditto.com

Dogpile
http://www.dogpile.com

Factbites
http://www.factbites.com

Findspot
http://www.findspot.com

The Front Page
http://www.thefrontpage.com

Galaxy
http://www.galaxy.com

Gigablast
http://www.gigablast.com

Google
http://www.google.com

Google Scholar
http://scholar.google.com

HotBot
http://www.hotbot.com

HotSheet
http://www.hotsheet.com

Itools
http://www.itools.com

KartOO
http://www.kartoo.com

Liszen
http://liszen.com

LookSmart
http://search.looksmart.com

Metacrawler
http://metacrawler.com

MSN
http://www.msn.com

Omgili
Search engine for discussion forums.
http://omgili.com

Singingfish
http://www.singingfish.com

Soople
http://www.soople.com

Starting Page
http://www.startingpage.com

Starting Point
http://www.stpt.com

WebCrawler
http://webcrawler.com

Wikipedia
http://en.wikipedia.org

WiseNut
http://www.wisenut.com

Yahoo
http://www.yahoo.com

B. EDUCATION WEB SITES

Academic Info—Educational Resources
http://www.academicinfo.net

American Universities
http://www.clas.ufl.edu/CLAS/
american-universities.html

Best Sites for Financial Aid
http://www.cslr.org

Career Education
http://educhoices.org

College and University Home Pages
http://www.mit.edu:8001/people/
cdemello/univ.html

CollegeNet
Guide to colleges, universities, and scholarships.
http://www.collegenet.com

College Search
http://www.utexas.edu/world/univ

College Xpress
http://www.collegeexpress.com

Education Index
http://www.educationindex.com

Education Web Sites
An extensive listing of education Web sites, including search engines.
http://ejw.18.com/educweb.htm

Google Directory—Education
http://www.google.com/Top/
Reference/Education

LearnNet
http://www.chemsoc.org/networks/
learnnet

The Library & Information Science Professional's Career Development Center
http://liscareer.com

Library Assistant Job Level Guide
http://libstaff.mit.edu/admin/
profdev/classification/lajoblevel.
doc

National Center for Education Statistics
http://nces.ed.gov

Petersons.com
http://www.petersons.com

The Princeton Review
http://www.princetonreview.
com/college/research/majors/
majorBasics.asp?majorID=174

San José State University, School of Library & Information Science—List of Library Schools in United States and Canada, with Internet Links
http://slisweb.sjsu.edu/resources/
libraryschools.htm

Worldwide Learn
http://www.worldwidelearn.com/
online-education-guide

Yahoo!—Education
Guide to courses and degrees in many fields.
http://degrees.education.yahoo.com

Yahoo's Colleges and Universities by States
http://dir.yahoo.com/Education/
Higher_Education

C. GOVERNMENT WEB SITES

Chief Information Officers Council
http://www.cio.gov

U.S. Department of Labor, Bureau of Labor Statistics: *Occupational Outlook Handbook*
http://www.bls.gov/oco/home.htm

U.S. Department of Labor, Office of Apprenticeship Training, Employer and Labor Services (OATELS)
http://www.dol.gov/dol/topic/
training/apprenticeship.htm

U.S. Department of Labor, State Apprenticeship Information
http://www.doleta.gov/atels_bat

D. JOB SEARCH, SALARY SURVEY, AND CAREER INFORMATION WEB SITES

Some of these Web sites require a subscription fee for their use.

Academic Employment Network
http://academploy.com

Academic Position Network
http://apnjobs.com

Academic360.com
http://www.academic360.com

American Library Association
joblist.ala.org

American Society of Information Science and Technology
http://careercenter.asisonline.org/search.cfm

American Theological Library Association
http://www.atla.com/Member/job_openings.html

America's CareerInfoNet
http://www.careerinfonet.org

America's Service Locator
http://www.servicelocator.org

B2B Jobs
http://www.b2byellowpages.com/jobs/index.cgi

CareerOneStop
http://www.careeronestop.org

Career Voyages
http://www.careervoyages.gov

Chronicle of Higher Education: Chronicle Careers
http://chronicle.com/jobs

Dev Bistro
http://www.devbistro.com

Dice
http://seeker.dice.com/jobsearch/genthree/index.jsp

Employnow
http://www.employnow.com

Federal Library Jobs
http://www.libraryjobpostings.org/federal.htm

Get Library Jobs
http://www.getlibraryjobs.com

Google
http://directory.google.com/Top/Regional/North_America/United_States/Business_and_Economy/Employment

Higher Education.com
http://www.higheredjobs.com

Hot Jobs
http://www.hotjobs.com

Internet Public Library Job Resources
http://ipl.org.ar/svcs/employment.html

Job Descriptions
http://www.job-descriptions.org

Job Hunt
http://www.job-hunt.org

Job Profiles
http://www.jobprofiles.org

Jobs.aol.com
http://jobs.aol.com/?sem=1&ncid=AOLCAR00170000000004

Jobs.net
http://jobs.net

JobSmart Salary Info
http://jobsmart.org/tools/salary/sal-prof.htm

Jobs Search
http://jobs.ea.com

JobStar Central
http://jobstar.org/tools/salary/sal-prof.php

The Library & Information Science Professional's Career Development Center
http://liscareer.com/jobhunting.htm

Library and Information Technology Association
http://www.lita.org/ala/lita/litaresources/litajobsite/litajobsite.cfm

Library Job Postings on the Internet
http://www.libraryjobpostings.org

Library Land
http://www.librarylandindex.org/out/job.htm

LibrarySupportStaff.com
http://librarysupportstaff.com/libjobs.html

Lisjobs.com
http://www.lisjobs.com

Monster
http://www.monster.com

MSN Careerbuilder
http://jobs.msn.careerbuilder.com/Custom/MSN/FindJobs.aspx

Nation Job
http://nationjob.com

The Networked Librarian
http://pw2.netcom.com/~feridun/libjobs2.htm

PayScale, Inc.
http://www.payscale.com

The Real Rate Survey
http://www.realrates.com/survey.htm

Roadtechs.com
http://www.roadtechs.com

Salary.com
http://www.salary.com

Salary Wizard
http://swz-hoovers.salary.com

School Library Journal
http://jobs.slj.com/jobbank.
    cfm?id=220

Sloan Career Corner
http://www.careercornerstone.org

Special Library Association
http://careercenter.sla.org

TheLadders
Job site for $100K+ job listings.
http://www.theladders.com

TopUSAjobs.com
http://topusajobs.com

True Careers
http://www.truecareers.com/
    jobseeker/careerresources/
    default.shtml

USAJobs
Career information on government
    jobs.
http://www.usajobs.opm.gov

Vault
http://www.vault.com

Wetfeet
http://www.wetfeet.com

Yahoo
http://careers.yahoo.com/
    employment/carrer_resources/
    salaries_and_benefits

E. NEWSLETTERS (E-MAIL) AND BLOGS

American Association of
    School Libraries
http://www.aasl.ala.org/aaslblog

American Library Association
    Blogs and RSS Feeds
http://wikis.ala.org/readwriteconnect/
    index.php/ALA_blogs

American Library Association
    Committee on the Status of
    Women in Librarianship
http://blogs.ala.org/coswlcause.
    php

American Library Association
    Smart Libraries
http://www.techsource.ala.org/sln

American Library Association
    TechSource
http://www.alatechsource.org/blog

Association for Library
    Collections and Technical
    Services
http://blogs.ala.org/digiblog.php

Association for Library Science
    and Education
http://www.alise.org/mc/page.do?sit
    ePageId=60153&orgId=ali

Association for Library
    Services to Children
http://blogs.ala.org/digiblog.php

Association of College and
    Research Libraries
http://acrlog.org

Beyond the Job
http://www.beyondthejob.org

Biblio Tech
http://www.ringgold.com/biblio-tech

Catalogablog
http://www.catalogablog.blogspot.
    com

Chief Technology Officer
    Weblog
http://www.ctoweblog.com

Christina's LIS Rant
http://christinaslibraryrant.
    blogspot.com

CyberSkeptic's Guide to
    Internet Research
http://www.cyberskeptic.com/cs

Designing Better Libraries
About the contents of and uses of a
    library.
http://dbl.lishost.org/blog

D-Lib
http://www.dlib.org

Elsevier Library Connect
http://libraryconnect.elsevier.com/
    lcn/0502/lcn050208.html

Federal Library and
    Information Center
    Committee
http://www.loc.gov/flicc/fn/fncurr.
    html

Free Range Librarian
http://freerangelibrarian.com

if:book
http://www.futureofthebook.org/
    blog

Info Career Trends
http://www.lisjobs.com/newsletter

INFOcus
http://lyponline.com/INFOCUS.
    aspx

Infopeople
http://www.infopeople.org

Information Adviser
http://www.informationadvisor.
    com

Information Technology and Telecommunication Services
http://blogs.ala.org/ittsupdate.php

Information Today, Inc. NewsLink
http://www.infotoday.com/ newslink/default.shtml

Infotoday
http://www.infotodayblog.com

Intelligent Agent
http://www.ia-blog.com

In the Bookroom
http://www.libraryjournal.com/ blog/770000077.html

Intranets Today
http://www.intranetstoday.com

It's All Good
http://scanblog.blogspot.com

The Kept-Up Academic Librarian
http://keptup.typepad.com

Librarian and Information Science News
http://www.lisnews.org

Librarian.Net
http://www.librarian.net

Librarian's Guide to Etiquette
http://libetiquette.blogspot.com

Library Administration and Management Association
http://blogs.ala.org/lamaleads.php

Library and Information Technology Association
http://litablog.org

Library Juice
http://libraryjuicepress.com/blog

LibraryLaw
http://blog.librarylaw.com

Libraryola
http://www.libraryola.com

LibrarySpot
http://www.libraryspot.com

Library Stuff
http://www.librarystuff.net

Library Web Chic
http://www.librarywebchic.net/ wordpress

NFAIS News
http://www.nfais.org/news/news.cfm

OA (Open Access) Librarian
http://oalibrarian.blogspot.com

Online Insider
http://www.onlineinsider.net

Public Library Association
http://plablog.org

ResourceShelf
http://www.resourceshelf.com

The Shifted Librarian
http://www.theshiftedlibrarian.com

Special Libraries Association
http://slablogger.typepad.com/ sla_blog

Special Libraries Association Blog Feeds
http://www.sla.org/content/Shop/ enewsletters/subscribe.cfm

Special Libraries Association: Internet Technology
http://sla-divisions.typepad.com/ itbloggingsection

Tame the Web
http://tametheweb.com

WebJunction
http://webjunction.org/do/Home

Young Adult Library Services Association
http://yalsa.ala.org/blog

F. RESOURCES

Academic Info: Library and Information Science Resources
http://www.academicinfo.net/ infosci.html

American Association of Law Librarians
http://www.aallnet.org/committee/ rllc/resources/education.asp

American Association of School Librarians Resources
http://www.ala.org/ala/aasl/ aaslproftools/resourceguides/ aaslresource.cfm

American Library Association: Library Support Staff Resource Center
http://www.acrl.org/ala/hrdr/library supportstaff/library_support_ staff_resource_center.cfm

American Library Association: Professional Tools
http://www.ala.org/ala/proftools/ professional.htm

Association of College and Research Libraries: Professional Tools
http://www.ala.org/ala/acrl/ acrlproftools/professional.cfm

Beyond the Basics: Interesting Features on Library Web Sites
http://marylaine.com/libsite.html

Chief Information Officer (CIO) News & Info
http://www.cioupdate.com

Chief Technology Officer Network
http://www.ctonet.org

Data Mining Forum
http://tech.groups.yahoo.com/ group/datamining2

Data Mining Resources
http://www.the-data-mine.com

Digital Library of Information Science and Technology
http://dlist.sir.arizona.edu

DMOZ Open Directory Project: Library and Information Science
http://www.dmoz.org/Reference/
Libraries/Library_and_
Information_Science

EServer TC Library: A Cooperative for Tech Communicators
http://tc.eserver.org/dir/
Information-Design

Friends of Libraries U.S.A.
http://folusa.org

Google Directory: Library and Information Science
http://directory.google.com/Top/
Reference/Libraries/Library_
and_Information_Science

The Information Architecture Institute
http://iainstitute.org

Information Technology World Resources
http://www.itworld.com

Internet Library for Librarians
http://itcompany.com/inforetriever

Internet Public Library
http://www.ipl.org

ItmWEB: Information Technology Resources
http://www.itmweb.com

Lib-Bling
http://www.lib-bling.com/home

LibDex: The Library Index
http://libdex.com

Librarian's Guide to Intranet Resources
http://slis.cua.edu/ihy/SP/KT.htm

Librarian's Resource Center
http://units.sla.org/toronto/
resources/lrc/cover.htm

Librarian's Toolbox
http://www.oclc.org/toolbox/
default.htm

Librarian's Yellow Pages
http://lyponline.com

Librarian Web Sites
http://www.angelfire.com/stars3/
education/library.html

Library Consultants Directory Online
http://www.rburgin.com/
libraryconsultants

Library of Congress Cataloging Distribution Service
http://www.loc.gov/cds

Library-related Glossaries
http://www.jkup.net/terms.html

LibraryResources—ReadyToGo
http://librarianresources-readytogo.
wikispaces.com

Library Spot
http://www.libraryspot.com

Library Success: A Best Practices Wiki
http://www.libsuccess.org/index.
php?title=Main_Page

Professional Associations in the Information Sciences
http://slisweb.sjsu.edu/resources/
orgs.htm

Public Library Association Resources
http://www.ala.org/ala/pla/
resources/resources.cfm

Resources for School Librarians
http://www.sldirectory.com/libsf/
resf/current.html

Society of Competitive Intelligence Professionals Resources
http://scip.org/Resources/
?navItemNumber=499

Special Libraries Association Resources
http://www.sla.org/content/
resources/inforesour/index.cfm

Yahoo: Library and Information Science Resources
http://dir.yahoo.com/Reference/
Libraries/Library_and_
Information_Science

GLOSSARY

Words in full uppercase within a definition have their own entries in the glossary.

abstract A summary of a book, article, speech, REPORT, DISSERTATION, standard, PATENT, or other writing.

abstracting and indexing (A&I) A category of DATABASE that provides bibliographic citations and ABSTRACTS of the literature of a DISCIPLINE or subject area, as opposed to a retrieval service that provides INFORMATION sources, usually in full-text.

abstracting journal A JOURNAL that specializes in providing summaries (called ABSTRACTS) of articles and other documents published within the scope of a specific academic DISCIPLINE or field of study.

acceptable use policy (AUP) Guidelines established by a library or library system concerning the manner in which its computer SYSTEMS and equipment may be used by patrons and staff. In most libraries, a printed copy of acceptable use policy is posted near the computer workstations to which–restrictions apply. Some libraries make their policy statements available electronically, and users may be required to assent to them by clicking on a small box or icon before access is granted.

accession To record in an accession list the addition of a bibliographic item to a LIBRARY COLLECTION, whether acquired by purchase, exchange, or as a gift.

accession number A unique number assigned to a bibliographic item in the order in which it is added to a LIBRARY COLLECTION, recorded in an ACCESSION record maintained by the technical services department of the library. Most libraries assign accession numbers in continuous numerical sequence, but some employ a code system to indicate type of material and/or year of accession in addition to order of accession.

accreditation The voluntary nongovernmental evaluation process by which an educational or service organization regularly establishes that its programs or the institution as a whole (or one of its schools or units) meets preestablished standards of quality and integrity. In higher education, accreditation is a collegial process based on self-assessment and peer evaluation for the improvement of academic quality and public accountability. In the United States, institutions of higher learning (and academic libraries) are evaluated by regional accrediting bodies. Graduate programs of library and INFORMATION SCIENCE are evaluated by the Committee on Accreditation (COA) of the American Library Association (ALA).

acquisitions The process of selecting, ordering, and receiving materials for library or archival collections by purchase, exchanges, or gift. May also refer to the department of the library tasked with selecting, ordering, and receiving new materials and for maintaining accurate RECORDS on such TRANSACTIONS.

affiliated library A library that is, by formal agreement, part of a larger library system but administered independently by its own board or management structure. Medical and law libraries at large universities often fall into this category.

album A BOUND or loose-leaf book containing blank pages for mounting stamps, photographs, quotations, newspaper clippings, or other memorabilia or for collecting autographs. Also, a book containing a collection of pictures with or without accompanying text.

analytical entry (also analytic) An entry in a library CATALOG for a part of a work (for example, a chapter in a book) or an entire work (such as a story, play, essay, or poem) contained in an item, such as an anthology or collection, for which a comprehensive entry in the catalog is also made. Because preparation of analytical entries is time consuming, the level of bibliographic description provided in a catalog depends on the administrative policy of the library and its assessment of its patrons' and researchers' needs.

***Anglo-American Cataloguing Rules* (AACR)** A detailed set of standardized rules for cataloging various types of library materials that had its origin in *Catalog Rules: Author and Title Entries*, published in 1908 under the auspices of the American Library Association (ALA) and the Library Association (UK), and the *A.L.A. Cataloging Rules for Author and Title Entries* (1949), with its companion VOLUME *Rules for Descriptive Cataloging in the Library of Congress.* Cooperation between the ALA, the Library Association, and the Canadian Library Association resumed with the joint publication in 1967 of *Anglo-American Cataloging Rules,* which is divided into two parts: rules for creating the bibliographic description of an item of any type and rules governing the choice and form of entry of headings (access points) in the CATALOG. A second edition (*AACR2*) was published in 1978 and revised in 1988 (*AACR2R*) to reflect changes in INFORMATION formats. Additional amendments were issued in 1999 and 2001. The current version, *Anglo-American Cataloguing Rules, Second edition, 2002 Revision* (*AACR2 2002*), includes extensive revisions on continuing resources (formerly known as SERIALS). *AACR2-e* is a HYPERTEXT version published by ALA Editions that includes all amendments through 2001.

annual A SERIAL publication, such as a REPORT, yearbook, or directory, issued once a year.

application software Computer software that allows the user to process data or perform calculations necessary to achieve a desired result, as opposed to the OPERATING SYSTEM designed to control the computer's hardware and run all other programs. Common applications include word processing, spreadsheets, e-mail, presentation graphics, desktop publishing, DATABASE management SYSTEMS, and Web browsers.

approval plan A formal arrangement in which a publisher or wholesaler agrees to select and supply, subject to return privileges specified in advance, publications exactly as issued that fit a library's pre-established collection development profile. Approval profiles typically specify subject areas, levels of specialization or reading difficulty, SERIES, formats, price ranges, languages, and so forth.

approved program A postgraduate program in library and INFORMATION SCIENCE recognized or certified by a state board or educational agency as meeting its standards of quality and professionalism. Some approved programs are also accredited by the American Library Association (ALA).

archives Public RECORDS or historical documents or the place where such records and documents are kept.

audiovisual materials Nonbook materials, such as filmstrips, recordings, films, records, video and audio cassettes, CDs, and DVDs. Sometimes they are referred to as AV materials.

AUP See ACCEPTABLE USE POLICY.

authorized use A purpose for which the VENDOR of an electronic DATABASE or other online resource allows its content to be used, usually stated explicitly in the licensing agreement signed by the library or INFORMATION service that provides access.

balanced A LIBRARY COLLECTION containing materials that present the full range of opinion on controversial issues and sensitive topics, for example, the "for" and "against" positions on legalized abortion or religious books representing a variety of faiths.

bar code A small label of closely spaced vertical bars that encode INFORMATION about an item and that can be read by a computer. Bar codes on books and library cards are used to charge out books from the library by quickly scanning the information in the bar code into a computer.

BCL See BOOKS FOR COLLEGE LIBRARIES.

bibliographic citation The INFORMATION that identifies a book, article, or other print or nonprint material. Information for a book generally includes the author, title, publisher, and date. The citation for an article contains the author, title of the article, title of the PERIODICAL, VOLUME, pages, and date.

bibliographic database A DATABASE that indexes and contains references to the original sources of INFORMATION, thus containing information about the documents in it rather than the documents themselves.

bibliographic record An entry representing a specific item in a library CATALOG or BIBLIOGRAPHIC DATABASE containing all the data elements necessary for a full description presented in a specific bibliographic format. Traditionally, the format was a catalog card, but in modern cataloging since the advent of computers, the standard format is machine readable.

bibliography A list of materials (books, articles, documents, DISSERTATIONS, videos, and so forth) arranged in a logical order and on one subject or geographic region or by one author or producer. Often a bibliography is found at the end of a book or an article, whereas a long bibliography may be published separately as a book.

bindery An establishment that performs one or more assorted types of binding. Some large libraries and library SYSTEMS have an in-house bindery typically handled by their centralized technical processing department. In smaller libraries, materials in need of binding or rebinding (such as back ISSUES of PERIODICALS or paperback editions) are sent to a commercial bindery.

blanket order An agreement in which a publisher or dealer supplies to a library or library system one copy of each title as issued on the basis of a profile established in advance by the purchaser. Blanket order plans are used primarily by large academic and public libraries to reduce the amount of time required for selection and acquisition and to speed the process of getting new titles into CIRCULATION. Unlike APPROVAL PLANS, most blanket order plans do *not* allow returns.

blueprint A photographic copy of the detailed plans for constructing a building or other structure, formerly printed in white against a blue ground by the cyanotype process. Blueprints are usually produced in sets, one for each floor for each phase of construction (including plumbing, electrical, and heating and air conditioning). They are collected by architecture libraries and by ARCHIVES and special collections for construction projects of historical significance.

bookmobile A large motorized van equipped with shelves to accommodate a small LIBRARY COLLECTION and a desk for a LIBRARIAN or a PARAPROFESSIONAL member of the library staff, that serves as a traveling branch library in neighborhoods and communities too remote to be easily served by the nearest public library.

books-by-mail CIRCULATION of library materials via the postal system to registered borrowers who request items by telephone, post, or e-mail, usually from a mail-order CATALOG, a service provided by public libraries that serve rural areas and homebound patrons.

Books for College Libraries (BCL) A list of approximately 50,000 titles recommended for a core collection for academic libraries serving undergraduates first published by the American Library Association (ALA) in 1967. In fall 2006, the Association of College and Research Libraries (ACRL) in association with R. R. Bowker Company, publisher of *Books in Print*, issued *Resources for College Libraries (RCL)*, a new core collection of recommended print and electronic titles, a successor to the third edition of *BCL*, published in 1988. The online edition of *RCL* is regularly updated.

Boolean searching A method of combining search terms by expressing the relationship of one concept to another generally using "and," "or," and "not." The expression "Value 1 and Value 2" requires both values to be in the grouping retrieved. "Value 1 or Value 2" will retrieve either of the values, and "Value 1 but not Value 2" will retrieve only Value 1 items without returning Value 2.

bound A term referring to pages, sheets, or ISSUES of PERIODICALS that have been covered by a binding, usually hardback, to create a single VOLUME. This process is used in libraries to preserve items for long-term usage.

branch library An auxiliary service outlet in a library system housed in a facility separate from the central library that has at least a basic collection of materials, a regular staff, and established hours, with a budget and policies determined by the central library. A branch library is generally managed by a branch LIBRARIAN who may have responsibility for more than one branch.

bricks-and-mortar The traditional library, functioning for millennia as a physical repository ("warehouse") for the permanent storage of tangible items, as opposed to the modern concept of the library as an institution dedicated to providing access to INFORMATION maintained on-site and remotely in print and nonprint formats.

brief record An abbreviated display of a BIBLIOGRAPHIC RECORD in an ONLINE CATALOG or DATABASE that omits data elements contained in some of the less essential fields and subfields, in contrast to the full record, which provides a complete bibliographic description of the item. In most CATALOGS and BIBLIOGRAPHIC DATABASES, search results can be displayed in both formats.

broader term (BT) In a hierarchical CLASSIFICATION system, a subject heading or descriptor that includes another term as a subclass, for example, "libraries" listed as a broader term under "school libraries."

browse To look through a LIBRARY COLLECTION, CATALOG, BIBLIOGRAPHY, INDEX, BIBLIOGRAPHIC DATABASE, or other search tool in a casual search for items of interest without clearly defined intentions. To facilitate browsing, libraries assign similar CALL NUMBERS to items on the same subject, which groups them together on a shelf. In INFORMATION RETRIEVAL, to conduct a directed search in a dynamic but casual way. A clearly formulated query may determine the initial point of entry into an index or DATABASE, but searches that begin systematically often give way to an exploratory approach as new terminology is revealed by the results retrieved. Also, to search for INFORMATION available on the INTERNET in a casual manner. HYPERTEXT is designed to facilitate online browsing by providing embedded links to related documents and electronic resources.

business intelligence (BI) The process of gathering INFORMATION about customer needs and decision-making processes; the competition and competitive pressures; industry conditions; and general economic, technological, cultural, and political trends affecting a company's success undertaken to gain sustainable advantage in the marketplace. BI involves the extraction and analysis of information from multiple sources of relevant data to gain strategic KNOWLEDGE on which to base risk assessment and decision making. BI applications include query and reporting, data mining, online analytical processing (OLAP), statistical analysis, forecasting, and decision support SYSTEMS. BI focused specifically on a company's external environment (markets and competitors) is COMPETITIVE INTELLIGENCE.

call number A unique code printed on a label affixed to the outside of an item in a LIBRARY COLLECTION and also printed or handwritten on a label inside the item. Assigned by the cataloger, the call number is also displayed in the BIBLIOGRAPHIC RECORD that represents the item in the library CATALOG to identify the specific copy of the work and give its relative location on the shelf. In most collections, a call number is composed of letters, numbers, and symbols (used separately or in combination) followed by additional NOTATION to make the call number unique. Generally, the class number is followed by an author mark to distinguish the work from others of the same class, followed by a work mark to distinguish the title from other works of the same class by the same author, and sometimes other INFORMATION such as publication date, VOLUME number, copy number, and location symbol. In the LIBRARY OF CONGRESS CLASSIFICATION (LCC), used by most academic and research libraries in the United States, class notation begins with letters of the English alphabet (for example, PN 2035.H336 1991). In the DEWEY DECIMAL CLASSIFICATION (DDC), used by most public and school libraries in the United States, class notation consists of Arabic numerals (for example, 480.0924 W3). U.S. federal government documents are assigned SUPERINTENDENT OF DOCUMENTS CLASSIFICATION SYSTEM (SuDocs) numbers (for example, L 2.2:M 76).

carrel Originally, a small stall or pew in a medieval cloister containing a desk for reading, writing, and semiprivate study. In modern libraries, a small room or alcove in the STACKS designed for individual study. Newer study carrels have built-in illumination and may be wired to provide NETWORK access for patrons using laptops.

catalog A comprehensive list of the books, PERIODICALS, maps, videos/DVDs, CDs, and other materials in a given LIBRARY COLLECTION arranged in systematic order to facilitate retrieval (usually alphabetically by author, title, and/or subject). In most modern libraries, the card catalog has been converted to machine-readable BIBLIOGRAPHIC RECORDS and is available online. The purpose of a library catalog is to offer the library patron a variety of approaches or access points to the INFORMATION contained in the collection.

catalog record In a manual card CATALOG, all the INFORMATION given on a library catalog card, including a description of the item, the main entry, any added entries and subject headings, notes, and the call number. In an ONLINE CATALOG, the screen display that represents most fully a specific edition of a work, including elements of description and access points derived from the complete machine-readable BIBLIOGRAPHIC RECORD as well as information about the holdings of the local library or library system (copies, location, call number, status, and so forth) taken from the item RECORDS attached to the bibliographic record.

CD (compact disc) A DIGITAL audio recording MEDIUM capable of storing up to 74 minutes of sound in a single spiral track on one side of a 4.75-inch disc.

CD-ROM (compact disc-read only memory) A small plastic optical disk similar to an audio compact disc used as a publishing MEDIUM and for storing INFORMATION in DIGITAL format. Stamped by the producer on the metallic surface, the data encoded on a CD-ROM can be searched and displayed on a computer screen but not changed or erased. CD-ROMs can be used to store soundtracks, still or moving images, and computer files as well as text. In libraries, CD-ROMs are used primarily as a storage medium for BIBLIOGRAPHIC DATABASES and full-text resources, mostly dictionaries, encyclopedias, and other reference works.

centralized cataloging The preparation of BIBLIOGRAPHIC RECORDS for books and other library materials by a central cataloging agency that distributes them in printed and/or machine-readable form to participating libraries, usually for a modest fee. Also refers to the cataloging of materials for an entire library system at one of its facilities, generally the central library, to achieve uniformity and economies of scale.

centralized processing   The practice of concentrating in a single location all the functions involved in preparing materials for library use, as opposed to technical processing carried out at multiple locations within a library or library system. Centralization allows processing methods to be standardized.

check-in   The ongoing process of recording the receipt of each ISSUE of a newspaper or PERIODICAL, a routine task accomplished by the SERIALS department of a library manually or with the aid of an automated serials control system. Some automated SYSTEMS allow the patron to view the check-in record for a given title.

check-in record   A separate record attached to the BIBLIOGRAPHIC RECORD for a SERIAL title in which the receipt of individual ISSUES or parts is entered on an ongoing basis, usually by an assistant working in the serials department. Most ONLINE CATALOGS allow users to view the CHECK-IN record to determine if a specific ISSUE or part has been received. The check-in record may also indicate whether an issue is missing, claimed, or at the BINDERY.

check out   To borrow library materials for use outside the library or library system.

chip   A shortened form of microchip, a high-speed, miniaturized integrated circuit etched in a semiconducting material (usually silicon) on the surface of a tiny, wafer-thin piece of metal for use as microprocessors and memory in computers and other electronic equipment. The design of increasingly powerful microchips has been the driving force behind the INFORMATION TECHNOLOGY revolution.

circulation   The process of checking books and other materials in and out of a library.

circulation desk   The service point at which books and other materials are checked in and out of a library. It may include a built-in book drop for returning borrowed materials. In small- and medium-sized libraries, items on HOLD or reserve are usually available at the circulation desk, which is normally staffed by one or more persons trained to operate the CIRCULATION SYSTEM and handle patron accounts.

circulation system   The methods used to record the loan of items from a LIBRARY COLLECTION by linking data in the patron record to the item record for each item loaned. Such a system provides means of identifying items on loan to a specific patron (including those that are overdue) and enables CIRCULATION staff to place HOLDS, recall items needed before the due date, and notify borrowers when items are overdue. An automated circulation system is capable of generating circulation statistics for planning and reporting purposes.

classification   The process of dividing objects or concepts into logically hierarchical classes, subclasses, and sub-subclasses based on the characteristics they have in common and those that distinguish them.

closed reserve   An item on reserve that may be checked out by a registered borrower but may not be removed from library premises. Also, a reserve collection shelved in a closed stack from which requested items must be retrieved by a member of the library staff.

CODEN   A system of alphanumeric codes developed to uniquely and permanently identify scientific and technical SERIAL and monographic publications. It is used in electronic INFORMATION SYSTEMS to process bibliographic data because it is more concise than the full title and less ambiguous than an abbreviated title.

collaborative collection development (CCD)   An agreement between two or more libraries to share the expense of COLLECTION DEVELOPMENT and management by allocating strengths in certain subject areas among the participating libraries, with the understanding that resource sharing will make materials accessible to users of all the libraries.

collection development   The process of planning and building a useful and balanced collection of library materials over a period of years based on an ongoing assessment of the INFORMATION needs of the library's clientele, analysis of usage statistics, and demographic projections, normally constrained by budgetary limitations. Collection development includes the formulation of selection criteria, planning for resource sharing, and replacement of lost and damaged items as well as routine selection and deselection decisions. Large libraries and library SYSTEMS may use an APPROVAL PLAN or BLANKET ORDER plan to develop their collections. In small- and medium-sized facilities, collection development responsibilities are typically shared by all the LIBRARIANS based on their interests and subject specializations, generally under the overall guidance of a written collection development policy.

company file   A collection of data about one or more commercial enterprises, usually maintained by a corporation or business library for the use of employees, business students, investors, career counselors, job seekers, and so forth. ANNUAL REPORTS, SEC filings, trade CATALOGS, ISSUES of house organs, news clippings, photographs, and the like are typically organized alphabetically by name of firm.

competitive intelligence (CI)   In business, the collection, analysis, and assessment of INFORMATION about a company's markets and competition for use in strategic decision making. CI involves monitoring the environment external to the company for information pertinent to the decision-making process, which is then analyzed into accurate, usable strategic KNOWLEDGE about the firm's markets and competitors, including position, performance, capabilities, and intentions.

computer output microform (COM)   Computer output produced directly on MICROFICHE or MICROFILM without ever having been printed on paper.

consortium   An association of independent libraries and/or library SYSTEMS established by formal agreement usually for the purpose of resource sharing. Membership may be restricted to a specific geographic region, type of library (public, academic, special), or subject specialization.

continuing resource   See SERIAL.

controlled vocabulary   An established list of preferred terms from which a cataloger or indexer must select when assigning subject headings or descriptors in a BIBLIOGRAPHIC RECORD to indicate the content of the work in a library CATALOG, INDEX, or BIBLIOGRAPHIC DATABASE. Synonyms are included as lead-in vocabulary, with instructions to *see* or *use* the authorized heading. Thus, a cross-reference to the heading "dogs" will be made from the term "canines" to ensure that anyone looking for INFORMATION about dogs under "canines" will be directed to the correct heading.

copyright   The exclusive legal rights granted by a government to an author, editor, compiler, composer, playwright, publisher, or distributor to publish, produce, sell, or distribute copies of a literary, musical, dramatic, artistic, or other work within certain limitations (fair use and first sale). Copyright law also governs the right to prepare derivative works, reproduce a work or portions of it, and display or perform a work in public. Such rights may be transferred or sold to others and do not necessarily pass with ownership of the work itself. Copyright protects a work in the specific form in which it is created, not the idea, theme, or concept expressed in the work, which other writers are free to interpret in a different way. A work never copyrighted or no longer protected by copyright is said to be in the PUBLIC DOMAIN.

corporation library   A type of special library established and maintained as a unit within an incorporated company or organization to meet the INFORMATION needs of its employees and facilitate the achievement of its mission and goals. Some corporation libraries also serve as the repository for the official RECORDS of the organization. For internal security reasons, most corporation libraries are closed to the public except by special appointment.

course reserves   Materials (such as books, PERIODICAL articles, DISSERTATIONS, and REPORTS) that instructors (teachers, professors, and so forth) set aside for students in their classes to read. These items are usually kept together in one area of the library, may be borrowed for a short period of time only, and have very high fines for late returns.

database   A large, regularly updated file of digitized INFORMATION (BIBLIOGRAPHIC RECORDS, ABSTRACTS, full-text documents, directory entries, images, statistics, and so forth) related to a specific subject or field. It consists of RECORDS of uniform format organized for ease and speed of search and retrieval and managed with the aid of database management system (DBMS) software. Content is created by the database producer, which often publishes a print version and leases the content to one or more database VENDORS that provide electronic access to the data after it has been converted to a machine-readable format. Most databases used in libraries are CATALOGS, PERIODICAL INDEXES, ABSTRACTING SERVICES, and full-text reference resources leased annually under licensing agreements that limit access to registered borrowers and library staff.

data conversion   The process of translating data from one form to another, usually from human-readable to machine-readable format (or vice versa), from one file type to another, or from one recording MEDIUM to another, for example, from film to DVD.

data processing   The systematic performance of a single operation or sequence of operations by one or more central processing units on data converted to machine-readable format to achieve the result for which the computer program that controls the processing was written (for example, the compilation of

CIRCULATION statistics from RECORDS of circulation transactions that occur in a library over a given period of time).

data set A logically meaningful collection or grouping of similar or related data usually assembled as a matter of record or for research.

decision tree A tree-shaped structure that represents a set of decisions. These decisions generate rules for the CLASSIFICATION of a DATA SET.

depository library A library legally designated to receive without charge all or a portion of the government documents provided by the U.S. Government Printing Office (GPO) and other federal agencies to the Superintendent of Documents for distribution through the Federal Depository Library Program (FDLP), having made a legal commitment to comply with federal regulations concerning maintenance and accessibility. Some federal depositories also collect publications issued by state government agencies.

Dewey decimal classification (DDC) A hierarchical system for classifying books and other library materials by subject. In Dewey decimal CALL NUMBERS, Arabic numerals and decimal fractions are used in the class NOTATION (for example, 996.9) and an alphanumeric book number is added to subarrange works of the same CLASSIFICATION by author and by title and edition (for example, 996.9 B3262h). In the United States, public and school libraries use DDC, but most academic and research libraries employ LIBRARY OF CONGRESS CLASSIFICATION (LCC) because it is more hospitable.

digital Data recorded or transmitted as discrete, discontinuous voltage pulses represented by the binary digits 0 and 1, called bits. In digitized text, each alphanumeric character is represented by a specific eight-bit sequence called a byte. The computers used in libraries transmit data in digital format.

digital asset management (DAM) SYSTEMS designed to organize and display DIGITAL content produced in a variety of MEDIA types. The content is usually locally owned and controlled, rather than licensed from a third party.

digital imaging The field within computer science that covers all aspects of the capture, storage, manipulation, transmission, and display of images in DIGITAL format, including digital photography, scanning, and bitmapped graphics. In libraries, images of text documents are created for electronic reserve collections and digital archives. They are also available in full-text BIBLIOGRAPHIC DATABASES and reference resources.

digital rights management (DRM) A system of INFORMATION TECHNOLOGY components (hardware and software) and services designed to distribute and control the rights to intellectual property created or reproduced in DIGITAL form for distribution online or via other digital media, in conjunction with corresponding law, policy, and business models. DRM SYSTEMS typically use data encryption, digital watermarks, user plug-ins, and other methods to prevent content from being distributed in violation of COPYRIGHT.

digitization The process of converting data to DIGITAL format for processing by a computer. In INFORMATION SYSTEMS, digitization usually refers to the conversion of printed text or images (including photographs, illustrations, and maps) into binary signals using some kind of scanning device that enables the result to be displayed on a computer screen.

discipline An organized branch of human KNOWLEDGE developed through study and research or creative endeavor constituting a division of the curricula at institutions of higher learning. A discipline may be divided into subdisciplines, for example, biology and zoology within the biological sciences. In Western scholarship, the disciplines are traditionally organized as arts and humanities, social sciences, and sciences. In the DEWEY DECIMAL CLASSIFICATION (DDC) system, the classes representing subjects are arranged according to discipline (for example, 150 for psychology).

dispersal In RECORDS MANAGEMENT, a method of ensuring the survival of RECORDS by maintaining duplicate copies in different physical locations, usually reserved for essential records because of the expense. Duplicates may be created on paper, MICROFILM, magnetic tape, or other permanent MEDIUM as part of regular operating procedure. If the records are electronic, the necessary hardware and software must be maintained to access them when needed. Vital records are often protected in this way because they provide direct evidence of legal status, ownership, obligations incurred, and so forth, making them irreplaceable in the event of disaster.

dissertation A lengthy, formal written treatise or thesis, often an account of scholarly investigation or original research on a specialized topic, submitted to a university in partial fulfillment of the requirements for a Ph.D. degree.

document delivery service (DDS) The provision of published or unpublished documents in hard copy,

MICROFORM, or DIGITAL format, usually for a fixed fee upon request. In most libraries, document delivery service is provided by the INTERLIBRARY LOAN office on a cost-recovery basis. The library patron is usually required to pick up printed material at the library, but electronic full-text may be forwarded via e-mail. Also refers to the physical or electronic delivery of documents from a LIBRARY COLLECTION to the residence or place of business of a library user upon request.

domain name   The address identifying a specific site on the INTERNET. In the United States, domain names usually consist of three parts separated by a period (full stop). In the address www.thisuniversity.edu, the first part (www) indicates the protocol or language used in accessing the address, the second part (.thisuniversity) represents the name of the institution or organization hosting the site, and the last part (.edu) is a top level domain code indicating type of entity serving as NETWORK host. For the United States, the six basic top level domain codes are .com for commercial enterprises, .edu for educational institutions, .gov for government agencies, .mil for military installations, .net for networks, and .org for nonprofit organizations.

due date   The date of the last day of a loan period, stamped or written by a library staff member on the date due slip affixed to an item when it is checked out at the CIRCULATION DESK. Fines may be charged for materials returned after the due date if they are not renewed. In the ONLINE CATALOG, the due date may be displayed to indicate the CIRCULATION status of an item currently checked out.

DVD   An abbreviation of DIGITAL videodisc, a type of optical disk of the same size as a CD (COMPACT DISC) but with significantly greater recording capacity.

electronic book   A DIGITAL version of a traditional print book designed to be read on a personal computer or an e-book reader (a software application for use on a standard-sized computer or a book-sized computer used solely as a reading device). Some libraries offer access to electronic books through their ONLINE CATALOGS.

electronic publications   Works in DIGITAL form capable of being read or otherwise perceived and made available to the general public electronically via the Web, e-mail, or other means of INTERNET access. The category includes electronic JOURNALS (e-journals) and e-prints, electronic MAGAZINES (e-zines) and newspapers, ELECTRONIC BOOKS and DISSERTATIONS, electronic NEWSLETTERS, Web sites, and blogs. Some electronic publications are online versions of print publications; others are strictly digital.

electronic resources management (ERM)   SYSTEMS developed to assist LIBRARIANS in the control of licensed third-party resources published electronically (such as DATABASES, e-books, and e-journals), including license management, renewal, legal use, access management, and COLLECTION DEVELOPMENT.

e-metrics   The systematic definition, collection, and analysis of statistical data about networked environments and the use of electronic resources, particularly useful in e-commerce.

encoding   In INFORMATION RETRIEVAL, the process of converting a message or data into electronic signals that can be processed by a computer or transmitted over a communications channel.

expert system (ES)   A computer system or application based on artificial intelligence designed to replicate the ability of a human expert to solve a problem or perform a specific task (or sequence of tasks), for example, financial analysis and forecasting. An expert system requires a KNOWLEDGE base (KB) composed of facts and rules bases plus an inference engine to run the KB.

extranet   A private computer NETWORK designed to serve the employees of a company or members of an organization (as in an INTRANET) and also to provide various levels of accessibility to selected persons *outside* the organization (business partners, customers, clients, and so forth) but *not* the general public.

fair use   Conditions under which copying a work or a portion of it does not constitute infringement of COPYRIGHT, including copying for purposes of criticism, comment, news reporting, teaching, scholarship, and research.

federal library   A library owned and operated by the U.S. federal government that usually contains a collection of government documents pertaining to the field(s) it is mandated to cover. The largest are the LIBRARY OF CONGRESS, the National Agricultural Library, the National Library of Education, and the National Library of Medicine.

folio and quarto   Oversized books too large for normal shelving in a library. They are generally housed in special cases.

free-text search   A search of a BIBLIOGRAPHIC DATABASE in which NATURAL LANGUAGE words and phrases that appear in the texts of the documents indexed or in their bibliographic descriptions are used as search terms, rather than terms selected from a list of CONTROLLED VOCABULARY (authorized subject headings or descriptors).

full-text search A search of a BIBLIOGRAPHIC DATABASE in which the entire text of each record or document is searched and the entry retrieved if the terms included in the search statement are present. Most Web search engines are designed to perform full-text searches.

geographic information system (GIS) A computer-based system consisting of hardware, software, geographic INFORMATION, and personnel designed to facilitate the efficient capture, storage, maintenance, manipulation, analysis, and display of spatially distributed data that provide an automated link between the data and its location in space, usually in relation to a system of coordinates (latitude, longitude, elevation or depth, and so forth). The data can be on any scale, from microscopic to global. A GIS differs from a map in being a DIGITAL rather than an analog representation. Each spatial feature is stored as a separate layer of data that can be easily altered using techniques of quantitative analysis. Any category of information that has a geographic component can be mapped in a GIS, allowing thematic maps to be constructed from layers of data representing traditional cartographic information and from DATA SETS supplied from other sources (census data, health statistics, economic data, law enforcement statistics, and so forth).

government archives A government agency authorized by legislation to provide centralized archival services for all or a portion of the agencies or units that administer a country's government (legislative, executive, and judicial). For the federal government of the United States, that agency is the National Archives and Records Administration (NARA). Each of the 50 U.S. state governments maintains its own state ARCHIVES, sometimes as a unit of the state library.

government documents Publications of the U.S. federal government, including transcripts of hearings and the texts of bills, resolutions, statutes, REPORTS, charters, treaties, PERIODICALS, statistics, and so forth. In libraries, federal documents are usually shelved in a separate section by their SUPERINTENDENT OF DOCUMENTS CLASSIFICATION SYSTEM (SuDocs) number. Also refers to publications of other governmental bodies (state, local, territorial, foreign).

government library In the United States, a library maintained by a unit of government at the local, state, or federal level that contains collections primarily for the use of its staff. Some government libraries have a wider mandate that includes accessibility to the general public (for example, the Smithsonian Institution Libraries).

GPO The U.S. Government Printing Office, the government agency responsible for collecting, publishing, and distributing federal government INFORMATION. The GPO publishes a printed INDEX to GOVERNMENT DOCUMENTS under the title *Monthly Catalog of U.S. Government Publications.* Its online equivalent is *GPO Access,* which provides free electronic access to more than 1,500 DATABASES containing information from the three branches of the federal government,

gray literature Documentary material in print and electronic formats, such as REPORTS, preprints, internal documents (memoranda, NEWSLETTERS, market surveys, and so forth), theses and DISSERTATIONS, conference PROCEEDINGS, technical specifications and standards, trade literature, and so forth not readily available through regular market channels because it was never commercially published/listed or was not widely distributed. Such works pose challenges to libraries in identification (indexing is often limited) and acquisition (availability may be uncertain). Absence of editorial control also raises questions of authenticity and reliability.

hit In INFORMATION RETRIEVAL, a record retrieved from a DATABASE that matches the INFORMATION need expressed in the query.

hold When a book or other item is currently on loan, most libraries permit another borrower to place a "hold" on it by contacting the CIRCULATION DESK. The patron who has the item checked out will not be permitted to renew it, and the person who placed the "hold" will be entitled to check it out after it has been returned. Some ONLINE CATALOGS allow the user to place an item on hold without staff assistance.

homework center A space set aside for study in a public library usually with established hours and assigned staff trained to provide clearly defined services to students in need of assistance with their homework assignments.

homework help Services provided by public libraries or library systems specifically designed to assist public school, private school, and home-schooled students, usually in grades four to 12, with their take-home assignments.

housekeeping records   In ARCHIVES, the RECORDS of an organization that are related to its budgetary, fiscal, personnel, supply, maintenance, and other administrative operations, as opposed to the program records related to the organization's primary functions.

house organ   A PERIODICAL issued by a commercial or industrial organization for distribution internally to its employees and/or externally to its customers and not intended for wider publication.

HTML   See HYPERTEXT MARKUP LANGUAGE.

hypertext   A method of presenting DIGITAL INFORMATION that allows related files and elements of data to be interlinked rather than viewed in linear sequence. Text links and icons embedded in a document written in HTML script allow INFORMATION to be browsed in nonlinear, associative fashion similar to the way the human mind functions by selecting with a pointing device or using a computer keyboard. Hypertext is the basic organizing principle of the World Wide Web.

hypertext markup language (HTML)   Used to create the HYPERTEXT documents accessible via the World Wide Web and INTRANETS, HTML script is a cross-platform presentation markup language that allows an author to incorporate into a Web page text, frames, graphics, audio, video, and links to other documents and applications.

independent librarian   A provider of library services who functions outside traditional library settings, for example, an INFORMATION broker who works from a home office.

index   An alphabetically (or numerically) arranged list of headings consisting of the personal names, places, and subjects treated or mentioned in a written work, with page numbers to refer the reader to the point in the text at which INFORMATION pertaining to the heading is found.

informatics   The formal study of INFORMATION, including its structure, properties, uses, and functions in society; the people who use it; and in particular the technologies developed to record, organize, store, retrieve, and disseminate it.

information   Data presented in readily comprehensible form to which meaning has been attributed within the context of its use.

information commons (IC)   A new type of technology-enhanced collaborative facility on college and university campuses that integrates library and computer application services (INFORMATION, technology, and learning) in a single floor plan, often equipped with a wireless NETWORK and, in some cases, equipment for MULTIMEDIA production. Most ICs are designed to support LIBRARIANS engaged in assisting individual students and in teaching research skills to groups, teaching assistants helping individuals and groups of students with class assignments, and individual students and groups independently accessing information in print and online.

information desk   A desk in a large public or academic library usually located near the main entrance staffed by a nonprofessional trained to screen questions, provide basic INFORMATION about library services and collections, and direct users to the reference desk or some other public service point when further assistance is needed.

information industry   A broad term covering all the companies and individuals in the business of providing INFORMATION and access to information for a profit, including the mass MEDIA, commercial publishers, software and DATABASE producers and VENDORS, indexing and abstracting services, and freelance information brokers. Public libraries, academic libraries, and many types of special libraries, while providing information to their patrons, function outside the information industry because they operate on a nonprofit basis.

information law   The regulation and control of INFORMATION by the state, including laws governing censorship, COPYRIGHT and intellectual property, forgery, freedom of information, intellectual freedom, privacy, computer crime, and public funding of information providers, such as libraries and museums.

information literacy (IL)   The skill to find needed INFORMATION, including an understanding of how libraries are organized, familiarity with the resources they provide (such as information formats and automated search tools), and KNOWLEDGE of commonly used research techniques. The concept also includes the skills required to critically evaluate information content and employ it effectively as well as an understanding of the technological infrastructure on which information transmission is based, including its social, political, and cultural contexts and impacts.

information management   The exercise of control over the acquisition, organization, storage, security, retrieval, and dissemination of the INFORMATION resources essential to the successful operation of a business, agency, organization, or institution, including documentation, RECORDS MANAGEMENT, and technical infrastructure.

information policy A governing principle, plan, or course of action concerning INFORMATION resources and technology adopted by a company, organization, institution, or government, for example, the political decision to use public funds to subsidize INTERNET access for schools and public libraries.

information retrieval (IR) The process, methods, and procedures employed to selectively recall recorded INFORMATION from a file of data. In libraries and ARCHIVES, searches are typically for a known item or for information on a specific subject, and the file is usually a human-readable CATALOG or INDEX or a computer-based information storage and retrieval system, such as an ONLINE CATALOG or BIBLIOGRAPHIC DATABASE. In designing such SYSTEMS, balance must be achieved between speed, accuracy, cost, convenience, and effectiveness.

information science The systematic study and analysis of the sources, development, collection, organization, dissemination, evaluation, use, and management of INFORMATION in all its forms, including the channels (formal and informal) and technology used in its communication.

information system (IS) A computer hardware and software system designed to accept, store, manipulate, and analyze data and to report results usually on a regular, ongoing basis. An IS generally consists of a data input subsystem, a data storage and retrieval subsystem, a data analysis and manipulation subsystem, and a reporting subsystem.

information technology (IT) A very broad term encompassing all aspects of the management and processing of INFORMATION by computer, including the hardware and software required to access it.

information theory The systematic statement of principles relating to the phenomenon of INFORMATION and its transmission based on the collection and analysis of quantitative and qualitative data as a means of testing hypotheses about its nature and properties.

integrated access An INFORMATION RETRIEVAL system that permits users to search for books, PERIODICAL articles, and electronic resources such as computer files and Web sites in one operation using a single interface, instead of searching ONLINE

CATALOGS, BIBLIOGRAPHIC DATABASES, and Web search engines separately.

interlibrary loan (ILL) A cooperative arrangement among libraries that allows books or other materials from one library to be loaned out to a patron from another library. A patron may submit a request by filling out a printed interlibrary loan request form at a service desk or electronically via the library's Web site. Some libraries also accept ILL requests via e-mail and telephone, usually under exceptional circumstances.

International Standard Book Number (ISBN) A unique 10-digit standard number assigned to identify a specific edition of a book or other monographic publication issued by a given publisher under a system recommended for international use by the International Organization for Standardization (ISO) in 1969. The four parts of the ISBN are group identifier (e.g., national, geographic, language, or other convenient group), publisher identifier, title identifier, and check digit. In the ISBN system, MEDIA such as audio recordings, video recordings, MICROFICHE, and computer software are considered monographic publications, but SERIALS, music sound recordings, and printed music are excluded because other identification SYSTEMS have been developed to cover them.

International Standard Serial Number (ISSN) A unique eight-digit standard number assigned by the International Serials Data System (ISDS) to identify a specific SERIAL title. The ISSN is generally provided in the masthead of each ISSUE or on the COPYRIGHT page of each VOLUME or part of a SERIES. The standard has been revised and is now known as the ISSN-L.

Internet The global NETWORK of computers linked together, accessible mainly via the World Wide Web. Originally started by government and international scientists to facilitate communication, it is now used by the public at large.

internship A limited period of supervised training in a library or other INFORMATION agency intended to facilitate the application of theory to practice following completion of formal course work toward a master's degree in library and INFORMATION SCIENCE. An intern may be paid and/or receive graduate credits based on the number of hours worked.

intralibrary loan The loan of an item by a library to another library within the same library system or directly to a patron of another library in the same system on request. In some ONLINE CATALOGS, the user may initiate this type of transaction without staff assistance.

intranet   An in-house computer NETWORK designed to be used only by the staff or employees of an organization, institution, or commercial enterprise.

invisible college   Researchers, scholars, and experts who have established communication links that are independent of the literature in the fields in which they work. People who are on the frontiers of research, regardless of the field, tend to communicate directly with one another about their work.

ISBN   See INTERNATIONAL STANDARD BOOK NUMBER.

ISSN   See INTERNATIONAL STANDARD SERIAL NUMBER.

ISSN-L   In April 2007, the International Standards Organization (ISO) revised its standard for the International Standard Serial Number (ISSN) to cover all continuing resources, including looseleaf services, updating DATABASES, and some Web sites. The new standard maintained the earlier structure of the ISSN and defined a new mechanism—the "linking ISSN," or ISSN-L, a single, labeled ISSN that brings together the various MEDIA versions of a SERIAL publication under one ISSN. Designated for each resource in the ISSN Register, regardless of how many media versions exist when first assigned, the ISSN-L is a separate data element tagged and stored separately in METADATA RECORDS. Creation of the ISSN-L was an attempt to resolve disagreement between publishers and LIBRARIANS over whether the ISSN identifies a product or a work.

issue   A single, uniquely numbered or dated part of a PERIODICAL or newspaper.

iterative search   A search for INFORMATION in which the researcher or investigator repeatedly poses questions until an answer or solution is found.

jobber   In the United States, a wholesaler that stocks large quantities of new books and nonprint materials (including audiobooks, videotapes, and music CDs) issued by various publishers and supplies them to retail bookstores and libraries on order, usually at a substantial discount (10 to 40 percent). Large jobbers also offer customized services such as continuation orders, APPROVAL PLANS, cataloging, technical processing, and so forth. Using a book jobber allows a library to operate more efficiently by consolidating orders.

journal   A PERIODICAL devoted to disseminating original research and commentary on current developments in a specific DISCIPLINE, sub-discipline, or field of study, usually published in quarterly, bimonthly, or monthly ISSUES sold by subscription. JOURNAL articles are usually written by the person (or persons) who conducted the research. Longer than most MAGAZINE articles, they almost always include a BIBLIOGRAPHY, or list of works cited, at the end. Most scholarly journals are reviewed by experts (peers) in the field for critical evaluation prior to publication. Articles from some journals are available in DIGITAL format in full-text BIBLIOGRAPHIC DATABASES, typically by licensing agreement. Some journal publishers also provide an electronic version accessible via the World Wide Web.

keyword(s)   A significant word or phrase in the title, subject headings (descriptors), contents note, ABSTRACT, or text of a record in an ONLINE CATALOG or BIBLIOGRAPHIC DATABASE that can be used as a search term in a FREE-TEXT SEARCH to retrieve all the RECORDS containing it.

knowledge   INFORMATION that has been understood and evaluated in the light of experience and incorporated into an individual's intellectual understanding of a subject.

LAN   See LOCAL AREA NETWORK.

librarian   A professionally trained person responsible for the care of a library and its contents, including the selection, processing, and organization of materials and the delivery of INFORMATION, instruction, and loan services to meet the needs of its users. In the online environment, the role of the librarian is to manage and mediate access to information that may exist only in electronic form.

librarianship (library science)   The profession devoted to applying theory and technology to the creation, selection, organization, management, PRESERVATION, dissemination, and use of collections of INFORMATION in all formats.

library card   A small paper or plastic card issued by a library in the name of a registered borrower to be presented at the CIRCULATION DESK when checking out materials from its collections. Identification is usually required of new applicants.

library collection   The total accumulation of books and other materials owned by a library, cataloged and arranged for ease of access and often consisting of several smaller collections (reference, circulating books, SERIALS, government documents, rare books, special collections, and so forth). The process of building a library collection over an extended period of time is called COLLECTION DEVELOPMENT.

Library of Congress (LC) Established by Congress in 1800 to function as a research library for the legislative branch of the federal government, the Library of Congress eventually became the unofficial national library of the United States. Located in Washington, D.C., the Library of Congress houses a collection of more than 120 million items and administers the U.S. COPYRIGHT system, serving as the nation's copyright depository.

Library of Congress classification (LCC) A system of classifying books and other library materials developed and maintained over the last 200 years by the LIBRARY OF CONGRESS. In LCC, human KNOWLEDGE is divided into 20 broad categories indicated by single letters of the roman alphabet, with major subdivisions indicated by a second letter and narrower subdivisions by decimal numbers and further alphabetic NOTATION.

Library of Congress subject heading (LCSH) A descriptive word or phrase selected by a subject specialist at the LIBRARY OF CONGRESS from the list of *Library of Congress Subject Headings* and assigned to a book or other item when first published to indicate its subject. Multiple subject headings are assigned when necessary or desirable. The complete list of subject headings is published annually in a multi-VOLUME set colloquially known as "the big red books," usually available in the reference sections of most large public and academic libraries and in the cataloging departments of smaller libraries.

library science The professional KNOWLEDGE and skill with which recorded INFORMATION is selected, acquired, organized, stored, maintained, retrieved, and disseminated to meet the needs of a specific clientele, usually taught at a professional library school qualified to grant the post-baccalaureate degree of M.L.S. or M.L.I.S. The term is used synonymously in the United States with LIBRARIANSHIP.

line-item budget A method of budgeting employed in some libraries and library SYSTEMS in which anticipated expenditures are divided into discrete functional categories called "lines" (salaries and wages, materials, equipment, and so forth) for the purpose of systematically allocating resources and tracking operating expenditures.

local area network (LAN) A communications NETWORK restricted to a relatively small geographic area, often within a single building or group of adja-

cent buildings such as a college, university, or corporate office, consisting of at least one high-speed server, client workstations, a NETWORK OPERATING SYSTEM, and a communications link.

machine-readable cataloging (MARC) An international standard DIGITAL format for the description of bibliographic items developed by the LIBRARY OF CONGRESS to facilitate the creation and dissemination of computerized cataloging from library to library within the same country and between countries. The MARC format has become both the national and international standard for dissemination of bibliographic data. There are several versions of MARC in use in the world, the most predominant being MARC 21. The MARC 21 family of standards now includes formats for authority RECORDS, holdings RECORDS, CLASSIFICATION schedules, and community INFORMATION in addition to formats for the BIBLIOGRAPHIC RECORD. Widespread use of the MARC standard has helped libraries acquire predictable and reliable cataloging data, make use of commercially available library automation SYSTEMS, share bibliographic resources, avoid duplication of effort, and ensure that bibliographic data will be compatible when one automation system is replaced by another.

magazine A popular interest PERIODICAL that usually contains articles on a variety of topics written by various authors in a nonscholarly style for a general readership. Most magazines are issued monthly or weekly for sale at newsstands, in bookstores, and by subscription.

management information system (MIS) A computer-based INFORMATION SYSTEM developed and maintained by a commercial enterprise to integrate data from all its departments (product development, production and inventory, marketing and sales, personnel administration, and so forth) to support managerial and supervisory decision making with real-time analysis. MIS SYSTEMS are designed to track progress toward achievement of a company's goals and objectives and to aid in identifying problems or obstacles that must be resolved or removed by upper-level management.

MARBI (Machine-Readable Bibliographic Information Committee) The body within the American Library Association (ALA) responsible for developing official ALA positions on standards for representing bibliographic INFORMATION in machine-readable formats.

MARC See MACHINE-READABLE CATALOGING.

markup language In computing, a predefined set of descriptors (symbols and tags) or a method of defining descriptors that is used to embed external INFORMATION in an electronic text document, usually to specify formatting or facilitate analysis. Markup languages were originally designed for use with a specific program, but in 1986, the STANDARD GENERALIZED MARKUP LANGUAGE (SGML) was adopted as an international standard. The HYPERTEXT MARKUP LANGUAGE (HTML) used in creating Web pages is derived from SGML.

media A generic term for nonprint library materials (films, filmstrips, slides, video recordings, audio recordings, CD-ROMs, machine-readable data files, computer software, and so forth). MICROFORMS are *not* considered media because they are reproductions of print documents. Also refers collectively to all the channels through which INFORMATION is broadcast, including radio, television, cable, and the INTERNET.

medium In INFORMATION storage and retrieval, the physical substance or material on which data is recorded (such as parchment, paper, film, magnetic tape or disk, optical disk, and so forth) or through which data is transmitted (optical fiber, coaxial cable, twisted pair, and so forth).

MEDLARS (Medical Literature Analysis and Retrieval Service) Originally responsible for maintaining and leasing a collection of National Library of Medicine DATABASES to libraries and research institutions, the MEDLARS Management System (MMS) has expanded its scope to include database development, management, testing, and quality assurance aimed at enhancing access to health INFORMATION for health professionals and the public.

metadata Literally, "data about data." Structured INFORMATION describing information resources and objects for an assortment of purposes.

microfiche A small, card-shaped flat sheet of photographic film designed for storing miniaturized text and/or microimages arranged sequentially in horizontal and vertical rows.

microfilm The use of 16mm or 35mm photographic film to store miniaturized text and/or microimages in a linear array consisting of a single row or double row of frames that can be magnified and reproduced only with the aid of specially designed equipment.

microform A generic term for a highly reduced photographic copy of text and/or images stored on a translucent MEDIUM (MICROFICHE or MICRO-FILM) or on an opaque medium such as card stock (microopaque or aperture card). Reader-printer machines are required to view and make hard copies.

M.L.I.S. In the United States, the postbaccalaureate degree of master of library and information science, granted by a library school upon completion of a required course of study. To be considered for a professional position in most public and academic libraries in the United States, a candidate must have earned either an M.L.I.S. or M.L.S. degree.

M.L.S. In the United States, the postbaccalaureate degree of master of library science, granted by a library school upon completion of a required course of study. To be considered for a professional post in most public and academic libraries in the United States, a candidate must have earned either an M.L.S. or M.L.I.S. degree.

monograph A relatively short book or treatise on a single subject complete in one physical piece usually written by a specialist in the field. Monographic treatment is detailed and scholarly but not extensive in scope.

morgue A library maintained by the publisher of a newspaper usually consisting of back ISSUES, reference materials, INDEXES and DATABASES, clippings, notes, photographs, illustrations, and other resources needed by reporters and staff to research, write, and edit articles for publication. The term originally referred to the repository of biographical materials collected on persons of interest for the purpose of writing obituaries.

multimedia A combination of two or more DIGITAL MEDIA (text, graphics, audio, animation, video, and so forth) used in a computer application or a data file, such as an online encyclopedia, computer game, or Web site. Multimedia applications are often interactive. In a more general sense, any program, presentation, or computer application in which two or more communication media are used simultaneously or in close association; for example, slides with recorded sound.

narrower term (NT) In a hierarchical CLASSIFICATION system, a subject heading or descriptor that represents a subclass of a class indicated by another term; for example, "music librarianship" under "librarianship."

natural language A human language in which the structure and rules have evolved from usage usually over an extended period time, as opposed to an artificial language based on rules prescribed prior to its development and use, as in a computer language. In computer search software designed to handle input expressed in natural language, the user may enter the query in the same form in which it would be spoken or written ("Where can I find information about Abraham Lincoln?" as opposed to the search statements "abraham lincoln" or "su:lincoln").

network A group of physically discrete computers interconnected to allow resources to be shared and data exchanged usually by means of telecommunication links and client-server architecture. Most networks are administered by an operations center that provides assistance to users. The largest "network of networks" in the world is the INTERNET, which allows users of computers of all types and sizes to communicate in real time. Also, two or more organizations engaged in an exchange of INFORMATION through common communication channels usually for the purpose of accomplishing shared objectives.

newsletter A SERIAL publication that consists of no more than a few pages devoted to news, announcements, and current INFORMATION of interest primarily to a specialized group of subscribers or members of an association or organization who receive it as part of their memberships.

notation The set of characters (numerals, letters of the alphabet, and/or symbols) used to represent the main classes and subdivisions of a CLASSIFICATION system. In library cataloging, the class notation assigned to a bibliographic item represents its subject and is the first element of the CALL NUMBER, which determines its position on the shelf relative to items on other subjects.

OCLC See ONLINE COMPUTER LIBRARY CENTER.

online catalog A library CATALOG consisting of a collection of BIBLIOGRAPHIC RECORDS in machine-readable format maintained on a dedicated computer that provides uninterrupted interactive access via terminals or workstations in direct, continuous communication with the central computer. Although the software used in online catalogs is proprietary and not standardized, most online catalogs are searchable by author, title, subject heading, and KEYWORDS, and most public and academic libraries in the United States provide free public access usually through a Web-based graphical user interface.

Online Computer Library Center (OCLC) The largest bibliographic utility in the world, which provides cataloging and ACQUISITIONS services, SERIALS and CIRCULATION control, INTERLIBRARY LOAN support, and access to online DATABASES. OCLC has become a major source of cooperative cataloging data for libraries around the world.

Online Programming for All Libraries (OPAL) A collaborative effort by libraries of all types to provide cooperative Web-based programming and training for library users and library staff from any location using Web conferencing software (synchronized browsing, text chatting, voice over INTERNET protocol, and so forth). OPAL public online programs include book discussions, interviews, memoir-writing workshops, virtual tours of selected DIGITAL LIBRARY COLLECTIONS, special events, and library training. OPAL is administered by the Alliance Library System, the Mid-Illinois Talking Book Center (MITBC), and the Illinois State Library Talking Book and Braille Service (ISLTBBS). Programs are free with no registration required.

Online Public Access Catalog (OPAC) A DATABASE composed of BIBLIOGRAPHIC RECORDS that describe the books and other materials owned by a library or library system accessible via public terminals or workstations usually concentrated near the reference desk to make it easy for users to request the assistance of a trained reference LIBRARIAN. Most ONLINE CATALOGS are searchable by author, title, subject, and KEYWORDS and allow users to print, download, or export RECORDS to an e-mail account.

open access INFORMATION content made freely and universally available via the INTERNET in an easy-to-read format, usually because the publisher maintains online ARCHIVES to which access is free or has deposited the information in a widely known open-access repository. Open access is a new model of scholarly publishing developed to free researchers and libraries from the limitations imposed by subscription price increases for peer-reviewed JOURNALS, particularly in the sciences and medicine. Open access makes access to scientific information easier and has the added advantage of allowing the author(s) to retain COPYRIGHT.

operating system (OS) Software designed to control the basic operation of a computer and the exchange of data between the central processing unit and any peripheral equipment, mainly input and output devices. Loaded whenever the computer is started, the OS controls the running of all other programs, including any security SYSTEMS designed to prevent unauthorized use. Commonly used PC operating SYSTEMS include DOS, Windows, Mac OS, and UNIX.

paraprofessional A member of the library support staff who usually holds at least a bachelor's degree and is trained to understand specific procedures and apply them according to preestablished rules under normal circumstances without exercising professional judgment. Library paraprofessionals are usually assigned high-level technical support duties. In smaller public library SYSTEMS in the United States, branch LIBRARIANS are sometimes paraprofessionals.

patent A legal document issued by the U.S. government or the government of another country in response to a formal application process in which the inventor or originator of a new product or process is granted the exclusive right to manufacture, use, and sell it for a designated period of time. The document is assigned a patent number by the patent office for future reference. Most large engineering libraries provide patent search DATABASES and services.

periodical A SERIAL publication with its own distinctive title that contains a mix of articles, editorials, reviews, columns, short stories, poems, or other short works written by more than one contributor issued in softcover more than once, generally at regular intervals of less than a year with no prior decision as to when the final ISSUE will appear. Although each issue is complete in itself, its relationship to preceding issues is indicated typically by the issue number and VOLUME number printed on the front cover. Content is controlled by an editor or editorial board.

pertinence In INFORMATION RETRIEVAL, the extent to which a document retrieved in response to a query actually satisfies the INFORMATION need based on the user's current state of KNOWLEDGE—a narrower concept than relevance. Although a document may be relevant to the subject of the inquiry, it may be already known to the searcher, written in a language the user does not read, available in a format the researcher is unable or unwilling to use, or unacceptable for some other reason.

PIN An acronym for personal identification number, a code used in automated SYSTEMS to identify authorized users. Whether the PIN is created by or issued to the user depends on the policy governing access to the system. The practice originated in the banking industry and is used in some libraries and library systems to verify that a patron is registered

to use electronic resources restricted by licensing agreement and other services to which the library prefers to restrict access.

practicum A limited period of hands-on work in a library or other INFORMATION service agency structured to provide an opportunity for a novice to relate theory to practical experience, usually in the student's field(s) of specialization.

preservation Prolonging the existence of library and archival materials by maintaining them in a condition suitable for use, either in their original format or in a more durable form, through retention under proper environmental conditions or actions taken after a book or collection has been damaged to prevent further deterioration. Single sheets may be encapsulated or laminated for protection. Materials printed on acidic paper may be deacidified if their value warrants the expense. However, when the original has deteriorated beyond the point of salvation, reformatting may be necessary. Publications with soiled or foxed leaves are sometimes washed before being rebound. Materials infected with mildew or mold may require fumigation. Insects and larvae can be eliminated by freezing the infested item. Rare books and manuscripts are usually stored in a darkened room with temperature and humidity strictly controlled. A broader term than conservation, preservation includes managerial and financial considerations, including storage and accommodation provisions, staffing, and policy decisions as well as the techniques and methods of maintaining materials in optimal condition.

procedure manual A systematic list that documents the tasks involved in a specific job, sometimes including a description of the manner in which they are to be performed, given in sufficient detail that after careful reading, someone unfamiliar with the job will be able to perform basic functions with a minimal amount of assistance. Procedure manuals are often maintained in loose-leaf format to facilitate revision.

proceedings The published record of a conference, congress, symposium, or other meeting sponsored by a society or association usually but not necessarily including ABSTRACTS or REPORTS of papers presented by the participants. When the entire text of the papers presented is included, the result is called TRANSACTIONS.

provenance A record of the origin and history of ownership or custodianship of a specific copy of a book, manuscript, or other work of art. Authentication of archival materials requires that provenance be determined with certainty.

public domain Works not protected by COPYRIGHT or for which copyright has expired that may be printed for distribution and sale, quoted, excerpted, reproduced, and made available online to the public without infringement (for example, a government document over which an agency decides not to exercise copyright in order to make its content widely known). The term also applies to computer software (freeware and shareware) that the designers make available at no charge as a public service.

quarto See FOLIO.

readers' advisory (RA) Services provided by an experienced public services LIBRARIAN who specializes in the reading needs of the patrons of a public library. A readers' adviser recommends specific titles and/or authors based on KNOWLEDGE of a patron's past reading preferences and may also compile lists of recommended titles and serve as liaison to other education agencies in the community.

records Documents in any form created or received by an agency or person, accumulated in the normal conduct of business or affairs, and retained as evidence of such activity permanently or for a limited period of time, usually arranged according to a discernible system of record keeping.

records management The field of management devoted to achieving accuracy, efficiency, and economy in the systematic creation, retention, conservation, dissemination, use, and disposition of the official RECORDS of a company, government agency, organization, or institution, whether in physical or electronic form, usually undertaken by a professionally trained records manager on the basis of a comprehensive and thorough records survey. Security and disaster preparedness are essential elements of a good records management program.

reference services All the functions performed by a trained LIBRARIAN employed in the reference section of a library to meet the INFORMATION needs of patrons (in person, by telephone, and electronically), including but not limited to answering substantive questions, instructing users in the selection and use of appropriate tools and techniques for finding information, conducting searches on behalf of patrons, directing users to the location of library resources, assisting in the evaluation of information, referring patrons to resources outside the library when appropriate, keeping reference statistics, and participating in the development of the reference collection.

related term (RT) In a hierarchical CLASSIFICATION system, a descriptor or subject heading closely related to another term conceptually but not hierarchically; for example, "media specialists" listed as a related term under "school libraries."

report A separately published record of research findings, research still in progress, or other technical findings usually bearing a report number and sometimes a grant number assigned by the funding agency. Also, an official record of the activities of a committee or corporate entity, the PROCEEDINGS of a government body, or an investigation by an agency, whether published or private, usually archived or submitted to a higher authority.

reprint A new impression of an existing edition often made by photographic means or a new edition made from a new setting of type that is a copy of a previous impression with no alterations in the text except perhaps the correction of typographical errors.

reprography A general term encompassing quick-service document reproduction or copying by any means except large-scale professional printing, including photography, microphotography, xerography, and photo duplication.

Research Libraries Information Network (RLIN) An INFORMATION MANAGEMENT and retrieval system consisting of an online union CATALOG of the holdings of members of the Research Libraries Group (RLG) (now part of the Online Computer Library Center) combined with the *English Short-Title Catalog (ESTC)* and authority files. The NETWORK contains more than 88 million RECORDS and is used by many libraries, ARCHIVES, and museums for cataloging, interlibrary loan, and control of manuscript and archival collections.

reserve materials See COURSE RESERVES.

residency A library employment program in which new graduates are offered a one-year full-time professional contract position, often with the opportunity for second-year renewal. Some academic libraries have adopted residency programs as a means of recruiting minorities into the profession. Residents may be encouraged to explore different areas of LIBRARIANSHIP on the job.

Resources for College Libraries (RCL) See BOOKS FOR COLLEGE LIBRARIES (BCL).

RLIN See RESEARCH LIBRARIES INFORMATION NETWORK.

scanner In DATA PROCESSING, a peripheral device that reads and converts handwritten or printed text, graphics, or BAR CODES into DIGITAL format (a bitmap) for processing or display on a computer screen. In libraries, optical scanners are used to create digital images of materials for INTERLIBRARY LOAN, document delivery, and electronic reserves and in CIRCULATION to read the bar code on a patron's library card and on items in the collection. Some bar code scanners require an external decoder.

Scholarly Publishing and Academic Resources Coalition (SPARC) An international alliance of approximately 200 universities, research libraries, and library associations whose purpose is to address the pricing practices and policies of scientific, technical, and medical (STM) JOURNAL publishers. The coalition seeks to educate faculty on academic SERIALS ISSUES, fosters competition in the scholarly communication market, and advocates fundamental changes in the system and culture of scholarly communication.

search strategy In INFORMATION RETRIEVAL, a systematic plan for conducting a search. In most cases, the first step is to formulate a clear and concise topic statement. The next step is to identify the main concepts in the topic. Then the most appropriate finding tools for the subject must be identified and located. Lists of authorized subject heading(s) and descriptors in the appropriate indexing SYSTEMS then can be consulted to find preferred terms to represent the main concepts. In computer-based information retrieval, keywords can be combined using BOOLEAN logic to form one or more queries expressed in syntax acceptable to the CATALOGS, BIBLIOGRAPHIC DATABASES, and search engines most likely to contain INFORMATION on the subject. If the initial results of a search are unsatisfactory, the user can modify the search statement by adding related terms or substituting broader terms to expand retrieval or by substituting narrower terms to restrict retrieval. In most systems, limiting can be employed to restrict retrieval to entries that meet specific parameters.

Sears List of Subject Headings A list of essential SUBJECT HEADINGS used by many small and medium-sized libraries instead of the LIBRARY OF CONGRESS SUBJECT HEADINGS (LCSH).

selection criteria The set of standards used by LIBRARIANS to decide whether an item should be added to a collection, which normally includes a list of subjects or fields to be covered, levels of specialization, editions, currency, languages, and formats (large print, nonprint, abridgments, and so forth).

Selection criteria usually reflect a library's mission and the INFORMATION needs of its clientele, but selection decisions are also influenced by budgetary constraints and qualitative evaluation in the form of reviews, recommended core lists, and other selection tools.

serial A publication in any MEDIUM issued under the same title in a succession of discrete parts usually numbered (or dated) and appearing at regular or irregular intervals with no predetermined conclusion. Serial publications include print PERIODICALS and newspapers, electronic MAGAZINES and JOURNALS, ANNUALS (including REPORTS and yearbooks), continuing directories, PROCEEDINGS and TRANSACTIONS, and numbered monographic SERIES cataloged separately. Most libraries purchase serials on subscription or continuation order. A specific serial title is identified by a unique INTERNATIONAL STANDARD SERIALS NUMBER (ISSN) and key title, assigned and maintained by the International Serials Data System (ISDS), a NETWORK of national serials data centers. Serials are commonly referred to as continuing resources.

series A group of separately published works related in subject and/or form issued in succession (numbered or unnumbered) by a single publisher or distributor usually in uniform style, each bearing, in addition to its own title, a collective or series title applied by the publisher to the group as a whole. The individual VOLUMES or parts may not share the same author or editor, nor is it necessary for them to be published at regular intervals. The series title is given on a separate series title page, but it may also appear at the top of the title page or on a page following the title page.

server A host computer on a NETWORK programmed to answer requests to download data or program files received from client computers connected to the same network. Also refers to the software that makes serving clients possible over a network. Servers are classified by the functions they perform (application server, DATABASE server, fax server, file server, INTRANET server, mail server, proxy server, terminal server, Web server, and so forth).

SGML See STANDARD GENERALIZED MARKUP LANGUAGE.

SPARC See SCHOLARLY PUBLISHING AND ACADEMIC RESOURCES COALITION.

stacks The area of a library where the main body of the collection (usually books and PERIODICALS) is stored when not in use, usually on rows of free-standing, double-faced shelving. In some libraries, the stacks are closed to the public, but most libraries in the United States permit patrons to BROWSE all or part of their primary collections in open stacks.

Standard Generalized Markup Language (SGML) SGML is an ISO computer standard governing the rules for defining tag sets that determine how machine-readable text documents are formatted. Not dependent on a specific computer system or type of software, SGML is widely used in preparing machine-readable text ARCHIVES. The HTML code used to create Web pages is an SGML markup language that uses a fixed set of predefined tags. XML is a subset of SGML in which the tags are unlimited and not predefined.

style manual A special handbook or VOLUME that covers the mechanics of writing (punctuation, capitalization, quotations, plagiarism, and so forth), formatting (spacing, headings, tables, and illustrations), and correct form of documentation (footnotes, endnotes, and bibliographies), usually including pertinent examples. Some style manuals are for general use, while others are published by professional associations as guides for writing articles for JOURNALS in that field of KNOWLEDGE and research.

subject heading The most specific word or phrase that describes the subject or one of the subjects of a work, selected from a list of preferred terms (CONTROLLED VOCABULARY) and assigned as an added entry in the BIBLIOGRAPHIC RECORD to serve as an access point in a library CATALOG. The process of examining the content of new publications and assigning appropriate subject headings is called subject analysis. In the United States, most libraries use LIBRARY OF CONGRESS SUBJECT HEADINGS (LCSH), but small libraries may use the SEARS LIST OF SUBJECT HEADINGS.

Superintendent of Documents Classification System (SuDocs) A system of arranging U.S. federal government publications in an alphabetical/numerical order based on the name of the major issuing government department (such as Agriculture Department or Commerce Department). Libraries that use SuDocs numbers shelve government documents in a separate location. Those that use LIBRARY OF CONGRESS CLASSIFICATION (LCC) or DEWEY DECIMAL CLASSIFICAITON (DDC) for government documents typically shelve them in reference or with the general collection.

systems All the computer hardware, software, and electronic resources on which a library or library system depends in its daily operations, including the ONLINE CATALOG and CIRCULATION system, BIBLIOGRAPHIC DATABASES, networked and stand-alone PCs, Web server(s) and Web site(s), application programs, and so forth. It is the responsibility of the systems LIBRARIAN to keep the various components running smoothly, including any connections to outside NETWORKS.

taxonomy The science of CLASSIFICATION, including the general principles by which objects and phenomena are divided into classes, which are subdivided into subclasses, then into sub-subclasses, and so on. Taxonomies have traditionally been used in the life sciences to classify living organisms, but the term has been applied more recently within the INFORMATION INDUSTRY to the classification of resources available via the World Wide Web.

technical services (TS) Library operations concerned with the acquisition, organization (bibliographic control), physical processing, and maintenance of LIBRARY COLLECTIONS, as opposed to the delivery of public services.

tenure The guarantee of permanent employment granted by an academic institution to a faculty member for satisfactory performance upon completion of a specified number of years of service, to be terminated only for adequate cause (such as incompetence, malfeasance, mental or physical incapacity, and genuine financial need). A position for which tenure is offered is classified as "tenure-track." Academic LIBRARIANS who have faculty status are eligible for tenure; those with academic status usually are not.

thesaurus A book of synonyms and near-synonyms in a written language usually arranged conceptually, although dictionary-style arrangement is not uncommon. Also refers to an alphabetically arranged lexicon of terms that constitutes the specialized vocabulary of an academic DISCIPLINE or field of study and shows the logical and semantic relations among terms, particularly a list of subject headings or descriptors used as preferred terms in indexing the literature of the field. In INFORMATION RETRIEVAL, a thesaurus may be used to locate broader terms and related terms if the user wishes to expand retrieval or narrower terms to make a search statement more specific. A well-designed thesaurus also enables an indexer to maintain consistency in the assignment of indexing terms to documents.

trade journal   A PERIODICAL devoted to disseminating news and INFORMATION of interest to a specific category of business or industry, often published by a trade association. Some trade JOURNALS are available in an online version as well as in print.

transactions   The published papers or ABSTRACTS of papers presented at a conference or meeting of a society, association, institution, or other organization usually including an account of what transpired. The term may also appear in the title of a scholarly JOURNAL that publishes articles that have not been presented orally. The term *transactions* is sometimes used as a synonym of PROCEEDINGS. A general distinction made between transactions and proceedings is that transactions are the papers presented and proceedings are the RECORDS of the meeting.

vendor   A company in the business of providing access to a selection of BIBLIOGRAPHIC DATABASES online or on CD-ROM by subscription or on a per-search basis usually under a licensing agreement. Providers of nonprint MEDIA are also commonly referred to as vendors. In a more general sense, any individual, company, or agency other than a publisher that provides products and/or services to a library or library system for a fee. A distinction is normally made between book vendors (such as booksellers, dealers, and JOBBERS) and SERIALS vendors (including subscription agents and continuation dealers). A vendor may also provide automated customer services such as management REPORTS and electronic transmission of bibliographic or invoice data. The term is also used for businesses that specialize in developing and marketing library SYSTEMS, such as ONLINE CATALOG software and library management systems.

virtual library   A "library without walls" in which the collections do *not* exist on paper, microform, or other tangible form at a physical location but are electronically accessible in DIGITAL format via computer NETWORKS. Such libraries exist only on a very limited scale, but in most traditional print-based libraries in the United States, CATALOGS and PERIODICAL INDEXES are available online, and some periodicals and reference works may be available in electronic full text. The term *digital library* is more appropriate because *virtual* suggests that the experience of using such a library is not the same as the "real" thing, when, in fact, the experience of reading or viewing a document on a computer screen may be qualitatively different from reading the same publication in print, but the data content is the same regardless of format.

volume   In the bibliographic sense, a major division of a work distinguished from other major divisions of the same work by having its own chief source of INFORMATION and, in most cases, independent pagination, foliation, or signatures, even when not BOUND under separate cover and regardless of the publisher's designation. In a set, the individual volumes are typically numbered, with any INDEXES at the end of the last volume. For a PERIODICAL, volume refers to all the ISSUES published during a given publishing period (usually a calendar year), bound or unbound. The volume number is usually printed on the front cover of each issue and on the same page as the table of contents. In bound periodicals, it is impressed on the spine.

WAN   See WIDE AREA NETWORK.

wide area network (WAN)   A communication NETWORK that covers an extensive geographic area such as a country, region, province, or state.

World Wide Web   A client-server INFORMATION SYSTEM that uses the INTERNET to access computers containing millions of HYPERTEXT documents.

Z39.50   Prepared by the National Information Standards Organization, an INFORMATION RETRIEVAL service definition and protocol specification for library applications. The standard defines how one computer SYSTEM can cooperate with other systems for the purpose of searching DATABASES and retrieving RECORDS.

BIBLIOGRAPHY

Arent, Wendi, and Candace R. Benedict, eds. *The Image and Role of the Librarian.* New York: Haworth Information Press/Haworth Press, 2002.

Bates, Mary Ellen. *Building and Running a Successful Research Business: A Guide for the Independent Information Professional.* Medford, N.J.: Information Today, 2003.

Bryson, Jo. *Managing Information Services: A Transformational Approach.* 2d ed. Burlington, Vt.: Ashgate Publishing, 2006.

Budd, John. *The Changing Academic Library: Operations, Culture, Environments.* Chicago: Association of College and Research Libraries, 2005.

Bureau of Labor Statistics, U.S. Department of Labor. *Occupational Outlook Handbook, 2007-08 Edition.*

   Bookbinders and Bindery Workers. Available online at http://www.bls.gov/oco/ocos020.htm.

   Computer and Information Systems Managers. Available online at http://www.bls.gov/oco/ocos258.htm.

   Computer Control Programmers and Operators. Available online at http://www.bls.gov/oco/ocos286.htm.

   Computer Programmers. Available online at http://www.bls.gov/oco/ocos110.htm.

   Computer Software Engineers. Available online at http://www.bls.gov/oco/ocos267.htm.

   Computer Support Specialists and Systems Administrators. Available online at http://www.bls.gov/oco/ocos268.htm.

   Data Entry and Information Processing Workers. Available online at http://www.bls.gov/oco/ocos155.htm.

   Education Administrators. Available online at http://www.bls.gov/oco/ocos007.htm.

   File Clerks. Available online at http://www.bls.gov/oco/ocos146.htm.

   Financial Managers. Available online at http://www.bls.gov/oco/ocos010.htm.

   Human Resources Assistants. Available online at http://www.bls.gov/oco/ocos150.htm.

   Librarians. Available online at http://www.bls.gov/oco/ocos068.htm.

   Library Assistants, Clerical. Available online at http://www.bls.gov/oco/ocos147.htm.

   Library Technicians. Available online at http://www.bls.gov/oco/ocos113.htm.

   Medical Records and Health Information Specialists. Available online at http://www.bls.gov/oco/ocos103.htm.

   Office and Administrative Support Worker Supervisors and Managers. Available online at http://www.bls.gov/oco/ocos127.htm.

   Office Clerks, General. Available online at http://www.bls.gov/oco/ocos130.htm.

   Public Relations Specialists. Available online at http://www.bls.gov/oco/ocos086.htm.

   Receptionists and Information Clerks. Available online at http://www.bls.gov/oco/ocos134.htm.

   Secretaries and Administrative Assistants. Available online at http://www.bls.gov/oco/ocos151.htm.

   Top Executives. Available online at http://www.bls.gov/oco/ocos012.htm.

Burke, John J. *Neal-Schuman Library Technology Companion: A Basic Guide for Library Staff.* New York: Neal-Schuman Publishers, 2000.

Cassell, Kay Ann, and Uma Hiremath. *Reference and Information Services in the 21st Century: An Introduction.* New York: Neal-Schuman Publishers, 2006.

Chan, Lois Mai, and Theodore L. Hodges. *Cataloging and Classification: An Introduction.* 3d ed. Lanham, Md.: Scarecrow Press, 2007.

Choo, Chan Wei. *The Knowing Organization: How Organizations Use Information to Construct Meaning, Create Knowledge, and Make Decisions.* New York: Oxford University Press, 1998.

Cohn, John M., Ann L. Kelsey, and Keith Michael Fields. *Planning for Integrated Library Systems and Technologies.* New York: Neal-Schuman Publishers, 2001.

Connor, Elizabeth, ed. *An Introduction to Reference Services in Academic Libraries.* New York: Routledge, 2006.

Curry, Adrienne, Ivan Hollingworth, and Peter Flett. *Managing Information and Systems.* New York: Routledge, 2006.

Dority, G. Kim. *Rethinking Information Work: A Career Guide for Librarians and Other Information Professionals.* Greenwood Village, Colo.: Libraries Unlimited, 2006.

Eberts, Marjorie, and Margaret Gisler. *Careers for Book Worms and Other Literary Types*. 3d ed. New York: VGM Career Books/McGraw-Hill, 2003.

Evans, G. Edward, and Margaret Zamosky Saporno. *Developing Library and Information Center Collections*. 5th ed. Greenwood Village, Colo: Libraries Unlimited, 2005.

Fourie, Denise K., and David R. Dowell. *Libraries in the Information Age: An Introduction and Career Exploration*. Greenwood Village, Colo: Libraries Unlimited, 2002.

Gordon, Rachel Singer. *The Accidental Systems Librarian*. Medford, N.J.: Information Today, 2003.

———. *The Nextgen Librarian's Survival Guide*. Medford, N.J.: Information Today, 2006.

———. *Teaching the Internet in Libraries*. Chicago: American Library Association, 2001.

———. *What's the Alternative? Career Options for Librarians and Info Pros*. Medford, N.J.: Information Today, 2008.

Gorman, Michael. *Our Enduring Values: Librarianship in the 21st Century*. Chicago: American Library Association, 2000.

Grady, Jenifer, and Denise Davis, project dirs. *ALA-APA Salary Survey Librarian–Public and Academic: A Survey of Library Positions Requiring an ALA-Accredited Master's Degree*. Chicago: American Library Association, 2007.

———. *ALA-APA Salary Survey Non-MLS–Public and Academic: A Survey of Library Positions Not Requiring an ALA-Accredited Master's Degree*. Chicago: American Library Association, 2007.

Gregory, Vicki L. *Selecting and Managing Electronic Resources: A How-To-Do-It Manual for Librarians*. New York: Neal-Schuman Publishers, 2000.

Grosch, Audrey N. *Library Information Technology and Networks*. New York: Marcel Dekker, 1995.

Kane, Laura Townsend. *Straight from the Stacks: A Firsthand Guide to Careers in Library and Information Science*. Chicago: American Library Association, 2003.

Luenberger, David G. *Information Science*. Princeton, N.J.: Princeton University Press, 2006.

Mason, Florence M., and Chris Dobson. *Information Brokering: A How-To-Do-It Manual*. New York: Neal-Schuman Publishers, 1998.

Matthews, Joseph. *Strategic Planning and Management for Library Managers*. Greenwood Village, Colo: Libraries Unlimited, 2005.

McCook, Kathleen de la Peña, and Margaret Myers. *Opportunities in Library and Information Science Careers*. Rev. ed. New York: VGM Career Books/McGraw-Hill, 2002.

McGonagle, John J., and Carolyn M. Vella. *The Manager's Guide to Competitive Intelligence*. New York: Praeger Publishers, 2003.

Miller, Joseph, and Barbara A. Bristow, eds. *Sears List of Subject Headings*. 19th ed. Bronx, N.Y.: H.W. Wilson, 2007.

Moorehead, Joe. *Introduction to United States Government Information Sources*. 6th ed. Greenwood Village, Colo: Libraries Unlimited, 1999.

Mount, Ellis, ed. *Opening New Doors: Alternative Careers for Librarians*. Washington, D.C.: Special Libraries Association, 1993.

Neely, Teresa Y., and Khafre K. Abif, eds. *In Our Own Voices: The Changing Face of Librarianship*. Lanham, Md.: Scarecrow Press, 1996.

Nesbeitt, Sarah L., and Rachel Singer Gordon. *The Information Professional's Guide to Career Development*. Medford, N.J.: Information Today, 2001.

Norton, Melanie J., ed. *Introductory Concepts in Information Science*. Medford, N.J.: Information Today, 2000.

Porter, Cathy A., and Elin B. Christianson. *Special Libraries: A Guide for Management*. 4th ed. Washington, D.C.: Special Libraries Association, 1997.

Raddon, Rosemary, ed. *Your Career, Your Life: Career Management for the Information Professional*. Burlington, Vt.: Ashgate Publishing, 2005.

Reitz, Joan M. *Dictionary for Library and Information Science*. Greenwood Village, Colo: Libraries Unlimited, 2004.

Rubin, Richard E. *Foundations of Library and Information Science*. New York: Neal-Schuman Publishers, 1998.

Rugge, Sue, and Alfred Glossbrenner. *The Information Broker's Handbook*. New York: McGraw-Hill, 1997.

Sabroski, Suzanne. *Super Searchers Make It on Their Own*. Medford, N.J.: Information Today, 2002.

Saye, Jerry. *Manheimer's Cataloging and Classification*. 4th ed. Boca Raton, Fla.: CRC Press, 1999.

Schement, Jorge Reina, ed. *Encyclopedia of Communication and Information, 3 Volume Set*. New York: Macmillan Library Reference, 2002.

Shontz, Priscilla K., ed. *The Librarian's Career Guidebook*. Lanham, Md.: Scarecrow Press, 2004.

Shontz, Priscilla K., and Richard A. Murray, eds. *A Day in the Life: Career Options in Library and Information Science*. Greenwood Village, Colo: Libraries Unlimited, 2007.

Shontz, Priscilla K., and Steven J. Oberg. *Jump Start Your Career in Library and Information Science*. Lanham, Md.: Scarecrow Press, 2002.

Shuman, Bruce A. *Beyond the Library of the Future: More Alternative Futures for the Public Library*. Greenwood Village, Colo: Libraries Unlimited, 1997.

———. *Issues for Libraries and Information Science in the Internet Age*. Greenwood Village, Colo: Libraries Unlimited, 2001.

Siess, Judith A., and Jonathan Lorig, compilers. *Out Front with Stephen Abrams: A Guide for Information Leaders*. Chicago: American Library Association, 2007.

Stueart, Robert D., and Barbara B. Moran. *Library and Information Center Management*. 7th ed. Greenwood Village, Colo: Libraries Unlimited, 2007.

Taylor, Arlene G. *Introduction to Cataloging and Classification*. 10th ed. Greenwood Village, Colo: Libraries Unlimited, 2006.

———. *The Organization of Information*. 2d ed. Greenwood Village, Colo: Libraries Unlimited, 2003.

White, Herbert S. *Librarianship—Quo Vadis? Opportunities and Dangers as We Face the New Millennium*. Greenwood Village, Colo: Libraries Unlimited, 2000.

———. *Managing the Special Library: Strategies for Success Within the Larger Organization*. Boston: G.K. Hall, 1984.

Wilson, Thomas C. *The Systems Librarian: Designing Roles, Defining Skills*. Chicago: American Library Association, 1998.

Woolls, Blanche. *The School Library Media Manager*. 3d ed. Greenwood Village, Colo: Libraries Unlimited, 2004.

INDEX

American Library Association—
Allied Professional Association
19, 25, 28, 40, 49
American Library Directory (book)
6, 11, 32, 41
American Management Association
(AMA) 32, 150, 153, 156
American Marketing Association
(AMA) 47
American Medical Information
Association (AMIA) 100
American Press Institute (API) 106
American Society for Information
Science and Technology (ASIS&T)
6, 9, 11, 14, 17, 20, 23, 26, 29, 32,
35, 41, 44, 47, 50, 53, 57, 60, 66, 69,
72, 78, 82, 85, 88, 91, 96, 106, 113,
115, 117, 120, 122, 128, 131, 134,
136, 141, 144, 150, 153, 156, 160,
162, 165, 169, 172, 175, 178, 192,
195–196, 199, 208, 212, 215, 218, 221
American Society for Training and
Development (ASTD) 34–35, 112,
113
Americans with Disabilities Act
(ADA) 35, 41
AMIA. *See* American Medical
Information Association
AMITHE. *See* Association for the
Management of Information
Technology in Higher Education
Anglo-American cataloging rules
(AACR2r) 94
*Anglo-American Cataloging Rules,
Second Edition (AACR2)* 129
APA. *See* Allied Professional
Association; Audio Publishers
Association
API. *See* American Press Institute
APRA. *See* Association of
Professional Researchers for
Advancement
APTL. *See* Association of Part-Time
Librarians
archival manager 7–9, 86–88
Archival Products News (periodical)
138
archives director 7–9
archivist **7–9,** 61, 176–178
ARL. *See* Association of Research
Librarians
ARLIS/NA. *See* Arts Libraries
Society of North America

ARMA. *See* Association for Records
Managers and Administrators
ARSC. *See* Association for Recorded
Sound Collections
art and design librarian 74–76
art catalog librarian 74–76
artificial intelligence programmer
167–169
art librarian **74–76**
Arts Libraries Society of North
America (ARLIS/NA) 76
ASA. *See* Association of Subscription
Agents
ASCD. *See* Association for Supervi-
sion and Curriculum Development
ASCLA. *See* Association of
Specialized and Cooperative
Library Agencies
ASIS&T. *See* American Society
for Information Science and
Technology
assistant cataloger 15, 129–131
assistant library director **10–11,** 27,
33, 39, 58, 61, 70
associate director, library human
resource 33–35
associate library director 10–11, 39
Association for Computing
Machinery (ACM) 66, 153, 156,
160, 165, 169, 172, 175, 181, 186,
189, 192, 195, 202, 205, 221
Association for Educational
Communications and Technology
(AECT) 44, 57, 66, 149
Association for Education
in Journalism and Mass
Communication (AEJMC) 106
Association for Financial
Professionals (AFP) 31–32
Association for Information and
Image Management (AIIM) 178
Association for Information Media
and Equipment (AIME) 85
Association for Information
Professionals (AIP) 208, 212
Association for Information Systems
(AIS) 165, 172
Association for Information
Technology Professionals (AITP)
172
Association for Library and
Information Science Education
(ALISE) 6, 41

Association for Library Collections
and Technical Services (ALCTS)
11, 17, 26, 29, 41, 60, 63, 66, 69, 78,
127–128, 131, 134, 136, 144
Association for Library Service to
Children (ALSC) 22–23, 57, 72
Association for Library Trustees and
Advocates (ALTA) 41
Association for Recorded Sound
Collections (ARSC) 88
Association for Supervision and
Curriculum Development (ASCD)
57
Association for the Management
of Information Technology in
Higher Education (AMITHE)
66
Association for Women in
Communications (AWC) 106
Association of Academic Health
Sciences Libraries (AAHSL) 100
Association of American
Geographers (AAG) 96
Association of Bookmobile and
Outreach Services (ABOS) 110
Association of College
Administration Professionals
(ACAP) 215
Association of College and Research
Libraries (ACRL) 6, 17, 50, 60,
62–63, 66, 128, 131, 136, 141, 215
Association of Computer Support
Specialists (ACSS) 181, 189
Association of Independent
Information Professionals (AIIP)
78, 208, 212
Association of Information System
Professionals (AISP) 141
Association of Management
Consulting Firms (AMCF) 38
Association of Part-Time Librarians
(APTL) 117, 120
Association of Professional
Researchers for Advancement
(APRA) 162
Association of Records Managers
and Administrators (ARMA) 11,
41, 94, 178, 198–199
Association of Research Libraries
(ARL) 17, 66
Association of Specialized and
Cooperative Library Agencies
(ASCLA) 63

Association of Subscription Agents (ASA) 60, 128
Audio Publishers Association (APA) 85
audiovisual specialist 83–85
automation librarian 64–66
automation specialist 64–66
AWC. *See* Association for Women in Communications

B

Barron's Marketing Dictionary (book) 45
Bates, Mary Ellen 208
bibliographer **12–14**
Bibliographical Society of America (BSA) 14
binder technician 137–138
binding and conservation technician 137–138
book binder technician 137–138
book conservator 137–138
bookmobile assistant librarian 108–110
bookmobile clerk/driver 108–110
bookmobile driver **108–110**
bookmobile librarian 108–110
book repair technician 137–138
BRASS. *See* Business and Reference and Services Section
Breeding, Marshall 65–66
BSA. *See* Bibliographical Society of America
Burwell World Directory of Information Brokers 209, 212
business analyst 36–38
Business and Reference and Services Section (BRASS) 78
business information specialist 77–78
business institutional librarian 77–78
business librarian **77–78**

C

cataloger **15–17,** 68, 129, 135
cataloger/classifier 135–136
cataloger/technical services specialist 142–144
cataloging assistant 129–131, 135–156

cataloging technician 121–123, **129–131**
catalog librarian 15–17, 129
CDO. *See* chief data officer
CFA. *See* chartered financial analyst
CFO. *See* chief financial officer
chair, department of library and information technology 219–221
chair, information science department **219–221**
chartered financial analyst (CFA) Institute 31
chief data officer (CDO) 152, 193–196
chief financial officer (CFO) 30–32, 149
chief information officer (CIO) xvii, 18, 24, 27, 42, 48, 79, **148–150,** 154, 157, 163, 170–171, 179, 200
Chief Information Officers (CIO) Council 150
Chief Information Officers (CIO) Executive Council, 150
chief knowledge officer (CKO) 148–150
chief librarian 4, **18–20**
chief officer, library 39–41
chief officer, library system 39–41
chief technical officer (CTO) 151–153
chief technology officer (CTO) 148, **151–153,** 154, 184
children's librarian **21–23**
children's media specialist 21–23
children's service librarian 21–23
children's service manager 21–23
CIO. *See* chief information officer
CIO Today 150
circulation aide 114–115
circulation assistant 118–120, 132–134
circulation clerk 114–117
circulation department director 24–26
circulation department head 24–26, 142
circulation/interlibrary loan librarian **24–26**
circulation librarian 132–133
circulation specialist 132–134
circulation supervisor 132–134
circulation technician 24, 27, 121–123, **132–134**

Cisco Company 165
CISM. *See* certified information security manager
CKO. *See* chief knowledge officer
classifier **135–136**
classifying technician 135–136
clinical medical librarian 98–100
CLIR. *See* Council on Library and Information Resources
CMA. *See* certified management accountant
CNA. *See* Certified Network Associate
collection management librarian 61–63
collections development director **27–29,** 61, 126, 135
collections development librarian 12, 27–29
collections development officer 27–29
collections director 7–9
collections librarian 61–63
collections manager 7–9
College and University Professional Association of Human Resources (CUPA-HR) 217
college librarian 4–6
COLT. *See* Council on Library/Media Technicians
Committee on Cataloging: Description and Access 131
Communications Workers of America (CWA) 181
computer communications specialist 184–186
computer engineer 184–186
computer research analyst 184–186
computer scientist **184–186**
computer support specialist **187–189**
computer systems manager 163–166, 178–181
computer technical support specialist 187–189
Computing Research Association (CRA) 172, 186, 202, 205, 221
Computing Technology Industry Association (CTIA) 153, 156, 160, 165, 169, 181, 186, 189, 192, 195, 202, 205, 221
conservation technician **137–138**
conservator 86–88, 137

information technology (IT) analyst 200–202

Information Technology and Libraries (journal) 66

information technology (IT) architect 157–160

Information Technology Association of America (ITAA) 139, 141, 150, 153, 156, 165, 192, 196, 203, 205

information technology (IT) director 170–172

information technology (IT) manager 163–166, 173–175

information technology (IT) specialist 54–57, 178–181, 187–189

information technology (IT) support technician 203–205

Information technology systems (ITS) manager 163–166

information technology (IT) technician 203–205

INFORMS. *See* Institute for Operations Research and Management Sciences

InfoWorld (periodical) 153, 204

in-house information specialist 77–78

Institute for Certification of Computing Professionals (ICCP) 186, 189, 192, 201, 204

Institute for Operations Research and Management Sciences (INFORMS) 172

Institute for the Management of Information Systems (IMIS) 172

Institute of Certified Records Manager (ICRM) 178

Institute of Electrical and Electronics Engineers (IEEE) Computer Society 153, 156, 165, 169, 175, 181, 186, 189, 192, 195, 202, 205, 221

Institute of Management Consultants USA (IMCUSA) 38

Institute of Operations Management (IOM) 172

interaction designer 157–160

interactive designer 157–160

interlibrary loan clerk 116–117

interlibrary loan coordinator 24–26

International Association of Business Communicators (IABC) 46

International Association of School Librarianship (IASL) 57

International Council on Archives (ICA) Committee on Electronic Records 176

International Federation of Library Associations and Institutions (IFLA) 50, 57, 82, 131, 138, 215

International Foundation of Employee Benefit Plans (IFEBP) 34

International Preservation News (periodical) 138

International Public Management Association for Human Resources (IPMA-HR) 35

International Society for Technology in Education (ISTE) 57

IOM. *See* Institute of Operations Management

IPMA-HR. *See* International Public Management Association for Human Resources

IRM. *See* information resource management; information resource manager

IS. *See* information systems

ISTE. *See* International Society for Technology in Education

IT. *See* information technology

ITAA. *See* Information Technology Association of America

ITS. *See* information technology systems

J

Jefferson, Thomas 16

Jobs for Librarians and Information Professionals (online resource) 23, 82

K

knowledge/content manager 167–169

knowledge engineer **167–169**

knowledge management specialist 167–169

knowledge manager 167–169

knowledge strategy analyst 167–169

knowledge systems analyst 167–169

L

LAMA. *See* Library Administration and Management Association

LAN/WAN Administrator 173–175

LAN/WAN Manager 173–175

Law and Technology Resources for Legal Professionals (LLRX) 94

law librarian **92–94**

law library cataloging librarian 92–94

law reference librarian 92–94

LCSH. *See* Library of Congress subject headings classification system

League of Professional System Administrators (LOPSA) 181

lecturer, library and information science 216–218

Library Administration and Management Association (LAMA) 6, 11, 20, 26, 134, 144

library administrator 10–11, 39, 42, 54

library aide **114–115,** 118, 121, 126, 129, 132, 139, 142

library and information science professor 216–218

Library and Information Technology Association (LITA) 20, 44, 66, 208, 212

library and information technology instructor 216–218

library assistant, clerical 116–117, 118–120

library assistant, paraprofessional 118–120

library assistant/bookmobile driver 108–110

library assistants 21, 27, 48, 79, 104, 108, 111, 114, 116, **118–120**, 129, 135, 137, 139, 142

Library Assistants and Technicians Group 117, 120, 122

library attendant 114–115, 118–120

library circulation specialist 132–134

library clerk 111, 114, **116–117,** 118, 121, 126, 139

library collections technician 126–128

library conservation technician 137–138

library consultant **36–38**

ABOUT THE AUTHORS

ALLAN TAYLOR, a freelance author, editor, indexer, and researcher, comes from a family long involved in the publishing and newspaper industries and, as a production manager, has participated in the computerization of bibliographic and scientific/technical databases. He is the coauthor of *Career Opportunities in Writing*; *Career Opportunities in Television and Cable*; *Career Opportunities in the Internet, Video Games, and Multimedia*; *Career Opportunities in the Energy Industry*; and *The Encyclopedia of Ethnic Groups in Hollywood* (all Facts On File) and has been a freelance editor and indexer for such publishers as Aurum Press, Belle Publishing, Contemporary Books, Hoover Institution Press, John Wiley & Sons, Kensington Books, McFarland & Company, Routledge, St. Martin's Press, Scarecrow Press, Seven Locks Press, and Thunder's Mouth Press. In addition, he has created special bibliographic indexes for such book titles as *Along the Roaring River: My Wild Ride from Mao to the Met*; *Angel and Demons: One Actor's Hollywood Journey, An Autobiography*; *The Great American Gamble: How the 1979 Daytona 500 Gave Birth to a NASCAR Nation*; *George: The Poor Little Rich Boy Who Built the Yankee Empire*; *The Great Spy Pictures*; *In the Same Voice: Men and Women in Law Enforcement*; *Questions and Answers about Community Associations*; *Soul of a People: The WPA Writers' Project Uncovers Depression America*; *Swim against the Current: Even a Dead Fish Can Go with the Flow*, and *Women Doctors Guide to Health and Healing*.

Mr. Taylor's publishing industry posts include tenures at R. R. Bowker Company (Bibliographic Services), Engineering Information, Inc. (Production Manager), and Graphic Typesetting Services (Proofreading/Technical Specifications Department Manager). He resides in Los Angeles, California. His Web site is at http://www.tataylor.net.

JAMES ROBERT PARISH, a former entertainment reporter, publicist, and book series editor, is the author of many published biographies and reference books about the entertainment industry, including *It's Good to Be the King: The Seriously Funny Life of Mel Brooks*, *The Hollywood Book of Extravagance*, *The Hollywood Book of Breakups*, *Fiasco: Hollywood's Iconic Flops*, *The American Movies Reference Book*, *The Complete Actors TV Credits*, *The Hollywood Songsters*, *The Hollywood Book of Scandals*, *The Hollywood Book of Death*, *The RKO Gals*, *Katharine Hepburn*, *Whitney Houston*, *Gus Van Sant*, and *Whoopi Goldberg*. With Allan Taylor, he coauthored *Career Opportunities in Writing*; *Career Opportunities in Television and Cable*; *Career Opportunities in the Internet, Video Games, and Multimedia*; *Career Opportunities in the Energy Industry*; and *The Encyclopedia of Ethnic Groups in Hollywood* (all Facts On File) and has written several entries in the Ferguson Young Adult biography series (including Gloria Estefan, Jim Henson, Twyla Tharp, Denzel Washington, Katie Couric, Stan Lee, Halle Berry, Steven Spielberg, Tom Hanks, and Stephen King).

Mr. Parish is a frequent on-camera interviewee on cable and network TV for documentaries on the performing arts in both the United States and the United Kingdom. He resides in Studio City, California. His Web site is at http://www.jamesrobertparish.com.